DANGEROUS
LIAISONS

CULTURAL ✌ POLITICS

A series from the Social Text Collective

Aimed at a broad interdisciplinary audience, these volumes seek to intervene in debates about the political direction of current theory and practice by combining contemporary analysis with a more traditional sense of historical and socioeconomic evaluation.

Cultural Politics, Volume 11

DANGEROUS LIAISONS

Gender, Nation, and Postcolonial Perspectives

Anne McClintock, Aamir Mufti,
and Ella Shohat, editors
(for the Social Text Collective)

University of Minnesota Press
Minneapolis
London

Published by the University of Minnesota Press
111 Third Avenue South, Suite 290
Minneapolis, MN 55401–2520
http://www.upress.umn.edu
Printed in the United States of America on acid-free paper

Second printing, 1998

Library of Congress Cataloging-in-Publication Data

Dangerous liaisons : gender, nation, and postcolonial perspectives /
  Anne McClintock, Aamir Mufti, Ella Shohat, editors (for the Social
  Text Collective).
      p.   cm. – (Cultural politics ; v. 11)
    Includes bibliographical references and index.
    ISBN 0-8166-2648-0. – ISBN 0-8166-2649-9 (pbk.)
    1. Minorities. 2. Minority women. 3. Nationalism. 4. Ethnic
  relations. 5. Race relations. 6. Decolonization. 7. Sex role.
  8. Multiculturalism.   I. McClintock, Anne, 1954-   . II. Mufti,
  Aamir. III. Shohat, Ella, 1959-   . IV. Social Text Collective.
  V. Series: Cultural politics (Minneapolis, Minn.) ; v. 11.
  JC312.D36 1997
  306.2–dc21   96-51991

Contents

Acknowledgments

We wish first to thank the members of the Social Text Collective, for it was during our editorial meetings that this book began. We also wish to thank all the contributors to this volume for giving so generously of their time, energy, and patience. Grateful **thanks go to Jaune Quick-to-See Smith for kindly allowing us use of *War Shirt* for** the cover, as well as to Jeanne Lee for her cover design. Our heartfelt thanks go to all the publishers and permissions editors for their generosity and cooperation in granting us permission rights.

Many friends gave their support at various stages of the project. Special thanks go to Andrew Ross and Bruce Robbins, coeditors of *Social Text*. We are especially grateful to Monica Marciczkiewicz, the journal's managing editor, for her unfailing good humor, cooperation, and hard work. John McClure offered us indispensable help and inspiration in the early stages of the book, as did Inderpal Grewal, Caren Kaplan, and Jyotsina Uppal.

We are deeply grateful to the editors and staff of the University of Minnesota Press, especially Lisa Freeman and Gretchen Asmussen, for their help. Our warm appreciation goes to Hank Schlau at ediType for his meticulous work and kind patience during the last stages of the project. We are also very grateful to Iannis Mentzas and Sreemala Nair for their scrupulous work proofreading sections of this book.

Finally, and above all, we wish to offer our deepest thanks to Saloni Mathur, Rob Nixon, and Robert Stam for their inspirational support, love, and friendship.

Introduction
Aamir Mufti / Ella Shohat

"There's no place like home," whispers a dislocated Dorothy as she and her lost dog, so far away from Kansas, hanker to get back home. Comforting words, written by L. Frank Baum in 1900 just as U.S. expansionism was yet again displacing Native America and denying its quest for a settled share of land, now met with a "vanishing-world" nostalgia.[1] Comforting words, at a time when the abolition of slavery had given way to African-Americans fighting against sexually panicked cross-burners. Reassuring words, filmed by Victor Fleming in 1939 at the brink of a new era in modern history, one that brought the United States an unprecedented central role in the affairs of the "ever-shrinking world." Hollywood's Kansas, displayed for billions of spectators around the world over the past five decades, has become no less of a magic land than Oz. For the powerful mythmaking machine of empire turned the image of Kansas's orderly tranquillity into the idea of home for war-torn regions where partitions engendered refugees crossing newly barbwired borders.

To the contemporary "postcolonial" critic, Dorothy's words have a doubly complicated meaning. On the one hand, they give expression to a Euro-American masculinist ideology of domesticity, verso to the recto of ideologies of imperial gregariousness, from the Monroe Doctrine to the new world order. On the other hand, they recall communities of mobilization against precisely that hegemonism, especially the antiracist and anticolonial nationalisms. It was in the name of home and homeland that the nonallied nations fought the imperial family embrace. In each case, the idea of home appears locked within a fundamental ambivalence: "home" — place or desire?[2]

Home, as a set of material, communal, and emotional securities, was often projected as a pastoral stability, free of the dissonance between place and desire. Cultural criticism today, however, has accentuated precisely that dissonance. To be critical implies not fudging over this ambivalence, not giving in to ruling ideas of total mobility and "universal abandon," but also not dreaming of permanent and secure dwellings.[3] The postcolonial critic resists putting on the ruby red shoes to click his/her heels three times, for in the context of strict border-surveillance and severe passport control, belonging cannot be housed simply within the material space of walls and roofs, of fenced topographies and well-drawn maps.

Is there still a place called home? How do the displaced and exiled get "there"?

Was there ever such a place? Home and the loss of home constitute a recurring motif of modernity. The post–world war era has seen it return, nourished on fresh historical experiences, imbued with new meanings. In the last decade, specifically, rearticulated notions of exile and diaspora have played an important role in a cultural critique that not only charted the history of communities displaced in the postindependence era but also employed that history as a condition and a trope for cultural criticism itself.[4] In the repeated mutual impacting of divergent trajectories, claims, and memories that constitute the cultural landscape of late capitalism, the loss of home and the struggle to reclaim and reimagine it are experiences fraught with tension. But whereas in the era of Third Worldist euphoria the limitation and repressions of the nation were often hushed, today they have been brought center stage within critical and cultural practices. Nation, community, race, class, religion, gender, sexuality — each names a site for the enactment of the great drama of origins, loyalty, belonging, betrayal; in short, of identity and identification.

The gradual eclipse of the revolutionary anticolonial era has been accompanied by the emergence of new forms of selfhood, political allegiance, capital accumulation, imperial power, and mass migration, forms whose contours are perhaps still only half-visible. Postcolonial criticism is now a familiar mode of cultural practice in the Anglo-American academy. The perspectives on imperialism produced within this new intellectual formation represent a perceptible shift relative to the critical positions that had developed out of and alongside anticolonial revolutionary movements for national liberation in the postwar era both in the Third and First Worlds. The anticolonial struggles have had their repercussions in the academy, seen in the efforts to decolonize Eurocentric culture. *Dangerous Liaisons: Gender, Nation, and Postcolonial Perspectives* brings together a set of essays on currently debated Third World and postcolonial issues within cultural studies. Located within a transitional moment in the history of "center-periphery" relations, they seek to address, from a wide range of perspectives and positions, the structure of inequalities inherent in the present moment. They also examine the dilemmas and contradictions of the ongoing critique of racism and imperialism at a moment when such politically mobilizing categories as "Third World" and even "nation" have lost their earlier liberationist clarity and thrust. But, above all, they represent an attempt at grappling with the meaning of location and belonging, of communities of interpretation and praxis, of home, in the increasingly diasporic panoramas of the contemporary world.

Some of the recently published collections on cultural studies do not give sufficiently complex attention to these debates. Furthermore, while multicultural volumes tend to focus on the U.S. context and postcolonial anthologies tend to ignore it, *Dangerous Liaisons* insists upon precisely the contrapuntal juxtaposition of these diverse yet related debates. Our editorial process was guided by a conceptual framework that refuses to separate the linked histories of race as well as the contemporary coimplication of communities within and across the borders of nation-states. In a world where Third World immigrants to the United States can participate in racist discourses and practices toward U.S. Native American and African-American communities, where U.S. racial "minorities" might join U.S. imperial wars, and where Third World national elites become complicit with the new world order being created by the World Bank and International Monetary Fund, it is impossible to discuss issues of nation and gender in national isolation. By no means comprehensive in scope, this volume does seek to remedy the lack of putting into "dialogue," as it were, these diverse intellectual contributions, and narratives of the nation, in post-colonial criticism. This volume takes as its starting point the interventions around these issues in the pages of the journal *Social Text*. As an interdisciplinary journal on the left, *Social Text* has, over the decade and a half of its existence, devoted substantial space to ongoing Third World struggles against imperialism in regions like Latin America and the Middle East. To perhaps a lesser degree, contributions to the journal also have examined the formations of colonialism within a gendered and racialized perspective, examining as well the historical aftermaths of different forms of colonialism, especially ethnic/racial and gender identities in the increasingly diasporic world of the postindependence era. As members of the journal's editorial collective, we wanted first of all to bring together in one volume some of the disparate interventions in these debates. But we also wanted to reach beyond the journal and draw on other published and nonpublished material, in order to give a somewhat fuller sense of the issues. We have sought, for instance, to compensate partially for the relative absence, in *Social Text,* of feminist interventions in the field in the past decade.

Dangerous Liaisons is shaped around four overlapping and only provisionally distinct areas of concern: colonial discourse and the question of the nation, diasporic identities and multicultural agendas, the intertwined politics of gender/sexuality and race within the double context of both nationalism and feminism, and, finally, the debate about "the postcolonial" as conjuncture and perspective. The rest of the introduction will outline the main issues, as we see them, in each of the areas, the links and overlaps between them, and, in the broadest terms possible, the contributions of this group of essays to the debates. In doing so, it is not our intention to suggest uniformity of conception and methodology, let alone political agreement, among the contributors. On the contrary, the point is precisely to bring to the fore the larger tensions and contradictions within which this work is being produced.

That the great era of national liberation in the Third World that began in the years following World War II is now over has become more or less obvious. This is evident in even those struggles for nation-statehood and self-determination that continue into the 1990s, struggles that have consequently been marked by a deep sense of belatedness and anachronism. In large regions of the Third World, the powerful framework of nationalism, which held such enormous liberationist promise even twenty years ago, has begun to fall apart. In these countries, the slogans of nationalism, its mythos of hearth and home, are now the property of national elites that have been increasingly revealed to be corrupt, capitulationist, undemocratic, patriarchal, and homophobic.

Dangerous Liaisons begins with a set of essays that highlight the problems (and problematic) of the nation as a lived form, and in particular as a form of struggle against imperialism. They do so from theoretical and political vantage points that are saturated with the historical specificities of the 1980s, including the ongoing struggles for national sovereignty in Palestine and South Africa. Despite the great range of positions they embody, however, the essays may be said to share one common tendency: the nation appears in them not as the embodiment of, in

Frantz Fanon's cautionary words, "the immemorial truth" of the people, but rather as a historically produced, unfinished, and contested terrain.[5] The nation and the signs of its cultural life emerge as necessarily littered with unresolved contradictions and dilemmas. Thus nationalism appears in some of the contributions as a *provisional* vantage point for a critical understanding of contemporary forms of imperialism (Said, Franco, McClintock, Prasad); and in others constructions of nationhood are revealed to be contradictory and crisis-riven, serving diverse forms of legitimation (in very different ways, in the essays by Shohat, Nixon, Stoler, Viswanathan).

A number of the essays in this volume therefore testify to the difficulties of re-defining and reestablishing a relationship to the icons, discourses, and symbolic complexes of anticolonial nationalism after the decline of its liberationist thrust. How do we reclaim the nation as a site for struggle when the primary function of the nation-state in the global economy is that of a terminal for the flows of transnational capital? How do we redefine "national interest" when the postcolonial nation-state has become a vehicle for national bourgeoisies increasingly integrated into the cul-ture of corporate transnationalism? How do we rethink the postindependence nation as a means of identification and mobilization, as the "home" of critical conscious-ness, given its clear discriminatory history, its inability to mobilize men and women, gays and lesbians, and ethnic and religious majorities and minorities on equal terms?

These are long-standing questions that are by no means unique to the "post-colonial" criticism being produced, for the most part, in the Anglo-American academy, but they have acquired their present form and urgency during the 1980s and 1990s. It is not an accident that they are being asked in this form, at this time, and at this site. For the last two decades have seen people of color and/or recent Third World origin entering, along with white women, the First World academy at an unprecedented level. And previously taboo questions concerning gender, race, and colonial discourse have acquired, despite continuing resistance from some en-trenched sectors, a certain respectability. We read as a sign of its coming of age that the discourse around "postcoloniality" has recently produced considerable contro-versy about its conceptual framework, its institutional locale, and its relationship to the middle-class emigrations from the Third World in the postindependence era. Part of that debate is reproduced here (Dirlik), and we shall return to it in the course of this introduction.[6] But here we wish to note that in keeping with our understand-ing of the politics of location in the contemporary world, we have brought together essays concerning specifically Third World issues with those dedicated to cognate questions in the First World itself. This is consonant with our conviction that these debates and sites, although distinct, are historically inseparable and even overlap-ping, mutually imbricated in contemporary global cultural politics. Both these "areas" represent contemporary efforts at analyzing the history of colonialism, imperialism, and racism and critiquing Eurocentric study of history and culture.

Whereas the postcolonial debate has been limited to the academic scene, one of the most pressing sets of public issues that came to prominence in the 1980s concerns the cultural agendas bundled under the name of "multiculturalism." The Eurocentrism and racism of institutions have become subject to debate at numerous sites — including the academy; school boards; federal, state, and local governing bodies; and of course the print and broadcast media. The university, however, has gained a central place in these debates, and its own versions of the issues — core curricula, faculty and student body composition, questions of language, power, and representation, caricatured in the mainstream media as the imposition of the "cult of sensitivity" — have often come metonymically to stand for the larger social questions involved. The ever-present danger in the formulation of multicultural agendas has been the risk of sliding into forms of liberal pluralism to which existing cultural regimes can easily prove hospitable: "Such pluralism tolerates the existence of salsa, it enjoys Mexican restaurants, but it bans Spanish as a medium of instruction in American schools. Above all it refuses to acknowledge the class basis of discrimination and the systematic economic exploitation of minorities that underlie postmodern culture."[7] Radical critiques of Eurocentric agendas must steer clear of this liberal "salad bar" vision of culture, insist upon analyzing the field of power and conditions of conflict within which cultural "encounter" takes place, and link their analyses explicitly to projects of political transformation. They must formulate a rigorous critique of the notion of diversity underlying the corporate/liberal espousal of multiculturalism, so vividly captured in the advertising slogan "The United Colors of Benetton."

The ongoing academic debates about the canon and the pedagogical controversies about school curricula have been fueled by an increasingly radical critique of "Europe" as the source of all cultural value and meaning. The multicultural challenge over the past decade has sought to break out of the institutional confinement of its impulses to ethnic studies in the 1960s and 1970s; it has meant looking critically at *all* disciplines in their continued privileging of Western cultural production. These radical perspectives and critical theories offer an explicit commitment to a different vision of education, knowledge, and social relations (Hanchard, Lubiano, Flores, and Yúdice). They seek to highlight the coimplicated multiplicity of community histories and perspectives, as well as the hybrid character of *all* communities in a world increasingly characterized by the "traveling" of images, sounds, goods, and people. Rather than imagine unconnected geographies of identities, postcolonial diasporic writings take as their starting point the cultural consequences of the worldwide movements and dislocations of people that have characterized the development of mass-mediated "global" or "transnational" capitalism.[8] In the era of globalization, furthermore, the old imperial hegemonies have become "dispersed" (Arjun Appadurai's term) and "scattered" (Inderpal Grewal and Caren Kaplan's term).[9] These processes have required a profound reconceptualization of power relations between cultural communities and a renewed emphasis on not only diverse, but even opposing, community interpretations of texts and historical experiences within and beyond the borders of the nation-state (Retamar). Furthermore, this reconceptualization has meant challenging the hierarchies that produce some communities as "ethnic" or otherwise "minor" and others as being "above" ethnicity, "major," and normative.

The debates over gender and sexuality, similarly, have transcended the institutional boundaries of women's studies programs, asserting their relevance to *all* disciplines and fields of inquiry. Multicultural and transnational feminism(s) inscribes the notion of race and (neo)colonialism into the debates about feminism, while simultaneously inscribing gender and sexuality into the debates about nation and race in the era of globalization. The formulation of gendered, multicultural, and transnational agendas across the social landscape is perhaps the most palpable sign of ongoing attempts to create bridges between communities of recent immigrants to this country (from Asia, Africa, and Latin America), relatively "new" communities of militant identification (such as gays, lesbians, and bisexuals), and "older" communities of struggle, in particular the Native American, African-American, and Chicano/a. But the work of criticism in these entirely salutary developments is also to guard against an easy conflation of sites. The danger of a uniform problematic of "race" in the United States, for instance, is that it allows implicit appropriation of the highly unique African-American history of pain, deprivation, and violent subjugation in the name of communities that, however marginalized by Anglo-American hegemony, can nevertheless not claim *that* racialized experience as their own within the U.S. context. At the same time, the African-American experience of trans-Atlantic slave trade, as Afro-diasporic-conscious writing suggests, cannot be limited to a U.S. nation-state frame of analysis. Such an experience virtually forces the critique to move beyond the nation-state as a sufficient unit for analysis. The highly hybrid nature of diverse colonial, neocolonial, and postcolonial displacements and diasporas, in this sense, must be historicized and contextualized, spoken about from, within, and in relation to specific locations.[10]

The essays collected here under the explicit rubric of multiculturalism focus on these questions of power and representation, continuing to give expression to the traditional concern of the left with the distribution of power, with empowering the disempowered, but seeking always to extend the struggle beyond the "material" realm. While some essays explicitly challenge the neoconservative backlash against multicultural pedagogy (Stam), all of the essays are ultimately concerned in a central way with the effects that institutionalized discourses and community identities have on the envisioning and formulation of more egalitarian social relations. But they also subject the notions of identity and culture themselves to radical critique, seeking to make visible their production within the problematics of power and representation (Hall): in other words, they seek to rethink culture not as primordial home but rather as a *conjunctural* alignment of needs and claims, forged in an inclusionary history of oppositional struggles.

Several essays in this volume also represent a consistent effort to inscribe the notion of gender into the debates about empire, race, and nation. Some of the essays grouped together explicitly under the rubric of gender make visible a coherent critique addressed not only to the patriarchal basis of colonial regimes, political as well as epistemological, and to the often male-dominated culture of nationalist or ethnic movements, but also to the First World and "Eurocentric" bias and often heterosexist assumptions of mainstream feminism itself. Critiquing such universalizing and homogenizing categories as woman, nation, race, and class, Third World and U.S. multicultural feminists have sought to shake the epistemological ground upon which Eurocentric feminist critique has been raised (Mohanty). Reflecting this engagement, these essays not only reject essentialist expressions of gender identity but, alive to the need for a truly coalitionary politics, also seek to point the way toward oppositional practices and alternative epistemologies and institutional strategies necessary for a diversified feminist empowerment.

The strength of this feminist critique has come in part from the fact that it has tried to free itself from the "dirty linen" defensiveness about not publicly criticizing one's "home" community — national, racial, ethnic — "in public" lest that be viewed as betrayal. And a great deal of feminist and gay/lesbian effort has been directed at making visible the exclusions, the instability, the fear that characterize the illusion of home. Such commitment to criticism is no small task, and therefore no mean accomplishment, when the life of the national or racial group is felt to be under a state of (political, economic, cultural) siege. Several of the contributors address with perfect candor the patriarchal nature of specific ethnic and national communities as well as the gender/sexual biases of communities of mobilization (Jaimes and Halsey, Alarcón, Butler, Mercer). This has involved not only documenting the distinct contribution of women (and to a lesser extent the contribution of gays and lesbians) to nationalist and racial struggles but also revealing the complicities between colonialism and nationalism around the figure of woman. Often made to metaphorize the nation, the image of the revolutionary woman carrying a bomb or waving a flag was celebrated precisely because her precarious position within the revolution called attention to its fissures. Thus, the same Third Worldist discourse that valorized the revolutionary female figure has also condemned Third World feminists as "traitors to the nation" in response to their critique of the masculinist narration of the nation. Emerging from the logic of political and cultural decolonization, the essays in part III ("Gender and the Politics of Race") seek to articulate an emancipatory vision beyond the gender and sexual repressions of the nation.

The essays in part III also reflect the fact that feminists of Third World and "minority" background have found no easy and all-encompassing "home" in the communities of First World white feminism.[11] They give shape to an ongoing critique of mainstream feminism for its silence about the gulfs that divide women precisely on the basis of race, class, and national positioning in the global relations between "sovereign" nation-states. This critique seeks to dismantle the unitary and uniform understanding of "woman" upon which so much of the feminist intervention of the 1960s and 1970s was based, and it foregrounds everywhere the *range* of gendered and racially distinct subjects and the practices within which they are produced (Lorde, Carby, hooks). Thus a significant portion of African-American feminist criticism, for instance, has been concerned with the writing out of black women from much of "white" feminism, raising such unaddressed issues as the semiotics (and politics) of the "black female body" in the patriarchal structures of American late-capitalist society. Furthermore, given the history of slavery and the continuing deprivation and oppression of the African-American community as a whole, the critique of patriarchal family structures and of male-female relations has taken a different form, and has had a different significance, for African-American women than it has for feminists "located" in white American society. And so important a feminist project as the demonstration that public and private forms of violence to the "female body" are inextricably linked and interdependent has come to have a different significance in the work of Third World feminists protesting the transnational dumping of reproductive technologies, exposing often opposing practices toward women in accordance with their national and racial positioning.

Within the academy, a major concern over the last decade has been the institutionalized marginalization within women's studies programs of feminist work that seeks to undo or to go beyond the universalizing discourse of "women's issues." The point here is not to suggest "women of color" as a uniform and univocal foil to the subject of "white" or mainstream feminism. On the contrary, this formulation of feminism(s) as "situated knowledge" (Donna Haraway) has also led to a concern with the contradictions between the positionings of diverse women of color themselves. In institutional terms, for example, the relative ease with which some women of recent Third World origin have been accepted in the academy, in sharp contrast to the long history of struggle behind the still minuscule Native American, African-American, and Chicana presence, is itself a significant fact, and one that cannot be papered over in the process of building a coalitionary feminist politics. Issues of location and coalition have thus become central in Third World and minority feminist critique. Focusing on these entangled questions of race, class, gender, and sexuality, the essays in part III look at the overlapping and contradictory worlds inhabited by women, given the multiple sites of power within and between communities. Therefore, despite their differences of location, the essays share a preoccupation with the social positionings of women and with their distinct historical experiences as important elements in the formation of coalitionary politics.

A concern with the politics and anxiety of location also marks the debates about the meaning of "postcoloniality" as such. In fact, much of "postcolonial theory" can be seen as an attempt to come to terms with its own location, to a large extent, in the First World academy. As we have already noted, the wider historical context for this location is the relatively recent middle-class and professional immigration to the West from the (broadly conceived) Third World, one of the strands in the global movements of people that characterize contemporary capitalism. And this immigration, together with greater (though highly uneven) access of racial "minorities" to cultural and educational institutions, also provides part of the context in which contemporary forms of multiculturalism should be understood. It should therefore not be surprising that the migrant as social type figures prominently in so much contemporary criticism, as subject and object of critical practice and as metaphor for the displacements, the terrors, the stubborn survivals that characterize social life under late capitalism. For, in the figure of the migrant, home, that place and time outside place and time, appears to mingle promiscuously with its opposite — exile, the outside, elsewhere. Hence its attraction for a critical practice that seeks to undo such binaries as belonging/unbelonging, loyalty/disloyalty, to unpack their ideological baggage, to make visible the multifarious ways in which they participate in the production of social relations as second nature. And perhaps we get a glimpse here of the double bind within which criticism is practiced today in a context where "home" is both a myth of belonging and the name of a state that criticism cannot avoid wanting to inhabit.

Some of the debate about the emergence of postcolonial criticism has centered around its relationship to French poststructuralist thought, in particular the Foucauldian theme of the power/knowledge nexus in discursive formations and the deconstructionist critique of representation.[12] This relationship has been extensively commented upon by proponents and critics alike (Appiah, Diawara, Dirlik, Prakash). As the great bulk of the essays collected in this volume testify, the thrust of postcolonial criticism has come, first, from its reading of the colonial archive *as* archive, a reading that seeks to displace the latter's (epistemological, political, ethical) author-ity.[13] The colonial appears from this reading as a figure of difference and hybridity, implying that apprehension of modernity in its colonial mediation necessitates com-plicating the "universal" narratives of the march of progress, reason, capital. Second, theoretical elaboration of "the postcolonial" has implied deconstruction of the na-tionalist claim — "the-people-as-one" — as a double structure of representation that fuses together the semiotic and the political, erasing any sign and memory of its own production. In this sense, the cluster of concerns denoted by "the postcolonial," and the *position(s)* they collectively signify, may perhaps be thought of as also post-nationalist, or, more precisely, "post–Third Worldist,"[14] as coming after the decline of Third World nationalism and after the erosion of the transparency of its claims.

Both these aspects of postcolonial criticism — its figuring of the colonial as a dis-ruption of the post-Enlightenment "grand narratives" and its self-distancing from the procedures and positions of high nationalism — figure centrally in what is perhaps its defining tension, sometimes latent and sometimes explicitly theorized, namely, its relationship to the legacy of Marxist thought and practice. The mutual links, influences, and overlaps between Marxism, on the one hand, and Third World na-tionalism (including within the First World), on the other, are both numerous and well known. From the revolutionary uprisings in China and Vietnam to the na-tionalist movement in India under largely bourgeois leadership, local histories of struggle against imperialism were deeply marked by the vocabulary and the prac-tices of Marxist politics. A great number of later attempts to disengage from imperial domination — Cuba, Angola, Mozambique, and Nicaragua come immediately to mind — are perhaps unimaginable without the sustained material and moral support of the Soviet Union and the COMECON countries. And no matter how one con-strues a postwar pantheon of nationalist *thinkers* — Mao, Nehru, Du Bois, James, Guevara, Fanon, Cabral, to name a few — it is difficult to examine their positions without engaging their appropriation of Marxist traditions of social critique and analysis.

It is this legacy that follows postcolonial criticism wherever it goes in its reexam-ination of the colonial encounter and of the contradictions of contemporary global realities. If our critical practices are to remain critical, that is, if they are to continue to intervene in ways that reveal them as produced, and hence as malleable, they cannot opt for strategies that seek merely to paper over or exorcise this legacy, a common feature of many varieties of poststructuralist criticism in the Euro-American setting. Oppositional criticism today must engage in a sustained evaluation of its relationship to Marxist analysis and to Marxism's deep history of involvement in anti-colonial and antiracist struggles at diverse locations around the globe. At the same time, the struggles of indigenous peoples force us also to reexamine the alliance between Marxism and Third World nationalism vis-à-vis indigenous, "fourth world" peoples, whose subsistence economies have formed a structuring absence in that alliance, one that masked the possibility of an indigenous critique both of the First World's colonial relation to Native Americans and of similar practices performed by the Third World postindependent nation-state. Some Native American critics have even argued that Marxism and capitalism share a productivist ideology of modern-ization in relation to work, land, and time. These critics thus lay the foundations for egalitarian social models that challenge the Third Worldist marriage between Marxism and nationalism.[15]

Such indeed is the thrust of several of the final set of essays in this volume, and they may perhaps be thought of as postcolonial criticism in its self-reflective mode. This is not to suggest that the rest of the writings in the volume lack such self-reflection; it is merely to note that this last group focuses in a more sustained theoretical fashion upon, and raises questions about, "the postcolonial" as perspective, historical moment, and mode of cultural criticism. What are the (varied) chronologies of the postcolonial? How are they linked to actual histories of decolonization and to feminist resistance to domination in different parts of the world? What is the relationship of contemporary criticism to the ideologies institutionalized in the post-independent nation-state? What political, ethical, and *epistemological* consequences follow from the critic's interpellation as gendered citizen of a "sovereign" nation-state rather than as colonial subject? What are the costs in political and ethical terms for a critical practice that is produced for the most part at the institutional site of the First World academy? In what ways can Marxist analyses of class be extended to account for "post-Fordist" productive relations and the specific place of women workers within them? Given its critique of "representation," in the double sense of the word, through what gestures of accountability does a "decolonizing" feminism gain the right to represent the struggles of the gendered subaltern? What kinds of communities of interpretation and praxis must we strive to imagine in this era of unprecedented globalizations (Bhabha, Trinh)? Can "home" be refashioned by criticism, and by cultural production as a whole, once its violent and exclusionary function vis-à-vis women and other "minorities" stands so unnervingly exposed? Such questions among others animate the essays presented here, and they represent the ongoing self-examination of emerging forms of criticism, attempts at rethinking the relationship of criticism to intellectual and political history, at formulating conceptual frameworks with greater precision, and at remaining alert to the dangers of losing the critical edge that is criticism's vocation.

It is in this spirit that we conceived the title of this volume, *Dangerous Liaisons.* In a world overwhelmingly linked by transnational capital and global media, this volume is far from celebrating a global village where we are all connected. The dangerous links made by diverse transnational capitalist corporations have not exactly created a stability of "at home in the world" for the global transnational workers — Filipina migrant maids, Guatemalan refugee farm laborers, Chinese illegal-immigrant sweatshop workers — displaced not only within the borders of the nation-state but also across them to the United States, the Gulf States, and Western Europe. They have not simply brought an equal mobilization of capital, of internationalization of trade, of ecological questions, and of information technologies and cultural production between nation-states, let alone between those on the margins of the nation-states (Spivak). They have, however, brought a complex realignment of social forces that engender an intense global-political, economic, and cultural interdependency. The term "dangerous liaisons" also refers, for us, to the evolving complicity between imperial and national elite interests and around diverse forms of class and gender. The UN Women's Conference in Beijing was an important site even for critical feminists in the effort to define agendas and make links vis-à-vis the collusion between diverse worldwide patriarchal and homophobic institutions. Multicultural and transnational critical coalitions can be empowering, envisioning discursive frameworks beyond the nation-state framework to chart the linked analogies between the experiences of marginalized communities as well as the possibility of allied resistant practices. On another level, our title embodies the reflexive thrust of a volume that attempts to link previously isolated areas of critical analysis between U.S. multicultural debates and colonial discourse outside the United States, between gender/sexuality and the nation, and between ethnic studies and postcolonial studies. Liaisons indeed can be dangerous when used by the critic as imaginary homes that transcend the boundaries separating segregated disciplines, discourses, and communities of identification and mobilization.

NOTES

1. L. Frank Baum, the author of *The Wizard of Oz*, even casually recommended genocide in 1891: "The best safety of the frontier settlements will be secured by the total annihilation of the few remaining Indians. Why not annihilation? . . . [B]etter that they should die than live the miserable wretches that they are" (quoted in David E. Stannard, *The American Holocaust: Columbus and the Conquest of the New World* [New York: Oxford University Press, 1992], 126).

2. Rather than the complete positive reading of displacement that Rushdie seems to offer, we are using the *Wizard of Oz* narrative in a more critical sense.

3. Andrew Ross, ed., *Universal Abandon? The Politics of Postmodernism* (Minneapolis: University of Minnesota Press, 1989).

4. For an account and analysis of the role of "displacement" in contemporary criticism, see Caren Kaplan's *Questions of Travel: Postmodern Discourses of Displacement* (Durham, N.C.: Duke University Press, 1996).

5. Frantz Fanon, "On National Culture," in *The Wretched of the Earth* (New York: Grove Press, 1979), 225–27.

6. The debate that largely began in the pages of *Social Text* has now gained serious momentum. See Ella Shohat, "Notes on the 'Post-colonial'"; Anne McClintock, "The Angel of Progress," both in *Social Text* 31/32 (1992); *Public Culture* 5 (fall 1992) and *Calaloo* 16, no. 4 (1993), both special issues devoted to the subject of postcolonialism; Ruth Frankenberg and Lata Mani, "Crosscurrents, Crosstalk," *Cultural Studies* 7, no. 2 (1993); Inderpal Grewal, "The Postcolonial, Ethnic Studies, and the Diaspora," *Socialist Review* 24, no. 4 (1994); Anne Ducille, "Postcolonialism and Afrocentricity," in *The Black Columbus,* ed. Werner Sollors and Maria Diedrich (Cambridge, Mass.: Harvard University Press, 1994).

7. Abdul R. JanMohamed and David Lloyd, "Introduction: Toward a Theory of Minority Discourse: What Is to Be Done?" in JanMohamed and Lloyd, eds., *The Nature and Context of Minority Discourse* (New York: Oxford University Press, 1990), 8.

8. Robert J. S. Ross and Kent C. Trachte, *Global Capitalism: The New Leviathan* (Albany: State University of New York Press, 1990). Also see Arjun Appadurai, "Global Ethnoscapes," in Richard Fox, ed., *Recapturing Anthropology* (Seattle: University of Washington Press, 1991).

9. See Arjun Appadurai, "Disjuncture and Difference in the Global Cultural Economy," *Public Culture* 2, no. 2 (1990); Inderpal Grewal and Caren Kaplan, "Introduction: Transnational Feminist Practices and Questions of Postmodernity," in Grewal and Kaplan, eds., *Scattered Hegemonies: Postmodernity and Transnational Feminist Practices* (Minneapolis: University of Minnesota Press, 1994).

10. See Shohat, "Notes on the 'Post-colonial,'" esp. 108–11.

11. See Chandra Talpade Mohanty and Biddy Martin, "Feminist Politics: What's Home Got to Do with It?" in Teresa de Lauretis, ed., *Feminist Studies/Critical Studies* (Bloomington: Indiana University Press, 1986), esp. 192.

12. For a discussion of these intersections, see Robert Young, *White Mythologies: Writing History and the West* (London: Routledge, 1990).

13. The pioneering text in this regard is of course Edward Said's *Orientalism* (New York: Vintage, 1978).

14. The term "post–Third Worldism," as proposed elsewhere by Ella Shohat, assumes the fundamental validity of the anticolonial movement but also interrogates the fissures that rend the Third World

nation, fissures having to do with gender, religion, class, race, and sexuality. Thus "post–Third Worldism" points to a move beyond the ideology of Third Worldism. Whereas the term "postcolonial" can ambiguously imply a movement both beyond anticolonial nationalist ideology *and* beyond a specific moment of colonial history, "post–Third Worldism" conveys a movement beyond a specific ideology, that is, Third Worldist nationalism. See Ella Shohat and Robert Stam's *Unthinking Eurocentrism: Multiculturalism and the Media* (New York: Routledge, 1994); and Ella Shohat, "Post–Third Worldist Culture: Gender, Nation, and the Cinema," in M. Jacqui Alexander and Chandra Talpade Mohanty, eds., *Feminist Genealogies, Colonial Legacies, Democratic Futures* (New York: Routledge, 1996).

15. See Ward Churchill, ed., *Marxism and Native Americans* (Boston: South End Press, 1984).

Part I

Contesting Nations

Chapter 1
Zionism from the Standpoint of Its Victims
Edward W. Said

All rulers are the heirs of those who conquered before them. Hence, empathy with the victor invariably benefits the ruler. Historical materialists know what that means.
Walter Benjamin, "Theses on the Philosophy of History"

The starting point of critical elaboration is the consciousness of what one really is, and is "knowing thyself" as a product of the historical process to date which has deposited in you an infinity of traces, without leaving an inventory. It is important therefore to make an inventory.
Antonio Gramsci, *Prison Notebooks*

Zionism and the Attitudes of European Colonialism

Every idea or system of ideas exists *somewhere;* it is mixed in with historical circumstances; it is part of what one may very simply call "reality." One of the enduring attributes of self-serving idealism, however, is the notion that ideas are just ideas and that they exist only in the realm of ideas. The tendency to view ideas as pertaining only to a world of abstractions increases among people for whom an idea is essentially perfect, good, uncontaminated by human desires or will. Such a view also applies when the ideas are evil, absolutely perfect in their evil, and so forth. When an idea has become effective — that is, when its value has been proved in reality by its widespread acceptance — of course some revision of it will seem to be necessary, since the idea must be viewed as having taken on some of the characteristics of brute reality. Thus it is frequently argued that such an idea as Zionism, for all its political tribulations and the struggles on its behalf, is at bottom a *constant* idea that expresses the yearning for Jewish political and religious self-determination — for Jewish national selfhood — to be exercised on the promised land. Because Zionism seems to have culminated in the creation of the state of Israel, it is also argued that the historical realization of the idea confirms its unchanging essence and, no less important, the means used for its realization. Very little is said about what Zionism entailed for non-Jews who happened to have encountered it; for that matter nothing is said about where outside Jewish history it took place and from what in the historical context of nineteenth-century Europe it drew its force. To the Palestinian, for

15

whom Zionism was somebody else's idea imported into Palestine and for which in a very concrete way he or she was made to pay and suffer, these forgotten things about Zionism are the very things that are centrally important.

In short, effective political ideas like Zionism need to be examined historically in two ways: (1) *genealogically,* in order that their provenance, their kinship and descent, their affiliation both with other ideas and with political institutions may be demonstrated; and (2) as practical systems for *accumulation* (of power, land, ideological legitimacy) and *displacement* (of people, other ideas, prior legitimacy). Present political and cultural actualities make such an examination extraordinarily difficult, as much because Zionism in the advanced capitalist West has acquired for itself an almost unchallenged hegemony in liberal "establishment" discourse as because in keeping with one of its central ideological characteristics Zionism had hidden, or caused to disappear, the literal historical ground of its growth, its political cost to the native inhabitants of Palestine, and its militantly oppressive discriminations between Jews and non-Jews.

Consider as a startling instance of what I mean, the symbolism of a former head of the Irgun terror gang, in whose autobiography there are numerous admissions of cold-blooded murder of Arab civilians,[1] being honored as Israeli premier at Northwestern University in May 1978 with a doctorate of laws *honoris causa,* a leader whose army a scant month before had created five hundred thousand new refugees in South Lebanon, who spoke constantly of "Judea and Samaria" as "rightful" parts of the Jewish state (claims made on the basis of the Old Testament and without so much as a reference to the land's actual inhabitants): and all this — on the part of the press or the so-called intellectual community — without one sign of comprehension that Menachem Begin's honored position came about literally at the expense of Palestinian Arab silence in the Western "marketplace of ideas," that the entire historical duration of a Jewish state in Palestine prior to 1948 was a sixty-year period two millennia ago, that the dispersion of the Palestinians was not a fact of nature but a result of specific force and strategies. The concealment by Zionism of its own history has by now therefore become institutionalized, and not only in Israel. To bring out its history as in a sense it was exacted from Palestine and the Palestinians, these victims on whose suppression Zionism and Israel have depended, is thus a specific intellectual/political task and an important part of the worldwide struggle against imperialism, against the techniques of secrecy and domination, against ahistorical rhetoric, and (in the United States at least) against liberal hegemony.[2]

The special, one might even call it the privileged, place of the United States in this struggle is impressive — for all sorts of reasons. In no other country, except Israel, is Zionism enshrined as an unquestioned good, and in no other country (also the world's leading imperialist power) is there so strong a conjuncture of powerful institutions and interests — the press, the liberal intelligentsia, the military-industrial complex, the academic community, labor unions — for whom uncritical support of Israel and Zionism enhances their domestic as well as international standing. Although there has recently been some modulation in this remarkable consensus — due to the influence of Arab oil, the emergence of countervailing Muslim right-wing states allied to the United States (Iran, Saudi Arabia, Egypt), and the redoubtable political and military visibility of the Palestinian people and their representative, the

PLO — the prevailing pro-Israeli bias persists. For not only does it have deep cultural roots in the West generally, and the United States in particular, but its *negative, interdictory* character vis-à-vis the *whole* historical reality is systematic. Both these things require brief exposition here, at least enough for us to grasp the true political meaning of a critical analysis of Zionism in the present circumstances.

Consider now the two attributes, one affirmative, the other negative and interdictory, that give Zionism its unique, almost unchallenged cultural force here. One is a long-standing commitment by Zionism, as an essentially Western ideology, to presenting itself to the world as legitimate, to legitimizing itself *internationally*. Everything the Zionists did in Palestine they did, of course, as settler-colonialists; yet everything they did in Palestine was enacted on the world stage, so to speak, in a rhetoric and costume fundamentally of the same sort as the cultural currency of the period. Thus Zionism initially portrayed itself as a movement bringing civilization to a barbaric and/or empty locale, and indeed from 1880 to 1918 the movement marketed itself to the Ottoman and British Empires as advancing their schemes for Palestine. Later, of course, Zionism transformed itself into a movement bringing Western democracy to the East, so much so that by the 1940s and 1950s major figures in the United States who had no particular connection with Middle Eastern politics — men and women like Reinhold Niebuhr, Edmund Wilson, and Eleanor Roosevelt[3] — could speak on behalf of Zionism and its *mission civilisatrice* with a sort of natural affirmation. The centrality of Zionism to the American experience, and not only because there existed in the United States a highly politicized Jewish community, became practically a fact of nature. Moreover, Zionism was a movement for acquiring land in the Orient during a period when in only one century (1815–1918) Europe's overseas territorial acquisitions increased from 35 percent to 85 percent of the earth's land.

The second proposition about Zionism is best derived, I think, from a remark made by Lord Balfour in 1919. As the author of the Balfour Declaration he found himself frequently reiterating his attitude toward Zionism:

> The contradiction between the Letter of the Covenant [the Anglo-French Declaration of 1918 promising the Arabs of former Ottoman colonies, including Palestine, that as a reward for supporting the Allies they would have their independence] is even more flagrant in the case of the independent nation of Palestine than in that of the independent nation of Syria. For in Palestine we do not propose even to go through the form of consulting the wishes of the present inhabitants of the country, though the American Commission has been going through the form of asking what they are. The four great powers are committed to Zionism and Zionism, be it right or wrong, good or bad, is rooted in age-long tradition, in present needs, in future hopes, of far profounder import than the desires and prejudices of the 700,000 Arabs who now inhabit that ancient land. In my opinion that is right.[4]

The difference between what Balfour considered to be important and what he dismissed as unimportant is accounted for by a complex network of values, power relations, and epistemological perspectives: on the one hand, there are superior Europeans, on the other, natives, inferior Orientals. Later in this essay I discuss this difference in some detail, and in a recent book I treat its considerable history at great length. Here I want only to comment on its consequences for any history of the subsequent conflict between native Palestinians and the Zionist colonists. Despite the Arab majority, both the Zionists and the British took as their point of departure the cultural judgment that the Arab Palestinians need not be heard from, and, indeed, as I show a little later, the Zionists set out systematically either to reduce the Palestinians to a nonexistent population or to strip down those who remained to the status of a silent coolie class.

The sheer mechanics of the process by which Zionism caused land and demographic alienation in Palestine requires study on its own, which is why in this essay I treat it as an autonomous subject. Nevertheless, such a subject is neither a fragment of antiquarian history nor a chapter in the by now familiar story of how the Third World has been exploited by Europe. In the case of Zionism and the Palestinians any attempt in the United States to give the Palestinian case some material substance — if only by writing about it — has to be seen as a concrete part of the struggle against Zionism, racism, and imperialism. For in essence Zionism and its partisans, because they command the resources of diffusion and representation in the West, have in the West effaced the Palestinian, his or her history, his or her actuality. Take as a simple instance of this effacement the fact that there exists in the United States not a single book on the Palestinians by a Palestinian. Articles appear from time to time in the press, but the accumulation, consideration, and gravity a text/book, as well as the vital testimonial sense of human struggle against oppression, are kept from the Palestinian case. Even the book from which this essay of mine is excerpted has been refused by the publisher who originally contracted for it, mainly because there is a consensus that except as nuisances, terrorists, or anonymous refugees, the Palestinians do not exist, have no history politically.

Therefore a historical study such as this must set out consciously and deliberately not only to provide the Palestinian history suppressed programmatically by Zionism and the liberal imperialism of the West but also, as an integral part of this counter-memory, to make available to Western radicals a counterarchive of material about settler-colonialism. The very fact that I *can* write and speak as a Palestinian, in however limited a way, is a sign that imperialist hegemony is at last beginning to be challenged. To put what Marx called the weapons of criticism to use in this way is also to narrow the distance between the luxuries of academic discourse and the processes of political struggle. Even the assertion of Palestinian identity therefore takes on the form of a political challenge, since in Israel Palestinians are identified formally only as "non-Jews," and elsewhere their existence is either doubted or considered to be disruptive.[5]

Yet there is no getting around the formidable historical reality that in writing about the Palestinian struggle against Zionist settler-colonialism one also abuts the entire disastrous problem of anti-Semitism, on the one hand, and, on the other, the complex interrelationship between the Palestinians and the Arab states. The task of criticism or — to put it in another way — the role of the critical consciousness is in such cases to be able to make distinctions, to produce differences where at present there are none. To oppose Zionism in Palestine has never meant, and does not now mean, being anti-Semitic; conversely, the struggle for Palestinian rights and self-determination does not mean support for the Saudi royal family, nor for the antiquated and oppressive state structure of most of the Arab nations.

One must admit, however, that all liberals, and even most "radicals," have been unable to overcome the Zionist maneuver of equating anti-Zionism with anti-Semitism. Any well-meaning person can thus oppose South African or American racism and tacitly support Zionist racial presentation of non-Jews in Palestine. The almost total absence of any handily available historical knowledge from non-Zionist sources, the dissemination by the media of malicious simplifications (e.g., Jews versus Arabs), the cynical opportunism of various Zionist pressure groups, the tendency endemic to university intellectuals uncritically to repeat cant phrases and political clichés (this is the role Gramsci assigned to traditional intellectuals, that of being "experts in legitimation"), the fear of treading upon the highly volatile terrain of what Jews did, in an age of genocidal extermination of Jews: all this contributes to the dulling, regulated enforcement of almost unanimous support for Israel. But, as I. F. Stone recently noted, this unanimity exceeds even the Zionism of most Israelis.

On the other hand, it would be totally unjust to neglect the power of Zionism as an idea for Jews or to minimize the complex internal debates characterizing Zionism, its true meaning, its messianic destiny, and so on. Even to speak about this subject, much less than attempting to "define" Zionism, is for an Arab quite a difficult matter. Let me use myself as an example. Most of my education, and certainly all my basic intellectual formation, are Western; in what I have read, in what I write about, even in what I do politically, I am profoundly influenced by mainstream Western attitudes toward the history of the Jews, anti-Semitism, the destruction of European Jewry. I have been directly exposed to those aspects of Jewish history and experience that have mattered singularly for Jews and for Western non-Jews reading and thinking about Jewish history. I know as well as any educated non-Jew can know, what anti-Semitism has meant for the Jews, especially in this century. Consequently I can understand the intertwined terror and the exultation out of which Zionism has been nourished, and I think I can at least grasp the meaning of Israel for Jews and even for the enlightened Western liberal. And yet, because I am an Arab Palestinian, I can also see and feel other things — and it is these that complicate matters considerably, that cause me also to focus on Zionism's *other* aspects. The result is, I think, worth describing, not because what I think is so crucial, but because it is useful to see the same phenomenon in two complementary ways, not normally associated with each other.

One can begin with a literary example, George Eliot's last novel, *Daniel Deronda* (1876). The unusual thing about the book is that its main subject is Zionism, although the novel's principle themes are recognizable to anyone who has read Eliot's earlier fiction. Seen in the context of Eliot's general interest in idealism and spiritual yearning, Zionism for her was one in a series of worldly projects for the nineteenth-century mind still committed to hopes for a secular religious community. In her earlier books Eliot had studied a variety of enthusiasms, all of them replacements for organized religion, all of them attractive to persons who would have been St. Teresas had they lived during a period of coherent faith. The reference to St. Teresa was originally made by Eliot in *Middlemarch;* in using it to describe the novel's heroine, Dorothea Brooke, Eliot intended to compliment her on her visionary and moral energy sustained despite the absence in the modern world of certain assurances for faith and knowledge. Dorothea emerges at the end of *Middlemarch* as a chastened woman, forced to concede her grand visions of a "fulfilled" life in return for a relatively modest domestic success as a wife and mother. It is this considerably diminished view of things that *Daniel Deronda,* and Zionism in particular, revise upward: toward a genuinely hopeful socioreligious project in which individual energies can be merged and identified with a collective national vision, the whole emanating out of Judaism.

The novel's plot alternates between the presentation of a bitter comedy of manners involving a surprisingly rootless segment of the British upper bourgeoisie, and the gradual revelation to Daniel Deronda — an exotic young man whose parentage is unknown but who is the ward of Sir Hugo Mallinger — of his Jewish identity and, when he becomes the spiritual disciple of Mordecai Ezra Cohen, his Jewish destiny. At the end of the novel Daniel marries Mirah, Mordecai's sister, and commits himself to fulfilling Mordecai's hopes for the future of the Jews. Mordecai dies as the young pair gets married, although it is clear well before his death that his Zionist ideas have been passed on to Daniel, so much so that among the newlyweds' "splendid wedding-gifts" is "a complete equipment for Eastern travel" provided by Sir Hugo and Lady Mallinger. For Daniel and his wife will be traveling to Palestine, presumably to set the great Zionist plan in motion.

The crucial thing about the way Zionism is presented in the novel is that its backdrop is a generalized condition of homelessness. Not only the Jews but even the wellborn Englishmen and women in the novel are portrayed as wandering and alienated beings. If the novel's poorer English people (e.g., Mrs. Davilow and her daughters) seem always to be moving from one rented house to another, the wealthy aristocrats are no less cut off from some permanent home. Thus Eliot uses the plight of Jews to make a universal statement about the nineteenth century's need for a home, given the spiritual and psychological rootlessness reflected in her characters' almost ontological physical restlessness. Her interest in Zionism therefore can be traced to the reflection, made early in the novel, that

> a human life, I think, should be well rooted in some spot of a native land, where it may get the love of tender kinship for the face of the earth, for the labours men go forth to, for the sounds and accents that haunt it, for whatever will give that early home a familiar unmistakable difference amidst the future widening of knowledge.[6]

To find the "early home" means to find the place where originally one was *at home,* a task to be undertaken more or less interchangeably by individuals and by a "people." It becomes historically appropriate therefore that those individuals and that "people" best suited to the task are Jews. Only the Jews as a people (and consequently as individuals) have retained both a sense of their original home in Zion and an acute, always contemporary, feeling of loss. Despite the prevalence of anti-Semitism, the Jews are a reproach to the Gentiles who have long since forsaken the "observance" of any civilizing communal belief. Thus Mordecai puts these sentiments positively as a definite program for today's Jews:

> They [the Gentiles] scorn our people's ignorant observance; but the most accursed ignorance is that which has no observance — sunk to the cunning greed of the fox, to which all law is no more than a trap or the cry of the worrying hound. There is a degradation deep down below the memory that has withered into superstition. In

the multitudes of the ignorant on three continents who observe our rites and make the confession of the divine Unity, the soul of Judaism is not dead. Revive the organic centre: let the unity of Israel which has made the growth and form of its religion be an outward reality. Looking towards a land and a polity, our dispersed people in all the ends of the earth may share the dignity of a national life which has a voice among the peoples of the East and the West — which will plant the wisdom and skill of our race so that it may be, as of old, a medium of transmission and understanding. Let that come to pass, and the living warmth will spread to the weak extremities of Israel, and superstition will vanish, not in the lawlessness of the renegade, ... but in the illumination of great facts which widen feeling and make all knowledge alive as the young offspring of beloved memories.[7]

"The illumination of great facts which widen feeling" is a typical phrase for Eliot, and there is no doubt that her approbation for her Zionists derives from her belief that they were a group almost exactly expressing her own grand ideas about an expanded life of feelings. Yet if there is a felt reality about "the peoples of the West," there is no such reality for the "peoples of the East." They are named, it is true, but are no more substantial than a phrase. The few references to the East in *Daniel Deronda* are always to England's Indian colonies, for whose people — as people having wishes, values, aspirations — Eliot expresses the complete indifference of absolute silence. Of the fact that Zion will be "planted" in the East, Eliot takes no very detailed account; it is as if the phrase "the peoples of the East and the West" covers what will, territorially at least, be a neutral inaugural reality. In turn that reality will be replaced by a permanent accomplishment when the newly founded state becomes the "medium of transmission and understanding." For how could Eliot imagine that even Eastern peoples would object to such grand benefits for all?

There is, however, a disturbing insistence on these matters when Mordecai continues his speech. For him Zionism means that "our race takes on again the character of a nationality, ... a labour which shall be a worthy fruit of the long anguish whereby our fathers maintained their separateness, refusing the ease of falsehood." Zionism is to be a dramatic lesson for humankind. But what ought to catch the reader's attention about the way Mordecai illustrates his thesis is his depiction of the land:

[The Jews] have wealth enough *to redeem the soil from debauched and paupered conquerors;* they have the skill of the statesman to devise, the tongue of the orator to persuade. And is there no prophet or poet among us to make the ears of Christian Europe tingle with shame at the hideous obloquy of Christian strife *which the Turk gazes at* [the reference here is to the long history of European disputes about the Holy Land] *as at the fighting of beasts to which he has lent an arena?* There is a store of wisdom among us *to found a new Jewish polity, grand, simple, just like the old* — a republic where there is equality of protection, an equality which shone like a star on the forehead of our ancient community, *and gave it more than the brightness of Western freedom amid the despotisms of the East.* Then our race shall have an organic centre, a heart and brain to watch and guide and execute; *the outraged Jew shall have a defence in the court of nations,* as the outraged Englishman or American. And the world will gain as Israel gains. For there will be a community in the van of the East which carries the culture and the sympathies of every great nation in its bosom; *there will be a land set for a halting-place of enmities, a neutral ground for the East as Belgium is for the West.* Difficulties? I know there are difficulties. But let the spirit of sublime achievement move in the grate among our people, and the work will begin. (emphases added)[8]

The land itself is characterized in two separate ways. On the one hand, it is associated with debauched and paupered conquerors, an arena lent by the Turk to fighting beasts, a part of the despotic East; on the other, with "the brightness of Western freedom," with nations like England and America, with the idea of neutrality (Belgium). In short, with a degraded and unworthy East and with a noble, enlightened West. The bridge between those warring representatives of East and West will be Zionism.

Interestingly, Eliot cannot sustain her admiration of Zionism except by seeing it as a method for transforming the East into the West. This is not to say that she does not have sympathy for Zionism and for the Jews themselves: she obviously does. But there is a whole area of Jewish experience, lying somewhere between longing for a homeland (which everyone, including the Gentile, feels) and actually getting it, that she is dim about. Otherwise she is quite capable of seeing that Zionism can easily be accommodated to several varieties of Western (as opposed to Eastern) thought, principal among them the idea that the East is degraded, that it needs reconstruction according to enlightened Western notions about politics, that any reconstructed portion of the East can with small reservations become as "English as England" to its new inhabitants. Underlying all this, however, is the total absence of any thought about the actual inhabitants of the East, Palestine in particular. They are irrelevant both to the Zionists in *Daniel Deronda* and to the English characters. Brightness, freedom, and redemption — key matters for Eliot — are to be restricted to Europeans and the Jews, who are themselves European prototypes so far as colonizing the East is concerned. There is a remarkable failure when it comes to taking anything non-European into consideration, although curiously all of Eliot's descriptions of Jews stress their exotic, "Eastern" aspects. Humanity and sympathy it seems are not endowments of anything but an Occidental mentality; to look for them in the despotic East, much less find them, is to waste one's time.

Two points need to be made immediately. One is that Eliot is no different from other European apostles of sympathy, humanity, and understanding for whom noble sentiments were either left behind in Europe or made programmatically inapplicable outside Europe. There are the chastening examples of John Stuart Mill and Karl Marx (both of whom I have discussed in my *Orientalism*),[9] two thinkers known doctrinally to be opponents of injustice and oppression. Yet both of them seemed to have believed that such ideas as liberty, representative government, and individual happiness must not be applied in the Orient for reasons that today we would call racist. The fact is that nineteenth-century European culture was racist with a greater or lesser degree of virulence depending on the individual: Ernest Renan, for instance, was an outright anti-Semite; Eliot was indifferent to races who could not be assimilated to European ideas.

Here we come to the second point. Eliot's account of Zionism in *Daniel Deronda* was intended as a sort of assenting Gentile response to prevalent Jewish-Zionist currents; the novel therefore serves as an indication of how much in Zionism was legitimated and indeed valorized by Gentile European thought. On one important issue there was complete agreement between the Gentile and Jewish versions of Zionism: their view of the Holy Land as essentially empty of inhabitants, not because there were no inhabitants — there were, and they were frequently described in numerous travel accounts, in novels like Disraeli's *Tancred,* even in the various nineteenth-century Baedekers — but because their status as sovereign and human inhabitants was systematically denied. While it may be possible to differentiate between Jewish and Gentile Zionists on this point (they ignored the Arab inhabitants for different reasons), the Palestinian Arab was ignored nevertheless. That is what needs emphasis, the extent to which the roots of Jewish *and* Gentile Zionism are in the culture of high capitalism and how the work of its liberals, like George Eliot, reinforced, perhaps also completed, that culture's less attractive tendencies.

None of what I have so far said applies adequately to what Zionism meant for Jews or what it represented as an advanced idea for enthusiastic non-Jews; it applies exclusively to those less fortunate beings who happened to be living on the land, people of whom no notice was taken. What has too long been forgotten is that while important European thinkers considered the desirable and later the probable fate of Palestine, the land was being tilled and villages and towns were being built and lived in by thousands of natives who, for want of knowing better, believed that it was *their* homeland. In the meantime their actual physical being was ignored; later it became a troublesome detail. Strikingly, therefore, Eliot sounds very much like Moses Hess, an important figure in the development of Marx's own early thought, who in his *Rome and Jerusalem* (1862) uses the same theoretical language to be given to Mordecai:

> What we have to do at present for the regeneration of the Jewish nation is, first, to keep alive the hope of the political rebirth of our people, and, next, to reawaken that hope where it slumbers. When political conditions in the Orient shape themselves so as to permit the organization of a beginning of the restoration of the Jewish state, this beginning will express itself in the founding of Jewish colonies in the land of their ancestors, to which enterprise France will undoubtedly lend a hand. France, beloved friend, is the savior who will restore our people to its place in universal history. Just as we once searched in the West for a road to India, and incidentally discovered a new world, so will our lost fatherland be rediscovered on the road to India and China that is now being built in the Orient.[10]

Hess continues his paean to France (since every Zionist saw one or another of the imperial powers as patron) by quoting at some length from Ernest Laharanne's *The New Eastern Question,* from which Hess draws the following passage for his peroration:

> A great calling is reserved for the Jews: to be a living channel of communication between three continents. You shall be the bearers of civilization to peoples who are still inexperienced and their teachers in the European sciences, to which your race has contributed so much. You shall be the mediators between Europe and far Asia, opening the roads that lead to India and China — those unknown regions which must ultimately be thrown open to civilisation. You will come to the land of your fathers decorated with the crown of age-long martyrdom, and there, finally, you will be completely healed from all your ills! Your capital will again bring the wide stretches of barren land under cultivation; your labor and industry will once more turn the ancient soil into fruitful valleys, reclaiming it from the encroaching sands of the desert, and the world will again pay its homage to the oldest of peoples.[11]

Between them Hess and Eliot concur that Zionism is to be carried out by the Jews with the assistance of major European powers; that Zionism will restore "a lost fatherland," and in so doing mediate between the various civilizations; that present-day Palestine was in need of cultivation, civilization, reconstitution; that Zionism would finally bring enlightenment and progress where at present there was neither. The three ideas that depend on each other in Hess and Eliot — and later in almost every Zionist thinker or ideologist — are (1) the nonexistent Arab inhabitants, (2) the complementary Western-Jewish attitude to an "empty" territory, and (3) the restorative Zionist project, which would repeat by rebuilding a vanished Jewish State and combine it with modern elements like disciplined, separate colonies, a special agency for land acquisition, and so on. Of course none of these ideas would have any force were it not for the additional fact of their being addressed to, shaped for, and formed out of an *international* (i.e., non-Oriental, and hence European) context. This context was the reality, not only because of the ethnocentric rationale governing the whole project but also because of the overwhelming facts of Diaspora realities and imperialist hegemony over the entire gamut of European culture. It needs to be remarked, however, that Zionism (like the view held by the Puritans of America as an empty land) was a colonial vision unlike that of most other nineteenth-century European powers, for whom the natives of outlying territories were *included* in the redemptive *mission civilisatrice*.

From the earliest phases of its modern evolution until it culminated in the creation of Israel, Zionism appealed to a European audience for whom the classification of overseas territories and natives into various uneven classes was canonical and "natural." That is why, for example, every single state or movement in the formerly colonized territories of Africa and Asia today identifies with, fully supports, and understands the Palestinian struggle. In many instances — as I hope to show presently — there is an unmistakable coincidence between the experiences of Arab Palestinians at the hands of Zionism and the experiences of those black, yellow, and brown people who were described as inferior and subhuman by nineteenth-century imperialists. For although it coincided with an era of the most virulent Western anti-Semitism, Zionism also coincided, as I said above, with the period of unparalleled European territorial acquisition in Africa and Asia, and it was as part of this general movement of acquisition and occupation that Zionism was launched initially by Theodor Herzl. During the latter part of the greatest period in European colonial expansion, Zionism also made its crucial first moves along the way to getting what has now become a sizable Asiatic territory. And it is important to remember that in joining the general Western enthusiasm for overseas territorial acquisition, Zionism *never* spoke of itself unambiguously as a Jewish liberation movement, but rather as a Jewish movement for colonial settlement in the Orient. To those Palestinian victims that Zionism displaced, it *cannot have meant anything by way of sufficient cause* that Jews were victims of European anti-Semitism, and, given Israel's continued oppression of Palestinians, few Palestinians are able to see beyond their reality, namely, that Occidental Jews in Israel, once victims themselves, have become oppressors — of Palestinian Arabs and Oriental Jews.

These are not intended to be backward-looking historical observations, for in a very vital way they explain and even determine much of what now happens in the Middle East. The fact that no sizable segment of the Israeli population has as yet been able to confront the terrible social and political injustice done the native

Palestinians is an indication of how deeply ingrained are the (by now) anomalous imperialist perspectives basic to Zionism, its view of the world, its sense of an inferior native other. The fact also that no Palestinian, regardless of political stripe, has been able to reconcile him/herself to Zionism suggests the extent to which, for the Palestinian, Zionism has appeared to be an uncompromisingly exclusionary, discriminatory colonialist praxis. So powerful, and so unhesitatingly followed, has been the radical Zionist distinction between privileged Jews in Palestine and unprivileged non-Jews there, that nothing else has emerged; no perception of suffering human existence has escaped from the two camps created thereby. As a result it has been impossible for Jews to understand the human tragedy that Zionism has caused for the Arab Palestinians; and it has been impossible for Arab Palestinians to see in Zionism anything except an ideology and a practice keeping them, and Israeli Jews, imprisoned. But in order to break down the iron circle of inhumanity we must see how it was forged, and there it is ideas and culture itself that play the major role.

Consider Herzl. If it was the Dreyfus Affair that first brought him to Jewish consciousness, it was the idea of overseas colonial settlement for the Jews that came to him at roughly the same time as an antidote for anti-Semitism. The idea of overseas settlement itself was very current at the end of the nineteenth century, even as an idea for Jews. Herzl's first significant contact was Baron Maurice de Hirsch, a wealthy philanthropist who had for some time been behind the Jewish Colonization Association and its work in helping Eastern Jews to emigrate to Argentina and Brazil. Later Herzl thought generally about South America, then about Africa as places for establishing a Jewish colony. Both areas were widely acceptable as places for European colonialism, and that Herzl's mind followed along the orthodox imperialist track of his period is perhaps understandable. The impressive thing, however, is the degree to which Herzl had absorbed and internalized the imperialist perspective on "natives" and their "territory."[12]

There could have been no doubt whatever in Herzl's mind that Palestine in the late nineteenth century was peopled. True, it was under Ottoman administration (and therefore already a colony), but it had been the subject of numerous travel accounts, most of them very famous, by Lamartine, Chateaubriand, Flaubert, and so on. Yet even if he had not read these authors, Herzl as a journalist must surely have looked at a Baedeker to ascertain that Palestine was indeed inhabited by (in the 1880s) 650,000 mostly Arab people. This did not stop him from regarding their presence as manageable in ways that, in his diary, he spelled out with a rather chilling prescience for what later took place. The mass of poor natives were to be expropriated, and, he added, "both the expropriation and the removal of the poor must be carried out discreetly and circumspectly." This was to be done by "spirit[ing] the penniless population across the border by procuring employment for it in the transit countries, while denying it any employment in our own country." With uncannily accurate cynicism Herzl predicted that the small class of large landowners could be "had for a price" — as indeed they were. The whole scheme for displacing the native population of Palestine far outstripped any of the then-current plans for taking over vast reaches of Africa. As Desmond Stewart aptly says:

Herzl seems to have foreseen that in going further than any colonialist had so far gone in Africa, he would, temporarily, alienate civilised opinion. "At first, incidentally," he writes on the pages describing "involuntary expropriation," "people will avoid us. We are in bad odor. By the time the reshaping of world opinion in our favor has been completed, we shall be firmly established in our country, no longer fearing the influx of foreigners, and receiving our visitors with aristocratic benevolence and proud amiability."

This was not a prospect to charm a peon in Argentina or a fellah in Palestine. But Herzl did not intend his Diary for immediate publication.[13]

One need not wholly accept the conspiratorial tone of these comments (whether Herzl's or Stewart's) to grant that world opinion had not been, until the 1960s and 1970s, when the Palestinians forced their presence on world politics, concerned with the expropriation of Palestine. I said earlier that in this regard the major Zionist achievement was getting international legitimization for its own accomplishments, thereby making the Palestinian cost of these accomplishments seem to be irrelevant. But it is clear from Herzl's thinking that that could not have been done unless there was a prior European inclination to view the natives as irrelevant *to begin with*. That is, those natives already fit a more or less acceptable classificatory grid, which made them sui generis inferior to Western or white men — and it is this grid that a Zionist like Herzl appropriated, domesticating it from the general culture of his time to the unique needs of a developing Jewish nationalism. One needs to repeat that what in Zionism served the no doubt fully justified ends of Jewish tradition, saving the Jews as a people from homelessness and anti-Semitism and restoring them to nationhood, also collaborated with those aspects of the dominant Western culture (in which Zionism exclusively and institutionally lived) that made it possible for Europeans to view non-Europeans as inferior, marginal, and irrelevant. For the Palestinian Arab, therefore, it is the collaboration that has counted, not by any means the fulfillment of Jewish nationalism. The Arab has been on the receiving end not of benign Zionism — which has been restricted to Jews — but of an essentially discriminatory and powerful culture, of which Zionism has been the agent in Palestine.

What did the victims feel as they watched the Zionists arriving in Palestine? What do they think as they hear Zionism described today? Where do they look in Zionism's history to locate its roots, and the origins of its practices toward them? These are the questions that are never asked — and they are precisely the ones that I am trying to raise, as well as answer, here in this examination of the links between Zionism and European imperialism. My interest is in trying to record the effects of Zionism on its victims, and these effects can only be studied genealogically in the framework provided by imperialism, even during the nineteenth century when Zionism was still an idea and not a state called Israel. For the Palestinian now who tries critically to see what his or her history has meant, and who tries — as I am now trying — to see what Zionism has been for the Palestinians, Gramsci's observation is relevant: "[T]he consciousness of what one really is . . . is 'knowing thyself' as a product of the historical process to date which has deposited in you an infinity of traces, without leaving an inventory." The job of producing an inventory is a first necessity, Gramsci continued, and so it must be now, when the "inventory" of what Zionism's victims (*not* its beneficiaries) endured is rarely exposed to public view.[14]

Imperialism was and still is a political philosophy whose aim and purpose for being are territorial expansion and its legitimization. A serious underestimation of imperialism, however, would be to consider territory in too literal a way. Gaining and holding an imperium means gaining and holding a domain, which includes a variety of operations, among them constituting an area, accumulating its inhabitants, having power over its ideas, its people, and, of course, its land, converting people, land, and ideas to the purposes and uses of a hegemonic imperial design — all this as a result of being able to treat reality appropriatively. Thus the distinction between an idea that one *feels* to be one's own and a piece of land that one claims by right to be one's own (despite the presence on the land of its working native inhabitants) is really nonexistent, at least in the world of nineteenth-century culture, out of which imperialism developed. Laying claim to an idea and laying claim to a territory — given the extraordinarily current idea that the non-European world was there to be claimed, occupied, and ruled by Europe — were considered to be different sides of the same, essentially constitutive activity, which had the force, the prestige, and the authority of *science*. Moreover, because in such fields as biology, philology, and geology the scientific consciousness was principally a reconstituting, restoring, and transforming activity, turning old fields into new ones, the link between an outright imperialist attitude towards distant lands in the Orient and a scientific attitude to the "inequalities" of race was that both attitudes depended on the European *will,* on the determining force necessary to change confusing or useless realities into an orderly, disciplined set of new classifications useful to Europe. Thus in the work of Linnaeus, Buffon, and Cuvier, the white race became scientifically different from reds, yellows, blacks, and browns, and, consequently, territories occupied by those races also newly became vacant, open to Western colonies, developments, plantations, settlers. Additionally, the less equal races were made useful by being turned into what the white race studied and came to understand as a part of its racial and cultural hegemony (see, e.g., the work of Gobineau and Spengler), or, following the impulse of outright colonialism, these lesser races were put to direct use in the empire. When in 1918 Clemenceau stated that he believed he had "an unlimited right of levying black troops to assist in the defense of French territory in Europe if France were attacked in the future by Germany," he was saying that by some scientific right France had the knowledge and the power to convert blacks into what Poincaré called an economical form of gun-fodder for the white Frenchman.[15] Imperialism of course cannot be blamed on science, but what needs to be seen is the relative ease by which science could be deformed into a rationalization for imperial domination.

Supporting the taxonomy of natural history, deformed into a social anthropology whose real purpose was social control, were the taxonomy of linguistics and the extension of ideas about language families into theories of human types. In 1808, as an instance, Schlegel discerned a clear rift between the Indo-Germanic (or Aryan) languages, on the one hand, and the Semitic-African languages, on the other. The former he said were creative, regenerative, lively, and aesthetically pleasing; the latter were mechanical in their operations, unregenerate, passive. From this kind of distinction Schlegel himself, and later Renan, went on to generalize about the great distance separating a superior Aryan and an inferior non-Aryan mind, culture, and society.

Perhaps the most effective deformation or translation of science into something more accurately resembling political administration took place in the amorphous field assembling together jurisprudence, social philosophy, and political theory. First of all, a fairly influential tradition in philosophic empiricism (studied by Harry Bracken)[16] seriously advocated a type of racial distinction that divided humankind into lesser and greater breeds of men. The actual problems (in England mainly) of dealing with a three-hundred-year-old Indian empire, as well as numerous voyages of discovery, made it possible "scientifically" to show that some cultures were advanced and civilized, others backward and uncivilized; these ideas, plus the lasting social meaning imparted to the fact of color (and hence of race) by philosophers like Locke and Hume, made it axiomatic by the middle of the nineteenth century that Europeans always ought to rule non-Europeans.

This doctrine was reinforced in other ways, some of which had a direct bearing, I think, on Zionist practice and vision in Palestine. Among the supposed juridical distinctions between civilized and noncivilized peoples was an attitude toward land, almost a doxology about land that noncivilized people supposedly lacked. A civilized man, it was believed, could cultivate the land because it meant something to him; on it accordingly he bred useful arts and crafts, he created, he accomplished, he built. An uncivilized people either farmed land badly (i.e., inefficiently by Western standards) or left it to rot. From this string of ideas, by which whole native societies who had lived on American, African, and Asian territories for centuries were suddenly denied their right to live on that land, came the great dispossessing movements of modern European colonialism, and with them all the schemes for redeeming the land, resettling the natives, civilizing them, taming their savage customs, turning them into useful beings under European rule. Land in Asia, Africa, and the Americas was there for European exploitation, because Europe understood the value of land in a way impossible for the natives. At the end of the century, Joseph Conrad dramatized this philosophy in *Heart of Darkness* and embodied it powerfully in the figure of Kurtz, a man whose colonial dreams for the earth's "dark places" were made by "all Europe." But what Conrad drew on, as indeed the Zionists drew on it also, was the kind of philosophy set forth by Robert Knox in his work *The Dark Races*,[17] in which men were divided into white and advanced (the producers) and dark, inferior wasters. Similarly, thinkers like John Westlake and before him Emer de Vattel divided the world's territories into empty (though inhabited by nomads and a low kind of society) and civilized — and the former were then "revised" as being ready for takeover on the basis of a higher, civilized right to them.

I very greatly simplify the transformation in perspective by which millions of acres outside metropolitan Europe were thus declared empty, their people and societies decreed to be obstacles to progress and development, their space just as assertively declared open to European white settlers and their civilizing exploitation. During the 1870s in particular new European geographical societies mushroomed as a sign that geography had become, according to Lord Curzon, "the most cosmopolitan of all the sciences."[18] Not for nothing in *Heart of Darkness* did Marlow admit to his

passion for maps. I would look for hours at South America, or Africa, or Australia, and lose myself in all the glories of exploration. At that time there were many blank spaces [populated by natives, that is] on the earth, and when I saw one that looked particularly inviting on a map (but they all look that) I would put my finger on it and say, when I grow up I will go there.[19]

Geography and a passion for maps developed into an organized matter mainly devoted to acquiring vast overseas territories. And, Conrad also said, this

> conquest of the earth, which mostly means taking it away from those who have a different complexion or slightly flatter noses than ourselves, is not a pretty thing when you look into it too much. What redeems it is the idea only. An idea at the back of it; not a sentimental pretence but an ideal — something you can set up, and bow down before, and offer a sacrifice to.[20]

Conrad makes the point better than anyone, I think. The power to conquer territory is only in part a matter of physical force: there is the strong moral and intellectual component making the conquest itself secondary to an idea, which dignifies (and indeed hastens) pure force with arguments drawn from science, morality, ethics, and a general philosophy. Everything in Western culture potentially capable of dignifying the acquisition of new domains — as a new science, for example, acquires new intellectual territory for itself — *could* be put at the service of colonial adventures. And *was* put, the "idea" always informing the conquest, making it entirely palatable. One example of such an idea spoken about openly as a quite normal justification for what today would be called colonial aggression is to be found in these passages by Leroi-Beaulieu, a leading French geographer in the 1870s:

> A society colonizes, when having itself reached a high degree of maturity and of strength, it procreates, it protects, it places in good conditions of development and it brings to virility a new society to which it has given birth. Colonization is one of the most complex and delicate phenomena of social psychology.

There is no question of consulting the natives of the territory where the new society is to be given birth. What counts is that a modern European society has enough vitality and intellect to be "magnified by this pouring out of its exuberant activity on the outside." Such activity must be good since it is believed in, and since also it carries within itself the healthy current of an entire advanced civilization. Therefore, Leroi-Beaulieu added,

> colonization is the expansive force of a people; it is its power of reproduction; it is its enlargement and its multiplication through space; it is the subjugation of the universe or a vast part of it to that people's language, customs, ideas, and laws.[21]

Imperialism was the theory, colonialism the practice, of changing the uselessly unoccupied territories of the world into useful new versions of the European metropolitan society. Everything in those territories that suggested waste, disorder, and uncounted resources was to be converted into productivity, order, and taxable and potentially developed wealth. You get rid of most of the offending human and animal blight — whether because it simply sprawls untidily all over the place or because it roams about unproductively and uncounted; you confine the rest to reservations, compounds, native homelands — where you can count, tax, and use them profitably; and you build a new society on the vacated space. Thus was Europe reconstituted abroad, its "multiplication in space" successfully projected and managed. The result was a widely varied group of little Europes scattered throughout Asia, Africa, and the Americas, each reflecting the circumstances, the specific instrumentalities of the parent culture, its pioneers, its vanguard settlers.[22] All of these were similar in one other major respect — despite the differences, which were considerable — and that was that their life was carried on with an air of *normality*. The most grotesque reproductions of Europe (South Africa, Rhodesia, etc.) were considered appropriate; the worst discriminations against and exclusions of the natives were thought to be normal because "scientifically" legitimate; the sheer contradiction of living a foreign life in an enclave many physical and cultural miles from Europe, in the midst of hostile and uncomprehending natives, gave rise to a sense of history, a stubborn kind of logic, a social and political state decreeing the present colonial venture as *normal,* justified, good.

These then are the gross points that must be made about the connections between Zionism and European imperialism or colonialism. Whatever it may have done for Jews, Zionism essentially saw Palestine as the European imperialist did, as an empty territory; it allied itself, as Chaim Weizmann quite clearly said after World War I, with the imperial powers in carrying out its plans for establishing a new Jewish state in Palestine, and it did not think in terms of "the natives" who were passively supposed to accept the plans made for their land; as even Zionist historians like Porath and Mandell have empirically shown, the idea of Jewish colonizers in Palestine (well before World War One) always met with quite unmistakable native resistance, not because the natives thought that Jews were evil but because no natives take kindly to having their territory settled by foreigners; moreover, in formulating the concept of a Jewish nation "reclaiming" its own territory, Zionism not only accepted the generic racial concepts of European culture but also banked on the fact that Palestine was actually peopled not by an advanced but by a backward people, over which it *ought* to be dominant. Thus that implicit *assumption* of domination led specifically to the practice of ignoring the natives for the most part as not entitled to serious consideration.[23] Zionism therefore developed with a unique consciousness of itself, but with little or nothing left over for the unfortunate natives. Maxime Rodinson is perfectly correct in saying that Zionist indifference to the Palestinian natives was

> an indifference linked to European supremacy, which benefited even Europe's proletarians and oppressed minorities. In fact, there can be no doubt that if the ancestral homeland had been occupied by one of the well-established industrialized nations that ruled the world at the time, one that had thoroughly settled down in a territory it had infused with a powerful national consciousness, then the problem of displacing German, French, or English inhabitants and introducing a new, nationally coherent element into the middle of their homeland would have been in the forefront of the consciousness of even the most ignorant and destitute Zionists.[24]

In short, all the constitutive energies of Zionism were premised on the excluded presence, that is, the functional absence of "native people" in Palestine: institutions were built deliberately shutting out the natives; laws were drafted when Israel came into being that made sure the natives would remain in their "nonplace," Jews in theirs, and so on. It is no wonder that today the one issue that electrifies Israel as a society is the problem of the Palestinians, whose negation is the most consistent thread running through Zionism. And it is this perhaps unfortunate aspect of Zionism that ties it ineluctably to imperialism — at least so far as the Palestinian is concerned. Rodinson again:

> The element that made it possible to connect these aspirations of Jewish shopkeepers, peddlers, craftsmen, and intellectuals in Russia and elsewhere to the conceptual orbit of imperialism was one small detail that seemed to be of no importance: Palestine was inhabited by another people.[25]

Zionist Population, Palestinian Depopulation

I have been discussing the extraordinary unevenness in Zionism between care for the Jews and an almost total disregard for the non-Jews or native Arab population in conceptual terms. Zionism and European imperialism are epistemologically, hence historically and politically, coterminous in their view of resident natives, but it is how this irreducibly imperialist view worked in the world of politics and in the lives of people for whom epistemology was irrelevant that justifies looking at epistemology at all. In that world and in those lives, among them several million Palestinians, the results can be detailed, not as mere theoretical visions, but as an immensely traumatic Zionist effectiveness. One general Arab Palestinian reaction towards Zionism is perfectly caught, I think, in the following sentence written by the Arab delegation's reply in 1922 to Winston Churchill's white paper: "[T]he intention to create the Jewish National Home is to cause the disappearance or subordination of the Arabic population, culture and language."[26] What generations of Palestinian Arabs watched therefore was an unfolding design, whose deeper roots in Jewish history and the terrible Jewish experience were necessarily obscured by what was taking place before their eyes and to them in Palestine. There the Arabs were able to see embodied,

> a ruthless doctrine, calling for monastic self-discipline and cold detachment from environment. The Jews who gloried in the name of socialist worker interpreted brotherhood on a strictly nationalist, or racial basis, for they meant brotherhood with Jew, not with Arab. As they insisted on working the soil with their own hands, since exploitation of others was anathema to them, they excluded the Arabs from their regime.... They believed in equality, but for themselves. They lived on Jewish bread, raised on Jewish soil that was protected by a Jewish rifle.[27]

The "inventory" of Palestinian experience that I am trying to take here is based on the simple truth that the exultant or (later) the terrorized Jews who arrived in Palestine were seen essentially as foreigners whose proclaimed destiny was to create a state for Jews. What of the Arabs who were there? is the question we must feel ourselves asking now. What we will discover is that everything positive from the Zionist standpoint looked absolutely negative from the perspective of the native Arab Palestinians.

For they could never be fitted into the grand vision. Not that this "vision" was merely a theoretical matter: it was later to determine the character and even the detail of Israeli government policy toward the native Arab Palestinians; and it was also the way Zionist leaders looked at the Arabs in order later (or perhaps at that moment) to deal with them. Thus, as I said earlier, I have in mind the whole dialectic between theory and actual day-to-day practice that determined and produced victorious Zionist effectiveness. My premise is that Israel developed as a social polity out of the Zionist thesis that Palestine's colonization was to be accomplished simultaneously for and by Jews, and by the displacement of the Palestinians; moreover, that in its conscious and declared ideas about Palestine, Zionism attempted first to minimize, then to eliminate, then, all else failing, finally to subjugate the natives as a way of guaranteeing that Israel would not be simply the state of its citizens (which included Arabs of course) but the state of the whole Jewish people, having a kind of sovereignty over land and peoples that no other state possessed or possesses. It is this anomaly that in their frequently ineffective ways the Arab Palestinians have since been trying both to resist and to provide an alternative for.

One can learn a great deal from pronouncements made by strategically important Zionist leaders whose job it was, after Herzl, to translate the design into action. Chaim Weizmann comes to mind at once, as much for his extraordinary personality as for his brilliant successes in bringing Zionism up from an idea to a conquering political institution. His thesis about the land of Palestine is revealing in the extent to which it repeats Herzl:

> It seems as if God has covered the soil of Palestine with rocks and marshes and sand, so that its real beauty can only be brought out by those who love it and will devote their lives to healing its wounds.[28]

The context of this remark, however, is a sale made to the Zionists by a wealthy absentee landlord (the Lebanese Sursuk family) of unpromising marshland. Weizmann admits that this particular sale was of *some,* by no means a great deal, of Palestine, yet the impression he gives is of a whole territory essentially unused, unappreciated, misunderstood (if one can use such a word in this connection). Despite the people who lived on it Palestine was therefore *to be made* useful, appreciated, understandable. The native inhabitants were believed curiously to be out of touch with history, and, it seemed to follow, they were not really present. In the following passage written by Weizmann to describe Palestine when he first visited there in 1907, notice how the contrast between past neglect and forlornness and present "tone and progressive spirit" (he was writing in 1941) is intended to justify the introduction of foreign colonies and settlements:

> A dolorous country it was on the whole, one of the most neglected corners of the miserably neglected Turkish Empire. [Here, Weizmann uses "neglect" to describe Palestine's native inhabitants, the fact of whose residence there is not a sufficient reason to characterize Palestine as anything but an essentially empty and patient territory, awaiting people who show a proper care for it.] Its total population was something above six hundred thousand, of which about eighty thousand were Jews. The latter lived mostly in the cities, . . . but neither the colonies nor the city settlements in any

way resembled, as far as vigor, tone and progressive spirit are concerned, the colonies and settlements of our day.[29]

One short-term gain was that Zionism "raised the value of the . . . land,"[30] and the Arabs could reap profits even if politically the land was being cut out from underneath them.

As against native neglect and decrepitude, Weizmann preached the necessity of Jewish energy, will, and organization for reclaiming, "redeeming," the land. His language was shot through with the rhetoric of voluntarism, with an ideology of will and new blood that appropriated for Zionism a great deal of the language (and later the policies) of European colonialists attempting to deal with native backwardness. "New blood had to be brought into the country; a new spirit of enterprise had to be introduced." The Jews were to be the importers of colonies and colonists whose role was not simply to take over a territory but also to be schools for a Jewish national self-revival. Thus if in Palestine "there were great possibilities," the question became how to do something about the fact that "the will was lacking. How was that to be awakened? How was a cumulative process to be set in motion?" According to Weizmann, the Zionists were saved from ultimate discouragement only because of "our feeling that a great source of energy was waiting to be tapped — the national impulse of a people held in temporary check by a misguided interpretation of historic method."[31] The "method" referred to was the Zionist tendency hitherto to rely on great foreign benefactors like the Rothschilds and "neglect" the development of self-sustaining colonial institutions on the land itself.

To do this it was necessary to visualize and then to implement a scheme for creating a network of realities — a language, a grid of colonies, a series of organizations — for converting Palestine from its present state of "neglect" into a Jewish state. This network would not so much attack the existing "realities" as ignore them, grow alongside them, and then finally blot them out, as a forest of large trees blots out a small garden. A main ideological necessity for such a program was acquiring legitimacy for it, giving it an archaeology and a teleology that completely surrounded and, in a sense, outdated the native culture that was still firmly planted in Palestine. One of the reasons Weizmann modified the conception of the Balfour Declaration from its favoring the establishment of a Jewish national home to favoring a "reestablishment" was precisely to enclose the territory with the oldest and farthest reaching of possible "realities." The colonization of Palestine proceeded always as a fact of repetition: the Jews were not supplanting, destroying, breaking up a native society. That society was itself the oddity that had broken the pattern of a sixty-year Jewish sovereignty over Palestine that had lapsed for two millennia. In Jewish hearts, however, Israel had always been there, an actuality difficult for the natives to perceive. Zionism therefore reclaimed, redeemed, repeated, replanted, and realized Palestine and Jewish hegemony over it. Israel was a return to a previous state of affairs, even if the new facts bore a much greater resemblance to the methods and the successes of nineteenth-century European colonialism than to some mysterious first-century forebears.

The dehumanization of the Arab, which began with the view that Palestinians were either not there or savages, or both, saturates everything in Israeli society. It was not thought too unusual during the 1973 war for the army to issue a booklet (with a preface by General Yona Efrati of the Central Command) written by the Central Command's rabbi, Abraham Avidan, containing the following key passage:

> When our forces encounter civilians during the war or in the course of a pursuit or a raid, the encountered civilians may, and by Halachic standards even must be killed, whenever it cannot be ascertained that they are incapable of hitting us back. Under no circumstances should an Arab be trusted, even if he gives the impression of being civilized.[32]

Children's literature in Israel is made up of valiant Jews who always end up killing low, treacherous Arabs with names like Mastoul (crazy), Bandura (tomato), or Bukra (tomorrow). As a writer for *Ha'aretz* (September 20, 1974) said, children's books "deal with our topic: the Arab who murders Jews out of pleasure, and the pure Jewish boy who defeats 'the coward swine!' " Nor are such enthusiastic ideas limited to individual authors who produce books for mass consumption; as I hope later to show, these ideas derive more or less logically from the state's institutions, whose other, benevolent side has the task of regulating Jewish life humanistically.

There are perfect illustrations of this duality in Weizmann, for whom such matters immediately found their way into policy, action, and detailed results. He admires Samuel Pevsner as "a man of great ability, energetic, practical, resourceful and, like his wife, highly educated." One can have no problem with this. Then immediately comes the following, without so much as a transition: "For such people, going to Palestine was in effect going into a social wilderness — which is something to be remembered by those who, turning to Palestine today, find in it intellectual cultural and social resources not inferior to those of the Western world."[33] Zionism was all foregrounding; everything else was background, and it had to be subdued, suppressed, lowered in order that the foreground of cultural achievement could appear as "civilizing pioneer work."[34] Above all, the native Arab had to be seen as an irremediable opposite, something like a combination of savage and superhuman, at any rate a being with whom it is impossible (and useless) to come to terms.

On another occasion, he recounts an experience that in effect was the germ of Tel Aviv, whose importance as a Jewish center derives in great measure from its having neutralized the adjacent (and much older) Arab town of Jaffa. In what Weizmann tells the reader, however, there is only the slightest allusion to the fact of Arab life already existing there, on what was to be the adjacent future site of Tel Aviv. What matters is the production of a Jewish presence, whose value appears to be more or less self-evident:

> I was staying in Jaffa when Ruppin called on me, and took me out for a walk over the dunes to the north of the town. When we had got well out into the sands — I remember that it came over our ankles — he stopped, and said, very solemnly: "Here we shall create a Jewish city!" I looked at him with some dismay. Why should people come to live out in this wilderness where nothing could grow? I began to ply him with technical questions, and he answered me carefully and exactly. Technically, he said, everything is possible. Though in the first years communication with the new settlement would be difficult, the inhabitants would soon become self-supporting and self-sufficient. The Jews of Jaffa would move into the new, modern city, and the Jewish colonies of the neighborhood would have a concentrated market for their products.

The Gymnasium would stand at the center, and would attract a great many students from other parts of Palestine and from Jews abroad, who would want their children to be educated in a Jewish high school in a Jewish city. Thus it was Arthur Ruppin who had the first vision of Tel Aviv, which was destined to outstrip, in size and in economic importance, the ancient town of Jaffa, and to become one of the metropolitan centers of the eastern Mediterranean.[35]

In time of course the preeminence of Tel Aviv was to be buttressed by the military capture of Jaffa. The visionary project later turned into the first step of a military conquest, the idea of a colony being later fleshed out in the actual appearance of a colony, of colonizers, and of the colonized. Weizmann and Ruppin, it is true, spoke and acted with the passionate idealism of pioneers; they also were speaking and acting with the authority of Westerners surveying fundamentally retarded, non-Western territory and natives, planning the future *for them*. Weizmann himself did not just think that as a European he was better equipped to decide for the natives what their best interests were (e.g., that Jaffa *ought to be* outstripped by a modern Jewish city); he also believed he "understood" the Arab *as he really was*. In saying that the Arab's "immense talent" was "in fact" for never telling the truth, he said what other Europeans had observed about non-European natives elsewhere, for whom, like the Zionists, the problem was controlling a large native majority with a comparative handful of intrepid pioneers:

> It may well be asked how it is that we are able to control, with absurdly inadequate forces, races so virile and capable, with such mental and physical endowments. The reply is, I think, that there are two flaws to be found: — the mental and moral equipment of the average African. . . . I say that inherent lack of honesty is the first great flaw. . . . Comparatively rarely can one African depend upon another keeping his word. . . . Except in very rare instances it is a regrettable fact that this defect is enlarged rather than diminished by contact with European civilization. The second is lack of mental initiative. . . . Unless impelled from the outside the native seldom branches out from a recognized groove and this mental lethargy is characteristic of his mind.[36]

This is C. L. Temple's *The Native Races and Their Rulers* (1918); its author was an assistant to Lugard in governing Nigeria, and like Weizmann he was less a proto-Nazi racist than a liberal Fabian in his outlook. The Zionist in Palestine or the Britisher in Africa was therefore realistic. He saw facts and dealt with them and knew the value of truth. Notwithstanding the "fact" of long residence on a native territory, the non-European was always in retreat from truth. European vision meant the capacity to see not only what was there but what *could* be there: hence the Weizmann-Ruppin exchange about Jaffa and Tel Aviv. The specific temptation before the Zionist in Palestine was to believe — and plan for — the possibility that the Arab natives would not *really* be there, which was doubtless a proven eventuality (1) when the natives would not acknowledge Jewish sovereignty over Palestine and (2) when after 1948 they became legal outsiders on their land.

But the success of Zionism did not derive exclusively from its bold outlining of a future state or from its ability to see the natives for the negligible quantities they were or might become. Rather, I think, Zionism's effectiveness in making its way against Arab Palestinian resistance to it lay *in its being a policy of detail*, not simply a general colonial vision. Thus Palestine was not only the promised land, a concept as elusive and as abstract as any that one could encounter. It was a specific territory, with specific characteristics, that was surveyed down to the last millimeter, settled on, planned for, built on, and so forth — in *detail*. From the beginning of the Zionist colonization this was something the Arabs had no answer to; they had no equally detailed counterproposal. They assumed that since they lived on the land and legally owned it, it was theirs. They did not understand that what they were encountering was a discipline of detail — indeed, a very culture of discipline by detail — by which a hitherto imaginary realm could be constructed on Palestine, inch-by-inch and step-by-step. The Palestinian Arabs always opposed a *general* policy on general principles: Zionism, they said, was foreign colonialism (which strictly speaking it was, as the early Zionist admitted); it was unfair to the natives (as some early Zionists, like Ahad Ha'am also admitted); and it was doomed to die of its various theoretical weaknesses.

Between Weizmann's epoch to our own, Zionism for the native Arabs in Palestine had been converted from an advancing encroachment upon their lives to a settled reality — a nation-state — enclosing them within it. For Jews after 1948, Israel not only realized their political and spiritual hopes: it continued to be a beacon of opportunity guiding those of them still living in Diaspora and keeping those who lived in former Palestine on the frontier of Jewish development and self-realization. For the Arab Palestinians, Israel meant one essentially hostile fact and several unpleasant corollaries. After 1948 every Palestinian disappeared nationally and legally. Some Palestinians reappeared juridically as "non-Jews" in Israel; those who left became "refugees," and later some of those acquired new Arab, European, or American identities. No Palestinian, however, lost his or her "old" Palestinian identity. This is because Israel — for what can now be seen as shortsighted ends — legislated the "non-Jew" into oppressive permanence and because the Arab states did much the same, supporting and yet stunting an independent Palestinian political identity. Out of such legal fictions as the nonexistent Palestinian in Israel and elsewhere, the Palestinian has finally emerged, and with this emergence a considerable amount of international attention prepared at last to take critical notice of Zionist theory and praxis.

The outcry in the West after the 1975 "Zionism is racism" resolution was passed in the United Nations was doubtless a genuine one. Israel's Jewish achievements — or rather its achievements on behalf of European Jews, less so for the Sephardic (Oriental) Jewish majority — stand before the Western world: by most standards they are considerable achievements, and it is right that they not sloppily be tarnished with the sweeping rhetorical denunciation associated with "racism." For the Palestinian Arabs who have lived and who have now studied the procedures of Zionism toward them and their land, the predicament is complicated, but not finally unclear. They know that the Law of Return allowing a Jew immediate entry into Israel just as exactly prevents the Palestinian from returning to his or her home; they also know that Israeli raids against Palestinian refugee camps inside Lebanon killed literally thousands of civilians, all on the acceptable pretext of fighting terrorism, but in reality because Palestinians as a race have become synonymous with unregenerate, essentially unmotivated terrorism; they understand, without perhaps being able to master, the intellectual process by which their violated humanity has been trans-muted, unheard and unseen, into praise for the ideology that has all but destroyed them. "Racism" is too vague a term: Zionism is Zionism. For the Arab Palestinian this tautology has a sense that is perfectly congruent with, but exactly the opposite of, what it says to Jews.

And just as no Jew in the last hundred years has been untouched by Zionism, so too no Palestinian has been unmarked by it. Yet it must not be forgotten that the Palestinian was not simply a function of Zionism. His or her life, culture, and politics have their own dynamic and ultimately their own authenticity.

NOTES

1. Menachem Begin, *The Revolt* (1948; reprint, Los Angeles: Nash Publishing, 1972), 162. Red Cross figures for the massacre at Deir Yassin specify about 250 civilians, mostly women and children. Of this group, Begin has the following to say: "The fighting was thus very severe. Yet the hostile propaganda, disseminated throughout the world, deliberately ignored the fact that the civilian population of Deir Yassin was actually given a warning by us before the battle began. One of our tenders carrying a loud speaker was stationed at the entrance to the village and it exhorted in Arabic all women, children and aged to leave their houses and to take shelter on the slope of the hill. By giving this humane warning our fighters threw away the element of complete surprise, and thus increased their own risk in the ensuing battle." Despite the Irgun's humane warning, these unfortunates were slaughtered. Of Begin, David Ben-Gurion said in May 1963: "Begin is a thoroughly Hitlerite type, ready to destroy all the Arabs for the wholeness, who devotes all his efforts for a holy purpose,...and it has a clear meaning: the murder of tens of Jews, Arabs, and Englishmen — in the explosion of the King David Hotel, the pogrom in Deir Yassin and the murder of Arab women and children....I have no doubt that Begin hates Hitler — but this hatred does not prove that he is different from him and when for the first time I heard Begin on the radio — I heard the voice and the screeching of Hitler" (quoted in *Israleft* 108; the text is from a letter by Ben-Gurion to Haim Guri). Perhaps one ought also to mention that the present secretary general of the Jewish Agency (executive of the World Zionist Congress) is one Shmuel Lehis, who was convicted as a criminal in 1948 for murdering at least thirty-five Arabs in cold blood in Hula village; Lehis was given an unconditional amnesty (his sentence was to have been seven years) and rose to the top of the Zionist hierarchy. See R. Barkan, "The Strange Case of Shmuel Lehis" *Al Hamishmar,* March 3, 1978.

2. See my account of this in "The Idea of Palestine in the West," *MERIP Reports* (September 1978). For a general description of liberal acrobatics, see Noam Chomsky, *Human Rights and American Foreign Policy* (London: Spokesman Books, 1978).

3. See Niebuhr's letter to the *New York Times,* November 21, 1947, and his "A New View of Palestine," *The Spectator,* August 6, 1946; for Wilson, see his *Black, Red, Blond, and Olive* (New York: Oxford University Press, 1956), 462–63, where he speaks about the "natural contempt" that Westerners (like himself presumably) have for Arabs and about "the rather stupid obstinacy of the Arab refugees in Jordan, who have refused the offers of UNRWA to accommodate them in other localities and continue to insist on returning to their villages and farms in Israel." Roosevelt's position is too well known to require documentation here.

4. Quoted in Christopher Sykes, *Crossroads to Israel, 1947–1948* (1965; reprint, Bloomington: Indiana University Press, 1973), 5.

5. See Golda Meir's famous remark in 1969: "The Palestinians don't exist." General (later Prime Minister) Rabin referred to them for decades as "so-called Palestinians."

6. George Eliot, *Daniel Deronda* (1876; reprint, London: Penguin, 1967), 50.

7. Ibid., 592.

8. Ibid., 594–95.

9. Edward W. Said, *Orientalism* (New York: Vintage, 1978), 153–57, 214, 228.

10. Quoted in Arthur Hertzberg, ed., *The Zionist Idea: A Historical Analysis and Reader* (New York: Atheneum, 1976), 133.

11. Ibid., 34.

12. See Philip D. Curtin, ed., *Imperialism* (New York: Harper, 1971), which contains a good selec-

tion from the imperialist literature of the last two hundred years. I survey the intellectual and cultural backgrounds of the period in *Orientalism,* chaps. 2 and 3.

13. Desmond Stewart, *Theodor Herzl* (Garden City, N.Y.: Doubleday, 1974), 192.

14. Antonio Gramsci, *The Prison Notebooks: Selections,* trans. and ed. Quintin Hoare and Geoffrey Nowell Smith (New York: International Publishers, 1971), 324.

15. See Hannah Arendt, *The Origins of Totalitarianism* (New York: Harcourt Brace, 1973), 129.

16. Harry Bracken, "Essence, Accident and Race," *Hermathena* 116 (winter 1973) 81–96.

17. See Curtin, *Imperialism,* 93–105, which contains an important extract from Temple's book.

18. George Nathaniel Curzon, *Subjects of the Day: Being a Selection of Speeches and Writings* (London: George Allen and Unwin, 1915), 155–56.

19. Joseph Conrad, *Heart of Darkness,* in *Youth and Two Other Stories* (Garden City, N.Y.: Doubleday, 1925), 52.

20. Ibid., 50–51.

21. Cited in Agnes Murphy, *The Ideology of French Imperialism* (Washington, D.C.: Catholic University Press, 1949), 189, 110, 136.

22. Amos Oz, a leading Israeli novelist (also considered a "dove"), puts it nicely: "[F]or as long as I live, I shall be thrilled by all those who came to the Promised Land to turn it either into a pastoral paradise or egalitarian Tolstoyan communes, or into a well-educated, middle-class Central European enclave, a replica of Austria and Bavaria. Or those who wanted to raise a Marxist paradise, who built kibbutzim on biblical sites and secretly yearned for Stalin to come one day to admit that 'Bloody Jews, you have done it better than we did' " (*Time,* May 15, 1978, 61).

23. See the forthright historical account of this in Amos Elon, *The Israelis: Founders and Sons* (New York: Bantam, 1972), 218–24.

24. Maxime Rodinson, *Israel: A Colonial-Settler State?* (New York: Anchor Foundation, 1973), 39.

25. Ibid., 38.

26. Quoted in David Waines, "The Failure of the Nationalist Resistance," in *The Transformation of Palestine,* ed. Ibrahim Abu-Lughod (Evanston, Ill.: Northwestern University Press, 1987), 220.

27. Ibid., 213.

28. *Trial and Error: The Autobiography of Chaim Weizmann* (New York: Harper, 1959), 371.

29. Ibid., 125.

30. Ibid., 253.

31. Ibid., 128–29.

32. Reproduced in *Haolam Hazeh,* May 15, 1974. Uri Avnery, the editor of *Haolam Hazeh,* has written an interesting, somewhat demagogic book, worth looking at for the light it sheds on Israeli politics: *Israel without Zionists: A Plea for Peace in the Middle East* (New York: Macmillan, 1968). It contains some vitriolic attacks on people like Moshe Dayan, whom Avnery describes essentially as "an Arab-fighter" (cf. Indian fighters in the American West).

33. *Trial and Error,* 130.

34. Ibid., 188.

35. Ibid., 130.

36. C. L. Temple, *The Native Races and Their Rulers* (1918; reprint, London: Frank Cass, 1968), 41.

Chapter 2
Sephardim in Israel: Zionism from the Standpoint of Its Jewish Victims
Ella Shohat

Alternative critical discourse concerning Israel and Zionism has until now largely focused on the Jewish/Arab conflict, viewing Israel as a constituted state, allied with the West against the East, whose very foundation was premised on the denial of the Orient and of the legitimate rights of the Palestinian people. I would like to extend the terms of the debate beyond earlier dichotomies (East versus West, Arab versus Jew, Palestinian versus Israeli) to incorporate an issue elided by previous formulations, to wit, the presence of a mediating entity, that of the Arab Jews or Mizrahi/Oriental Jews, those Sephardi Jews coming largely from the Arab and Muslim countries. A more complete analysis, I will argue, must consider the negative consequences of Zionism not only for the Palestinian people but also for the Sephardim who now form the majority of the Jewish population in Israel. For Zionism not only undertakes to speak for Palestine and the Palestinians, thus "blocking" all Palestinian self-representation, but also presumes to speak for Oriental Jews. The Zionist denial of the Arab-Muslim and Palestinian East, then, has as its corollary the denial of the Jewish "Mizrahim" (the "Eastern Ones"), who, like the Palestinians, but by more subtle and less obviously brutal mechanisms, have *also* been stripped of the right of self-representation. Within Israel, and on the stage of world opinion, the hegemonic voice of Israel has almost invariably been that of European Jews, the Ashkenazim, while the Sephardi/Mizrahi voice has been largely muffled or silenced.

Zionism claims to be a liberation movement for *all* Jews, and Zionist ideologists have spared no effort in their attempt to make the two terms "Jewish" and "Zionist" virtually synonymous. In fact, however, Zionism has been primarily a liberation movement for European Jews (and that, as we know, problematically) and more precisely for that tiny minority of European Jews actually settled in Israel. Although Zionism claims to provide a homeland for *all* Jews, that homeland was not offered to all with the same largess. Sephardi Jews were first brought to Israel for specific European-Zionist reasons, and once there they were systematically discriminated against by a Zionism that deployed its energies and material resources differentially, to the consistent advantage of European Jews and to the consistent detriment of Oriental Jews. In this essay, I would like to delineate the situation of structural oppression experienced by Sephardi Jews in Israel, to trace briefly the historical origins of that oppression, and to propose a symptomatic analysis of the discourses —

historiographic, sociological, political, and journalistic — that sublimate, mask, and perpetuate that oppression.

Superimposed on the East/West problematic will be another issue, related but hardly identical, namely, that of the relation between the "First" and the "Third" Worlds. Although Israel is not a Third World country by any simple or conventional definition, it does have affinities and structural analogies to the Third World, analogies that often go unrecognized even, and perhaps especially, within Israel itself. In what sense, then, can Israel, despite the views of it offered by official spokesmen, be seen as partaking in "Third Worldness"? To begin, in purely demographic terms, a majority of the Israeli population can be seen as Third World or at least as originating in the Third World. The Palestinians make up about 20 percent of the population while the Sephardim, the majority of whom have come, within very recent memory, from countries such as Morocco, Algeria, Egypt, Iraq, Iran, and India, countries generally regarded as forming part of the Third World, constitute another 50 percent of the population, thus giving us a total of about 70 percent of the population as Third World or Third World–derived (and almost 90 percent if one includes the West Bank and Gaza). European hegemony in Israel, in this rereading of the demographic map, is the product of a distinct numerical minority, a minority in whose interest it is to downplay Israel's "Easternness" as well as its "Third Worldness."

Within Israel, European Jews constitute a First World elite dominating not only the Palestinians but also the Oriental Jews. The Sephardim, as a Jewish Third World people, form a semicolonized nation-within-a-nation. My analysis here is indebted to anticolonialist discourse generally (Frantz Fanon, Aimé Césaire) and specifically to Edward Said's indispensable contribution to that discourse, his genealogical critique of Orientalism as the discursive formation by which European culture was able to manage — and even produce — the Orient during the post-Enlightenment period.[1] The Orientalist attitude posits the Orient as a constellation of traits, assigning generalized values to real or imaginary differences, largely to the advantage of the West and the disadvantage of the East, so as to justify the former's privileges and aggressions. Orientalism tends to maintain what Said calls a "flexible positional superiority," which puts the Westerner in a whole series of possible relations with the Oriental, but without the Westerner ever losing the relative upper hand. My essay concerns, then, the process by which one pole of the East/West dichotomy is produced and reproduced as rational, developed, superior, and human, and the other as aberrant, underdeveloped, and inferior, but in this case as it affects Oriental Jews.

The Zionist Master Narrative

The view of the Sephardim as oppressed Third World people goes directly against the grain of the dominant discourse within Israel and disseminated by the Western media outside of Israel. According to that discourse, European Zionism "saved" Sephardi Jews from the harsh rule of their Arab "captors." It took them out of "primitive conditions" of poverty and superstition and ushered them gently into a modern Western society characterized by tolerance, democracy, and "humane values," values with which they were but vaguely and erratically familiar due to the "Levantine environments" from which they came. Within Israel, of course, they have suffered not simply from the problem of "the gap," that between their standard of living and that of European Jews, but also from the problem of their "incomplete integration" into Israeli liberalism and prosperity, handicapped as they have been by their Oriental, illiterate, despotic, sexist, and generally premodern formation in their lands of origin, as well as by their propensity for generating large families. Fortunately, however, the political establishment, the welfare institutions, and the educational system have done all in their power to "reduce this gap" by initiating the Oriental Jews into the ways of a civilized, modern society. Fortunately as well, intermarriage is proceeding apace, and the Sephardim have won new appreciation for their "traditional cultural values," their folkloric music, their rich cuisine and warm hospitality. A serious problem persists, however. Due to their inadequate education and "lack of experience with democracy," the Jews of Asia and Africa tend to be extremely conservative, even reactionary, and religiously fanatic, in contrast to the liberal, secular, and educated European Jews. Antisocialist, they form the base of support for the right-wing parties. Given their "cruel experience in Arab lands," furthermore, they tend to be "Arab-haters," and in this sense they have been an "obstacle to peace," preventing the efforts of the "peace camp" to make a "reasonable settlement" with the Arabs.

I will speak in a moment of the fundamental falsity of this discourse, but I would like first to speak of its wide dissemination, for this discourse is shared by right and "left," and it has its early and late versions as well as its religious and secular variants. An ideology that blames the Sephardim (and their Third World countries of origin) has been elaborated by the Israeli elite, expressed by politicians, social scientists, educators, writers, and the mass media. This ideology orchestrates an interlocking series of prejudicial discourses possessing clear colonialist overtones. It is not surprising, in this context, to find the Sephardim compared, by the elite, to other "lower" colonized peoples. Reporting on the Sephardim in a 1949 article, during the mass immigration from Arab and Muslim countries, the journalist Arye Gelblum wrote:

> This is immigration of a race we have not yet known in the country.... We are dealing with people whose primitivism is at a peak, whose level of knowledge is one of virtually absolute ignorance, and worse, who have little talent for understanding anything intellectual. Generally, they are only slightly better than the general level of the Arabs, Negroes, and Berbers in the same regions. In any case, they are at an even lower level than what we knew with regard to the former Arabs of Eretz Israel.... These Jews also lack roots in Judaism, as they are totally subordinated to the play of savage and primitive instincts.... As with the Africans you will find card games for money, drunkenness and prostitution. Most of them have serious eye, skin and sexual diseases, without mentioning robberies and thefts. Chronic laziness and hatred for work, there is nothing safe about this asocial element.... "Aliyat HaNoar" [the official organization dealing with young immigrants] refuses to receive Moroccan children and the Kibbutzim will not hear of their absorption among them.[2]

Sympathetically citing the friendly advice of a French diplomat and sociologist the conclusion of the article makes clear the colonial parallel operative in Ashkenazi attitudes toward Sephardim. Basing his comments on the French experience with its African colonies, the diplomat warns:

> You are making in Israel the same fatal mistake we French made. . . . You open your gates too wide to Africans. . . . [T]he immigration of a certain kind of human material will debase you and make you a levantine state, and then your fate will be sealed. You will deteriorate and be lost.[3]

Lest one imagine this discourse to be the product of the delirium of an isolated retrograde journalist, we have only to quote then prime minister David Ben-Gurion, who described the Sephardi immigrants as lacking even "the most elementary knowledge" and "without a trace of Jewish or human education."[4] Ben-Gurion repeatedly expressed contempt for the culture of the Oriental Jews: "We do not want Israelis to become Arabs. We are in duty bound to fight against the spirit of the Levant, which corrupts individuals and societies, and preserve the authentic Jewish values as they crystallized in the Diaspora."[5] Over the years Israeli leaders constantly reinforced and legitimized these Eurocentric ideas, which encompassed both Arabs and Oriental Jews. For Abba Eban, the "object should be to infuse [the Sephardim] with an Occidental spirit, rather than allow them to drag us into an unnatural Orientalism."[6] Or again: "One of the great apprehensions which afflict us . . . is the danger lest the predominance of immigrants of Oriental origin force Israel to equalize its cultural level with that of the neighboring world."[7] Golda Meir projected the Sephardim, in typical colonialist fashion, as coming from another, less developed time, for her, the sixteenth century (and for others, a vaguely defined "Middle Ages"): "Shall we be able," she asked, "to elevate these immigrants to a suitable level of civilization?"[8] Ben-Gurion, who called the Moroccan Jews "savages" at a session of a Knesset committee and who compared Sephardim, pejoratively (and revealingly), to the blacks brought to the United States as slaves, at times went so far as to question the spiritual capacity and even the Jewishness of the Sephardim.[9] In an article entitled "The Glory of Israel," published in the government's annual, the prime minister lamented that "the divine presence has disappeared from the Oriental Jewish ethnic groups," while he praised European Jews for having "led our people in both quantitative and qualitative terms."[10] Zionist writings and speeches frequently advance the historiographically suspect idea that Jews of the Orient, prior to their "ingathering" into Israel, were somehow "outside of" history, thus ironically echoing nineteenth-century assessments, such as those of Hegel, that Jews, like blacks, lived outside of the progress of Western civilization. European Zionists in this sense resemble Fanon's colonizer who always "makes history"; whose life is "an epoch," "an Odyssey" against which the natives form an "almost inorganic background."[11]

Again in the early 1950s, some of Israel's most celebrated intellectuals from Hebrew University in Jerusalem wrote essays addressing the "ethnic problem." "We have to recognize," wrote Karl Frankenstein, "the primitive mentality of many of the immigrants from backward countries," suggesting that this mentality might be profitably compared to "the primitive expression of children, the retarded, or the mentally disturbed." Another scholar, Yosef Gross, saw the immigrants as suffering from "mental regression" and a "lack of development of the ego." The extended symposium concerning the "Sephardi problem" was framed as a debate concerning the "essence of primitivism." Only a strong infusion of European cultural values, the scholars concluded, would rescue the Arab Jews from their "backwardness."[12] And in 1964, Kalman Katznelson published his frankly racist *The Ashkenazi Revolution,* where he protested the dangerous admission into Israel of large numbers of Oriental Jews and where he argued the essential, irreversible genetic inferiority of the Sephardim, fearing the tainting of the Ashkenazi race by mixed marriage and calling for the Ashkenazim to protect their interests in the face of a burgeoning Sephardi majority.

Such attitudes have not disappeared; they are still prevalent, expressed by Euro-Israelis of the most diverse political orientations. The "liberal" Shulamit Aloni, head of the Citizen's Rights Party and a member of the Knesset, in 1983 denounced Sephardi demonstrators as "barbarous tribal forces" that were "driven like a flock with tom-toms" and chanting like "a savage tribe."[13] The implicit trope comparing Sephardim to black Africans recalls, ironically, one of the favored topics of European anti-Semitism, that of the "black Jew." (In European-Jewish conversations, Sephardim are sometimes referred to as *schwartze chaies* or "black animals.") Amnon Dankner, a columnist for the "liberal" daily *HaAretz,* favored by Ashkenazi intellectuals and known for its presumably high journalistic standards, meanwhile, excoriated Sephardi traits as linked to an Islamic culture clearly inferior to the Western culture "we are trying to adopt here." Presenting himself as the anguished victim of an alleged official "tolerance," the journalist bemoans his forced cohabitation with Oriental subhumans:

> This war [between Ashkenazim and Sephardim] is not going to be between brothers, not because there is not going to be war but because it won't be between brothers. Because if I am a partner in this war, which is imposed on me, I refuse to name the other side as my "brother." These are not my brothers, these are not my sisters, leave me alone, I have no sister. . . . They put the sticky blanket of the love of Israel over my head, and they ask me to be considerate of the cultural deficiencies of the authentic feelings of discrimination. . . . [T]hey put me in the same cage with a hysterical baboon, and they tell me "OK, now you are together, so begin the dialogue." And I have no choice; the baboon is against me, and the guard is against me, and the prophets of the love of Israel stand aside and wink at me with a wise eye and tell me: "Speak to him nicely. Throw him a banana. After all, you people are brothers."[14]

Once again we are reminded of Fanon's colonizer, unable to speak of the colonized without resorting to the bestiary, the colonizer whose terms are zoological terms.

The racist discourse concerning Oriental Jews is not always so overwrought or violent, however; elsewhere it takes a "humane" and relatively "benign" form. Read, for example, Dr. Dvora and Rabbi Menachem Hacohen's *One People: The Story of the Eastern Jews,* an "affectionate" text thoroughly imbued with Eurocentric prejudice.[15] In his foreword, Abba Eban speaks of the "exotic quality" of Jewish communities "on the outer margins of the Jewish world." The text proper, and its accompanying photographs, convey a clear ideological agenda. The stress throughout is on "traditional garb," on "charming folkways," on premodern "craftsmanship," on cobblers and coppersmiths, on women "weaving on primitive looms." We learn of a "shortage of textbooks in Yemen," and the photographic evidence shows only sacred writings on the *ktuba* or on Torah cases, never secular writing. Repeatedly, we are reminded that some North African Jews inhabited caves (intellectuals such as Albert Memmi and Jacques Derrida apparently escaped this condition), and an entire chapter is devoted to "the Jewish cave-dwellers."

The actual historical record, however, shows that Oriental Jews were overwhelmingly urban. There is, of course, no intrinsic merit in being urban or even any intrinsic fault in living in "cave-like dwellings." What is striking, on the part of the commentator, is a kind of "desire for primitivism," a miserabilism that feels compelled to paint the Asian and African Jews as innocent of technology and modernity. The pictures of Oriental misery are then contrasted with the luminous faces of the Orientals in Israel itself, learning to read and mastering the modern technology of tractors and combines. The book forms part of a broader national export industry of Sephardi "folklore," an industry that circulates (the often expropriated) goods — dresses, jewelry, liturgical objects, books, photos, and films — among Western Jewish institutions eager for Jewish exotica. In this sense, the Israeli Ashkenazi glosses the enigma of the Eastern Jews for the West — a pattern common as well in academic studies. Ora Gloria Jacob-Arzooni's *The Israeli Film: Social and Cultural Influences, 1912–1973,* for example, describes Israel's "exotic" Sephardi community as having been plagued by "almost unknown tropical diseases" — the geography here is somewhat fanciful — and as "virtually destitute." The North African Jews, we are told — in language that surprises so long after the demise of the Third Reich — were hardly "racially pure," and among them one finds "witchcraft and other superstitions far removed from any Judaic law."[16] We are reminded of Fanon's ironic account of the colonialist description of the natives: "torpid creatures, wasted by fevers, obsessed by ancestral customs."[17]

The Theft of History

An essential feature of colonialism is the distortion and even the denial of the history of the colonized. The projection of Sephardim as coming from backward rural societies lacking all contact with technological civilization is at best a simplistic caricature and at worst a complete misrepresentation. Metropolises such as Alexandria, Baghdad, and Istanbul, in the period of Sephardi emigration, were hardly the desolate backwaters without electricity or automobiles implied by the official Zionist account, nor were these lands somehow miraculously cut off from the universal dynamism of historical processes. Yet Sephardi and Palestinian children, in Israeli schools, are condemned to study a history of the world that privileges the achievements of the West, while effacing the civilizations of the East. The political dynamics of the Middle East, furthermore, are presented only in relation to the fecundating influence of Zionism on the preexisting desert. The Zionist master narrative has little place for either Palestinians or Sephardim, but while Palestinians possess a clear counternarrative, the Sephardi story is a fractured one embedded in the history of both groups. Distinguishing the "evil" East (the Muslim Arab) from the "good" East (the Jewish Arab), Israel has taken upon itself to "cleanse" the Sephardim of their Arabness and redeem them from their "primal sin" of belonging to the Orient. Israeli historiography absorbs the Jews of Asia and Africa into the monolithic official memory of European Jews. Sephardi students learn virtually nothing of value about their particular history as Jews in the Orient. Much as Senegalese and Vietnamese children learned that their "ancestors the Gauls had blue eyes and blond hair," Sephardi children are inculcated with the historical memory of "our ancestors, the residents of the shtetls of Poland and Russia," as well as with a pride in the Zionist founding fathers for establishing pioneer outposts in a savage area. Jewish history is conceived as primordially European, and the silence of historical texts concerning the Sephardim forms a genteel way of hiding the discomfiting presence of an Oriental "other," here subsumed under a European-Jewish "we."

From the perspective of official Zionism, Jews from Arab and Muslim countries appear on the world stage only when they are seen on the map of the Hebrew state, just as the modern history of Palestine is seen as beginning with the Zionist renewal of the biblical mandate. Modern Sephardi history, in this sense, is presumed to begin with the coming of Sephardi Jews to Israel, and more precisely with the "Magic Carpet" or "Ali Baba" operations (the latter refers to the bringing to Israel of the Jews of Iraq in 1950–51, while the former refers to that of Yemeni Jews in 1949–50). The names themselves, borrowed from *A Thousand and One Nights,* evoke Orientalist discourses by foregrounding the naive religiosity and the technological backwardness of the Sephardim, for whom modern airplanes were "magic carpets" transporting them to the promised land. The Zionist gloss on the Exodus allegory, then, emphasized the "Egyptian" slavery (Egypt here being a synecdoche for all the Arab lands) and the beneficent death of the (Sephardi) "desert generation." European Zionism took on the patriarchal role in the Jewish oral tradition of fathers passing to sons the experiences of their peoples (*vehigadeta lebinkha bayom hahu...*). And the stories of the Zionist pater drowned out those of the Sephardi fathers and mothers whose tales thus became unavailable to the sons and daughters.

Filtered through a Eurocentric grid, Zionist discourse presents culture as the monopoly of the West, denuding the peoples of Asia and Africa, including Jewish peoples, of all cultural expression. The multilayered culture of Jews from Arab and Muslim countries is scarcely studied in Israeli schools and academic institutions. While Yiddish is prized and officially subsidized, Ladino and Judeo-Arabic dialects are neglected ("Those who do not speak Yiddish," Golda Meir once said, "are not Jews"). Yiddish, through an ironic turn of history, became for Sephardim the language of the oppressor, a coded speech linked to privilege.[18] While the works of Sholem Aleichem, Y. D. Berkowitz, and Mendle Mocher Sfarim are examined in great detail, the works of Anwar Shaul, Murad Michael, and Salim Darwish are ignored, and when Sephardi figures are discussed, their Arabness is downplayed. Maimonides, Yehuda HaLevi, and Iben Gabirol are viewed as the product of a decontextualized Jewish tradition, or of Spain, that is, Europe, rather than of what even the Orientalist Bernard Lewis recognizes as the "Judeo-Islamic symbiosis." Everything conspires to cultivate the impression that Sephardi culture prior to Zionism was static and passive and, like the fallow land of Palestine, lying in wait for the impregnating infusion of European dynamism. Although Zionist historiography concerning Sephardim consists of a morbidly selective "tracing of the dots" from pogrom to pogrom (often separated by centuries), part of a picture of a life of relentless oppression and humiliation, in fact the Sephardim lived, on the whole, quite comfortably within Arab-Muslim society. Sephardi history can simply not be discussed in European-Jewish terminology; even the word "pogrom" derives from and is reflective of the specificities of the European-Jewish experience. At the same time, we should not idealize the Jewish-Muslim relationship as idyllic. While it is true that Zionist propaganda exaggerated the negative aspects of the Jewish situation in Muslim countries, and while the situation of these Jews over fifteen centuries was undeniably better than in the Christian countries, the fact remains that the status of *dhimmi,* applied to both Jews and Christians as "tolerated" and "protected" minorities, was intrinsically inegalitarian. But this fact, as Maxime Rodinson points out, was quite explicable by the sociological and historical conditions of the time and was not the product of a pathological European-style anti-Semitism.[19] The Sephardi communities, while retaining a strong collective identity, were generally well integrated and indigenous to their countries of origin, forming an inseparable part of their social and cultural life. Thoroughly Arabized in their traditions, the Iraqi Jews, for example, used Arabic even in their hymns and religious ceremonies. The liberal and secular trends of the twentieth century engendered an even stronger association of Iraqi Jews and Arab culture, allowing Jews to achieve a prominent place in public and cultural life. Jewish writers, poets, and scholars played a vital role in Arab culture, translating, for example, books from other languages into Arabic. Jews distinguished themselves in Iraqi Arabic-speaking theater, in music, as singers, as composers, and as players of traditional instruments. In Egypt, Syria, Lebanon, Iraq, and Tunisia, Jews became members of legislatures, of municipal councils, of the judiciary, and even occupied high economic positions; the finance minister of Iraq, in the 1940s, was Ishak Sasson, and in Egypt, Jamas Sanua — higher positions, ironically, than those usually achieved by Sephardim within the Jewish state.

The Lure of Zion

Zionist historiography presents the emigration of Arab Jews as the result of a long history of anti-Semitism, as well as of religious devotion, while Zionist activists from the Arab-Jewish communities stress the importance of Zionist ideological commitment as a motivation for the exodus. Both versions neglect crucial elements: the Zionist economic interest in bringing Sephardim to Palestine/Israel, the financial interest of specific Arab regimes in their departure, historical developments in the wake of the Arab/Israeli conflict, as well as the fundamental connection between the destiny of the Arab Jews and that of the Palestinians. Arab historians, as Abbas Shiblak points out in *The Lure of Zion,* have also underestimated the extent to which the policies of Arab governments in encouraging Jews to leave were self-defeating and ironically helpful to the Zionist cause and harmful both to Arab Jews and to Palestinians.[20] It is important to remember that Sephardim, who had lived in the Middle East and North Africa for millennia (often even before the Arab conquest), cannot be seen as simply eager to settle in Palestine and in many ways had to be "lured" to Zion. Despite the messianic mystique of the Land of Zion, which formed an integral part of Sephardi religious culture, they did not exactly share the European-Zionist desire to "end the diaspora" by creating an independent state peopled by a new archetype of Jew. Sephardim had always been in contact with the promised land, but this contact formed a "natural" part of a general circulation within the countries of the Ottoman Empire. Up through the 1930s, it was not uncommon for Sephardim to make purely religious pilgrimages or business trips to Palestine, at times with the help of Jewish-owned transportation companies. (Although the Zionist geographical mindset projected the Sephardi lands of origin as remote and distant, in fact they were, obviously, closer to Eretz Israel than Poland, Russia, and Germany.)

Before the Holocaust and the foundation of Israel, Zionism had been a minority movement among world Jewry. Although both enthusiasm and hostility were expressed toward the Zionist project, the majority of Sephardi Jews were quite indifferent to it. The Iraqi-Jewish leadership, for its part, cooperated with the Iraqi government to stop Zionist activity in Iraq; the chief rabbi of Iraq even published an "open letter" in 1929 denouncing Zionism and the Balfour Declaration.[21] In Palestine, some of the leaders of the local (Sephardi) Jewish community made formal protests against Zionist plans. In 1920, they signed an anti-Zionist petition organized by Palestinian Arabs, and in 1923 some Palestinian Jews met in a synagogue to denounce Ashkenazi-Zionist rule (some even cheered the Muslim-Christian Committee and its leader Mussa Hassam al-Husseini), an event that the National Jewish Committee managed to prevent from being discussed in the newspapers.[22] Zionism, in this period, created wrenching ideological dilemmas for the Palestinian Jewish, Muslim, and Christian communities alike. The national Arab movement in Palestine and Syria carefully distinguished, in the early phases, between the Zionist immigrants and the local Jewish inhabitants (largely Sephardim) "who live peacefully among the Arabs."[23] The first petition of protest against Zionism by the Jerusalem Palestinian Arabs stated in November 1918: "We want to live ... in equality with our Israelite brothers, long-standing natives of this country; their rights are our rights and their duties are our duties."[24] The all-Syrian convention of July 1919, attended by a Sephardi Arab-Jewish representative, even claimed to represent all Arab Syrians, Muslims, Christians, and Jews. The manifesto of the first Palestinian convention in February 1919 also insisted on the local Jewish/Zionist distinction, and in March 1920, during the massive demonstrations against the Balfour Declaration, the Nazareth area petition spoke only against Zionist immigration and not against Jews in general: "The Jews are people of our country who lived with us before the occupation, they are our brothers, people of our country, and all the Jews of the world are our brothers."[25]

At the same time, however, there were real ambivalences and fears on the part of both Arab Jews and Arab Muslims and Christians. While some Muslim and Christian Arabs rigorously maintained the Zionist/Jewish distinction, others were less cautious. The Palestinian Anglican priest of Nazareth deployed anti-Semitic theological arguments against "the Jews" in general, while Arab demonstrators, in bloody rebellions both in 1920 and in 1929, did not distinguish between Zionist targets per se and the traditional communities quite uninvolved in the Zionist project.[26] Zionism, then, brought a painful binarism into the formerly relatively peaceful relationship between diverse Palestinian religious communities. The Sephardi Jew was prodded to choose between anti-Zionist "Arabness" and a pro-Zionist "Jewishness." For the first time in Arab-Jewish history, Arabness and Jewishness were posed as antonyms. The situation led the Palestinian Muslims and Christians, meanwhile, to see all Jews as at least potential Zionists. With the pressure of waves of Ashkenazi-Zionist immigration and the swelling power of its institutions, the Jewish/Zionist distinction was becoming more and more precarious, much to the advantage of European Zionism. Had the Arab nationalist movement maintained this distinction, as even the Zionist historian Yehoshua Porath has recognized, it would have had significant chances for enlisting Sephardi support in the anti-Zionist cause.[27]

Outside of Palestine, meanwhile, it was not an easy task for Zionism to uproot the Arab-Jewish communities. In Iraq, for example, despite the Balfour Declaration in 1917, despite the tensions generated by Palestinian/Zionist clashes in Palestine, despite Zionist propaganda among Sephardi Jews in Arab-Muslim lands, despite the historically atypical attacks on Iraqi Jews in 1941 (attacks inseparable from the geopolitical conflicts of the time), and even after the proclamation of Israeli statehood, most Arab Jews were not Zionist and remained reluctant to emigrate. Even subsequent to the foundation of the state, the Jewish community in Iraq was constructing new schools and founding new enterprises, clear evidence of an institutionalized intention to stay. When the Iraqi government announced in 1950 that any Jews who wanted to leave were free to do so contingent upon relinquishing their citizenship and property, and set a time limit for the exodus, only a few families applied for exit permits. Since the carrot was insufficient, therefore, a stick was necessary. A Jewish underground cell, commanded by secret agents sent from Israel, planted bombs in Jewish centers so as to create hysteria among Iraqi Jews and thus catalyze a mass exodus to Israel.[28] In one case, on January 14, 1951, a bomb was thrown into the courtyard of the Mas'ouda Shemtob Synagogue in Baghdad, at a time when hundreds were gathered.[29] Four people, including a boy of twelve, were killed, and a score were wounded. These actions appear to have been the product of a collusion between two groups — Israeli Zionists (including a small group of Iraqi Zionists) and factions in the Iraqi government (largely those around the British-oriented ruler Nuri Said) who were pressured by the international Zionist-led campaign of denunciation and who had an immediate financial interest in the expulsion of the Iraqi Jews.[30] Caught in the vice of Iraqi government–Zionist collaboration, the Sephardi community panicked and was virtually forced to leave. What its proponents themselves called "cruel Zionism" — namely, the idea that Zionists had to use violent means to dislodge Jews from exile — had achieved its ends.

The same historical process that dispossessed Palestinians of their property, lands, and national-political rights was linked to the process that dispossessed Sephardim of their property, lands and rootedness in Arab countries (and within Israel itself, of their history and culture). This overall process has been cynically idealized in Israel's diplomatic pronouncements as a kind of "spontaneous population exchange" and a justification for expelling Palestinians, but the symmetry is factitious, for the so-called "return from exile" of the Arab Jews was far from spontaneous and in any case cannot be equated with the condition of the Palestinians, who have been exiled from their homeland and wish to return there. In Israel itself, as the Palestinians were being forced to leave, the Sephardim underwent a complementary trauma, a kind of image in negative, as it were, of the Palestinian experience. The vulnerable new immigrants were ordered around by arrogant officials, who called them "human dust," and crowded into *ma'abarot* (transient camps), hastily constructed out of corrugated tin. Many were stripped of their "unpronounceable" Arab, Persian, and Turkish names and outfitted with "Jewish" names by Godlike Israeli bureaucrats. The process by which millennial pride and collective self-confidence and creativity were to be destroyed was inaugurated here. This was a kind of Sephardi "middle passage" where the appearance of a voluntary "return from exile" masked a subtle series of coercions. But while Palestinians have been authorized to foster the collective militancy of nostalgia in exile (be it under an Israeli, Syrian, or Kuwaiti passport or on the basis of *laissez-passer*), Sephardim have been forced by their no-exit situation to repress their communal nostalgia. The pervasive notion of "one people" reunited in their ancient homeland actively disauthorizes any affectionate memory of life before the state of Israel.

"Hebrew Work": Myth and Reality

The Zionist "ingathering from the four corners of the earth" was never the beneficent enterprise portrayed by official discourse. From the early days of Zionism, Sephardim were perceived as a source of cheap labor that had to be maneuvered into immigrating to Palestine. The economic structure that oppresses Sephardim in Israel was set in place in the early days of the *yishuv* (prestate Zionist settlement in Palestine). Among the orienting principles of the dominant socialist Zionism, for example, were the twin notions of *avoda ivrit* (Hebrew work) and *avoda atzmit* (self-labor), suggesting that a person, and a community, should earn from their own, not from hired, labor, an idea whose origins trace back to the Haskalah, or eighteenth-century Hebrew Enlightenment. Many Jewish thinkers, writers, and poets, such as Mapu, Brenner, Borochov, Gordon, and Katznelson, highlighted the necessity of transforming Jews by "productive labor," especially agricultural labor. Such thinkers advanced *avoda ivrit* as a necessary precondition for Jewish recuperation. The policy and practice of *avoda ivrit* deeply affected the historically positive self-image of the Hebrew pioneers and later of Israeli as involved in a noncolonial enterprise, which unlike colonialist Europe did not exploit the "natives" and was, therefore, perceived as morally superior in its aspirations.

In its actual historical implication, however, *avoda ivrit* had tragic consequences, engendering political tensions not only between Arabs and Jews but also between Sephardim and Ashkenazim as well as between Sephardim and Palestinians. At first, the European-Jewish settlers tried to compete with Arab workers for jobs with previously settled Jewish employers; "Hebrew work" then meant in reality the boycotting of Arab work. The immigrants' demands for relatively high salaries precluded their employment, however, thus leading to the emigration of a substantial proportion. At a time when even the poorest of Russian Jews were heading toward the Americas, it was difficult to convince European Jews to come to Palestine. It was only after the failure of Ashkenazi immigration that the Zionist institutions decided to bring in Sephardim. Ya'acov Tehon, from the Eretz Israel Office, wrote in 1908 about this problem of "Hebrew workers." After detailing the economic and psychological obstacles to the goal of *avoda ivrit* as well as the dangers posed by employing masses of Arabs, he proposed, along with other official Zionists, the importation of Sephardim to "replace" the Arab agricultural workers. Since "it is doubtful whether the Ashkenazi Jews are talented for work other than in the city," he argued, "there is a place for the Jews of the Orient, and particularly for the Yemenites and Persians, in the profession of agriculture." Like the Arabs, Tehon goes on, they "are satisfied with very little" and "in this sense they can compete with them."[31] Similarly, in 1910, Shmuel Yavne'eli published in *HaPoel HaTzair* (The young worker, the official or-gan of the Zionist Party of the Workers in Eretz Israel, later part of the Labor Party) a two-part article entitled "The Renaissance of Work and the Jews of the Orient" in which he called for an Oriental-Jewish solution for the "problem" of the Arab workers. *HaTzvi,* a newspaper, gave expression to this increasingly disseminated position:

> This is the simple, natural worker capable of doing any kind of work, without shame, without philosophy, and also without poetry. And Mr. Marx is of course absent both from his pocket and from his mind. It is not my contention that the Yemenite element should remain in its present state, that is, in his barbarian, wild present state.... [T]he Yemenite of today still exists at the same backward level as the Fellahins.... [T]hey can take the place of the Arabs.[32]

Zionist historiographers have recycled these colonialist myths, applied both to Arabs and to Arab Jews, as a means of justifying the class positioning into which Sephardim were projected. Yemeni workers have been presented as "merely work-ers," socially "primeval matter," while Ashkenazi workers have been described as "creative" and "idealists, able to be devoted to the ideal, to create new moulds and new content of life."[33]

Regarded by European Zionists as capable of competing with Arabs but refractory to more lofty socialist and nationalist ideals, the Sephardim seemed ideal imported laborers. Thus the concept of "natural workers" with "minimal needs," exploited by such figures as Ben-Gurion and Arthur Ruppin, came to play a crucial ideological role, a concept subtextually linked to color; to quote Ruppin: "Recognizable in them [Yemeni Jews] is the touch of Arab blood.... [T]hey have a very dark color."[34] The Sephardim offered the further advantage of generally being Ottoman subjects, and thus, unlike most Ashkenazim, without legal difficulties in entering the country, partially thanks to Jewish (Sephardi) representation in the Ottoman parliament.[35]

Tempted by the idea of recruiting "Jews in the form of Arabs," Zionist strategists agreed to act on "the Sephardi option." The bald economic-political interest moti-vating this selective "ingathering" is clearly discernible in emissary Yavne'eli's letters from Yemen, where he states his intention of selecting only "young and healthy people" for immigration.[36] His reports about potential Yemeni laborers go into great detail about the physical characteristics of the different Yemeni regional groups, de-scribing the Jews of Dal'a, for example, as "healthy" with "strong legs," in contrast with the Jews of Ka'ataba, with their "shrunken faces and skinny hands."[37] These policies of a quasi-eugenic selection were repeated during the 1950s in Morocco, where young men were chosen for aliya on the basis of physical and gymnastic tests.

Often deluding Sephardim about realities in the "land of milk and honey," Zion-ist emissaries engineered the immigration of over ten thousand Sephardim (largely

Yemenis) before World War I. They were put to work mainly as agricultural day laborers in extremely harsh conditions to which, despite Zionist mythology, they were *decidedly not* accustomed. Yemeni families were crowded together in stables, pastures, windowless cellars (for which they had to pay) or simply obliged to live in the fields. Unsanitary conditions and malnutrition caused widespread disease and death, especially of infants. The Zionist Association employers and the Ashkenazi landowners and their overseers treated the Yemeni Jews brutally, at times abusing even the women and children who labored over ten hours a day.[38] The ethnic division of labor, in this early stage of Zionism, had as its corollary the sexual division of labor. Tehon wrote in 1907 of the advantages of having "Yemenite families living permanently in the settlements," so that "we could also have women and adolescent girls work in the households instead of the Arab women who now work at high salaries as servants in almost every family of the colonists."[39] Indeed, the "fortunate" women and girls worked as maids; the rest worked in the fields. Economic and political exploitation went hand in hand with habitual European feelings of superiority. Any treatment accorded to the Sephardim was thought to be legitimate, since they were bereft, it was assumed, of all culture, history, or material achievement. Sephardim were excluded, furthermore, from the socialist benefits accorded European workers.[40] Labor Zionism, through the Histadrut (the General Federation of Labor), managed to prevent Yemenis from owning land or joining cooperatives, thus limiting them to the role of wage earners. As with the Arab workers, the dominant "socialist" ideology within Zionism thus provided no guarantee against ethnocentrism. While presenting Palestine as an empty land to be transformed by Jewish labor, the founding fathers presented Sephardim as passive vessels to be shaped by the revivifying spirit of Promethean Zionism.

At the same time, the European Zionists were not enthralled by the prospect of "tainting" the settlements in Palestine with an infusion of Sephardi Jews. The very idea was opposed at the first Zionist Congress.[41] In their texts and congresses, European Zionists consistently addressed their remarks to Ashkenazi Jews and to the colonizing empires that might provide support for a national homeland; the visionary dreams of a Zionist Jewish state were not designed for the Sephardim. But the actual realization of the Zionist project in Palestine, with its concomitant aggressive attitude toward all the local peoples, brought with it the possibility of the exploitation of Sephardi Jews as part of an economic and political base. The strategy of promoting a Jewish majority in Palestine in order to create a Jewish national homeland entailed at first the purchase and later the expropriation of Arab land. The policy, favored by *tzionut ma'asit* (practical Zionism), of creating de facto Jewish occupation of Arab land formed a crucial element in Zionist claims on Palestine. Some Zionists were afraid that Arab workers on Jewish lands might someday declare that "the land belongs to those who work it," whence the need for Jewish (Sephardi) workers. This skewed version of *avoda ivrit* generated a long-term structural competition between Arab workers and the majoritarian group of Jewish (Sephardi) workers, now reduced to the status of a subproletariat.

It was only after the failure of European immigration — even in the post-Holocaust era most European Jews chose to immigrate elsewhere — that the Zionist establishment decided to bring Sephardi immigrants en masse. The European-Zionist rescue fantasy concerning the Jews of the Orient, in sum, masked the need to rescue European Zionism from possible economic and political collapse. In the 1950s, similarly, Zionist officials continued to show ambivalence about the mass importation of Sephardi Jews. But once again demographic and economic necessities — settling the country with Jews, securing the borders, and having laborers to work and soldiers to fight — forced the European-Zionist hand. Given this subtext, it is instructive to read the sanitized versions promoted even by those most directly involved in the exploitation of Sephardi labor. Yavne'eli's famous *shlihut* (Zionist mission promoting aliya) to Yemen, for example, has always been idealized by Zionist texts. The gap between the "private" and the more public discourse is particularly striking in the case of Yavne'eli himself: his letters to Zionist institutions stress the search for cheap labor, but his memoirs present his activity in quasi-religious language, as bringing "to our brothers Bnei-Israel [Sons of Israel], far away in the land of Yemen, tidings from Eretz Israel, the good tidings of Renaissance, of the Land and of Work."[42]

The Dialectics of Dependency

These problems, present in embryonic form in the time of the prestate era, came to their bitter "fruition" after the establishment of Israel, but now explained away by a more sophisticated set of rationalizations and idealizations. Israel's rapid economic development during the 1950s and 1960s was achieved on the basis of a systematically unequal distribution of advantages. The socioeconomic structure was thus formed contrary to the egalitarian myths characterizing Israel's self-representation until the last decade. The discriminatory decisions of Israeli officials against Sephardim began even before Sephardi arrival in Israel and were consciously premised on the assumption that the Ashkenazim, as the self-declared "salt of the earth," deserved better conditions and "special privileges."[43]

In contrast with Ashkenazi immigrants, Sephardim were treated inhumanely already in the camps constructed by the Zionists in their lands of origin as well as during transit. A Jewish Agency report on a camp in Algiers speaks of a situation in which "more than fifty people were living in a room of four or five square meters."[44] A doctor working in a Marseilles transit camp for North African Jewish immigrants noted that as a result of the bad housing and the recent decline in nutrition, children had died, adding that "I can't understand why in all the European countries the immigrants are provided with clothes while the North African immigrants are provided with nothing."[45] When information about anti-Sephardi discrimination in Israel filtered back to North Africa, emigration from North Africa declined. Some left the transit camps in order to return to Morocco, while others, to quote a Jewish Agency emissary, had virtually "to be taken aboard the ships by force."[46] In Yemen, the journey across the desert, exacerbated by the inhuman conditions in the Zionist transit camps, led to hunger, disease, and massive death, resulting in a brutal kind of natural selection. Worrying about the burden of caring for sick Yemenis, Jewish Agency members were reassured by their colleague Itzhak Refael (of the Nationalist Religious Party) that "there is no need to fear the arrival of a large number of chronically ill, as they have to walk by foot for about two weeks. The gravely ill will not be able to walk."[47]

The European-Jewish scorn for Eastern-Jewish lives and sensibilities — at times projected onto the Sephardim by Ashkenazi Orientalizing "experts," who claimed that death for Sephardim was a "common and natural thing" — was evident as well in the notorious incident of "the kidnapped children of Yemen."[48] Traumatized by the reality of life in Israel, some Sephardim, most of them Yemenis, fell prey to a ring of unscrupulous doctors, nurses, and social workers who provided, according to some estimations, several thousand Sephardi babies for adoption by Ashkenazi families (some of them outside of Israel, largely in the United States), while telling the natural parents that the children had died. The conspiracy was extensive enough to include the systematic issuance of fraudulent death certificates for the adopted children and to ensure that over several decades Sephardi demands for investigation were silenced and information was hidden and manipulated by government bureaus.[49] On June 30, 1986, the Public Committee for the Discovery of the Missing Yemenite Children held a massive protest rally. The rally, like many Sephardi protests and demonstrations, was almost completely ignored by the media, but a few months later Israeli television produced a documentary on the subject, blaming the bureaucratic chaos of the period for unfortunate "rumors" and perpetuating the myth of Sephardi parents as careless breeders with little sense of responsibility toward their own children.

Ethnic discrimination against Sephardim began with their initial settling. Upon arrival in Israel the various Sephardi communities, despite their will to stay together, were dispersed across the country. Families were separated; old communities disintegrated; and traditional leaders were shorn of their positions. Oriental Jews were largely settled in *ma'abarot,* remote villages, agricultural settlements, and city neighborhoods, some of them only recently emptied of Palestinians. As the absorption facilities became exhausted, the settlement authorities constructed *ayarot pituha* (development towns) largely in rural areas and frontier regions, which became, predictably, the object of Arab attack. The declared policy was to "strengthen the borders," implying not only against Arab military attacks but also against any attempt by Palestinian refugees to return to their homeland. Although Israeli propaganda lauded the better-protected Ashkenazi kibbutzim for their courage in living on the frontiers, in fact their small number (about 3 percent of the Jewish population, and half that if one considers only border settlements) hardly enabled them to secure long borders, while the settlement of the more numerous Sephardim on the borders did ensure a certain security. Sephardi border settlements lacked, furthermore, the strong infrastructure of military protection provided to Ashkenazi settlements, thus leading to Sephardi loss of life. The ethnic segregation that tends to characterize Israeli urban housing also dates from this period. While Ashkenazim tend to live in the more prosperous "northern" zones, Sephardim are concentrated in the less wealthy "southern" zones. Despite this quasi-segregation, the two communities are generally linked in a relation of dependency, whereby the poor neighborhoods serve the privileged neighborhoods, a relational structure that mirrors that between the "socialist" kibbutzim and the neighboring development towns.

In cases where Sephardim were moved into preexisting housing — and in Israel preexisting housing means Palestinian housing — the Sephardim often ended up by living in promiscuous conditions because the Orientalist attitudes of the Israeli authorities found it normal to crowd many Sephardi families into the same house, on the assumption that they were "accustomed" to such conditions. These poor Sephardi neighborhoods were then systematically discriminated against in terms of infrastructural needs, educational and cultural advantages, and political self-representation. Later, when some of these neighborhoods became obstacles to urban gentrification, the Sephardim were forced, against their will and despite violent demonstrations, to other "modern" poor neighborhoods. In Jaffa, for example, the authorities, after the removal of the Sephardim, renovated the very same houses that they had refused to renovate for their Sephardi dwellers, thus facilitating the transition by which sections of "Oriental" Jaffa became a "bohemian" touristic locale dotted with art galleries. More recently, the Sephardi neighborhood of Musrara in Jerusalem has been undergoing a similar process. Now that the neighborhood is no longer near the pre-1967 border, the authorities have been trying to remove its Sephardi residents and force them to relocate to settlements on the West Bank, again under the pretense of improving their material conditions. The pattern is clear and systematic. The areas forcibly vacated by the Sephardim soon become the object of major investments, leading to Ashkenazi gentrification; in these areas the elite enjoy living within a "Mediterranean" mise-en-scène but without the inconvenience of a Palestinian or Sephardi presence, while the newly adopted Sephardi neighborhoods become decapitalized slums.

As a cheap, mobile, and manipulable labor-force, Sephardim were indispensable to the economic development of the state of Israel. Given the need for mass housing in the 1950s, many Sephardim became ill-paid construction workers. The high profits generated by the cheap labor led to the rapid expansion of construction firms, managed or owned by Ashkenazim. Recruited especially into the mechanized and nonskilled sectors of agricultural production within large-scale government projects, Sephardim provided much of the labor force for settling the land. In the case of agricultural settlements, they received less and poorer lands than the various Ashkenazi settlements such as the kibbutzim and much less adequate means of production, resulting in lower production, lower income, and gradually the economic collapse of many of the Sephardi settlements.[50] After agricultural development and construction work reached a saturation point in the late 1950s and early 1960s, the government acted to industrialize the country, and Sephardi workers once again were crucial to Israel's rapid development. A large section of the Sephardim came to form, in this period, an industrial proletariat. (In recent years, the monthly wage of production-line workers in textile factories has hovered around $150–200, roughly equivalent to that earned by many Third World workers.)[51] In fact, Israel's appeals for foreign (largely Jewish) investment were partially based on the "attraction" of local cheap labor. The low wages of workers led to a widening gap between the upper and lower salary ranges in the industry. Development towns, essential to industrial production, became virtual "company towns" in which a single factory became the major single provider of employment for a whole town, whose future became inextricably linked to the future of the company.[52]

While the system relegated Sephardim to a futureless bottom, it propelled Ashkenazim up the social scale, creating mobility in management, marketing, banking, and technical jobs. Recent published documents reveal the extent to which discrimination was a calculated policy that knowingly privileged the European immigrants, at times creating anomalous situations in which educated Sephardim became unskilled laborers, while much less educated Ashkenazim came to occupy high administrative positions.[53] Unlike the classical paradigm where immigration is linked to a desire for individual, familial, and community improvement, in Israel this process, for Sephardim, was largely reversed. What for Ashkenazi immigrants from Russia or Poland was a social *aliya* (literally "ascent") was for Sephardi immigrants from Iraq or Egypt a *yerida* (a "descent"). What was for persecuted Ashkenazi minorities a certain solution and a quasi-redemption of a culture was for Sephardim the complete annihilation of a cultural heritage, a loss of identity, and a social and economic degradation.

The Facade of Egalitarianism

These discriminatory policies were executed under the aegis of the Labor Party and its affiliates, whose empire included a tentacular set of institutions, the most important of which was the General Federation of Labor (Histadrut). The Histadrut controls the agricultural sector, the kibbutzim, and the largest labor unions in the industrial sector. With its own industries, marketing cooperatives, transportation systems, financial institutions, and social-service network, it exercises immense power. (Solleh Boneh, a Histadrut construction company, for example, could easily "freeze out" private builders from the Likud Party.) As a kind of caricature of trade unionism, the Histadrut, despite its professed socialist ideology, generally wields its vast power for the benefit of the elite, consistently favoring Ashkenazim for white-collar management positions and Sephardim for blue-collar skilled and unskilled labor, leaving the latter most vulnerable in situations where factories are closed or workers are laid off. The same relational structure of oppression operates in the process whereby regional factories (even government-owned regional factories) tend to be managed by the largely Ashkenazi kibbutzim while the workers are largely Sephardi or Palestinian. The dominant institutions, and more specifically the "socialist"-Zionist elite, have thus virtually forced the Sephardim into underdevelopment, and this contrary both to Ashkenazi denials that such processes have been taking place and to the claims that those processes were unconscious and uncalculated.

   The dominant socialist-humanist discourse in Israel hides this negative dialectic of wealth and poverty behind a mystifying facade of egalitarianism. The Histadrut and the Labor Party, claiming to represent the workers, monopolize socialist language. Their May Day celebrations, the flying of red flags alongside the blue and white, and their speeches in the name of the "working class" mask the fact that the Labor network really represents only the interests of the Euro-Israeli elite, whose members nevertheless still refer to themselves nostalgically as *Eretz Israel HaOvedet* (working Eretz Israel). The Sephardim and the Palestinians, the majority of workers in Israel, have been represented by special Histadrut departments called, respectively, the Oriental Department and the Minority Department. (The Histadrut is not preoccupied, it goes without saying, with the economic exploitation of West Bank and Gaza Strip workers). The manipulation of syndicalist language and the co-optation of socialist slogans have thus served as a smoke screen for classed, racialized, and gendered inequalities. As a consequence, Sephardi militants have had to confront a kind of visceral aversion, on the part of working-class Sephardim, to the very word "socialist," associated, for them, with oppression rather than liberation.

Although the official meliorative discourse suggests a gradual lessening of the "gap" between Sephardim and Ashkenazim, in fact the inequalities are more glaring now than they were two generations ago.[54] The system continues to reproduce itself, for example, in the differential treatment accorded to present-day European immigrants versus that accorded to "veteran" Mizrahim. While second-generation Sephardim stagnate in substandard housing in poor neighborhoods, newly arrived Russian immigrants (with the exception of Asian-Soviets, such as Georgian Jews) are settled by the government into comfortable housing in central areas. (I do not examine here the racism suffered by the Ethiopian Jews, now undergoing what the Sephardim experienced in the 1950s, supplemented by the added humiliation of religious harassment.) Indeed, the ethnic allegiances of the establishment become especially clear with regard to immigration policy. While supposedly promoting universal aliya and the end to the Diaspora, the establishment, given its (unnamed) fear of a Sephardi demographic advantage, energetically promotes immigration by Soviet Jews — a majority of whom would prefer to go elsewhere — while dragging its feet in response to the Ethiopian Jews (Falashas), who wish to go and whose very lives have been endangered.

The largely segregated and unequal educational system in Israel also reproduces the ethnic division of labor through a tracking system that consistently orients Ashkenazi pupils toward prestigious white-collar positions requiring a strong academic preparation while pointing Sephardi pupils toward low-status blue-collar jobs. Euro-Israelis have double the representation in white-collar occupations. The schools in Ashkenazi neighborhoods have better facilities, better teachers, and higher status. Ashkenazim have on the average three more years of schooling than Sephardim. Their attendance rate in academic high school is 2.4 times as high, and it is 5 times as high in universities.[55] Most Mizrahi children, furthermore, study in schools designated by the Ministry of Education as schools for the *teunei tipuah* (literally, "those who need nurture," or "the culturally deprived"), a designation premised on the equation of cultural difference with inferiority. The educational system functions, as Shlomo Swirski puts it, as "a huge labelling mechanism that has, among other things, the effect of lowering the achievement and expectations of Oriental children and their parents."[56]

On whatever level — immigration policy, urban development, labor policy, or government subsidies — we find the same pattern of a racialized discrimination that touches even the details of daily life. The government, for example, subsidizes certain basic dietary staples, one of them being European-style bread; the pita favored as a staple by both Sephardim and Palestinians, meanwhile, is not subsidized. These discriminatory processes, which were shaped in the earliest period of Zionism, are reproduced every day and on every level, reaching into the very interstices of the Israeli social system. As a result, the Sephardim, despite their majority status, are underrepresented in the national centers of power — in the government, in the Knesset, in the higher echelons of the military, in the diplomatic corps, in the media, and in the academic world — and they are overrepresented in the marginal, stigmatized regions of professional and social life.

The dominant sociological accounts of Israel's "ethnic problem" have attributed the inferior status of Oriental Jews not to the classed and raced structure of Israeli society but rather to their origins in "premodern," "culturally backward" societies. Borrowing heavily from the intellectual arsenal of American functionalist studies of development and modernization, Shumuel Eisenstadt and his many social-scientist disciples gave ideological subterfuge the aura of scientific rationality. The influential role of this "modernization" theory derived from its perfect match with the needs of the establishment.[57] Eisenstadt borrowed from American structural functionalism (Parsons) its teleological view of a "progress" that takes us from "traditional" societies, with their less complex social structures, to "modernization" and "development." Since the Israeli social formation was seen as that entity collectively created during the *Yishuv* period, the immigrants were perceived as integrating themselves into the preexisting dynamic whole of a modern society patterned on the Western model. The underlying premise of Zionism, the "ingathering of the exiles," was thus translated into the sociological jargon of structural functionalism. The "absorption" (*klita*) of Sephardi immigrants into Israeli society entailed the acceptance of the established consensus of the "host" society and the abandonment of "premodern" traditions. While European immigrants required only "absorption," the immigrants from Africa and Asia required "absorption through modernization." For the Eisenstadt tradition, the Oriental Jews had to undergo a process of "desocialization" (i.e., erasure of their cultural heritage) and of "resocialization" (i.e., assimilation to the Ashkenazi way of life). Thus cultural difference was posited as the cause of maladjustment. (The theory would have trouble explaining why other Sephardim, coming from the same "premodern" countries, at times from the very same families, suffered no particular maladjustment in such "postmodern" metropolises as Paris, London, New York, and Montreal.) At times the victim is even blamed for blaming an oppressive system. Here is sociologist Yosef Ben David: "In such cases ethnic difficulties will render yet more acute the immigration crisis.... The immigrant will tend to rationalize the failure by putting the blame openly or implicitly on ethnic discrimination."[58]

The Ashkenazim, however, hid behind the flattening term "Israeli society," an entity presumed to embody the values of modernity, industry, science, and democracy. As Swirski points out, this presentation camouflaged the actual historical processes by obscuring a number of facts: first, that the Ashkenazim, not unlike the Sephardim, had also come from countries on the periphery of the world capitalist system, countries that entered the process of industrialization and technological-scientific development roughly at the same time as the Sephardi countries of origin; second, that a peripheral *Yishuv* society had *also* not reached a level of development comparable to that of the societies of the "center"; and, third, that Ashkenazi "modernity" was made possible thanks to the labor force provided by Oriental mass immigration.[59] The ethnic/racial basis of this process is often elided even by most Marxist analysts who speak generically of "Jewish workers," a simplification roughly parallel to speaking of the exploitation of "American" workers in Southern cotton plantations.

The Ordeals of Civility

The Oriental Jew clearly represents a problematic entity for European hegemony in Israel. Although Zionism collapses the Sephardim and the Ashkenazim into the single category of "one people," at the same time the Sephardi's Oriental "difference" threatens the European ideal-ego that fantasizes Israel as a prolongation of Europe "in" the Middle East but not "of" it. Ben-Gurion, we may recall, formulated his visionary utopia for Israel as that of a "Switzerland of the Middle East," while Herzl called for a Western-style capitalist-democratic miniature state, to be made possible by the grace of imperial patrons such as England or even Germany. The leitmotif of Zionist texts is the cry to form a "normal civilized nation," without the myriad "distortions" and forms of pariahdom typical of the Diaspora. (Zionist revulsion for shtetl "abnormalities," as some commentators have pointed out, is often strangely reminiscent of the very anti-Semitism it presumably so abhors.) The Ostjuden, perennially marginalized by Europe, realized their desire of becoming Europe, ironically, in the Middle East, this time on the back of their own "Ostjuden," the Eastern Jews. Having passed through their own "ordeal of civility," as the "blacks" of Europe, they now imposed their civilizing tests on "their own" blacks.[60]

The paradox of secular Zionism is that it attempted to end the Diaspora, during which Jews suffered intensely in the West and presumably had their heart in the East — a feeling encapsulated in the almost daily repetition of the phrase "next year in Jerusalem" — only to found a state whose ideological and geopolitical orientation has been almost exclusively turned toward the West. It is in this same context that we must understand the oppression of Sephardi not only as Middle Eastern people but also as embodying, for the Sabra-Zionist mind, what it erroneously perceived as a reminiscence of an "inferior" shtetl Jewishness. (This attitude was at times expressed toward Ashkenazi newcomers as well.) The immigrants or refugees from the Third World, and especially from Arab-Muslim countries, provoked "anti-Jewish" feelings in the secularly oriented Sabra culture both because of the implicitly threatening idea of the heterogeneity of Jewish cultures and because of the discomforting amalgam of "Jewishness" and what was perceived as "backwardness." This latter combination was seen as a malignancy to be eradicated, and this ideological impulse was manifested in measures taken to strip Sephardi Jews of their heritage: religious Yemenis shorn of their sidelocks, children virtually forced into Euro-Zionist schools, and so forth. The openness toward Western culture, then, must be understood within the relational context of a menacing heteroglossia, as a reaction against the vestiges of shtetl culture as well as against a projected penetration of "alien" Oriental Jews. The Sephardi cultural difference was especially disturbing to a secular Zionism whose claims for representing a single Jewish people were premised not only on common religious background but also on common nationality. The strong cultural and historical links that Sephardim shared with the Arab-Muslim world, stronger in many respects than those they shared with the Ashkenazim, threatened the conception of a homogeneous nation akin to those on which European nationalist movements were based.

Those Sephardim who came under the control of Ashkenazi religious authorities, meanwhile, were obliged to send their children to Ashkenazi religious schools, where they learned the "correct" Ashkenazi forms of practicing Judaism, including Yiddish-accented praying, liturgical-gestural norms, and sartorial codes favoring the dark colors of centuries-ago Poland. Some Oriental Jews, then, were forced into the Orthodox mold. The caricatural portrayal of Sephardim as religious fanatics, when not the product of *mauvaise foi,* is linked to a Eurocentric confusion between religiousness and Orthodoxy. In fact, however, the wrenching dechirement of the secular-Orthodox split, so characteristic of the European-Jewish experience, has been historically quite alien to Sephardi culture. Among Sephardim, Jewishness has generally been lived in an atmosphere of flexibility and tolerance, downplaying both abstract laws and rabbinical hierarchy. It is not uncommon, among Sephardim, to find coexisting within the same family diverse ways of being Jewish without this diversity entailing conflict. In Israel, the clash that pits secular against Orthodox Jews largely divides Ashkenazim rather than Sephardim, the majority of whom, whether religious or secular, feel repelled by the rigidity of both camps while being mindful of the ways both camps have oppressed them, albeit in different ways.

As an integral part of the topography, language, culture, and history of the Middle East, Sephardim were necessarily close to those who were posited as the common enemy for all Jews — the Arabs. Fearing an encroachment of the East upon the West, the establishment repressed the Middle Easternness of Sephardim as part of an attempt to separate and create hostility between the two groups. Arabness and Orientalness were consistently stigmatized as evils to be uprooted. For the Arab Jew, existence under Zionism has meant a profound and visceral schizophrenia, mingling stubborn self-pride with an imposed self-rejection, typical products of a situation of colonial ambivalence. The ideological dilemmas of Sephardim derive from the contradictions inherent in a situation where they are urged to see Judaism and Zionism as synonyms and Jewishness and Arabness as antonyms (for the first time in their history), when in fact they are both Arab and Jewish, and less historically, materially, and emotionally invested in Zionist ideology than the Ashkenazim.

Sephardim in Israel were made to feel ashamed of their dark olive skin, of their guttural language, of the winding quarter tones of their music, and even of their traditions of hospitality. Children, trying desperately to conform to an elusive Sabra norm, were made to feel ashamed of their parents and their Arab countries of origins. At times the Semitic physiognomies of the Sephardim led to situations in which they were mistaken for Palestinians and therefore arrested or beaten. Since Arabness led only to rejection, many Sephardim internalized the Euro-Israeli perspective and turned into self-hating Sephardim. Thus not only did the "West" come to represent the "East," but also, in a classic play of colonial specularity, the East came to view itself through the West's distorting mirror. Indeed, if it is true, as Malcolm X said, that the white man's worst crime was to make the black man hate himself, then the establishment in Israel has much to answer for. In fact, Arab-hatred when it occurs among Oriental Jews is almost always a disguised form of self-hatred. As research from 1978 indicates, Sephardi respect for Arabs rises with their own self-esteem.[61]

Sephardi hostility to Arabs, to the extent that it does exist, is very much "made in Israel."[62] Oriental Jews had to be taught to see the Arabs, and themselves, as other. The kind of *selbst-hass* that sometimes marked the post-Enlightenment Ashkenazi community had never been a part of Sephardi existence in the Muslim world; for the Sephardim, *selbst-hass* (of themselves as Orientals) had to be "learned" from the Ashkenazim, who themselves had "learned" self-hatred at the feet and among the ranks of the Europeans. Here too we are confronted with problematic antonyms, in this case that opposing the words "Zionism" and anti-Semitism." (But that subject merits separate discussion.)

The Demonization of Sephardim

The "divide and conquer" approach to Sephardi/Palestinian relations operated, as we have seen, by turning Sephardim into the most accessible targets for Arab attacks as well as in the deformation of the ideal of "Hebrew work." But the everyday power mechanisms in Israeli society also foster concrete economic pressures that generate tension between the two communities. Those Sephardim who continue to constitute the majority of the Jewish blue-collar workers are constantly placed in competition with the Palestinians for jobs and salaries, a situation that allows the elite to exploit both groups more or less at will. The considerable government expenditures for West Bank settlements, similarly, prod some Sephardim to move there for economic reasons — rather than ideological reasons that motivate many Ashkenazi settlers — and thus provoke Palestinians. Finally, because of the segregation between the two, Sephardim and Palestinians in Israel tend to learn about each other through the Euro-Israeli-dominated media, with little direct contact. Thus the Sephardim learn to see the Palestinians as "terrorists," while the Palestinians learn to see Sephardim as "Kahanist fanatics," a situation that hardly facilitates mutual understanding and recognition.

Although liberal left discourse in Israel has in recent years taken a small step toward recognizing the "Palestinian entity," it continues to hermetically seal off the Sephardi issue as an internal social problem to be solved once peace is achieved. Just as this discourse elides the historical origins of the Palestinian struggle and thus nostalgically looks back to an imagined prelapsarian past of "beautiful Israel," so it also elides the historical origins of Sephardi resentment and thus constructs the myth of "reactionaries." One problem is compartmentalized as political and foreign and the other as social and internal; the mutual implication of the two issues and their common relation to Ashkenazi domination are ignored. In fact the Sephardi movement constitutes a more immediate threat to Ashkenazi privilege and status than the abstract, perpetually deferred, future solution to the Palestinian question. Whereas the "Palestinian problem" can be still presented as the inevitable clash of two nationalities, acknowledgment of the exploitation and deculturalization of Sephardim in a putatively egalitarian Jewish state implies the indictment of the Israeli system itself as incorrigibly oppressive toward all peoples of the Orient.

Peace Now leaders such as General Mordechai Bar-On attribute the lack of Sephardi enthusiasm for Peace Now to "strong rightist tendencies" and "excited loyalty to the personal leadership of Menahem Begin," symptomatic of the Sephardim's "natural and traditional tendency . . . to follow a charismatic leader," all compounded with a "deep-rooted distrust in the Arabs."[63] The Sephardi other is portrayed as uncritical, instinctual, and, in accord with Oriental-despotic traditions, easily manipulated by patriarchal demagogues. The Sephardim, when not ignored by the Israeli "left," appear only to be scapegoated for everything that is wrong with Israel: "they" have destroyed beautiful Israel; "they" are turning Israel into a right-wing, antidemocratic state; "they" support the occupation; "they" are an obstacle to peace. These prejudices are then disseminated by Israeli "leftists" in international conferences, lectures, and publications. The caricatural presentation of Sephardim is a way for the Israeli left to enjoy a self-celebratory we-of-the-liberal-West image before international public opinion (at a time when Israel has undeniably lost its progressive allure and past unquestioned status) while continuing to enjoy, in Israel itself, a comfortable position as an integral part of the establishment. This facile scapegoating of Sephardim for a situation generated by Ashkenazi Zionists elides the reality of significant Sephardi pro-Palestinian activities as well as the lack of Sephardi access to the media and the consequent inability to counter such charges, which are then taken seriously by Palestinians and public opinion around the world. The demonization of Sephardim also has the advantage of placing the elite protesters in the narcissistic posture of perpetual seekers after peace who must bear the hostility of the government, the right wing, the Sephardim, and recalcitrant Palestinians. This martyrdom of the "shoot-and-cry" public-relations left contributes almost nothing to peace, but it does create the optical illusion of a viable oppositional peace force. Even the progressive forces in the peace camp that support a Palestinian state alongside Israel seldom abandon the idea of a Jewish Western state whose subtext inevitably is the ethnic/racial and class oppression of Sephardim. Within such a context, it is hardly surprising that the membership of Peace Now is almost exclusively Ashkenazi, with almost no Sephardi, or for that matter, Palestinian, participation.

Sephardi hostility toward Peace Now, rather than being discussed in class and racial terms, is conveniently displaced by Ashkenazi liberals onto the decoy-issue of a presumed general Sephardi animosity toward Arabs. This formulation ignores a number of crucial points. First, anti-Arabism forms an integral part of Zionist practice and ideology; Sephardim should not be scapegoated for what the Ashkenazi establishment itself has promoted. Second, Ashkenazim form the leadership of the right-wing parties, and many Euro-Israelis vote for these parties. (Polls taken during the 1981 elections showed that 36 percent of foreign-born Ashkenazim and 45 percent of Israeli-born Ashkenazim opted for Likud.[64] Sephardim, for their part, have also voted for Labor and other liberal parties, including the Communist Party.) In fact, however, the relatively high Sephardi vote for Likud has little to do with the latter's policies toward the Arabs; it is, rather, a minimal and even misplaced expression of Sephardi revolt against decades of Labor oppression. Since Sephardim cannot really represent themselves within the Israeli political system, a vote for the opposition interests within the ruling class becomes a way, as some Sephardi militants put it, of "strengthening the hyena in order to weaken the bear." Some independent leftist Sephardi activists viewed Likud, for example, as "an overnight shelter" where Oriental Jews could find temporary refuge while beginning to forge a powerful Sephardi revolt. The difference between Likud and Labor with regard to the

Palestinians, in any case, has not been one of practice but rather one of discourse, one aggressive-nationalist and the other humanist-liberal. The difference between the two parties with regard to Sephardim, similarly, is less one of policy than one of a contrast between populist appeals (Likud) and elitist condescension (Labor).

From Kahane to the Communists, the ideologies of the Israeli parties — from non-Zionist religious Orthodoxy dating back to Eastern European anti-Zionist opposition, through religious nationalism that foregrounds the "holiness of the land" (a religious variant on a common topos of European nationalism), to the dominant secular-humanist Zionism, based on European Enlightenment ideals — "translate" on a political register the various Jewish-European identity dilemmas. Founded, led, and controlled by Ashkenazim, these parties are the locus of struggle over the share of power among the various Ashkenazi groups. Within this structure there is little place for Sephardi aspirations. The Jewish-Sephardi majority has been politically marginalized, in other words, in a Jewish state, and in what is ritually and erroneously referred to as the "only democracy in the Middle East." The historical reasons for this marginalization are complex and can hardly be detailed here, but they include the following: the historical legacy of the Ashkenazi domination of the institutional party apparati prior to the arrival en masse of the Sephardim; the inertia of a hierarchical top-down structure that leaves little room for major shifts in direction; the delegitimization of the traditional Sephardi leadership; objectively harsh conditions, in the 1950s and 1960s, which left little time and energy for effective political and communal reorganization; and the repression as well as the co-optation of Sephardi revolts.

Political manipulation of Sephardi immigrants began virtually on their arrival, and at times even before, when Israeli party recruiters competed for Sephardi allegiance in the diverse countries of origins of Sephardim. In Israel, the immigrants or refugees were met in the airports not only by the officials in charge of arrival procedures but also by representatives of the various parties, who parceled out the Sephardim along the existing political spectrum. In the *ma'abarot,* as in Palestinian villages, the government controlled the populace through the intermediary of "notables" authorized to dispense favors in exchange for votes. At the time of the foundation of the state, there was some discussion of having a token Sephardi among the first twelve cabinet members, and considerable energy was expended on finding a sufficiently insignificant post ("The Sephardi minister," said David Remez of the Labor Party, "cannot have any grandiose pretensions").[65] At the same time, the Ashkenazi institutional apparatus has always claimed to represent the interests of all Jewish people, including Sephardim, as demonstrated by the proliferation of "Oriental departments." Unlike Palestinians, Sephardim were never denied official access to any Israeli institutions, and they were allowed, even encouraged, to find refuge in existing organizations. Class resentments could thus be exorcised through "socialist" organizations, while traditional Jewish activities could be entertained through religious institutions.

Signs of Sephardi Rebellion

Despite these obstacles, Sephardi revolt and resistance have been constant. Already in the transient camps there were "bread-and-jobs" demonstrations. David Horowitz, then general director of the Ministry of Finance, during a political consultation with Ben-Gurion, described the Sephardi population in the camps as "rebellious" and the situation as "incendiary" and "dynamite."[66] Another major revolt against misery and discrimination began in Haifa, in the neighborhood of Wadi-Salib, in 1959. Israeli authorities suppressed the rebellion with military and police terror. The Labor Party (Mapai), furthermore, tried to undermine the political organization that emerged from the riots by obliging slum residents to join the party if they hoped for a job. Another large-scale rebellion broke out again in the 1970s, when the Israeli Black Panthers called for the destruction of the regime and for the legitimate rights of all the oppressed without regard to religion, origin, or nationality. This alarmed the establishment, and the movement's leaders were arrested and placed under administrative detention. At that moment, the Black Panthers launched demonstrations that shook the entire country. In a demonstration that has since become famous (May 1971), tens of thousands, in response to police repression, went into the streets and threw Molotov cocktails against police and government targets. The same evening, 170 activists were arrested; 35 were hospitalized; and more than 70 policemen and officers were wounded. Taking their name from the American movement, the Black Panther revolt was led by the children of the Arab-Jewish immigrants, many of them having passed through rehabilitation centers or prisons. Gradually becoming aware of the political nature of their "inferiority," they sabotaged the myth of the melting pot by showing that there is in Jewish Israel not one but two peoples. They often used the term *dfukim vesheborim* (screwed and blacks) to express the racial/class positioning of Sephardim and viewed the American black revolt as a source of inspiration. (The choice of the name "Black Panthers" also ironically reverses the Ashkenazi reference to Sephardim as "black animals.") More recently, in December 1982, riots broke out in response to the police murder of a Mizrahi slum resident whose only crime was to build an illegal extension to his overcrowded house.

The establishment, meanwhile, has consistently tried to explain away all manifestations of Sephardi revolt. The "bread-and-jobs" demonstrations in the transient camps were dismissed as the result of the agitational work of leftist Iraqi immigrants; the demonstrations of Wadi-Salib and the Black Panthers were the expression of "violence-prone Moroccans"; individual acts of resistance were the symptoms of "neurosis" or "maladjustment." Golda Meir, prime minister during the Black Panther revolts, complained maternalistically that "they are not nice kids." Demonstrators were described in the press and in academic studies as lumpen proletarian deviants, and the movements were caricatured in the media as "ethnic organizing" and an attempt to "divide the nation." Class and ethnic antagonisms were often suppressed in the name of a supposedly imminent national-security disaster. In any case, all attempts at independent Sephardi political activity have faced the carrot-and-stick countermeasures of the establishment, measures that range on a spectrum from symbolic gestures toward token "change" channeled via the welfare infrastructure, through systematic co-optation of Sephardi activists (offering jobs and privilege is a major source of power in a small centralized country), to harassment, character assassination, imprisonment, torture, and, at times, pressures to leave the country.

The orchestrated attacks on Sephardi independent political activities — including by the "left" — were executed in the name of national unity in the face of the Arab threat. The assumption throughout was that the dominant parties were *not* "ethnic" — the very word, here as often, reflects a marginalizing strategy premised on the implicit contrast of "norm" and "other" — when in fact the existing Israeli institutions were *already* ethnically based according to countries of origins, a reality masked by a linguistic facade that made the Ashkenazim "Israelis" and the Sephardim *Bnei Edot haMizrah* (sons of the Oriental ethnic communities). The plural here covered the fact of the Sephardi numerical superiority, emphasizing plurality of origin, in contrast with a presumed preexisting (Ashkenazi) Israeli unity, and disguised the fact that the Sephardim, whatever their country of origin, have come in Israel to form a collective entity based both on cultural affinities and on the shared experience of oppression. Like many other ethnically/racially based dominating groups, the Israeli Ashkenazim have a kind of *pudeur* about being named; they rarely refer to themselves, or their power, as Ashkenazi; they do not see themselves as an ethnic group (partially because "Ashkenazi" evokes the "unflattering" memory of shtetl Jews). The Sephardim, however, do not share this *pudeur*. Sephardim, whatever their superficial political allegiance, often refer to the "Ashkenazi state," "the Ashkenazi newspapers," "the Ashkenazi television," "the Ashkenazi parties," "the Ashkenazi court," and at times even "the Ashkenazi army." The overwhelming majority of army deserters is to be found in the Sephardi community, particularly among the very working class, whose behavior reveals a reluctance to "give anything to this Ashkenazi state," and this in a society whose very structure sends the subliminal message: "Fight the Arabs and then we will accept you." A recent editorial in a Sephardi-neighborhood newspaper, entitled "Forty Years of the Ashkenazi State," summed up Sephardi feelings after four decades of statehood:

> This is the 40th year of independence for the Ashkenazi state called Israel, but who is going to celebrate? Our Oriental brothers who sit in jails? Our prostitute sisters from Tel Baruch? Our sons in schools, will they be celebrating the decline in the level of education? Will we celebrate the Ashkenazi theater of Kishon's Sallah? Or the rising fanaticism in our society? The flight from peace? The Oriental music broadcast only in the ghettoes of the media? The unemployment in development towns? It seems that the Orientals have no reason to celebrate. The joy and light are only for the Ashkenazim, and for the glory of the Ashkenazi state.[67]

Although effaced or overshadowed by the Israeli/Arab conflict, and despite official harassment, Sephardi resistance is always present, going through transformations, changing organizational forms. Despite the attempts to engender hostility between Sephardim and Palestinians, there have always been Sephardi activities in favor of justice for the Palestinians. Many members of the older Sephardi generation, both inside and outside of Israel, were eager to serve as a bridge of peace to the Arabs and to the Palestinians, but their efforts were consistently refused or undercut by the establishment.[68] The Black Panthers, seeing themselves as a "natural bridge" for peace, called in the 1970s for a "real dialogue" with the Palestinians, who are "an integral part of the political landscape of the Middle East" and whose "representatives must be allowed to take part in all meetings and discussions which seek a solution to the conflict."[69] The Panthers were also among the first Israeli groups to meet with the PLO. In the 1980s, movements such as East for Peace and the Oriental Front in Israel and Perspectives Judeo-Arabes in France — the names themselves point to the shedding of self-shame and the vision of integration into the political and cultural East — have called for an independent Palestinian state led by the PLO. The Oriental Front stresses that Sephardim are not Zionists in the conventional sense, but rather "in the Biblical meaning of 'Zion,' of a Jewish life in the birthplace of the Jewish people." It stresses as well the "debt of respect to Arab countries that gave [us] protection during centuries" and the strong Sephardi love and respect for Arab culture, since "there is no alienation between the Arab existence and the Oriental [Jewish] one."[70]

Epilogue

In many respects, European Zionism has been an immense confidence trick played on Sephardim, a cultural massacre of immense proportions, an attempt, partially successful, to wipe out, in a generation or two, millennia of rooted Oriental civilization, unified even in its diversity. *My* argument here, I hasten to clarify, is not an essentialist one. I am not positing a new binarism of eternal hostility between Ashkenazim and Sephardim. In many countries and situations, the two groups, despite cultural and religious differences, have coexisted in relative peace; it is only in Israel that they exist in a relation of dependency and oppression. (In any case, only 10 percent of Ashkenazi Jews are in Israel.) Obviously, Ashkenazi Jews have been the prime victims of the most violent kinds of European anti-Semitism, a fact that makes it more delicate to articulate not only a pro-Palestinian point of view but also a pro-Sephardi point of view. A Sephardi critique is expected to be suppressed in the name of the menaced "unity of the Jewish people" in the post-Holocaust era (as if within all unities, especially those of recent construction, there were not also differences and dissonances). My argument is also not a moralistic or characterological one, positing a Manichaean schematism contrasting good Oriental Jews with evil Ashkenazi oppressors. My argument is structural, an attempt to account theoretically for the "structure of feeling," the deep current of rage against the Israeli establishment that unites most Sephardim independent of their declared party affiliation. My argument is situational and analytical; it claims that the Israeli sociopolitical formation continually generates the underdevelopment of the Mizrahim.

A specter haunts European Zionism, the specter that all of its victims — Palestinians, Sephardim (as well as critical Ashkenazim, in and outside Israel, stigmatized as "self-hating" malcontents) — will perceive the linked analogies between their oppressions. To conjure this specter, the Zionist establishment in Israel has done everything in its power: the fomenting of war and the cult of national security, the simplistic portrayal of Palestinian resistance as terrorism; the fostering of situations that catalyze Sephardi-Palestinian tension; the caricaturing of Sephardim as Arab-haters and religious fanatics; the promotion, through the educational system and the media, of Arab-hatred and Sephardi self-rejection; the repression or co-optation of all those who might promote a progressive Palestinian-Sephardi alliance. I in no way mean to equate Palestinian and Sephardi suffering — obviously Palestinians are those most egregiously wronged by Zionism — or to compare the long lists of crimes against both. The point is one of affinity and analogy rather than perfect identity of interests or experience. I am not asking Palestinians to feel sorry for the Sephardi soldiers who might be among those shooting at them. It is not Sephardim, obviously, who are being killed, time after time, in the streets of Gaza or in the refugee camps of Lebanon. What is at stake, in any case, is not a competition for sympathy but a search for alternatives. Until now both Palestinians and Sephardim have been the objects and not the subjects of Zionist ideology and policies, and until now they have been played against each other. But it was not the Sephardim who made the crucial decisions leading to the brutal displacement and oppression of the Palestinians — even if the Sephardim were enlisted as cannon fodder after the fact — just as it was not the Palestinians who uprooted, exploited, and humiliated the Sephardim. The present regime in Israel inherited from Europe a strong aversion to respecting the right of self-determination of non-European peoples; whence the quaint vestigial, out-of-step quality of its discourse, its atavistic talk of the "civilized nations" and "the civilized world." As much as it is impossible to imagine peace between Israel and the Arabs without recognizing and affirming the historical rights of the Palestinian people, so a real peace must not overlook the collective rights of Mizrahim. It would be shortsighted to negotiate only with those in power or embraced by it, dismissing the subjection of Jews from Arab and Muslim countries as an "internal Jewish" problem; that position would be analogous to taking the Zionist attitude that the Palestinian question is an "internal" Arab problem. I am not suggesting, obviously, that all Sephardim would ascribe to my analysis, although most would endorse much of it. I am suggesting, rather, that only such an analysis can account for the complexities of the present situation and the depth and extent of Sephardi rage. My analysis hopes, finally, to open up a long-range perspective that might aid in a larger effort to move beyond the present intolerable impasse.

NOTES

Throughout this essay, all translations from the Hebrew are mine.

1. Edward Said, *Orientalism* (New York: Vintage, 1978), 31.
2. Arye Gelblum, *HaAretz,* April 22, 1949.
3. Ibid.
4. David Ben-Gurion, *Eternal Israel* (Tel Aviv: Ayanot, 1964), 34.
5. Quoted in Sammy Smooha, *Israel: Pluralism and Conflict* (Berkeley: University of California Press, 1978), 88.
6. Abba Eban, *Voice of Israel* (New York, 1957), 76, as quoted in Smooha, *Israel.*
7. Quoted in Smooha, *Israel,* 44
8. Quoted in ibid., 88–89.
9. Quoted in Tom Segev, *1949: The First Israelis* (New York: Free Press, 1986), 156–57.
10. Quoted in Tom Segev, *1949: The First Israelis* (Jerusalem: Domino Press, 1984), 156 (in Hebrew).
11. See Frantz Fanon, *The Wretched of the Earth* (New York: Grove Press, 1964), 51.
12. Quotations taken from Segev, *1949,* 157 (Hebrew).
13. Quoted in David K. Shipler, *Arab and Jew* (New York: Times Books, 1986), 24.
14. Amnon Dankner, "I Have No Sister," *HaAretz,* February 18, 1983.
15. Dr. Devora and Rabbi Menachem Hacohen, *One People: The Story of the Eastern Jews* (New York: Adama Books, 1986).
16. Ora Gloria Jacob-Arzooni, *The Israeli Film: Social and Cultural Influences, 1912–1973* (New York: Garland, 1983), 22, 23, 25. For a critique of Israeli colonial discourse, see Ella Shohat, *Israeli Cinema: East/West and the Politics of Representation* (Austin: University of Texas Press, 1989).

17. See Fanon, *Wretched of the Earth,* 51.

18. On the various forms of encouragement given to Yiddish in Israel, see Itzhak Koren (of the World Council for Yiddish and Jewish Culture), "Letter to the Editor," *Ma'ariv,* December 4, 1987.

19. See Maxime Rodinson, "A Few Simple Thoughts on Anti-Semitism" in *Cult, Ghetto, and State* (London: Al Saqi, 1983).

20. See Abbas Shiblak, *The Lure of Zion* (London: Al Saqi, 1986).

21. Yosef Meir, *Beyond the Desert* (Israel: Ministry of Defence, 1973), 19, 20 (in Hebrew).

22. Yehoshua Porath, *The Emergence of the Palestinian-Arab National Movement, 1919–1929* (Tel Aviv: Am Oved, 1976), 49 (in Hebrew).

23. Ibid., 48.

24. Ibid.

25. Ibid., 48–49.

26. Ibid., 49.

27. Ibid., 22, 23, 24.

28. See *HaOlam HaZe,* April 20, 1966 (Hebrew); *The Black Panther,* November 9, 1972 (Hebrew); Wilbur Crane Eveland, *Ropes of Sands: America's Failure in the Middle East* (New York: Norton, 1980), 48–49; Shiblak, *Lure of Zion;* Uri Avnery, *My Friend, the Enemy* (Westport, Conn.: Lawrence Hill, 1986), 133–40.

29. Segev, *1949,* 167 (Hebrew).

30. See "Denaturalization" and "Exodus," in Shiblak, *Lure of Zion,* 78–127.

31. Quoted in Yosef Meir, *The Zionist Movement and the Jews of Yemen* (Tel Aviv: Afikim Library, 1983), 43 (Hebrew).

32. Quoted in ibid., 48.

33. See Yaakov Zerubavel, *Alei-haim* (Tel Aviv: Y. L. Peretz Library Publication, 1960) (Hebrew).

34. Arthur Ruppin, *Chapters of My Life* (Tel Aviv: Am Oved, 1968), pt. 2, p. 27 (Hebrew).

35. Yaakov Rabinovitz, *HaPoel HaTzair,* July 6, 1910.

36. Shmuel Yavne'eli, *A Journey to Yemen* (Tel Aviv: Ayanot, 1963), 106 (Hebrew).

37. Ibid., 83–90.

38. Meir, *Zionist Movement,* 97–98.

39. Quoted in ibid., 44.

40. See Meir, *Zionist Movement,* esp. 113–21. Cf. Niza Droyan, *And Not with a Magic Carpet* (Jerusalem: Ben-Tzvi Institute for Research into the Communities of Israel in the East 134–48 (in Hebrew).

41. Meir, *Zionist Movement,* 58.

42. Quoted in ibid., 65.

43. Segev, *1949,* 171–74 (Hebrew).

44. Quoted in Segev, *1949,* 169 (English).

45. Quoted in ibid., 166 (Hebrew).

46. Ibid., 167, 328.

47. Ibid., 330.

48. Ibid., 178.

49. See Dov Levitan, "The *Aliya* of the 'Magic Carpet' as a Historical Continuation of the Earlier Yemenite *Aliyas"* (M.A. thesis, Bar Ilan University [Israel], 1983) (Hebrew); Segev, *1949,* 185–87, 331 (Hebrew).

50. Segev, *1949,* 172–73 (Hebrew).

51. Shlomo Swirski and Menaham Shoushan, *Development Towns in Israel* (Haifa: Breirot Publishers, 1986), 7.

52. See ibid.

53. For citations from some of the documents, see Segev, *1949* (English) particularly pt. 2: "Between Veterans and Newcomers," 93–194.

54. Ya'acov Nahon, *Patterns of Education Expansion and the Structure of Occupation Opportunities: the Ethnic Dimension* (Jerusalem: Jerusalem Institute for the Research of Israel, 1987).

55. Smooha, *Israel,* 178–79.

56. Shlomo Swirski, "The Oriental Jews in Israel," *Dissent* 31, no. 1 (winter 1984): 84.

57. Shlomo Swirski, *Orientals and Ashkenazim in Israel* (Haifa: Mahbarot LeMehkar UleBikoret, 1981) (Hebrew).

58. Yosef Ben David, "Integration and Development," in S. N. Eisenstadt, Rivkah Bar Yosef, and Haim Adler, eds., *Integration and Development in Israel* (Jerusalem: Israel Universities Press, 1970), 374.

59. Swirski, *Orientals,* 53–54.

60. For a discussion of the secular European-Jewish encounter with Protestant culture, see John Murray Cuddihy, *The Ordeal of Civility* (Boston: Beacon Press, 1974).

61. See *The Sephardic Community in Israel and the Peace Process* (New York: Institute for Middle East Peace and Development, CUNY, 1986), directed by Harriet Arnone and Ammiel Alcalay.

62. See Hashem Mahameed and Yosef Gottman, "Autostereotypes and Heterostereotypes of Jews and Arabs under Various Conditions of Contact," *Israeli Journal of Psychology and Counseling in Education* (Jerusalem: Ministry of Education and Culture) 16 (September 1983).

63. Mordechai Bar-On, *Peace Now: The Portrait of a Movement* (Tel Aviv: HaKibbutz HaMeuchad, 1985), 89–90 (Hebrew).

64. Swirski, "Oriental Jews," 89–90.

65. Segev, *1949,* 174 (Hebrew).

66. Ibid., *1949,* 161.

67. Beni Zada, "Forty Years of the Ashkenazim State," *Pa'amon* 16 (December 1987).

68. Abba Eban, for example, opposed "regarding our immigrants from Oriental countries as a bridge toward our integration with the Arabic-speaking world" (quoted in Smooha, *Israel,* 88).

69. Cited from a Black Panther press conference held in Paris, March 1975.

70. Quotations are taken from several speeches of the Oriental Front delivered in their meeting with the PLO in Vienna, July 1986.

Chapter 3
Of Balkans and Bantustans: Ethnic Cleansing and the Crisis in National Legitimation
Rob Nixon

Let me say something briefly about the so-called black-on-black violence in our country. . . . What we are confronted with here is a problem of violent resistance to democratic change, and not a situation of ethnic conflicts that are supposedly inherent in African societies. South Africa is not Bosnia-Herzegovina.
Nelson Mandela, Speech to NAACP convention, Indianapolis, 1993

The word pollution is often on the lips of the violent.
— Natalie Z. Davis, *Society and Culture in Early Modern France*

An academic prophecy can seldom have been so instantly superannuated as the closing words to Eric Hobsbawm's book *Nations and Nationalism since 1780.* For Hobsbawm, writing in 1989, progress in the analysis of nationalism signaled that "the phenomenon is past its peak. The owl of Minerva which brings wisdom, said Hegel, flies out at dusk. It is a good sign that it is now circling round nations and nationalism."[1] Hobsbawm's owl seems to have been lured out less by the twilight of nationalism than by its bloody new dawn.

Eminent theorists of nationalism like Hobsbawm, Benedict Anderson, Ernest Gellner, and Tom Nairn, who established their reputations on the subject in the late 1970s or 1980s, could not have anticipated the unprecedented proliferation of nation-states since 1990. In the past few years, more new states have arisen in Eastern Europe and Eurasia than during those high eras of European national birthing, 1848 and 1917 to 1921. German reunion, the fracturing of the Soviet Union, the splitting of Czechoslovakia, and Yugoslavia's sanguinary disintegration have all signaled an upsurge in ethnic nationalisms bent on redrawing the boundaries of nation-states — whether through irredentism or, more commonly, by carving large states into more ethnically homogeneous polities.

These developments have sharply raised the stakes of ethnic nationalism by creating, through the power of immediate precedent, a land-grabbing atmosphere in which national boundaries appear to be more elastic. Only a smattering of recognized states can claim ethnic homogeneity, yet the belief that a state should bring in train a unitary lineage of culture, tradition, ethnicity, and nation retains a lingering international prestige. In the current climate of border changes, this residual prejudice in favor of "sameness" encourages the destabilizing pursuit of that *ignis fatuus,* ethnic consistency. This point has been demonstrated with brutal force by the assault on Bosnia-Herzegovina: amid a resurgent view that people who are the "same" deserve and require ethnic self-rule, a history of multicultural tolerance can be transformed into a liability.

During the early 1990s, the combination of imperial collapse, state proliferation, and ascendant ethnic nationalism has brought on a crisis in the procedures for national legitimation. If national claims resting on ethnic foundations appear desta-bilizing, how else are aspirant states to mount their appeals? Arguments based on historical occupation resolve little in the myriad cases of layered possession; only a minority of states display linguistic unity; and economic viability carries little weight in a world of microstates like Andorra, Gambia, and St. Vincent. Other than simply freezing the status quo — which would be catastrophic for the Palestinians, among others — there appear to be inadequate internationally sanctioned counters to the redrawing of national boundaries along ethnic lines.

The train of logic that idealizes the alignment of culture, ethnicity, and the nation-state provides a powerful means of staking a territorial claim; read in the opposite direction, the same logic explains violence as a "natural" explosion of primordial ethnic differences — the revenge of the past, in the purported manner of Yu-goslavia. The Balkan conflicts have, in many quarters, given weight to this perilous assumption that ethnic differences "naturally" produce conflict and, conversely, that ethnicity offers a "natural" basis for national community.[2] This reversible argument threatens to become an axiom of nationalist politics in the 1990s. It has found favor with advocates of "immigrant" expulsion, population "transfer," ethnic segregation, "ethnic cleansing," and/or ethnic secession in societies as varied as Israel, France, Zaire, Azerbaijan, South Africa, Bosnia-Herzegovina, India, Iraq, Kuwait, Israel, and Germany.

The revival of ethnic nationalism has given focus not just to the unstable pro-cedures for national legitimation but also to the equivocal character of the term of ethnicity. If ethnicity is conventionally associated with cultural attributes as opposed to the biological constructs of race, it would seem to be the more accommodating of the two categories — admitting a looser, more conditional image of identity achieved through socialization, not genes. Yet, particularly in the context of nationalism, the cultural markers of ethnicity may become invested with a surrogate determinism that achieves a neobiological intensity.

The efforts to sanctify ethnicity as an impermeable, inescapable identity have been intensified during the transitional crises in South Africa and the former Yu-goslavia. The assumption that ethnic difference is the fount of South Africa's violence reinforces suggestions that the conflict is the predictable outcome of mixing in-compatible "ethnic nations." This belief can in turn be used to brace arguments for a federal constitution that reinforces the old racially ordered inequities. And, as in Bosnia-Herzegovina, the view that the conflict is at heart an interethnic blood feud weakens the case for decisive international involvement — an issue of press-ing importance with regard to the monitoring of South Africa's first democratic elections.[3]

To those whose economic and political calculations cannot accommodate sym-biosis, cosmopolitanism — be it in Sophiatown or Sarajevo — stands as a symbolic provocation to a system premised on inviolable ethnic difference. The project of "cleansing" such places may be vindicated by the contention, among others, that "improving" a community's ethnic consistency requires short-term violence for the ends of long-term peace. But the claim that ethnic homogeneity enhances the prospects of social stability remains wholly unsubstantiated. Moreover, in both South Africa and the former Yugoslavia, this misguided assumption has produced an inverted account of a violence that has its source less in ethnic incompatibility than in the futile, infinite, and bloodstained labor of seeking to divide the indivisible. Ethnic difference is not the wellspring of "ethnic violence," which flows instead from (among other things) historical efforts to impose categorical ethnic identities. Thus a symptom of the violence — the defensive production of brittle ethnicities — is readily misconstrued as its cause.

The Amplification of Ethnic Nationalism

Over one hundred new states have emerged during the post–World War II era, the majority of them in the *soi-disant* "Third World" following the breakup of the European empires. But almost all of these states — barring a handful of exceptions like India, Pakistan, Lebanon, and the Cameroon — have remained circumscribed by territorial boundaries inherited from the colonial epoch. Since then, secessionist movements representing the Palestinians, Kurds, Kashmiris, Western Saharans, and others have campaigned for the redrawing of international borders. But rarely have their efforts met with success.

However, the perception that the early 1990s offer a uniquely propitious moment for publicizing minority nationalist causes has spread westward and southward from the former communist bloc. In Western Europe, events to the east didn't so much catalyze new claims as enhance the visibility of old ones by representing them as part of an international drive. Thus, Breton, Walloon, Scottish, Basque, Catalan, Sardinian, Gibraltan, and Tyrol nationalisms all sought to capitalize on the political atmosphere, particularly in 1991, when the (now wavering) prospect of European unity held out the promise of an autobahn running from regional to European Community polities and bypassing centralized states.

While these European developments have drawn extensive comment, there has been little discussion of the reverberations of the newly fortified idiom of ethnic nationalism beyond Europe and Eurasia's borders. Dissidents in Zaire, for instance, have sought to advance their secessionist campaign against Mobutu's kleptocracy by calling for the birth of "the Baltic states of Zaire: Katanga, Kasai, and Kivu."[4] And Jacques Parizeau, leader of Parti Quebecois, has invoked the fall of the Soviet empire as proof that Quebec's separatists had been "visionaries, nearly prophets all along."[5]

The amplification of ethnic-nationalist discourse has set up dangerous echoes in South Africa, where right-wing forces ranged against the African National Congress (ANC) have alighted, with dismaying speed, on the political kudos to be gained from Soviet and Yugoslavian analogies. The European-led resurgence of the ethnic-nationalist idiom has coincided with two developments that will have a critical impact on the long-term character of South Africa's transformation. These are the upswing in violence and negotiations toward a democratic constitution.

Between 1986 and 1993, more South Africans died in conflict than in any comparable period this century — since what Gerhard Mare sardonically calls the "white-on-white violence" of the Anglo-Boer War.[6] Ironically, it is European conflicts that have fortified ethnic interpretations of South Africa's violence; yet such explanations can be conveniently fused to the colonial charge that "tribal" warfare is an immanent, atavistic African failing.[7] If the towering issue of violence in South Africa is projected as the result of "natural" hostilities between innately different ethnic nations, this strengthens the hand of those who maintain that ethnic fault lines are "natural" divides that ought to play a leading role in the reorganization of the South African state. This in turn would retard efforts to redress apartheid's central legacy, the racial imbalances in access to resources and institutional power.

Apartheid and the Dismemberment of Yugoslavia

In 1989, Leroy Vail could begin a book he edited, *The Creation of Tribalism in Southern Africa,* by questioning whether socialism could furnish African states with a transcendent "pan-ethnic class consciousness." It was, in his view, improbable that "Africa would be a continent of new Yugoslavias."[8]

More recently, the specter of Yugoslavia has returned to haunt South African politics. But it now looks very different. Yugoslavia has metamorphosed from a symbol of a pan-ethnic socialism ostensibly beyond African emulation into a reminder of what might lie ahead for South Africa if it spurns a federal model of government responsive to "ethnic awakenings." This fashionable analogy has found particular favor among conservatives partial to the Inkatha Freedom Party and hostile to the ANC. It has been upheld by, among others, Chief Mangosuthu Gatsha Buthelezi, Andries Treurnicht (leader of the Conservative Party), and the Oxford political scientist R. W. Johnson. Writing in the *Times* (London), Johnson has warned that "without federalism, South Africa might simply split apart like a huge African Yugoslavia....As Yugoslavia has shown, once the dominoes begin to fall it is a matter of *sauve qui peut*."[9]

But how salient is this comparison? And what is the political cost of accepting it?

The views of Treurnicht, a die-hard ring-winger, reveal some of the unsettling implications of brisk analogies between South Africa and Eastern Europe. Treurnicht has hailed the secessionist aftermath of communism's fall as a belated vindication of "separate development." "The ethnic awakening and demand for self-determination in Eastern Europe," he opined,

> has been political practice in South Africa for the past four decades, but is now being betrayed [by the pressure to democratize according to majority rule]....South Africa has a deeply divided population — along racial, ethnic, cultural, language and religious lines....To force together such largely disparate people, cultures and races, will amount to a form of tyranny, the very opposite of democratic freedom....[Instead we must promote] the development of separate freedoms for the various peoples, ethnic groups, in their own territories, or homelands.[10]

This is back to the future with a vengeance: the Bantustan system as the fin de siècle's fast lane to democracy.

However, it is Buthelezi who has most energetically worked the possibilities of Eastern European and Balkan analogies. Although he represents only a minority of Zulus, Buthelezi has become the torchbearer of an at times neobiological vision of the "Zulu nation" as a primordially vindicated, historically sanctified ethnic community. Through a sleight of hand, he has then equated his political organization, Inkatha, with this inviolable ethnic nation. Buthelezi is also South Africa's most vocal advocate of a federal "solution" with ethnic-nationalist overtones. For these reasons, he stands to gain symbolically from the upheavals in the former Eastern bloc. He has, for instance, threatened to "lead his homeland of KwaZulu to secession," thereby taking what he calls the "Yugoslavia option."[11] Buthelezi develops this threat in a document that he calls (in an echo of Ian Smith's "Unilateral Declaration of Independence") his "Unilateral Declaration of Autonomy."

As the antagonists in the Bosnian war argued over ethnically charged plans for regional autonomy and states-within-a-state, so too, in South Africa, opponents of the ANC's vision of a unitary, nonracial state aired schemes that would produce an ethnic carve-up. Buthelezi's declining fortunes, together with the secessionist mood in Eastern Europe, have emboldened him in his long-standing efforts to establish Natal/KwaZulu as an embryonic state. Buthelezi has proposed that this "state" draw up its own autonomous constitution — replete with opt-out clauses — *prior* to negotiating membership in a federal South African state. The Inkatha leader posits an Afrikaner homeland and the parlous homelands of the Ciskei and Bophuthatswana as "potential states" along parallel lines — a de facto cementing of apartheid's Bantustan legacy.[12]

In one of his wilder posturings, Buthelezi has maintained that the ANC and the National Party are jointly prosecuting a policy of "ethnic cleansing" against his "Zulu nation."[13] This is a risible claim: as the Inkathagate scandal proved in 1992, Buthelezi's forces have enjoyed the financial and logistical support of the country's police and military elite.[14] Moreover, the majority of political killings in recent years have resulted from inter-Zulu violence — between Zulu supporters of the ANC and its allies, and Zulu supporters of Inkatha.[15] Polls consistently show that more Zulus back the ANC than Inkatha, yet Buthelezi persists in projecting his organization and the Zulu nation as isomorphic. The ANC possesses a deep history of Zulu support, particularly, though not exclusively, among urban workers. The eminent Zulu chief Albert Luthuli stands as one of Mandela's most honored precursors, both as president of the ANC and as a fellow recipient of the Nobel Peace Prize. Yet Buthelezi papers over such complexities in his efforts to portray his political party, alias the "Zulu nation," as the target of ethnic cleansings.

Conservatives like Buthelezi and Johnson who read Yugoslavia's disintegration as an omen for South Africa flatter the country's secessionist potential. The appeal of their contention rests partly on its graphic and topical simplification: the South African violence becomes instantly more intelligible if it is recast as an intimation of a Balkan scenario. But more than simplification is at stake. To predict successive ethnic and regional secessions is to inflate Inkatha's importance by projecting it as a bellwether of future defections from South Africa.

To cast Inkatha in this role requires that Buthelezi, Johnson, and others maintain a symptomatic silence about the dissimilar histories of ethnic engineering in Yugoslavia and South Africa. Very stark differences pertain. Yugoslavia's socialist rulers saw the containment of ethnic-nationalist claims as a condition of the state's survival, while in South Africa the central order sought to safeguard its authority by deepening ethnic divides and fostering multiple ethnic nationalisms. The apartheid regime's efforts to kick-start ten Bantustans was, for several decades, a defining feature of the centralized apartheid state.

Ethnic nationalism thus became firmly associated with apartheid's paradoxical attempts to consolidate power through the illusion of dispersing it. The appeal of ethnic secession in South Africa remains muted by its association with cynical state efforts to impose ersatz "independent ethnic nation-states" in the absence of popular impulses sustaining such constructs from below. Resistance to the Bantustan legacy of *divide et impera* does not guarantee the unity of those whom it oppressed; nor can the raw memories of that system halt the violence per se. However, apartheid's calamitous attempts to fabricate ethnic "homelands" has shrouded ethnic-nationalist politics in suspicion for the foreseeable future, thus curbing its centrifugal power.

That much is manifest from South Africa's and Yugoslavia's contrasting experiences of ethnic cleansing. In the former Yugoslavia, this policy was prosecuted by Radovan Karadzic's forces *after* the central state had unraveled. The Serbian clampdown in Kosovo notwithstanding, ethnic cleansing was a post-Yugoslavian phenomenon.[16] In South Africa, however, "ethnic cleansing" was a hallmark of the old order. While that repellent phrase was never featured in apartheid's lexicon, the process was systematic and long-standing. For proof, one need only recall the notorious pronouncement by Connie Mulder, minister of Bantu administration and development, in 1978: "If our policy is taken to its logical conclusion as far as the black people are concerned, there will not be one black man with South African citizenship."[17] The perception of this policy as a kind of cleansing became explicit in references to the need to eradicate "black spots" from "white" South Africa — an image that drew on the discourses of epidemiology and domestic labor for a project of ethnic engineering.[18]

Black South Africans may not have endured the precise equivalent of the Bosnian camps, but they suffered over several decades all the other brutalities that comprise ethnic cleansing: collective expulsion; forced migration; the bulldozing, gutting, or seizure of homes; the mandatory carrying of "passes" detailing the holder's putative ethnicity and movements; and the corralling into rural ghettos of people decreed to be "illegal squatters," "surplus," "idle," "alien," or "unassimilable." These removals, in the South African case, were conducted under the guise of a spurious repatriation.[19]

The apartheid version of ethnic cleansing was cynically and transparently packaged as the fruition of ethnic self-determination. The regime sought — with almost no internal or international success — to present its actions as a species of decolonization. It argued that "separate development" was "not a policy of discrimination on the ground of race or colour, but a policy of differentiation on the ground of nationhood, ... granting to each self-determination within the borders of their homelands."[20] The completion of this argument required several legerdemains, exemplified by the utterances of another Nationalist MP, Louis Nel. Nel declared that "while no umbrella nationalism exists among the black people, there are strongly rooted ethnic nationalisms."[21] Not only does this utterance gainsay the history of black resistance, but it posits ethnic nationalisms that are largely the conceptual offspring of the regime's reinvention of ethnic difference.

Nel's second vindication of the "Bantustan" policy, although voiced in 1977, achieves a grim resonance in the 1990s:

> The more heterogeneous a society the greater the potential for conflict and even bloodshed. The reverse of this argument is also true, namely that the more homogeneous a society the greater the potential for conflict and even bloodshed.[22]

This unfounded, indeed incendiary, assumption now echoes across Europe and beyond. Just as South Africa's Nationalists could forcibly drive 3.5 million people from their homes under the guise of creating harmonious pockets of homogeneity, a similarly circular argument is being popularized by Karadzic and his cohorts — that violent "cleansings" serve as a prophylactic against violence.

When the Bantustan policy was most ruthlessly implemented in the 1960s and 1970s, the South African regime sought to link its actions imaginatively not just to a decolonizing Africa but to European precedents as well. A contest over analogies took shape: the regime sought to assimilate the Bantustans to the idea of "cantonization," while the liberation movement condemned them as attempts to "balkanize" African nationalism.[23] For those who lived through this shoot-out between analogies, Western euphemisms for Bosnia's dismemberment have acquired a macabre familiarity. While the Serbs carved up the internationally recognized state of Bosnia-Herzegovina and the Croats opportunistically grabbed bits for themselves, Lord Carrington urged that this particular Balkan conflict be resolved through "cantonization."[24] Not for the first time were territorial plunder and ethnic "purification" graced with a Swiss name.[25]

Pollution and Biological Nationalism

Karadzic, together with his allies in Belgrade and the Yugoslav People's Army, adopted a genocidal policy toward Bosnia's Muslims that exposed the lurking biologism in the very ideal of the "healthy" nation. For the intelligibility of the noxious metaphor of ethnic cleansing depends on the prior, seemingly innocent figure of the nation as body politic. Karadzic's forces have pursued this idiom with a bloody literalness, reminding us of the insidious danger of representing nations as healthy or ailing. Such an idiom readily serves, in economic and ideological crises, as a bridge to the discourse of national pathologies. The "ailments" or "degeneration" of the national body can then be readily ascribed to the presence of "alien bodies" and "parasites," the antidote for which is cleansing, purification, or a *cordon sanitaire* to prevent further "contamination" — all on the assumption that "disinfecting" the nation is a precondition for its "convalescence" or "recovery."[26]

On the cultural front, the baleful consequences of the tyranny of cleanliness were not restricted to Serbian nationalism. The Croatian writer Dubravka Ugresic recounts how in the euphoric aftermath of Croatia's independence empty cans bearing Croatia's red and white coat of arms and the label "Clean Croatian Air" became all the rage. The popularity of such nationalist kitsch was a stimulus to and a symptom of a broad campaign to purify school curricula, genealogies, libraries, and towns of "Serbo-Byzantine" history, blood, books, and houses.[27]

The glaring offensiveness of the idiom of national sanitation has, by now, been repeatedly remarked upon. However, the "cleansing" may serve as a decoy for our outrage, distracting us from questioning its "ethnic" designation. Plainly, the goal of ethnic cleansing can only proceed on the basis of ethnic definition and recognition, yet much of the media has acquiesced in the assumption that categorical ethnic differences predated, indeed, detonated, the Bosnian conflict. Even those with only a passing knowledge of the former Yugoslavia can recognize an asymmetry in the naming of the principal antagonists: Serbs, Croats, and Muslims. Yet, in most reporting on the conflict, "Muslim" has come to serve as an ersatz ethnic category. It ought to have signaled that, while Bosnia-Herzegovina is crossed-hatched with religious and cultural differences, it requires a sleight of hand to classify these as firm ethnic divides. Muslims, Serbs, and Croats are, after all, all Slavs who speak mutually intelligible variants of Serbo-Croatian.[28] Lejla Somum, formerly of Sarajevo, has argued that prior to the war, most of the city's Bosnian Serbs did not believe in their ethnic difference and even during the siege many continued to refuse that designation.[29] However, the idea of ethnic incompatibilities has been institutionalized through a dialectic between the military enforcement of difference, on the one hand, and, on the other, the West's accession to the notion of this as an ethnic war.

The unquestioned assumption that the target of the "cleansing" is a discrete ethnicity reinforces the link between an essentialist theory of ethnicity and the notion of "natural" conflicts. Such reasoning has proved catastrophic for Bosnia-Herzegovina, reducing a politically complex war to a force of nature — a conflagration or a tornado, best left to burn or blow itself out. This obscures the political calculations at stake along with the moral distinctions between territorial aggressors and defenders. Ethnicity serves as an ethical leveler. Thus the apparently mitigating ethnic factor in Bosnia has helped excuse the temporizing and virtual quietism of Western leaders. In short, the combustible "nature" of ethnic difference and the geopolitical "nature" of the Balkans have allowed the West what Mark Thompson has aptly called "the comforts of fatalism."[30]

A version of this process is evident in representations of the South African conflict. Nelson Mandela has complained that by failing to marshal its military resources to contain the violence, the de Klerk regime treated black lives as cheap. If the conflict can be designated as "ethnic" — as a blood feud between "*the* Zulus" and "*the* Xhosas" — it can be smoothly dismissed as "natural," thereby cheapening the lives at stake.

The currently ascendant assumption that there are "natural" national communities — and by extension "natural" conflicts between them — rests on a crucial ambiguity in the very idea of ethnicity. The term wavers between the poles of culture and biology, between the contingencies of socialization and the fixity of genetic determinism. In the liberal aftermath of World War II, it became less acceptable to enunciate racism in racial terms. Yet, as Paul Gilroy and Stuart Hall have observed in Britain and Etienne Balibar in France, the retreat of articulated racism did not diminish the power of what Balibar calls "racism without race."[31] While the rhetoric of racial determinism — the idiom of bloodlines, degeneration, genetic purity, and physical stigmata — declined, racism was readily admitted through the open fanlight of ethnic culturalism.

Thus the distinction between a paradigm foregrounding physical features and one emphasizing cultural contingencies is by no means absolute. That much was manifest in the South African regime's representations of the Bantustans as, by turns, "ethnic nation-states" and "biologically demarcated tribal states."[32] This latter conceptual omelet is indicative of the tendency, common among ethnic nationalists, to inflate the authority of the nation-state by straining to portray it as a genetic rather than a merely cultural institution.

However, the biological assumptions underpinning the nation-state are seldom so self-defeatingly explicit. What one witnesses instead is biology by other means, most often through the surrogacy of ethnic cultural or primordial claims. Ethnicity, as one among many aspects of our identity, lacks the uncompromising closure of a genetic pedigree: for those who would raise mere ethnic consciousness to the pitch of ethnic nationalism, the porousness of cultural identity becomes a liability. If ethnicity is to be mobilized on behalf of national destiny, cultural differences must be internalized as inbred and inviolate.

Hence, among nationalists, the cultural instability of ethnicity often gives way to the kind of ethno-geneticism that suffuses the official pronouncements of Karadzic in Bosnia and Buthelezi in KwaZulu. That much is apparent from Buthelezi's insistence that Zuluness is genetic and membership in Inkatha determined at birth (notwithstanding the fact that only a minority of Zulus have joined his organization).[33] Thus Buthelezi has decreed that "all members of the Zulu nation are automatically members of Inkatha if they are Zulus. There may be people who are inactive members, but no one escapes being a member as long as he or she is a member of the Zulu nation."[34] In keeping with this sentiment, Buthelezi and Karadzic have condemned Zulu and Serbian members of rival political parties as blood-traitors. Both men have sought to seal off the exits from *Blud und Boten* nationalism by insisting that their political parties are primordially vindicated — a neogenetic attempt at shielding their ethnic organizations against the complicating claims of historical identities.

As Deniz Kandiyoti and Anne McClintock have observed, in nationalist quests for airtight, invariant identities, women are often assigned symbolically crucial roles as reproducers of the nation and as upholders of its innermost values.[35] Women may thus serve in a double sense as the bearers of the nation, carrying in their wombs the hope of perpetuity while also incarnating national values. Moreover, women are ordinarily institutionalized as male property; they come to mark the borders between ethnicities. Thus ethnic biology, ethnic culture, and ethnic territory converge in their beings.

During a war of dispossession, this symbolic freight can become costly indeed — as evidenced by the Serbian enlistment of rape as a strategy for ethnic cleansing.[36] Caught in the crossfire of a male war, women find themselves unenviably cast as first-class icons but second-class citizens. They are denied the arms to defend themselves while weighed down with symbolic responsibilities as guarantors of homeland, ethnos, and lineage.

The mapping of the ideas of ethnic continuity, purity, and territory onto women makes such militarized rape brutally overdetermined. Rape is commonly coded by law as a crime, not against a woman's person, but against male property. If women are projected as the inner sanctum of the patriarchal homeland, for Serbian men to invade Muslim women is symbolically and legally continuous with the gutting, looting, and seizure of Muslim property. Such defilement becomes the mark of a homeland that, in every sense, is no longer impregnable.

Mass rape is, among other things, organized insemination, men's way of interfering with the lineage of the enemy. In their campaign of ethnic cleansing the Bosnian Serbs have deployed rape obstructively to prevent the "mothers of the nation" from reproducing a "pure" Muslim "nation." Any ensuing children will be vulnerable to rejection as the living embodiments of personal and national violations. Thus the Serbian strategy threatens not just to seed unwanted children but to implant, as well, a mentality of ethnic purity among people who have previously had little reason to think in such constricting terms.

The Multiple Origins of Violence

Most academic, as opposed to media, analysts of South Africa's violence resist the view that the country is experiencing the tectonic rumblings of buried ethnic nationalisms. There is no "Yugoslavian" scenario in the offing. Instead, studies by Shula Marks, Lauren Segal, Mike Morris, and Doug Hindson suggest that any limited, reactive retreat into ethnicity must be viewed alongside the effects of chaotic urbanization, epidemic unemployment, economic recession, generational conflict, the legacy of migrant labor, and the attendant crises in masculinity.[37]

Since the abolition of apartheid's influx-control laws in 1986, the growth-rate of South African cities has ranked among the highest in the world. Yet the de Klerk regime did not even attempt to provide the civic structures or housing to accommodate these changes. These pressures have been exacerbated by the discrepancy between the four hundred thousand new workers who are entering the labor force annually, of whom only forty thousand are finding work in the formal sector.[38] In such conditions, new class tensions arise between a relatively elite working class who possess housing and a swelling ring of squatters vulnerable to the brutal, exploitative patronage of warlords.

To refute the view that the South African conflict is at heart ethnic-nationalist is not to gainsay the power of ethnic consciousness as one facet of social identity. Nor is it to deny that violently affirmed identities readily provoke equally powerful counteridentities. In circumstances where Zulu-speaking migrant workers have been killed on the sometimes unwarranted supposition that they are Inkatha members, this can stir non-Inkatha Zulus into embracing the allegiance wrongly ascribed to them.[39] A similar spiral of action and reaction has dogged the Yugoslavian crisis. If you risk being raped, tortured, or killed for being a Muslim on ascriptive grounds of accent, appearance, or belief, you might as well — in circumstances that deny you the option of upholding multiculturalism or cosmopolitanism — avail yourself of the resources of Muslim solidarity.

However, to acknowledge the reactive hardening of exclusive identities amid a crisis is not in the least synonymous with designating ethnicity as the overweening, most "natural" of identities, and therefore as a fundamental factor in the remapping of a country and its constitution. As Marks points out, ethnic interpretations of South Africa's violence fail to address the fact that the majority of the six thousand people killed in political violence during the late 1980s and early 1990s died in feuds between Zulus. It was only later, when the violence was carried into the ethnically symbiotic heartland of the Transvaal, that ethnicity could even be posited — by those who found such explanations politically expedient — as the wellspring of the problem.[40]

To insist on a farrago of causes may be intellectually unwieldy and journalistically inconveniencing, but it is a necessary acknowledgment of tensions between South Africa's residual and emergent orders. Those who see ethnic incompatibility as the source of clashes between hostel-dwellers and surrounding urban communities tend to bypass apartheid's disabling institutional legacy — not least the congested barracks for male migrant workers.

Ironically, the evidence suggests that the violent feuding in the Transvaal resulted more from a shortage than an excess of interethnic contact. Apartheid's self-enclosed hostels for migrants inserted into the cities vast enclaves of men who retained predominantly rural allegiances. These workers often remained on the periphery of the processes of urban synthesis — cultural transfer, poly-lingualism, intermarriage, and civic organization — that encourage more elastic conceptions of ethnicity. Among hostel-dwellers, recession, political uncertainty, and the lifting of constraints on urbanization have triggered desperate male competition over jobs, women, and territory. The violence should thus be seen not as expressive of primordial ethnic differences but as a response to unstable historical conditions that catalyze essentialist identities — be they ethnic, generational, gender, class, or urban-rural ones.

Ethnically slanted explanations obscure a further critical factor: the security forces' zealous funding, fueling, and fanning of violence in a manner that invented an ethnic aspect in some circumstances, exaggerated it in others.[41] By December 1992, reports by the Goldstone Commission and others had pressured de Klerk into sacking some of his highest officers whom the press, military defectors, and the ANC had long accused of fomenting "third force" violence (whether with or without de Klerk's knowledge). Far from being the work of rogue wild men, this campaign was meticulously orchestrated from within the Directorate of Military Intelligence. Strategies included hit-squad assassinations, the staging of train massacres, disinformation against the ANC, the hiring of RENAMO "contras" from Mozambique, the secret training of Inkatha police, and the bankrolling of Inkatha rallies and trade unions. After February 1990, the "third force" devised contingency plans for a military coup, a fact that crystallized de Klerk's dilemma — how to weaken the ANC's support but in a manner that did not simultaneously increase the political leverage of the Conservative Party, which, according to one estimate, held the allegiances of 90 per cent of the police and the military.[42]

To stress the scale of this conspiracy is not to imply that it accounted directly for all or even most of the violence. This is unnecessary. Under the tinder-dry conditions of 1990s South Africa, it was far easier to spark a conflict than to douse it. And those who stood to gain most from the violence — Inkatha, the Nationalist regime, and the security forces — had little motive for controlling it. All these forces, in their diverse ways, had reason to discredit the ANC's vision of a unitary, nonracial state. There was, moreover, a partial but significant community of interest between the security forces and the Inkatha leadership, both of whom had benefited materially from the apartheid legacy of neofederal, neoethnic politics. Government support for the KwaZulu Bantustan as a bulwark against the ANC had given Buthelezi access to state slush funds, the support of the ruthless KwaZulu Police, and the administrative authority and financial means to dispense patronage — jobs, housing, and the like. Hence the leaders of Inkatha and of South Africa's security forces were equally fearful of their power atrophying under a new, democratic order.

Whatever limited comparisons can be made between the Balkan and South African conflicts are best sought not in ethnic nationalism but elsewhere: in the contest over dwindling resources amid local and global recessions; in ideological bewilderment following the implosion of old certitudes (be they apartheid, socialist, communist, or anticommunist); and in the uncertain promise of the elusive, often rhetorical idea of democracy.

Perhaps most significantly of all, both the former Yugoslavia and South Africa face the labor of emerging from beneath decades of inflated militarization that, as a proportion of GNP, has dwarfed the spending of even heavily militarized Western countries like Britain and the United States. As a result of these buildups, both the former Yugoslavia and southern Africa are saturated with arms and military personnel who have every motive for forestalling their own obsolescence. The dissipation of the enemy constructs that secured their employment and the waning of the old regimes have rendered many professional soldiers violently insecure, as they ponder fates ranging from tribunals and prison to unemployment and evaporating pensions.

In seeking to shore up their precarious power, the military relics of the decaying orders in ex-Yugoslavia and South Africa have found the discourse of ethnic nationalism highly serviceable. The ethnic-nationalist adventurism of the Bosnian Serbs would have stalled without the considerable backing of the Yugoslavian National Army. And in South Africa, the campaign for an ethnically slanted federalism would have achieved little resonance without, on the one hand, support from the South African Defense Force and the KwaZulu Police and, on the other, politically contrived analogies to the campaigns for greater ethnic autonomy in the former Yugoslavia and the Commonwealth of Independent States.

Militarized Memory

"I am always fascinated," the Scottish historian Neal Ascherson once observed, "when people talk about 'the forging of a nation.' Most nations are forgeries, perpetrated in the last century or so. Some nationalisms relied on literal forgeries: the epics of Ossian in Scotland, the phony 'Libuse' manuscripts supposed to date from the Czech past, the ancient Welsh literature which was actually written by Iolo Morganwg in the King Lud pub at the bottom of Fleet Street."[43] Ascherson's exposé of national forgeries is consistent with the current trend toward theorizing the nation through the idiom of artifice — inventing, crafting, imagining. This tendency marks a decided advance over theories of natural nations, but it does harbor dangers of

its own. For the ethereal idiom of national imaginings can distract us from the institutional solidity of their effects. Perhaps even more insidious is the temptation
to assume that all nations or aspirant nations have available to them a past that is
equally susceptible to effective reinvention.

For ethnic-nationalist politicians, the decisive challenge is not whether they can
generate random reimaginings but whether they can reconceive the past in a manner
that guarantees it a popular purchase. The invention of an illustrious ethnic patrimony is of nugatory political value unless it rallies prospective adherents to the
ethnic-nationalist cause. That much is manifest from the divergent fates of Zulu nationalism under Buthelezi and Ciskeian nationalism under "President" Lennox Sebe.
When South Africa goaded the Ciskeian Bantustan to "independence" in 1982, Sebe
faced a critical difficulty. How was he to manufacture even superficially plausible
myths of ethno-genesis in circumstances where there were no cultural, linguistic, or
historical grounds for distinguishing Ciskeian Xhosas from their Xhosa neighbors in
the Transkei? Despite the ministrations of government ethnologists, and the erection
of a national shrine (inspired by a visit to Israel's Mount Massad), all Sebe's ethno-
genetic flights of fancy crashed on takeoff. There was no concealing the fact that
the idea of "Ciskeiness" as an ethnic nationality lacked any imaginative resonance
prior to the 1970s. Sebe's reimaginings were risibly transparent as top-down impo-
sitions; he was thus incapable of rousing in his subjects any ethnic-nationalist sense
of felt antiquity.[44]

Buthelezi faced no such obstacles in seeking to mobilize ethno-history for political gain. The quest for hegemony over the idea of Zuluness has been bitterly
contested since the mid–nineteenth century by forces within Zulu society and by
settler interests.[45] Buthelezi has been tirelessly inventive in straightening the vagaries
of Zulu history, in suppressing the contingencies of Zulu identity, and, above all, in
enshrining his political party, Inkatha, as the sole repository of Zulu nationhood.[46]
While Buthelezi's methods have often been coercive, he could not have established
a following through coercion alone.

Inkatha's militant ethnic nationalism has been mounted not just for the purposes
of territorial control but for control over a past that is particularly susceptible to
reinvention in epic-heroic terms. In the bitter contest over the idea of "Zuluness," the
preeminent sanctities are military battles and military leaders, above all, the towering
figure of Shaka, arguably the most renowned and mythologized of all nineteenth-
century African leaders.

The iconography and history that Inkatha has sought to commandeer are relentlessly male and militaristic. The insistence on a warrior blood-lineage and a history
narrated through battlefield victories and defeats has meant that Buthelezi repeatedly
characterizes the state of "his" Zulu nation in terms of virility or emasculation. Thus,
for instance, he and other Inkatha leaders have consistently portrayed the ANC's
criticisms of Inkatha's so-called "traditional cultural weapons" as an attempt to im-
pugn Zulu manhood and, thereby, the essence of Zulu identity.[47] To be Zulu, in
these terms, is to exhibit a martial, "manly" pride that is at once an expression and a
defense of the past, an attitude that fuels South Africa's violence.

Buthelezi has obsessively advanced the idea of an indivisible Zulu nation seam-
lessly descended from Shaka, the imperial warrior-king. To this end, he (and his

cheerleaders in the right-wing media) has been party to all kinds of genetic chicanery and gestures of fake primordialism. Typically, one South African newspaper depicts Buthelezi as "Chief Minister of KwaZulu — a position filled by his family since the days of Shaka."[48] Such an illustrious military pedigree is the fruit of some fantastically inventive topiary on Buthelezi's family tree. Moreover, it overlooks the fact that KwaZulu — as opposed to the differently circumscribed Zululand — did not exist prior to the early 1970s. Sometimes, not content with nineteenth-century beginnings, Buthelezi lays claim to a prehistoric ethnic cohesion. "We were a people," he affirms, "long before those who snipe at us had any identity. We were a people since the beginning of time."[49]

Yet the very terms in which Buthelezi defines "Zuluness" testify to the instability of the claimed ethnic-nationalist identity. That much is apparent from his startling plunge into the debates over the invention of tradition. Buthelezi chose to enter the intellectual fray not in some fusty, smoke-filled seminar room but in an open-air stadium where he could vent his theories before tens of thousands of assembled warriors who, we can assume, were not au courant with the niceties of Hobsbawm and Ranger, Anderson, Mudimbe, Appiah, and Marks.

On this occasion — the 1991 Shaka Day celebrations — Buthelezi set aside one-third of his speech to assail Shula Marks for having the temerity to suggest that "we actually reinvented history so that we could paint a picture of Zulu unity" and that the warfare in Natal "has been between Zulus over what it means to be a Zulu."[50] Buthelezi had acquired a video of a Channel 4 documentary, "Age to Age," in which Marks expatiated on the politically charged reinventions of Zulu authenticity. The chief proceeded to regale his forces with a catalog of Marks's "errors," which he condemned as symptoms of "a campaign to scale down Zulus as Zulus, and a concerted effort to re-invent Zulu history. . . . Nothing on God's earth is powerful enough to destroy the identity of the Zulu people. We are here because history brought us here."[51] Yet what kind of historical deliverance is this? Buthelezi spends the bulk of his speech detailing Shaka's military conquests — "We know this because we have learnt it from our grandparents who learnt it from their grandparents who learnt it from those who were alive when King Shaka conquered and united and established his empire."[52] Buthelezi's Shaka Day speech constructs a version of Zuluness wherein the violent incorporation of others stands as a fundamental, historically vindicated expression of the national character. Thus, paradoxically, for Zulu nationalism to stay the same it must remain faithful to Shaka's putative legacy of conquest.

Buthelezi's most powerful ally, King Goodwill Zwelethini, adopts a related logic in goading Inkatha to attack the considerable numbers of Zulus who have identified with the ANC, the United Democratic Front, and the Congress of South African Trade Unions: "I command you to eliminate from your midst all those disgusting usurpers of our dignity. . . . Rout them out only to make them one of us. Thrash them, if necessary, only to purge them into becoming better Zulus."[53] King Goodwill thus sanctions violence for enforcing an unconditional equation between Inkatha as a political party and Zuluness as an ethnically pure bloodline. His call for purgation is the language not of ethnic cleansing but of ethnic self-cleansing.

Inkatha's monopoly over the vernacular repertoire of Zulu culture has been amply contested, as *Black Mamba Rising,* an anthology of trade union performance poetry, and Liz Gunner and Mafika Gwala's fine collection, *Musho! Zulu Popular Praises,* both testify.[54] As Gunner, Gwala, and Ari Sitas document, Zulu poets aligned with the progressive Congress of South African Trade Unions have molded Zulu poetic and historical material into something more plastic, more accommodating of an inclusive, nonethnic vision of national belonging. Sitas distinguishes between the way Zulu traditions of poetic praise have been taken up by Inkatha's chauvinist "authoritarian populism" and by a broader "popular democratic culture." Yet even inclusive adaptations of Zuluness struggle to extricate themselves from a patriarchal ethno-history that has been conventionally narrated through male warrior triumphs and defeats, the aggrandizement of warrior values, and the founding presence of an imperial warrior-king.

The dangers of a nationalist iconography whose dominant images are those of men at war become equally manifest in the quite different context of Serbian history. A BBC documentary by Paul Palinowski gave focus to the epic-heroic verse of Karadzic, self-proclaimed president of the Serbian Republic of Bosnia and Herzegovina and self-styled warrior-poet.[55] Karadzic's compositions and performances on the *gusle* invoke a nationalist history of lost grandeur, returning above all to the Serbs' conquest by the Ottomans in the fourteenth-century Battle of Kosovo. Idiosyncratically, the crucible of Serbian ethno-genesis is not a martial victory but a cataclysmic battle-field defeat; all the same, the legacy of that founding moment — compounded by massive Serbian casualties in World War II — is a tradition of militant remembrance that easily tilts into ethno-fabulism. (One symptom of this resurgent martial imagination has been the sudden proliferation of Battle of Kosovo kitsch, what one critic has called "papier-mâché medievalism.")[56] The bellicose, patriarchal, epic-heroic impulse behind Serbian nationalism has found particularly forceful expression in the novels of Dobrica Cosic, president of rump Yugoslavia. Cosic's romantic portraits of the Serbs' epic sufferings have been seized upon as a primary inspiration by that predatory wing of Serbian nationalism responsible for ethnic cleansing.[57]

The violence in South Africa and Bosnia suggests that, in periods of economic and ideological crisis, distinctive dangers may arise when an ethnic-nationalist political party possesses an obsessive military mythology backed by contemporary military might. Leaders in both instances have relied, for their popular support, on an avalanche of inventive remembrance. The Serbs, backed by the Yugoslav National Army, have been egged on to reprisal slaughters fifty or six hundred years deferred. On a smaller scale, Buthelezi's *impis,* bolstered by the KwaZulu Police and the South African Defense Force, was emboldened by the fantasy that Shaka the Great — he who defeated the British army and a host of African societies — sired Inkatha.[58]

The role of militarized memory in the brutal chauvinisms of Buthelezi's and Karadzic's forces complicate efforts, such as Etienne Balibar's, to discriminate categorically between legitimate and illegitimate nationalisms. Balibar has sought to make the issue of power decisive: "We have no right," he maintains, "to equate the nationalism of the dominant with that of the dominated, the nationalism of liberation with the nationalism of conquest."[59] Yet this assumes an absolute divide. What of those many circumstances where an ethnic-nationalist ideology is constructed from layered memories of subjection and dominance? What, for instance, of the Palestinian predicament? The Palestinians stand, in Edward Said's lapidary phrase, as "the victims of the victims," oppressed by people who can mobilize in their defense memories of their own persecution.

Thus the power of ethnic memory enables presently oppressive ethnic nationalisms — be they Israeli, Afrikaner, or Serbian — to continue to fixate on past sufferings, whether at the hands of Germany or the British or Ottoman Empires. Sometimes power relations among nationalisms are triangulated — the Quebecois, for instance, can be projected as colonized and colonizing in relation to Anglo-Canadians and indigenous Canadian peoples. Afrikaners, while busy subjugating black South Africans, elaborated an ethnic-nationalist narrative that centered on their own territorial dispossession and sufferings at British hands, including the death of twenty-eight thousand of their people in British concentration camps during the Anglo-Boer War.[60] When Italy occupied Ethiopia, the dominant Amhara viewed them as European oppressors while many other Ethiopian ethnicities — themselves conquered by the Amharic empire in the nineteenth century — embraced the Italians as liberators.[61]

These impacted narratives of ethnic-nationalist self-perception admit a broader perspective on the power struggles waged by the Serbian and Inkatha ethnic-nationalist leadership. Both groups were relative beneficiaries of the old, now-declining orders. Yet the Serbs' current concentration of military and political might has not allayed their fears of Ottoman and papal tyrannies revisited. And in striving to monopolize the idea of Zuluness, the Inkatha leadership has reanimated the Zulus' ambiguous status as a colonized empire, a people subjugated by white settlers but also — as their grand history putatively testifies — the "natural" overlords of other African peoples. Thus, from the perspective of ethnic nationalists, the question of domination or subjection is often unanswerable on the basis of present power alone and becomes, instead, subject to the militant, manipulative politics of ethnic remembrance.

South Africa enjoys two decisive advantages over the former Yugoslavia in the effort to keep pseudo-commemorative ethnic nationalisms at bay. For most South Africans, such political practices have been discredited in advance by apartheid efforts to mobilize ethnicity through the Bantustans. Moreover, much the strongest current of nationalism in South Africa — that represented by the ANC — is inclusive, nonracial, and premised on a conciliatory unity, not an enforced ethnic homogeneity.

The ANC has a far-from-unblemished record: as the torture and summary executions in the Quatro guerrilla camp and the organization's implication in the ongoing violence have confirmed. Yet, mercifully, of the myriad forms of corruption open to the ANC, ethnic absolutism does not rank among them. For the ANC is a broad church whose ethnic and ideological ecumenicism is of incalculable worth in the current epoch. Indeed, of the decisive political contestants in South Africa — the ANC, the National Party, Inkatha, and the Pan-Africanist Congress — the ANC alone can claim a durable record of ethnic inclusion: for more than a quarter of a century, the organization has accepted members from every South African ethnicity. As the visceral zealotries of ethnic nationalism threaten to become *the* malaise of the 1990s on a sweeping international front, South Africans should find solace in the fact that their most powerful nationalist party has long defined itself in terms that preclude any recourse to an ethnic pedigree. It is a party that offers no joy whatsoever to the purveyors of ethnic "authenticity," the crafters of primordial memory, and all the other ethno-antiquarians.

Conclusion

These past few years have brought to a crisis point the profound international confusion in the procedures for national legitimation. A major factor in this crisis has been the persistent assumption that ideally nationalisms should correspond to ethnic cultures. This view is implicit, for instance, in Ernest Gellner's portrait of nationalism as "the striving to make culture and polity congruent, to endow culture with its own political roof, and not more than one roof at that."[62] Even if one set aside the always approximate character of ethnic identity, only a few micro–nation-states could meet this exacting criterion. However, the rift between principle and practice does not appear to have weakened the incentives for invoking a putatively cohesive ethnicity as primary evidence in claiming statehood.

How can the world "community" arrest this potentially regressive process without implicitly favoring the historical status quo? The blood-and-soil arguments that have fortified France or Sweden as nation-states are no more logical than those later mounted in favor of statehood for Palestine or East Timor or Croatia. Such appeals all resort in one way or another to the idiom of antiquity, tradition, cultural authenticity, linguistic uniqueness, ethnicity, and territorial integrity. Thus the division lies not between authentic and inauthentic nation-states but between nations whose statehood achieved early international recognition and those from whom statehood was withheld.

Thus aspirant nation-states find themselves in a catch-22: despite the rarity of ethnically homogeneous states, prospective states find themselves held to an archaic and potentially destabilizing vision of what constitutes a nation. Yet in seeking to reinvent themselves as singular and homogeneous they cannot legitimately resort to the conquests and "cleansings" that countries like France, Britain, Germany, Turkey, and Spain once used to secure the internationally sanctified statehood they now enjoy.

The bloody consequences of this unresolved procedural dilemma were exemplified by Germany's hasty recognition of Slovenia's and Croatia's — but not Bosnia's — claims to independence. While Germany's decision may have helped check the Serbian onslaught against Croatia, it simultaneously precipitated the dismembering of Bosnia-Herzegovina on the altar of blood-and-soil nationalism. Complex historical allegiances lay behind the German decision, but it was prompted partly by a prejudice in favor of would-be states that purport to ethnic homogeneity. Thus, the lingering prestige of sameness in the execution of such claims becomes an incentive for the violent measures required to produce a facade of uniformity.

That canny nineteenth-century philosopher of nationalism, Ernest Renan, recognized this temptation: "Unity," he remarked, "is always effected by means of brutality."[63] While this may not be wholly true of "unity," it certainly holds for homogeneity. In the current world climate, the rewards for the pursuit of homogeneity remain explosively high. Far from resolving minority-majority tensions the pursuit of homogeneity is liable to provoke ever-smaller microethnic claims in a spiral of action and reaction, destroying, in the process, precious legacies of intercommunal forbearance.

NOTES

1. Eric J. Hobsbawm, *Nations and Nationalism since 1780: Programme, Myth, Reality* (Cambridge: Cambridge University Press, 1990), 183.

2. If Hitler personifies the horrors of ethnic cleansing, it is less often remembered that Churchill and Roosevelt embraced a weak version of one of his assumptions, namely, that homogeneous nation-states are more desirable and stable than heterogeneous ones. To this end the Allies oversaw the forced removal of millions of Europeans after World War II.

3. Indeed, Buthelezi and his allies have maintained that, on account of the persistent violence, democratic elections should be ruled out. Meanwhile, they say, a constitution ought to be drawn up that partitions South Africa into strongly autonomous regions with ethnic majorities of Zulus, Afrikaners, Tswanas, Xhosas, and so forth, each possessing the right of secession. Such a scheme would defer indefinitely the advent of democracy and exacerbate the bloodshed.

4. "Expatriates' Sun Sinks with Zaire," *Guardian,* October 8, 1991.

5. Patrick Wright, "Quebec's Tainted Separatist Dream," *Guardian,* September 3, 1992.

6. Gerhard Mare, "History and Dimension of the Violence in Natal: Inkatha's Role in Negotiating Political Peace," *Social Justice* 18, nos. 1–2 (spring/summer 1991): 187. The portrait of the Anglo-Boer War as "white-on-white" could only be ironic; otherwise it would occlude the considerable numbers of black soldiers and civilians killed during that war.

7. Rupert Taylor gives an excellent account of such atavistic interpretations of South Africa's violence. He cites, for example, *Time* magazine's ascription of the conflict to "tribal-based animosities [between Zulus and Xhosas] that date back centuries." This despite the fact that a clash in 1827 is the solitary record of such a Zulu-Xhosa conflict. See Taylor, "The Myth of Ethnic Division: Township Conflict on the Reef," *Race and Class* 33, no. 2 (1991): 3–5.

8. Leroy Vail, ed., *The Creation of Tribalism in Southern Africa* (London: James Currey, 1989), 2.

9. R. W. Johnson, "The Danger of Majority Rule," *Times* (London), September 4, 1992, 10. See his related views in "What Buthelezi Wants," *London Review of Books,* December 19, 1991, 14–15. Johnson's prophetic zeal seems undented by his spectacular failures in this sphere in the past, as in the final chapter of *How Long Will South Africa Survive?* (London: Macmillan, 1977).

10. Andries Treurnicht, *International Herald Tribune,* March 2, 1990. I am grateful to Preben Kaarsholm for drawing my attention to this utterance in his paper "The Ethnicisation of Politics and the Politicisation of Ethnicity: Culture and Political Development in South Africa," presented at the Institute of Commonwealth Studies, November 13, 1992.

11. Radio 4 (Britain), six o'clock news, October 6, 1992. See also *Guardian,* September 28, 1992.

12. " 'Governor' Buthelezi's Tail Wags a National Party Dog," *Southern Africa Report* 4 (December 1992): 2.

13. "Mangosuthu Buthelezi: Message of the Drums," *Financial Mail* (Johannesburg), October 23, 1992, 26.

14. See "Pretoria and Inkatha: Evidence of a Conspiracy," *Independent on Sunday,* July 28, 1991, and "Pretoria Admits Giving Inkatha Financial Help," *Independent,* July 20, 1991.

15. On this point, see especially Shula Marks's incisive article, "The Origins of Ethnic Violence in South Africa," in Norman Etherington, ed., *Peace, Politics and Violence in the New South Africa* (London: Hans Zell, 1992).

16. Despite the Serbs' draconian measures against Albanians in Kosovo during the late 1980s, ethnic cleansing was not instituted there.

17. Connie Mulder, *Hansard* (South Africa), February 7, 1978, col. 579.

18. On the subject of "black spots," see, for example, Verwoerd's speeches of December 5, 1950, and April 14, 1961, in A. N. Pelzer, ed., *Verwoerd Speaks: Speeches 1948–1966* (Johannesburg: APB Publishers, 1966), 27, 591.

19. See Lauren Platsky and Cheryl Walker, *The Surplus People — Forced Removals in South Africa*

(Johannesburg: Ravan, 1985), and Elaine Unterhalter, *Forced Removal: The Division, Segregation and Control of the People of South Africa* (London: International Defence and Aid Fund, 1987).

20. G. F. van L. Froneman, chairman of the Bantu Affairs Commission, speaking in 1968. Quoted in J. D. Omer-Cooper, *History of Southern Africa* (London: Heinemann, 1987), 213.

21. Louis Nel, in a letter to the *Sunday Times* (Johannesburg), July 10, 1977.

22. Ibid.

23. See, for example, No Sizwe, *One Azania, One Nation: The National Question in South Africa* (London: Zed, 1979), 1; Colin Bundy, *Re-making the Past* (Cape Town: University of Cape Town Press, 1986), 54.

24. For one account of Carrington's recommendations, see Christopher Hitchens, "Why Bosnia Matters," *London Review of Books,* September 10, 1992, 6–7.

25. "Balkanization," one should add, is also an unfortunate term, for it perpetuates the reductive image of the Balkans as a barbarous place that gives rise to small, vicious nationalist animosities.

26. For one brief but suggestive reflection on this metaphor, see Neil Ascherson, "The Tragically Easy Path to 'Ethnic Cleansing,' " *Independent on Sunday,* August 9, 1991, 23.

27. Dubravka Ugresic, "Dirty Tyranny of Mr. Clean," *Independent on Sunday,* December 6, 1992, 22.

28. For some emphatic arguments against the view that the Serbs, Croats, and Muslims constitute discrete ethnicities, see Robert Fisk, "The Lie That Leaves Bosnia in the Lurch," *Independent on Sunday,* December 6, 1992, 13; Hitchens, "Why Bosnia Matters," 6–7; and Mark Thompson, "Comforts of Fatalism," *Guardian,* November 13, 1992, 327.

29. Lejla Somum, "Fifth Column," a documentary shown on BBC2, December 16, 1992.

30. Thompson, "Comforts of Fatalism."

31. Paul Gilroy, *There Ain't No Black in the Union Jack* (London: Unwin Hyman, 1987); Stuart Hall, "New Ethnicities," in James Donald and Ali Rattansi, eds., *"Race," Culture and Difference* (London: Sage, 1992), 252–59; Etienne Balibar and Immanuel Wallerstein, *Race, Nation, Class: Ambiguous Identities* (London: Verso, 1991), 23.

32. J. A. Coetzee, *Nasieskap en Politieke Groepering in Suid-Afrika (1652–1968)* (Pretoria: Transvaalse Uitgewersmaatskappy, 1969), 322–23.

33. With an eye to forthcoming national elections, Buthelezi found himself in a dilemma. Regionally, his political trump card is his claim that Inkatha represents the Zulu nation; nationally, this same claim is a liability. Thus, particularly since 1990, Buthelezi has tended to vacillate between incompatible visions of Inkatha as embodying an exclusive ethnic nationalism and as accommodating the kind of inclusive, multiethnic nationalism that would be a prerequisite if he hopes to build a constituency in South Africa at large.

34. Quoted in Gerhard Mare, *Brothers Born of Warrior Blood* (Johannesburg: Ravan, 1992), 75–76.

35. Anne McClintock, "Family Feuds: Gender, Nation, and the Family," *Feminist Review* (spring 1993), and Deniz Kandiyoti, "Identity and Its Discontents: Women and the Nation," *Millennium: Journal of International Studies* 20, no. 3 (1991): 429–43. See also Cynthia Enloe, *Bananas, Beaches, and Bases: Making Feminist Sense of International Politics* (Berkeley: University of California Press, 1990), 42–64.

36. For an account of the rape camps, see Maggie O'Kane, "Forgotten Women of Serb Rape Camps," *Guardian,* December 19, 1992. See also Catherine Bennett's discussion of masculinity and rape in "Ordinary Madness," *Guardian,* January 20, 1993.

37. For some incisive commentary on this issue, see Catherine Campbell, "Learning to Kill? Masculinity, the Family and Violence in Natal," *Journal of Southern African Studies,* 18, no. 3 (September 1992): 614–22.

38. Leslie Maasdorp, "The Internal Economic Situation in South Africa," paper presented at the Institute of Commonwealth Studies, London, November 23, 1991.

39. For an excellent account of these complex, compound tensions, see Lauren Segal, "The Human Face of Violence: Hostel Dwellers Speak," *Journal of Southern African Studies* 18, no. 3 (September 1992).

40. Marks, "Origins of Ethnic Violence," 25.

41. On this subject, see Kaarsholm, "Ethnicisation of Politics," 9, and Mike Morris and Doug Hindson, "The Disintegration of Apartheid: From Violence to Reconstruction," in Glenn Moss and Ingrid Obery, eds., *South African Review* 6 (Johannesburg: Ravan, 1992), 152–70.

42. *Africa Confidential* 33, no. 4 (February 21, 1992).

43. Neal Ascherson, *Games with Shadows* (London: Radius Books, 1988), 281.

44. For an instructive account of Ciskei's problems see "Ethnicity and Pseudo-ethnicity in the Ciskei," in Vail, *Creation of Tribalism,* 395–413.

45. For a detailed analysis of these rivalries, see especially Shula Marks, *The Ambiguities of Dependence: Race, Class, and Nationalism in Twentieth Century South Africa* (Baltimore: Johns Hopkins University Press, 1986).

46. For a suggestive account of Buthelezi's efforts, see Mare, *Brothers Born of Warrior Blood.*

47. In a speech in 1991, Buthelezi argued that "the call to ban the bearing of cultural weapons by Zulus is an insult to my manhood. It is an insult to the manhood of every Zulu man" (quoted in Mare, *Brothers Born of Warrior Blood,* 68). Cf. King Goodwill Zwelethini's insistence that "the ANC seeks to deprive Zulu men of their manhood by taking away their cultural weapons" (*Weekly Mail,* May 31, 1991). For a very suggestive analysis of the Inkatha premium on manliness against the backdrop of changes in the family, see Campbell, "Learning to Kill?" 614ff.

48. "Mangosuthu Buthelezi: Message of the Drums," *Financial Mail,* October 23, 1992.

49. Speech delivered on September 23, 1990 (quoted in Gerhard Mare, "History and Dimension of the Violence in Natal: Inkatha's Role in Negotiating Political Peace," *Social Justice* 18, nos. 1–2 [1991], 190).

50. Mangosuthu Buthelezi, "Inkatha, 'Zuluness' and the Historians," *Passages: Newsletter of the Program for African Studies at Northwestern University* 4 (1992): 9.

51. Ibid.

52. Ibid.

53. Quoted Mare, "History and Dimension," 72–73.

54. Liz Gunner and Mafika Gwala, eds., *Musho! Zulu Popular Praises* (East Lansing: Michigan State University Press, 1991); Ari Sitas, "'Class, Nation, Ethnicity in Natal's Black Working Class," in Shula Marks, ed., *The Societies of Southern Africa in the 19th and 20th Centuries,* vol. 15 (London: Institute of Commonwealth Studies, 1990), 257–78.

55. Paul Palinowski, "Serbian Epics," BBC2, December 16, 1992.

56. Thompson, "Comforts of Fatalism," 145.

57. See T. D. Allman, "Serbia's Blood War," *Vanity Fair* (March 1993): 34.

58. There has, of late, been considerable revisionist debate over the rise of the Zulu Empire. See Carolyn Hamilton, "The Character and Objects of Chaka: A Reconsideration of the Making of Shaka as Mfecane 'Motor,'" and Julian Cobbing, "The Mfecane: A Rejoinder," both in *Journal of African History* (1992). See also Carolyn Hamilton and John Wright, "The Beginnings of Zulu Identity," and Mary de Haas and Paulus Zulu, "Ethnic Mobilisation: KwaZulu's Politics of Secession," both in *Indicator South Africa* 10, no. 3 (winter 1993): 43–46, 47–52.

59. Etienne Balibar, "Racism and Nationalism," in Etienne Balibar and Immanuel Wallerstein, *Race, Nation, and Class: Ambiguous Identities* (London: Verso, 1991), 45.

60. The memory of Afrikaners' territorial dispossession and of the twenty-eight thousand who died in British concentration camps during the Anglo-Boer War became psychologically crucial to the Afrikaners elaboration of an ethnic-nationalist narrative of themselves as a suffering, colonized people. But it was not only Afrikaners who died in those camps: there were fourteen thousand recorded concentration camp deaths among Afrikaners' African workers — predominantly tenant farmers — who were interned in large numbers. See Dougie Oakes, ed., *Illustrated History of South Africa* (Cape Town: Reader's Digest, 1992), 256.

61. The non-Amharas had themselves been conquered by the Ethiopian Empire in the late nineteenth century and had suffered under the Amharas' policy of Christianization and coercive assimilation. I am indebted to the Ethiopian anthropologist Alex Naty for drawing my attention to the complexity of Ethiopia's layered imperialisms.

62. Ernest Gellner, *Nations and Nationalism* (Oxford: Basil Blackwell, 1983), 32. If the United States, Australia, and some Caribbean states stand as exceptions to this generalization, even their eclecticism may become insitutionalized as a decisive trait of *the* national culture.

63. Ernest Renan, "What Is a Nation?" trans. Martin Thom, in Homi K. Bhabha, ed., *Nation and Narration* (London: Routledge, 1990), 11.

Chapter 4
"No Longer in a Future Heaven": Gder, Race and Nationalism

Anne McClintock

The tribes of the Blackfoot confederacy, living along what is now known as the United States/Canadian border, fleeing northward after a raiding attack, watched with growing amazement as the soldiers of the United States army came to a sudden, magical stop. Fleeing southwards, they saw the same thing happen, as the Canadian mounties reined to an abrupt halt. They came to call this invisible demarcation the "medicine line."

Sharon O'Brien

All nationalisms are gendered; all are invented; and all are dangerous — dangerous, not in Eric Hobsbawm's sense of having to be opposed but in the sense that they represent relations to political power and to the technologies of violence.[1] As such, nations are not simply phantasmagoria of the mind; as systems of cultural representation whereby people come to imagine a shared experience of identification with an extended community, they are historical practices through which social difference is both invented and performed.[2] Nationalism becomes in this way constitutive of people's identities through social contests that are frequently violent and always gendered. Yet if, following Benedict Anderson, the invented nature of nationalism has recently found wide theoretical currency, explorations of the gendering of the national imaginary have been conspicuously paltry.

Nations are contested systems of cultural representation that limit and legitimize people's access to the resources of the nation-state, but despite many nationalists' ideological investment in the idea of popular *unity,* nations have historically amounted to the sanctioned institutionalization of gender *difference.* No nation in the world grants women and men the same access to the rights and resources of the nation-state. Yet, with the notable exception of Frantz Fanon, male theorists have seldom felt moved to explore how nationalism is implicated in gender power. As a result, as Cynthia Enloe remarks, nationalisms have "typically sprung from masculinized memory, masculinized humiliation and masculinized hope."[3]

Not only are the needs of the nation typically identified with the frustrations and aspirations of men, but the representation of male *national* power depends on the prior construction of *gender* difference. All too often in male nationalisms, gender difference between women and men serves to symbolically define the limits of national difference and power between *men.* Even Fanon, who at other moments knew better, writes: "The look that the native turns on the settler town is a look of

89

lust . . . to sit at the settler's table, to sleep in the settler's bed, with his wife if possible. The colonized man is an envious man."[4] For Fanon, both colonizer and colonized are here unthinkingly male, and the Manichaean agon of decolonization is waged over the territoriality of female, domestic space.

Excluded from direct action as national citizens, women are subsumed symbolically into the national body politic as its boundary and metaphoric limit: "Singapore girl, you're a great way to fly." Women are typically constructed as the symbolic bearers of the nation but are denied any direct relation to national agency. As Elleke Boehmer notes, the "motherland" of male nationalism thus may "not signify 'home' and 'source' to women."[5] Boehmer notes that the male role in the nationalist scenario is typically "metonymic"; that is, men are contiguous with each other and with the national whole. Women, by contrast, appear "in a metaphoric or symbolic role."[6] Yet it is also crucial to note that not all men enjoy the privilege of political contiguity with each other in the national community.

In an important intervention, Nira Yuval-Davis and Floya Anthias identify five major ways in which women have been implicated in nationalism:

1. As biological reproducers of the members of national collectivities

2. As reproducers of the boundaries of national groups (through restrictions on sexual or marital relations)

3. As active transmitters and producers of the national culture

4. As symbolic signifiers of national difference

5. As active participants in national struggles[7]

Nationalism is thus constituted from the very beginning as a gendered discourse and cannot be understood without a theory of gender power. Nonetheless, theories of nationalism reveal a double disavowal. If male theorists are typically indifferent to the gendering of nations, feminist analyses of nationalism have been lamentably few and far between. White feminists, in particular, have been slow to recognize nationalism as a feminist issue. In much Western, socialist feminism, as Yuval-Davis and Anthias point out, "[i]ssues of ethnicity and nationality have tended to be ignored."[8]

A feminist theory of nationalism might thus be strategically fourfold: investigating the gendered formation of sanctioned male theories; bringing into historical visibility women's active cultural and political participation in national formations; bringing nationalist institutions into critical relation with other social structures and institutions; and at the same time paying scrupulous attention to the structures of racial, ethnic, and class power that continue to bedevil privileged forms of feminism.

The National Family of Man: A Domestic Genealogy

A paradox lies at the heart of most national narratives. Nations are frequently figured through the iconography of familial and domestic space. The term "nation" derives from *natio:* to be born. We speak of nations as "motherlands" and "fatherlands." Foreigners "adopt" countries that are not their native homes and are naturalized into the national "family." We talk of the "family of nations," of "homelands" and "native" lands. In Britain, immigration matters are dealt with at the Home Office; in the United States, the president and his wife are called the first family. Winnie Mandela was, until her fall from grace, honored as South Africa's "mother of the nation." In this way, despite their myriad differences, nations are symbolically figured as domestic genealogies. Yet, as I have argued elsewhere, since the mid–nineteenth century, at least in the West, the family itself has been figured as the antithesis of history.[9]

The family trope is important for nationalism in at least two ways. First, it offers a "natural" figure for sanctioning national *hierarchy* within a putative organic *unity* of interests. Second, it offers a "natural" trope for figuring national time. After 1859 and the advent of social Darwinism, Britain's emergent national narrative took shape increasingly around the image of the evolutionary family of man. The family offered an indispensable metaphoric figure by which national difference could be shaped into a single historical genesis narrative. Yet a curious paradox emerged. The family as a *metaphor* offered a single genesis narrative for national history while, at the same time, the family as an *institution* became void of history and excluded from national power. The family became, at one and the same time, both the *organizing figure* for national history and its *antithesis*.

In the course of the nineteenth century, the social function of the great service families was displaced onto the national bureaucracies, while the image of the family was projected onto these nationalisms as their shadowy, naturalized form. Because the subordination of woman to man and child to adult was deemed a natural fact, hierarchies within the nation could be depicted in familial terms to guarantee social difference as a category of nature. The metaphoric depiction of social hierarchy as natural and familial — the "national family," the global "family of nations," the colony as a "family of black children ruled over by a white father" — depended in this way on the prior naturalizing of the social subordination of women and children within the domestic sphere.

In modern Europe, citizenship is the legal representation of a person's relationship to the rights and resources of the nation-state. But the putatively universalist concept of national citizenship becomes unstable when seen from the position of women. After the French Revolution, women were incorporated into European nation-states not directly as citizens but only indirectly, through men, as dependent members of the family in private and public law. The Code Napoléon was the first modern statute to decree that the wife's nationality should follow her husband's, an example other European countries briskly followed. A woman's *political* relation to the nation was thus submerged as a *social* relation to a man through marriage. For women, citizenship in the nation was mediated by the marriage relation within the family. This essay is directly concerned with the consequences for women of this uneven gendering of the national citizen.

The Gendering of Nation-Time

A number of critics have followed Tom Nairn in naming the nation "the modern Janus."[10] For Nairn, the nation takes shape as a contradictory figure of time: one face gazing back into the primordial mists of the past, the other into an infinite future. Deniz Kandiyoti expresses the temporal contradiction with clarity: nationalism "presents itself both as a modern project that melts and transforms traditional attachments in favour of new identities and as a reflection of authentic cultural values culled from the depths of a presumed communal past."[11] Homi K. Bhabha, following Nairn and Anderson, writes: "Nations, like narratives, lose their origins in the myths of time and only fully realize their horizons in the mind's eye."[12] Bhabha and Anderson borrow here on Walter Benjamin's crucial insight into the temporal paradox of modernity. For Benjamin, a central feature of nineteenth-century industrial capitalism was the "use of archaic images to identify what was historically new about the 'nature' of commodities."[13] According to Benjamin, the mapping of progress depends on systematically inventing images of archaic time to identify what is historically new about enlightened, national progress. Anderson can thus ask: "Supposing 'antiquity' were, at a certain historical juncture, the *necessary consequence* of 'novelty'?"[14]

What is less often noticed, however, is that the temporal anomaly within nationalism — veering between nostalgia and the impatient, progressive sloughing off of the past — is typically resolved by figuring the contradiction in the representation of *time* as a natural division of *gender*. Women are represented as the atavistic and authentic body of national tradition (inert, backward-looking, and natural), embodying nationalism's conservative principle of continuity. Men, by contrast, represent the progressive agent of national modernity (forward-thrusting, potent, and historic), embodying nationalism's progressive, or revolutionary, principle of discontinuity. Nationalism's anomalous relation to time is thus managed as a natural relation to gender.

In the nineteenth century, the social evolutionists secularized time and placed it at the disposal of the national, imperial project. The axis of *time* was projected onto the axis of *space,* and history became global. Now not only natural space but also historical time was collected, measured, and mapped onto a global science of the surface.[15] In the process, history, especially national and imperial history, took on the character of a spectacle.

Secularizing time has a threefold significance for nationalism. First, figured in the evolutionists' global family tree, the world's discontinuous nations appear to be marshaled within a single, hierarchical European ur-narrative. Second, national history is imaged as naturally teleological, an organic process of upward growth, with the European nation as the apogee of world progress. Third, inconvenient discontinuities are ranked and subordinated into a hierarchical structure of branching time — the progress of "racially" different nations mapped against the tree's self-evident boughs, with "lesser nations" destined, by nature, to perch on its lower branches.

National time is thus not only *secularized* but also *domesticated.* Social evolutionism and anthropology gave to national politics a concept of natural time as familial. In the image of the family tree, evolutionary progress was represented as a series of anatomically distinct family types, organized into a linear procession, from the "childhood" of "primitive" races to the enlightened "adulthood" of European imperial nationalism. Violent national change took on the character of an evolving spectacle under the organizing rubric of the family. The merging of the racial evolutionary tree and the gendered family into the family tree of man provided scientific racism with a simultaneously gendered and racial image through which it could popularize the idea of linear national progress.

Britain's emerging national narrative gendered time by figuring women (like the colonized and the working class) as inherently atavistic — the conservative repository of the national archaic. Women were seen not as inhabiting history proper but as existing, like colonized peoples, in a permanently anterior time within the modern nation. White, middle-class men, by contrast, were seen to embody the forward-thrusting agency of national progress. Thus the figure of the national family of man reveals a persistent paradox. National progress (conventionally the invented domain of male, public space) was figured as familial, while the family itself (conventionally the domain of private, female space) was figured as beyond history.

One can safely say, at this point, that there is no single narrative of the nation. Different groups (genders, classes, ethnicities, generations, and so on) do not experience the myriad national formations in the same way. Nationalisms are invented, performed, and consumed in ways that do not follow a universal blueprint. At the very least, the breathtaking Eurocentrism of Hobsbawm's dismissal of Third World nationalisms warrants sustained criticism. In a gesture of sweeping condescension, Hobsbawm nominates Europe as nationalism's "original home," while "all the anti-imperial movements of any significance" are unceremoniously dumped into three categories: mimicry of Europe, anti-Western xenophobia, and the "natural high spirits of martial tribes."[16] By way of contrast, it might be useful to turn at this point to Frantz Fanon's quite different analysis of the gendering of the national formation.

Fanon and Gender Agency

As male theorists of nationalism go, Frantz Fanon is exemplary, not only for recognizing gender as a formative dimension of nationalism but also for recognizing — and immediately rejecting — the Western metaphor of the nation as a family. "There are close connections," he observes in *Black Skin, White Masks,* "between the structure of the family and the structure of the nation." Refusing, however, to collude with the notion of the familial metaphor as natural and normative, Fanon instead understands it as a cultural projection ("the characteristics of the family are projected onto the social environment") that has very different consequences for families placed discrepantly within the colonial hierarchy. "A normal Negro child, having grown up within a normal family, will become abnormal on the slightest contact with the white world."[17]

The challenge of Fanon's insight is threefold. First, he throws radically into question the naturalness of nationalism as a domestic genealogy. Second, he reads familial normality as a product of social power — indeed, of social violence. Third, Fanon is remarkable for recognizing, in this early text, how military violence and the authority of a centralized state borrow on and enlarge the domestication of gender power within the family: "Militarization and the centralization of authority in a country automatically entail a resurgence of the authority of the father."[18]

Perhaps one of Fanon's most provocative ideas is his challenge to any easy relation of identity between the psychodynamics of the unconscious and the psychodynamics of political life. The audacity of his insight is that it allows one to ask whether the psychodynamics of colonial power and of anticolonial subversion can be interpreted by deploying (without mediation) the same concepts and techniques used to interpret the psychodynamics of the unconscious. If the family is not "a miniature of the nation," then are metaphoric projections from family life (the Lacanian "Law of the Father," say) adequate for an understanding of colonial or anticolonial power? Fanon himself seems to say no. Relations between the individual unconscious and political life are, I argue, neither separable from each other nor reducible to each other. Instead, they comprise crisscrossing and dynamic mediations, reciprocally and untidily transforming each other, rather than duplicating a relation of structural analogy.

Even in *Black Skin, White Masks,* the most psychological of Fanon's texts, he insists that racial alienation is a "double process." First, it "entails an immediate recognition of social and economic realities." Then, it entails the "internalization" of inferiority. Racial alienation, in other words, not only is an "individual question" but also involves what Fanon calls a "sociodiagnostic."[19] Reducing Fanon to a purely formal psychoanalysis, or a purely structural Marxism, risks foreclosing precisely those suggestive tensions that animate, in my view, the most subversive elements of his work. These tensions are nowhere more marked than in his tentative exploration of the gendering of national agency.

Gender runs like a multiple fissure through Fanon's work, splitting and displacing the "Manichaean delirium" to which he repeatedly returns. For Fanon, the colonial agon appears, at first, to be fundamentally Manichaean. In *Black Skin, White Masks,* he sees colonial space as divided into "two camps: the white and the black."[20] Nearly a decade later, writing from the crucible of the Algerian resistance in *The Wretched of the Earth,* Fanon once again sees anticolonial nationalism as erupting from the violent Manichaeanism of a colonial world "cut in two," its boundaries walled by barracks and police stations. Colonial space is split by a pathological geography of power, separating the bright, well-fed settler's town from the hungry, crouching casbah: "This world . . . cut in two is inhabited by two different species."[21] As Edward Said puts it: "From this Manichean and physically grounded statement Fanon's entire work follows, set in motion, so to speak, by the native's violence, a force intended to bridge the gap between white and non-white."[22] Yet the fateful chiaroscuro of race is at almost every turn disrupted by the crisscrossings of gender.

Fanon's Manichaean agon appears at first to be fundamentally male: "There can be no further doubt that the real Other for the white man is and will continue to be the black man." As Homi Bhabha writes: "It is always in relation to the place of the Other that colonial desire is articulated."[23] But Fanon's anguished musings on race and sexuality disclose that "colonial desire" is not the same for men and women: "Since he is the master and more simply the male, the white man can allow himself the luxury of sleeping with many women. . . . But when a white woman accepts a black man there is automatically a romantic aspect. It is a giving, not a seizing."[24] Leaving aside, for the moment, Fanon's complicity with the stereotype of women as romantically rather than sexually inclined, as giving rather than taking, Fanon opens race to a problematics of sexuality that reveals far more intricate entanglements than a mere doubling of "the Otherness of the Self." The psychological Manichaeanism of

Black Skin, White Masks and the more political Manichaeanism of *The Wretched of the Earth* are persistently inflected by gender in such a way as to radically disrupt the binary dialectic.

For Fanon, the envy of the black man takes the form of a fantasy of territorial displacement: "The fantasy of the native is precisely to occupy the master's place." This fantasy can be called a *politics of substitution.* Fanon knows, however, that the relation to the white woman is altogether different: "When my restless hands caress those white breasts, they grasp white civilization and dignity and make them mine."[25] The white woman is seized, possessed, and taken hold of, not as an act of *substitution,* but as an act of *appropriation.* However, Fanon does not bring this critical distinction between a politics of substitution and a politics of appropriation into explicit elaboration as a theory of gender power.

As Bhabha astutely observes, Fanon's *Black Skin, White Masks* is inflected by a "palpable pressure of division and displacement" — although gender is a form of self-division that Bhabha himself fastidiously declines to explore. Bhabha would have us believe that "Fanon's use of the word 'man' usually connotes a phenomeno-logical quality of humanness, inclusive of man and woman."[26] But this claim is not borne out by Fanon's texts. Potentially generic terms like "the Negro" or "the na-tive" — syntactically unmarked for gender — are almost everywhere immediately contextually marked as male: "Sometimes people wonder that the native, rather than giving his wife a dress, buys instead a transistor radio"; " . . . the Negro who wants to go to bed with a white woman"; " . . . the Negro who is viewed as a penis symbol." The generic category "native" does not include women; women are merely pos-sessed by the (male) native as an appendage: "When the native is tortured, when his wife is killed or raped, he complains to no one."[27]

For Fanon, colonized men inhabit "two places at once." If so, how many places do colonized women inhabit? Certainly, Bhabha's text is not one of them. Except for a cursory appearance in one paragraph, women haunt Bhabha's analysis as an elided shadow — deferred, displaced, and dis-remembered. Bhabha concludes his eloquent meditation on Fanon with the overarching question: "How can the human world live its difference? how can a human being live Other-wise?"[28] Yet immediately appended to his foreword appears a peculiar note. In it Bhabha announces, without apology, that the "crucial issue" of the woman of color "goes well beyond the scope" of his foreword. Yet its scope, as he himself insists, is bounded by nothing less than the question of *humanity:* "How can the human world live its difference? how can a human being live Other-wise?" Apparently, the question of the woman of color falls beyond the question of human difference, and Bhabha is content simply to "note the importance of the problem" and leave it at that. Bhabha's belated note on gender appears after his authorial signature, after the time and date of his essay. Women are thus effectively deferred to a no-where land, beyond time and place, outside theory. If, indeed, "the state of emergency is also a state of emergence," the question remains whether the national state of emergency turns out to be a state of emergence for women at all.[29]

To ask "the question of the subject" ("What does a man want? What does the black man want?") while postponing a theory of gender presumes that subjectivity itself is neutral with respect to gender.[30] From the limbo of the male afterthought, however, gender returns to challenge the male question not as women's "lack" but as that excess that the masculine "otherness of the self" can neither admit nor fully elide. This presumption is perhaps nowhere more evident than in Fanon's remarkable meditations on the gendering of the national revolution.

At least two concepts of national agency shape Fanon's vision. His anticolonial project is split between a Hegelian vision of colonizer and colonized locked in a life-and-death conflict and an altogether more complex and unsteady view of agency. These paradigms slide against each other throughout his work, giving rise to a number of internal fissures. These fissures appear most visibly in his analysis of gender as a category of social power.

On one hand, Fanon draws on a Hegelian metaphysics of agency inherited, by and large, through Jean-Paul Sartre and the French academy. In this view, anticolonial nationalism erupts violently and irrevocably into history as the logical counterpart to colonial power. This nationalism is, as Edward Said puts it, "cadenced and stressed from beginning to end with the accents and inflections of liberation."[31] It is a liberation, moreover, that is structurally guaranteed, immanent in the binary logic of the Manichaean dialectic. This metaphysics speaks, as Terrence Eagleton nicely phrases it, "of the entry into full self-realization of a unitary subject known as the people."[32] Nonetheless, the privileged national agents are urban, male, vanguardist, and violent. The progressive nature of the violence is preordained and sanctioned by the structural logic of Hegelian progress.

This kind of nationalism can be called an *anticipatory nationalism*. Eagleton calls it nationalism "in the subjunctive mood," a premature utopianism that "grabs instinctively for a future, projecting itself by an act of will or imagination beyond the compromised political structures of the present."[33] Yet, ironically, anticipatory nationalism often claims legitimacy by appealing precisely to the august figure of inevitable progress inherited from the Western societies it seeks to dismantle.

On the other hand, alongside this Manichaean, mechanical nationalism appears an altogether more open-ended and strategically difficult view of national agency. This nationalism stems not from the inexorable machinery of Hegelian dialectics but from the messy and disobliging circumstances of Fanon's own activism, as well as from the often dispiriting lessons of the anticolonial revolutions that preceded him. In this view, agency is multiple rather than unitary, unpredictable rather than immanent, bereft of dialectical guarantees, and animated by an unsteady and nonlinear relation to time. There is no preordained rendezvous with victory; no single, undivided national subject; no immanent historical logic. The national project must be laboriously and sometimes catastrophically invented, with unforeseen results. Time is dispersed and agency is heterogeneous. Here, in the unsteady, sliding interstices between conflicting national narratives, women's national agency makes its uncertain appearance.

In "Algeria Unveiled," Fanon ventriloquizes — only to refute — the long Western dream of colonial conquest as an erotics of ravishment. Under the hallucinations of empire, the Algerian woman is seen as the living flesh of the national body, unveiled and laid bare for the colonials' lascivious grip, revealing "piece by piece, the flesh of Algeria laid bare."[34] In this remarkable essay, Fanon recognizes the colonial gendering of women as symbolic mediators, the boundary markers of an agon that is fundamentally male. The Algerian woman is "an intermediary between obscure forces and the group" (37). "The young Algerian woman ... establishes a link" (53), he writes.

Fanon understands brilliantly how colonialism inflicts itself as a *domestication* of the colony, a reordering of the labor and sexual economy of the people, so as to divert female power into colonial hands and disrupt the patriarchal power of colonized men. Fanon ventriloquizes colonial thinking: "If we want to destroy the structure of Algerian society, its capacity for resistance, we must first of all conquer the women" (37–38). His insight here is that the dynamics of colonial power are fundamentally, though not solely, the dynamics of gender: "It is the situation of women that was accordingly taken as the theme of action" (38). Yet, in his work as a whole, Fanon fails to bring these insights into theoretical focus.

Long before Anderson, Fanon recognizes the inventedness of national community. He also recognizes the power of nationalism as a *scopic* politics, most visibly embodied in the power of sumptuary customs to fabricate a sense of national unity: "It is by their apparel that types of society first become known" (35). Fanon perceives, moreover, that nationalism, as a politics of visibility, implicates women and men in different ways. Because, for male nationalists, women serve as the visible markers of national homogeneity, they become subjected to especially vigilant and violent discipline. Hence the intense emotive politics of dress.

Yet a curious rupture opens in Fanon's text over the question of women's agency. At first, Fanon recognizes the historical meaning of the veil as open to the subtlest shifts and subversions. From the outset, colonials tried to grant Algerian women a traitorous agency, affecting to rescue them from the sadistic thrall of Algerian men. But, as Fanon knows, the colonial masquerade of giving women power by unveiling them was merely a ruse for achieving "a real power over the man" (39). Mimicking the colonial masquerade, militant Algerian women deliberately began to unveil themselves. Believing their own ruse, colonials at first misread the unveiled Algerian women as pieces of "sound currency" circulating between the casbah and the white city, mistaking them for the visible coinage of cultural conversion (42). For the *fidai,* however, the militant woman was "his arsenal," a technique of counter-infiltration, duplicitously penetrating the body of the enemy with the armaments of death.

So eager is Fanon to deny the colonial rescue fantasy that he refuses to grant the veil any prior role in the gender dynamics of Algerian society. Having refused the colonial's desire to invest the veil with an essentialist meaning (the sign of women's servitude), he bends over backward to insist on the veil's semiotic innocence in Algerian society. The veil, Fanon writes, was no more than "a formerly inert element of the native cultural configuration" (46). At once the veil loses its historic mutability and becomes a fixed, "inert" element in Algerian culture: "an undifferentiated element in a homogeneous whole" (47). Fanon denies the "historic dynamism of the veil" and banishes its intricate history to a footnote, from where, however, it displaces the main text with the insistent force of self-division and denial (63).

Fanon's thoughts on women's agency proceed through a series of contradictions. Where, for Fanon, does women's agency begin? He takes pains to point out that women's militancy does not precede the national revolution. Algerian women are not self-motivating agents, nor do they have prior histories or consciousness of revolt from which to draw. Their initiation in the revolution is learned, but it is not learned from other women or from other societies, nor is it transferred analogously from local feminist grievances. The revolutionary mission is "without apprenticeship, without briefing" (50). The Algerian woman learns her "revolutionary mission instinctively" (50). This theory is not, however, a theory of feminist spontaneity, for women learn their militancy only at men's invitation. Theirs is a *designated agency* — an agency by invitation only. Before the national uprising, women's agency was null, void, inert as the veil. Here Fanon not only colludes with the stereotype of women as bereft of historical motivation but also resorts, uncharacteristically, to a reproductive image of natural birthing: "It is an authentic birth in a pure state" (50).

Why were women invited into the revolution? Fanon resorts immediately to a mechanistic determinism. The ferocity of the war was such, the urgency so great, that sheer structural necessity dictated the move: "The revolutionary wheels had assumed such proportions; the mechanism was running at a given rate. The machine would have to be complicated" (48). Female militancy, in short, is simply a passive offspring of male agency and the structural necessity of the war. The problem of women's agency, so brilliantly raised as a question, is abruptly foreclosed.

Women's agency for Fanon is thus agency by designation. It makes its appearance not as a direct political relation to the revolution but as a mediated, domestic relation to a man: "At the beginning, it was the married women who were contacted. Later, widows or divorced women were designated" (51). Women's first relation to the revolution is constituted as a domestic one. But domesticity, here, also constitutes a relation of possession. The militant was, in the beginning, obliged to keep "his woman" in "absolute ignorance" (48). As designated agents, moreover, women do not commit themselves: "It is relatively easy to commit oneself. . . . The matter is a little more difficult when it involves designating someone" (49). Fanon does not consider the possibility of women committing themselves to action. He thus manages women's agency by resorting to contradictory frames: the authentic, instinctive birth of nationalist fervor; the mechanical logic of revolutionary necessity; male designation. In this way, the possibility of a distinctive feminist agency is never broached.

Once he has contained women's militancy in this way, Fanon applauds women for their "exemplary constancy, self-mastery and success" (54). Nonetheless, his descriptions of women teem with instrumentalist similes and metaphors. Women are not women: they are "fish"; they are "the group's lighthouse and barometer," the *fidai*'s "women-arsenal" (58, 54). Most tellingly, Fanon resorts to a curiously eroticized image of militarized sexuality. Carrying the men's pistols, guns, and grenades beneath her skirts, "the Algerian woman penetrates a little further into the flesh of the Revolution" (54). Here, the Algerian woman is not a victim of rape but a masculinized rapist. As if to contain the unmanning threat of armed women — in their dangerous crossings — Fanon masculinizes the female militant, turning her into a phallic substitute, detached from the male body but remaining, still, the man's "woman-arsenal." Most tellingly, however, Fanon describes the phallic woman as penetrating the flesh of the "Revolution," not the flesh of the colonials. This odd image suggests an unbidden fear of emasculation, a dread that the arming of women might entail a fatal unmanning of Algerian men. A curious instability of gender power is here effected as the women are figured as masculinized and the male revolution is penetrated.

Fanon's vision of the political role of the Algerian family in the national uprising likewise proceeds through contradiction. Having brilliantly shown how the family constitutes the first ground of the colonial onslaught, Fanon seeks to reappropriate it as an arena of nationalist resistance. Yet the broader implications of the politicizing of family life are resolutely naturalized after the revolution. Having recognized that women "constituted for a long time the fundamental strength of the occupied," Fanon is reluctant to acknowledge any gender conflict or feminist grievance within the family prior to the anticolonial struggle, or after the national revolution (66). Although he admits that in "the Algerian family, the girl is always a notch behind the boy," he quickly insists that she is assigned to this position "without being humiliated or neglected" (105). Although the men's words are "Law," women "voluntarily" submit themselves to "a form of existence limited in scope" (66).

The revolution shakes the "old paternal assurance" so that the father no longer knows "how to keep his balance," and the woman "cease[s] to be a complement for man" (109). It is telling, moreover, that in Fanon's analysis of the family, the category of mother does not exist. Women's liberation is credited entirely to national liberation, and it is only with nationalism that women "enter into history." Prior to nationalism, women have no history, no resistance, no independent agency (107). And since the national revolution automatically revolutionizes the family, gender conflict naturally vanishes after the revolution. Feminist agency, then, is contained by and subordinated to national agency, and the heterosexual family is preserved as the "truth" of society — its organic, authentic form. The family is revolutionized, taken to a higher plane through a Hegelian vision of transcendence, but the rupturing force of gender is firmly foreclosed: "The family emerges strengthened from this ordeal" (116). Women's militancy is contained within the postrevolutionary frame of the reformed, heterosexual family, as the natural image of national life.

In the postrevolutionary period, moreover, the tenacity of the father's "unchallengeable and massive authority" is not raised as one of the "pitfalls" of the national consciousness (115). The Manichaean dialectic — as generating an inherent, resistant agency — does not, it seems, apply to gender. Deeply reluctant as he is to see women's agency apart from national agency, Fanon does not foresee the degree to which the Algerian National Liberation Front (FLN) will seek to co-opt and control women, subordinating them unequivocally once the revolution is won.

A feminist investigation of national difference might, by contrast, take into account the dynamic social and historical contexts of national struggles; their strategic mobilizing of popular forces; their myriad, varied trajectories; and their relation to other social institutions. We might do well to develop a more theoretically complex and strategically subtle genealogy of nationalisms.

With these theoretical remarks in mind, I wish now to turn to the paradoxical relation between the invented constructions of family and nation as they have taken shape within South Africa in both black and white women's contradictory relations to the competing national genealogies. In South Africa, certainly, the competing Afrikaner and African nationalisms have had both distinct and overlapping trajectories, with very different consequences for women.

Nationalism as Fetish Spectacle

Until the 1860s, Britain had scant interest in its unpromising colony at the southern tip of Africa. Only upon the discovery of diamonds (1867) and gold (1886) were the Union Jack and the redcoats shipped out with any real sense of imperial mission. But very quickly, mining's needs for cheap labor and a centralized state collided with traditional farming's interests, and out of these contradictions, in the conflict for control over African land and labor, exploded the Anglo-Boer War of 1899–1902.

Afrikaner nationalism was a doctrine of crisis. After their defeat by the British, the bloodied remnants of the scattered Boer communities had to forge a new counter-culture if they were to survive in the emergent capitalist state. From the outset, this counter-culture had a clear *class* component. When the Boer generals and the British capitalists swore blood brotherhood in the Union of 1910, the ragtag legion of "poor whites" with few or no prospects, the modest clerks and shopkeepers, the small farmers and poor teachers, the intellectuals and petit bourgeoisie, all precarious in the new state, began to identify themselves as the vanguard of a new Afrikanerdom, the chosen emissaries of the national *Volk*.[35]

However, Afrikaners had no monolithic identity to begin with, no common historic purpose, and no single unifying language. They were a disunited, scattered people, speaking a medley of High Dutch and local dialects, with smatterings of the slave, Nguni, and Khoisan languages — scorned as the *Kombuistaal* (kitchen-language) of house-servants, slaves, and women. Afrikaners therefore had, quite literally, to invent themselves. The new, invented community of the *Volk* required the conscious creation of a single print-language, a popular press, and a literate populace. At the same time, the invention of tradition required a class of cultural brokers and image-makers to do the inventing. The "language movement" of the early twentieth century, in a flurry of poems, magazines, newspapers, novels, and countless cultural events, provided just such an invention, fashioning the myriad Boer vernaculars into a single, identifiable Afrikaans language. In the early decades of the twentieth century, as Isabel Hofmeyer has brilliantly shown, an elaborate labor of "regeneration" was undertaken as the despised Hotnotstaal (Hottentot's language) was revamped and purged of its rural, "degenerate" associations and elevated to the status of the august mother tongue of the Afrikaans people. In 1918, Afrikaans achieved legal recognition as a language.[36]

At the same time, the invention of Afrikaner tradition had a clear gender component. In 1918, a small, clandestine clique of Afrikaans men launched a secret society with the express mission of capturing the loyalties of dispirited Afrikaners and fostering white male business power. The tiny, white brotherhood swiftly burgeoned into a secret countrywide Mafia that came to exert enormous power over all aspects of Nationalist policy.[37] The gender bias of the society, as of Afrikanerdom as a whole, is neatly summed up in its name: the Broederbond (the Brotherhood). Henceforth, Afrikaner nationalism would be synonymous with white male interests, white male aspirations and white male politics. Indeed, in a recent effort to shore up its waning power, the Broederbond has decided to admit so-called colored Afrikaans speakers into the Brotherhood. All women will, however, continue to be barred.

In the voluminous Afrikaner historiography, the history of the *Volk* is organized around a male national narrative figured as an imperial journey into empty lands. As I have discussed elsewhere, the myth of the empty land is simultaneously the myth of the virgin land — effecting a double erasure.[38] But the empty lands are in fact peopled, so the contradiction is contained by the invention, once more, of anachronistic space. The colonial journey is figured as proceeding forward in *geographical* space, but backward in *racial* and *gender* time, to a prehistoric zone of linguistic, racial, and gender degeneration. At the heart of the continent, a historic agon is staged as degenerate Africans "falsely" claim entitlement to the land. A divinely organized military conflict baptizes the nation in a male birthing ritual, which grants to white men the patrimony of land and history. The white nation emerges as the progeny of male history through the motor of military might. Nonetheless, at the center of the imperial gospel stands the contradictory figure of the *Volksmoeder,* the mother of the nation.

Inventing the Archaic: The Tweede (Second) Trek

The animating emblem of Afrikaner historiography is "the Great Trek," and each trek is figured as a family presided over by a single, epic patriarch. In 1938, two decades after the recognition of Afrikaans as a language, an epic extravaganza of invented tradition inflamed Afrikanerdom into a delirium of nationalist passion. Dubbed the Tweede Trek (Second Trek), or the Eeufees (Centenary), the event celebrated the Boers' first mutinous Great Trek in 1838 away from British laws and the effrontery of slave emancipation. The Centenary also commemorated the Boer massacre of the Zulus at the Battle of Blood River. Nine replicas of Voortrekker wagons were built — a vivid example of the reinvention of the archaic to sanction modernity. Each wagon was literally baptized and named after a male Voortrekker hero. No wagon was named after an adult woman, although one was called, generically, Vrou en Moeder (Wife and Mother). This wagon, creaking across the country, symbolized woman's relation to the nation as indirect, mediated through her social relation to men, her national identity lying in her unpaid services and sacrifices, through husband and family, to the *Volk*.

Each wagon became the microcosm of colonial society at large: the whip-wielding white patriarch prancing on horseback, black servants toiling alongside, white mother and children sequestered in the wagon — the women's starched white bonnets signifying the purity of the race, the decorous surrender of their sexuality to the patriarch, and the invisibility of white female labor.

The wagons rumbled along different routes from Cape Town to Pretoria, sparking along the way an orgy of national pageantry and engulfing the country in a four-month spectacle of invented tradition and fetish ritual. Along the way, white men grew beards and white women donned the ancestral bonnets. Huge crowds gathered to greet the trekkers. As the wagons passed through the towns, babies were named after trekker heroes, as were roads and public buildings. Not a few girls were baptized with the improbable but popular favorites: Eeufesia (Centenaria) or Ossewania (from *ossewa*, ox wagon). Children scrambled to rub grease from the wagon axles onto their handkerchiefs. The affair climaxed in Pretoria in a spectacular marathon with Third Reich overtones, led by thousands of Afrikaner Boy Scouts bearing flaming torches.

The first point about the Tweede Trek is that it invented white nationalist traditions and celebrated unity where none had existed before, creating the illusion of a collective identity through the political staging of vicarious *spectacle*. The second point is that the Nationalists adopted this ploy from the Nazis. The Tweede Trek was inspired not only by the Nazi creed of *Blut und Boden* but by a new political style: the Nurenberg politics of fetish symbol and cultural persuasion.

In our time, national collectively is experienced preeminently through spectacle. Here I depart from Anderson, who sees nationalism as emerging primarily from the Gutenberg technology of print capitalism. Anderson neglects the fact that print capital has, until recently, been accessible to a relatively small literate elite. Indeed, the singular power of nationalism since the late nineteenth century, I suggest, has been its capacity to organize a sense of popular, collective unity through the management of mass, national *commodity spectacle*.

In this respect, I argue, nationalism inhabits the realm of fetishism. Despite the commitment of European nationalism to the idea of the nation-state as the embodiment of rational progress, nationalism has been experienced and transmitted primarily through fetishism — precisely the cultural form that the Enlightenment denigrated as the antithesis of reason. More often than not, nationalism takes shape through the visible, ritual organization of fetish objects (flags, uniforms, airplane logos, maps, anthems, national flowers, national cuisines, and national architectures) as well as through the organization of collective fetish spectacle (in team sports, military displays, mass rallies, the myriad forms of popular culture, and so on). Far from being purely phallic icons, fetishes embody crises in social value, which are projected onto, and embodied in, what can be called impassioned objects. Considerable work remains to be done on the ways in which women consume, refuse, or negotiate the male fetish rituals of national spectacle.

The Eeufees was, by anyone's standards, a triumph of fetish management, from the spectacular regalia of flags, flaming torches, and patriotic songs to incendiary speeches, archaic costumes, and the choreographing of crowd spectacle, while everywhere visible was the unifying fetish of the wagon. More than anything, the Eeufees revealed the extent to which nationalism is a theatrical performance of invented community: the Eeufees was a calculated and self-conscious effort by the Broederbond to paper over the myriad regional, gender, and class tensions that threatened it. As a fetishist displacement of difference, it succeeded famously, for the Tweede Trek's success in mobilizing a sense of white Afrikaner collectively where none before existed was a major reason, though certainly not the only one, for the Nationalists' triumphant sweep to power in 1948.[39]

Yet, as Albert Grundlingh and Hilary Sapire note, historians have shown scant interest in explaining the overwhelming emotional euphoria elicited by the celebrations, tending instead to collude with the mythologizing of Afrikaners as inherently atavistic and temperamentally given to quaint anthropological rituals.[40] Certainly, as Grundlingh and Sapire suggest, "it was economic insecurity...that made Afrikaners susceptible to the cultural and political blandishments of the Second Trek.[41] The idea of the symbolic trek had originated among the recently urbanized Afrikaner railway workers, who had very good reason to feel that their position was precarious in the new English-dominated state. Very quickly, moreover, the insecure scattering of Afrikaans-speaking petit bourgeois professionals and intellectuals — teachers, civil servants, lawyers, members of the clergy, writers, and academics — eagerly embraced their vocation of choreographing the symbolic trek, with all the renewed prominence and prestige that attended their status as cultural brokers imbued with the mission of unifying the *Volk.*

Nonetheless, the Tweede Trek was not simply the lurid, melodramatic offspring of ethnic insecurity and class fission. Grundlingh and Sapire point out that there were rival mythologies — socialism and "South Africanism" being the most prominent — that were as eager to capture the loyalties of the poor whites. The Tweede Trek, however, enjoyed a number of stunning advantages. For those dispirited and disoriented Afrikaners, who had so recently trekked from the rural areas to the mines, rail yards, and sweatshops of urban South Africa, the Tweede Trek offered a potent symbolic amalgam of disjointed times, capturing in a single fetish spectacle the impossible confluence of the modern and the archaic, the recent displacement and the ancestral migration.

Rather than being viewed as enacting a backward-looking, atavistic ceremony of ancestral cult worship, the Tweede Trek can be read as an exemplary act of modernity: a theatrical performance of Benjamin's insight into the evocation of archaic images to identify what is new about modernity. Photographs of the Eeufees vividly capture the doubling of time consequent upon this evocation of the archaic, as anachronistic ox-wagons jostle among the motorcars, and women in white *kappies* mingle with the modern urban crowd. Unlike socialism, then, the Tweede Trek could evoke a resonant archive of popular memory and a spectacular iconography of historical travail and fortitude, providing not only the historical dimension necessary for national invention but also a theatrical stage for the collective acting out of the traumas and privations of industrial dislocation.

The Tweede Trek also dramatized a crisis in the poetics of historical time. The ox-wagon embodied two distinct notions of time. First, it represented the linear time of imperial progress, figured as a forward-thrusting journey traced across the space of the landscape, obedient to the unfolding telos of racial advance and the rational mapping of measurable space. Second, it embodied in the same fetish object of the wagon a quite different notion of recurring, nonlinear time: the divinely preordained event rehearsed once more in the zone of historical nature. For recently urbanized Afrikaners, these two overlapping, but conflictual, figures of time — pastoral, cyclical time (the time of rural nostalgia) and modern, industrial time (the time of mechanical simulacrum and repetition) — were marvelously embodied in the single icon of the ox-wagon.

As they passed through towns, the wagons were driven through wet concrete to memorialize their tracks, petrifying history as an urban fossil — exemplifying the modern compulsion to collect time in the form of an object; history as palimpsest:

"in such a way," as Theodor Adorno put it, "that what is natural emerges as a sign for history and history, where it appears most historical, appears as a sign for nature."[42]

The Tweede Trek had another advantage. Tom Nairn has pointed out, in the British context: "Mobilization had to be in terms of what was there; and the whole point of the dilemma was that there was nothing there — none of the economic and political institutions of modernity. The middle-classes, therefore, had to function through a sentimental culture sufficiently accessible to the lower strata now being called to battle."[43] Lacking control of the institutions of modernity, Afrikaners mobilized through the one institution with which they were intimate and over which they still held precarious control: the family. Not only was much of the folk-memory and sentimental culture of the Great Trek fostered through the family, but its centralizing iconography and the epic social unit was familial. Perhaps this also goes some way toward explaining the zest with which Afrikaner women participated in the national pageantry that would soon write them out of power.

From the outset, as the Eeufees bore witness, Afrikaner nationalism was dependent not only on powerful constructions of racial difference but also on powerful constructions of gender difference. A racial and gendered division of national creation prevailed whereby white men were seen to embody the political and economic agency of the *Volk*, while women were the (unpaid) keepers of tradition and the *Volk*'s moral and spiritual mission. This gendered division of labor is summed up in the colonial gospel of the family and the presiding icon of the *Volksmoeder*. In photographs in the *Gedenkboek*,[44] women serve as boundary markers visibly upholding the fetish signs of national difference and visibly embodying the iconography of race and gender purity. Their starched white bonnets and white dresses set a stark chiaroscuro of gender difference against the somber black of the men's clothes. Photographic captions hail women in the Victorian iconography of cleanliness, purity, and maternal fecundity as the gatekeepers to the nation.

The *Volksmoeder*, however, is less a biological fact than a social category. Nor is it an ideology imposed willy-nilly on hapless female victims. Rather, it is a changing, dynamic ideology rife with paradox, under constant contest by men and women and adapted constantly to the pressures arising from African resistance and the conflict between Afrikaner colonialists and British imperialists.

The Invention of the *Volksmoeder*

The Anglo-Boer War (fundamentally a war over African land and labor) was in many respects waged as a war on Boer women. In an effort to break Boer resistance, the British torched the Boers' farms and lands and herded thousands of women and children into concentration camps, where twenty-five thousand women and children perished of hunger, desolation, and disease. Yet after the Anglo-Boer War, the political power of the fierce Boer women was muted and transformed. In 1913, three years after Union, the Vrouemonument (Women's Monument) was erected in homage to the female victims of the war. The monument took the form of a circular domestic enclosure, where women stand weeping with their children.

Here, women's martial role as fighters and farmers was purged of its indecorously militant potential and replaced by the figure of the lamenting mother with babe in arms. The monument enshrined Afrikaner womanhood as neither militant nor political, but as suffering, stoic, and self-sacrificing.[45] Women's disempowerment was figured not as expressive of the politics of gender difference, stemming from colonial women's ambiguous relation to imperial domination, but as emblematic of national (that is, male) disempowerment. By portraying the Afrikaner *nation* symbolically as a weeping woman, the mighty male embarrassment of military defeat could be overlooked and the memory of women's vital efforts during the war washed away in images of feminine tears and maternal loss.

The icon of the *Volksmoeder* is paradoxical. On the one hand, it recognizes the power of (white) motherhood; on the other hand, it is a retrospective iconography of gender containment, containing women's mutinous power within an iconography of domestic service. White women are defined as weeping victims of African menace, and their activism is thus overlooked and their disempowerment thereby ratified.

Yet, in the early decades of this century, as Hofmeyer shows, women played a crucial role in the invention of Afrikanerdom. The family household was seen as the last bastion beyond British control, and the cultural power of Afrikaner motherhood was mobilized in the service of white nation-building. Afrikaans was a language fashioned very profoundly by women's labors, within the economy of the domestic household. "Not for nothing," as Hofmeyer notes, "was it called the 'mother tongue.'"

In Afrikaner nationalism, motherhood is a political concept under constant contest. It is important to emphasize this for two reasons. First, erasing Afrikaner women's historic agency also erases their historic complicity in the annals of apartheid. White women were not the weeping bystanders of apartheid history but active, if decidedly disempowered, participants in the invention of Afrikaner identity. As such they were complicit in deploying the power of motherhood in the exercise and legitimation of white domination. Certainly, white women were jealously and brutally denied any formal political power, but they were compensated by their limited authority in the household. Clutching this small power, they became implicated in the racism that suffuses Afrikaner nationalism. Second, because of all this, black South African women have been justly suspicious of any easy assumption of a universal, essential sisterhood in suffering. White women are both colonized and colonizers, ambiguously complicit in the history of African dispossession.

"No Longer in a Future Heaven": Gender and the African National Congress

African nationalism has roughly the same historical vintage as Afrikaner nationalism. Forged in the crucible of imperial thuggery, mining capitalism, and rapid industrialization, African nationalism was, like its Afrikaner counterpart, the product of conscious reinvention, the enactment of a new political collectively by specific cultural and political agents. But its racial and gender components were very different, and African nationalism would describe its own distinct trajectory across the century.

In 1910, the Union of South Africa was formed, uniting the four squabbling provinces under a single legislature. Yet at the "national" convention, not a single black South African was present. For Africans the Union was an act of profound betrayal. A color bar banished Africans from skilled labor, and the franchise was denied to all but a handful. And so, in 1912, African men descended on Bloemfontein from all over South Africa to protest a union in which no black person had a voice. At this gathering, the South African Natives National Congress (SANNC) was launched, soon to become the African National Congress (ANC).

At the outset the ANC, like Afrikaner nationalism, had a narrow class base. Drawn from the tiny urban intelligentsia and petit bourgeoisie, its members were mostly mission-educated teachers and clerks, small businessmen and traders, the kind of men whom Fanon described as "dusted over with colonial culture." As Tom Lodge shows, they were urban, antitribal, and assimilationist, demanding full civic participation in the great British Empire rather than confrontation and radical change.[46] Although Lodge does not mention this fact, they were also solidly male.

For the first thirty years of the ANC, black women's relation to nationalism was structured around a contradiction: their exclusion from full political membership within the ANC contrasted with their increasing grassroots activism. As Frene Ginwala has argued, women's resistance was shaped from below.[47] While the language of the ANC was the *inclusive* language of national unity, the ANC was in fact *exclusive* and hierarchical: there was an upper house of chiefs (which protected traditional patriarchal authority through descent and filiation), a lower house of elected representatives (all male), and an executive (all male). Indians and so-called coloreds were excluded from full membership. Wives of male members could join as "auxiliary members" but were denied formal political representation as well as the power to vote. Their subordinate, service role to nationalism was summed up in the draft constitution of the SANNC (later the ANC), which presented women's political role within nationalism as mediated by the marriage relation and as replicating wives' domestic roles within marriage: "All the wives of the members ... shall ipso facto become auxiliary members. ... It shall be the duty of all auxiliary members to provide suitable shelter and entertainment for delegates to the Congress."

In 1913, the white state saw fit to impose passes on black women in an effort to preempt their migration to the cities. In outraged response, hundreds of women marched mutinously on Bloemfontein to fling back their passes and for their temerity met the full brunt of state wrath in a barrage of arrests, imprisonment, and hard labor. Women's insurgence alarmed both the state and not a few African men. Nonetheless, the climate of militancy gave birth to the Bantu Women's League of the African National Congress, which was launched in 1918, drawing by and large, but not solely, on the tiny, educated, Christian elite. Thus, from the outset, women's organized participation in African nationalism stemmed less from the invitation of men than from their own politicization in resisting the violence of state decree.

At this time, however, women's potential militancy was muted and their political agency domesticated by the language of familial service and subordination. Women's volunteer work was approved insofar as it served the interests of the (male) "nation," and women's political identity was figured as merely supportive and auxiliary. As Pixley KaIsaka Seme, founder and president of the ANC, said: "No national movement can be strong unless the women volunteers come forward and offer their services to the nation." Nonetheless, women's national mission was still triv-ialized and domesticated, defined as providing "suitable shelter and entertainment for members or delegates." At women's own insistence, the ANC granted women full membership and voting rights in 1943. It had taken thirty-one years.

After the Urban Areas Act of 1937, which severely curtailed black women's move-ments, new insistence began to be voiced for a more militant and explicitly political national women's organization: "We women can no longer remain in the back-ground or concern ourselves only with domestic and sports affairs. The time has arrived for women to enter the political field and stand shoulder to shoulder with their men in the struggle."[48] In 1943, the ANC decided that a women's league should be formed, yet tensions would persist between women's calls for greater autonomy and men's anxieties about losing control.

During the turbulent 1950s, however, the ANC Women's League thrived. This was the decade of the Defiance Campaign, the Freedom Charter, the Congress Alliance, and the Federation of South African Women. In 1956, thousands of women marched on Pretoria to once more protest passes for women, and the Women's Charter was formed, calling for land redistribution; workers' benefits and union rights; housing and food subsidies; the abolition of child labor; universal education; the right to vote; and equal rights with men in property, marriage, and child custody. It is sel-dom noted that this charter preceded the Freedom Charter and inspired much of its substance.

Within African nationalism, as in its Afrikaans counterpart, women's political agency has been couched in the presiding ideology of motherhood. Winnie Man-dela has long been hailed as "mother of the nation," and the singer Miriam Makeba is reverently addressed as "Ma Africa." The ideologies of motherhood in Afrikaner and ANC nationalism differ, however, in important respects.[49] In ANC nationalism, motherhood is less the universal and biological quintessence of womanhood than it is a social category under constant contest. African women have embraced, trans-muted, and transformed the ideology in a variety of ways, working strategically within traditional ideology to justify untraditional public militancy. Unlike Afrikaans women, moreover, African women have appealed to a racially inclusive image of motherhood in their campaigns to fashion a nonracial alliance with white women. A Federation of South African Women pamphlet of 1958 exhorted white women: "In the name of humanity, can you as a woman, as a mother, tolerate this?" In 1986, Albertina Sisulu appealed impatiently to white women: "A mother is a mother, black or white. Stand up and be counted with other women."

Over the decades, African women nationalists, unlike their Afrikaans counterparts, have transformed and infused the ideology of motherhood with an increasingly insurrectionary cast, identifying themselves more and more as the "mothers of rev-olution." Since the 1970s, women's local rites of defiance have been mirrored on a national scale in rent and bus boycotts, organized squatter camps, strikes, antirape protests, and community activism of myriad kinds. Even under the State of Emer-gency, women everywhere enlarged their militancy, insisting not only on their right to political agency but also on their right of access to the technologies of violence.

Black women's relation to nationalism has thus undergone significant historical changes over the years. At the outset, black women were denied formal representation; then their volunteer work was put at the service of the national revolution, still largely male. Gradually, as a result of women's own insistence, the need for women's full participation in the national liberation movement was granted, but their emancipation was still figured as the handmaiden of national revolution. Only recently has women's empowerment been recognized in its own right as distinct from the national, democratic, and socialist revolution. Nonetheless, the degree to which this rhetorical recognition will find political and institutional form remains to be seen.

Feminism and Nationalism

For many decades, African women have been loath to talk of women's emancipation outside the terms of the national liberation movement.[50] During the 1960s and 1970s, black women were understandably wary of the middle-class feminism that was sputtering fitfully to life in the white universities and suburbs. African women raised justifiably skeptical eyebrows at a white feminism that vaunted itself as giving tongue to a universal sisterhood in suffering. At the same time, women's position within the nationalist movement was still precarious, and women could ill afford to antagonize the embattled men, who were already reluctant to surrender whatever patriarchal power they still enjoyed.

In recent years, however, a transformed African discourse on feminism has emerged, with black women demanding the right to fashion the terms of nationalist feminism to meet their own needs and situations.[51] On May 2, 1990, the National Executive of the ANC issued a historic document entitled "Statement on the Emancipation of Women," which forthrightly proclaimed: "The experience of other societies has shown that the emancipation of women is not a by-product of a struggle for democracy, national liberation or socialism. It has to be addressed within our own organisation, the mass democratic movement and in the society as a whole." The document is unprecedented in placing South African women's resistance in an international context; in granting feminism independent historic agency; and in declaring, into the bargain, that all "laws, customs, traditions and practices which discriminate against women shall be held to be unconstitutional." If the ANC remains faithful to this document, virtually all existing practices in South Africa's legal, political, and social life will be rendered unconstitutional.

A few months later, on June 17, 1990, the leaders of the ANC Women's Section, recently returned to South Africa from exile, insisted on the strategic validity of the term "feminism": "Feminism has been misinterpreted in most third world countries... [T]here is nothing wrong with feminism. It is as progressive or reactionary as nationalism. Nationalism can be reactionary or progressive. We have not got rid of the term nationalism. And with feminism it is the same." Feminism, they believed, should be tailored to meet local needs and concerns.

Yet very real uncertainties for women remain. So far, theoretical and strategic analyses of South Africa's gender imbalances have not run deep. There has been little strategic rethinking of how, in particular, to transform labor relations within the household, and women are not given the same political visibility as men. At a Congress of South African Trade Unions (COSATU) convention, trade union women called for attention to sexual harrassment in the unions, but their demand was brusquely flicked aside by male unionists as a decadent symptom of "bourgeois imperialist feminism." Lesbian and gay activists have been similarly condemned as supporting lifestyles that are no more than invidious imports of empire.[52]

There is not only one feminism, nor is there one patriarchy. Feminism is imperialist when it puts the interests and needs of privileged women in imperialist countries above the local needs of disempowered women and men, borrowing from patriarchal privilege. In the last decade, women of color have been vehement in challenging privileged feminists who don't recognize their own racial and class power. In an important article, Chandra Mohanty challenges the appropriation of women of color's struggles by white women, specifically through the use of the category "Third World woman" as a singular, monolithic, and paradigmatically victimized subject.[53]

Denouncing all feminisms as imperialist, however, erases from memory the long histories of women's resistance to local and imperialist patriarchies. As Kumari Jayawardena notes, many women's mutinies around the world predated Western feminism or occurred without any contact with Western feminists.[54] Moreover, if all feminisms are derided as a pathology of the West, there is a very real danger that Western, white feminists will remain hegemonic, for the simple reason that such women have comparatively privileged access to publishing, the international media, education, and money.

A good deal of this kind of feminism may well be inappropriate to women living under very different situations. Instead, women of color are calling for the right to fashion feminism to suit their own worlds. The singular contribution of nationalist feminism has been its insistence on relating feminist struggles to other liberation movements.

All too frequently, male nationalists have condemned feminism as divisive, bidding women hold their tongues until after the revolution. Yet feminism is a political response to gender conflict, not its cause. To insist on silence about gender conflict when it already exists is to cover, and thereby ratify, women's disempowerment. Asking women to wait until after the revolution serves merely as a strategic tactic to defer women's demands. Not only does it conceal the fact that nationalisms are from the outset constituted in gender power, but, as the lessons of international history portend, women who are not empowered to organize during the struggle will not be empowered to organize after the struggle. If nationalism is not transformed by an analysis of gender power, the nation-state will remain a repository of male hopes, male aspirations, and male privilege.

All too often, the doors of tradition are slammed in women's faces. Yet traditions are both the outcome and the record of past political contests as well as the sites of present contest. In a nationalist revolution, both women and men should be empowered to decide which traditions are outmoded, which should be transformed, and which should be preserved. Male nationalists frequently argue that colonialism or capitalism has been women's ruin, with patriarchy merely a nasty second cousin destined to wither away when the real villain expires. Yet nowhere has a national or socialist revolution brought a full feminist revolution in its train. In many nationalist or socialist countries, women's concerns are at best paid lip service, at worst greeted with hilarity. If women have come to do men's work, men have not come to share women's work. Nowhere has feminism in its own right been allowed to be more than the maidservant to nationalism.

A crucial question thus remains for progressive nationalism: Can the iconography of the family be retained as the figure for national unity, or must an alternative, radical iconography be developed? In South Africa currently, critical questions for women remain. The Freedom Charter promises that the land will be given to those who work it. Since, in South Africa, women do much of the farming, will the land be given to them? Or, as in so many other postindependence countries, will the property rights, the technology, the loans, and the aid be given to men? Will men become the principal beneficiaries of the rights and resources of the new nation-state? When these questions are answered, perhaps we can begin to talk about a new South Africa.

Frantz Fanon's prescient warnings against the pitfalls of the national consciousness were never more urgent than now. For Fanon, nationalism gives vital expression to popular memory and is strategically essential for mobilizing the populace. At the same time, no one was more aware than Fanon of the attendant risks of projecting a fetishist denial of difference onto a conveniently abstracted "collective will." In South Africa, to borrow Fanon's phrase, national transformation is "no longer in a future heaven." Yet the current situation gives sober poignancy, especially for women, to the lines from Giles Pontecorvo's famous film on the Algerian national war of liberation, *The Battle of Algiers*: "It is difficult to start a revolution, more difficult to sustain it. But it's later, when we've won, that the real difficulties will begin."

NOTES

1. See Eric Hobsbawm's critique of nationalism in *Nations and Nationalism since 1780* (Cambridge: Cambridge University Press, 1990); Ernest Gellner, *Thought and Change* (London: Weidenfeld and Nicholson, 1964); and idem, *Nations and Nationalism* (Oxford: Blackwell, 1983).

2. Benedict Anderson, *Imagined Communities* (London: Verso, 1983), 6.

3. Cynthia Enloe, *Bananas, Beaches, and Bases: Making Feminist Sense of International Politics* (Berkeley: University of California Press, 1989), 44.

4. Frantz Fanon, *The Wretched of the Earth*, trans. Constance Farrington (London: Penguin, 1963), 30.

5. Elleke Boehmer, "Stories of Women and Mothers: Gender and Nationalism in the Early Fiction of Flora Nwapa," in Susheila Nasta, ed., *Motherlands: Black Women's Writing from Africa, the Caribbean and South Asia* (London: Women's Press, 1991), 5.

6. Ibid., 6.

7. Nira Yuval-Davis and Floya Anthias, eds., *Women-Nation-State* (London: Macmillan, 1989), 7.

8. Ibid., 1.

9. See Anne McClintock, *Imperial Leather: Race, Gender, and Sexuality in the Colonial Contest* (New York: Routledge, 1995).

10. Tom Nairn, *The Break-up of Britain* (London: New Left Books, 1977).

11. Deniz Kandiyoti, "Identity and Its Discontents: Women and the Nation," *Millennium: Journal of International Studies* 20, no. 3 (1991): 431.

12. Homi K. Bhabha, ed., *Nation and Narration* (London: Routledge, 1991), 1.

13. See Susan Buck-Morss, *The Dialectics of Seeing: Walter Benjamin and the Arcades Project* (Cambridge, Mass.: MIT Press, 1990), 67.

14. Ibid., xiv.

15. For further discussion, see McClintock, *Imperial Leather*, chap. 1.

16. Hobsbawm, *Nations and Nationalism,* 151.

17. Frantz Fanon, *Black Skin, White Masks,* trans. Charles Lam Markmann (London: Pluto Press, 1986), 141, 142, 143.

18. Ibid., 141–42.

19. Ibid., 13.

20. Ibid., 10.

21. Fanon, *Wretched of the Earth,* 29, 30.

22. Edward Said, *Culture and Imperialism* (London: Chatto and Windus, 1993), 326.

23. Homi K. Bhabha, foreword to Fanon, *Black Skin, White Masks,* ix.

24. Fanon, *Black Skin, White Masks,* 46.

25. Ibid., 46, 63.

26. Bhabha, foreword to Fanon, *Black Skin, White Masks,* ix, xxvi.

27. Fanon, *Black Skin, White Masks,* 81, 16, 159, 92.

28. Bhabha, foreword to Fanon, *Black Skin, White Masks,* xxv.

29. Ibid., xi.

30. Ibid.

31. Said, *Culture and Imperialism,* 89.

32. Terrence Eagleton, "Nationalism, Irony, and Commitment," in Terrence Eagleton, Fredric Jameson, and Edward Said, *Nationalism, Colonialism, and Literature* (Minneapolis: University of Minnesota Press, 1990), 28.

33. Ibid., 25.

34. Frantz Fanon, "Algeria Unveiled," in *A Dying Colonialism,* trans. Haakon Chevalier (New York: Grove Press, 1965), 42; all further references to this work will be given in the text.

35. For accounts of the rise of Afrikanerdom, see Dunbar T. Moodie, *The Rise of Afrikanerdom: Power, Apartheid, and the Afrikaner Civil Religion* (Berkeley: University of California Press, 1975), and Dan O' Meara, *Volkskapitalisme: Class, Capital and Ideology in the Development of Afrikaner Nationalism 1934–1948* (Cambridge: Cambridge University Press, 1983).

36. Isabel Hofmeyer, "'Building a Nation from Words': Afrikaans Language, Literature and Ethnic Identity, 1902–1924," in Shula Marks and Stanley Trapido, eds., *The Politics of Race, Class and Nationalism in Twentieth Century South Africa* (London: Longman, 1987), 105.

37. See Moodie, *Rise of Afrikanerdom,* and O'Meara, *Volkskapitalisme.*

38. See McClintock, *Imperial Leather,* chap. 1.

39. The degree to which the Eeufees papered over fatal divisions within the white populace became most manifest in 1988, when during the height of the State of Emergency two competing Treks set out to reenact the reenactment, each sponsored by two bitterly rivalrous white nationalist parties.

40. Albert Grundlingh and Hilary Sapire, "From Feverish Festival to Repetitive Ritual? The Changing Fortunes of the Great Trek Mythology in an Industrializing South Africa, 1938–1988," *South African Historical Journal* 21 (1989): 19–37.

41. Ibid., 24.

42. Theodor Adorno, *Gesammelte Schriften,* 1:360–61 (quoted in Buck-Morss, *Dialectics of Seeing,* 59).

43. Nairn, *Break-up of Britain,* 340.

44. H. J. Klopper, *Gedenkboek, Eeufees: 1838–1939* (Cape Town: Nasionale Pers, 1940).

45. See Elsabie Brink, "Man-made Women: Gender, Class and the Ideology of the *Volksmoeder,*" in C. Walker, ed., *Women and Gender in Southern Africa to 1945* (London: James Currey, 1990), 273–92.

46. See Tom Lodge, "Charters from the Past: The African National Congress and Its Historiographical Traditions," *Radical History Review* 46, no. 7 (1990): 161–89.

47. Frene Ginwala, *Agenda* 8 (1990): 77–93.

48. J. Mpama, *Umsebenzi,* June 26, 1937.

49. See Deborah Gaitskell and Elaine Unterhalter, "Mothers of the Nation: A Comparative Analysis of Nation, Race and Motherhood in Afrikaner Nationalism and the African National Congress," in Yuval-Davis and Anthias, eds., *Women-Nation-State.*

50. The ANC delegation to the Nairobi Conference on Women in 1985 declared: "It would be suicidal for us to adopt feminist ideas. Our enemy is the system and we cannot exhaust our energies on women's issues."

51. At a seminar titled "Feminism and National Liberation," convened by the Woman's Section of the ANC in London in 1989, a representative from the South African Youth Congress exclaimed: "How

good it feels that feminism is finally accepted as a legitimate school of thought in our struggles and is not seen as a foreign ideology."

52. For a groundbreaking book on the history, politics, and culture of lesbian and gay life in South Africa, see Edwin Cameron and Mark Gewisser, eds., *Defiant Desire: Gay and Lesbian Lives in South Africa* (New York: Routledge, 1994).

53. Chandra T. Mohanty, "Under Western Eyes: Feminist Scholarship and Colonial Discourses," in Chandra T. Mohanty, Ann Russo, and Lourdes Torres, eds., *Third World Women and the Politics of Feminism* (Bloomington: Indiana University Press, 1991), 52.

54. Kumari Jayawardena, *Feminism and Nationalism in the Third World* (London: Zed Press, 1986).

Chapter 5
Currying Favor:
The Politics of British Educational
and Cultural Policy in India, 1813–54
Gauri Viswanathan

Antonio Gramsci illuminates the relations of culture and power through the useful insight that cultural domination works by consent and often precedes conquest by force. Power, operating concurrently at two clearly distinguishable levels, produces a situation where "the supremacy of a social group manifests itself in two ways, as 'domination' and as 'intellectual and moral leadership. . . .' It seems clear . . . that there can, and indeed must, be hegemonic activity even before the rise to power, and that one should not count only on the material force which power gives in order to exercise an effective leadership."[1]

The importance of moral and intellectual suasion in matters of governance is readily conceded on theoretical grounds as an implicit tactical maneuver in the con- solidation of power. There is an almost bland consensus in post-Arnoldian cultural criticism that the age of ideology begins when force gives way to ideas. But the precise mode and process by which cultural domination is ensured are less open to scrutiny as historically documented fact. Current approaches have gotten around this problem somewhat by treating ideology as a form of masking, and the license given to speculative analyses as a result is sometimes great enough to suspend, at least temporarily, the search for actual intentions.

Arguably, detailed records of self-incrimination are not routinely preserved in state archives. But where such records do exist, the evidence is often compelling enough to suggest that the Gramscian notion is not merely a theoretical construct but an uncannily accurate description of historical process, howsoever subject it may be to the vagaries of particular circumstances. A case in point is British India, whose checkered history of cultural confrontation conferred a sense of urgency to volun- tary cultural assimilation as the most effective form of political action. The political choices are spelled out in the most chilling terms: "The Natives must either be kept down by a sense of our power, or they must willingly submit from a conviction that we are more wise, more just, more humane, and more anxious to improve their condition than any other rulers they could possibly have."[2]

Implicit in this statement by a high-ranking British official in the Bombay adminis- tration is a recognition of the importance of self-representation, or the production of an image of the "ideal" Englishman. Logically, there were two sources from which the colonial subjects could derive an idea of the humaneness and justness of their

rulers, one actual (i.e., through British actions and behavior) and the other representational. Of the two, the former posed more serious problems of control and
consistency. The East India Company's servants who were sent to India were often
charged by Englishmen themselves with intemperance and rapacity. Their actions in
India belied the fondest hope that colonial subjects would be convinced of the superiority of English ideals. Since the actual image could not supply the appropriate
model, representational sources increasingly came to be relied on to do the work.
This essay deals with the ways in which the literature and arts of England were
gradually put to use to convey an image of the "ideal" Englishman.

•

English literature came into India, howsoever imperceptibly, with the passing of the
Charter Act of 1813. This act, which renewed the East India Company's charter for
commercial operations in India, produced two major changes in Britain's role with
respect to its Indian subjects: one was the assumption of a new responsibility toward native education, and the other was a relaxation of controls over missionary
work in India.

The pressure to assume a more direct responsibility for the welfare of the natives
came from several sources. The earlier and perhaps more significant one, decisively
affecting the future course of British administrative rule in India, was the English
Parliament. Significantly, the goal of civilizing the natives was far from being the
central motivation in these first official efforts at educational activity. Parliamentary
involvement with Indian education had a rather uncommon origin in that it began
with the excesses of the parliamentarians' own countrymen in India. The extrav-
agant and demoralized lifestyles of the East India Company's servants, combined
with their ruthless exploitation of native material resources, had begun to raise serious and alarming questions in England about the morality of British presence in
India. It was an issue that was too embarrassing for Parliament to ignore — avoiding
the matter would have appeared to be an endorsement of the company's excesses.
But unable to check the activities of these highly placed nabobs, or wealthy Europeans whose huge fortunes were amassed in India, Parliament sought instead to
remedy the wrongs committed against the natives by attending to their welfare and
improvement.

Yet however much parliamentary discussions of the British presence in India may
have been couched in moral terms, there was no obscuring the real issue, which
remained political, not moral. The English Parliament's conflict with the East India
Company was a long-standing one, going back to the early years of trading activity
in the East Indies when rival companies clashed repeatedly in a bid to gain exclusive
rights to trade in the region. Besides, the English Parliament was becoming alarmed
by the danger of having a commercial company constituting an independent political power in India. By 1757 the East India Company had already become virtual
master of Bengal, and its territorial influence was growing steadily despite numerous
financial problems besetting it. But in the absence of any cause for interference in
the activities of the company, the British Crown could conceivably do little to reorga-
nize the company's system of administration and win control of its affairs. Not until
the last quarter of the eighteenth century, when reports of immorality and depravity
among company servants started pouring in, did Parliament find an excuse to inter-

vene, at which point, in the name of undertaking responsibility for the improvement of the natives, it began to take a serious and active interest in Indian political affairs. It was a move that was to result in a gradual erosion of the unchallenged supremacy of the company in India.

One cannot fail to be struck by the peculiar irony of a history in which England's initial involvement with the education of the natives derived not from a conviction of native immorality, as the later discourse might lead one to believe, but from the depravity of England's own administrators and merchants. In Edmund Burke's words, steps had to be taken to "form a strong and solid security for the natives against the wrongs and oppressions of British subjects resident in Bengal."[3] While the protectiveness contained in this remark may seem dangerously close to an attitude of paternalism, its immediate effect was beneficial, as it led to a strengthening of existing native institutions and traditions to act as a bulwark against the forces of violent change unleashed by the British presence.

This mission to revitalize Indian culture and learning and protect it from the oblivion to which foreign rule might doom it merged with the then current literary vogue of Orientalism and formed the mainstay of that phase of British rule in India known as the Orientalist phase. Orientalism was adopted as an official policy partly out of expediency and caution and partly out of an emergent political sense that an efficient Indian administration rested on an understanding of Indian culture. It grew out of the concern of Warren Hastings, governor-general from 1774 to 1785, that British administrators and merchants in India were not sufficiently responsive to Indian languages and Indian traditions. The distance between ruler and ruled was perceived to be so vast as to evoke the sentiment that "we rule over thorn and traffic with them, but they do not understand our character, and we do not penetrate theirs. The consequence is that we have no hold on their sympathies, no seat in their affections."[4] Hastings's own administration was distinguished by a tolerance for the native customs and by a cultural empathy unusual for its time. Underlying Orientalism was a tacit policy of reverse acculturation, whose goal was to train British administrators and civil servants to fit into the culture of the ruled and to assimilate them thoroughly into the native way of life.

Opposing Orientalism was the countermovement of Anglicism, which gained ascendancy in the 1830s. Briefly, Anglicism grew as an expression of discontent with the policy of promoting the Oriental languages and literatures in native education. In its vigorous advocacy of Western instead of Eastern learning, it came into sharp conflict with Orientalism, whose proponents vehemently insisted that such a move would have disastrous consequences, the most serious being the alienation of Indians from British rule. To understand the forces enabling the shift from Orientalism to Anglicism, it is necessary to distinguish the various political and commercial groups entering the Indian scene. Warren Hastings was succeeded in the governor-generalship by Lord Cornwallis (1786–93), who found himself at the helm of a government seriously compromised by financial scandals and deteriorating standards. For this state of affairs the new governor-general squarely laid the blame on the earlier policy of accommodation to the native culture. In his view the official indulgence toward Oriental forms of social organization, especially government, was directly responsible for the lax morals of the East India Company's servants. If the company had sorely abused its power, what better explanation was there than the fact that the model of Oriental despotism was constantly before the eyes of its functionaries? To Cornwallis, the abuse of power was the most serious of evils afflicting the East India Company, not only jeopardizing the British hold over India but, worse still, dividing the English nation on the legitimacy of the colonial enterprise.

The most pressing task, therefore, was to ensure that no further abuse would occur. In the process of working toward this end, Cornwallis evolved a political philosophy that he believed would be consistent with British commercial aims. His theoretical position was that a good government was held together not by men but by political principles and laws, and in these alone rested absolute power. Dismissing the Oriental system as deficient in a strong political tradition (and in this belief Cornwallis was doing no more than echoing a view that was common currency), he turned to English principles of government and jurisprudence for setting the norms of public behavior and responsibility by which administrators were to function. Determined to run a government that would remain free of corrupting influences from the native society, Cornwallis concentrated his entire energies on the improvement of European morals on English lines. The natives engaged his attention only minimally; for the most part, he appeared wholly content to leave them in their "base" state, in the belief that their reform was well beyond his purview.

Clearly, the first steps toward Anglicization were aimed at tackling the problem of corruption within the ranks. To this extent, Anglicism began as an entirely defensive movement. But even in this form it was not without elements of aggression toward the native culture, as is apparent in certain measures that Cornwallis adopted to streamline the government. Convinced that contact with natives was the root cause of declining European morals, he resolved to exclude all natives from appointment to responsible posts, hoping by this means to restore the Englishman to his pristine self and rid him once and for all of decadent influences. Predictably, the exclusion of Indians from public office had serious repercussions on Anglo-Indian relations. The personal contact that Englishmen and Indians had enjoyed during Hastings's administration vanished with Cornwallis, and the result was that a more rigidified master-subject relationship set in. One historian, Percival Spear, has gone so far as to suggest that this event marks the point at which there developed "that contempt for things and persons Indian...which produced the views of a Mill or a Macaulay."[5]

With Cornwallis charting an apparently serious course for administrative rule on English principles, one would expect Anglicism as a cultural movement to have triumphed much earlier than it actually did (i.e., the 1830s). Its momentum was badly shattered, however, by the cultural policy of his immediate successors, a group of skilled and politically astute administrators who had all at one time served under Lord Wellesley, a governor-general (1798–1805) noted for his caution and reserve, and later under the Marquess of Hastings, under whose governor-generalship (1812–23) British rule was more firmly consolidated. Conservative in their outlook and fiercely Romantic in their disposition, these accomplished officers — John Malcolm, Thomas Munro, Charles Metcalf, and Mountstuart Elphinstone — had no use for the impersonal bureaucratic system of government carved out for India by Cornwallis. While Cornwallis had no particular interest in either promoting or discouraging Oriental learning, as long as Englishmen were not compelled to study it, his successors by no means shared his indifference. Indeed, they were shrewd enough to see that it was entirely in their interest to support Orientalism if it meant the preservation of the feudal character of British rule. At the same time they were too conscious of England's by-then-strengthened position in India to resort to the promotion of native culture as a purely defensive measure. Rather, Orientalism represented for them the logical corollary of a precise and meticulously defined scheme of administration. In that scheme, the British government was to function as a paternal protectorate governing India not by direct rule (i.e., through the force of British law) but through various local functionaries. In other words, the Cornwallis system of centralized administration was spurned in favor of one that was more diffuse and that operated through a network of hierarchical relationships between British officers at one level and between the British and the Indians on another. In order to draw the Indians into this hegemonic structure, it was imperative for the British administration to maintain an alliance with those who formed the traditional ruling class. This was essential partly to conciliate the indigenous elite for their displaced status but also partly to secure a buffer zone for absorbing the effects of foreign rule, which, if experienced directly by the masses, might have an entirely disastrous impact.

This scheme of administration was at once more personal and more rigidly stratified in its conception. It was further bolstered by the philosophy that no political tradition could be created anew or superimposed on another without a violent rejection of it by the preexisting society. It was argued that for a new political society to emerge, the native tradition and culture had to provide the soil for its growth. The imagery of grafting that permeated the discourse around this time pointed to an emerging theory of organicism that conceived of political formation as part of a process of cultural synthesis.[6]

This phase of British rule, roughly spanning the first two decades of the nineteenth century, acquires a special significance in this narrative for marking the historical moment when political philosophy and cultural policy converged to work toward clearly discernible common ends. The promotion of Orientalism no less than Anglicism became irrevocably tied from this point onward to questions of administrative structure and governance: for example, How were Indian subjects to be imbued with a sense of public responsibility and honor? By what means could the concept of a Western-style government best be impressed on their minds to facilitate the business of state?

Such questions also implied that, with the reversal of the Cornwallis policy of isolationism from Indian society and the hierarchical reordering of the Indian subjects for administrative purposes, the problem of reform was no longer confined to the British side but extended more actively to the Indian side as well. The more specialized functions devolving upon a government now settling down to prospective long-term rule brought the Indians as a body of subjects more directly into the conceptual management of the country than was the case in either Hastings's or Cornwallis's time. As a result, the "Indian character" suddenly became a subject of immense importance, as was the question of how it could best be molded to suit British administrative needs.

But curiously it was on this last point that Orientalism began to lose ground to Anglicism. For even though it appeared to be the most favorable cultural policy for a feudal-type administration, its theoretical premises were seriously undermined by the gathering tide of reform that accompanied the restructuring of government. It is well worth remembering that this was a government that had grown acutely aware of both its capacity for generating change (thus far internally) and its own vested authority over the natives. The Orientalist position was that a Western political tradition could be successfully grafted upon the native tradition without having to direct itself toward the transformation of that society along Western lines. But as a theory it found itself at odds with the direction of internal consolidation along which British rule was moving. The strengthening of England's position in India, as exemplified by a recently coordinated and efficient administrative structure, put the rulers under compulsion less to direct change inward than to carry over the reformist impulse to those over whom they had dominion.

That tendency was reinforced by two outside developments. One was the opening of India to free trade in 1813, which resulted in the Private Trade and City interests steadily exerting stronger influence on the Crown at the expense of Indian interests. The "Private Traders" had no tradition of familiarity with India behind them and were prone to make decisions that reflected their own biases and assumptions about what was good for their subjects rather than decisions that took account of what the existing situation itself demanded.

A second and more important influence in the thrust toward reform was exerted by a group of missionaries called the Clapham Evangelicals, who played a key role in the drama of consolidation of British interests in India. Among them were Zachary Macaulay, William Wilberforce, Samuel Thornton, and Charles Grant, and to these men must be given much of the credit for supplying British expansionism with an ethics of concern for reform and conversion. Insisting that British domination was robbed of all justification if no efforts were made to reform native morals, the missionaries repeatedly petitioned Parliament to permit them to engage in the urgent business of enlightening the Indians. Unsuccessful in influencing the Act of 1793, which renewed the East India Company's charter for a twenty-year period, the missionaries were more triumphant by the time of the 1813 resolution, which brought about the other major event associated with the Charter Act: the opening of India to missionary activity.

Although chaplains had hitherto been appointed by the East India Company to tend to the needs of the European population residing in India, the English Parliament had consistently refused to modify the company charter to allow missionary work in India. The main reason for government resistance had been an apprehension that the Indians would feel threatened and eventually cause trouble for England's commercial ventures. Insurrections in various areas around the country had been invariably blamed on proselytizing activity in those areas. The fear of further acts of hostility on religious grounds had grown so great that it had prompted a temporary suspension of the Christianizing mission. In keeping with the government policy of religious neutrality, the Bible had been proscribed and scriptural teaching forbidden.

The opening of India to missionaries, along with the commitment of the British to native improvement, might appear to suggest a victory for the missionaries, encouraging them perhaps to anticipate official support for their evangelizing mission.

But if they had such hopes, they were to be dismayed by the continuing checks on their activities, which grew impossibly stringent. Publicly, the English Parliament demanded a guarantee that large-scale proselytizing would not be carried out in India. Privately, though, it needed little persuasion about the distinct advantages that would flow from missionary contact with the Indians and their "many immoral and disgusting habits."

Although they represented a convergence of interests, these two events — British involvement in Indian education and the entry of missionaries — were far from being complementary or mutually supportive. On the contrary, they were entirely opposed to each other both in principle and in fact. The inherent constraints operating on British educational policy were apparent in the central contradiction of a government committed to the improvement of the people while being restrained from imparting any direct instruction in the religious principles of the English nation. The encouragement of Oriental learning, seen initially as a way of fulfilling the ruler's obligations to the subjects, seemed to accentuate rather than diminish the contradiction. For as the British swiftly learned to their dismay, it was impossible to promote Orientalism without exposing the Hindus and Muslims to the religious and moral tenets of their respective faiths — a situation that was clearly not tenable with the stated goal of "moral and intellectual improvement."

This tension between increasing involvement in Indian education and enforced noninterference in religion was productively resolved through the introduction of English literature. Significantly, the direction to this solution was present in the Charter Act itself, which ambiguously stated that "a sum of not less than one lac of rupees shall be annually applied to the revival and improvement of literature, and the encouragement of the learned natives of India."[7] While the use of the word "revival" may weight the interpretation on the side of Oriental literature, the almost deliberate imprecision suggests a more fluid government position in conflict with the official espousal of Orientalism. Over twenty years later Macaulay was to seize on this very ambiguity to argue that the phrase clearly meant Western literature, and he denounced in no uncertain terms attempts to interpret the phrase as a reference to Oriental literature:

> It is argued, or rather taken for granted, that by literature, the Parliament can have meant only Arabic and Sanskrit literature, that they never would have given the honourable appellation of a learned native to a native who was familiar with the poetry of Milton, the Metaphysics of Locke, the Physics of Newton; but that they meant to designate by that name only such persons as might have studied in the sacred books of the Hindoos all the uses of cusa-grass, and all the mysteries of absorption into the Deity.[8]

Macaulay's plea on behalf of English literature had a major influence on the passing of the English Education Act in 1835, which officially required the natives of India to submit to the study of that literature. But English was not an unknown entity in India at that time, for rudimentary instruction in the language had been introduced more than two decades earlier. Initially, English did not supersede Oriental studies but was taught alongside it. Yet it was clear that it enjoyed a different status, for there was a scrupulous attempt to establish separate colleges for its study. Even when it was taught within the same college, the English course of studies was kept separate from the course of Oriental studies and was attended by a different set of students. The rationale was that if the English department drew students who were attached only to that department and to no other (that is, the Persian or the Arabic or the Sanskrit), the language might then be taught "classically" in much the same way that Latin and Greek were taught in England.

Although based on literary material, the early Indian curriculum in English was primarily devoted to language studies. However, by the 1820s the atmosphere of secularism in which these studies were conducted became a major concern to the missionaries, who had been permitted to enter India after 1813. One missionary in India, the Reverend William Keane, argued that while European education had done much to destroy "heathen" superstition, it had not substituted any moral principle in its place. The exclusion of the Bible had a demoralizing effect, he claimed, for it tended to produce evils in the country and to give the native

> mind unity of opinion, which before it never had, . . . and political thoughts, which [the Indians] get out of our European books, but which it is impossible to reconcile with our position in that country, political thoughts of liberty and power, which would be good if they were only the result of a noble ambition of the natural mind for something superior, but which when they arise without religious principles, produce an effect which, to my mind, is one of unmixed evil.[9]

The missionaries got further support from an unexpected quarter. The military officers who testified in the parliamentary sessions on Indian education joined hands with them in arguing that a secular education in English would increase the natives' capacity for evil because it would elevate their intellects without providing the moral principles to keep them in check. Major General Rowlandson of the British army warned: "I have seen native students who had obtained an insight into European literature and history, in whose minds there seemed to be engendered a spirit of disaffection towards the British Government."[10] While the missionaries and the military obviously had different interests at stake, with the latter perhaps not quite as interested in the souls of the heathen as the former, they were both clearly aiming at the same goal: the prevention of situations leading to political disunity or lawlessness. The alliance between the two undoubtedly proved fruitful insofar as it loosened the British resistance to the idea of religious instruction for the natives and made British leaders more conscious of the need to find alternate modes of social control.

In England, the function of providing authority for individual action and belief and of dispensing moral laws for the formation of character had traditionally been carried out through church-controlled educational institutions. The aristocracy maintained a monopoly over access to church-dominated education and instituted a classical course of studies that it shared with the clergy, but from which the middle and working classes were systematically excluded. The classical curriculum under church patronage in England became identified as a prerequisite for social leadership and, more subtly, as the means by which social privilege was protected. This alliance between church and culture consecrated the concept of station in life and directly supported the existing system of social stratification: while the classical curriculum served to confirm the upper orders in their superior social status, religious instruction was given to the lower orders to fit them for the various duties of life and to secure them in their appropriate station. The alliance between church and culture was thus equally an alliance between ideas of formative education and of social control.

As late as the 1860s, the "literary curriculum" in British educational establishments remained polarized around classical studies for the upper classes and religious studies for the lower. As for what is now known as the subject of English literature, the British educational system had no firm place for it until the last quarter of the nineteenth century when the challenge posed by the middle classes resulted in the creation of alternative institutions devoted to "modern" studies.

It is quite conceivable that educational development in British India may have run the same course as it did in England, were it not for one crucial difference: the strict controls on Christianizing activities. Clearly, the texts that were standard fare for the lower classes in England could not legitimately be incorporated into the Indian curriculum without inviting violent reactions from the native population, particularly the learned classes. And yet the fear lingered that without submission of the individual to moral law or the authority of God, the control the British upper classes were able to secure over the lower classes in their own country would elude them in India. Comparisons were on occasion made between the situation at home and in India, between the "rescue" of the lower classes in England, "those living in the dark recesses of our great cities at home, from the state of degradation consequent on their vicious and depraved habits, the offspring of ignorance and sensual indulgence," and the elevation of the Hindus and Muslims, whose "ignorance and degradation" required a remedy not adequately supplied by their respective faiths.[11] Such comparisons served to intensify the search for other social institutions to take over from religious instruction the function of communicating the laws of the social order.

Provoked by missionaries, on the one hand, and fears of native insubordination, on the other, British administrators discovered an ally in English literature to support them in maintaining control of the natives under the guise of a liberal education. With both secularism and religion appearing as political liabilities, literature appeared to represent a perfect synthesis of these two opposing positions. The idea evolved in alternating stages of affirmation and disavowal of literature's derivation from and affiliation with Christianity as a social institution. What follows is a description of that process as reconstructed from the minutes of evidence given before the British Parliament's Select Committee, and recorded in the 1852–53 volume of the Parliamentary Papers. These proceedings reveal not only an open assertion of British material interests but also a mapping out of strategies for promoting those interests through representations of Western literary knowledge as objective, universal, and rational.

•

The first stage in the process was an assertion of structural congruence between Christianity and English literature. Missionaries had long argued on behalf of the shared history of religion and literature, of a tradition of belief and doctrine creating a common culture of values, attitudes, and norms. They had ably cleared the way for the realization that as the "grand repository of the book of God" England had produced a literature that was immediately marked off from all non-European literatures, being "animated, vivified, hallowed, and baptized" by a religion to which

Western man owed his material and moral progress. The difference was rendered as a contrast between

> the literature of a world embalmed with the Spirit of Him who died to redeem it, and that which is the growth of ages that have gloomily rolled on in the rejection of that Spirit, as between the sweet bloom of creation in the open light of heaven, and the rough, dark recesses of submarine forests of sponges.[12]

This other literature was likened to Plato's cave, whose darkened inhabitants were "chained men ... counting the shadows of subterranean fires."

If not in quite the same eloquent terms, some missionaries tried to point out to the government that though they pretended to say they taught no Christianity, they actually taught a great deal, for it was virtually impossible to take Christianity out of an English education, and much more of scriptural teaching was imparted than was generally admitted. The Reverend Keane tried to persuade officials that

> Shakespeare, though by no means a good standard, is full of religion; it is full of the common sense principles which none but Christian men can recognize. Sound Protestant Bible principles, though not actually told in words, are there set out to advantage, and the opposite often condemned. So with Goldsmith, Abercrombie on the Mental Powers, and many others books which are taught in the schools; though the natives hear they are not to be proselytized, yet such books have undoubtedly sometimes a favourable effect in actually bringing them to us missionaries.[13]

The missionary description was appropriated in its entirety by government officers. But while the missionaries made such claims in order to force the government to sponsor teaching of the Bible, the administrators used the same argument to prove English literature made such direct instruction redundant. Several steps were initiated to incorporate selected English literary texts into the Indian curriculum on the claim that these works were supported in their morality by a body of evidence that also upheld the Christian faith. In their official capacity as members of the Council on Education, Macaulay and his brother-in-law Charles Trevelyan were among those engaged in a minute analysis of English texts to prove what they called the "diffusive benevolence of Christianity" in them. The process of curricular selection was marked by weighty pronouncements on the "sound Protestant Bible Principles" in Shakespeare, the "strain of serious Piety" in Joseph Addison's *Spectator* papers, the "scriptural morality" of Francis Bacon and John Locke, the "devout sentiment" of John Abercrombie, and the "noble Christian sentiments" in Adam Smith's *Theory of Moral Sentiments* (which was hailed as the "best authority for the true science of morals which English literature could supply").[14] The cataloguing of shared features had the effect of convincing detractors that the government could effectively cause voluntary reading of the Bible and at the same time disclaim any intentions of proselytizing.

But while these identifications were occurring at one level, at another level the asserted unity of religion and literature was simultaneously disavowed, as evidenced in a series of contradictory statements. The most directly conflicting of these maintained, on the one hand, that English literature is "imbued with the spirit of Christianity" and "interwoven with the words of the Bible to a great degree" so that "without ever looking into the Bible one of those Natives must come to a considerable knowledge of it merely from reading English literature."[15] On the other hand, in the same breath a counterclaim was made that English literature "is not interwoven to the same extent with the Christian religion as the Hindoo religion is with the Sanskrit language and literature."[16] Charles Cameron, who succeeded Macaulay as president of the Council on Education, attempted to provide an illustration for the latter position by arguing that although Milton assumed the truth of Christianity, his works did not bear the same relation to the doctrines of Christianity as did Oriental literature to the tenets of the native religious systems. But when pressed by his examiners to explain the point further, he refused to elaborate, admitting only "a difference in degree."[17]

It is certainly possible to interpret the contradiction as an unimportant and inconsequential instance of British ambivalence or inconsistency of policy. But to do so is to ignore a subtle but palpable shift in emphasis from the centrality of universal Christian truths to the legitimacy and value of British authority. Mediating this shift was a relativization of the notion of truth, producing a heightened emphasis upon the intellectual motive in literary instruction. The difference that Cameron hesitated to specify had long before been named by several missionaries when they termed Western literature a form of intellectual production, in contrast to Oriental literature, which, they claimed, set itself up as a source of divine authority. The Serampore Baptist missionary William Carey best expressed the missionary viewpoint when he lamented, in comparing the Hindu epic the *Mahabharata* to Homer, that "[were] it, like his *Iliad,* only considered as a great effort of human genius, I should think it is one of the first productions in the world, but alas! it is the ground of Faith to Millions of men; and as such must be held in the utmost abhorrence."[18]

The distinction served to emphasize the arbitrariness of the Oriental conception of truth, which derived its claims from the power of the explicator (that is, the *maulvis* and the pundits, the class learned in Arabic and Sanskrit) to mediate between the popular mind and sacred knowledge. From the viewpoint of a government seeking entry into the native system, the distinction had a powerful political appeal, for it proposed an idea that turned into an effective political strategy: if the native learned classes had arrogated all power to decipher texts unto themselves by blurring the lines between literature and religion, an erosion of that power base was bound to ensue, so the reasoning went, if the authority vested in the explicator were relocated elsewhere — that is, if authority were reinvested in a body of texts presented as objective, scientific, rational, empirically verifiable truth, the product not of an exclusive social or political class but of a consciousness that spoke in a universal voice and for the universal good.

The Protestant Reformation provided a historical model for the relocation of authority in the body of knowledge represented by English literary texts. In its deliberations on the curriculum, the Council on Indian Education seized on the analogy between the British presence in India and the Reformation in Europe to make two related arguments, which are here summarized from the reports issued from 1840 to 1853. First, the characterization of English literature as intellectual production suggested a different process of reading, requiring the exercise of reason rather than unquestioning faith. The history of the "despotic Orient" was adequate proof from the British viewpoint that a literature claiming to provide divine revelation diluted the capacity of the individual mind to resist the manipulations of a priestly caste. By the terms of this argument, not only did Oriental literature lull the individual into a passive acceptance of the fabulous incidents as actual occurrences; more alarmingly, the acceptance of mythological events as factual description stymied the mind's capacity to extrapolate a range of meanings for analysis and verification in the real world. The logic of associating reason with an approach to literary texts as types of human activity was a simple one: the products of human conscious-ness must submit to interpretation because their creating subject is man, not God, man in all his imperfection and fallibility. Because interpretation by definition en-tails a plurality of response, the receiving mind is pressured all the more to weigh the truth-value of each possibility, thereby activating rational processes of discrimi-nation and judgment — intellectual skills unanimously held to be utterly alien to a literature conceived as divine agency.

Second, as an example of human invention drawing its material from a rationally perceived world, English literature disciplined the mind to think and reason from the force of evidence. The Cartesian influence is especially strong in this description, particularly in the argument that the element of doubt attending upon the senses sets the mind in a state of intellectual ferment, forcing it to do battle with error until a full knowledge of the truth is reached. Since an individually realized truth would have proceeded through the stages of rational investigation — of detached observation, analysis, verification, and application — its claims to universal, objective knowledge were unquestionably greater, it was concluded, than the claims to truth of received tradition.

The movement toward an affirmation of British authority that such a characteriza-tion of Western knowledge implied appears as willed event in a report filed by the president of the Board of Education at Bombay in April 1853:

> For my own part, I believe that Providence dictated this policy [of religious neutrality] as the means of riveting the power of England over this country; but it is clear that we cannot expect a blessing to rest upon a violation of the public faith, solemnly pledged by conquerors to those submitting to their authority.
>
> And what, I would ask, is the course to be followed by a great and generous country under such circumstances? Its faith is pledged, and the opinion of its scrupulous good faith is the keystone of the arch which supports its mighty power over these lands. Surely, surely, there is but one course open.
>
> We have the subtle Brahmin, the ardent Mahomedan, the meek, though zealous, Christian missionary, each and all relying on this promise of noninterference, and pressing the evidence of his respective faith on the attention of the people of India; and when this people look up to the Government and say, "You tolerate all religions; all cannot be true; show us what is truth," the Government can only answer, "Our own belief is known to you; we are ready to give a reason for the faith that is in us; and we will place you in a situation by which you may judge whether those reasons are convincing or not. We will teach you History by the light of its two eyes, Chronology and Geography; you will therein discover the history and system of every religion. We will expand your intellectual powers to distinguish truth from falsehood by the aid of Literature and Logic; we will...lay open to you all we know of the firmament above, of the nature of the earth on which we live, and the organization of the flowers which enamel its surface; and with your perceptions of the power and wisdom of

your God and ours, thus cleared and enlarged, we may safely leave you to distinguish truth for yourselves. . . ." Each one, be he Christian, Mahomedan, Hindoo or Parsee, is engaged in one common object; viz., the advancement of truth. We differ only as to that which is truth, and, like other discreet men, we never talk on that respecting which we are sure to differ.[19]

Though a policy of noninterference may have been originally adopted for reasons of expediency, it was rapidly transformed into a medium of self-representation. As a symbol of free intellectual inquiry, religious noninterference generated an image of the Englishman as benign, disinterested, detached, impartial, and judicious. Indeed, British authority depended vitally on the stability of the image and on the consistency with which it was preserved and relayed to the native mind. From this standpoint, violations of the policy of religious neutrality were of more than military consequence: in more far-reaching ways, by breaching the "good faith" through which the British exercised their authority over the natives, they threatened to unmask the illusions that British rule in India required for its legitimation — illusions of trust, honor, obligation.

And yet in a land where, as the missionary Joshua Marshman said, Indians were known to attach a high religious feeling even to secular education, it was political folly to leave British noninterference to be interpreted by the Indians in their own way, such that it might be construed "not as liberty of conscience but as carelessness about any religion."[20] Interpreted so, religious toleration had the potential of earning for the British not the image of benevolence and noncoerciveness but its very converse — of irresponsibility, indifference, and disdain of duty. If the rulers' faith was perceived to be shallow, much the same could be expected of their oaths. There was little self-deception on the part of the report's author: he realized that pledges of respect for the beliefs of British subjects would be viewed as having no content, no value, if the inference to be drawn from neutrality was that no discernible belief system lay behind those pledges.

The only escape from this predicament, albeit one fraught with risks, was to convince the natives, as the report advised, "that the government cultivate[d] its own religion." To do this without seeming to coerce this religion on the Indians was the recurrent problem, and it was precisely where the role of English literature as subject of study and as method of analysis was preeminent. Literary study served as the means through which, simultaneously, the claims of Western belief were asserted and the grounds of its truthfulness vindicated. What made this twofold activity possible, as the president's report implied, was literature's double stance toward reason and faith, utility and tradition, empiricism and revelation — a stance obscuring its affiliations with institutional religion (and the entire system of social and political formation of which it was a part) through its appeal to an objective, empirical reality. Charles Cameron's reticence before his examiners may take on more meaning in this context, for his reluctance to affirm unambiguously literature's relation to Christianity stemmed from an awareness of the operational value of his double stance in reinforcing the validity of the knowledge to be imparted and, by extension, of the authority of those imparting it. Further, it enabled the validation of Christian belief by the disciplinary techniques of European learning while at the same time deflecting attention from its self-referential, self-confirming aspects. Its power rested on the idea that European disciplines, being products of human reason, were independent of systems of belief based on pure faith. Therefore, by proving what faith merely proposed, they confirmed far more than the mere truthfulness of Christian belief; more importantly, they demonstrated the power and authority of the Western mind to penetrate the mysteries of the natural and phenomenal world.

I'd like now to give an example of a prescribed text in the British Indian literature curriculum that provided a theoretical grounding for representations of English literature as intellectual authority. Adam Smith's *Theory of Moral Sentiments* (1759) remained a central text in the Indian curriculum throughout the nineteenth century, both in government and in missionary institutions — it was still listed in the *Calcutta University Commission Report of 1919* as part of the prescribed course of studies. Though it was well over a century before his proposals were implemented, Adam Smith was evidently among the first to propose the study of selections from the works of English prose writers as a social and moral corrective for dangers that he believed were inherent in laissez-faire capitalism, particularly dangers associated with the potential for a morally corrupted concept of individualism.[21]

In *Moral Sentiments,* Adam Smith argued the need for a broad academic program that would encourage and direct a process of self-evaluation and self-enlightenment. His work can be read as a systematic argument for the education of the man of intellect, who is also a man of good conduct and virtue. Smith began by noting a principle inherent in man's nature, which he called the impartial spectator, that makes him responsive to how others think and behave. Those who are able to direct our sentiments are models of intellectual virtue: the "man of taste," for instance, "who distinguishes the minute and scarce perceptible differences of beauty and deformity" or the "experienced mathematician who unravels with ease the most intricate and perplexed proportions."[22] Smith believed that through the admiration of the sentiments of these "others," these learning models, we come to realize the existence of intellectual virtues. The impartial spectator, the spectator within us, as Smith referred to him, "enters by sympathy into the sentiments of the master" and "views the object under the same agreeable aspect." The task before us, he claimed, if we truly wish to realize the intellectual virtues, is to cultivate the impartial spectator within us, to develop the ability to place ourselves in the context of those sentiments. The study of literature, Smith argued, provides the formative structures that will determine the development of this spectator within. Through literature, he wrote, "we endeavour to examine our own conduct as we imagine any other fair and impartial spectator would examine it. If, upon placing ourselves in his situation, we thoroughly enter into all the passions and motives which influenced it, we approve of it, by sympathy with the approbation of this supposed equitable judge. If otherwise, we enter into his disapprobation, and condemn it."[23]

Smith's concept of the impartial spectator was embedded in the rationale of literary instruction in India, which presupposed a divided self-consciousness. Smith had written that "when I endeavour to examine my own conduct, when I endeavour to pass sentence upon it, . . . either to approve or condemn it, it is evident that, in all such cases, I divide myself as it were into two persons; and that I, the examiner and judge, represents a different character from that other I, the person whose conduct is examined and judged of." The first person *I* becomes the half he called the "spectator"; the second person is the one whose conduct the first person (working "under the character of a spectator") "endeavours to form some opinion [of]."[24] This concept was of instrumental value in disengaging the Indian from his own society in order that he might observe it critically from the viewpoint of the other, that impartial *I*.

Nowhere was the objective better achieved than through the written examination. The missionary institutions in particular converted the examination into a powerful complement to the work performed by literary instruction in developing the impartial spectator. In many instances the topics on which students were asked to write were worded in such a way as to predetermine the response, as with the following: "On the disadvantages of Caste, and the benefits of its abolition"; "On the internal marks of Falsehood in the Hindu Shastras"; "On the Physical Errors of Hinduism"; "The best Contrast between Christianity and Hinduism, morally considered"; "Essay, illustrative of the manner in which the Law of the Hindu Caste is opposed to the Principles of Political Economy"; "The Evidences of the Antiquity of the New Testament, and the bearing of this question on the General Argument for the Truth of Christianity"; "On the Merits of Christianity, and the Demerits of Hinduism." The topics in the government institutions shied away from direct reference to religion, but they were no less oriented toward making the students conscious of the benefits of British rule, as with these topics: "The Effects upon India of the New Communication with Europe by means of Steam"; "The Advantages India derives in regard to commerce, security of property, and the diffusion of knowledge, from its Connexion with England"; "The Diffusion of Knowledge through the Medium of the English Language in India."[25]

Needless to say, the students wrote exactly what their examiners wanted to read, as in this conclusion of a student's essay on "The Influence of sound General Knowledge on Hinduism":

> But alas! alas! our countrymen are still asleep — still sleeping the sleep of death. Rise up, ye sons of India, arise, see the glory of the Sun of Righteousness! Beauty is around you; life blooms before you; why, why will ye sleep the sleep of death? And shall we who have drunk in that beauty — shall we not awake our poor countrymen? Come what will, ours will be the part, the happy part of arousing the slumber of slumbering India.[26]

To the extent that this student's essay can be read as an honest response to the English education he received, British literary instruction achieved the intended effect. The Indian response confirmed what Macaulay's brother-in-law Charles Trevelyan maintained all along: that the Indians' greatest desire was to raise themselves to the level of moral and intellectual refinement of their masters; their most driving ambition, to acquire the intellectual virtues that confirmed their rulers as lords of the earth. Already, he declared, the Indians had an idea that "we have gained everything by our superior knowledge; that it is this superiority which has enabled us to conquer India, and to keep it; and they want to put themselves as much as they can upon an equality with us."[27]

•

In effect, the strategy of locating authority in English texts all but effaced the often sordid history of colonialist expropriation, material exploitation, and class and race oppression behind European world dominance. Making the Englishman known to the natives through the products of his mental labor removed him from the plane of ongoing colonialist activity — of commercial operations, military expansion, administration of territories — and deactualized and diffused his material presence in the process. In a crude, parodic reworking of the Cartesian formula, production of thought defined the Englishman's true essence, overriding all other aspects of his identity — his personality, actions, behavior. His material reality as subjugator and alien ruler was dissolved in his mental output; the blurring of the man and his works effectively removed him from history. The English literary text functioned as a surrogate Englishman in his highest and most perfect state; to quote again from Trevelyan: "[The Indians] daily converse with the best and wisest Englishmen through the medium of their works, and form ideas, perhaps higher ideas of our nation than if their intercourse with it were of a more personal kind."[28] The split between the material and the cultural practices of colonialism is nowhere sharper than in the progressive rarefaction of the rapacious, exploitative, and ruthless actor of history into the reflective subject of literature.

NOTES

1. Antonio Gramsci, *Selections from the Prison Notebooks of Antonio Gramsci,* ed. Quintin Hoare and Geoffrey N. Smith (London: Lawrence and Wishart, 1971), 57.

2. Minutes of J. Farish, dated 28 August 1838; Poll. Dept., vol. 20/795, 1837–39 (Bombay Records) (quoted in B. K. Boman-Behram, *The Cultural Conquest of India under British Imperialism* [Bombay: Taraporevala Sons and Co., 1942], 239).

3. *Ninth Report of Select Committee on the Affairs of India, 1783* (quoted in Eric Stokes, *The English Utilitarians and India* [Oxford: Clarendon Press, 1959], 2).

4. William Adam, *Reports on Vernacular Education in Bengal and Bihar, Third Report* (Calcutta: Calcutta University Press), 340.

5. Percival Spear, *Oxford History of Modern India 1740–1975* (Oxford: Oxford University Press, 1965), 89.

6. "To allure the learned natives of India to the study of European science and literature, we must, I think, engraft this study upon their own established methods of scientific and literary institutions, and particularly in all the public colleges or schools maintained or encouraged by government, good translations of the most useful European compositions on the subjects taught in them, may, I conceive, be introduced with the greatest advantage" (paper by J. H. Harington, June 19, 1814 [quoted in Adam, *Reports on Vernacular Education in Bengal and Bihar,* 310]).

7. United Kingdom, *Parliamentary Papers* (1831–32), vol. 9, appendix 1, p. 486, "Extract of Letter in the Public Department, from the Court of Directors to the Government-General-in-Council."

8. Thomas B. Macaulay, *Speeches* (London: Oxford University Press, 1935), 345.

9. United Kingdom, *Parliamentary Papers* (1852–53), vol. 32, p. 301, evidence of the Reverend W. Keane.

10. Ibid.

11. United Kingdom, *Parliamentary Papers* (1852–53), vol. 29, p. 190, minutes of Marquess of Tweeddale on education, July 4, 1846.

12. *Madras Christian Instructor and Missionary Record* 2, no. 4 (September 1844): 195.

13. United Kingdom, *Parliamentary Papers* (1852–53), vol. 32, p. 302, evidence of the Reverend W. Keane.

14. All references are from ibid.

15. Ibid., p. 185, evidence of Charles Trevelyan.

16. Ibid., p. 287, evidence of Charles Cameron.

17. Ibid.

18. Northampton MS: William Carey to Andrew Fuller, April 23, 1796 (quoted in M. A. Laird, *Missionaries and Education in Bengal 1793–1837* [Oxford: Clarendon Press, 1972], 56).

19. United Kingdom, *Parliamentary Papers* (1852–53), vol. 32, appendix B, p. 380, report of Mr. Warden, president of the Board of Education at Bombay, April 1853.

20. United Kingdom, *Parliamentary Papers* (1852–53), vol. 32, p. 119, evidence of Joshua Marshman.

21. This view has been advanced most recently by Franklin Court in his article "Adam Smith and the Teaching of English Literature," *History of Education Quarterly* (fall 1985): 325–41.

22. Adam Smith, *The Theory of Moral Sentiments* (London: Henry G. Bohn, 1853), 214.

23. Ibid., 257–58.

24. Ibid.

25. United Kingdom, *Parliamentary Papers* (1852–53), vol. 32, appendix G, pp. 452–53, "Statement of the Progress and Success of the General Assembly (Now Free Church) Institution at Calcutta."

26. Ibid., 450.

27. United Kingdom, *Parliamentary Papers* (1852–53) vol. 32, p. 187, evidence of Charles Trevelyan.

28. Charles E. Trevelyan, *On the Education of the People of India* (London: Longman, 1838), 176.

Chapter 6
The Nation as Imagined Community
Jean Franco

On the eve of Mexican independence, the Mexican writer José Joaquín Fernández de Lizardi published a letter purportedly from a brother who had been shipwrecked and washed ashore on an island whose multiracial population resembled that of Mexico. The brother, who had unexpectedly become the ruler of the island, appeals to Lizardi to "imagine a kingdom in your head and give it laws and a constitution."[1] Lizardi responded not in a letter but with a novel, *El periquillo sarniento* (The itching parrot [1816]), in which he included an episode depicting just such an imaginary kingdom. The link between national formation and the novel as genre was not fortuitous: well into the twentieth century, the intelligentsia would appropriate the novel and there work out imaginary solutions to the intractable problems of racial heterogeneity, social inequality, and urban versus rural society. It was in the novel that different and often conflicting programs for the nation were debated either by "typical" characters in the Lukácsian sense (for instance, the peasants of Mariano Azuela's *Los de abajo* [The underdogs (1816)]) or by more properly allegorical figures like the wandering hero in Eugenio María de Hostos's *La peregrinación de Bayoán* [1863]).

Yet it is one thing to recognize that not only the novel but also the essay and the "great poem" have been deeply implicated in the process of national formation and its attendant problems of national and cultural identity and quite another to claim, as Fredric Jameson has done, that the "national allegory" characterizes Third World literature at the present time, that is, in "the era of multinational capitalism."[2] Indeed, not only is "the nation" a complex and much contested term, but in recent Latin American criticism it is no longer the inevitable framework for either political or cultural projects.[3] Further, the privileging of a particular genre — national allegory — is a risky enterprise in a continent where literary genres and styles are inevitably hybridized and where the novel, in particular, has often "bled" into other genres such as the essay or the chronicle.

Jameson is particularly interested in "the era of multinational capitalism" and in the Third World response to Americanization in certain "embattled" societies such as China and Cuba.[4] He is surprised that in such countries key questions should be formulated in national terms and that intellectuals should have a major investment in political life. He believes that the novel-as-national-allegory is a response to the

130

"embattled" situation of these countries, which are then taken as representative of the Third World. What I propose in this essay is not to refute Jameson's generalization, which like all generalizations provokes us to think of exceptions, but rather to consider whether the term "national allegory" can be any longer usefully applied to a literature in which "nation" is either a contested term or something like the Cheshire cat's grin — a mere reminder of a vanished body.[5]

The new social movements that have sprung up on the margins of the nation-state no longer couch cultural or political projects in national terms. This disaffection is not only a response to military or other authoritarian regimes that have appropriated national discourse but also the result of a long historical process. It has to be understood in relation to the fact that in Latin America nation-states were vehicles for (often enforced) capitalist modernization. The stabilization of the nation-state (often built on colonial, bureaucratic infrastructures) occurred for the most part without grassroots participation or any form of democratic debate and was often promoted by autocratic or populist/authoritarian regimes. Most recently, military regimes furthered modernization while banning political parties, censoring the press, and crushing unions and any form of opposition.

This cyclical conjunction of modernity and repression in the name of national autonomy or development has been vigorously contested in literature but in terms that are far too complex to be labeled "national allegory." In the 1940s and 1950s, the novel, which in the nineteenth century had offered blueprints of national formation, more and more became a skeptical reconstruction of past errors. The novel made visible the absence of any signified that could correspond to the nation. Individual and collective identity, social and family life were like shells from which life had disappeared. Consider novels such as Carlos Fuentes's *La muerte de Artemio Cruz* (The death of Artemio Cruz [1962]) and Juan Rulfo's *Pedro Páramo* (1955), in which the names of the protagonists — Cruz (Cross) and Páramo (Wasteland) — suggest an allegorical reading, or novels such as Mario Vargas Llosa's *La casa verde* (The green house [1966]) and Alejo Carpentier's *Los pasos perdidos* (The lost steps [1953]), which use generic names such as the Sergeant or the Goldseeker. It quickly becomes evident that the names are signifiers pried loose from any signified and are intended more as indicators of loss or absence than as clues to an allegorical reading. In place of an identifiable microcosm of the nation, such novels offer a motley space in which different historical developments and different cultures overlap. What they enact is the unfinished and impossible project of the modernizing state.

This is strikingly borne out by the recurrence of one particular motif in several novels written between the 1940s and early 1960s — the motif of the dying community or the wake around the body. This motif occurs in José Revueltas's *El luto humano* (Human mourning [1943]), Juan Carlos Onetti's *El astillero* (The shipyard [1961]), Ernesto Sábato's *Sobre héroes y tumbas* (Of heroes and tombs [1961]), and Gabriel García Márquez's *La hojarasca* (Leaf storm [1955]). In José Revueltas's *El luto humano,* a group of peasants slowly and violently sink to death during a flood that halts the linear time of progress and thrusts the protagonists back into the ritual time of death and vengeance. In Mario Vargas Llosa's *La casa verde,* a series of individual stories are recounted within the framework of a river journey that transports the dying entrepreneur Fushía to his last resting place in a leper colony, thus suggesting the death and corruption of a class that but for dependency might have revitalized the nation. In Carlos Fuentes's *La muerte de Artemio Cruz*, the dying of the protagonist marks the end of some libidinal force that had become displaced from productive national goals and had spent itself in personal satisfaction. Many such novels center on the life and death of an "imagined" community — García Márquez's Macondo, Onetti's Santa María, Fushía's island (in *La casa verde*), the communities in *El luto humano* and *El astillero* — and all of these communities represent in their different ways doomed enterprises. In fact, the novels describe alternative nations dreamed up by writers whose kingdoms in the head founder on the hard rock of realpolitik. In Onetti's novel, the tragedy of the entrepreneurial protagonist is played out in a shipyard and a city where the nation has been reduced to a few nostalgic signs — the statue of a founding father and a hitching post that is the last remnant of the long-vanished rural culture on which the nation had been founded.

No Latin American writer has so persistently parodied and pilloried the nation as García Márquez. Indeed, he has even written the allegory of the transition from colony to nation to nation-state in a short story, "Blacaman the Good, Salesman of Miracles" (1968). The story is a Nietzschean account of legitimation that is told by the victor, the self-styled Blacaman the Good, once apprentice to Blacaman the Bad, a magician who had invented a snakebite cure that could bring him back from the dead after being bitten. But modern magic proves more potent than these old superstitions. Blacaman the Good, with the help of the American marines, seizes control of the state and becomes a tropical dictator in the manner of Batista or Trujillo. When Blacaman the Bad dies, Blacaman the Good has him resuscitated so that the people can hear his wailing in the mausoleum where he is entombed. This modern magic controls the past, which is useful as long as it reminds people of how much better off they are in the present. In this brief tale, the modern state is a kind of illusionist that needs the past only as a lament and whose miracle is the economic miracle of dependency.

García Márquez returned to the problem of legitimation and the identification of the dictator with the nation-state in *El otoño del patriarca* (The autumn of the patriarch [1975]), in which the dictator/protagonist epitomizes a grotesque modernization that has been achieved through murder and oppression. Yet the nation and the dictator are clearly shown to be producers of and produced by a particular discursive formation. In one episode, for example, the dictator tries to legitimate his rule by claiming that he was born miraculously of a virgin birth. The papal nuncio sent to investigate the improbable claim is shot as he rides over the mountains on his mule and falls headlong — not through a landscape but through pastiche:

> The nuncio fell into a bottomless vertigo, from the mountains covered with *perpetual snow,* through different and simultaneous climates, through the engravings of natural history books, down the precipices and over the tiny springs from which *the great navigable waters flow,* over the escarpments over which European scientists climb on the backs of Indians in search of secret herbal remedies, down the plateau of wild magnolias on which sheep grazed *whose warm wool gives us generous protection* as well as *setting us a good example* and past the coffee plantation mansions with their solitary balconies and their interminable invalids, past the perpetual roar of turbulent rivers and past *the beginnings of the torrid zone.* [my translation and emphasis]

The italicized passages expose the way the nation-state is legitimized through pedagogical discourse — for example, the geography textbook. The papal nuncio falls
through this secular landscape constituted by a positivist discourse that identifies the
nation with natural regions (and exploitable resources) and with a literary canon
(the image of invalids in houses probably refers to Columbia's classic nineteenth-
century sentimental novel, *María,* by Jorge Isaacs). But as soon as the nation is
described as discourse, it simply becomes a provisional framework, a fiction that
will disappear once the dictator is shown to be mortal. García Márquez underscores
the role of nationalism in homogenizing disparate texts that together come to make
up our idea of the "nation"; at the same time he shows how national allegory itself
is complicit in a legitimizing ideology. This leads to the realization that the problems that national discourse engendered — problems of patriarchy and of power
and its attendant techniques of exclusion and discrimination — could not be resolved by a genre that was implicated in these very procedures. His most recent
novel, *El amor en los tiempos del cólera* (Love in the time of cholera [1985]), can
no longer be read in Jamesonian terms at all. It is the private that has become central, a private that cannot be allegorized or transposed into an exemplary national
story because there is disjunction between the public and the private. The apocalyptic landscape of decay and cadavers bears the scars of modernization and progress,
of old national battles and ancient conquests, but the protagonists enacting their
anachronistic love story can no longer represent anything beyond their own mortal passion. *El amor en los tiempos del cólera* thus marks the dissolution of a once
totalizing myth that is now replaced by private fantasies lived out amid public disaster. And the novel, rather than an allegory, has become the terrain of conflicting
discourses.

   In such novels, it is precisely the disappearance of the nation, its failure to provide systems of meaning and belief, that undermines referential reading. It is true
that they capture the continued resonance of certain historical events, such as the
conquest and the impact of succeeding waves of modernization, visible in the fragmented life-forms they have left in their wake. For this untimeliness is the condition
of Latin American modernity, giving one a sense of reliving the past. Or it is as if the
past can speak in the present tense. In Augusto Roa Bastos's *Yo el supremo* (I, the
supreme [1978]), which the author describes as a compilation of "twenty thousand
unpublished documents as well as journals, tape-recorded interviews and letters,"
the compiler (who declines to be the author) observes that "unlike the usual text,
this one has been read first and written afterwards." The protagonist of the novel
is the nineteenth-century dictator, Dr. Gaspar Rodríguez de Francia, founder of the
Paraguayan nation, a man who can be known only through historical documents.
Roa Bastos, however, is interested not in historical reconstruction but in reading
the past in terms of the present, because the past has never been transcended and
the problems with which Francia struggled — problems of national autonomy, racial
diversity, the unrepresented masses — are those of contemporary Paraguay. He
therefore transforms third-person historical writing, translating the documents into
a first-person narrative in which the "I" is both the nation embodied in Dr. Francia
and a personal, mortal "I." As representative of the nation, the supreme "I" is immortal, disembodied, continuous — yet this transcendent "I" is continually undermined

by the "I" of the mortal Dr. Francia that is always in a relationship with a reader or listener and whose language is always inflected by the presence of the other. But the personal is represented as voice, and voice can be recorded only in writing that, like fatherhood, is putative. Thus while the novel itself is motivated by a document apparently written in the dictator's "own" handwriting and bearing his signature, this "authentic" document is also a reproduction since it is reproduced in the published text we read. The document reads as follows:

> I, the Supreme Dictator of the Republic, order that upon my death, my body shall be decapitated, the head placed upon a lance for three days in the main square of the Republic to which the people will be summoned by the sound of tolling bells.
>   All my civil and military servants will be hanged. Their bodies will be buried outside the city walls without a cross or mark to commemorate their names. At the end of the said period, I command that my remains be burned and the ashes thrown into the river. [my translation]

The lampoon poses a problem of attribution, for the author is not a person but discourse. In addition, by using the first person in a document in which the first person is inappropriate, it underlines the difference between the impersonal discourse of the state and the "I" of the living "dictator" who cannot control meaning after his own death (nor even during his lifetime). For even what appears to be "living" speech in the novel is constantly revealed to be writing. The dictator's "speech" often breaks off in midsentence, and the accompanying gloss exposes the fact that it is not said but written — "manuscript burned," "torn," "the next folios are missing." The supreme "I" speaks both as a person and as a nation, as the supreme "I" of an immortal, ungendered, abstract state and as a human being, a human being who cannot, however, be present in the written word. Further, the illocutionary force of the decree is lodged not in the living Dr. Francia but only in the imaginary body of the nation. The nation as the locus of secular immortality is here shown to be incompatible with the person who momentarily embodies statehood. Once this living person attempts to speak as the impersonal and public "I," the disparity is foregrounded.

Dr. Francia represents the impossible conjunction of the person and writing, a conjunction that is made plausible by the grammatical category of the subject. Roa Bastos transforms the impersonality of historical writing into a speaking subject who is argumentative, plaintive, and resentful because excluded from the discourse of the state. The mortal Francia wants to be a Cartesian cogito, a cogito that can abstract itself from the material world and endure as idea. Yet the "I" is forced to take into account the decomposition of the material body that supports it and the invasion of flies that will devour the corpse. As the body decomposes, the "I" is still hungering for food, for a cooked egg — the egg that like Francia's nation will never generate new life.

Roa Bastos is able to represent Latin American nationalist discourse as an enactment of contradictions — the struggle to tell historical truth when that "truth" is always written from a partisan point of view, the struggle to maintain purity of boundaries when that purity means the exclusion of the heterogeneous. Although *Yo el supremo* is often described as a novel of dictatorship, it goes far beyond the representation of authoritarianism to show the complicity of language in the constitution of the nation. In other words, Roa Bastos attacks the very basis on which national identity is constructed, making visible the gap — which discourse conceals — between person and institution.

A reverse strategy is exemplified by the Puerto Rican author Edgardo Rodríguez Juliá in his novel *La noche oscura del Niño Avilés* (The dark night of Niño Avilés [1984]). Whereas Roa Bastos tries to invent the living speaker of existing texts, Rodríguez Juliá restores the documents that would correspond to the oral myths, legends, dreams, and pornographic nightmares that have never been part of official history.

The novel uses a Borgesian device of describing a city that is mentioned only in apocryphal documents. The city is founded by the Blessed Avilés, who, as a child, had been found floating like Moses on the waves. The bulk of the novel consists of rival documents and chronicles describing a campaign, led by Bishop Trespalacios, against the heretical Avilés sect. One of the chronicles is written by Gracián, who is on the side of the bishop, and the other is written by a renegade Spaniard, one of the captains of the black leader Obatal. Yet these chronicles are also digressions. They constantly stray from the campaign in order to pause over a particular succulent feast and the farts that follow it, over drug trips (the bishop is a drug "aficionado"), and, in the case of the renegade, there is a prolonged incursion into the realm of the senses and his love affair with an African queen. Inserted in the chronicles is also the story of Obatal's obsession with the construction of a glass city, a city of forgetting whose entrance is in the form of a vagina.

The period to which the documents supposedly refer dates from the end of the eighteenth century, that is, the period of the great slave rebellions that liberated Haiti from the French. Puerto Rican history records no such uprising, and its black culture was largely "hidden from history" by a ruling class that was mainly concerned with "whitening" the island. Rodríguez Juliá's novel restores the body to history, rather as Roa Bastos restored the living person to the abstract dictatorship. The two Spanish chroniclers who interpret Puerto Rican history regard it either as a perpetual feast or as a perpetual orgy, reading into it the history of their own repressions. That is why their classical language is again and again rudely interrupted by the fart.[6]

The juxtaposition of disparate discourses and the use of pastiche perhaps help explain why U.S. critics so eagerly embrace Latin American novels as postmodern.[7] But incorporation into postmodernism is no more satisfactory than being labeled with Jameson's notion of Third World national allegory. Indeed, the two recuperative gestures seem to be motivated by the same operation of extrapolation. Extrapolation reduces the complexity of intertextual allusions and deprives texts of their own historical relations to prior texts. It implies a view of Latin American literature either in opposition to the metropolis or as part of the metropolis's postmodern repertoire. Yet novels such as Augusto Roa Bastos's *Yo el supremo* and Edgardo Rodríguez Juliá's *La noche oscura del Niño Avilés,* which defy facile recuperation as national allegory or as the postmodern, demand readings informed by cultural and political history.

Hybrid genres have always abounded in Latin America. Thus, both "national allegory" and "postmodern" imply an impoverishment, for they overlook an entire cultural history in which essay, chronicle, and historical document have been grafted onto novels, a history of rereadings and rewritings that give rise to voluminous compendia — such as José Donoso's *El obsceno pájaro de la noche* (*The obscene bird of night* [1970]), Lezama Lima's *Paradiso* (Paradise [1966]), and Carlos Fuentes's *Terra Nostra* (1972) — that defy categorization, as well as to texts such as *Yo el supremo* in which the rancorous voice of posthumous knowledge mingles with the murmur of the fictional characters. Such texts may seem "postmodern" because of a sum of characteristics — pastiche, nostalgia, and the like — and because they reflect dissolution of any universal system of meaning or master discourse, a dissolution that clearly affects Latin America's relation to metropolitan discourse.

Yet just as "national allegory" fails to describe adequately the simultaneous dissolution of the idea of the nation and the continuous persistence of the local and oral culture, so "postmodernism" cannot adequately describe those texts that use pastiche and citation not simply as style but as correlatives of the continent's uneasy and unfinished relationship to modernity. Indeed, it is significant that the 1980s and 1990s have witnessed a proliferation of testimonial fiction and chronicle as well as novelized histories and historical novels that seem to suggest that generic boundaries cannot easily contain the bizarre overlappings of cultures and temporalities. I shall cite one outstanding example — Edgardo Rodríguez Juliá's *El entierro de Cortijo* (The funeral of Cortijo [1983]), which is a "chronicle" of the author's attendance at the wake and funeral of a *plena* musician, Cortijo. The writer is one of a mass of people who crowd the funeral home in a popular quarter of San Juan for a last glimpse of the singer, who lies in an open coffin with a guard of honor. The writing moves backward and forward between reminiscence, observation, and snatches of conversation and song. What we have is a kaleidoscope of minute gestures; of myriads of individuals, each one different, unclassifiable; of transient contact; of fragments of an event that is clearly an event but defies classification, for it is properly speaking neither a Catholic ritual nor a patriotic demonstration. As the church, the state, and opposition politicians in turn try to take over the funeral, pluralism always reasserts itself. One man pays homage by straightening the crucifix in the hand of the dead man; another embraces the body. Styles clash — from the 1950s, the 1960s, and the 1980s. Does anything unite this crowd apart from the corpse? The kaleidoscope constantly shifts to form different and unreconcilable patterns. The author concludes: "We live in a period of costly intentions, and unburied gestures; tradition breaks up into a thousand conflicting fragments. How can so much volatility be reconciled with such depth of feeling?"

What is at stake here is precisely the impossibility of the typical, the representative, the Puerto Rican (except as the sum of idiosyncrasies). The only unity is mortality; the only way to resist death is to play Cortijo's music. There is no way of converting this into national allegory, but neither will it do simply to sweep it under the carpet of postmodernism. *El entierro de Cortijo* presents in the form of a simultaneous kaleidoscope all the unfinished problems of modernity in Puerto Rico, projects that cannot be totalized or simply celebrated. It is also thick with political allusions and therefore forces those of us not familiar with Puerto Rico to do some homework.

Each piece of clothing, the name of a street, a manner of walking represent traces not only of the past but of the past's relationship to modernity. It is the refusal to totalize, however, rather than heterogeneity that distinguishes Rodríguez Juliá from his modernist and nineteenth-century predecessors. What used to be a source of embarrassment to the intelligentsia — the imitation of the metropolis, the recourse to pastiche — has now come to be seen as an irrepressible process of appropriation and defiance.

In this light, the proliferation of "historical" novels, testimonials, and chronicles and the emergence of women writers in Latin America highlight not only a celebration of heterogeneity but also the efforts to contain it by state violence and repression. Although pluralism of style is not equivalent to democratic participation, those texts that open up to the multiple and often antagonistic discourses of the Latin American continent represent a political as well as an aesthetic choice, one that no longer needs the nation for its realization.

NOTES

1. The letters are included in José Joaquín Fernández de Lizardi, *El pensador Mexicano* 2, 3, and 4 (January–February 1814), in *Obras,* vol. 3 (Mexico City: UNAM, 1968), 386–99.

2. Fredric Jameson, "Third-World Literature in the Era of Multinational Capitalism," *Social Text* 15 (fall 1986): 65–88. There is a response to this article — see Aijaz Ahmad, "Jameson's Rhetoric of Otherness and the 'National Allegory,'" *Social Text* 17 (fall 1987): 3–25.

3. See, for instance, Carlos Monsivais, *Entrada libre, crónicas de la sociedad que se organiza* (Mexico: Era, 1988), in which new social movements spring up on the margins of the hegemonic national project.

4. Jameson, "Third-World Literature," 69, defines the Third World text thus: "[T]he story of the private individual destiny is always an allegory of the embattled situation of the public third-world culture and society."

5. Benedict Anderson, *Imagined Communities: Reflections on the Origin and Spread of Nationalism* (London: Verso, 1983).

6. On the fart as response, see Peter Sloterdijk, *Critique of Cynical Reason* (Minneapolis: University of Minnesota Press, 1987), esp. 150–51.

7. For Jameson, postmodernism is part of the logic of late capitalism in the First World and especially the United States; see his "Postmodernism, or the Cultural Logic of Late Capitalism," *New Left Review* 146 (July–August 1984): 53–92. For the inclusion of Latin American literature in the postmodern, see Brian McHale, *Postmodernist Fiction* (London: Methuen, 1987).

Part II

Multiculturalism and Diasporic Identities

Chapter 7
On the Question of
a Theory of (Third) World Literature
Madhava Prasad

I

Critical theory, by opening up a field of inquiry into the production and reproduction of subjectivities, transformed the object of literary/cultural studies. It became possible to think cultural studies not as a means of selecting and preserving the quintessence of a society's cultural production by lavishing a fetishist labor of veneration upon it, but instead as an investigation of the cultural domain for the purpose of making visible the ideological processes by which meaning in culture is produced and naturalized. This work posed a serious challenge to the orthodoxies that reigned in cultural studies, and many ways of escaping the consequences of theoretical knowledge have since been devised. One "grand narrative" that has served this increasingly hostile tendency well is the one that posits an epic battle between conceptuality and its unnamable opposite. In the recent debate about "Third World literature" that began in the pages of *Social Text* and has since spread to other spaces, this conflict over the origins, aims, and consequences of theory surfaced once again and seemed to have produced a consensus of sorts about the need to "live and let live," so to speak. This expression captures well the ideological role of antitheory today. My purpose in what follows is to raise some questions about the conditions of possibility of the new neighborliness in the cultural academy by reading some texts implicated, directly or indirectly, in that debate.

In his response to Fredric Jameson's attempt to produce a theory of Third World literature, Aijaz Ahmad raises many objections to the very idea of such a project. Of these objections, the easiest to deal with are those based on empirical evidence against Jameson's claim that "all" Third World literary texts are national allegories. Ahmad points out, for instance: "I cannot think of a single novel in Urdu between 1935 and 1947 . . . which is in any direct or exclusive way about 'the experience of colonialism and imperialism'" (Ahmad, 21). This remark is based on a commonsensical assumption that the object of a theory must exist in its fullness prior to its theoretical articulation, the latter being understood as the *restatement* of a latent meaning in another language. But theory's project is to bring to the surface the naturalized, concealed frames of intelligibility that enable cultural enunciation and

141

also to develop new conceptual frames that, by providing new perspectives on the problem, enable (re)thinking with the goal of social transformation.

The more significant contention in Ahmad's text is that, besides being impossible, such a theory is objectionable on political grounds. Ahmad writes: "[C]ognitive aesthetics rests . . . upon a suppression of the multiplicity of significant difference among and within both the advanced capitalist countries and the imperialist formations" (4). This argument is accompanied by a declaration of allegiance to Marxism. And indeed, Ahmad's essay offers an extended critical account of global political economy, only to return to a nationalist position on the question of cultural theory. The conditions that make possible the coexistence of these two opposed positions have themselves something to do with Jameson's claim that all Third World literature is national allegory. In pursuing our investigations it will be useful to remember that the inaugural question, that of a theory of Third World literature, is not our direct or only concern here. Rather, it functions in the space of this text as an *instrument* for an examination of the directions that the struggle over meaning has taken in the postmodern intellectual space.

Before we turn to that matter, it would be useful to note that a theoretical proposition such as Jameson's cannot simply be verified by reference to an existing body of texts directly or indirectly dealing with the question of national identity or of the experience of colonialism. If we begin with the premise that what is at stake is the (re)production of subject-positions, the point to be made is not only that texts betray a preoccupation with nation/collectively but also that a labor of *comparison* accompanies cultural production and reception so consistently as to form an integral element of "Third World" subjectivity. The "Third World" also requires definition: it is to be understood as a time-space of subject-formation, necessarily determined by imperialism, colonialism, developmentalism, and experimentation with bourgeois democracy and other forms of nation-statehood. Not just a geographical zone with its millennia of cultural history — not, for instance, "India," from its Vedic past to its new-Vedic present, but the one that came into being after and through its occupation and transformation by British despotic rule (although pre-British determinations continue to play a part in this time-space).

"[W]hen I was on the fifth page of [Jameson's] text . . . I realized that what was being theorized was, among other things, myself" (Ahmad, 3–4). Here in a nutshell is a common postcolonial nightmare that is a very important determining element in Ahmad's resistance to the idea of a theory of Third World literature. To examine its implications it will be useful to turn to a more dramatic fictional representation of it, in a Kannada short story by A. K. Ramanujan called "Annayya's Anthropology." The protagonist of this story, born in a South Indian Brahmin village, arrives in the United States as a student, thereby gaining access to a whole body of knowledge that was out of reach of the former "native." Of course, this passage to America has the allegorical significance of the successful re-formation of a precapitalist subject into a bourgeois individual; the physical relocation is not a necessary condition of such knowledge. Access to the archive also implies that the subject is a fully formed self capable, in the global political economy of knowledge, of occupying the position of producer as well as consumer. But while fulfilling the role that this position enables, the protagonist finds himself forced to recall and to reoccupy the position of an object of knowledge. To be precise, he discovers, in a journal devoted to anthropology, an article dealing with Brahmin ritual practices — illustrated with photographs of his family, including his mother.

On the one hand, it is not necessary to discount the trauma associated with that moment in order to recognize its class origins. Nor would such a recognition preclude a critique of the systems of representation — anthropological, historical, literary, scientific — developed and deployed by the imperialist West as part of its machinery of control and domination. On the other hand, the native, *as* native, has no access to that position from which the trauma can be encountered.[1] It is only through acquiring the class privilege of access to knowledge and the position of producer/consumer within the dominant economy of knowledge that it is possible to encounter a former "self" alienated from the current one by the representational apparatus whose tools are now within the latter's reach. But having arrived at this stage, a critique of those systems of representation could proceed in two ways. First, critique could take as its aim the reclamation and protection of a lost identity, in which case what is being defended is privacy, a space beyond the limits of the public discourses, to which reason has no access. The moment of revelation shatters the illusion of self-possession and exposes the fragility of the postcolonial subject's assumption of sovereignty. In response, the subject compensates for this disillusionment by projecting a lost sovereignty onto the (re)discovered past. "Postcoloniality" thus is signaled by the historic moment in which the coveted "private" realm is created as the zone of "noninterference" that is off-limits to the "public." The public realm, in this case, is the *inter*national sphere, a neutral space, real or hypothetical. The defense of this privacy would be a defense of that very position that rendered visible the contradictions involved in the erasure of multiple subjectivities, for it is that position that gives to the figures of the past an "identity" that the intellectual now defends against it. The adoption of "discovered" identities requires the erasure of the machineries of representation that did the work of "discovering." Second, the alternative to such a surrender (which is what it is, in spite of a strong connotation of resistance) would be an interrogation of the very history that, by providing access to the "neutral" position of knowledge, enables the critique. The challenge is to overcome individualist ideology, not by embracing its by-products — native individualisms — but by going beyond it.

It is the domain of literature, where the "self" is produced and elaborated, that Ahmad wants to protect from the encroachments of theory: "[W]hat was being theorized was ... myself." Ahmad's claim that the differences between nations/literatures in the Third World are beyond the reach of a single theory, in its repetition of a poststructuralist truism, is faithful to a fantasy on which all national-cultural identities are based. He asserts: "[T]his phrase, 'the third world,' is, even in its most telling deployments, a polemical one, with no theoretical status whatsoever." Thus he will argue "that there is no such thing as a 'third world literature' which can be constructed as an internally coherent object of theoretical knowledge" (4). But it is equally true that there is not *one* capitalism but several distinct capitalist social formations, a fact that does not prevent us from speaking of an abstraction called "capitalism." Nor is the "aesthetic," which lies behind our very ability to speak of something called "literature," a more stable concept than the "Third World." Ahmad's argument rests on the presupposition that the countries that are together designated the Third World have little in common with one another. The suggestion that "the experience of colonialism and imperialism" has commensurable material effects on the futures of different, unrelated peoples does not impress him at all. His first major objection to this is that while the First and Second Worlds are defined in terms of modes of production, the Third is defined in terms of an experience. This is indeed problematic (where it is the case: theories of dependency provide more than a subjective, experiential basis for classification of the poor countries of the world together) not because it is a matter of cultural justice but because of a lack of clarity and consistency in the definition, leading to a neglect of the relational aspect of global economic segregation. However, in Jameson's text the term "Third World" receives a new meaning. A scholastic insistence on the "pure" meaning of the term is less useful than a demand for a clearer enunciation of the new meaning, which, although not presented in isolation, clearly means to indicate a brief time-space with specific features associated with the history of the unification of the globe by, and in the interests of, (North Atlantic) capitalism.

Ahmad proceeds to examine the case of India. By the criterion supplied — the experience of imperialism — there is no problem of identification. But Ahmad serves up a vision of political and economic progress that, while complicating the analysis, does absolutely nothing to explain hundreds of observable phenomena: the nation-state; the parliamentary system; the laws and bureaucracy inherited from the British, by which the people continue to be governed; the continuing effects of "divide and rule"; clubs' dress codes inherited from military cantonments; the role of English (which partly explains the occurrence of this debate in the United States); the role of capitalist literary forms in reforming precapitalist subjectivities; the "transfer of power" from a foreign power to an indigenous coalition of old and new ruling classes; neo-Brahmanism's meritocracy; and so on. Ahmad's narrative is not incorrect, but the developments he mentions have not wiped out the legacy of imperialism. This is not a "presumably pre- or non-capitalist third world" (7) but a part of the capitalist world marked by uneven and combined development.

Ahmad is right to insist that "we live not in three worlds but one." But this is somewhat contradictory coming after a call to acknowledge radical heterogeneity on the cultural plane. In Ahmad's terms the world is one because, for instance, one would pose similar questions to several different literatures. This in turn can be done because each is characterized by the same class differentiation, the same aspirations to socialism, and so on. In other words, the world is one because one social structure repeats itself in almost identical fashion across the globe! This is a picture of abstract equality, the same abstract equality that the "social contract" bestowed on "all" adults, while real inequality, as Marx put it, was blamed on the fact that "long, long ago there were two sorts of people; one, the diligent, intelligent and above all frugal elite; the other, lazy rascals" (Marx, 873). What Ahmad finds objectionable is Jameson's suggestion that the independent nation-states of the world, who all sit side by side in the United Nations, are nevertheless linked to one another by a complex structure of *hierarchization* enabled by the history of primitive accumulation.

Ahmad claims that the countries of Asia, Africa, and Latin America have "historically" had no close ties. This is not entirely true: the world before European hegemony was still an actively interdependent world. While Ahmad admits that metropolitan mediation is the common element of these countries' relations with one another, he does not regard this as significant enough to be constitutive of enunciatory possibilities. Where subjectivity is the object of investigation, the importance of metropolitan mediation cannot be overstated. Indeed, even as Ahmad denies any reality to nonpositive factors, his mode of enunciating the critique reproduces the effects of metropolitan mediation: the argument is inscribed in the *comparative* space of the discourse of the colonized, here figured as the injured party presenting a case before a court: the court of Western liberal justice. Of course, there is as yet no space for the colonial subject outside this space of comparison and competition. But to begin the work of undoing it, it is imperative to make that ground itself the constant object of investigation.[2]

The differences among nations that Ahmad invokes are suspiciously similar to the arguments for the uniqueness of individual texts offered by neopragmatist antitheorists against the possibility of a theory of literature. Neopragmatists, by privileging a theological notion of authorial intention, attempt to preserve the "self" as the sole source of meaning and teach the reader to read the text "on its own terms" and in search of an intended meaning. Any theoretical attempt to overcome the literal, physical autonomy of a text from other texts or an author from other authors is deemed "illegitimate" by a school whose concepts are derived predominantly from legal discourse.[3] The reductive pragmatist definition of theory is that it is "the attempt to govern interpretations of particular texts by appealing to an account of interpretation in general" (Mitchell, 11). The real is composed of "particular texts," each of which must generate its own principles of interpretation (although, paradoxically, all of them will bear their producer's intention). Theory does not respect the distinction between texts or, in Ahmad's case, between national literatures. Bourgeois individualism thus finds an ally in nationalist arguments for the autonomy of national cultures. Ahmad is aware of the possible linkages here. He says: "But there is, I believe, a considerable space where one could take one's stand between (a) the postmodernist cult of utter non-determinacy and (b) the idea of a unitary determination which has lasted from Hegel up to some of the most modern of marxist debates" (22–23). In this formulation the difference between the two "extreme" positions is one of degree, as if there were a spectrum of choices ranging from total fragmentariness to absolute unity. But the celebration of difference remains an ideological move, directly opposed to, not distantly related to, the conceptual. Besides, Marxisms do not negate all differences any more than festive postmodernisms undo unity when they proclaim the finality of fragmentation. What is *unitary* is not the determination but the system of social relations, the features of whose unity are not already given but need to be theorized. What postmodernisms rely on is a theory of difference; Marxisms, on the contrary, have produced more or less successful theories of the relatedness of apparently distinct and autonomous zones of the social. A theory of cultural autonomy along national or linguistic lines is disenabling because it is blind to the participation of the nation-state in the hierarchization of the globe along class lines.

Theories of dependency are useful in understanding this aspect of the nation-state. Enrique Dussel, for instance, has reiterated the argument about the transfer of surplus value from one national capital to another as the basis of dependency. When two national capitals of unequal strength confront each other on the world market, the transfer, as opposed to the creation, of surplus value takes place "because the average international price is less than the national value of the same commodity."[4] This is possible wherever different values reside in the same product in different places due to the difference in the organic composition of capital and in wages. The *national* determination is indispensable, for it alone enables the transfer of surplus value. Even in the context of the rise of transnational corporations, what is involved is not the fading of national boundaries but their consolidation in new ways: "These corporations do not suppress national entities; rather they assume them, to such a degree that if there were not total national capitals of different levels of development they could not exist" (Dussel, 90).[5]

In order for individual capitals to transcend national boundaries, those boundaries must continue to remain in place. A national capital can be identified only on the basis of the reach of state power. Thus the nation-state is an administrative unit that is integral to capitalism. Nations enter this order only by attaining statehood, which can now be defined as a prize in the competition of capitals. Nations may not even emerge except in the shadow of a struggle to establish a state or to challenge an established distribution of state power. To come back to Ahmad's text, the interdependency of nation-states and their inscription in a single world order, whatever the regional and cultural differences, are lost sight of in the anxiety to preserve inviolate an interiority that the nation-state claims for itself and that Ahmad grants to it uncritically. Ahmad's is the first in a series of texts (others are considered below) that are all characterized by the understanding that the notion of a dominant system implies that its limits are to be found *outside* it, in an *alternative* that resides elsewhere and is resistant to the encroachments of the dominant system. That outside is also endowed with its own *inside,* that being the true mark of autonomous existence. But as we have seen above, such an outside is itself a product of the dominant system's machinery of representation that then becomes reified.

Henry Schwarz's contribution to the debate, "Provocations toward a Theory of Third World Literature," is more vividly illustrative of the problem. Schwarz's text is critical of Ahmad for some of the same reasons that I have stated above, but Schwarz finds a "limit" to theory ready-made in the poststructuralist theme of unintelligibility via a reading of the manifesto of the Subaltern Studies project. The notion of the object's "own" identity, the theme that runs through Ahmad's text and neopragmatist theory, is also a concern of this manifesto, from which Schwarz derives his theory of the Third World text. Bourgeois historiography, the main target of the Subaltern Studies critique, inscribed the bourgeois leadership of the independence movement as the subject of Indian history and the masses as its faithful followers. Historians of the empire had earlier engaged in an elaborate and systematic coding of events in India in accordance with colonial interests. Against these two trends the Subaltern Studies project sought to foreground the underside of the anticolonial struggle — the unwritten history of the struggle of peasants, tribes, and other groups against domination by both external and internal masters. This project, as presented in Ranajit Guha's introduction to volume 1 of *Subaltern Studies,* involves the critique of problematic existing conceptual frameworks as well as the resolve to avoid developing new ones. While subaltern historians employed a Marxist discourse, the theory posited a realm of struggle that was outside all rational systems and was resistant not only to existing conceptual frames but to conceptualization per se. Enabling the subaltern to speak and to be heard was itself to be the political intervention. In place of the bourgeoisie and the elusive working class as the competing subjects of the history of the new nation, Subaltern Studies historiography offered multiple, localized sites of resistance. The subaltern historian therefore finds him/herself in the self-effacing role of a facilitator unwilling to articulate a counterhegemonic project that is "extraneous" to the histories unearthed. By default, the nationalist frame of reference, which was the target of the project, becomes the order of meaning in and against which these histories operate. The demand for authenticity that the histories made on their material is symptomatic of the persistence of nationalist frames of reference and of a faith in the *discovery* of an already existing political program in the rebel consciousness of the subaltern.

This is not an exhaustive description of the great variety of research undertaken under the Subaltern Studies banner. I have only summarized that part of its internal logic that now finds a welcome in the postmodern regime of unintelligibility in the U.S. academy. Schwarz's misreadings of the early Subaltern Studies texts are suggestive of the ways in which the failure to explicitly retheorize the Marxist paradigm as the basis of the subalternist intervention has led to its appropriation by a kind of politics that finds its meaning and effectivity in self-effacement and regards celebration of the other as the only possible source of a new politics. Schwarz writes, for instance, in a summary of Guha's argument in the introduction to volume 1 of *Subaltern Studies,* that "both Marxist and bourgeois accounts of nationalism and anti-colonialism write the story of rebellion 'from above' " (Schwarz, 185). To write a story from above is to write it from the point of view of the elite. Guha's introduction begins with this statement: "The historiography of Indian nationalism has for a long time been dominated by elitism — colonialist elitism and bourgeois-nationalist elitism" (Guha, "On Some Aspects," 1). Schwarz, in a symptomatic gesture, reads "colonialist" to mean "Marxist" (or fails to read "colonialism," putting "Marxism" in its place). Guha's text itself does not mention Marxism (by any name), nor is the claim made anywhere else that Marxist historiography wrote the story of rebellion "from above," even though a strong critique of idealist tendencies in Marxist historiography is part of the general *Subaltern Studies* critique of existing historiography.[6] This overreading is a symptom of the currently privileged axes of opposition that the unwary intellectual brings to the task "naturally" in these times.

It is on the basis of a reading of "subaltern politics" as "largely unknowable" (Schwarz, 186) that Schwarz proceeds to read the literary texts of Mahasweta Devi as representations of the unrepresentable or unintelligible, which leads him to the conclusion that the political object of a theory of Third World literature is to enable the First World to contemplate its own mistakes as they unfold in that literature. Schwarz writes: "The thematics of this story revolve around two systems of unintelligibility" (193). "Like the jungle's blackness, the insurgent mind is impenetrable by the rationality of the *Army Handbook* followed by the police" (195). "Dopdi, as an allegory of the inscrutability of the sign, is reduced and constrained to rational signification by her capture, interrogation, and representation at the hands of the expert" (197).

Before looking at the shared desire of Guha's and Schwarz's texts to render their own systems of representation invisible along with the historical origins of those systems, it is necessary to remind ourselves that Guha's text does not ascribe inscrutability to the subaltern's actions. Guha's critique of left historiography is quite specific; it is not a question of indeterminacy but of *knowledge:*

> The purpose of...tertiary discourse is quite clearly to try and retrieve the history of insurgency from that continuum which is designed to assimilate every jacquerie to "England's Work in India," and arrange it along the alternative axis of a protracted campaign for freedom and socialism. However, as with colonialist historiography, this too amounts to an act of appropriation which excludes the rebel as the conscious subject of his own history and incorporates the latter as only a contingent element in another history with another subject. Just as it is not the rebel but the Raj which is the real subject of secondary discourse and the Indian bourgeoisie that of tertiary discourse of the History-of-the-Freedom-Struggle genre, so is an *abstraction* called Worker-and-Peasant, *an ideal rather than the real historical personality of the insurgent,* made to replace him in the type of literature discussed above. (Guha, "On Some Aspects," 33)

The "abstraction" called Worker-and-Peasant, when adopted as the subject of history, is problematic insofar as by that means the past is redefined in terms produced in the present as if the past in its entirety were the missing content of those terms. Thus, since the ideal consciousness of the Worker-and-Peasant "is supposed to be one hundred percent secular in character, the devotee tends to look away when confronted with the evidence of religiosity as if the latter did not exist or explain it away as a clever but well-intentioned fraud perpetrated by enlightened leaders on their moronic followers — all done of course, 'in the interests of the people'!" (39). The revolutionary working class, in other words, which has to be produced in the political realm, is "discovered" in history by a certain idealist historiography. But in the course of this critique Guha also makes two counterassertions: (1) that history can be written without the aid of any "abstractions" (and that subaltern historiography is an example of such writing); and (2) that the subaltern groups are agents of their "own" history, which is recoverable/must be recovered as such. If there is a suggestion that the discourse in/through which this rescue will take place is transparent, it is rendered very complicated by the very next paragraph:

> To say this of course is not to deny the political importance of such appropriation. Since every struggle for power by the historically ascendant classes in any epoch involves a bid to acquire a tradition, it is entirely in the fitness of things that the revolutionary movements in India should lay a claim to, among others, the Santal rebellion of 1855 as a part of their heritage. But however noble the cause and instrument of such appropriation, it leads to the mediation of the insurgent's consciousness by the historian's — that is, of a past consciousness by one conditioned by the present. The distortion which follows necessarily and inevitably from this process is a function of that hiatus between event-time and discourse-time which makes the verbal representation of the past less than accurate in the best of cases....
>
> There is nothing historiography can do to eliminate such distortion altogether, for the latter is built into its optics. (33)

This and the previous passage together give us, first, a contrast between an *ideological* distortion and the aspiration to be free of distortion that marks the Subaltern

Studies project and, second, the mutation of distortion into a purely nonideological, "necessary" one that cannot be avoided. It is very unclear what is being conceded and what defended here. Is Guha conceding that the "subaltern" is as much of an "abstraction" as the "Worker-and-Peasant"? That the shift in terminology represents not the movement toward a more accurate representation but a different representation with a different political agenda? If the imposition of a "Worker-and-Peasant" mold on the material of the past constitutes an "appropriation" indistinguishable from the appropriative gestures of the national bourgeoisie, in what way does the imposition of the "subaltern" mold on the same material *not* constitute an appropriation? Guha's text makes no attempt to answer such questions and is content to regard "discursive appropriation" as somehow unjust in itself, an assumption that, interestingly, does not come into operation when subalternist discourse is in question. The neopragmatists, as we have seen, object to a general theory that attempts to "govern" the reading of particular texts, while retaining "authorial intention" as the general principle of particular interpretation. Guha's critique of abstractions similarly fails to acknowledge the "abstract" character of the term "subaltern."

Gayatri Spivak's "Deconstructing Historiography," along with "Can the Subaltern Speak?" remains the most thoroughgoing critique of the Subaltern Studies project undertaken so far. Spivak, however, reads the "subject-effect" produced by the writing "as a *strategic* use of positivist essentialism in a scrupulously visible political interest" (Spivak, 205). The difficulty here stems from the implicit suggestion that strategy is necessarily one step behind theory, that theory itself is not a strategic necessity. "I am suggesting . . . that although the group does not wittingly engage with the poststructuralist understanding of 'consciousness,' our own transactional reading of them is enhanced if we see them as *strategically* adhering to the essentialist notion of consciousness, that would fall prey to an anti-humanist critique, within a historiographic practice that draws many of its strengths from that very critique" (206–7). "Strategy" is at work at two levels here: the group's strategic backward step into essentialism is matched by Spivak's own strategic negotiation of a coexistence of poststructuralism with strategic essentialism. Spivak's text is acutely aware of its location at the intersection of two complexly related intellectual traditions, and it insists on the necessity of a critical operation that brings these traditions into productive conflict. But an "unwitting" tendency to position historians as themselves "subaltern" in the intellectual field intervenes to produce the effect of a contrast between two kinds of writing, one taking place in the trenches and the other in a more leisurely space of philosophical speculation.[7]

In the new mode of intellectual contestation that has emerged in recent years, the contest is over which groups are the true subjects of history. Imperialist forces and bourgeois nationalists wrote themselves as subjects, against which left historiography inscribed the working class in the same place. The current tendency is to find new and multiple subjects of fragmented histories, so that history itself is divided up into any number of independent, self-propelled trajectories, each with its own share of the "homogeneous, empty time" of capitalism. If the subject in all these instances is understood as the locus of an intention, we see how the smallest intention-bearing unit, the neopragmatist "author," is the logical precursor of all the other intentional formations, large or small. Behind the theological "intention" of any specified entity, lies, of course, the more strictly relevant notion of "property," of possession, which defines the entity. Intention is simply the theological verification of secular possession.

Poststructuralist theoretical advances often seem to "overtake" political struggles and produce "academics supposedly 'marginated' by the 'advanced' state of their intellectual sophistication" (Morton, 101). Political intervention thus always requires a strategic climb-down from the advanced state. And since new conceptual frameworks are avoided like a disease, celebration of others' struggles is the only option. In this way poststructuralism often comes to rest beside pragmatism and other status-quoist tendencies as a reluctant but helpless ally. Some of the contributors to a volume entitled *Postmodernism/Jameson/Critique* offer poststructuralist defenses of intentional units that are helpful in mapping the wider antitheoretical network in which the texts we are here concerned with are situated.

One of these, by R. Radhakrishnan, claims, for a start, that "contemporary realities themselves are marked by a certain poststructuralist 'difference'" (Radhakrishnan, 302). Thus poststructuralism is offered to us not, as it used to be, as a theory that problematizes the real and the "natural" but as the expression of the spirit of the age, the natural discursive reflection of a "differentiated" reality. In place of what he calls Jameson's "universal and anthropological Subject of history," Radhakrishnan posits "the realities of different and globally unequal histories" (305). Once again, one subject has been replaced by many subjects. But in addition to their "difference" from one another, Radhakrishnan recognizes something called inequality. Unlike difference, however, inequality resists reification and preserves its relationality. How to reconcile, then, these two contradictory effects? Is there difference in spite of inequality? Is there difference *in order to conceal* inequality? What is the basis of the decision to focus on difference, to the exclusion of inequality? Is it the belief that the achievement of difference will automatically erase inequality? If the regime of difference has already been inaugurated in a reality that is itself poststructuralist, has inequality, then, ended?

On the assumption that there are many autonomous histories, time itself is said to be fragmented accordingly, with each group possessing its own time. In a footnote commenting on Jameson's theory of Third World literature, Radhakrishnan elaborates this notion:

> During the course of this essay, Jameson talks all too glibly about "the return of nationalism" in the Third World as though nationalism were enjoying a re-run in the Third World. The confident use of the term 'return' suggests that within the universal synchronicity of Western time, nationalism is repeating itself in the Third World, whereas, historically, "nationalism" is new to the Third World. Throughout this essay (in spite of an initial gesture of unease), Jameson has little difficulty in maintaining his official conviction that the Third World histories are a predictable repetition of the histories of the "advanced world"; hence, the masterly confidence with which he "allegorizes" the Third World on its own behalf. (329)

According to one way of reading world history (a totalizing one), nationalism, having emerged in the West as a mechanism of postfeudal integration of contiguous populations under an authority with monopoly over foreign policy and trade, *repeats* itself in the struggles of the colonized against the colonizers. But Radhakrishnan proposes another model, whereby nationalism will forever maintain its novelty — every time a new geographical space claims national identity, it is making a *new* claim from its own perspective. A deliberate erasure of the memory of the global history of nationalism has to be effected in order to arrive at this liberating position. But this is a classic instance of commodity fetishism: my Ford, once it is in my possession, is no longer just like any other Model T. While at the moment of encounter with the commodity on the market no one can escape the lure of commodity fetishism (as Alfred Sohn-Rethel points out), here even the *knowledge* of mechanical reproduction is banished from the sphere of intellectual activity. According to this approach, the task of intellectuals is to keep the demystifying knowledge about nationalism from reaching the ears of the nationalists.

Later in the essay Radhakrishnan recommends a coalition politics based on the example of the Rainbow Coalition. But there are some "unwitting" remarks elsewhere, as in the passage above, that indicate the approach to politics that is really being promoted here. The quotation marks around "advanced world" and, in a part of the same passage that I have not quoted, the reference to a "so-called First World" are the first clues. Add to them the attribution of "the best of intentions" to Jameson's project; his applause for Jameson's "rare, inaugural *generosity*" (305; emphasis added); and, finally, this interim conclusion: "Unfortunately then, Jameson ends up dehistoricizing the very constituencies that he had set out to *befriend and understand*" (306; emphasis added). These are the symptoms of a coalitionism that wants relations based on "generosity," "goodwill," and "understanding." Whose generosity? For whom? Is it not the "generosity" of the liberal-pluralist sanctioning of "difference" that poses the greater danger today — the danger that representative elites will accept this generosity "on behalf of" their "natural" constituencies and "forgive," out of a reciprocal generosity, the oppression and exploitation that continue elsewhere? By way of a critique of the natural, of an "attack on identity and totality," once more, we arrive at a very old bourgeois solution to all crises — coalitionism.

But what, in any case, is the rationale of the coalition? The contemporary situation demands "the creation of a *non-aggressive, non-coercive, and generous* space where different and multiple constituencies may meet *collectively*" (323; emphasis added). The Rainbow Coalition is just such a space, besides being an instance of the practical implementation of the theory of poststructuralism. Coalitions are "opportunistic structures" to be used and discarded "as soon as power is seized" (326). But here, following upon that vision, is another one:

> Built into the coalition is the insight that *a common world* is thinkable only when we can divest ourselves from interests that are merely and obsessively regional and that it is the ethical and political responsibility of the advanced [no deprecatory quotation marks this time round] and developed sectors within a country or the world *to practice some form of sacrifice and askesis* so that the underdeveloped sectors may *catch up* and *be redressed* of their *grievances*. I say "responsibility" since underdevelopment in one area has always the result of overdevelopment elsewhere [an interesting inversion of the cause-effect relation: underdevelopment *causes* — "has the result of" — overdevelopment, no doubt because of sacrifices made voluntarily and "ethically" by the autonomous subjects of the underdeveloped nations?]; we need only to look *briefly*

at the history of colonialism, imperialism, racism, and sexism to reach this conclusion. (326–27; emphasis added)

This is the real meaning of coalition: no occasion here for any "seizure of power." All autonomous underdeveloped subjects must await the charity of their overdeveloped neighbors, whom they will continue to love in true Christian spirit until they begin to make the necessary sacrifices. Developed and underdeveloped, bourgeoisie and working class, can and must enter into coalitions.

Haynes Horne, another contributor to the same volume, builds the case for fragmentation on a Lyotardian foundation. "Only when it will be possible to speak of Marxist *philosophies of histories* and be understood, without being accused of some [any?] liberal pluralism, will Marxism have emerged from the hegemony of enlightenment schemes of totality and offered itself anew as a vehicle for transforming — not reproducing — the given social order" (Horne, 269). This is the place to take up again Radhakrishnan's notion of "western time" and "other times," which was left unexamined above, since Horne's notion of multiple philosophies of histories refers to the same desire for a plurality of homogeneous empty times. Horne's vision of the world is stated with equal vehemence, as when, against Jameson's notion of history, he declaims:

> [T]here is a . . . question Jameson utterly fails to ask, namely, "*whose* history?" Africa's or China's? No, Euramerika's! Blacks' history or Orientals'? No, Caucasians'! Women's history? No, Men's! What Jameson reduces to "practitioners of alternate codes" are more properly in his own terms "livers of alternate histories." As such they have every reason to expect that their histories *be taken seriously by Jameson,* which, however, will not be possible under the regime of a metanarrative in which the single "logic of capital" dictates *the temporality as well as the space* of each narrative." (283; emphasis added)

Note the unwitting(?) deification of "Jameson" in the words emphasized, before we move on to the question of time. The discourse of the supplicant, the injured party, once again serves as the identifying mark of the postcolonial other. When, soon after this, Horne criticizes Jameson's notion of the "sectoral validity" of various "alternate codes" for the signs it bears of a paternal attitude, he does not remember the demand that he makes here for precisely such paternalism. To return to "time," however: it is clear from Radhakrishnan's and Horne's formulations that autonomous histories can only be theorized in the context of a developmental model of the globe where backward but autonomous sectors will be able, thanks to someone's generosity, to "catch up" with the advanced sectors. Why all these autonomous sectors should want to catch up with the same model of economic well-being is a question that does not occur to the specialists of difference. In any case, "western time" or the global capitalist "philosophy of history" is there, in that developmental model that lies at the base of Lyotardian fragmentation and its repetitions. The grand narratives are not pure discursive formations but philosophies whose material existence is the institutionalized developmental logic of capitalism in which "autonomous" nation-states are the primary institutions. It is within one, single, unidirectional capitalist time-space that all existing differences are recognized. To celebrate that order of difference, then, is to celebrate that time-space as the eternal ground of existence. It is only through the destruction of that time-space that a new order, enabling new conceptions of heterogeneity, can be produced. That time-space, in which is inscribed the history of all histories, whose representational machinery asserts its preeminence at every site (so that, e.g., all histories will have to posit, for themselves, a subject of history as the very condition of their autonomy), is the signified of the concept of totality.

Ahmad's argument against a theory of "Third World" literature is an instance of the return, by complicated ways, to an ultimately nationalist position that falls within the developmental philosophy of history. By claiming that "there is no such thing as a 'third world' literature" (4), Ahmad implies that there *is,* in unproblematic ways, a Nigerian, an Indian, an Urdu, or a black American literature. This assertion is by no means self-evident: it depends on a naturalized understanding of "literature" as a random body of work produced in specific linguistic, cultural, national domains. Such a definition — assuming as it does that because it refuses to theorize, it is free from theory — participates in the naturalizing ideology of bourgeois nationalist-cultural understanding. If there is a determinable institutionalized "Urdu literature," to assert which Ahmad's text has to adopt without explicit acknowledgment a position in linguistic nationalism, its status as a representational apparatus, its institutional role in culture as a machinery of social cohesion, has to be examined. In formulations like the following, the contradictions of a Marxist position moored in nationalist/essentialist "cultural soils" becomes clear: "These various countries, from three continents [Africa, Latin America, and Asia], have been assimilated into the global structure of capitalism not as a single cultural ensemble but highly differentially, each establishing its own circuits of (unequal) exchange with the metropolis, each acquiring its own very distinct class formations" (Ahmad, 10). "These various countries," however, are constructions that do not necessarily possess a natural rationality or internal coherence — their constitution as nation-states is determined by many factors, but their principal common feature is that they predominantly constitute themselves or are constituted as *structures of administration by representation* on the model of the bourgeois democracies of Europe. The nation-state, with a representative rule approximating in varying degrees to the primary models, is the politically, economically, and ideologically privileged mode of participation in the global order.

Literature, or a national culture in general, is one of the representational machineries that serve to consolidate the nation-state. Its historical emergence in Europe is tied to the rise of the primary capitalist nation-states, and in this sense literature is "national." Of course this claim is of little value by itself, but a Marxist theory of literature cannot begin anywhere else. Ahmad's own arguments point in this direction (12–13), but a residual nationalist disdain for globalizing theories prevents him from attempting a more rigorous, extensive, and complex theorization of literature than the one Jameson has put forward.

II

A concern that the very possibility of agency is dependent on the existence of irreducible, autonomous selves seems to be shared by the texts of Guha, Schwarz, and

Ahmad. The threat to such agency is variously seen as arising from the incursions of theory (Ahmad), historiography (Guha), and (instrumental) reason (Schwarz). But there is a point of divergence: while Guha and Schwarz, positioned on the familiar side of the epistemic barrier, are anxious to avoid doing violence to the objects on the other side, Ahmad positions himself *as* that object, protesting the violence done to it by theory. In other words, while Ahmad's text marks a resistance to theory on the part of a subject who considers it an attempt to objectify him, Guha's and Schwarz's texts, as if in response to this complaint, are anxious to eliminate from their intellectual work the offending theoretical apparatus. In Guha's text the failure to adequately specify one of its concerns — the need for a materialist historiography to overcome the tendency to impose an ideal of Worker-and-Peasant on the class struggles of the past — leads to an equally idealist faith in the rebellious groups' "internal principle of elaboration." In Schwarz there is an equation of the (instrumental) reason of the *Army Handbook* (196) with reason per se or with the very attempt to comprehend. This leads him to conclude: "As Guha remarks on the impossibility of fully knowing the consciousness of the Other, the distance between these two perspectives can never be reconciled, but rather it must be acknowledged that the 'distortion is parametric'; reading Third World literature can only be a political practice of reflection on our own situation, a reflection that makes us aware of the gaps and blind spots within the strategic model we have developed, and of what we are doing about them" (198). The call for a self-critique that is heard in this passage is one thing; quite another is the imperative to produce and protect an unintelligibility as the measure of "our" failures and crimes. It is hard to avoid the suspicion that this gesture of withdrawal and contemplation is a concession to Ahmad's demand.

If the institution of literature is closely bound up with the history of the nation-state, there is no reason to take, as Jameson does, the predominance of "private," "libidinal" preoccupations in the literature of advanced capitalist nations as indicative of a loss of that capacity for collective expression that, it would seem, distinguishes Third World literature.[8] Another way of thinking about the differences between these two categories has to be found. The concept of "national allegory" that Jameson has introduced can be a useful component of such a rethinking, but first it has to be freed from its moorings in an Orientalist paradigm (as Ahmad recognizes) that some Marxist theory has shared with the dominant intellectual tradition. As Bryan Turner has shown, drawing on the extensive debates over the theory of modes of production, Marxism owes the notion of an "Asiatic mode of production" to the Orientalist tradition (Turner, 31–32). Ahmad's charge against Jameson is that "a literary theorist who sets out to formulate 'a theory of the cognitive aesthetics of third-world literature' shall be constructing ideal types, in the Weberian manner, duplicating all the basic procedures which orientalist scholars have historically deployed in presenting their own readings of a certain tradition of 'high' textuality as *the* knowledge of a supposedly unitary object which they call 'the Islamic civilization'" (4). Jameson takes the Weberian route but in a different sense than Ahmad seems to imply. One can turn to Turner again for his account of the internalist (Weberian) and externalist explanatory models that compete with each other in the social sciences. Internalist explanations are theories of development that treat the main problems of "backward societies" as a question of certain characteristics internal to societies considered in isolation from any international societal context. . . . Another important dimension of internalist theory is that development is conceptualized in terms of a set of contrasts between dichotomous ideal types — *Gemeinschaft/Gesellschaft,* tradition/modernity, religious/secular. Alternatively development is treated as a process through a series of necessary stages — primitive, premodern, modern, post-industrial — which lead to an end-state society. . . . The outcome of development is the achievement of a stationary end-state which is a faithful replica of the liberal democracies of Western capitalism. (Turner, 10–11)

What we are dealing with in the case of Ahmad and others is a sort of internalized internalism: in Ahmad we have a cultural internalism, in Radhakrishnan and Horne an unreconstructed general internalism, and in Jameson an internalism of modes of production, all three purporting to serve oppositional intellectual projects. In thus internalizing libidinal preoccupations as "Western" and collective awareness as "Third World," the "limits" of the libidinal are located *outside* the "West." It would be more accurate to reinscribe all literatures in their national context and then begin the analysis of the invisibility of the national framework in the Western context and its hypervisibility in the Third World context.

The argument in this case would be, not that Third World literature is more expressive of the political realities of this world, but that for historical reasons, its critical focus is on a collective social reality more than on (say) an individual's existential crisis; and, further, that even the literary representations of existential crises in the Third World context cannot be read in isolation from the national/collective framework. What all this means is that there cannot be two distinct theories of literature, one specific to the Third World and the other to the First World. In this sense, the turn in the revised version of Jameson's text to "world" rather than "Third World" literature may be an advance (though restricted to the title) toward the proper point of departure in the general that would enable an approach to the concrete.

The question of the proper place to begin is important enough to require further elaboration. It is curious that, at the moment of producing a theory of Third World literature, Jameson should find it necessary to embrace the essentialist self-image of the West as a homogeneous entity and, in existentialist terms, lament "our" failure to keep alive a sense of collectively. We have seen this gesture in Schwarz to be partly the result of a caution exercised against the easy tendency to presume to speak for the Third World. But as we also noted above, that gesture at once locates the resistance to the "West" outside it. Even Jameson temporarily forgets the class struggle in the West. On the question of the status of the political, Jameson finds that in the First World the split between private and public ("Freud versus Marx") has a powerful hold over "individual and collective lives" (141). In the Third World, in contrast, an allegorical dimension makes even the personal political. Of course Jameson is making the latter argument only about Third World *texts,* while the former is extended to cover both First World lives and texts. But when the extra emphasis on the line from Sembene Ousmane's novel — "Its life was based on the principles of community interdependence" — is recalled (Jameson, 152), it becomes clear that the allegorical dimension of textual representations is being extended to the nondiscursive realm as well. Thus, Jameson locates the limits of individualism in the precapitalist societies that have been invoked as the limits of "economic man" as well.[9] Indeed, here these two arguments come together, because economic man and individualist ideology are aspects of the same type of social formation. Jameson's argument thus falls into the mold of some of the other texts that we have been considering; it evokes a certain nostalgia for the cohesiveness of precapitalist communities (this is not the case in the reading of Lu Xun, where "nation" is used in a more strictly modern sense). Jameson is using two models of difference, one based on differences between modes of production, which perforce invites internalist explanations, and the second based on the split within the capitalist mode of production between exploiter and exploited. Because of this, the distinguishing features of the West, the once imperialist East, and Africa become inherent differences. On the other hand, like Schwarz, Jameson reads Third World literature as a mirror in which "a more unvarnished and challenging image of ourselves" can be discerned (140).

The question of the nation and community has to be investigated further: in the nation-states of the West, the destruction of "community interdependence" in feudal society preceded the formation of the national collection of individual citizens that was the achievement of the bourgeois revolution. The nation-state's citizenry, whose private and public domains were constituted for them by the bourgeois revolution, already contained the principles of new forms of solidarity — class solidarity in the main. The class for whom politics is a pistol shot in the middle of a concert is most at home in the idea of a nation as a community of private individuals. All classes, however, do not find that position of free, self-interested citizen as hospitable as the bourgeoisie. For the new nation-states, whose survival depends on "voluntary" participation in the international economy, the adoption of a hierarchical structure of representative administration brings conflicts that are read by a Weberian sociology as the result of a clash of modern and precapitalist consciousness. While such analyses have hitherto tended to look for ways to hasten the march into modernity, certain postmodernisms read the conflicts in celebratory ways as signs of resistance to modernity. Jameson's reading is partly informed by this latter strategy, but the more valuable part of his text is the one that suggests that the reassertion of precapitalist communal solidarity is an oppositional deployment of collective identity as a weapon of class struggle, to which we must add that the question of the adequacy of this weapon remains to be posed.

A theory of (Third) World literature cannot be produced from any already available position. This specific question of theory, moreover, affords an opportunity to rethink the question of the locus of articulation of theory in general in the postmodern world. Here it would be useful to recall the epistemic barrier and the positions that the theorists we have considered so far have taken up on either side of it. Ahmad, for instance, like the anthropologist in the story, finds himself on both sides, even though he speaks, for the most part, from one side. Schwarz, Guha, and the poststructuralist theorists find themselves on the more privileged side of the barrier, attempting to conceal or neutralize the privilege by strategies of self-effacement and celebration of the other side's autonomy from their conceptual frameworks. A somewhat unusual version of this latter dilemma is what Jameson is also stuck with and what leads his theoretical project into Orientalist pitfalls. To clarify the problem, a brief detour into Edward Said's understanding of the role of the intellectual will be useful. In an interview with Bruce Robbins, Said talks about his notion of intellectual "affiliation":

> BR: Since you mention Raymond Williams, he makes an interesting distinction, as I'm sure you know, between alignment and commitment, the latter being more intentional. Alignment is what you are stuck with. I wonder whether you could locate "affiliation" in relation to that distinction.
>
> ES: The point is of course intention. If you want to put it in a Freudian context, it's the move from unaware alignment to active commitment that he's interested in, the bringing of social relationships to consciousness.
>
> BR: I didn't ask my question well. I guess I always wondered how much intention there was in affiliation, how close it was to alignment and how close it was to commitment.
>
> ES: Oh I see. That's a tough one. Well, I suppose it's closer to the notion of alignment than it is to commitment. It has also to do with larger degrees of involuntary association, complicity, and so forth than it does with active commitment. The problem of commitment is a very difficult one. It's not difficult in England, where there's a settled political tradition. Here, the notion of commitment is necessarily tactical. There is really no discourse of the left here. There is no left formation of any sort, unless you think the Democratic Party is the left. So the notion of commitment becomes a very difficult one to use. That's why it struck me as not possible to employ it in the American context, except within a very limited compass. (Robbins, 48)

The significance of this passage lies in the way in which Said's response collapses the distinction that Raymond Williams's terms are meant to signify. Williams would seem to be distinguishing between a relationship to a cause that is theorized, as opposed to one that is taken for granted, one that one finds oneself in. In pointing to the absence of a "left formation," a settled political tradition, in the United States, Said effectively thinks commitment itself as a form of alignment/affiliation. On the one hand, to be part of an already existing constituency, whether it is race, nation, gender, or a left formation, is to be not committed at all but affiliated. On the other hand, any of these affiliations, when historicized and retheorized, would give us, in Williams's sense, the basis for a commitment. The difference lies in the historicizing break that the intellectual has to make with natural affiliations.

In a way, Jameson can be understood to be in search of "already existing" left formations. For this reason, when he sets out to produce a theory, he ends up with a left literary anthropology or a typology of collective struggles. Thus an unexpected but real affinity between Jameson and Ahmad begins to reveal itself, which I would suggest is the chief obstacle in the way of Jameson's theoretical project. The dominant modes of knowledge production thus get reproduced in the most unlikely spaces, a fact that is indicative of the immensity of the task of rethinking, especially given the various versions of the concrete.

For the anthropologization of the left also proceeds from the continued occupation of the western humanist subject-position as the point of articulation of the theory. Thus Jameson launches his search for a theory as a disillusioned Western reader of libidinal literary texts that have exhausted their interest for him. But a theory of literature in the late-capitalist world, like a theory of capitalism in general, cannot proceed from one position *in* capitalist discourse and take as its object another region also within it: the structure of anthropology is already evident in this schematic formulation. Marx undertook the critique of political economy neither from the position of bourgeois political economists nor from some real or hypothetical "existing" working-class position. *There the position occupied by the theorist was itself produced by the theory and elaborated at the same time as it was occupied.* In the same way, a theory of (Third) World literature cannot be produced either from the position of a Western reader or from that of a "native," for even the former is a kind of nativism. The theory has to overcome both these and produce a new position, which for the present can only be a potentiality, that it will occupy and elaborate. Thus a global theory of literature as a "repeatable" institution becomes possible only after an analysis of literature as a nationalist institution and accounting for the different degrees of visibility of the national framework in various clusters of national literatures.

The first task, then, is to investigate the reasons for the greater visibility of the national frame of reference in Third World literatures than in those of the North Atlantic alliance. The extension of the primary capitalist nations' frame of reference to universal proportions in the imperialist era and the consequent fragmentation and reconstruction of this overstretched frame at the moment of withdrawal forced by anti-imperialist movements may be at the heart of the effect of "freedom from national determinations" that is widely installed in those nations. Another direction taken by nationalism in the West is toward a historically determined redefinition of a European cultural identity as subsuming and preserving French, English, or other national identities. This cohesion of nationalities takes place in the imperialist era in a sort of second-mirror stage, when the colonies in their perceived despotic/primitive homogeneity as other reflect back to the West its essential unity in spite of economic competition. The First World comes into being in this way as a recognizable concentration of globally dominant forces enjoying privileged access to a very large portion of the global surplus through the process of transfer of surplus value. This factor is the cohesive force that enables the production of the West as a self-identical cultural entity. The West, in other words, is a name for the class solidarity of imperialist capital.

Third World nationalisms, in contrast, are primarily counternationalisms, which produced national identities on the model of, but also against the domination of, the primary capitalist nation-states. Their efforts to attain subjecthood (the effect of a self-generated historical momentum) were due not to any internal necessity but to external pressure — it is a requirement for "voluntary" and "self-interested" participation in the global economy. For this reason, the nation as a frame of reference is a constant presence in cultural production. As Ahmad points out, the indigenous bourgeoisies of Third World nations do achieve the private/public, libidinal/political division characteristic of Western social formations. As he also argues, such divisions need not prevent the reading of the "libidinal" text as a cultural-expressive system of signification. But a reading of, say, an Indian "libidinal-private" text on its own terms is only possible from within a nationalist framework, that is, from a position in which the national framework is invisible as a result of complete assimilation into the ideology of national subjectivity. What appears as libidinal-private to the hypothetical (and in the case of the counternationalities, never fully realizable) fully assimilated citizen-subject would necessarily seem, to the "Western" reader, equipped with Orientalist and developmentalist frameworks, to be expressive of the nation's essence. The institutionalization of developmentalism ensures this effect because while defining counternationalities in collective terms, the center defines itself as a "free" space occupied by free individuals. The postcolonial intellectual, moreover, shares this perspective because of his/her location in a ground of *comparison* that is inescapable without a radical transformation of the global order. It is a partial adoption of this developmental apparatus of representation that leads to Jameson's division of world literature into national allegory, on the one hand, and "libidinal-private," on the other. The only way out of this model is to begin by redefining the libidinal-private in its allegorical status (its relation to particular nations but especially to particular classes — a class allegory) and collapsing the distinction that originates in capitalist ideology.

The greater visibility of the national frame of reference in Third World literature may be a function primarily of the historical conditions under which these nations came into being. The developmental paradigm under whose aegis "independence" for colonized regions became possible in the capitalist era creates the temporal order in which the contemporaneity of various social formations appears to be structured by a time lag. The appearance of a fortuitous developmental gap that serves to conceal the *necessity* of the uneven and combined development of regions of the globe for capitalism is part of the nation-state's ideology. Moreover, insofar as a global order, with its implicit value allocations, is a constant and active element of postcolonial subjectivity, internal comparison/competition is always accompanied by a comparison/competition at the international level. The tension between these two levels of articulation is a constitutive element of Third World literature — whether that tension is itself part of the representation (giving rise to allegory) or whether it functions as a determinant of reading practices — that the term "national allegory" may usefully signify.[10]

This is where the contemporary interest in allegory might prove to be of some interest. Craig Owens, in "The Allegorical Impulse: Toward a Theory of Postmodernism," argues that there was a "critical suppression of allegory" that is "one legacy of romantic art theory that was inherited uncritically by modernism" (Owens, 209). He also states:

> From the [French] Revolution on, [allegory] had been enlisted in the service of historicism to produce image upon image of the present *in terms of* the classical past. This relationship was expressed not only superficially, in details of costume and physiognomy, but also structurally, through a radical condensation of narrative into a single, emblematic instant . . . in which the past, present, and future, that is, the *historical* meaning, of the depicted action might be read. . . . Syntagmatic or narrative associations were compressed in order to compel a vertical reading of (allegorical) correspondences. (210)

Without falling into the trap of siding with one of these opposed tendencies against the other, as being inherently good or bad, we can note that Owens's characterization of a historic conflict of aesthetic modes suggests that the issues were clearly political. Owens goes on to suggest, through a reading of Benjamin on Baudelaire, that "in practice at least, modernism and allegory are *not* antithetical, that it is in theory alone that the allegorical impulse has been repressed" (212). In this theory, allegory and symbol are distinguished with a positive valence to the latter term, as in Coleridge: "The Symbolical cannot, perhaps, be better defined in distinction from the Allegorical, than that it is always itself *a part of* that, of the whole of which it is the representative" (Owens, 213). This "expressive theory of the symbol" relates "the symbol with aesthetic intuition and allegory with conven- tion" (214). In Benedetto Croce, a further advance toward the total aestheticization of the art work is made by treating allegory as a supplement, in order to preserve the unity of form and content. What is valuable for our analysis in Owens's dis- cussion is the suggestion that allegory's capacity for including (self)critical layers of discourse is one of the main reasons for its suppression. If this is linked to the role Owens believes romantic art theory played in the suppression, a strong suggestion emerges that the suppression of allegory was necessary for the successful institu- tionalization, to keep to our case, of the study of literature. The critical function is reserved for art's superstructure, that discipline that makes the art work its object. It is not just that romantic art theory aestheticizes the art work, de-allegorizes it: af- ter all, as Owens himself points out, this can only occur in theory and does not always affect the allegorical dimension of the text itself (which remains dependent on the artist's and the viewer/reader's positions). The more important conclusion is that in the process of theorizing the symbolic rather than allegorical status of the text, art theory *creates itself as a legitimate and necessary domain*. In insisting on the artistic text's unity with its context, theory establishes its own autonomy from it. The well-fortified establishments of literary criticism in the North Atlantic countries are a contrast to their relatively weak and devalued counterparts in a country like India. These establishments properly belong to the order of "ideological state appa- ratuses" because they take over the function of regulation — explication, selection, canonization, hierarchization, and so on. Meaning becomes their exclusive domain.[11]

The extent to which the national-allegorical dimension of a literary text is *visible* can now be seen as a function of a variety of factors. What we call the "libidinal/ individualist" text is one whose meaning is the responsibility of the institution of literary studies. Which is not to say that that text is free of allegorical signification but that the very idea of a text being free of "allegory" and therefore "individualistic" is an idea that only arises with the separation of the aesthetic from the theoretical/ critical functions. An important consequence is the isolation of the aesthetic function from the political.

In contrast to the global bourgeois solidarity whose emblem is the "First World," the absence of solidarity among the "differentially integrated" and exploited peoples of the Third World is painfully evident. Such a solidarity has been attempted by Third World nations in reformist forums such as the Non-Aligned Movement. If, as Ahmad points out, "an average Nigerian who is literate about his own country would know infinitely more about England and the United States than about any country of Asia or Latin America or . . . Africa," the reasons may lie in the reality of metropolitan me- diation, in the fact that competitive nation-states have to concentrate all their efforts on "catching up" with the West, which has yet to make the sacrifices that have been demanded of it. And the compulsive collective mediation of individual utterances that is characteristic of this condition of postcolonial competitive nation-statehood may prove to be a suitable point of departure for a global cultural critique.

NOTES

I wish to thank Donald Morton for his critique of earlier versions of this text.

1. A psychoanalytic approach may seize upon the potential here for a reading in terms of Oedipal politics, with the First World anthropologist and the native intellectual figuring as rivals in a struggle over the mother(land)'s body. But while such a narrative could well be a structuring element in the microsocial manifestations of the conflict, the reality of class struggle cannot be captured by this mythical grid of intelligibility. However, pursued with attention to history and to questions of property and sovereignty, such an analysis could certainly throw additional light on the patriarchal roots of nationalist cultural studies.

2. Jameson's project, in its essentials, closely resembles another theoretical undertaking — the Third Cinema Movement, whose theory was written by Latin American intellectuals. Indeed both projects could be said to belong to that history of the Third World as political concept that has only recently come to an end. But the important point here is that Jameson's project shares much more with its parallel in cinema theory than with the metropolitan drive for dominion to which Ahmad seems to want to link it (see Pines and Willemen, esp. 1–64). It is problematic, to say the least, to banish this project to the wrong side of racial and gender politics (as Ahmad does on p. 24) on the basis of unfounded speculations concerning the true inclinations of oppressed subjects.

3. See Mitchell, esp. 11–30, 48–52, 95–105, 106–31.

4. Marx, *Manuscripts of 1861–63*, quoted in Dussel, 85.

5. Another point of interest of the text is its demonstration that this theory had already been partially developed in Marx's *Economic Manuscripts of 1861–63*, which are currently being published.

6. In the other text that Schwarz quotes from extensively, "The Prose of Counter-insurgency," Guha includes in his "tertiary" category of historiography those writings that present "an ahistorical view of the history of insurgency" in which "all moments of consciousness are assimilated to...an Ideal Consciousness,...regrettably, in the name of Marxism" (Guha, "Prose," 39).

7. On the question of "strategic essentialism," see Dhareshwar, whose conclusions I quote here: "The strategic essentialist subscribes in principle to the critique of essentialism and the unspecified and unspecifiable ideal that it posits but feels that to act on that ideal would mean deserting struggles of resistance organized around essentialist categories. Strategic essentialism turns out to be an awkward resolution of a false problem generated by the theorist's attempt to use the vocabularies and figures of theory as foundational" (Dhareshwar, 152). The casualty in this oscillation between theoretical advances and political compromises is the domain of explanation, where the interest in struggles derives not from a desire to adequate them to an independently developed theoretical knowledge but from the necessity of explaining their historical conditions of possibility and producing new knowledges out of a critique of those conditions and limitations.

8. Here one may recall Volosinov's remarks on individualism: "A special kind of character marks the individualistic self-experience.... The individualistic experience is fully differentiated and structured. Individualism is a special ideological form of the 'we-experience' of the bourgeois class (there is also an analogous type of individualistic self-experience for the feudal aristocratic class).... The structure of the conscious, individual personality is just as social a structure as is the collective type of experience" (Volosinov, 89).

9. As Arun Patnaik has pointed out, first, Marx recognized the "limits" of economic (Smithian, self-seeking, individualistic) man to lie *within* the capitalist system and not outside it; second, precapitalist formations are integrated into the capitalist system through alliances between the respective elites — "a substantial section of the newly formed economic man emerges from within the pre-capitalist sectors which co-exist with the capitalist sector" (Patnaik, 13, 14).

10. "Western or First World theorists privilege their subject-positions unreflectively, for they do not (cannot?) theorize the background practices and the institutional authority that enables their theoretical productions, their 'statements.' Postcolonials cannot help noticing the conditions of possibility of their theory" (Dhareshwar, 145).

11. A further exploration of the points briefly touched upon here about artistic texts' imagining of a political order as their ground of enunciation and other questions concerning the relation between political structure and cultural form may be found in my "The State and Culture: Hindi Cinema in the Passive Revolution."

WORKS CITED

Ahmad, Aijaz. "Jameson's Rhetoric of Otherness and the 'National Allegory.' *Social Text* 17 (fall 1987): 3–25.

Dhareshwar, Vivek. "Toward a Narrative Epistemology of the Postcolonial Predicament." *Inscriptions* 5 (1989): 135–57.

Dussel, Enrique. "Marx's Economic Manuscripts of 1861–63 and the 'Concept' of Dependency." *Latin American Perspectives* 65 (17/2) (spring 1990): 62–101.

Guha, Ranajit. "The Prose of Counter-insurgency." In Ranajit Guha, ed., *Subaltern Studies*. Vol. 2, *Writings on South Asian History and Society*. Delhi: Oxford University Press, 1983, 1–42.

———. "On Some Aspects of the Historiography of Colonial India." In Ranajit Guha, ed., *Subaltern Studies*. Vol. 1, *Writings on South Asian History and Society*. Delhi: Oxford University Press, 1982, 1–8.

Horne, Haynes. "Jameson's Strategies of Containment." In Douglas Kellner, ed., *Postmodernism/Jameson/Critique*. Washington, D.C.: Maisonneuve Press, 1989, 268–300.

Jameson, Fredric. "World Literature in an Age of Multinational Capitalism." In Clayton Koelb and Virgil Lokke, eds., *The Current in Criticism*. West Lafayette, Ind.: Purdue University Press, 1987, 139–58. Revised version of "Third World Literature in an Age of Multinational Capitalism." *Social Text* 15 (fall 1986): 65–88.

Madhava Prasad. "The State and Culture: Hindi Cinema in the Passive Revolution." Ph.D. dissertation, University of Pittsburgh, 1994.

Marx, Karl. *Capital*. Vol. 1. New York: Vintage, 1977.

Mitchell, W. J. T., ed. *Against Theory: Literary Studies and the New Pragmatism*. Chicago: University of Chicago Press, 1985.

Morton, Donald. "The Politics of the Margin: Theory, Pleasure, and the Postmodern *Conferance*." *The American Journal of Semiotics* 5, no. 1 (1987): 95–114.

Owens, Craig. "The Allegorical Impulse: Toward a Theory of Postmodernism." In Brian Wallis, ed., *Art after Modernism*. New York: New Museum of Contemporary Art, 203–35.

Patnaik, Arun K. "Reification of Intellect." *Economic and Political Weekly: Review of Political Economy* (January 27, 1990): 12–19.

Pines, Jim, and Paul Willeman. *Questions of Third Cinema*. London: BFI, 1989.

Radhakrishnan, R. "Poststructuralist Politics: Towards a Theory of Coalition." In Douglass Kellner, ed., *Postmodernism/Jameson/Critique*. Washington, D.C.: Maisonneuve Press, 1989, 301ff.

Robbins, Bruce. "American Intellectuals and Middle East Politics: An Interview with Edward Said." *Social Text* 19/20 (fall 1988): 37–53.

Schwarz, Henry. "Provocations toward a Theory of Third World Literature." *Mississippi Review* 49/50 (1989): 177–201.

Spivak, Gayatri Chakravorty. *In Other Worlds: Essays in Cultural Politics*. New York: Methuen, 1987.

Turner, Bryan S. *Marx and the End of Orientalism*. London: George Allen and Unwin, 1978.

Volosinov, V. N. *Marxism and the Philosophy of Language*. Trans. Ladislav Matejka and I. R. Titunik. Cambridge, Mass.: Harvard University Press, 1986.

Chapter 8
Caliban Speaks Five Hundred Years Later
Roberto Fernández Retamar

In this essay, I will speak about Caliban, and frequently *through* him. Years ago I proposed mythical Sycorax's son as an image of the culture pertaining to what José Martí called "our America," which has worldwide roots. But the powerful "concept-metaphor" (to use Gayatri Chakravorty Spivak's words) of Caliban (a *concept-metaphor,* I insist, an instrument for understanding, by no means just a name in a play) will refer in these pages not only to Latin America and the Caribbean but, as has so frequently been the case, to the wretched of the earth as a whole, whose existence has reached a unique dimension since 1492.

My task here, as I have said, is to speak *through* Caliban, not always necessarily about him. This is what Caliban's eyes see, what Caliban's voice says five hundred years later. After all, it is the look and not the looked-at object that implies maturity. That look's genuineness, to mention an example from another important zone of the world, explains the fact that there is not a more English writer than he whose stories take place not only in his small country but also in Verona, in Venice, in Rome, in Denmark, in Athens, in Troy, in Alexandria, on the tempest-ridden shores of the "American Mediterranean," in bewitched forests, in the nightmares induced by the lust for power, in the heart, in madness, nowhere, everywhere.

Now, half a millennium after 1492, let us put an end to the already boring sport of going back five hundred years and take part in the less frequent one of going back a millennium. Europe in 992 was quite a poor little thing, wasn't it? Just as the Egyptians, at the time they practiced a millenary Egyptocentrism, looked over their shoulders at the — to them — childlike and impure Greeks, in what other manner could the refined Arabs or Byzantines (perhaps the very refined Chinese and certainly the Mayas did not even suspect the rudimentary Europeans existed), in what other manner, I was saying, could they consider their blurry and insignificant coeval Europeans?

And if this was so, how is reality such a different matter only one thousand years later? Once more 1492 must be mentioned. It is a relevant date because Columbus's arrival in this hemisphere, unlike Leif Eriksson's five hundred years before, was part of a vast project burgeoning in a zone of the European society of the time. It is well known that what was teeming in the 1492 European society was capitalism, which, among other things, needed for its development the pitiless plundering of the rest of the planet. But since "capitalism" and "bourgeois society" are not very beautiful names, some European-born intellectuals, those busy Ariels, stimulated names of geographical origins, but with the prestige of imperial and ecclesiastical glitter: "the West," "the Western world," and "Western culture" are the robes with which capitalism parades itself (see José Carlos Mariátegui and Leopoldo Zea).

In relation to the birth of capitalism, several facts must be pointed out. First, the European invasion of America following 1492; the conquest and the genocide, monstrous as they are; the millions wrenched from Africa, and later from other places, enslaved and sent to work like beasts; the diverse ulterior ways of direct or indirect exploitation: all this played (and some are still playing) a *decisive* role in the growth of capitalism, of the West, whose roots could not have been more cruel. *Time,* a magazine not given to radicalism, published in the fall of 1992 a special issue titled *Beyond the Year 2000: What to Expect in the New Millennium.*[1] One can there read: "The triumph of the West was in many ways a bloody shame — a story of atrocity and rapine, of arrogance, greed and ecological despoliation, of hubristic contempt for other cultures and intolerance of non-Christian faiths." Only one point should be altered in these eloquent lines: the use of the past tense. Such "a bloody shame" is not only *what was:* it is also *what is* the West's history, as it was suffered yesterday, *and is being suffered today,* by the rest of the planet.

Second, that in spite of the evidence that the first Europeans to settle in America were Iberian and that the Iberian countries greatly contributed to the capitalist development of *other* European countries, they themselves, for well-known reasons, as for example the deplorable expulsion of the Jews from Spain also five hundred years ago, did not develop likewise, and, in spite of being geographically the most Western countries of the European continent, they were left on the periphery of the "West," as paleo-Western countries. A fortiori this was going to be the case of various countries of central and eastern Europe.

Outside Europe, really great capitalist development would be known only by a few former British colonies, whose metropolis took the place of the Netherlands as the capitalist country par excellence, until the beginnings of this century. These few colonies (not all of them, certainly not those in Asia, Africa, or the Caribbean) are those in which the British practically wiped out the aborigines, reproduced and magnified the metropolis structures (I am of course referring to countries like the United States, Canada, and Australia — transplanted peoples, Darcy Ribeiro would call them). Nevertheless, there is one great exception: Japan, which has managed, for diverse reasons, as Paul A. Baran has shown, to establish its own original and powerful capitalism, thus becoming the only non-"white" country (putting aside the too recent and as yet undefined cases of Asia's "little tigers" or "little dragons") where such a feat has occurred. In this fashion, while the two geographically most Western continental European countries (Spain and Portugal) are not wholly "Western" but paleo-Western, a so-called Far East country (Japan) is not only "Western" but, with its computerized kimono, one of the seven Big Brothers of developed capitalism, whose spokesmen meet from time to time to talk about the best way to share the world's cake; and it is even, with the United States and Germany, one of the three countries that form the West's very core. Need I add that Eurocentric expressions like "Far East," "Middle East," "Near East," or *là bas* mean nothing, except that the one who uses these words is not there?

And if in two former British colonies on American soil a vigorous capitalism akin to that of their mother country flourished, it is not strange that in Ibero-America, following the impoverished paths of Spain and Portugal, *no* vigorous capitalism developed, but only a secondhand, puny, peripheral capitalism. It has been impossible to know what a developed capitalism would be like in our countries for the simple reason that it has not existed, does not exist, and will never exist *even in one country* in our America, if present conditions do not change. Two centuries after the initiation of our wars of independence (in 1791 in French St. Domingue, which became Haiti), we have, as a whole, a so-called political independence, memories of authentic heroes, shining constitutions, anthems, flags, shields, presidents, parliaments, statues of the fathers of the country and of horse thieves (sometimes they are one and the same), armies, and other similar attributes. But we do not have a Latin American Japan, however modest, that could have escaped the great powers in order to create a real capitalism.

I must now make an apparent but necessary digression. It is clear that we must reject the term "discovery" for what happened in 1492, because at the time there were in these lands tens of millions of human beings and several great cultures. As a matter of fact, it seems that the most populous city at the time was not in Europe but in what was going to be known as America: Tenochtitlán, now called Mexico City, again the most populous city on the planet. (The author of these lines first arrived in the United States forty-five years ago. Have you ever heard that this huge country was discovered by me in 1947?) But in order to be coherent, it is absolutely necessary to proceed in a similar way with the terminological/conceptual *system* to which that word "discovery" belongs; that is to say, we have to object to Prospero's ideology. Even more so today, when the death of ideologies is proclaimed, among many other deaths, by those who take for granted that Western ideology is totally triumphant, an ideological oversaturation often called by the astonishing name of "deideologization."

As I have neither the time nor the space to dwell upon the many falsehoods Prospero has brought forth, I will only mention some delusions. To begin, I might mention that the Western world is not Western, the Discovery was no discovery, and the so-called American Indians are not Indians; these are only hors d'oeuvres, for, likewise, the presumed ancestor par excellence of the Western world, "classical" Greece, is in fact Afro-Asiatic (see Martin Bernal, Samir Amin). Christianity, the Western world's proclaimed (and battered) religion, was, as is well known, an Oriental sect. Not only did the famous horrors of the year 1000 never happen (see Edmond Pognon, Georges Duby), but, had they happened, they would have affected only a handful of Europeans (the world population was then more or less the present population of the United States), for the time divisions of the epoch's humanity differed greatly. The term "race" was forged by the West in the sixteenth century (see Fernando Ortiz, Baran, Paul M. Sweezy, Raymond Williams) when, not existing yet in any language, it was borrowed — so it has been said — from zoological terminology. If this were so, no further comment is necessary. This brand new word, "race," became very important, for, although human beings have always been aware of their notorious and irrelevant somatic differences (think of the beautiful Song of Solomon, dedicated to a black woman), it was only after 1492, in trying to justify the West's plundering of the world, that it was proclaimed that such differences implied the set signifiers of no less set signifieds, and that these last were positive for those of "white" skin (more realistically, Shaw and Chesterton used words like "light brown" or "rosy," because who the hell has ever seen a phantomlike white human being?) and negative for the rest. The term "civilization," created in mid–eighteenth-century Europe, as Lucien Febvre and Émile Benveniste have shown, implies that the real human being lives in the city, while the practically nonhuman — the savage — lives in the jungle. This so-called civilization was located in the Western world at the time and was said to be the *only* really human way of life: the planet's other communities, many of which had great cultures before the West's arrival and their subsequent mutilation or destruction, were pushed to the presumed condition of savages or barbarians. As for colonization being the way to civilization (the preposterous *white man's burden* mocked at by Basil Davidson in his book *The Black Man's Burden*),[2] the notion is so absurd that it is not even worth refuting.

Let us consider some peculiar syntagmas invented by technicians of the emerging United Nations (see J. L. Zimmerman) to rebaptize Caliban's lands euphemistically. After disdainfully calling us "barbarians" and "colored peoples," and not wanting to use the proper denomination of colonies, semicolonies, or neocolonies (the epoch encouraged at least verbal equalities), more neutral and even hopeful denominations were proposed: first, "economically underdeveloped zones"; later, "underdeveloped countries" or even "developing" ones. These are, like in previous examples, terms of relation (civilization/barbarism, white people/colored people, colonizing countries/ colonized countries), which make it necessary to know their opposite pole. And it was then assured that the opposite was "developed countries." The relation would thus be "developed" countries/"underdeveloped" or "developing" ones. And the inference is that if the latter behaved well, learned their lessons, and so on, they could become like the former, the big ones, the adults. This candid or malicious (according to the user) aberration was named *desarrollismo* (developmentalism). As has recently been seen, good behavior means, for example, obedience to the drastic solutions, the crash policy of the International Monetary Fund, which under the lethal banner of the so-called neoliberalism is again devastating Caliban's lands.

However, everything becomes clear if we realize that the opposite pole of "underdeveloped" or "developing" is *not* "developed" but "underdeveloping"; with this only real polarization, the truth becomes evident. The fact is not that some countries have sturdily developed while, in an independent and parallel way, others have lagged behind because their peoples were (are) young or old, lazy, clumsy, vicious, or the like (a host of such empty words have been used). What has actually happened is that a few countries, in a vampire-like way, grew *at the cost of* many others, that the underdeveloping countries underdeveloped the others. On this question, Walter Rodney's *How Europe Underdeveloped Africa* is an already classic reference.[3]

And here we come again to 1492, for the division between a small, growingly rich group of underdeveloping countries and a huge, growingly poor group of countries, underdeveloped by the former, was born precisely after that date, though this was only established, we hope temporarily, during the nineteenth century, when the planet was divided between countries that were "winners" and those that were "losers," to use Eric Hobsbawm's and Paul Kennedy's terms. The first, of course, are those where an authentic capitalism was developed; and the second, the ones who contributed to *that* development at the cost of their own, making their weak, peripheral capitalism — as I have pointed out — their only possible one. Let us recall but two areas in which that already mentioned vampire-like relationship is still alive: the unequal terms of trade and the external debt.

Subsequent denominations, like the also metaphorical division proposed in 1952 by Alfred Sauvy of First, Second, and Third Worlds, or the later division between countries of the North and of the South, do not add greatly to the issue, though, for practical reasons (for instance, the so-called Second World has vanished), the latter tends to become predominant. In any case, it should be remembered that when we speak of countries of the North (the underdeveloping ones) and countries of the South (the ones they underdevelop), North/South, like, until recently, West/East (in this case with a strong political connotation), are denominations dealing with extra-geographical, socioeconomic realities. Because of this, what was yesterday called West is today increasingly called North.

Now, five hundred years after 1492, what else can Caliban say about our century, about our own days? If the thesis according to which the 1980s was a lost decade for Latin America and the Caribbean is already commonly accepted, should we not ask if, in a similar way, the already dying twentieth century will be seen as a lost century? Let us first recall the most incomparably devastating and bloody war of all time, which started in 1914 and certainly cannot be considered as ended. We all know the rather foolish joke about the character who says: "Good-bye, dear, I'm off to the One Hundred Year War." But a similar foolishness is not usually felt when one looks at the world conflagration that broke out in 1914. To begin with, it is obvious that the war that took place between 1914 and 1918 was not then known as the *First* World War: it was simply called the World War or the Great War. Only in 1939, when a new war period began, was the former one named *First,* since there was then a *Second* one. Besides, regarding them as two different wars, and not as two different periods of the same war, is only another pretension of our mediocre and boastful era, fiddled by a present-day jargon that tries to erase or arrange the past and usurp the place of the future, thus self-naming itself. Moreover, not only the Middle Ages, as is evident, but also the Renaissance did not use the names by which they would later be known. More sensibly, Jean Cocteau explained that the stars that form the Big Dipper ignore that the Earth sees them in that shape. The so-called (a posteriori, of course) One Hundred Year War (which, by the way, lasted even longer) was not an uninterrupted secular war but a series of periods historians would so later name, without ignoring the differences between those periods, but all the while still underlining their similarities. In an equivalent way, the lightly named First and Second World Wars were more similar than different, and the common qualifying adjective, *World,* reveals a unique resemblance. Besides, the reason that led to the war in 1914, a new allotment of an already allotted world among a few hegemonic powers, is still very much alive. I shall come back to this.

Out of the hell-on-earth created by the war begun in 1914, and with the intention, among others, of cutting it down at its roots, the most ambitious and long-lasting socialist experiment ever undertaken was initiated in 1917 in the archaic Russian Empire (the first ten days of which had in Harvard's John Reed an incomparable chronicler). This experiment that shook the world awakened hope in many, and, although it knew great difficulties, and numerous crimes and aberrations were committed in its name, it achieved, at a truly terrible price, the modernization of a backward country that would decisively contribute to the defeat of Nazi fascism and later to an ample process of decolonization. The recent fall of the Soviet regime implied the fall of regimes it imposed (according to the 1945 Yalta agreements) in European countries near the former Soviet Union. That experiment's deformations after the isolation imposed upon it and Lenin's premature death; the violent quarrels between his possible successors; the bloody tyranny of the triumphant Stalin; the spectacular failure of the experiment and the chaotic efforts that have followed it for the reestablishment of capitalism, with clumsy methods that worried John Kenneth Galbraith, and whose consequences are in the newspapers — all these could not but rudely strike the hardest blow known to socialist hopes.

Since 1945, the West/East polarity, which strongly came to life with its new meaning after the 1917 Russian Revolution (see Spengler's *The Decline of the West*)[4] and was strengthened with the surging of fascism and Nazism as capitalism's violent reactions to that revolution and its possible world consequences, posed the threat of a different war that could have put humanity to an end. However, the East's evaporation has not meant an entry into the dreamed-of *pax perpetua* but rather, as has already been said, the return to a stage similar to that which preceded 1914. Caliban does not at all wish to be apocalyptic, and he trusts he is totally in the wrong, but since the United States is pretty worried about things like the presence on its soil of so many Sony, Mitsubishi, Toyota, or Datsun products, and even more by Japanese capital buying up its enterprises, will this great country come to feel a shiver comparable to that felt by poor Spanish America at the beginning of this century, when our poet Rubén Darío wrote his verse "¿Tantos millones de hombres hablaremos inglés?" (Are so many millions of us to speak English?). Things have so changed that this line, which was a cry of alarm from Spanish Americans, seems today to have become a Berlitz (or any similar) School of Languages advertisement. But at the beginning of the next century, will a poet (hopefully not a post-postmodern one) of the United States write something like, "Are so many millions of us to speak Japanese?" My God, may the possible terrible consequences of such a shiver, and other similar ones, be spared to our grandchildren. In any case, when Caliban learned of the existence of books like Jeffrey E. Garten's *America, Japan, Germany, and the Struggle for Supremacy* and Lester Thurow's *Head to Head: The Coming Economic Battle among Japan, Europe, and America,* we can be sure that he was not amused.[5]

Above I mentioned the extended decolonization that followed the second period of the World War; it must be added now that this decolonization came to be another of this century's fiascoes. For many countries, in this process, were separated from their old metropolis, only to be recolonized, under the guise of neocolonialism, mainly by the great winner, at a very low cost, of that war period. Consequently, to speak of our neocolonial age as a postcolonial one, mistaking superficial political features for profound and decisive socioeconomic structures and their consequences, may be the acceptance, perhaps involuntarily, of another of Prospero's resonant falsehoods.

We have also witnessed the initial wars after the end of the so-called Cold War: hot wars that bode no good for a future where the very disagreeable and dangerous equilibrium of terror has been followed by the much more disagreeable and danger-ous lack of equilibrium of sheer arrogance and preponderance. Proof of this was the 1989 Panama invasion, incredibly presented as the hunting down of a man in order to bring him to trial outside his own country, in a new manifestation of imperialism, the judicial one, denounced by such an authority in the matter as Ramsey Clark.

And if that invasion was part of a long list of twentieth-century aggressions charac-teristic of the big stick or the gunboat policies in our American Mediterranean, then the 1991 Gulf War seems to be the first of a new type. Unleashed by the unaccept-able Iraqi invasion of Kuwait — similar to the Panama invasion that enjoyed total impunity — the Gulf War, approved by the UN ("les nations dites unies," de Gaulle once said), counted with a very ample coalition whose nature was denounced by Noam Chomsky, that admirable Bartolomé de las Casas of his own empire. In con-trast, if it is not true, as Jean Baudrillard (in Jean Anouilh's wake) has suggested, that such a war did not exist, then it certainly was a battleless one, in which coalition forces, at a prudent distance, proceeded to destroy the enemy forces and, above all, to methodically massacre the civilian population until surrender was obtained (see Edward W. Said).

Among the peculiar hot wars that have followed the Cold War, I must also mention the interethnic battles that are taking place in shattered European states like the for-mer Soviet Union and Yugoslavia. Those battles are not only dreadful in themselves but may have disastrous world consequences, especially now that the Sarajevo ghost has come to the forefront.

There are other facts that are no less desolating. Today, five hundred years after 1492, throughout the impoverished world, in a brief time span, a number of chil-dren equivalent to the number of the human beings killed in 1945 at Hiroshima and Nagasaki die of hunger or curable diseases; this goes on while millions of other homeless children wander about and survive, through thieving or prostitu-tion, in countries where there often are enterprises dedicated to buying them in order to sell their body organs or exterminate them as if they were rats. For some time now, epidemics thought of as medieval have been making a comeback and are spreading. Furthermore, not only have innumerable animal species already been extinguished by the human animal (especially in its Western or Northern variety), but fishless oceans and rivers, birdless skies, "silent springs" (see Rachel Carson), galloping deserts, and polluted atmospheres are all growing and provoking sur-roundings where even the fairly human animal that we are finds survival difficult. "Green" movements have been rightly fighting against all this, and the situation was *almost* unanimously understood at the UN's ECO '92 in Rio de Janeiro.

In such a general scene, the worst situation is of course that of Caliban's realm, that of those who are in the South. As I write this essay, they constitute more than two-thirds of the human beings now living; by the beginning of the twentieth-first century (which is to say, tomorrow), they will be three-fourths of the world, and by the middle of that century, nine-tenths. Taking into account the numerous poor in the North (who often come from the South), and of course not the rather thin layer of those who are wealthy in the South, frequently because they are the accomplices of the North and feel part of it and not of their own people, in the world today two out of three persons are poor, very poor, or miserable; if things do not change, in less than ten years, the proportion will be three out of four; in sixty years — my grandson's age then — nine out of ten, the great majority of them in the South. The proportion grows geometrically in a frightening way, and it explains why the poor from the South, trying to raise their standard of living and often as their only way of survival, are moving to the North. As this process develops overwhelmingly and because it is already raising enormous problems, the North is building barriers to stop new entries and, at times, when they have already occurred, is organizing paramilitary forces for the extermination of the undesired people from the South.

In Spain, a beloved country we would like to believe is nonracist (the gypsies there would like to believe it even more), a few years ago the word *sudaca* was derogatorily created in reference to Spanish Americans. The word may perhaps be proudly revindicated by those who are so called (I am immediately going to do so, thinking of the South as a whole) and may even become international, like other similar terms: the Italian "ghetto," the French "chauvinism," the Russian "pogrom," the English "lynching." After all, the North's chauvinists project or already carry out pogroms in order to lynch the *sudacas,* when they have not managed to keep them outside the walls of the North's citadels. This last goal is not an easy one, for waves of *sudacas* push forward like burning tides of lava. And those waves reveal the stigma that the North, in order to develop itself, provoked — and still provokes — in those whose countries it underdeveloped and is underdeveloping right now. It is often the case with famished creatures who — speaking languages frequently unknown in the North, most of them illiterate or with poor learning, with no training for the complex instruments that are part of the North's appealing life, possessing beliefs and habits that seem barbarian to the North — have little hygiene, exhibit promiscuous behavior (they are demographically exploding all the time), and carry illnesses already eliminated in the North, whose inhabitants therefore lack the proper antibodies, in a way similar to what happened to this hemisphere's original inhabitants when the European conquerors arrived.

And so, now that the North finally considers itself the winner all along the line, and it even has lackeys (bad readers of Hegel and even worse ones of reality) who whisper in its ear that what Stephen Dedalus called the nightmare of history has come to an end, its citadels' walls are surrounded by noisy, multicolored, earthy beings who come from another nightmare: from the South, not from the past.

If the North keeps its threats and, instead of plundering the growing South even more, decides to dispense with it, substituting its fabricated materials for the raw materials of the South, or augmenting its aggressive protectionism, then sickness, hunger, ignorance, despondency, and fanaticism will grow in the South, and its people's tidal waves will grow immensely in an inevitable, unstoppable, and somber march toward the aseptic North. Considering this, if the North decides to depopulate the South and hurls deadly atomic, chemical, or bacteriological weapons at it, could it avoid the lethal clouds they would provoke from reaching the bacterialess, birdless, and pitiless skies of the North, so proud of its ferocious capitalism?

When we know all this, even if we cowardly pretend to ignore or forget it, is it not urgent that the descendants of the necessary mating of Caliban and Miranda, that the people of clear vision and goodwill, who, in spite of everything, are plentiful in the South as well as in the North, compel, with inventiveness, valor, and energy, the ending of prejudice, hatred, sectarianism, greed, and general foolishness? Is it not necessary that we struggle together, all of us, in order to stop a race whose end is evident and all too close? Because humanity is also an ecosystem, neither the South nor the North can save itself separately. Either they manage to arrive at a post-Western society, authentically planetary, brotherly and sisterly, or human beings, for whom society is consubstantial, will have proved to be, to Teilhard de Chardin's horror, a vain, closed road, much worse than the dinosaurs, because they (we) were given infinitely more numerous and richer forces and virtualities.

Five hundred years after the discovery that was no such thing, but that surely was the beginning of the indispensable encounter of all human beings, let us say, from this brave(?) New World we share from pole to pole, from this world whose original inhabitants saw, in 1492, the arrival of the three caravels — along with the cross on which the Son of Man died once and a million times and keeps on dying and the crosslike sword — that our only chance, our only choice, is to culminate (and to compel forgiveness for) that terrible beginning with a real encounter, a real discovery, similar to what the Greeks named *anagnorisis*. This will be the human being's discovery of him/herself, the discovery of the total human being, man, woman, pansexual, yellow, black, redskin, paleface, *mestizo,* producer (creator) rather than consumer, inhabitant of humanity, the only real mother country ("Patria es humanidad," Martí said, restating a Stoic idea), without East or West, North or South, for its center will certainly also be its periphery. Religions, philosophies, arts, dreams, utopias, and deliriums, have so announced. It will be the end of prehistory and the beginning of the almost virginal history of the soul. If not, it will certainly be the premature end of us human beings, who would have precipitated ahead of time the end of the tiny fragment of cosmic existence that was allotted us. But such precipitation is not inevitable. Einstein, Sagan, and Hawking have made us all (even us laymen) familiar with the imagination of cosmos; Darwin, von Uexküll, and Gould with the imagination of life; Freud, the surrealists, and Jameson with the imagination of the unconscious; and Marx openly postulated that History has more imagination than we do. We could perhaps summarize this idea with Einstein's statement: "Imagination is more important than knowledge."

In face of the apparently insurmountable challenges of social reality, that in a previous stage drove figures like Romain Rolland and Antonio Gramsci to speak about the skepticism of intelligence, to which they opposed the optimism of willpower, let us also oppose to it the confidence in imagination, that essentially poetic device. And so we could fearlessly prepare to enter the menaced house of the future, although it would not yet be Walter Pater's House Beautiful; we must prepare to enter that house made of time and hope, to whose edification were dedicated the lives and deaths of human beings like Ernesto Che Guevara, the most Calibanesque of the Ariels I have ever personally met and loved. If we struggle together with courage, intelligence, passion, and compassion to deserve it, in such a house, to gloss Heraclitus the Obscure and Saint Teresa the illuminated, the gods will also dwell.

NOTES

Invited by New York University to talk on the present subject, in a panel titled "Encounter with the Other" (which I did on October 1, 1992, with Kamau Brathwaite and Serge Gruzinski), I later received invitations from other U.S. universities. In several of them (Iowa, Illinois at Champaign-Urbana, California at Berkeley, Stanford, New York at Purchase), I offered more ample versions of the original text. I used some passages in other essays, also written in 1992, and made public in Buenos Aires, Xalapa, Veracruz, Madrid, Florence, Havana, and Tokyo. I am grateful to the generous friends who invited me and to the institutions that gave me the opportunity to communicate my preoccupations and hopes. I am particularly grateful to Adelaida de Juan (with whom I shared my U.S. trip, as I have shared my life during more than forty years) for her many keen suggestions and her essential aid in putting these pages in tolerable English. An augmented version of the text, with numerous footnotes and returned to Spanish, appeared in the Stanford University journal *Nuevo texto crítico*, 11 (first semester 1993).

1. *Beyond the Year 2000: What to Expect in the New Millennium,* special edition of *Time* (fall 1992).
2. Basil Davidson, *The Black Man's Burden* (New York: Random House, 1992).
3. Walter Rodney, *How Europe Underdeveloped Africa* (Washington, D.C.: Howard University Press, 1982).
4. Oswald Spengler, *The Decline of the West* (New York: Random House, 1945).
5. Jeffrey E. Garten, *America, Japan, Germany, and the Struggle for Supremacy* (New York: Morrow, 1992); and Lester Thurow, *Head to Head: The Coming Economic Battle among Japan, Europe, and America* (New York: Morrow, 1992).

Chapter 9
The Local and the Global: Globalization and Ethnicity
Stuart Hall

The debate about globalization and its consequences has been going on now in a variety of different fields of intellectual work for some time. What I am going to try to do here is to map some of the shifting configurations of this question, of the local and the global, particularly in relation to culture and in relation to cultural politics. I am going to try to discover what is emerging and how different subject-positions are being transformed or produced in the course of the unfolding of the new dialectics of global culture. Later in this essay I shall address the question of new and old identities and the question of ethnicity.

I am going to look at this from what might be thought of as a very privileged corner of the process, though a declining one — that is, from the United Kingdom, and particularly, England. Certainly from the perspective of any historical account of English culture, globalization is far from a new process. Indeed, it is almost impossible to think about the formation of English society, or of the United Kingdom and all the things that give it a kind of privileged place in the historical narratives of the world, outside of the processes that we identify with globalization.

So when we are talking about globalization in the present context, we are talking about some of the new forms, some of the new rhythms, some of the new impetuses in the globalizing process. For the moment, I do not want to define it more closely than that, but I do want to suggest that it is located within a much longer history; we suffer increasingly from a process of historical amnesia in which we think that just because we are thinking about an idea, it has only just started.

As an entity and national culture, the United Kingdom rose with, and is declining with, one of the eras, or epochs, of globalization: that era when the formation of the world market was dominated by the economies and cultures of powerful nation-states. It is that relationship between the formation and transformation of the world market and its domination by the economies of powerful nation-states that constituted the era within which English culture took its existing shape. Imperialism was the system by which the world was engulfed in and by this framework, and the world was further engulfed through the intensification of world rivalries between imperial formations. In this period, one sees the construction of a distinct cultural identity that I want to call the identity of Englishness. Certain formative conditions must exist if a national culture like this is to aspire to and then acquire a world historical identity of this sort; the conditions have a great deal to do with a nation's position as a leading commercial world power, with its position of leadership in a highly international and industrializing world economy, and with the fact that this society and its centers have long been placed at the core of a web of global commitments.

But it is not my purpose to sketch that out. I intend, rather, to try to answer this question: What is the nature of cultural identity that belongs with that particular historical moment? And I have to say that, in fact, it has been defined as a strongly centered, highly exclusive, and exclusivist form of cultural identity. Exactly when the transformation to Englishness took place is quite a long story. But one can see a certain point at which the particular forms of English identity feel that they can command, within their own discourses, the discourses of almost everybody else: not quite everybody, but almost everyone else at a certain moment in history.

Certainly, the colonized other was constituted within the regimes of representation of such a metropolitan center. Those colonized persons were placed in their otherness, in their marginality, by the nature of the "English eye," the all-encompassing "English eye." The "English eye" sees everything else but is not so good at recognizing that it is itself actually looking at something. It becomes coterminous with sight itself. It is, of course, a structured representation nevertheless and it is a cultural representation that is always binary. That is to say, English identity is strongly centered; knowing where it is, what it is, it places everything else. And the thing that is extraordinary about English identity is that it didn't only place the colonized other — it placed *everybody* else.

To be English is to know yourself in relation to the French, to the hot-blooded Mediterraneans, and to the passionate, traumatized Russian soul. You know that you are what everybody else on the globe is not. Identity is always, in that sense, a structured representation that achieves its positive only through the narrow eye of the negative. It has to go through the eye of the needle of the other before it can construct itself. It produces a very Manichaean set of opposites. When I speak about this way of being in the world, being English in the world, with a capital "E" as it were, it is not only grounded in a whole history, a whole set of histories, a whole set of economic relations, a whole set of cultural discourses, but is also profoundly grounded in certain forms of sexual identity. In the heyday of the empire, the notion of the liberties of a true-born English *woman* was unthinkable. A freeborn English person was clearly a freeborn English *man*. And the notion of fully buttoned-up, stiff-upper-lip, corseted English masculinity is one of the means by which this particular cultural identity was very firmly stitched into place. This kind of Englishness belongs to a certain historical moment in the unfolding of global processes. It is, in itself, a kind of ethnicity.

It has not been polite until recently to call it this. One of the things that is happening in England is a discussion, which is just beginning, meant to try to convince the English that they are, after all, just another ethnic group — a very interesting ethnic group, just hovering off the edge of Europe, with their own language, their own peculiar customs, their rituals, their myths. Like any other native peoples, they have something that can be said in their favor, and of their long history. But English ethnicity — in the sense that it views itself as encompassing everything within its range — is, after all, a very specific and peculiar form of ethnic identity. It is located in a place, in a specific history. It could not speak except out of a place, out of those histories. It is located in relation to a whole set of notions about territory, about where is home and where is overseas, what is close to us and what is far away. It is mapped out in all the terms in which we can understand what ethnicity is. For the English, it is, unfortunately, for a time, the ethnicity that places all the other ethnicities; in short, it is an ethnicity defined in its own terms.

However, if one looks carefully and deeply at English identity, one sees what one always sees when one examines or opens up an ethnicity. It represents itself as perfectly natural: born an Englishman, always will be, condensed, homogenous, unitary. What is the point of an identity if it isn't one thing? That is why we keep hoping that identities will come our way: because the rest of the world is so confusing; everything else is turning, but identities ought to be some stable points of reference that were like that in the past, are now and ever shall be, still points in a turning world.

But Englishness never was and never could be that still, unitary point. It was not that in relation to those societies with which it was deeply connected, both as a commercial and global political power overseas. And one of the best-kept secrets of the world is that it was not that in relation to its own territory either. It was only by dint of excluding or absorbing all the differences that constituted Englishness, the multitude of different regions, peoples, classes, and genders that composed the people gathered together in the Act of Union, that Englishness could stand for everybody in the British Isles. It was always negotiated against difference. It always had to absorb all the differences of class, of region, of gender, in order to present itself as a homogenous entity. And that is something that we are only now beginning to see the true nature of, when we are beginning to come to the end of it. Because with the processes of globalization, that form of relationship between a national-cultural identity and a nation-state is now beginning, at any rate in Britain, to disappear. And one suspects that it is not only there that it is beginning to disappear. That notion of a national formation, of a national economy, that could be represented through a national-cultural identity is under considerable pressure. It is important here for me to very briefly elucidate what is happening that makes that formation an untenable configuration to keep in place for very much longer.

To begin, in the British case, the untenable nature of the configuration results from a long process of economic decline. From being the leading economic power in the world, at the pinnacle of commercial and industrial development, the first industrializing nation, Britain has become simply one among other, better, stronger, competing, new industrializing nations. It is certainly no longer at the forefront, or at the cutting edge, of industrial and economic development.

The trend toward the greater internationalization of the economy, rooted in the multinational firm, built on the foundations of Fordist models of mass production, and mass consumption long outran some of the most important leading instances of this in the British economy. From the position of being in the forefront, Britain has increasingly fallen behind as the new regimes of accumulation, production, and consumption have created new leading nations in the global economy.

More recently, the capitalist crisis of the 1970s has accelerated the opening up of new global markets, both commodity markets and financial markets, to which Britain has been required to harness itself if it were not to be left behind in the race. In the context of deindustrialization, Britain is trying to ground itself somewhere close to the leading edge of the new technologies that have linked production and markets in a new surge of international global capital. The deregulation of the City is simply one sign of the movement of the British economy and the British culture to enter the new epoch of financial capital. And new multinational production, the new international division of labor, not only links backward sections of the Third World to so-called advanced sections of the First World but increasingly tries to reconstitute the backward sectors *within* the First World: as evidenced by the processes of contracting out, of franchising, which are beginning to create small, dependent, local economies that are linked into multinational production. All of these have broken up the economic, political, and social terrain on which those earlier notions of Englishness prospered.

Those are things that are clearly evident. They are the constituent elements of globalization. I want to add some other things to them because I think we tend to think about globalization in too unitary a way. In a moment it will become clear why I want to insist on that point.

The enormous, continuing migrations of labor in the postwar world is another factor contributing to the breakup of the older, unitary formation. There is a tremendous paradox here that I cannot help relishing: the very moment Britain finally convinced itself it had to decolonize, that it had to get rid of the colonies, the colonized began flooding into England. As they hauled down the flag, the former colonized peoples got on the banana boat and sailed right into London. That is a powerful paradox because the British had ruled the world for three hundred years, and when they had made up their minds to climb out of that role, at least the others ought to have stayed out there in the rim, behaved themselves, gone somewhere else, or found some other client state. No, they had always said that this was really home, that the streets were paved with gold, and, bloody hell, the people from the margins decided to check out whether that was so or not. I am the product of that. I came right in. Someone said, "Why don't you live in Milton Keynes, where you work?" I said no: I wanted to live in London. If you come from the sticks, the colonial sticks, you want to live on Eros Statue in Piccadilly Circus. You don't want to go and live in someone else's metropolitan sticks. You want to go right to the center of the hub of the world. You might as well. You have been hearing about that ever since you were one month old. When I first got to England in 1951, I looked out and there were Wordsworth's daffodils. Of course, what else would you expect to find? That's what I knew about. That is what trees and flowers meant. I didn't know the names of the flowers I'd just left behind in Jamaica. One has also to remember that Englishness has been decentered not only by the great dispersal of capital to Washington, Wall Street, and Tokyo, but also by this enormous influx that is part of the cultural consequences of the labor migrations, the migrations of peoples, which go on at an accelerated pace in the modern world.

Another aspect of globalization comes from a quite different direction, from increasing international interdependence. This can be looked at in two quite different ways.

First, there is the growth of monetary and regional arrangements that link Britain into NATO, the Common Market, and similar organizations. There is the growth of these regional, supranational organizations and connections that simply make it impossible to conceive of what is going on in English society as if it only had an internal dynamic. And this is a very profound shift, a shift in the conceptions of sovereignty and of the nation-state. It is a shift in the conception of what the English government can do, what is in its control, what transformations it could bring about by its own efforts. These things increasingly are seen to be interdependent with the economies, cultures, and polities of other societies.

Second, there is the enormous impact of global ecological interdependence. When the ill winds of Chernobyl came our way, they did not pause at the frontier, produce their passports, and say, "Can I rain on your territory now?" They just flowed on in and rained on Wales and on places that never had known where Chernobyl was. Recently, we have been enjoying some of the pleasures and anticipating some of the disasters of global warming. The sources and consequences are miles away. We could begin to do something about it only on the basis of a form of ecological consciousness that has to have, as its subject, a base larger than the freeborn Englishman. The freeborn Englishman, on his own, can do very little about the destruction of the rain forest in Brazil. And he hardly knows how to spell ozone.

So something is escaping from this older unit that was the linchpin of globalization of an earlier phase; it is beginning to be eroded. We will come to look back at this era in terms of the importance of the erosion of the nation-state and the national identities that are associated with it.

The erosion of the nation-state, national economies, and national-cultural identities is a very complex and dangerous moment. Entities of power are dangerous when they are ascending and when they are declining, and it is a moot point whether they are more dangerous in the second or the first moment. The first moment, they gobble up everybody, and in the second moment, they take everybody down with them. So when I refer to the decline or erosion of the nation-state, I do not mean that the nation-state is bowing off the stage of history. "I'm sorry, I was here for so long. I apologize for all the things that I did to you — nationalism, jingoism, ferocious warfare, racism. I apologize for all that. Can I go now?" It is not backing off like that. Rather, it goes into an even deeper trough of defensive exclusivism.

Consequently, at the very moment when the so-called material basis of the old English identity was disappearing over the horizon of the West and the East, Thatcherism brought Englishness into a more firm definition, a narrower but firmer definition than it ever had before. Now we are prepared to go to anywhere to defend it: to the South Seas, to the South Atlantic. If we cannot defend it in reality, we will defend it in mime. What else can you call the Falklands episode? Living the past entirely through myth. Reliving the age of the dictators, not just as farce but as myth. Reliving the whole of that past through myth, a very defensive organization. We have never been so close to an embattled defensiveness of a narrow, national definition of Englishness, of cultural identity. And Thatcherism was grounded in that. When Thatcherism spoke, it frequently asked the question, Are you one of us? And the response from most quarters was no. The number of people who are not one of us would fill a book. Hardly anybody is one of us any longer. The people of Northern Ireland are not one of us because they are bogged down in sectarian warfare.

The Scots are not one of us because they did not vote for us. The Northeast and the Northwest are not one of us because they are manufacturing areas and are declining, and they have not jumped on to the enterprise culture; they are not on the bandwagon to the South. No blacks are, of course, truly English, not quite. There may be one or two who are "honorary," but they cannot really be English. Women can be English only in their traditional roles because if they get outside their traditional roles, they are clearly beginning to edge to the margins.

The question, Are you one of us? is still asked in the expectation that it might be answered with the same large confidence with which the English have always occupied their own identities. But the identity cannot be occupied in that way any longer. It is produced with enormous effort. Huge ideological work has to go on every day to produce this mouse that people can recognize as the English. You have to look at everything in order to produce it. You have to look at the curriculum, at the Englishness of English art, at what is truly English poetry, and you have to rescue that from all the other things that are not English. Everywhere, the question of Englishness is in contention.

The important point here is that when nation-states begin to decline in the era of globalization, they regress to a very defensive and highly dangerous form of national identity that is driven by a very aggressive form of racism.

Thus far I have been concentrating on questions of ethnicity and identity in an older form of globalization. What Thatcherism and other European societies are trying to come to terms with now is how to enter new forms of globalization.

The new forms of globalization are rather different from the ones I have just described. One of the things that happens when the nation-state begins to weaken, becoming less convincing and less powerful, is that the response seems to go in two ways simultaneously. It goes above the nation-state, and it goes below it. It goes global and local in the same moment. Global and local are the two faces of the same movement from one epoch of globalization, the one that has been dominated by the nation-state, the national economies, the national-cultural identities, to something new.

What is this new kind of globalization? The new kind of globalization is not English; it is American. In cultural terms, the new kind of globalization has to do with a new form of global mass culture, very different from that associated with English identity and the cultural identities associated with the nation-state in an earlier phase. Global mass culture is dominated by the modern means of cultural production, dominated by the image that crosses and recrosses linguistic frontiers much more rapidly and more easily and that speaks across languages in a much more immediate way. It is dominated by all the ways in which the visual and graphic arts have entered directly into the reconstitution of popular life, of entertainment, and of leisure. It is dominated by television, by film, and by the image, imagery, and styles of mass advertising. Its epitome is all those forms of mass communication that satellite television is the prime example of. Not because it is the only example but because one could not understand satellite television without understanding its grounding in a particular advanced national economy and culture, and yet its whole purpose is precisely that it cannot be limited any longer by national boundaries.

We have just, in Britain, opened up a satellite television link called Sky Channel, owned by Rupert Murdoch. It sits just above the English Channel. It speaks across to all the European societies at once, and as it went up all the older models of communication in our society were being dismantled. The notion of the British Broadcasting Corporation, of a public-service interest, was rendered anachronistic in a moment.

All this harbored a contradiction: just as Thatcherism sent the "Sky Channel" satellite aloft, it decided it needed to keep a close watch on what it broadcasts. Thus it created the Broadcasting Standards Committee to make sure that the satellite does not immediately communicate soft pornography to all of us after eleven o'clock, when the children are in bed.

So this is not an uncontradictory phenomenon. One side of Thatcherism, the respectable, traditional side, watches the free-market side. This is the bifurcated world that we live in, and this kind of technology — contradictions and all — is what is likely to carry the new international global mass culture back into the old nation-states, the national cultures of European societies; it is very much at the leading edge of the transmitters of the image. And as a consequence of the explosion of these new forms of cultural communication and cultural representation, there has opened up a new field of visual representation itself.

It is this field that I am calling global mass culture. Global mass culture has a variety of different characteristics, but I would identify two. First, it remains centered in the West. That is to say, Western technology, the concentration of capital, the concentration of techniques, the concentration of advanced labor in the Western societies, and the stories and the imagery of Western societies: these remain the driving powerhouse of this global mass culture. In that sense, it is centered in the West, and it always speaks English. However, this particular form does not speak the Queen's English any longer. It speaks English as an international language, which is quite a different thing. It speaks a variety of broken forms of English: English as it has been invaded, and as it has hegemonized a variety of other languages without being able to exclude them. It speaks Anglo-Japanese, Anglo-French, Anglo-German, or Anglo-English. It is a new form of international language, not quite the same old class-stratified, class-dominated, canonically secured form of standard or traditional highbrow English. That is what I mean by "centered in the West." It is centered in the languages of the West, but it is not centered in the same way.

Second, the most important feature of this form of global mass culture is its peculiar form of homogenization. It is enormously absorptive, as it were, but the homogenization is never absolutely complete, and it does not work for completeness. It is not attempting to produce miniversions of Englishness everywhere or little versions of Americanness. It wants to recognize and absorb those differences within the larger, overarching framework of what is essentially an American conception of the world. That is to say, it is very powerfully located in the increasing and ongoing concentration of culture and other forms of capital. But it is now a form of capital that recognizes that it can rule only through other local capitals, rule alongside and in partnership with other economic and political elites. It does not attempt to obliterate them; it operates through them. It has to hold the whole framework of globalization in place and simultaneously police that system: it stage-manages independence within it, so to speak. The relationship between the United States and Latin America demonstrates how those forms that are different, that have their own specificity, can nevertheless be repenetrated, absorbed, reshaped, negotiated, without absolutely destroying what is specific and particular to them.

Some people used to think that if they could simply identify the logic of capital, then it could be managed so it would gradually engross everything in the world. It would translate everything in the world into a kind of replica of itself, everywhere; all particularity would disappear; capital in its onward, rationalizing march would not in the end care whether you were black, green, or blue so long as you could sell your labor as a commodity. It would not care whether you were male or female, or a bit of both, provided it could deal with you in terms of the commodification of labor.

But the more we understand about the development of capital itself, the more we understand that this is only part of the story. Indeed, alongside that drive to commodify everything, which is certainly one part of its logic, is another critical part of its logic that works in and through specificity. Capital has always been quite concerned with the question of the gendered nature of labor power. It has always been able to work in and through the sexual division of labor in order to accomplish the commodification of labor. It has always been able to work between the different ethnically and racially inflected labor forces. Thus, the notion of an overarching, ongoing, totally rationalizing capital has been a very deceptive way of persuading ourselves of the totally integrative and all-absorbent capacities of capital itself.

As a consequence, we have lost sight of one of the most profound insights in Marx's *Capital* — capitalism only advances, as it were, on contradictory terrain. The contradictions it has to overcome produce their own forms of expansion. And until we can see the nature of that contradictory terrain — precisely how particularity is engaged, how it is woven in, how it presents its resistances, how it is partly overcome, and how those overcomings then appear again — we will not understand it. That is much closer to how we ought to think about the so-called logic of capital in the advance of globalization itself.

Until we move away from the notion of this singular, unitary logic of capital, which does not mind where it operates, we will not fully understand it. As a consequence of reading *Capital* in that way, we have not been able to understand a number of things about capital. We have not been able to understand why anybody is still religious at the end of the twentieth century. Religion ought to have gone; it is one of the forms of particularity. We have not been able to understand why nationalism, an old form of particularism, is still around. All those particularisms ought by now to have been modernized out of existence. And yet what we find is that the most advanced forms of modern capital on a global scale are constantly splitting old societies into their advanced and their not-so-advanced sectors. Capital is constantly exploiting different forms of labor, constantly explaining the sexual division of labor in order to accomplish its commodification of social life.

I think it is extremely important to see this more contradictory notion, this whole line of development that is leading to different phases of global expansion, because otherwise we do not understand the cultural terrain that is in front of us.

I have tried to describe the new forms of global economic and cultural power that are apparently paradoxical: multinational but decentered. This is what we are moving into: not the unity of the singular corporate enterprise that tries to encapsulate the entire world within its confines, but much more decentralized and decentered forms of social and economic organization.

In some of the most advanced parts of the globalization process one finds new regimes of accumulation, much more flexible regimes founded not simply on the logics of mass production and of mass consumption but on new, flexible accumulation strategies, on segmented markets, on post-Fordist styles of organization, on lifestyle and identify — specific forms of marketing, driven by the market, driven by just-in-time production, driven by the ability to address not the mass audience, or the mass consumer, but penetrating to the very specific smaller groups, to individuals, in its appeal.

From one point of view, one might ask: Is this just the old enemy in a new disguise? Is this the ever-rolling march of the old form of commodification, the old form of globalization, fully in the keeping of capital, fully in the keeping of the West, which is simply able to absorb everybody else within its drive? Or is there something important about the fact that, at a certain point, globalization cannot proceed without learning to live with and working through difference?

One can begin to get an answer to the questions by examining new forms of advertising. If you look at the new ads, you see that certain forms of modern advertising are still grounded on the exclusive, powerful, dominant, highly masculinist, old Fordist imagery of a very exclusive set of identities. But side by side with them are ads for something more sophisticated: the new exotica. To be at the leading edge of modern capitalism is to eat fifteen different cuisines in any one week. It is no longer popular to have boiled beef and carrots and Yorkshire pudding every Sunday. Who needs that? If you are just jetting in from Tokyo, via Harare, you come in not with the sense of how everything is the same but with the sense that everything is different. In one trip around the world, you could, in short order, see every wonder of the ancient world. You could take them in as you go by, all in one swoop, living with difference, wondering at pluralism, this concentrated, corporate, overcorporate, overintegrated, overconcentrated, and condensed form of economic power that lives culturally through difference and that is constantly teasing itself with the pleasures of the transgressive other.

This differs sharply from the form of identity that I was describing earlier: embattled Britain, in its corseted form, rigidly tied to the Protestant ethic. In England, for a very long time, certainly under Thatcherism, even now, you can only harness people to your project if you promise them a bad time. You can't promise them a good time that will come right away. You promise them a good time later on. Good times will come. But you first of all have to go through a thousand hard winters for six months of pleasure. Indeed, the whole rhetoric of Thatcherism constructed the past in exactly that way. That is what was wrong about the 1960s and 1970s. All that swinging, all that consumption, all that pleasurable stuff: you know, it always ends in a bad way. You always have to pay for it in the end.

The second regime I am talking about does not have this pleasure/pain economy built into it. It promises endless pleasure. Pleasure to begin with, pleasure in the middle, pleasure at the end, nothing but pleasure: the proliferation of difference, of gender and sexuality. It lives with the new man. It produced the new man before anyone was convinced he even existed. Advertising produced the image of the postfeminist man. Some of us cannot find him, but he is certainly there in the advertising. I do not know whether anybody is living with him currently, but he's there, out there in the advertising.

In England, it is these new forms of globalized power that are most sensitive to questions of feminism and multiculturalism. Those promoting these forms say: "Of course, there'll be women working with us. We must think about the question of daycare. We must think about equal opportunities for black people. Of course, we all know somebody of different skin color. How boring it would be just to know people like us. We can go anywhere in the world, and we have friends who are Japanese, you know. We were in East Africa last week, and then we were on safari, and we always go to the Caribbean . . ."

This is the world of the global postmodern. Some parts of the modern globalization process are producing the global postmodern. The global postmodern is not a unitary regime because it is still in tension within itself and with an older, embattled, more corporate, more unitary, more homogenous conception of its own identity. That struggle is being fought within itself, and so it is difficult to see. But it is important to see it, to hear the way in which, in American society, in American culture, those two voices speak at one and the same time; on the one hand, the voice of infinite pleasurable consumption, the voice of "the exotic cuisine," and, on the other hand, the voice of the moral majority, the more fundamental and traditional, conservative ideas. They are not coming out of different places; they are coming out of the same place. It is the same balancing act that Thatcherism tried to conduct by releasing Rupert Murdoch and Sir William Rees Mogg at one and the same time, in the hope that they would restrain each other, that an old petit bourgeois morality would constrain the already deregulated Rupert Murdoch. Somehow, these two people were supposed to live in the same universe — together.

Given that, I simply do not believe in the notion of globalization as a noncontradictory, uncontested space in which everything is fully within the keeping of institutions that know where globalization is going. I think the story points to something else: that in order to maintain its global position, capital has had to negotiate, has had to incorporate and partly reflect the differences it was trying to overcome. It has had to try to get hold of, and neutralize, to some degree, the differences. It is trying to constitute a world in which things are different. Some seem to take pleasure in that, but, for capital, in the end, the differences do not matter.

Now the question becomes: Is this simply the final triumph, the closure of history by the West? Is globalization nothing but the triumph and closure of history by the West? Is this the final moment of a global postmodern, a moment in which it gets hold of everybody, of everything, where there is no difference that it cannot contain, no otherness it cannot speak, no marginality that it cannot take pleasure out of?

I have used the term "the exotic cuisine." The term has meaning only in the West, of course. In Calcutta, Indian food is not exotic. It is exotic in Manhattan. So we should not imagine that the effects of globalization are evenly and equally spread throughout the world. Globalization is a process of profound unevenness. But we shouldn't dismiss it too quickly. "It is just another face of the final triumph of the West," some say. I know that position. I know it is very tempting. It is what I call ideological postmodernism: I can't see round the edge of it, and so history must have just ended. That form of postmodernism I don't buy. It is what happens to ex-Marxist French intellectuals when they head for the desert.

There is another reason we should not see this form of globalization as simply unproblematic and uncontradictory. I have been talking about what is happening within its own regimes, within its own discourses. I have not yet talked about what is happening outside it, what is happening at the margins. So in the conclusion of this essay, I want to look at the process from the point of view, not of globalization, but of the local. I want to discuss two forms of globalization, still struggling with one another: (1) an older, corporate, enclosed, increasingly defensive one that has to go back to nationalism and national-cultural identity in a highly defensive way and to try to build barriers around it before it is eroded; and (2) a form of the global postmodern that is trying to live with — and at the same moment overcome, sublate, get hold of, and incorporate — difference.

What has been happening out there in the local? What about the people who did not go "above" the globalization but went underneath, to the local?

The return to the local is often a response to globalization. It is what people do when, in the face of a particular form of globalization that I have described, they opt out of that and say: "I don't know anything about that any more. I can't control it. I know no politics that can get hold of it. It's too big. It's too inclusive. Everything is on its side. There are some terrains in between, little interstices, the smaller spaces within which I have to work." One of course has to see globalization always in terms of the relationship between unevenly balanced discourses and regimes, but that is not all that we have to say about the local.

Indeed, the most profound cultural revolution in this part of the twentieth century has come about as a consequence of the margins coming into representation — in art, in painting, in film, in music, in literature, in the modern arts everywhere, in politics, and in social life generally. Our lives have been transformed by the struggle of the margins to come into representation — not just to be placed by a dominant, imperializing regime but to reclaim some form of representation for themselves.

Paradoxically, marginality has become a powerful space. It is a space of weak power, but it is a space of power, nonetheless. Anybody who cares for what is creatively emergent in the contemporary arts will find that it has something to do with the languages of the margin, and this trend is increasing. New subjects, new genders, new ethnicities, new regions, and new communities — all hitherto excluded from the major forms of cultural representation, unable to locate themselves except as decentered or subaltern — have emerged and have acquired through struggle, sometimes in very marginalized ways, the means to speak for themselves for the first time. And the discourses of power in our society, the discourses of the dominant regimes, have been certainly threatened by this decentered cultural empowerment of the marginal and the local.

As with other new forms of the dominant cultural postmodern — such as homogenization and absorption, plurality and diversity — so forms of local opposition and resistance are going through a transformative phase.

Face-to-face with a culture, an economy, and a set of histories that seem to be written or inscribed elsewhere, and that are so immense, transmitted from one continent to another with such extraordinary speed, the subjects of the local, of the margin, can only come into representation by, as it were, recovering their own hidden histories. They have to try to retell the story from the bottom up, instead of from the top down. And this moment has been of such profound significance in the postwar world that one cannot describe the postwar world without it. One cannot describe the movements of colonial nationalism without that moment when the unspoken discovered that they had a history that they could speak, that they had languages other than the languages of the master. It is an enormous moment. The world begins to be decolonized at that moment. Indeed, the movements of modern feminism cannot be understood outside the recovery of hidden histories.

These are the hidden histories of the majority, which had never been told — histories without the majority, as a minority event. One cannot discover, or try to discuss, the black movements, civil rights movements, the movements of black cultural politics in the modern world, without that notion of the rediscovery of where people came from, the return to some kind of roots, the speaking of a past that previously had no language. The attempt to snatch from the hidden histories another place to stand in, another place to speak from — that moment is extremely important. It is a moment that always tends to be overrun and to be marginalized by the dominant forces of globalization.

But do not misunderstand me. I am not talking about some ideal free space in which everybody says, "Come on in. Tell us what you think. I'm glad to hear from you." The dominant culture did not say that, but in the last twenty years it has been impossible to silence the languages and the discourses from the margins.

Those movements have an extraordinarily complex history. At some time, in the histories of many of them over the last twenty years, they have become locked into counteridentities of their own. We do not understand this respect for local roots that is brought to bear against the anonymous, impersonal world of the globalized forces. "I can't speak of the world, but I can speak of my village. I can speak of my neighborhood. I can speak of my community." The face-to-face communities are knowable, are locatable, can be given a place. One knows what the voices are. One knows what the faces are. Through the reconstruction of imaginary, knowable places in the face of the global postmodern, globalized forces have, as it were, destroyed the identities of specific places, absorbed them into a postmodern flux of diversity. So one understands the moment when people reach for those groundings, and that reach is what I call ethnicity.

Ethnicity is the necessary place or space from which people speak. It is a very important moment in the birth and development of all the local and marginal movements that have transformed the last twenty years. But just as, when one looks at the global postmodern, one sees that it can go in either an expansive or a defensive way, in the same sense one sees that the local, the marginal, can also go in two different ways. When the movements of the margins are so profoundly threatened by the global forces of postmodernity, they can themselves retreat into their own exclusivist and defensive enclaves. And at that point, local ethnicities become as dangerous as national ones. We have seen that happen: the refusal of modernity that takes the form of a return, a rediscovery of identity that constitutes a form of fundamentalism.

But that is not the only way in which the rediscovery of ethnicity has to go. Modern theories of enunciation always oblige us to recognize that enunciation comes from somewhere. It cannot be unplaced; it cannot be unpositioned; it is always positioned in a discourse. It is when a discourse forgets that it is placed that it tries to speak for everybody else. This is exactly what happens when Englishness claims to be a world identity, to which everything else is an insignificant ethnicity. That is the moment when it mistakes itself for a universal language. But, in fact, it comes from a place, out of a specific history, out of a specific set of power relationships. It speaks within a tradition. Discourse, in that sense, is always placed. And the moment of the rediscovery of a place, of a past, of one's roots, of one's context, is a necessary moment of enunciation. The margins could not speak up without first grounding themselves somewhere.

But the problem is this: Do those on the margins have to be trapped in the place from which they begin to speak? Will the identities on the margins become another exclusive set of local identities? My answer to that is, probably, but not necessarily so. A local example may help elucidate that answer.

I was involved in a photographic exhibition that was organized in London by the Commonwealth Institute. The Commonwealth Institute had gotten money from one of the very large, ex-colonial banks that was anxious to pay a little guilt money back to the societies that it had exploited for so long. The bankers said: "We'll give a series of regional prizes for photography; we know that everybody in these societies doesn't have access to photography, but photography is still a widespread medium. Lots of people have cameras; it reaches a much wider audience. And we'll ask the different societies that used to be linked together under the hegemonic definition of the Commonwealth to begin to represent their own lives, to begin to speak about their own communities, to tell us about the differences, the diversities of life, in these different societies that used to be all threaded together by the domination of English imperialism. That's what the Commonwealth was, the harnessing of a hundred different histories within one singular history, the history of the Commonwealth." The idea was to use the cultural medium of photography to explode that old unity, to proliferate new images, to diversify, to see how the people in the margins represented themselves photographically. The exhibition was judged in the far regions of the world where there are Commonwealth countries, and then it was judged centrally.

In assembling the exhibition, we found that enormous resources can be released when peoples on the margins are empowered, in however small a way. They came forth with extraordinary stories, pictures, images of people looking at their own societies with the means of modern representation for the first time. Suddenly, the myth of unity, the unified identity of the Commonwealth, was simply exploded. Forty different peoples, with forty different histories, all located in a different way in relation to the uneven march of capital across the globe, harnessed at a certain point with the birth of the modern British Empire — all these had been brought into one place and stamped with an overall identity. They had all been told they should be unified, should contribute to one overall system. That is what the system was, the harnessing of these differences. And now, as that center begins to weaken, so the differences begin to pull away. That was an enormous moment of the empowering of difference and diversity. It is the moment of what I call the rediscovery of ethnicity, of people photographing their own homes, their own families, their own pieces of work.

We discovered two other things. First, in our naïveté, we had thought that the moment of the rediscovery of ethnicity, in this sense, would be a rediscovery of what we called "the past," of people's roots. But the past in these places has not been sitting around waiting to be discovered. People from the Caribbean went home to Africa to photograph the past, but what explodes through the camera is twentieth-century Africa, not seventeenth-century Africa. The homeland is not waiting back there for the new ethnics to rediscover it. There is a past to be learned about, but the past is now seen, and has to be grasped, as a history, as something that has to be told. It is narrated. It is grasped through memory. It is grasped through desire. It is grasped through reconstruction. It is not just a fact that has been waiting to ground our identities. What emerges from this is nothing like an uncomplicated, dehistoricized, undynamic, uncontradictory past. Nothing like that is caught in the image of the moment of return.

Second, we discovered that people wanted to speak out of that most local moment. What did they want to talk about? They wanted to tell about how they had come from the smallest village in the deepest recesses of wherever and went straight by New York to London. They wanted to talk about what the metropolis, what the cosmopolitan world, looked like to an ethnic. They were not prepared to come on as "ethnic artists." They weren't saying, "I will show you my crafts, my skills; I will dress up, metaphorically in my traditions; I will speak my language for your edification." They had to locate themselves somewhere, but they wanted to address problems that could no longer be contained within a narrow version of ethnicity. They did not want to go back and defend something that was ancient, that had stood still, that had refused the opening to new things. They wanted to speak right across those boundaries, and across those frontiers.

Earlier I asked: Is globalization the cleverest story the West has ever told, or is it a more contradictory phenomenon? Now I ask exactly the opposite: Does the notion of "the local" refer merely to exceptions located on the margins, to what used to be called a blip in history? Is the local simply something that does not register anywhere, does not do anything, is not very profound? Is it just waiting to be incorporated, eaten up by the all-seeing eye of global capital as it advances across the terrain? Or is it also, itself, in an extremely contradictory state? Is it also moving, historically being transformed, speaking across older and new languages? To answer these questions, one need only think about the languages of modern contemporary music and ask: Are there still traditional musics that have never been influenced by modern music? Are there any musics left that have not heard some other music? All the most explosive modern musics are crossovers. The aesthetics of modern popular music is the aesthetics of the hybrid, the aesthetics of the crossover, the aesthetics of the diaspora, the aesthetics of creolization. It is the mix of musics that is exciting to a young person who comes out of what Europe is pleased to think of as some ancient civilization, a civilization Europe wants to control. But the West can control it only if the people stay there, only if they remain simple tribal folks. The moment they want to leap right over the nineteenth-century technology — leap over making all the mistakes the West made — and get hold of some of the modern technologies to speak their own tongue, to speak of their own condition, then they are out of place. Then the other is not where it is supposed to be. The primitive has somehow escaped from control.

I am not trying to say that all is well, that the revolution throbs down at the margins, that it's living, that it's all OK, that we merely have to wait for the local to erupt and disrupt the global. I am, rather, asking that we not think of globalization as a pacific and pacified process. It's not a process at the end of history. It is working on the terrain of postmodern culture as a global formation, which is an extremely contradictory space. Within that, we have, in entirely new forms that we are only just beginning to understand, the same old contradictions, the same old struggle. These are the continuing contradictions of things that are trying to get hold of other things, and things that are trying to escape from their grasp. That old dialectic is not at an end. Globalization does not finish it off.

With the story about the Commonwealth Institute Photography Exhibition I tried to speak about questions of new forms of identity. But I have just barely touched on that. How can we clarify the notion of what these new identities might be? What will these identities be like, these identities constructed through things that are different rather than things that are the same? These are questions we need to work toward answering.

Chapter 10
Multiculturalism and the Neoconservatives
Robert Stam

My purpose in this essay will be to sketch a view of multiculturalism in order to deconstruct certain neoconservative misrepresentations about multiculturalism. I am thinking less of the innumerable factual errors proliferating in the diverse neoconservative diatribes by Arthur Schlesinger, Dinesh D'Souza, Richard Bernstein, William A. Henry III, and others than of fundamental conceptual confusions reflected in the right-wing portrayals of the multiculturalist project.

What, first of all, is multiculturalism? We can begin provisionally by distinguishing between the multicultural "fact" and the multicultural "project." In a strictly literal and indexical sense, the term "multiculturalism" points to the multiplicity of the world's cultures, and this in three distinct senses, in increasing order of nuance and complexity. The term points simultaneously to (1) the existence of multiple cultures in the world; (2) the coexistence of multiple cultures within particular nation-states; and (3) the existence of mutually impacting cultures both within and beyond the single nation-state. Conservatives can easily support the first two of these versions of the multicultural fact, although some might have a problem with the idea of "mutually impacting cultures," in that they might either reject mutual impact or acknowledge it only in order to deplore it. In any case, multiculturalism in this factual sense is difficult to deny because virtually all countries and regions are multicultural. The Americas generally, for example, feature polyphonic orchestrations of major constellations of cultures: Native American, African, European, and Asiatic, each strain itself being multiple and internally contradictory. Outside of the Americas, a country like Egypt melds pharaonic, Arab and Muslim, Jewish, Christian/Coptic, and Mediterranean influences, while India, with its fifteen official languages, is riotously plural in language and religion. The Mediterranean has long been multicultural, and now more than ever thanks to the colonial karma by which Europe absorbs the reflux of its own former colonized peoples — Arabs in France, Indians in England, Indonesians in the Netherlands. Multiculturalism as historical fact, then, is as banal as it is indisputable.

It is clearly not the multicultural fact that provokes the neoconservative howls of execration, however, but the multiculturalist project. The multiculturalist project unleashes virulent polemics because it calls for decisive changes, changes in the way we write history, the way we teach literature, the way we make art, the way we program films, the way we organize conferences, and the way we distribute cultural resources. Taken globally, multiculturalism is a pluri-dimensional project (most strongly developed within the United States but with analogous movements elsewhere), involving diverse ethnicities (Native Americans, African-Americans, Latino Americans, European Americans) and diverse activities (scholarship, creative writing, curatorial work, community activism). To speak only of scholarship, it includes revisionist histories (e.g., those of Richard Slotkin, Donald Grinde, Oren Lyons, Richard Drinnon, Francis Jennings), comparative and Atlanticist studies of Afro-diasporic culture (Paul Gilroy, Robert Farris Thompson), philosophical and literary essays on the variegated forms of oppression (Cornel West, Toni Morrison, bell hooks), analyses of stereotypical imagery in the media (Ward Churchill, Ed Guerrero, Donald Bogle, Charles Ramírez Berg), and countless other forms of adversarial knowledge. The neoconservative attacks on multiculturalism, curiously, almost never reference this vast body of work, resorting instead to invective and the endless recycling of the same corpus of anecdotal *fabulae,* now become the self-sustaining legends of the neocolonial tribe.

"Behind" all these diverse proposals for change lies the democratizing stance of multiculturalism as a philosophical and political position. Radically egalitarian, polycentric multiculturalism sees world history and contemporary social life from the theoretical perspective of the fundamental equality of peoples in status, intelligence, and rights. But this project does not emerge from nowhere; it is the local manifestation of a deeper and long ongoing "seismological shift" — the decolonization of global culture. In the wake of centuries of colonial domination, multiculturalism aspires to decolonize representation not only in terms of cultural artifacts but also in terms of power relations between the communities "behind" the artifacts. Its task is double, at once one of deconstructing Eurocentric and racist norms and of constructing and promoting multicultural alternatives.

It is important to say that "multiculturalism" is in one sense merely a new name for a venerable phenomenon. Throughout its history, colonialism has generated its own critics, whether in the form of its unceasingly critical victims or in the form of its own renegades and dissident voices. Thus when Michel de Montaigne in the late sixteenth century argued in "Des Cannibales" that civilized Europeans were ultimately more barbarous than cannibals, since cannibals ate the flesh of the dead only in order to appropriate the strength of their enemies, while Europeans tortured and murdered in the name of a religion of love, he might be described as a multiculturalist avant la lettre. When Denis Diderot in the eighteenth century, in his contributions to Reynal's *Histoire des deux Indes,* called for African insurrection against European colonialists, he too might be seen as a proleptic incarnation of multicultural thinking. And when Frantz Fanon in the twentieth century spoke of the goal of accepting "the reciprocal relativism of different cultures, once colonialism is excluded,"[1] he gave us an excellent working definition of multiculturalism.

One can also point to proleptic incarnations of multicultural practice. The seventeenth-century maroon republic Palmares, located in what is now called Brazil, was the very prototype of a multicultural democracy in the Americas. Recent archaeological research has confirmed earlier speculations that Palmares welcomed, along with the black majority, Indians, mestizos, renegade whites, Jews, and Muslims, ultimately becoming a refuge for the persecuted of Brazilian society.[2] Palmares lasted almost a century in the face of repeated assaults from both the Dutch and the Portuguese, withstanding on the average one Portuguese expedition every fifteen months.[3] At its height, the republic counted twenty thousand inhabitants spread over numerous villages in the northeastern interior of Brazil, covering an area roughly one-third the size of Portugal. Palmares bears witness to the capacity of Afro-Brazilians and their allies not only to revolt against slavery but also to imagine and mobilize an alternative life. Economically self-sufficient, Palmares rejected the monoculture farming typical of colonial Brazil in favor of the diversified agriculture the freed Afro-Brazilians remembered from Africa, planting corn, beans, manioc, potatoes, and sugarcane on communally shared land. Palmarino kings were kings in the African sense of consensus ruler — not absolute monarchs but custodians of the commonwealth, and Palmarinos enjoyed basic civic and political equality. The point is obviously not to suggest that Palmares provides a blueprint for multicultural democracy in the contemporary United States, but only to point to the fact that very early in the history of the colonized Americas we find a utopian model for a multiracial society, long before the term "multiculturalism" had been coined.[4]

The concept of multiculturalism is not only historically situated but also polysemically open to various interpretations and subject to diverse political force-fields; it has become a slippery signifier onto which diverse groups project their hopes and fears. In its more co-opted version, it easily degenerates into a state- or corporate-managed United-Colors-of-Benetton pluralism whereby established power markets and packages difference for commercial or ideological purposes. In its liberal-pluralist form, it develops a patronizing etiquette of tolerance and inclusiveness, a paternalistic exhortation to "be nice to minorities," what Peter Sellers once satirized as the spirit of "Take an Indian to lunch this week." In other national contexts, it takes on different colorations. In Canada, it designates official, largely cosmetic government programs designed to placate the Quebecois, native Canadians, blacks, and Asians. In Latin America, progressive intellectuals worry about a new Americanocentric multiculturalism, as simply another cultural export from the powerful neighbor to the north. The word "multiculturalism" thus has no essence; it simply points to a debate. While being aware of the term's ambiguities, our goal is to prod multiculturalism in the direction of a radical critique of power relations, turning it into a rallying cry for a more substantive and reciprocal intercommunalism.

First Misunderstanding: Multiculturalism Is Anti-European

Among the neoconservative misconceptions concerning multiculturalism is the idea that multiculturalism is systematically, reflexively anti-European. (I will be using "Europe" to refer not only to Europe per se but also to the neo-Europeas of the Americas, Australia, and elsewhere). Neoconservative tracts portray multiculturalism as calling for the abrupt jettisoning of European classics and of "western civilization as an area of study."[5] For William Bennett, the West is "under attack."[6] For Roger Kimball, multiculturalism implies "an attack on the . . . idea that, despite our many differences, we hold in common an intellectual, artistic, and moral legacy, descending largely from the Greeks and the Bible, [that] preserves us from chaos and barbarism. And it is precisely this legacy that the multiculturalist wishes to dispense with."[7] For William Phillips, "politically correct teachers" are "denouncing the traditions and values of the West. . . . [T]hey would substitute African and Asian traditions and values."[8] In fact, however, multiculturalism is an assault not on Europe or Europeans but on Eurocentrism. Rather than attack Europe, an anti-Eurocentric multiculturalism relativizes Europe, seeing it as a geographical fiction that flattens the cultural diversity even of Europe itself. Multiculturalism points out that ancient Greece, supposedly the fount of universal civilization, was not a proto-Europe; Greece was itself African, Semitic, and Asian, looking both east and west. Europe itself is in fact a synthesis of many cultures, Western and non-Western. The notion of a "pure" Europe originating in classical Greece is premised on crucial exclusions, from the African and Semitic influences that shaped classical Greece itself to the osmotic Sephardic-Judeo-Islamic culture that played such a crucial role in the Europe of the so-called Dark Ages (a Eurocentric designation for a period of Oriental ascendancy) and even in the Middle Ages and the Renaissance. Europe never came "pure." As Jan Pieterse points out, all the celebrated "stations" of European progress — Greece, Rome, Christianity, the Renaissance, the Enlightenment — are "moments of cultural mixing."[9] Western Art has always been indebted to and transformed by non-Western art, whence the Moorish influence on the poetry of courtly love, the African influence on modernist painting, the impact of Asian forms (Kabuki, Noh drama, Balinese theater, ideographic writing) on European theater and film, and the influence of Africanized dance forms on such choreographers as Martha Graham and George Ballanchine.[10] The "West," then, is itself a collective heritage, an omnivorous mélange of cultures; it did not simply "take in" non-European influences; "it was constituted by them."[11]

According to the neoconservative caricature, multiculturalists want to jettison all cultural artifacts produced by "dead white males." In the case of Shakespeare, for example, multiculturalists would presumably want to (1) throw him out completely or (2) study him only in order to trash him as racist, sexist, and colonialist. In my view, however, multiculturalism suggests nothing of the kind. A course in Shakespeare is not per se Eurocentric. Rather than either throw out Shakespeare or simply denounce him, a multicultural approach to Shakespeare would call attention to the multicultural reverberations of the Shakespearean text itself. Shakespeare's capacious Globe, within this perspective, not only displays European culture in all its exuberant diversity but also invokes the ethnic relationality of Moor and Venetian in *Othello,* of Egyptian and Roman in *Antony and Cleopatra,* of European and African/ Native American in *The Tempest,* and of Jew and Gentile in *The Merchant of Venice.* A multicultural approach might point out that in *Othello,* Shakespeare took the cowardly murderer of his Italian source play and turned him into a tragic hero, said to be modeled on the real-life Earl of Essex. It might point out that in the time of Jim Crow, *Othello* could not be performed in the South, since it showed a black man as hero.[12] A multicultural pedagogy might animate a kind of retroactive teleconference or Internet dialogue between Caliban and Shylock, for example, in which they share their anger about having been "buked and scorned." Or a multicultural approach might address the diverse anticolonialist reinvoicings of Shakespeare, for example, Aimé Césaire's rewriting of *The Tempest,* or might speak of the wedding of multiracial performance and the Shakespearean text, as, for example, in Orson Welles's *Voodoo Macbeth* in 1936 or in contemporary Central Park Public Theatre productions. What is it about Shakespeare that makes it so easy to rewrite *The Tempest* as anticolonialist or to see *The Merchant of Venice* as potentially sympathetic to Shylock or to cast actors of all races in his plays? A multicultural approach to Shakespeare might also explore the international repercussions of Shakespeare, for example, the energizing role of his plays within Polish nationalism or their reception in India (portrayed in the film *Shakespeare Wallah*). A film course might examine the Shakespearean parodies in the Brazilian *chanchadas*, where a black male actor (Grande Otelo) plays the balcony scene as Juliet in drag, or in the Israeli film *Avanti Popolo,* where an Egyptian character, played by a Palestinian, is presented as a professional actor who has always wanted to play Shylock on the Egyptian stage and who declaims "Hath not a Jew eyes" to the Israeli soldiers.[13] At the same time, it is not impossible to teach Shakespeare in a Eurocentric manner, if the European and extra-European multiculturalism of the Shakespearean text is ignored or if Shakespeare is used as a stick with which to beat down other cultures, as in the presumptuous question: Where is *your* Shakespeare? Or where is *your* Proust? Questions that have as much legitimacy as, Where is *your* Book of the Dead? Or, Where is *your* Mahabharata? Or, Where is *your* Yoruba dance pageant? Or, Where is *your* James Brown?

A multicultural analysis points out, further, that Europe itself, as the Shakespearean example demonstrates, has always had its own peripheralized regions and stigmatized ethnicities, classes, and genders (Jews, Irish, Gypsies, Huguenots, peasants, women). Europe itself served as a proving ground for colonialist ideas and practices. English colonialism was practiced against the Irish before it was applied to Africans and Native Americans. In 1609, Sir Charles Cornwallis, addressing the Spanish Lords of Council in Madrid, asserted that the Irish were "so savage a people" that they deserved the same treatment "used by the Kings of Spain in the Indies, or those employed with the Moors, . . . scattering them in other parts."[14] Racism was practiced by Christian Spaniards against Jews and Muslims, to take another example, before it was extended across the Atlantic. Anti-Semitism, along with "anti-infidelism," provided a conceptual and disciplinary apparatus that, after being turned against Europe's internal "other" (the Jews), was then projected outward against Europe's external others (the indigenous peoples of Africa and the Americas).[15] Preexisting forms of ethnic and religious otherizing were transferred from Europe to its colonies, the presumed "godlessness" and "devil worship" of the indigenous people becoming a pretext for enslavement and dispossession.

Nor does multiculturalism endorse a Europhobic attitude; that it emphasizes the "underside" of European history does not mean that it does not assume or recognize an "overside" of scientific, artistic, and political achievement. And since Eurocentrism is a historically situated discourse and not a genetic inheritance, Europeans can be anti-Eurocentric, just as non-Europeans can be Eurocentric. Europe has always spawned its own critics of empire. Some of the European cultural figures most revered by today's neoconservatives, such as Samuel Johnson and Adam Smith, ironically, themselves condemned European colonialism. Yet when contemporary multiculturalists make the same points, they are accused of "Europe-bashing."[16]

Often Europeans and Euro-Americans have a knee-jerk response to the criticism implied in the word "Eurocentric." They take it personally, as suggesting that they, and the culture that they on some level represent, are, in some unclarified way, being called "bad." The very word "Eurocentrism" at times triggers a kind of rushing-to-the-defense-of-Europe syndrome. But this reaction represents a misunderstanding on a number of levels. First, multiculturalism does not condemn Europe; it only criticizes the assumption of a "natural" European right to dominate others, whether through force, as in colonial times, or through domineering financial institutions and ethnocentric media, as in the present. A polycentric multiculturalism questions the universalization of Eurocentric norms, the idea that one race, in Aimé Césaire's words, "holds a monopoly on beauty, intelligence, and strength." The critique of Eurocentrism is addressed not to Europeans as individuals but rather to dominant Europe's historically oppressive relation to its internal and external others. The term does not suggest, obviously, that non-European people are somehow better than Europeans or that Third World and minoritarian cultures are inherently superior. Nor does it imply the existence of an inverted European narcissism that posits Europe as the source of all social evils in the world. Such an approach remains Eurocentric ("Europe exhibiting its own unacceptability in front of an anti-ethnocentric mirror," in Derrida's words) and also exempts Third World patriarchal elites from all responsibility.[17] Such "victimology" reduces non-European life to a pathological response to Western penetration. It merely turns colonialist claims upside down. The vision remains Promethean, but here Prometheus has brought not fire but the Holocaust, reproducing what Barbara Christian calls the "West's outlandish claim to have invented everything, including Evil."[18] Our focus here, in any case, is less on intentions than on institutional discourses, less on "goodness" and "badness" than on historically configured relations of power. The question, as Talal Asad puts it, is not "how far Europeans have been guilty and Third World inhabitants innocent but, rather, how far the criteria by which guilt and innocence are determined have been historically constituted."[19] Yet the frequency with which neoconservative attacks on multiculturalism attribute words such as "bad" and "good" to multiculturalist discourse carries with it the unpleasant odor of offended narcissism, the sense that for some the mere decentering and relativizing of Europe are in themselves sufficient cause for hurt pride and angry recrimination.

But contrary to neoconservative thinking, the antitheses of multiculturalism are not civility, democracy, patriotism, and integration but rather monoculturalism, and, more specifically, Eurocentric monoculturalism. Multiculturalism is an attack not on Europe but on Eurocentrism, the view that places Europe at the symbolic center of the world, a view that sees Europe as the privileged source of meaning, as the world's center of gravity, as the ontological "reality" to the rest of the world's shadow. Eurocentric thinking attributes to the West an almost providential sense of historical destiny. Like Renaissance perspective in painting, it envisions the world from a single privileged point. It maps the world in a cartography that centralizes and augments Europe while literally "belittling" Africa.[20] It bifurcates the world into the "West and the Rest"[21] and organizes everyday language into binaristic hierarchies implicitly flattering to Europe: *our* nations, *their* tribes; *our* religions, *their* superstitions; *our* culture, *their* folklore; *our* defense, *their* terrorism.

Eurocentrism first emerged as a discursive rationale for colonialism, the process by which the European powers reached positions of hegemony in much of the world. Indeed, J. M. Blaut calls Eurocentrism "the colonizer's model of the world."[22] As an ideological substratum common to colonialist, imperialist, and racist discourse, Eurocentrism is a form of vestigial thinking that permeates and structures *contemporary* practices and representations even after the formal end of colonialism. Eurocentrism enshrines the hierarchical structures inherited from colonialism as if they were natural and inevitable. Although colonialist discourse and Eurocentric discourse are intimately intertwined, the terms have a distinct emphasis. While the former explicitly justifies colonialist practices, the latter embeds, takes for granted, and "normalizes" the hierarchical power relations generated by colonialism and imperialism, without necessarily even thematizing those issues directly. Although generated by the colonizing process, Eurocentrism's links to that process are obscured in a kind of buried epistemology.

Although Eurocentrism is often assumed to be synonymous with "European," in fact it is not, anymore than "patriarchy" is synonymous with men, or "heterosexism" with heterosexuals. The word "Eurocentric" sometimes provokes apoplectic reactions because it is taken as a synonym for "racist." But although Eurocentrism and racism are historically intertwined, they are in no way equatable, for the simple reason that Eurocentrism is the "normal" view of history that most First Worlders and even many Third Worlders learn at school and imbibe from the media. As a result of this normalizing operation, it is quite possible to be antiracist at both a conscious and practical level, and still be Eurocentric. Eurocentrism is not a conscious political stance taken by people in the world but an implicit positioning; people do not announce themselves as Eurocentric anymore than men go around saying: "Hi. I'm Joe. I'm a phallocrat." This point is often misunderstood, as in David Rieff's breathless claim that "there is no business establishment any more that is committed...to notions of European superiority."[23] But corporate executives are the last people who need to consciously worry about European superiority; it is enough that they inherit the structures and perspectives bequeathed by centuries of European domination.[24]

Second Misunderstanding: Multiculturalism Is "Disuniting America"

Arthur M. Schlesinger Jr. is the most active proponent of the perspective that multiculturalism disunites America. It was not a coincidence that he was also an opponent of the multicultural "Rainbow Curriculum" designed for New York State schools. The view of multiculturalism as fractious and segregationist surfaces in the frequency of words like "Balkanization," "separatism," and "tribalism" in neoconservative discussions. Neoconservatives accuse multiculturalists of pulling people apart, of emphasizing what divides people rather than what brings them together, of summoning "ethnic" communities to form hermetically sealed enclaves, each with its own real or symbolic "militias." (Television images of strife in Los Angeles and New York reinforce such fears.) Thus George Bush in May 1991 publicly denounced the "political extremists" who "[set] citizens against one another on the basis of their class or race." For Charles Krautheimer, multiculturalism "poses a threat that no outside agent in this post-Soviet world can match — the setting of one ethnic group against another, the fracturing not just of American society but of the American idea."[25] The most extreme form of this accusation is to speak of ethnic war as a logical end-product of multiculturalism, as when P. J. O'Rourke claims that "multiculturalism is that which is practiced today in the former Yugoslavia."[26] From the neoconservatives, one has the impression that the Serbs, the Bosnians, and the Croats, fresh from their readings of Cornel West and bell hooks, are rushing deliriously into fratricidal slaughter in the name of multiculturalism.[27]

Apart from the fact that the neoconservative critics never manage to cite any multiculturalists who actually call for separatism — most call for coalition and collaboration — the talk of Balkanization confuses the messenger with the message. The social tensions are there; multiculturalism assumes them and even calls attention to them but only in order to transcend them through a realignment of cultural and political power. Neoconservative formulations in which the "common culture" is threatened by ethnic difference come dangerously close to implying that difference per se causes social strife. What is forgotten in the discussion is that the inequitable distribution of power itself generates divisiveness. Multiculturalism, by proposing a more egalitarian vision of social relations, seeks to heal these divisions. Multiculturalism implies notions of ethnic relationality and community answerability; it calls for a profound restructuring and reconceptualization of the power relations between cultural communities. Refusing a ghettoizing discourse, it sees the intense "co-implication" (Chandra Mohanty's term) of dominant and dominated communities, but it also discerns links between minoritarian communities. Indeed, it challenges the hierarchy that makes some communities "minor" and others "major" and "normative." Thus what neoconservatives in fact find threatening about the more radical forms of multiculturalism is the intellectual and political regrouping by which different "minorities" become a majority seeking to move beyond being tolerated to forming active intercommunal[28] coalitions.

Multiculturalism, far from being separatist, is relentlessly relational and anti-segregationist. Multiculturalism assumes that communities, societies, nations, and even entire continents exist not autonomously but rather in a densely woven web of relationality. Social communities and utterances "dialogue" with one another; they are "aware of and mutually reflect one another" within the communality of the sphere of speech communication.[29] Racial and national diversity is therefore fundamental to every utterance, even to that utterance that on the surface ignores or excludes the groups with which it is in relation. A dialogical, intercommunal multiculturalism is in this sense profoundly antisegregationist, not only in racial and communitarian terms but also in disciplinary terms. Although segregation can be temporarily imposed as a sociopolitical arrangement, it can never be absolute, especially on the level of culture. All utterances inescapably take place against the background of the possible responding utterances of other social and ethnic points of view.

Thus critics like Schlesinger are wildly off-target. One can maintain and even celebrate cultural difference while respecting the political ground rules of democracy, even if the interpretation of those ground rules, and the narratives concerning their origins and history, might differ. When phrases like "life, liberty, and the pursuit of happiness" were coined, they were not meant to include blacks, women, or people without property. The social contract delineated by such philosophers as Locke, Rousseau, and Mill, which legitimized the establishment of the government of the United States, was doubled by what Y. N. Kly calls the "antisocial contract" in which the idea of "equality among equals" came to entail an equal opportunity to disappropriate and exploit. Indeed, few texts illustrate Walter Benjamin's aphorism that "there is no document of civilization which is not at the same time a document of barbarism" better than the American Constitution. The principles enshrined there established two transcripts, one public and written, for Americans of European descent, and the other, largely unwritten, for non-European "minorities."[30] The liberal theses of the founding fathers, progressive as they were, were not meant to apply to "lesser peoples," just as Wilsonian self-determination, in a later period, was not meant to apply to non-European nations.

A polycentric multiculturalism suggests that the only real road to peace between ethnicities passes through *more* democracy, *more* equality, *more* justice, *more* reciprocal knowledge, through *more* awareness of very different histories and very different perspectives on history. (Multicultural education, similarly, is not about "lowering standards" but about raising them, about requiring knowledge of more cultures, more languages.) The Schlesinger version relays the myth of a unified America supposedly fractured by multiculturalism, but the United States, like other nations, has always been the site of tensions and conflicts. Repeating the litany of a "single nation" doesn't lessen the conflicts; it merely covers them up. And here it is not the multicultural left that creates divisions but rather the right. In 1984 David Duke published a map showing ethnic groups segregated across the country living in states with names like "Minoria," "West Israel," and "New Africa."[31] It has usually been conservative Republicans, similarly, who invoke "Southern strategies," "wedge issues," and "culture wars." And it has always been slavery, segregation, discrimination, and racial scapegoating that have disunited America, not multiculturalism.

Third Misunderstanding: Multiculturalism Is "Therapy for Minorities"

This third misunderstanding also proliferates in the neoconservative texts. Arthur Schlesinger ridicules revisionist multicultural history texts as "underdog" and "compensatory" history and as symptomatic of a "there's-always-a-black-man-at-the-bottom-of-it" approach to historiography. According to Schlesinger, multiculturalism sees history "not as an intellectual discipline but rather as social and psychological therapy whose primary function is to raise the self-esteem of children from minority groups."[32] Lynne Cheney dismisses Afrocentrism as "what people think is important for [students'] self-esteem."[33] Richard Bernstein speaks of "special-interest history" where "one's scholarly activity seems to derive directly from one's personal circumstances and affiliations."[34] The suggestion is that these revisionist histories have rewritten "true" history with the sole purpose of flattering insecure minorities, of making them feel good about themselves despite the unpalatable fact of their historical inferiority. It is worth pointing out, at the outset, that if it is indeed true that minorities have been traumatized by their experience in dominant educational institutions, then "therapy" for minorities is certainly better than "trauma" for minorities. The notion of a historical inferiority being "covered up," furthermore, is itself racist. Why should only the dominant Euro-American group have its narcissism massaged while others drink the bitter brew of marginalization and stereotype? The diatribes, significantly, rarely name specific offensive texts; we are not told precisely which historical texts are being criticized or exactly how they are inadequate. In any case, a truly multicultural history would not be designed to flatter one group: it simply proposes a multiperspectival history. It does not claim to proffer an immaculate truth to replace European "lies." It proposes, more modestly, a counterpoint of perspectives. Going beyond the long-standing monopoly by one group (with all its internal contradictions) on the recounting of history, it calls for a relational, contrapuntal, poly-communal, multiperspectival history, from which some sort of contingent, interested, pragmatic "truth" is more likely to emerge.

Fourth Misunderstanding: Multiculturalism Is the "New Puritanism"

One of the public relations feats of neoconservatives has been to associate individual attributes (self-righteousness, censoriousness, p.c. attitudes) that are democratically spread along the political spectrum with one group alone — the multicultural left. Thus "politically correct" thinking, hardly the monopoly of any single political group, and hardly alien to the likes of William Bennett, Jesse Helms, Newt Gingrich, and Lynne Cheney, came to be seen as pertaining only to those who called for more egalitarian relations between races, genders, and ethnicities. The same broad-brush approach constructed the image of the multicultural left as systematically favoring euphemisms in the name of the "cult of sensitivity," whence terms like "vertically challenged" for "short" and "nonhuman animal companion" for "pet" and so forth, all endlessly satirized in books like *The Official Politically Correct Dictionary and Handbook.* Apart from the fact that it is virtually impossible to locate anyone in the real world who actually talks that way, it is also obvious that "euphemization" is in no sense the monopoly of the multicultural left. Euphemism is the property of bureaucracies everywhere, and certainly of the Pentagon with its penchant for such prettifying terms as "collateral damage." And when the political right uses code words like "welfare queen," "criminals," "inner city," and "underclass" when they actually mean "black," is that not also a form of euphemism?

But the most devastating feature of this broad-brush strategy has to do with a constant leitmotif that portrays multiculturalists as puritanical party poopers, as unpleasant people anxious to spoil the good times of fun-loving Americans. (At the same time, paradoxically, the neoconservatives portray multiculturalists as irresponsible hedonists, the heirs of the permissive 1960s with its credo of "sex, drugs, and rock 'n' roll.") Thus words like "self-righteous," "censorious," "pious," "cranky," "sanctimonious," and "grim" constantly recur in neoconservative discourse, part of a portrait of a "culture of resentment" (Harold Bloom) and a "culture of complaint" (Robert Hughes). For Richard Bernstein, multiculturalism represents the "dictatorship of virtue," leading to an "excessive, fussy, self-pitying sort of wariness that induces others to spout pieties."[35] Amplifying the preexisting association of the left with moralistic self-righteousness and puritanical antisensuality, the right-wing por-trayed all politicized critique as the neurotic effluvium of whiny malcontents, the product of an uptight subculture of morbid guilt-tripping.

Like postmodernism, which is often said to exist simply because the discourse it-self exists, the "p.c." rubric has generated its own ontology; it has taken on a life of its own. Thus people say "what I hate about p.c. is . . ." when they mean "what I hate about what is represented as p.c. is . . ." The anti-p.c. discourse is even exported to the Third World, where neoliberal newsmagazines "indigenize" neoconservative thinking. In Brazil, weekly newsmagazines like *Isto E* and *Veja* disseminate the for-mulaic anecdotes of neoconservative discourse. The image of Communist Party–style "ideological patrols" merges with the Brazilian image of North American society as rigid, rule-bound, and puritanical. As a result, virtually all literate Brazilians know and use the phrase *politicamente correto* (politically correct), yet few could cite the name of even one multiculturalist thinker.[36]

But how does one respond to such charges? On one level, it seems that those who criticize are always seen, on some level, as a "drag" by those being criticized. It is doubtless annoying for the racist to have the multiculturalist not find his jokes funny, just as it was doubtless annoying for Hitlerians to be called to account for the crematoria. What is striking in the diatribes, however, is the emphasis on what can only be called personality traits (whininess, self-righteousness, crankiness, and so forth — hardly the monopoly of the left) being used as a diversion from what is really an argument about political and intellectual positions.

More importantly, what is missed in all this is both (1) the pleasurable possibil-ities inherent in multiculturalism itself and (2) the real sources of puritanism and antipleasure in our society. In relation to the first point, multiculturalism suggests that the dominant culture can learn from other cultures, including in terms of living more pleasurably. The multiculturalist critique is not only political but also cultural. A leitmotif in the valorization of Native American culture by some philosophically in-clined Europeans was that the indigenous way of life was *happier* than the European way of living. In *History of America* (1777), William Robertson described Indians as self-confident in their way of life and critical of that of Europeans: "[T]hey re-gard themselves as the standard of excellence, as beings the best entitled, as well as the most perfectly qualified, to enjoy real happiness. Unaccustomed to any restraint upon their will or actions, they behold with amazement the inequality of rank, and the subordination which takes place in civilized life."[37] Arguing for public ownership of land, Tom Paine pointed to Native American society as lacking "those spectacles of human misery which poverty and want present to our eyes in all the towns and streets of Europe."[38] Thomas Jefferson, in the same vein, was "convinced that those societies [e.g., Indian societies] which live without government enjoy in their general mass an infinitely greater degree of happiness than those who live under European governments."[39] Western culture can also learn from the very religious traditions that colonialism suppressed, traditions that are not so haunted by notions of sin, the fall, guilt, the devil, and hell. Yoruban trance religions, to take just one example, feature Exu, the messenger of the crossroads, but no devil, and display a ceremonial prac-tice in which pleasure, dance, and music are not prescribed by the religion but an integral part of it.

I have argued elsewhere the need for a "dialogic" and "carnivalesque" theory of politics and popular culture, one that endorses pleasure, including mass-mediated pleasure, and that eschews guilt and redemption and other forms of sublimated religiosity, and I will not rehearse those ideas here.[40] But I would like to give just one example of a propleasure critique that is at once political and cultural. In the 1920s, the Brazilian modernists also turned to indigenous culture, using the trope of cannibalism as the basis of an insurgent aesthetic, calling for a creative synthesis of European avant-gardism and Brazilian "cannibalism," and invoking an "anthropophagic" devouring of the techniques and information of the superdeveloped countries in order the better to struggle against domination. As exploited by the modernists, the cannibalist metaphor had a negative and a positive pole. The negative pole deployed cannibalism to expose the exploitative social Darwinism of class society. But the positive pole was ultimately more suggestive: radicalizing the Enlightenment valorization of indigenous Amerindian freedom, it highlighted aboriginal matriarchy and communalism as a utopian model. "The Indian," Oswald de Andrade wrote, "had no police, no repression, no nervous disorders, no shame at being nude, no class struggle, no slavery."[41] Synthesizing insights from Montaigne, Nietzsche, Marx, and Freud, along with what he knew of native Brazilian societies, he portrayed indigenous culture as offering a more adequate social model than the European one, a model based on the full enjoyment of leisure. Playing on the Portuguese word *negocio* — "business," but literally "neg-ocio," or the negation of leisure — de Andrade offered a proto-Marcusean encomium to *sacer-docio,* or "sacred leisure."

This revalorization of a ludic life must be seen against the backdrop of capitalist modernity's productivist and pleasure-denying work ethic and its historical aversion to "subsistence" cultures — a term that itself translates hostility by evoking a desperate struggle for a meager living rather than a proud self-sufficiency within abundance.[42] It is as if any relatively pleasurable life based on communally held land could provoke irritation on the part of "progressive," hardworking puritans. For some thinkers, the capital offense of non-European tribal peoples was not that they lived differently but that they lived enjoyably.[43] Renata Salecl, in an argument that recalls George Bernard Shaw's definition of puritanism as "that terrible fear that someone, somewhere is having a good time," argues that this ludophobia arises when an inhibition of one's own pleasure assumes the symptomatic form of attacks on the pleasures of others.[44]

Apart from the potentially pleasure-multiplying aspects of multiculturalism, what is forgotten in the portrayal of multiculturalists as humorless and resentful is the real historical sources of antipleasure and sexophobic attitudes in our society. Is it the right or the left that is more concerned with controlling women's bodies and the sexuality of young people? Who invented "Just Say No" as the talismanic solution to the socially generated drug problem? Who is it that censures the transracial homoerotic pleasure implied by the photographs of Robert Mapplethorpe or the films of Marlon Riggs? Who is it that sees AIDS as divine vengeance against homosexuals? Who is out fishing for obscenity on the Internet? Are the electronic evangelists, the right-wing radio talk show hosts, the partisans of pleasure? Is the Christian Coalition lots of fun? In a certain sense, many of the key ideas of the new right can be traced back not only to colonialist discourse (as in the link between nineteenth-century "scientific racism" and the latest tracts of Charles Murray) but also to the puritanical origins of the country. The Puritans who left Holland for these shores in 1608 founded an exclusivist democracy already obsessed with national unity and ethnic purity. They punished renegades like Thomas Morton, author of *New Canaan* (1636), who danced with Indians around the maypole and who found them "more full of humanity than the Christians."[45] Like the Puritans, the new rightists are fond of witch-hunts, and in their discourse "crime," presumably always committed by people of darker hue, becomes simply an updated version of "sin." New England Puritans also placed great faith in the death penalty, especially in cases of adultery, theft, and homosexuality. With both the old and the new Puritans, one finds the same concatenation of sexophobia and racism, along with the same suspicious attitude toward fiction and the arts. In Newt Gingrich's cybernetic Salem, there is no place for the National Endowment for the Arts, for Karen Finley or Marlon Riggs. Jesse Helms's pronouncements about the "blasphemy" and the "pornography" sponsored by the National Endowment for the Arts would have made perfect sense to the right-thinking inhabitants of Massachusetts back in 1636. And the scapegoated figure of Hester Prynne, not to mention Tituba the black witch of Salem, has been resuscitated in the form of the much-excoriated welfare queen, the teenage mother, and the abortionist. In the New Jerusalem of the new right, the very rich are God's elect. Wealth has once again become the sign of God's blessing, and poverty the sign of the Devil's curse. The homeless, far from deserving alms, are nothing less than the embodiment of man's fallen state.

Polycentric multiculturalism, in contrast, calls for a kind of diasporization of desire, the multiplication, the cross-fertilization, and the mutual relativization of social energies. I am not suggesting that multiculturalism is simply "fun," a culinary delight where one wanders from falafel one week to sushi the next, with some salsa dancing on Friday night and samba on Saturday. Nor can a radical, polycentric multiculturalism simply be "nice," like a suburban barbecue to which a few token people of color are invited. Any substantive multiculturalism has to recognize the political realities of injustice and inequality and the consequent existential realities of pain, anger, and resentment, since the multiple cultures invoked by the term "multiculturalism" have not historically coexisted in relations of equality and mutual respect. It is therefore not merely a question of communicating across borders but of discerning the forces that generate the borders in the first place. Multiculturalism has to recognize not only difference but even bitter, irreconcilable difference. The descendants of the slave ships and the descendants of the immigrant ships cannot look at the Washington Monument, or Ellis Island, through exactly the same viewfinder. But these gaps in perception do not preclude alliances, dialogical coalitions, intercommunal identifications, and affinities. Multiculturalism and the critique of Eurocentrism, I have tried to show, are inseparable concepts; each becomes impoverished without the other. Multiculturalism without the critique of Eurocentrism runs the risk of being merely accretive — a shopping mall boutique summa of the world's cultures — while the critique of Eurocentrism without multiculturalism runs the risk of simply inverting existing hierarchies rather than profoundly rethinking and unsettling them.

Central to multiculturalism is the notion of *mutual and reciprocal relativization,* the idea that the diverse cultures placed in play should come to perceive the limitations of their own social and cultural perspective. Each group offers its own exotopy (Bakhtin), its own "excess seeing," hopefully coming not only to "see" other groups but also, through a salutary estrangement, to see how it is itself seen. The point is not to completely embrace the other perspective but at least to recognize it, acknowledge it, take it into account, see oneself through it, and even be transformed by it. At the same time, historical configurations of power and knowledge generate a clear asymmetry within this relativization. The powerful and the conservative are not accustomed to being relativized; the world's institutions and representations are tailored to the measure of their narcissism. Thus a sudden relativization by a less flattering perspective is experienced as a shock, an outrage, giving rise to the hysterical neoconservative discourse of besieged civility and reverse victimization. Disempowered groups, in contrast, not only are historically accustomed to being relativized but often display a highly relativizing, even disdainful, attitude toward the dominant cultures. Those who have known in their bodies the violence of the system are less inclined to be deluded by its idealizations and rationalizations. But what I have been calling polycentric multiculturalism is not a favor, an act of charity, or "therapy for minorities," although it might provide therapy for the nation. Multiculturalism makes a cognitive, epistemological contribution. More than a response to a demographic challenge, it is a long overdue course correction, a gesture toward historical lucidity, a matter not of charity but of justice.

NOTES

1. See Frantz Fanon, *Toward the African Revolution* (New York: Monthly Review Press, 1967), 447.

2. For more on recent archaeological research into Palmares, see Ricardo Bonalume Neto, "O Pequeno Brasil de Palmares: Escavacoes arquelogical sugerem que o quilombo de Zumbi era multietnico como um pequeno Brasil," *Folha de São Paulo* (June 4, 1995): 5–16. Palmares has great contemporary resonance in Brazil, as black nationalists invoke Quilombismo and celebrate "Black Consciousness Day" on the anniversary of the death of the Palmarino leader Zumbi. Indeed, black farmers still cultivate the land that their ancestors settled, and a "Quilombo clause" could give land titles to five hundred thousand descendants of the free black communities. Musical groups from Bahia, specifically Olodum and Ile Aiye, have organized support for the present-day descendants of the Quilombos, composing lyrics such as "Quilombo, here we are/my only debt is to the Quilombo/my only debt is to Zumbi." See James Brooke, "Brazil Seeks to Return Ancestral Lands to Descendants of Runaway Slaves," *New York Times,* Sunday, August 15, 1993, 3.

3. R. K. Kent, "Palmares: An African State in Brazil," *Journal of African History* 6, no. 2 (1965): 167–69.

4. Palmares has been celebrated in two Brazilian films by Carlos Diegues, *Ganga Zumba* (1963) and *Quilombo* (1983).

5. Roger Kimball, *Tenured Radicals: How Politics Has Corrupted Higher Education* (New York: HarperCollins, 1990), postscript.

6. Quoted in "The Great PC Scare: Tyrannies of the Left, Rhetoric of the Right," in Jeffrey Williams, ed., *PC Wars: Politics and Theory in the Academy* (New York: Routledge, 1995), 69.

7. See Kimball, *Tenured Radicals,* postscript.

8. William Phillips, "Comment," *Partisan Review* 59 no. 1 (1992): 12.

9. Jan Pieterse, "Unpacking the West: How European Is Europe?" unpublished paper given to me by the author, 1992.

10. On the African influence on modern dance, see Brenda Dixon, "The Afrocentric Paradigm," *Design for Arts in Education* 92 (January/February 1991): 15–22.

11. Pieterse, "Unpacking the West," 16.

12. See Winthrop Jordan, *White over Black* (Baltimore: Penguin, 1968), 405.

13. For an analysis of *Avanti-Popolo,* see Ella Shohat, *Israeli Cinema: East/West and the Politics of Representation* (Austin: University of Texas Press, 1989).

14. Quoted in Theodore W. Allen, *The Invention of the White Race: Racial Oppression and Social Control* (London: Verso, 1994), 31.

15. Jan Pieterse makes the more general point that many of the themes of European imperialism traced antecedents to the European and Mediterranean sphere. Thus the theme of civilization against barbarism was a carry over from Greek and Roman antiquity; the theme of Christianity against pagans was the keynote of European expansion culminating in the Crusades; and the Christian theme of "mission" was fused with "civilization" in the *mission civilisatrice.* See Jan Pieterse, *Empire and Emancipation: Power and Liberation on a World Scale* (Westport, Conn.: Greenwood, 1989), 240.

16. Thomas Jefferson, similarly, called in his own time for the study of Native American culture and languages in schools, yet the multiculturalist call for a "curriculum of inclusion" is caricatured as "therapy for minorities." On Jefferson's interest in Native Americans, see Donald A. Grinde Jr. and Bruce E. Johansen, *Exemplar of Liberty: Native America and the Evolution of Democracy* (Los Angeles: American Indian Studies Center, 1991).

17. See Jacques Derrida, *De la grammatologie* (Paris: Minuit, 1967), 168.

18. Barbara Christian, from a paper presented at the "Gender and Colonialism Conference" at the University of California, Berkeley (October 1989).

19. Talal Asad, "A Comment on Aijaz Ahmad's *In Theory,*" *Public Culture* 6, no. 1 (fall 1993).

20. The world map designed by German historian Arno Peters corrects the distortions of traditional maps. The text of the map, distributed by the UN Development Programme and published by Friendship Press, New York, points out that traditional maps privilege the Northern Hemisphere (these maps have it occupying two-thirds of the world), that they make Alaska look larger than Mexico (when in fact Mexico is larger), Greenland larger than China (although China is four times larger), Scandinavia larger than India (which is in fact three times larger than Scandinavia).

21. The phrase "the West and the Rest," to the best of my knowledge, goes back to Chinweizu's *The West and the Rest of Us: White Predators, Black Slaves, and the African Elite* (New York: Random House, 1975). It is also used in Stuart Hall and Bram Gieben, eds., *Formations of Modernity* (Cambridge: Polity Press, 1992).

22. J. M. Blaut, *The Colonizer's Model of the World: Geographical Diffusionism and Eurocentric History* (New York: Guilford Press, 1993), 10.

23. See David Rieff, "Multiculturalism's Silent Partner," *Harper's* 287, no. 1719 (August 1993).

24. For a much more elaborated discussion of Eurocentrism, see Ella Shohat and Robert Stam, *Unthinking Eurocentrism: Multiculturalism and the Media* (London: Routledge, 1994).

25. See Charles Krautheimer, "An Insidious Rejuvenation of the Old Left," *Los Angeles Times,* December 24, 1990, B5.

26. Quoted in the Brazilian newsmagazine *Isto É* (February 1, 1995): 61.

27. A more relevant model for multiculturalists might be Sarajevo before the war, as a place where Jew and Muslim and Christian lived in peace.

28. The term "intercommunalism," to the best of my knowledge, was first used by the Black Panthers.

29. M. M. Bakhtin, "The Problem of Speech Genres," in *Speech Genres and Other Late Essays* (Austin: University of Texas Press, 1986), 91.

30. See Y. N. Kly, *The Anti-social Contract* (Atlanta: Clarity Press, 1989).

31. See Tom Reiss, "Home on the Range," *New York Times,* May 26, 1995, A11.

32. Arthur Schlesinger, *The Disuniting of America* (Knoxville: Whittle, 1991), 35.

33. Quoted in Barbara Kantrowitz, "A Is for Ashanti, B Is for Black," *Newsweek,* September 23, 1991, 46.

34. Richard Bernstein, *Dictatorship of Virtue* (New York: Knopf, 1994), 49.

35. Ibid., 8.

36. In Brazil, where I taught for five months, the neoconservative portrayal of politically correct leftists coincides with the general Brazilian image of North American society as puritanical and anti-sensual. Both left and right, furthermore, have a certain resistance to multiculturalism. For the right, it is a "black thing" and therefore to be censured, while for the white left it is just one more cultural export from the metropole.

37. William Robertson, *Works* (London, 1824), 9:94–95, quoted in Roy Harvey Pearce, *Savagism and Civilization* (Berkeley: University of California Press, 1988), 88.

38. Tom Paine, *Complete Writings,* ed. Foner, 1:610, quoted in Grinde and Johansen, *Exemplar of Liberty,* 153.

39. Quoted in Bruce E. Johansen, *Forgotten Founders: How the American Indian Helped Shape Democracy* (Boston: Harvard Common Press, 1982), 98.

40. See my *Subversive Pleasures: Bakhtin, Cultural Criticism, and Film* (Baltimore: Johns Hopkins University Press, 1989), and, with Ella Shohat, *Unthinking Eurocentrism: Multiculturalism and the Media* (London: Routledge, 1994), especially the chapter entitled "Esthetics of Resistance."

41. Oswald de Andrade's various manifestoes are collected in *Do Pau-Brasil a antropofagia às utopias* (Rio de Janeiro: Civilização Brasileira, 1972); translations mine.

42. On European hostility to "subsistence societies," see Jerry Mander, *In the Absence of the Sacred: The Failure of Technology and the Survival of the Indian Nations* (San Francisco: Sierra Club Books, 1991), and Marshall Sahlins, *Stone Age Economics* (Chicago: Aldine, 1972).

43. See Dean MacCannell, *Empty Meeting Grounds* (New York: Routledge, 1992).

44. See Renata Salecl, "Society Doesn't Exist," *American Journal of Semiotics* 7, nos. 1/2 (1987): 45–52.

45. The Thomas Morton story is well told by Richard Drinnon in *Facing West: The Metaphysics of Indian Hating and Empire Building* (New York: Schocken, 1980).

Chapter 11
Shuckin' Off the African-American Native Other: What's "Po-Mo" Got to Do with It?
Wahneema Lubiano

Remember the time when stories had a beginning, a middle, and an end?
  In that order...
  Three things made Britain great. A strong navy. The white race. And narrative closure. Don't let's throw them away.

The Sun, June 12, 1988

When Goebbels, the brain behind Nazi propaganda, heard culture being discussed, he brought out his revolver. That shows that the Nazis — who were and are the most tragic expression of imperialism — ...had a clear idea of the value of culture as a factor of resistance to foreign domination.

Amilcar Cabral

Minority texts, like all literary texts, exist simultaneously as determinate objects and as rhetorical practices. ...However, in the context of the neutralizing hegemonic pressures, they will never become effective rhetorical practices until a minority critical discourse articulates them as such.

Abdul R. JanMohamed

First, a polemic: in this moment, postmodern or not, African-American literature and cultural production are being read, consumed, and criticized against a cacophony of voices, from various points of the U.S. academy's political spectrum, bleating that "theory," "postmodernism," and "critiques of race, gender, class, and sexuality" (subtract class from the left version of this complaint) have gone too far. I've tried to understand what such disparate voices might have in common, and it seems to me that what I've been hearing is some version of old narratives (from the right and the left) that delimit the discursive or material space available for particular concerns that are held not to matter by the speakers compared to other concerns that just as obviously do matter. Those speaking, I presume, know who (or what) at any moment has "gone too far." And who (or that which) has gone too far is always some variety of the marginalized, unwilling to stay out of the "center," who transgresses, who "goes too far," who behaves, in this moment, as though she or he has a right to lay claim to a place in the discursive spotlight. While reading my way angrily through the mountains of prose that demand my silence, demand it in the name of the "others" of my group (the "real" others I suppose, since the minute I speak I stop being one) who "cannot speak" (at least not in forums where academics listen) because they (and not I) live in the "real" world, I was stopped cold by a sentence (of Jon Wiener's): "Tell that to the veterans of foreign texts."[1] Because some of the voices complaining of "things" (racialized persons, women, gays, and lesbians?) having "gone too far" evoke a "real" world — much in the way that Wiener's language does — I felt myself drawn into these discussions out of my conviction that African-American cultural practices, texts that come out of those cultural practices, and interpretations/readings of those texts are things that do matter. They matter in the academy and in a "real" world of prisons and bombs. Besides, if the other "others" cannot speak, and I (who at least under some circumstances used to be an "other") allow myself to be admonished into silence, then who is left speaking? And who or what will interrupt business-as-usual?

This essay explores why the debates around postmodernism, "theory," and particular kinds of critiques matter; it uses as an exemplar of the theoretical possibilities of African-American postmodern literary production a short story that scripts the relation of aesthetic notions to raw events of power, the aesthetic as the gloss for an imperializing moral certainty. That story and this essay are answers to the demand implied by "tell that to the veterans of foreign texts": the demand that texts be made as "real" as war.

Gayatri Chakravorty Spivak articulates in "The Post-modern Condition: The End of Politics?" a similar response in more general terms:

> But when they [Derrida, etc.] talk about there is nothing but text, etc., they are talking about a network, a weave — you can put names on it — politico-psycho-sexual-socio, you name it.... The moment you name it, there is a network broader than that.... [That] is very different from saying that everything is language. And to an extent if we are exterminated within the next 5 minutes, it will be a textual event, because it would not come about without the history that we are speaking of at great length here. And if that is not a text, nothing is. (25)

It is perhaps arrogant to suggest that a short story, talking about a short story, is a way to insist that one is "talking back to history," but I am reminded by Spivak and Bruce Robbins that an intellectual grounds herself specifically because there is work to be done in institutions and because the split between the academy and the "real" world is an imposition that keeps nostalgically before us all a harking back to those golden never-never-land moments when "we" were either all working-class, white, revolutionary men storming the Winter Palace or white culture-aristocrats properly mindful of the sacredness of ivory towers. Robbins (in *Intellectuals: Aesthetics, Politics, Academics*) states:

> In the context of gender politics, it requires no paranoia to see attacks on the inadequate "publicness" of the contemporary academy from left and right as a covert means of undermining the specific (though still fragile) gains scored by feminism there. Such attacks are understandable enough from the right, but there is no excuse for anyone else. As if for women, even getting out of the home and into the labor market (not to speak of getting into the academy, *where so much of the content of socialization is determined*) were not to take even the smallest step in a "public" direction! Even in the worst instance, professionalization is always partly achievement from below as well as co-optation from above. (xviii; my emphasis)

I would add only that what Robbins holds for gender politics, for women, holds also for African-Americans. African-American studies (in both its "on and off campus eras" — as Russell Adams terms it) has operated for roughly two hundred years on the assumption that wherever the sites for knowledge production, reproduction, and dissemination were, those were the places on which to take a stand, for oneself and for one's group. An old African-American truism runs thusly: being where they give out education must mean something or they (whites) wouldn't try so hard to keep us out. Of course, getting an education must be extended to giving one too: so I begin here with the debate around postmodernism as an ubiquitous presence from which African-American voices have been largely absent.

Generally, I derive much pleasure at the discursive spectacle of men out of control — even if "real" power and wealth have not yet been redistributed across gender and race as well as class lines — so, if for no other reason than that, postmodernism, as a sign of that lack of control, seems like a good idea to me. That this talk of a "crisis" is now routine makes compelling Alice Jardine's argument for the name that she gives it: "Gynesis" — "a movement away from" identity in the direction of "a concern with difference," that is, a name for males "acting out" anxiety over constraints that have always trapped women (36).

With displays of typical patriarchal arrogance, however, some men continue to agonize over postmodernism's implications: "What is to be done?" (although a more honest version of this question would be "What can *I* do?" or, "Where am *I* in all of this?") is the rallying cry that results from their realization that authority is not stable. A response articulated by feminists, and shared by African-Americans, is to figure out what happens when the idea of metanarratives is up for grabs. One must try to understand what differences do, although in the midst of this kind of postmodernist project African-American men have to re/learn the idea that "difference" for African-Americans includes gender. Still, it is necessary to be able to see when color hangs us all as well as when gender or sexuality adds weight to the tree limb. Such is the political African-American postmodernist project.[2]

I

> *for the embattled*
> *there is no place*
> *that cannot be*
> *home*
> *nor is*

Audre Lorde,
"School Note"

Postmodernism is, according to Dick Hebdige, "a term that gets stretched in all directions across different debates" — from interior design through the "collective chagrin and morbid projections of a post-War generation of baby boomers" to "discussions of global media consumer commodifications" (181–82). While I am not interested in rehearsing everything that has gone on in the debate over postmodernism, nor in staking out a particular yet comprehensive position on a general postmodernism, negotiating with the term is a way to draw attention to where African-American texts write themselves and are written (or are not) in the midst of this debate, especially given the "worldliness" of postmodernism, as Jonathan Arac puts it (281). He adds the caveat, however, that postmodernist criticism is not "urbane" because "this is not a world in which one can or should be too easily at home" (281). What a difference race makes! Given the inhospitality of the United States to African-Americans, there are few of us who need such a reminder. Perhaps that is one of the things that an African-American presence in postmodernism generally can offer: constantly reinvigorated caution.

In his very useful study *The Condition of Postmodernity,* David Harvey warns us against postmodernism's abuses:

> Worst of all, while it opens up a radical prospect by acknowledging the authenticity of other voices, postmodernist thinking immediately shuts off those other voices from access to more universal sources of power by ghettoizing them within an opaque otherness, the specificity of this or that language game. It thereby disempowers those voices (of women, ethnic and racial minorities, colonized peoples, the unemployed, youth, etc.) in a world of lopsided power-relations. The language game of a cabal of international bankers may be impenetrable to us, but that does not put it on par with the equally impenetrable language of inner-city blacks from the standpoint of power-relations. (117)

Prior to postmodernism, however, what or who was responsible for ghettoizing African-Americans — inner-city and otherwise? Was modernism so good to/for/about us? When Gayatri Spivak says "you might want to entertain the notion that you cannot consider all other subjects [and] you should look at your own subjective investment in the narrative that is being produced," she is speaking to those who seek to stand confidently on those "more *universal* sources of power" (29; my emphasis).

Harvey is somewhat attentive to the ways in which postmodernism, according to him, "fits in with the emergence since 1970 of a fragmented politics of divergent special and regional interest groups" (302). But he warns that "regional resistances," bound as they are to particular *spaces* and to the work of "oppositional groups — racial minorities, colonized people, women, etc." — while "excellent bases for political action,... cannot bear the burden of radical historical change alone. 'Think globally and act locally' was the revolutionary slogan of the 1960s. It bears repeating" (303). Certainly. What also bears sustained attention are the particularities, the specifics, of what that slogan means applied to those groups whose politics are delimited by the description "regional resistances." Some "racial minorities, colonized people, women, etc." have proven themselves able to "think globally and act locally" — Frantz Fanon, Amilcar Cabral, Anna Cooper, W. E. B. Du Bois, Malcolm X, Angela Davis, and even Jesse Jackson (despite the constraints that have accompanied his attempt to act in the realm of electoral politics) come most immediately to mind — at the same time they were acting on regional concerns: whether focused on the specifics of colonialism, as was the case with Cabral and Fanon, or on domestic political resistance, cultural internationalism, and the relation between U.S. foreign policy and domestic racism, as has been the case with the others.

Nonetheless, one can make the argument that global metanarratives, "master" narratives (like modernism), have been used to recognize, make a place for, and engage with the specifics of African-Americans, at particular moments. Two cases in point: in "The Dilemma of the Black Intellectual," Cornel West argues that the "Marxist model, despite its shortcomings, is more part of the solution than part of the problem for black intellectuals" (119), and Robin Kelly (in "Comrades, Praise Gawd for Lenin and Them!") examines a period when African-Americans in Alabama manipulated or transformed Marxism in such a way as to make it part of African-American cultural practice, connecting Communist Party analysis and practice with local concerns, mores, and manners, including religious beliefs and practices.

Metanarratives, including Marxism, however, have also often "translated" those who make up "regional resistances" into more politically "universal" categories as part of their more general political deployments. The record on "racism" among those who have articulated their theories and strategies from modernism, Marxism, or other metanarratives has been problematic, as even Harvey is at pains to delineate throughout his study.

Against Harvey's questioning of "regional resistances" with their *space* emphases, Robert Fox has argued that "perhaps it is only minority strategies that can offer an alternative, that can preserve spaces in which difference may operate" (10). Perhaps this is because within the context of postmodernism, those of us who are part of marginalized groups and who also occupy institutional space within the academy are able to consider, in more intent fashion than before, the announcement of postmodernism, *how* difference operates, as opposed to only considering *what* difference is, and want to do so as a way to spread and share the burden of radical change to which Harvey alludes.

Still, in his attempt to be fair to the possibilities of postmodernism and about the problems of metanarratives, Harvey lists the horrors that shattered the optimism of believers in the Enlightenment and modernism, such as the writers Condorcet and Jürgen Habermas, respectively (13). But his list of *twentieth*-century horrors ("with its death camps and death squads, its militarism and two world wars, its threat of nuclear annihilation and its experience of Hiroshima and Nagasaki") passes over slavery and the genocide of the indigenous American population — examples of the on-the-ground facts of history for two marginalized groups in the United States, which means that at least 350 years ago some of us were already in training to be both cynical about the Enlightenment and less than optimistic about modernism.

My awareness of this history, then, tempers any enthusiasm I might feel either for those harangues against postmodernism that want simply to recuperate the idea of metanarratives or for celebrations of postmodernism that, as Cornel West puts it, want to replace modernism with a celebration of "everybody's" marginality: "American attacks on universality in the name of differences, these postmodern issues of 'Otherness' (Afro-Americans, Native Americans, women, gays) are in fact an implicit critique of certain French postmodern discourses about Otherness that really serve to hide and conceal the power of voices and movements of Others" (see Stephanson, 273).[3] West here is concerned with what I call another manifestation of the privileged's ability to exoticize themselves selectively. Against this new universal "otherness," West wants to remind us that specific postmodernisms cost specific "others" their lives, such as African-Americans existing in the cauldron of inner cities or, sometimes (regardless of place, or price, of residence), stopped by the police for traffic violations. Craig Owens also warns against the idea of postmodernism as a kind of free-floating pluralism — a pluralism that "reduces us to being an other among others" and, therefore, "interchangeable" (58). Hal Foster reminds us, however, that seeing postmodernism as pluralism is simplistic, although he too recognizes differing positions in and deployments of postmodernism (xi).

Owens fastens his argument against pluralist postmodernism to recognition of the political edge that inheres in unequal, in politically loaded and oppressed, difference. He argues that feminism recognizes not just "difference" but politics (77). Owens's discussion of feminism and postmodernism is a considerable advance over the thinly disguised hostility toward feminism (and other sites of "regional resistances") that emerges from Harvey's criticism of postmodernism's privileging of difference (about which I say more below). It is an advance called for by Nancy Fraser and Linda Nicholson, who argue that postmodernism and feminism have much to learn from each other (84). Such an advance, however, also comes close, as Laura Kipnis puts it, to colonizing feminism as the currently politically empowering, peripheral "other" against the "center" of patriarchal Marxism (161).

The pitfalls of postmodernist celebration seem easy to fall into: Fox moves to a too general celebration of African-American postmodernism when he says that it has a "strong ethical basis rooted in the demand for, the need for justice" (8) and that "nowhere in the universe of black writing is there such a thing as a purely amoral text" (8). One needs to exercise caution in the matter of affirmations of general ideas of justice — especially "within the group," as many of us who are African-American women would be happy to attest — and morality: morality for whom, when, and under what circumstances? It seems to me more useful to think of African-American postmodernism as a way to negotiate particular material circumstances in order to attempt some constructions of justice.

Nonetheless, while I am cynical about some aspects of postmodernism, about the alleged "newness" of postmodernism's break with the past, for example, it is a "name" that allows certain of us African-Americans to organize our response to modernism's blind spot in regard to people of color, at least as part of a new attention to the politics of difference.

Stuart Hall argues that postmodernism says "this is the end of the world. History stops with us and there is no place to go after this" (47). Perhaps. Maybe for a certain subset of Euro-Americans with privilege to protect, which both stems from history and insulates them from the vacillations of the present, it is possible to say postmodernism and mean what Hall says — although Foster argues that one must not make of postmodernism a conservative monolith. African-American postmodernism, however, insists on the representation of history in the present moment.

But to return to Harvey's cautionary notes: he warns that "any postmodern novel focuses on masks without commenting directly on social meanings other than the activity of masking itself" (101). Well, there's masking and there's masking; within the terms of African-American vernacular, which often moves along lines of indirection — what we can call verbal masking — *commenting directly on* has often been a luxury denied us and, in the mouths of others, has meant being the object of a particular convention's imposition, a convention ignorant of, or which ignores the uses (depending on historical moment and circumstances) of, indirect commentary. Further, African masks, for example, exist in the world as commodities *and* as cultural markers with a wide range of meanings — again, both within specific groups and as political practices "speaking back to" or against domination and hegemony. Double deployment constitutes a primary mode of African-American masking in language and behavior, although as a strategy it is available for misuse as well: one "masks" oneself sometimes to live — striking poses, resisting other poses — and, unfortunately, one sometimes injures with or is injured by poses.

We can consider African-American postmodernism as not simply a historical moment when modernism's intellectual and cultural hegemony is at least being questioned, but as a general epistemological standpoint for engaging/foregrounding what has been left out of larger discourses, a consideration of certain kinds of difference and the reasons for their historical absences. It theorizes ways that prevent engagement with differences from concretizing into intellectually and politically static categories. That is to say, my interest, along with that of others — Hortense Spillers's "Mama's Baby, Papa's Maybe" comes to my mind — is in working over the conflicted ground of discourse genealogies in order to prevent difference from cohering into essentials that are then placed in the service of someone's theorizing.

I insist that African-American postmodernism has to include the kind of narrative flexibility demonstrated by James Alan McPherson's "Elbow Room." So, while I find West's discussion of postmodernism generally excellent and useful, he occasionally gives in to modernist nostalgia: "There used to be a set of stories that could convince people that their absurd situation was one worth coping with, but the passivity is now overwhelming" (in Stephanson, 286). Both passivity and active oppositionality historically have been part of African-American cultural and political practice and are present now. Our presence in this postmodern moment, our deployments of postmodern strategies, and our interventions in postmodern discourse will allow us to complicate those stories in the histories being written now.

I find useful Diane Elam's description of Foster's postmodernism, a postmodernist theorizing that

> allows us to recognize the limitations of the critic's own political role, a limitation we recognize as Foster goes on to explain what he means by postmodernism's resistance. [Instead of] proposing a "reality" outside of ideology,... Foster argues for a theory of resistance that would consider the historical circumstances, the context in which we are necessarily located, at the same time as it acknowledges the difficulty of defining those circumstances. (217)

"Think globally, act locally," then, in cultural resistance terms, might require some lack of sureness, confidence, some awareness of what Spivak calls "vulnerability" (18), or, to paraphrase Foster, a willingness to recognize that a representation may "mean" differently in place, in moment, and in particular minds.

The African-American presence in this postmodern moment is not a given. When Fredric Jameson (in his most recent and massive study of postmodernism) describes those postmodern productions of which he is a "relatively enthusiastic consumer," he lists, among other things, the novel, "the weaker of the new cultural areas," but states that the "subgeneric narratives, however, are very good, indeed; *in the Third World of course all this falls out very differently*" (*Postmodernism,* 298; my emphasis). Where does African-American fiction fit in this? Are we part of the category named by Third World, by subgeneric narrative? His assertion, in an earlier essay, "Modernism and Imperialism," more accurately places some African-American fiction:

> [W]e have come to think of the emergence of an internal Third World and of internal Third World voices, as in black women's literature or Chicano literature for example. When the other speaks, he or she becomes another subject, which must be consciously registered as a problem by the imperial or metropolitan subject — whence the turn of what are still largely Western theories of imperialism in a new direction, toward that other, and toward the structures of underdevelopment and dependency for which we are responsible. (49)

Jameson is not required to talk about the complexities of "internal Third World" cultural production or politics, but what is interesting for my purposes is that the discourse of postmodernism presents itself as a site for thinking about difference — it is possible, then, for some of us to elbow our way onto that site. And if postmodernism marks an "incredulity toward metanarratives" (Lyotard, xxiv), it is certainly an appropriate name for African-Americans (whose "status" in Eurocentric metanarratives has been at least more problematic than not and at worst has justified our repression): our histories show that we've maintained a fairly consistent level of incredulity; perhaps it is time that the "West" caught up with us.

No, the ending of various kinds of cultural authorities (Jameson in his *New Left Review* article) is not a crisis for African-Americans. First slavery and then the continuing manifestation and operation of racism — a meta- or master narrative on the ground of the United States — have demanded that African-Americans see themselves as incapable of constructing and complicating their subjectivity, of positing some versions of value. Objecting to and/or resisting meta- or master narratives — either as part of a project that reconstructs more specific narratives or as practitioners of cultural practices that resemble what is called "postmodernist" — allow us to be seen as postmodernist, although we can call, and have called, what we do by other names. In other words, depending upon where I find myself, I might both articulate and complicate "African-American cultural practices" or notions of "African-American literary traditions."

An African-American feminist postmodernism, a name for internal critiques of African-American postmodernism, is attuned to valorizing African-American cultural practices but is not blind to their transgressions against within-the-group differences. African-American postmodernism, then, to be politically nuanced in a radical way, has to focus on such differences' implications, especially in moments of oppositional transgressions: it is not just attention to assertions of presence, but attentiveness to responsibilities and strategies that have to change *given* certain presences.

Our experience of history as sloppily and inconsistently, but saliently, present in this moment, as Toni Morrison's *Beloved* so thoroughly demonstrates, suggests that the collage modality of postmodernism is one way to refuse the dangerous pleasures of coherence by instead demanding constant reconstructing.

If we are willing to consider *a* postmodernist (I am again being careful here not to try to account for a general postmodernism) concern with deconstructing the hegemonic ideologies of the West, insofar as they construct a universal human subject, metaphysical grounding, and "truth," then African-American cultural practice and cultural artifacts can be "read" within such an economy. And that is the claim I make for "Elbow Room."

I chose this male-authored and largely male-centered text to discuss because it represents marriage and families as the ground for rereading, deconstructing, the relationship between power and aesthetics. In the story's dramatization (1) of a deconstruction of narrative convention, (2) of complications of social constructions of race, and (3) of the nexus of the political and the personal, its representation of a struggle over aesthetic imperialism and its agenda for certain "native others" offer a reason to read and talk about African-American literature, a reason that goes beyond positivist "pluralist" reasons, that is, variations of the position that texts of marginalized groups should be read because we read those of the dominant group.

"Elbow Room" is both a specific theoretical text and an exemplar that functions to expose the way in which Eurocentric, particularly Enlightenment/modernist, gatekeepers have read/framed African-American texts. Thus, it suggests itself as a site for engagement with at least one project of the African-American theoretical discourse: exploration of counterhegemonic possibilities of narrative construction and interpretation that a minority critical discourse can address along the lines that Jan-Mohamed articulates in "Humanism and Minority Literature: Toward a Definition of Counter-hegemonic Discourse" (quoted in the epigraph). It is an example of politically engaged African-American postmodernism that derails narrative conventions in order to specify a connection between aesthetics and politics.

II

"Elbow Room" revolves around four people: an unnamed African-American male narrator, a married couple — including Virginia, an African-American woman, and Paul, a Euro-American man — and an editor. The plot follows the narrator's intervention into the couple's lives, his editorial battles with the editor, and the interstices between the couple's personal details and families, the issue of race, and literary/aesthetic convention. The story is framed by an epigraph that equates Daniel Boone's conquest of Kentucky with aesthetic morality; the plot follows the narrator's resistance to the editor's attempts to impose a particular set of conventions in perusing the narrator's final draft. In this way, the reader "sees" the mechanics of "literary gatekeeping" via the editor's demands for overexplanation and repeated insistence that the narrator delete crucial segments "impeding" (in the editor's opinion) the "realistic narrative flow" of the story. His[4] inability to "read" the narrator's story is paralleled by Paul's inability to "read" race. "Elbow Room" foregrounds the means of its own production — demystifying the aesthetic against which it intervenes.

The text foregrounds indeterminacy as an act of resistance to external pressure to translate and nail down racial consciousness; it delegitimates the master codes of narrative in the power struggle between the black narrator and the white editor; it parodies conventional literary modes in its play with the representations of romance; and it consistently draws attention to itself as a narrative in its metacommentary on the structure, demands, expectations, and failures of storytelling. The story exploits the political possibilities of postmodernist technique by juxtaposing problems of racism and imperialism (cultural and material) with arguments about aesthetics and narrative form.

At the same time that "Elbow Room" subverts expectations of traditional concepts of narrative, its language and structure provide a site for seeing the interplay between the discourse of colonialism and anticolonialism and the discourse of the African-American literary-critical tradition. In this regard my study draws on the terms that Houston Baker delineates.[5] And when I speak of African-American texts and African-Americans in terms of colonialist discourse, I am drawing on Frantz Fanon's theory that African-American culture has the same relationship to the dominant culture as a colonialized culture has to the colonialists, a relationship that he describes in *The Wretched of the Earth:*

> The Negroes who live in the United States . . . experience the need to attach themselves to a cultural matrix. Their problem is not fundamentally different from that of the Africans. The whites of America did not mete out to them any different treatment from that of the whites who ruled over the Africans. We have seen that the whites were used to putting all Negroes in the same bag. (215)

The story foregrounds the material struggles generally glossed over in the name of aesthetics by placing a matrix of overdeterminations — racial identity, racism, territoriality, a discussion of internal and external aesthetics, societal relations, and political upheavals — at the heart of what is also an almost ruthlessly formulaic story of boy meets girl, boy marries girl, boy and girl have baby, all against a background of parental disapproval. It also explores the pervasiveness and perniciousness of ideas of "race" and the "racial other," exemplifying the ways in which African-American texts (and marginalized texts generally) undermine notions of the world constructed according to, and by, the hegemonic culture of Euro-America. Through explicit and implicit problematizing of the possible range of meanings of "nigger," the story also "signifies" (in the vernacular sense)[6] on the terms of the discourse of African-American literary-critical tradition.[7]

What I find most interesting about "Elbow Room," however, is the fact that it is one of the very few male-authored African-American texts to center on what has historically been trivialized as "women's concerns" — the realm of marriage, domesticity, and private relations. Things conventionally considered public and political — race and imperialism — cohere in that private and personal realm. This text combines an anticolonialist reimagining of the world with content that embodies the tie between sexual attraction and politics. That tie manifests itself, within this narrative, in the construction of an interracial marriage; the tension implicit in the politics of aesthetics is embodied in the problematized domesticity of the protagonists of this story.

Feminist theory has argued for decades that the split between the personal and the political was always a chimera, and feminist practice has made the personal another site for political engagement — hence the slogan that equates the two. And while

Arac has argued that "one reason the personal has become the political is because of the agitation for public remedies in areas long considered private" (306), I would add that the political (or public) is both reified and made "real" in the realm of the personal or private, that the "chickens" of the public/political come "home" to roost in the personal (or private). The story dramatizes this.

III

According to JanMohamed, "race" or racial difference is transformed "into a moral and even metaphysical difference" within the logocentric system of the Western tradition or culture ("Economy," 80). He argues that "colonialist literature is an exploitation and a representation of a world at the boundaries of 'civilization,'...[a world] perceived as uncontrollable, chaotic, unattainable, and ultimately evil" (83). Within this economy a civilizing project is demanded that introduces the "native" to the benefits of Western culture (63).

"Elbow Room" turns such traditional and colonialist propositions of "race" or the "racial other" on their heads through the vehicle of the narrator, who appropriates the "civilizing function" in regard both to the editor of the story and to the story's white male protagonist, while he repeatedly interrupts the attempts of the editor to impose conventional narrative form on this story. At the same time, the story itself decenters traditional realistic narrative forms by replacing such forms, and reader expectation of such modes of presentation, with a narration that only initially suggests itself as "native other" to the expectations of the editor, but ultimately subverts both that editor's and its own potential control of the content. And through its explicit questioning of narrative form, and its implicit questioning of what is meant by "art," the story addresses the terms of the discourse of the African-American literary-critical tradition.

"Elbow Room" encourages theoretical analysis because it narrates a story of rebellion against imposed form as an analogue to its other, more customarily political, subject matters. The story refuses to explain itself, and that refusal critiques the "civilizing function" of such self-commentary. That is to say, its break with such forms is analogous to disrupting the colonizer positions such forms maintain in the literature of the colonized. The story represents a struggle that Hazel Carby (drawing on Hall) has described as "the struggle within and over language" that reveals "the nature of the struggle of social relations and the hierarchy of power" (17). I argue that this narrative is explicitly and implicitly a resisting narrative. In order to frame the issues at stake in this narrative, however, it is necessary to juxtapose African-American literary history to the larger Euro-American literary history.

IV

The idea of realism as the proper mode of narration goes back, at least, to Aristotle and comes down to us via the articulation of any number of critics and writers in the Western tradition. In "The Art of Fiction," for example, Henry James places the logocentric seal of approval on representation and its marriage to realism: "[T]he only reason for the existence of a novel [and, by extension, fiction] is that it represents life" (378). And, as John Ruskin asserts, the painter [or poet]

> must always have two great and distinctive ends: the first, to induce in the spectator's [reader's] mind the faithful conception of any natural objects; . . . the second, to guide the spectator's mind to those objects most worthy of its contemplation, and to inform him of the thoughts and feelings with which these were regarded by the artist himself. (133)

We get the point. Realistic technique is its own system of universal morality. What Ruskin's language does not admit is that such morality depends upon acceptance of a larger narrative that "explains" what is "worthy." Realism, then, according to Catherine Belsey, "evokes a world we already seem to know" and "offers itself as transparent" — thus performing the work of ideology, offering consistent subjects who originate meaning (51–52). Such realism, described by Wilson Harris as "obsessive centrality," can be subverted by the exercise of language, or as Harris asserts, the imposed centrality of something called realism can be undermined by the properties of language itself, an "interior and active expedition through and beyond what is already known" (77). I am talking here not about specific representations of a particular "real" but about a notion that a truthful, consensual real exists, a notion that is loaded with unacknowledged ideology about realism.

Of course, the privileging of realism is not restricted to British and Euro-American literary discourse; the effect of hegemony is that the concerns of the dominant culture are internalized, to some extent, by the "others." So it follows that African-American literary critics of the first two eras of African-American criticism, the integrationist poetics critics and the black aesthetic critics, also privilege realism as the key mode for narration without reflecting on their hegemonic compliance. Both eras of critics internalized to some degree the demands of Euro-American culture: the integrationist critics in their assumption that the forms of English and American literature had universal application, and the black aesthetic critics, black cultural nationalists, in their insistence upon the imposition of another "truth," another realism — a monolithic, absolutist, and essentialist "black truth" or "black reality" to counteract the big white "lies" about black culture and history. James Stewart (in Larry Neal and Amiri Baraka's *Black Fire*) puts it bluntly indeed: "The Black artist must construct models which correspond to his [*sic*] reality" (3) because "the [other] reality model was incongruous. It was a white reality model" (8).

I do not ignore here the constraints of material and historical oppression. The critics of both eras were beset by vicious distortions of African-Americans and their culture on the part of the dominant culture — distortions that had to be addressed. I agree with West when he states: "The fight for representation and recognition highlighted moral judgements regarding Black 'positive' images over and against White supremacist stereotypes" ("New Cultural Politics," 103). I refer only to the fact that their attempts at correction often responded in terms that remained on the ground of the racist and sexist Euro-American discourse. Edward Said argues: "[T]hat is one problem with nationalism: its results are written across the formerly colonized world, usually in the fabrics of newly independent states whose pathologies of power, as Eqbal Ahmad has called them, bedevil political life even as we speak" (74). While African-Americans as a group are not trying to constitute them-selves as a state (although some African-Americans do rally around such a desire) — here African-American nationalism is a cultural strategy and desire — Said's language does describe, to some degree, the traps built into uncomplicated African-American cultural nationalism.

Not an easily assimilable text for either integrationist or black nationalist read-ings, "Elbow Room" intervenes against preconstructions. Of course, the text has its own "real," its own world. And in that world characters are given histories by the text. Nonetheless, its narrator's insistence, within that "world," that he is looking for stories is the way in which the text attempts, at least, not to lay claim to a single monolithic "reality," a way to suggest that narrative is multiple, that others construct them also. "Elbow Room" calls the narrative conventions of monolithic or stable ideas of representation and realism into question from its beginning by refusing to state a "truth," a "general" truth in a form that pretends to be disinterested — al-though the editor never admits that any form he demands comes out of a particular aesthetic history. The narrator not only resists editorial authority — he shatters the illusion of accurate and controlled representation by interrupting the story to argue *against* the imposition of a single narrative form, reminding the reader that he is not telling his story along the lines or within the boundaries that would reassure the editor or reinstate a "white" aesthetic in "black" face. Additionally, by the end of the story, he even admits out loud his own narrative inadequacy in the face of storytelling "material" as complex as racialized human beings in their particularity.

This narrative constantly resists attempts to be read as a *unified* and organized whole even as it flagrantly displays the trappings of linear plot. It starts and stops as a result of false beginnings, vicissitudes of the friendship between the narrator and the characters, the editor's and narrator's passages of arms, and, most importantly, as a result of the difficulties, limitations, inadequacies, and intricacies of narration itself. The compromised omniscient, playful knowledge and interventions of the narrator of "Elbow Room" violate James's manifesto of the importance of intensity of illusion and pretense of bewilderment in constructing realistic prose that presents itself as unmediated (*Art of the Novel,* 66). It is not that the narrator has no investment in realism at all; rather, it is that he refuses to pretend that the stories he recounts are uninformed by his mediation, a mediation that takes a different form from that which the editor attempts to impose. The narrator continually reminds us of his presence as narrator through his decisions to continue the indirect mode of his "political" subtext. McPherson, as author, will not stay out of this text, nor will that narrator fall back within the lines the editor continually draws. The story interrupts the pretense of an "unauthored" narrative (Belsey, 52). While narrative interruptions are not inherently antirealistic, his interruptions shatter the illusion that the story is going on under its own momentum.

The idea of form confronted in the text is an analogue for the idea of Western civilization and its ideology of beauty and morality. The first lines of the text set up the struggle:

Narrator is unmanageable. Demonstrates a disregard for form bordering on the paranoid. Questioned closely, he declares himself the open enemy of conventional narrative categories. When pressed for reasons, narrator became shrill in insistence that "border," "structures," "frames," "order," and even "form" itself are regarded by him with the highest suspicion. Insists on unevenness as a virtue. Flaunts an almost barbaric disregard for the moral mysteries, or integrities, of traditional narrative modes. (215)

The disapproving voice of the editor ties conventions to morality — disregard of form is "almost barbaric" disregard for "moral mysteries" or "integrities" of traditional narrative form. The message is clear: certain aesthetics equal moral good. Indeed, these lines are a parody of received ideas about the sacredness of form. The editor goes on to assume the role of the civilizer who will present the refined "essence" of the story: "Editor speaks here of a morality of morality, of that necessary corroboration between unyielding material and the discerning eye of absolute importance in the making of a final draft. This is the essence of what he said" (256). The story itself, however, comes from the hands (or mouth) of an "unmanageable" black narrator and as such relentlessly undermines its own authority. The opening frame, however, is spoken by the nonnarrating editorial voice and sets up a journalistic distance; that editor attempts to make the reader complicit in prejudgment of the narrator, and while disavowing his ownership of the narration, the editor retains the power to deliver the "essence" — a crude reduction — of that story. He attempts to repeat the colonizer's trope: "native" caricature.

The "story" begins with a microhistory of two individuals it then places immediately in the larger political history of their time. In fact, we know the time and the characters in terms of political and social oppression. By the end of the story, we realize that through this narration of a microhistory (a "personal" relationship), we've been "reading" the macro- ("political") history of the construction of race in America.

But the confusion evoked by the story's refusal to "behave" makes it hard for the editor to read the words on the page: expectations of some forthcoming clarity get in the way. The editor finally can "see" neither the story taking shape before him nor the relationship between that failure and his "duty" to restrain the story and the "barbaric" narrator. Ironically, then, given the history of "whites' " encounters with "blacks," the narrator is there to "civilize" the editor, who has tried to set up a civilizing project directed at the narrative: an inversion of the colonialist ur-text. The text and the narrator, in African-American vernacular terms, deconstruct the terms of history. The two "talk back" and turn the tables, then, on a dynamic that Said describes as "one of the salient traits of modern imperialism," that "in most places it set out quite consciously to modernize, develop, instruct, and civilize the natives" (74).

The narration proper begins from an omniscient point of view (an omniscience that has been problematized already by the text and challenged by the editor), introducing characters and questions, presenting plausible information within conventional-enough metaphors — in short, setting us up to expect something or some things recognizable in symbolic terms we already understand:

Paul Frost was one of thousands of boys who came out of those little Kansas towns back during that time.
     Virginia Valentine had come out of Warren some ten years before, on the crest of that great wave of jailbreaking peasants.... Virginia's quest was an epic of idealism. (215–17)

We are introduced in greater detail to Paul, who represents the quintessential liberal humanist whose war protest took the form of conscientious objection and whose personal political statement takes the form of interracial marriage with Virginia, a black peasant, who, while on a voyage of international "discovery" (the typical romantic quest adventure made atypical and political by its context, the Peace Corps), had made an important finding not usually part of the conventional apparatus of the conventional "hero": a perspective that makes the sign "nigger" a symbol of self-affirmation (217), an inversion of an old hierarchy.

The temporal setting of the story focuses on the 1960s and a temporary new international egalitarianism (in some quarters) that could not, however, be sustained. The egalitarianism is undermined by reassertions of old conventions at home and forces Virginia and Paul out to the territory — to California — for new possibilities, just as the narrator is forced to the territory because he needs to find new narratives.

From the beginning, Virginia and Paul's marriage inverts the conventional hierarchy: Virginia, child of a rural African-American Tennessee farmer family, is the "rural lumpen" aristocrat, and Paul, the child of a Euro-American bourgeois, entrepreneurial family, is the consort who needs remaking. The inverted hierarchy here is based on political consciousness.

Almost immediately, however, the control of the narrative breaks down. The stories that had allowed for the beginning of connection among people begin to disappear, and a nascent internationalist perception (an internationalism that had empowered Virginia) recedes back into simplistic divisions of "black and white" (218), back into conventionalism — imperialist "form" inscribed in the flesh of individuals.

It is then that we are lulled by the entrance of the black, male, first-person narrator — no more customary (but behind-the-scenes) authorial omniscience guides the story — who seems to be the "native other" to the editor. This "I" "tells" the remainder of the narration, but his assumption of control has been complicated by the editor's prior presentation of him — the reader hears the echo of the words "unmanageable," "barbaric," and "uncontrollable" at his entrance; the struggle between these two voices is set up. The reader steps into a tug-of-war between the editor, who insists upon closure, and the narrator, holding out for indeterminacy or (in some cases) a turnabout of form and meaning.

This would-be civilizing function of the editor is manifested in his attempt to control the story: the narrator's story generates "too much" indeterminacy, which in turn threatens to undermine the certainty of conventional symbols and constructs. The editor's attempt, however, is turned on its head. His demand for narrative clarity and traditionally stated realism is decentered. In the first interruption (following the various beginnings of the story) the editor questions and the narrator answers with a nonanswer that nonetheless foregrounds the hidden demand made on the text by the editor:

A point of information. What has form to do with caste restrictions?

Everything.

You are saying you want to be white?

A narrator needs as much access to the world as the advocates of that mythology.

You are ashamed then of being black?

Only of not being nimble enough to dodge other people's straight-jackets.

Are you not too much obsessed here with integration?

I was cursed with a healthy imagination.

What have caste restrictions to do with imagination?

Everything.

A point of information. What is your idea of personal freedom?

Unrestricted access to new stories forming.

Have you paid sufficient attention to the forming of this present one?

Once upon a time there was a wedding in San Francisco. (220)

The editor's first interruption asks a question about explicit statements, about explicit explanations, that the narrator refuses to make. Throughout such interruptions, the narrator carries out both his resistance to the attempts of the editor to impose form on him as well as his own more subtle civilizing project in regard to the editor. The resistance itself, as in this case, often takes the shape of what seems to be a non sequitur, a seemingly direct answer that nonetheless refuses to answer the question: "Once upon a time there was a wedding in San Francisco" — a response so direct that it skips the metalanguage of an answer to the editor's question and goes so directly to a conventional narrative form that it parodies the demand of the editor's question. After all, what does "once upon a time" mean? Is it here? Is it true? Is it now? What could "there was" possibly mean in this context? It introduces a "dummy" topic that demonstrates that conventional and privileged forms do not "tell" us anything and that suppresses the principals of the wedding while introducing a conventional ritual in place of answering the editor's demand to make the story conventional. It cuts off a discussion with a narrative "red herring."

Here and elsewhere, the narrator, while resisting the pressure to impose control on this narrative and to clarify it, "teaches" the editor. While refusing to alter his mode of discourse, he forces the editor either to accept his own ignorance (his inability to "read" the narrator's language) or to "read" (or at least indicate his consciousness of) the narrator's indirectness. By the end of the story the editor's inability to do either makes him break down into unanswered hysteria. His final line (and that of the story also) is one last reiteration of his customary refrain: "Comment is unclear. Explain. Explain" (241). To this exhortation there is no response. The editor is outside of the text's discourse — left in the darkness of his uninterrogated whiteness. The editor "believes in" conventional form and can't accept the narrator's advocacy of other constructs; he refuses to acknowledge the surfacing of formerly repressed "otherness."

The narrator's more directly civilizing project comes into play with his interaction with Paul, the white male protagonist who is the new "native other," who needs the "light" of darkness, of knowledge of black people, of black culture. The nar-

rator reverses the colonizer/native relationship and describes Paul in the protective
language (normally associated with the "other") reminiscent of that which Ralph Ellison uses in order to establish invisibility as a beachhead for subversive activity.
The narrator (now the black colonizer) sets out to the "territory," to the frontier —
to California — repeating in North American terms the journey across the borders of
civilization to a more fluid, less civilized place, a place where social formations have
not yet cohered into the "old ways."

It is here, in the territory's fluid possibilities, that the text turns a spotlight on
the tendency of members of the dominant group to turn an exoticizing and com-
modifying gaze on the "native" and artifacts of that "native's" culture — a gaze that
nonetheless remains completely blind to the political and material reality of the "native." Paul, a man of the prairie, with "dead Indians living in his eyes" (263), must
remake himself in international terms in order to see past his own exoticizing gaze.
He has to learn to "see" Virginia (get an earlier set of dead "natives" out of his eyes)
in order to save his marriage to her — a black figure of power, a teller of stories with
an international flavor, and the figure who names and defines.

The narrator undertakes to bring to Paul's attention the assumptions underlying his
way of seeing and his refusal of sight — an intrasubjective evaluation. Such politicization is absolutely necessary if the marriage is to withstand the pressure from
Paul's conventionally racist father. The narrator attempts a warning:

> I said, "Someone is coming here to claim you. Soon you may surprise even yourself.
> While there is still time, you must force the reality of your wife into your father's mind
> and run toward whatever cover it provides."
>
> I felt bad for having intruded into his story, but there was a point I wanted very
> much for him to see. I pointed toward a Nigerian ceremonial mask nailed to the wall
> just over the kitchen door. The white light from the bulbs above us glowed on the
> brown polished wood of the mask. "Do you think it's beautiful?" I asked.
>
> Paul sipped his wine. He said, "It's very nice. Ginny bought it from a trader in
> Ibadan. There's a very good story behind it." I said, "But do you think it's beautiful?"
>
> Then he looked at me with great emotion in his eyes. "It's nice," he said. I said,
> "You are a dealer in art. You have extraordinary taste. But your shop is in a small
> town. You want to sell this mask by convincing your best customer it is beautiful and
> of interest to the eye. Every other dealer in town says it is ugly. How do you convince
> the customer and make a sale?"
>
> I said to Paul, "You have enlisted in a psychological war." (228)

Paul fails. At that time, he could not remake his aesthetic judgment even within the
terms of commodity culture. He would attempt to "sell" the mask by virtue of an
exotic narrative — it has "a very good story behind it" — but his "values" do not
allow him to "see" that it is beautiful. By allegorical extension, Paul fails to communicate Virginia's value to his middle-class, provincial father. Out of his frustration
and anger he asks the narrator what "nigger" *really* means to him and hangs up
angrily when the narrator answers: "A descendant of Proteus, an expression of the
highest form of freedom" (233). The narrator has responded with a version of the
truth: there isn't *one* or *a* nigger, but a Protean mass of definitions, a historically
specific set of deployable constructions. Yet Paul must generate a narrative about
the mask (or, at least, generate a sales pitch) that can explain its beauty, so as to

teach his entrepreneurial father to complicate his notions of "blackness," to "see" Virginia.

Paul's making of himself represents more than a bourgeois individualistic journey to a better self. His racial politicization, which is the thing at stake here, is part of the text's attempt to deconstruct his "innocence," the political privilege of the power-ful — an innocence that allows the ideology of white racial stratification to remain unchallenged while certain white individuals simply parade their idiosyncratic toler-ance, a tolerance incongruent with racism's history. The explicit ground upon which Paul's remaking is engaged is the need for him to understand and communicate a new set of aesthetics. A system of aesthetics, however, is only the artistic arm of the dominant culture's law. At stake in his increased consciousness is the undermining of the construction of race.

The narrative foregrounds the sign "nigger" as an ideological construction and reclaims it as a sign of affirmation. Aimé Césaire describes a similar moment in his explanation of the origins of "negritude": "That's when we adopted the word negre, as a term of defiance. It was a defiant name. To some extent it was a reaction of enraged youth. Since there was shame about the word negre, we chose the word negre" (74). Reconstructing "nigger" is part of the landscape of African-American self-imagining and an indication of deployments of rhetorical art. When Paul shouts accusingly at the narrator that "nigger" is what the narrator is when he thinks of himself as a work of art, Paul is speaking more truth than he knows. Yes, "nigger" is art, participatory art, creative manipulation of available materials with political intent. The focus is not on what a "nigger" is (classic or otherwise) but on what a "nigger" does — definition by practice, by relation to sociopolitical requirements. In a sharp piece of vernacular indirection, the text tells us that "nigger" equals art, a notion that eventually literally "gags" the editor.

Paul must act in this discursive work or his and Virginia's domesticity, as well as what their domesticity represents — a personally and politically engaged world order — is threatened. He has to learn to be part of a meditation that can form the necessary background for a "classic kind of nigger" and to be a fit consort for Vir-ginia — a woman complicated enough to resist the reification implied in the state of "honorary whiteness" for her soon-to-be-born child, a state offered by the strin-gently conditioned initial response to her of Paul's father (281). She realizes her own ability to "make enough elbow room" for herself and for her complexities, including her blackness (281), and it is she who decenters the colonial sign "nigger," but she alone cannot make that marriage.

Virginia, Paul, and their relationship are part of the text's play with notions of "star-crossed lovers" (a category into which interracial mésalliances conventionally fall). The narrator attempts to alert Paul to the conventional narrative formulas for such relationships: "I can understand your father's worry. According to convention, one of you is supposed to die, get crippled for life, or get struck down by a freak flash of lightning while making love on a sunny day" (226). But what resonates are the political ramifications and possibilities represented by an interracial marriage. The text ironically presents the ingredients of the old formula with a fascinating twist: the black, male narrator, while aware of his own vulnerabilities in matters of story-telling, still attempts to mold the white male's political consciousness in order to help this couple maintain the kind of relationship that foregrounds some of black and white America's most salient fears in order to subvert those fears. Within the terms of white supremacy, what is race, finally, if it is not completely delineated and contained by biological difference? An interracial relationship that results in children is at least the heterosexual deconstruction of a false metanarrative. Moving outside of that economy, the story asks another question: What is the meaning of race as a legal and geographical construct? And, given race as a construct, what is being represented in an interracial marriage and its issue — the mulatto? This relationship is the troubled ground for a consideration of the effects of the public and political hegemonic pressure of racism (and its manifestation in aesthetics) on something as private and personal as a romantic relationship, and for a consideration of the demands on private identity of increased racial consciousness. At the same time, the story critiques individual postures of defensive reaction. When Paul snaps at the narrator in anger, "You think I'm a racist," reinscribing a conventional political narrative, the required response is far more complicated than a simple yes or no could be.

V

The story's deliberate subversion of itself remains constant. Within its frame, stories have potential to save lives and allow for connection. But the narrative self-consciously admits its own inadequacies as well as the narrator's own inadequacies and occasional lack of vision or interest: "I did not think they had a story worth telling," he says at one point (227). In the face of his inadequacy, he falls back on an assertion of disdain based on personal aesthetics. He tries to pull back from the narration, at the point where Virginia reduces her own history to conventional rugged bourgeois individualism, by recourse to the prop of all inept narrators — a cliché: "Life is tough all right" (237).

Neither this narrative nor this narrator is part of a pattern for unproblematic and centered control, for a unified subject. The story is, however, a sure ground for exploration, for problematizing, and for decentering. The narrative decenters the authority of Western tradition and declines to replace it with another authority, not even narrative authority. It suggests, instead, the power and problems of attempts to create indeterminate space for the enactment of human imagination.

"Elbow Room" is not only an anticolonialist text that deconstructs the Manichaean dichotomies that posit the "native other" as a savage in need of the civilizing benefits of Western culture; it does so within the African-American vernacular "signifying" structure to which I referred above. Such a structure undoes the idea of a narrative even as it generates one; it engages the notion of a narrator telling a story that is the site of struggle within an editor.

Finally, who is telling this story? The narrator? Or the editor, who is attempting to deliver the "essence" of a story told by a black narrator about an interracial marriage, a story that questions notions of racial essence? Trying to both deliver and restrain something as slippery as essence is tricky, and the editor delivers more than he knows. And whose story is it? That of the protagonists? That of the editor, who demands constant translation, clarification, and commentary? Does the story belong to the narrator who resists certain narrative demands and questions even as he signifies on those demands and delivers, after a fashion, a story? Or does it slip out of everyone's grasp?

VI

From the idea that the self is not given to us, I think that there is only one practical consequence: we have to create ourselves as a work of art.

Michel Foucault

Indirection and playfulness characterize African-American signifying and the story "Elbow Room." The story constitutes the ground on which the battle over narrative aesthetics is yet another staging area for the same imperialist appropriations that govern land seizures and racial constructions. It indirectly states its intention of challenging the power of dynamics of conquest and aesthetics in the beginning with the epigraph taken from William Carlos William's "The Discovery of Kentucky":

> Boone's genius was to recognize the difficulty as neither material nor political but one purely moral and aesthetic.

Where this epigraph argues that questions of aesthetics not only are morally binding but are the *only real* questions, the *Sun's* language (quoted at the beginning of this essay) gives the game away: stories with narrative closure are as responsible for maintaining power as navies and white supremacy. And "Elbow Room" signifies on the idea of "Boone's genius" and unmasks it as a gloss for appropriation; to consider questions of aesthetics, or race, and not admit the power dynamics or material imperialism masked by such considerations — the message of Boone's discovery — is to leave the metanarrative unchallenged.

The nexus of class power and aesthetics is thematized at the point where the narrator, after visiting a recent prison parolee who has internalized prison, attends a prison reform party given by a female member of the bourgeoisie:

> This woman looked me straight in the eye while denouncing prisons with a passionate indignation. Periodically, she swung her empty martini glass in a confident arc to the right of her body. There, as always, stood a servant holding a tray at just the point where, without ever having to look, my hostess knew a perfect arc and a flat surface were supposed to intersect. . . . I began to laugh. (233–34)

The passage emphasizes the lock that order and constraint have on the interaction between the privileged and the objects of their largess, between aesthetics and politics. In other words, "Elbow Room" brings together narrative conventions, racial construction, aesthetics, and the dynamic of imperialist appropriativeness that is their subtext.

And this story vernacularly "loudtalks" in the presence of "the man" — the powerful white restrictor of other-than-conventional forms. The narrator addresses race issues that literally are outside the purview of this white gaze, a gaze finally made powerless because, while the editor simply does not "get it" (does not understand), the story is told anyway.

The narrative comments indirectly on imposed notions of reality and argues against the imposition of form, doing so by parodying such form: "Once upon a time there was a wedding." As part of its mode of indirection, it signifies on or revises tropes of other African-American texts.[8] From the beginning, "Elbow Room" pays tribute to Ralph Ellison's theorizing about the stranglehold of apolitical American modernism when it restates the phrase "morality of technique" (taken from Ellison's "Twentieth Century Fiction and the Black Mask of Humanity") in order to foreground form as the aesthetic arm of Anglo-American hegemony. Further, it tropes or revises the unnamed narrator of *Invisible Man* by making its own unnamed narrator the vehicle of other persons' stories while keeping him extraordinarily and didactically visible, and makes of "nigger" — the Protean shape-changer — a revised trope of Ellison's "invisibility": "nigger" here is "an expression of freedom." The idea of a Protean "nigger" is the theoretical equivalent of Ellison's Rinehart. And finally, the narrative revises Ishmael Reed's *Mumbo Jumbo* by unnaming the Western tradition parodied more directly by Reed: the Wallflower Order, the Atonists. In this text, however, that tradition is never described in its various named (or even renamed) aspects; it is left conspiratorially anonymous, but fought as the shadow everyone always already knows.

"Elbow Room" signifies on the concerns of the earlier integrationist poetic critics whose guiding assumption was that black content could be simply reclothed in traditional (i.e., Euro-American "civilized") forms. In the terms of "Elbow Room" such cross-dressing would be tantamount to the designation of Virginia Valentine's baby as an "honorary white." Instead, the narrative rejects the elimination of the black-white problem via black transformation into "honorary status."

The story indirectly calls into question the concerns of the black aesthetic critics by complicating notions of "blackness" or "nigger" and suggesting instead that such ideas rest on more than simple reaction to white culture or tradition. True to its decentering mode, however, "Elbow Room" does not offer an answer, only grounds for the discussion of component parts.

The narrative speaks more directly to the concerns of African-American theorists as it questions the big issues addressed above in terms of material about which we can theorize within or outside the form of a text. And it explores the materials in terms of who is, or what social categories are, changed by the form. The phrase written on the back of the photograph of the American family gothic turned on its head (black woman, white male, mulatto child) — "He will be a *classic* kind of nigger" — theorizes about intentionality, artisticness.

If "nigger" is a societal construct, then "classic kind of nigger" reconstructs, or unfixes, what "nigger" has been in the heart of the hegemonic culture. "Nigger," according to Kimberly Benston, "is a mechanism of control" that "subsumes the complexities of human existence into a tractable sign" (156–57). Reclaiming "nigger," reconstructing it by unmasking its constructedness, is a way to unmake the category; it is what Virginia does. "Classic kind of nigger" is both a new and an old story, a result of a dialectical engagement with political history. It alludes to the

classic grandfather of *Invisible Man* who knew the power of folk wisdom to create, within a racist culture, a screen behind which maneuverability was possible. But
the phrase also alludes to the consequences of a new attempt to resist definitions:
a "classic kind of nigger." It is a discursive entity that encourages an examination of
the question behind the pretense of a shared history, a mythology about the American black "other." "Classic kind of nigger" subverts the expectations evoked by the
sign "nigger" by forcing an awareness of intentioned difference: a black undermining of a Eurocentric sense of what such a sign represents. It also takes "nigger"
back to its older (i.e., African) terrain not as the nostalgic nationalist dream against
which Fanon warns, but as a way, as *Beloved* puts it, to re-remember a particular
history and its implication: a classic tenacity like that of African-Americans who lived
through centuries of slavery or faced down racist sheriffs, attack dogs, and tear gas;
a classicism like that of the African mask — one that demands a change in the gaze
of the onlooker for recognition to occur, the kind of change apparent in Paul at the
end, a father "who sees with both eyes." Classic niggers can see around corners.
"Elbow Room" is paradigmatic in its exploration of the subversive possibilities that
inhere in its reappropriation.

If interracial sexual relations have been the nightmare that embodies the sexual
and racial paranoia of a white patriarchal society, then the "happy family" ending
is vernacular signifying at its most surgical. The mulatto is reclaimed by the black
half of the newly constructed interracial "family" as "nigger," and the notion of race
as a societal construction is further complicated by biological combination. Or, as
Hazel Carby argues in regard to Frances E. Harper's *Iola Leroy:* "[H]istorically the
mulatto, as narrative figure, has two primary functions: as a vehicle for an exploration of the relationship between the races and, at the same time, an *expression* of
the relationship between the races. The figure of the mulatto should be understood
and analyzed as a narrative device of mediation" (89). The mulatto is finally a sign.
The representation of a possibly nontragic mulatto allows the issue of race to escape the containment implied by physical difference and permits a burlesque of the
Manichaean dichotomy of colonizer subject and colonized other, especially ironic
in view of the historical context of the black woman as the producer of the essential slave "goods." Virginia Valentine, herself an heir to the complicated, rhetorically
powerful, and subversive African-American populist techniques of folk culture, produces, in the context of American racial politics, the embodiment of semantic and
material complexity: a mulatto child born into his mother's troping possibility — "a
classic kind of nigger."

Naming this child Daniel, then, is the text's mulatto reappropriation of the impe-
rialistic mission of Daniel Boone, which was referred to in the epigraph that begins
the story. It is an act that exproprates the explorer/conqueror position and name
and that underscores the text's "play" with Euro-American territorial and cultural will
to power. Daniel Boone, the great American mythic, imperialist figure who is domesticated by this text, becomes Daniel P. Frost, a "classic nigger" who deconstructs
"nigger" as a social construction — classic in expressing the relationship between
the two parts of the racial dyad. Daniel Frost = Daniel Boone is an equation that
describes an act of counterimperialism: taking back the group's consciousness and
the "white" father's patrimony as well.

VII

According to Homi Bhabha, within the colonialist/European literary tradition, it is the discovery of the book that marks the intrusion of light into darkness; the world of God, truth, or art creates the conditions for a beginning, a practice of history of narrative (145).[9] Within the terms of this economy, the book is the supreme signifier of authority, culture, light, and reason (146). "Elbow Room" is not the "book," the narrative, the ur-text. It is antinarrative if by narrative we mean a form that poses as its own supreme signifier.

Houston Baker has written: "Fixity is a function of power. Those who maintain place, who decide what takes place and dictate what has taken place, are power brokers of the traditional. The 'placeless,' by contrast, are translators of the non-traditional.... Their lineage is fluid, nomadic, transitional" (202). "Elbow Room" is a text of such flux; it moves along an axis of guerrilla-like mobility.

I refer to "shuckin' off" in my title. By that I mean the story shrugs aside, refocuses, jive talks the *narrative* other, complicates the "native other," and, in fact, reconstitutes that "other" object as shifting and fragmentary subject, all of which deconstructs the grounds for attribution of an "other" as a form or as an idea that results from the imposition of civilization. In *other* words, the texts makes some elbow room for the work of resisting the imperialism disguised in aesthetics.

VIII

"Elbow Room" is, in many ways, still a text about boys talking to boys and about competing to be "father"; while the narrator seems to revere Virginia, the real skeleton of this text comprises the narrator, the editor, Paul, and his father. It is, however, more complicated than — or at least different from — a buddy cop film. One does not need to call it counterhegemonic in the fullest sense to be able to map its resistances. It has its own limitations: as I pointed out earlier, while it does focus on a romantic and domestic heterosexual relationship as a site for political representation, the male narrator *assists* the female in *her* nurturing — after her marriage he does not imagine her doing anything else. And while it tropes bourgeois entrepreneurial capitalism by continuing the flow of Paul's father's "capital" through a mulatto grandson — thereby representing a moment of revenge against white-supremacist, patriarchal anxieties about the purity of "bloodlines," ironically twisting the patrimonial procession of flesh and assets — it stops short of any radical, general redistribution of the wealth. Paul and Virginia exist in an opaque world that excludes both the details of their respective employments and their reactions to the possibility of inheritance from the father. Still, the end of the "story" places them in rural Tennessee, where Virginia's folks live — the rural lumpen — and leaves open its and their resolution.

My intention in "reading" this story was to reclaim an underread (even within African-American literary circles) literary artifact as a way of describing possible African-American deployments of postmodernism in cultural practice as well as African-American strategies for revising a discourse that, notwithstanding the tendentiousness of voices on all its sides, has yet to speak to various differences as much as it speaks "about" the idea of them.

NOTES

1. Weiner's piece was originally written for the *Nation* as part of his discussion of the Paul de Man affair. Weiner's language was recently repeated by Lipsitz.

2. I am not always sanguine about that project: I understand the motivating force behind Michele Wallace's question, "[C]an black women survive another dose of 'Black Pride'?" (106) — or, I might add, another dose of black male anxiety over the loss (and for them it was always illusory) of their authority?

3. While I agree with West generally, I do not draw the line that divides politically inflected and nonpolitically inflected postmodernism at national boundaries — we have homegrown conservative postmodernist villains, and I cannot believe that the French do not number among them those engaged in politically inflected postmodernism.

4. I choose to gender the editor as male, given that the function of the editor in this text is colonizer of the narrative and gatekeeper for literary master tropes, keeper of the word(s).

5. These are Baker's categories. He describes the first era of African-American critical tradition as the era of "integrationist poetics," an era that privileged African-American literary formal indistinguishability from Euro-American literature as the proper mode for African-American production. The second era of the critical tradition was that of the black aesthetic critics who privileged representation of the lower and working classes of African-American people as the source and core of black art. This era represented an important paradigm shift, according to Baker, in which "blackness" was posed as a fundamental condition of "artisticness." The third and current era is that of the "reconstructionist" critics who involve themselves with cultural, anthropological, historical, and language matters in terms of theoretical frameworks. These three eras of criticism are, of course, strategies and responses to hegemonic culture and politics. I use "hegemony" here to mean a state of affairs in which the "natives" (or the "native others") accept and participate in, to varying degrees, some version of the colonizer's system of values, attitudes, morality, and institutions. The first era (albeit with some important exceptions) centered on an internalization of Euro-American aesthetics and the second (again, with important exceptions) on confrontation with those aesthetics and attempts to work out alternatives from the marginalized perspective. The third and present era, it seems to me, is one in which many critics of African-American literature are attempting to delineate counterhegemonic literary poetics that do not reduce themselves to celebrations of romantic essentials of a single African-American cultural practice or tradition.

6. I refer here to Henry Louis Gates's history, delineation, and theory of African-American signifying articulated in *The Signifying Monkey*. Gates's analysis is useful as a way to specify African-American cultural practice, although he places his analysis in the service primarily of uncovering intertextual "histories" while I am also interested in using vernacularity as a way to describe African-American language play as theory-making in this text and in others. Additionally, Gates's study glosses over the politics of the vernacular both between African- and Euro-American cultures and within African-American culture — across gender lines, for example.

7. That the African-American literary-critical tradition has been male-centered, predominantly male-articulated, and male-restrictive in terms of literary production and criticism has been a truism the complexities of which critics such as Hazel Carby, Hortense Spillers, Gloria Hull, Deborah McDowell, Mary Helen Washington, and others are presently exploring.

8. Lee Quinby's work on American aesthetics brought the epigraph from Foucault to my attention. I think it especially apt here.

9. See Gates, *The Signifying Monkey,* for explanation of tropes of African-American intertextual revision.

10. I find this aspect of Bhabha's work very useful, although I agree generally with JanMohamed that this study does not take seriously enough the power differentials between colonial subject and colonial "object" or "native other."

WORKS CITED

Arac, Jonathan. *Critical Genealogies: Historical Situations for Postmodern Literary Studies.* New York: Columbia University Press, 1987.

Baker, Houston. *Blues, Ideology, and Afro-American Literature.* Chicago: University of Chicago Press, 1984.

Belsey, Catherine. "Constructing the Subject: Deconstructing the Text." In *Feminist Criticism and Social Change,* ed. Judith Newton and Deborah Rosenfelt, 45–64. New York: Methuen, 1985.

Benston, Kimberly. "I Yam What I Yam: The Topos of (Un)naming in Afro-American Literature." In *Black Literature and Literary Theory,* ed. Henry Louis Gates Jr., 151–72. New York: Methuen, 1984.

Bhabha, Homi. "Signs Taken for Wonders: Questions of Ambivalence and Authority under a Tree Outside Delhi, May 1817." *Critical Inquiry* 12, no. 1 (1985): 145–65.

Cabral, Amilcar. *Return to the Source: Selected Speeches of Amilcar Cabral.* Ed. African Information Service. New York: Monthly Review, 1973.

Carby, Hazel V. *Reconstructing Womanhood: The Emergence of the Afro-American Woman Novelist.* New York: Oxford University Press, 1987.

Césaire, Aimé. *Discourse on Colonialism.* Trans. John Pinkham. New York: Monthly Review, 1972.

Elam, Diane. "Irresistible Resistance." *Novel: A Forum for Fiction* 23, no. 2 (winter 1990): 212–17.

Fanon, Frantz. *The Wretched of the Earth.* New York: Grove, 1968.

Foster, Hal, ed. *The Anti-aesthetic: Essays on Postmodern Culture.* Port Townsend, Wash.: Bay, 1983.

Fox, Robert. *Conscientious Sorcerers: The Black Postmodernist Fiction of LeRoi Jones/Amiri Baraka, Ishmael Reed, and Samuel R. Delaney.* Westport, Conn.: Greenwood Press, 1987.

Fraser, Nancy, and Linda Nicholson. "Social Criticism without Philosophy: An Encounter between Feminism and Postmodernism." In *Universal Abandon: The Politics of Postmodernism,* ed. Andrew Ross, 83–104. Minneapolis: University of Minnesota Press, 1988.

Gates, Henry Louis, Jr. *The Signifying Monkey: A Theory of Afro-American Literary Criticism.* New York: Oxford University Press, 1988.

Hall, Stuart. "On Postmodernism and Articulation: An Interview with Stuart Hall." *Journal of Communication Inquiry* 10, no. 2 (summer 1986): 45–60.

Harris, Wilson. "Fossil and Psyche." In *Explorations: A Selection of Talks and Articles, 1966–1981,* ed. Hena Maes-Jelinek, 96–112. Mundelstrup, Denmark: Dangaroo, 1981.

Harvey, David. *The Condition of Postmodernity: An Inquiry into the Origins of Cultural Change.* Cambridge: Basil Blackwell, 1989.

Hebdige, Dick. *Hiding in the Light: On Images and Things.* New York: Routledge, 1988.

James, Henry. "The Art of Fiction." In *Partial Portraits,* 377–408. Westport, Conn.: Greenwood Press, 1970.

———. *The Art of the Novel: Critical Prefaces.* Ed. R. P. Blackmur. London: Scribner's, 1948.

Jameson, Fredric. "Modernism and Imperialism." In *Nationalism, Colonialism, and Literature,* ed. Terry Eagleton, Fredric Jameson, and Edward W. Said, 43–68. Minneapolis: University of Minnesota Press, 1990.

———. *Postmodernism: Or, the Cultural Logic of Late Capitalism.* Durham, N.C.: Duke University Press, 1991.

———. "Postmodernism: Or, the Cultural Logic of Late Capitalism." *New Left Review* 146, no. 1 (July–August 1984): 53–92.

JanMohamed, Abdul. "The Economy of Manichean Allegory: The Function of Racial Difference in Colonialist Literature." In *"Race," Writing, and Difference.* Ed. Henry Louis Gates Jr. Chicago: University of Chicago Press, 1986.

———. "Humanism and Minority Literature: Toward a Definition of Counter-hegemonic Discourse." *Boundary 2* 13, no. 1 (1984): 281–99.

Jardine, Alice. *Gynesis: Configurations of Woman and Modernity.* Ithaca, N.Y.: Cornell University Press, 1985.

Kelly, Robin G. " 'Comrades, Praise Gawd for Lenin and Them!' Ideology and Culture among Black Communists in Alabama, 1930–1935." *Science and Society* 52, no. 1 (spring 1988): 59–82.

Kipnis, Laura. "Feminism: The Political Conscience of Postmodernism?" In *Universal Abandon: The Politics of Postmodernism,* ed. Andrew Ross, 149–66. Minneapolis: University of Minnesota Press, 1988.

Lipsitz, George. "Listening to Learn and Learning to Listen: Popular Culture, Cultural Theory, and American Studies." *American Quarterly* 2, no. 4 (December 1990): 615–36.

Lyotard, Jean-François. *The Postmodern Condition: A Report on Knowledge*. Trans. Geoff Bennington and Brian Massumi. Minneapolis: University of Minnesota Press, 1984.

McPherson, James Alan. *Elbow Room*. Boston: Little, Brown, and Co. 1977.

Neal, Larry, and Amiri Baraka, eds. *Black Fire: An Anthology of Afro-American Writing*. New York: William Morrow, 1968.

Owens, Craig. "The Discourse of Others: Feminists and Postmodernism." In *The Anti-aesthetic: Essays on Postmodern Culture,* ed. Hal Foster, 57–82. Port Townsend, Wash.: Bay Press, 1983.

Robbins, Bruce, ed. *Intellectuals: Aesthetics, Politics, Academics*. Minneapolis: University of Minnesota Press, 1990.

Ruskin, John. *The Works of John Ruskin*. Vol. 3. Ed. E. T. Cook and Alexander Wedderburn. London: George Allen; New York: Longman, Green, 1903.

Said, Edward W. "Yeats and Decolonialization." *Nationalism, Colonialism, and Literature,* ed. Terry Eagleton, Fredric Jameson, and Edward W. Said, 69–95. Minneapolis: University of Minnesota Press, 1990.

Spillers, Hortense J. "Mama's Baby, Papa's Maybe: An American Grammar Book." *Diacritics* 17, no. 2 (summer 1987): 65–81.

Spivak, Gayatri. "The Post-modern Condition: The End of Politics?" In *The Post-colonial Critic: Interviews, Strategies, Dialogues,* ed. Sarah Harasym, 17–34. New York: Routledge, 1990.

Stephanson, Anders. "Interview with Cornel West." In *Universal Abandon? The Politics of Post-modernism,* ed. Andrew Ross, 269–87. Minneapolis: University of Minnesota Press, 1988.

Wallace, Michele. "Michael Jackson, Black Modernisms and 'The Ecstasy of Communication.'" In *Invisibility Blues: From Pop to Theory,* 77–110. New York: Verso, 1990.

West, Cornel. "The Dilemma of the Black Intellectual." *Cultural Critique* 1 (fall 1985): 109–24.

———. "The New Cultural Politics of Difference." *October* 53 (summer 1990): 93–109.

Chapter 12
Identity, Meaning, and the African-American
Michael Hanchard

[T]his independent Negro Movement is able to intervene with terrific force upon the
general social and political life of the nation, despite the fact that it is waged under
the banner of democratic rights, and is not led necessarily either by the organized
labor movement or the Marxist party.
  C. L. R. James, "The Revolutionary Answer to the Negro Problem in the U.S."

In the industrial era, El Dorado is the United States, and the United States is America.
  Eduardo Galeano, *Century of the Wind*

The second edition of Webster's *New International Dictionary* defines "America"
as follows: "1) Either continent of the Western Hemisphere; 2) The United States of
America; 3) The characteristic features of American life, collectively."[1] This definition illustrates the multiple incongruities we face in attempting to identify America
or Americans, its individual subjects. The elements of the definition clash with one
another. They suggest claims to American identity based on (1) residence in North
or South America, (2) citizenship in the United States, or (3) a mode of existence
across two continents that is, somehow, characteristically "American."

The shift from noun of place to noun of person (America, American) leads to
greater confusion. When the three components of the dictionary's definition are considered as facets of a single definition, several questions are raised. First, why does
the United States require a separate meaning in (2) when it is a part of the land
designated in (1)? Second, is it possible to describe people of different racial and
ethnic groups, social classes, religious convictions, and sexual preferences in North
America, South America, Mesoamerica, and the Caribbean in terms of "characteristic
features of American life, collectively"? Last, how is it that the secondary definition
of America is generally taken to be the primary and indeed the only definition (in
the United States and, indeed, in parts of Latin America, "America" and the "United
States" have become interchangeable terms)?

For my purposes, the last query is the most important one. Assuming a correlation between the politics of language, the politics of meaning, and realpolitik, the
emergence of the United States of America as the primary and dominant meaning
of "America" writ large must have resulted from the dialectical relation between the
hegemony of the United States and the residual location of the "other" nations of
the Western Hemisphere. This in itself is not a novel insight. It is one that has been

ably explicated in the fiction, prose, and poetry of José Marti, Pablo Neruda, Derek Walcott, and others. Yet it is important to rearticulate these narratives within the debate over the term "African-American," for this struggle over nomenclature reflects broader cultural and material struggles of U.S. blacks over their paradoxical location within the most powerful nation-state in the "New World."

While the quest for a more historically specific nomenclature for the descendants of African slaves who reside in the United States is an important step toward a renewed cultural awareness, the quest would remain unfulfilled, or worse, dishonest, if "American" as adjective and noun were not subject to intense critical scrutiny. Clearly "Africa," in its continental and etymological form, is far from a settled, monolithic site of symbolic and political discourse. Yet "America" too is a cacophony of unmanageable narratives. It is crucial that proponents of the term "African-American" avoid the inadvertent and implicit acceptance of the hegemonic notion of the United States as America, with its manipulative construction of individual and collective identities within the ambit of "Americana." To put this another way, the addition of "African" as adjective to "American" as noun should be neither effected nor clamored for without a consideration of its internal ambiguities and contradictions.

Many articles and essays concerning the naming of U.S. blacks have appeared over the past few years; a good number of these came in response to Jesse Jackson's use of "African-American" during a tour of African states. Others that were written years or even decades ago have been reissued now in an effort to lend historical perspective to the current debate. A selection of these essays, written by authors with divergent critical outlooks, gives evidence of an eager acceptance of "America" as collective subject and singular cultural form. What these articles reveal are the broader social and political conflicts that inform the discursive struggles over the meaning and identity of black life in the United States.

The recurrent theme in Ralph Ellison's *Going to the Territory,* an ensemble of essays, lectures, and speeches given over the course of his literary career, is the tension inherent in the relationship between the Negro American (to use his term) and pluralist society. Ellison stresses the impact of Negro Americans upon American culture, despite the barriers of Jim Crow, slavery, and other forms of oppression. His assumptions are given succinct expression in the following passage from the essay "What America Would Be Like without Blacks":

> If we can resist for a moment the temptation to view everything having to do with Negro Americans in terms of their racially imposed status, we become aware of the fact that for all the harsh reality of the social and economic injustices visited upon them, these injustices have failed to keep Negroes clear of the cultural mainstream; Negro Americans are in fact one of its major tributaries. If we can cease approaching social reality in terms of such false concepts as white and nonwhite, black culture and white culture, and think of these apparently unthinkable matters in the manner of western pioneers confronting the unknown prairie, perhaps we can begin to imagine what the United States would have been, or not been, had there been no blacks to give it ... color.[2]

Clearly Ellison has reduced America to the geographical and attitudinal realm of the United States, shifting from continent to nation-state within this passage while employing an identical meaning for both. What is most striking about his remarks, however, is his implicit acceptance of a notion of liberal pluralism. Through a suspension of the Manichaean scheme of U.S. society in a manner characteristic of liberal-pluralist ideology, Ellison implies that *all things being equal,* Negro Americans have had a profound impact upon U.S. culture, to the extent that it would be hard to imagine the country without them. Ellison describes Negro Americans as part of the "cultural mainstream" and as one of the "major tributaries" of American culture. Absent from his metaphors is a recognition of the terms of membership in U.S. culture and the invariably subordinate location of Negro Americans within it.

Ellison's lapses are regrettable yet characteristic of his politics. While economic liberalism excuses the suppression of wages and the repression of organized labor as "market imperfections," its justifying ideologies neglect "the influence of social power upon the encounter of voices."[3] Ellison discusses the encounter of whites and blacks in terms of our "pluralistic and easily available popular culture."[4] Yet if we acknowledge the dynamic of power and powerlessness lurking behind the interface of white and nonwhite cultures in the United States, we will recognize that U.S. blacks are represented as they are in popular culture not in spite of their marginality, as Ellison posits, but *because* of it.

Ellen Rooney characterizes liberal pluralism in its critical form as a "heterogeneous yet hegemonic discourse."[5] It masks the struggle for voice inherent in symbolic encounters with a myth of egalitarian representation. This myth serves to divert attention from the process of incorporation and sublimation of difference into something easily accessed and popular. One has only to gauge the spatial and symbolic distance between young black rappers performing during commercial time-outs and the communities in which their rhymes and rhythms are produced to recognize the drastic neutralization of context that occurs before those televisual images hit the screen.

Ellison asks us to forget about the black/white dichotomy and think of U.S. social reality "in the manner of western pioneers confronting the unknown prairie." Yet this purportedly resolute metaphor, full of conventional masculinity, only distorts the contextualization of black experience and identity. I was forced to ask myself after reading this passage if the prairie was really *unknown* to native peoples or if they had in fact known it by another name. Ellison buys into the notion of the expansive "American" spirit ever seeking out new areas to stretch out its (or perhaps "his") limbs. Yet the underside of this notion of early American expansion harbors the process of decimation inflicted upon native peoples. The pioneering spirit was at the same time the harbinger of dislocation, plunder, and brutality.

Finally, even if we accept the western pioneers on Ellison's terms, we must ask ourselves if their experience is a viable parallel to that of blacks who were transported, as mere chattel, from Africa to the New World; or if the subsequent passage of Europeans through Ellis Island could be compared to the northward migration of southern blacks after World War II or the influx of blacks from the Caribbean and Latin America to the already delimited spaces of the United States. If we ask these questions, I believe we will come to the conclusion that neither Ellison's brand of pluralism nor his metaphor of confrontation and pioneering is a tenable basis for considering the peculiarities of black experience in the United States.

Bayard Rustin's essay on the subject of nomenclature was published one year after Ellison's. It offers a counterpoint to the metaphors of the latter and furnishes a historical context for the "name game" that has been lacking in most recent commentary. Rustin traces the appellative transitions from "Africans" to "Free Africans" in the seventeenth and eighteenth centuries and then to "Colored Americans" in the nineteenth century. Rustin points out that "Negro" was a collectively self-chosen word reflecting the Negro's "Americanization and self-realization."[6] He cites a long passage from a 1928 letter W. E. B. Du Bois wrote to a fifteen-year-old correspondent about "Negro" as a noun. Rustin concurs with Du Bois's belief that "Negro is a fine word. Etymologically and phonetically much better and more logical than 'African' or 'Colored' or any of the various hyphenated circumlocutions."[7]

He admits that "Negro" is not historically accurate, but then neither are any of the words used to describe Europeans (Jews, Nordics, whites, etc.). Rustin concludes that personal changes in name, dress, or hairstyle will not change the Negro condition: "We should not be fooled by names or appearances. The real problems lie beneath the surface."[8] In a similar but flippant tone, writer Trey Ellis announced in the *Village Voice* that "this current black semantic brouhaha is a waste of time. . . . This is a topic to take up Sunday afternoon over barbecue, reward for a week of wrestling with real problems."[9]

Thus for Rustin and Ellis "real problems" are the base; "names and appearances" are the superstructure of black social experience. This dichotomy, however, is a false one. As Raymond Williams has argued, the conventional distinction between the material and symbolic does not correspond to the social reality of "language and signification as indissoluble elements of the material process itself."[10] The analytic space between "names and appearances" and "real problems" is socially traversed by collective and individual narratives engaged in discourse. How can one separate a racial epithet, for example, from the social context in which it is uttered? Certainly an *n, i,* double *g, e,* and *r* in unlinear sequence has not, in itself, harmed anyone. What has brought harm are the violent intentions that this linguistic ensemble mediates and the physical violence that often accompanies its use. This best exemplifies why Rustin's dichotomy is false. Moreover, the donning of "Afro" hairstyles and "African" dress are indicators of collective identification. Like the debates over nomenclature, this is but another example of the two-tiered discourse embedded within social relations, illustrating the fluidity of discursive relations between and within communities. As for Ellis's simplistic binary opposition of semantics versus real problems, work versus play, well, they speak for themselves precisely because naming and identity are "real problems" that should be discussed over barbecues as well as in work-spaces, classrooms, and committee rooms.

Nevertheless, Rustin does not follow Ellison in lauding the pluralistic/democratic uniqueness of the U.S. polity (at least not in this particular essay). By providing the historical memory of the names black people in the United States have used to refer to themselves, Rustin's essay serves the valuable purpose of displaying the intersection of identity, naming, and meaning despite the inconsistent usage of the real problems/appearances dichotomy. He notes that by the nineteenth century " 'American' signified an adamant refusal to be sent back to Africa (at the time the people urging emigration were mostly white) and an assertion of a new sense of American identity."[11] Here we can see the correlation between self-naming and social struggle. The linkage of African and American was part of an incipient narrative formulated by blacks about themselves that presented an alternative to the dominant myth of an America without non-Europeans.

Ruskin might have added that with the adoption of new meanings, old ones are suppressed. At the historical junctures of "colored" and "Negro," "Negro" and "black," the former nomenclatures were overtaken by the emergent ones in such a way that the connotations of "colored" and "Negro" as well as their location within the cultural lexicon were transformed. Negro (Stanley Crouch notwithstanding) is now commonly understood by blacks as a pejorative term signifying conciliation with whites, where it once stood as a signifier of self-definition and demarcation. To call someone black in the 1950s could have (and sometimes did) lead to a fight. In the early 1960s the term "black" resurfaced as a positive self-reference, linked to black nationalism, challenging the dominant culture in general and the acquiescent Negro in particular.

The interface of "black" and "Afro-American" in the 1960s and 1970s was not contentious. I suspect the encounter of "black" or "Afro-American" with "African-American" will be milder still. This meeting of terms and epochs does suggest, however, that "African-American" will alter other meanings as it comes into its own, and may even render some meanings culturally obsolete. Yet if we have recognized one tendency in this process of appellative transition, it is that each purportedly definitive term has been succeeded by another making similar claims. In addition, each term was superseded when its definition no longer corresponded to the shifting identity of the communities it was intended to represent.

The linkage of "African" with "American" holds this tension as well. Indeed, this new union rearticulates another set of contradictions that have persisted through this century and the one preceding it, because once linked each word symbolizes the inverted contradiction of the other. Africa has been canonized as a monolithic entity and not as a continent, while America as either continent or New World has been reduced to a single country. Consequently we are left with an elliptical designation that confuses as it seeks to clarify, that compresses the odysseys of nonwhite peoples into the singular experience of blacks in the United States.

Perhaps the most revealing exchange regarding the term "African-American" took place on a special segment of the *McNeil-Lehrer Report* on March 22, 1989, a panel discussion that included Kwame Toure (formerly Stokely Carmichael), black businessman Bruce Llewellen, Ramona Edelin of the National Urban Coalition, and Leon Wynter, an editor for the *Wall Street Journal*. Toure and Edelin favored the name change. Wynter and Llewellen seemed indifferent to it. Llewellen, using a beverage can as a metaphor for people of African descent in the United States, summed up his position by stating that "a can is a can. It doesn't matter what you call it. It's what's inside the can that counts." This metaphor epitomized two principal features of the commodification undergone by much of the black petit bourgeoisie. First, in the attempt to draw a parallel between an inanimate object (a can) and a social collective (blacks), Llewellen deprives the latter of human agency and shifts the responsibility of self-reference from blacks to someone else. In other words, if his metaphor were to have a truly relational utility, the can would have to speak and name itself. In any event, the can ain't saying. Second, there is Llewellen's materialistic distinction between form and substance, which is tragically ironic in light of the fact that it has been the perceived somatic form of black women, children, and men that has obscured (for many whites) the reality of their existence as species beings. The production and skills argument put forth by Llewellen was problematic over one hundred years ago when first exposed by Booker T. Washington. It is certainly problematic now.

Wynter echoed Llewellen's statements with depressing similarity. In response to Toure's claim that socialism was the only solution to the exploitation of black people, he sarcastically retorted that the last time he heard, blacks in the bustling city of Lagos, Nigeria, "still liked things." The message was clear from both Wynter and Llewellen. Capitalism was the only game in town, and black folk needed to get with it. In today's marketplace, skills and competence would provide the only saving graces.

The battle lines were drawn, much in the same manner that they have been over the course of the twentieth century, between W. E. B. Du Bois and Booker T. Washington, between Du Bois and Marcus Garvey, and between Malcolm X and Martin Luther King, Jesse Jackson, and Andrew Young. Each discussant's position on the term "African-American" was greatly influenced by, first, whether he or she was a patriot or, on the contrary, had decided that the United States was a sinking ship not worth saving and, second, whether he or she believed in integration rather than separatism, in economic nationalism or Pan-Africanist socialism as the path to progress.

Sounding both anachronistic and shrill, Toure declared that U.S. blacks were Africans, pure and simple. Their only hope as a people would be to discard the useless notion of being an "American" and embrace Africa and an African brand of socialism. Toure, who himself underwent a name change, now lives in Jerry Rawling's Ghana, where loans from multinational financial institutions coincide with socialist rhetoric. Toure had the courage of his conviction to leave the United States and reside elsewhere. Yet for most blacks in this country, exile or exodus is neither a probable nor a desired solution to their problems. Toure made no attempt to deal with this very "American" facet of "African" modes of existence in the United States, which made his comments sound perversely apolitical and resonant with exile. In the broadest sense, the three other discussants represented elements of social activity (entrepreneurial, media-related, political) generated by the black middle classes that would have to be accounted for in any calculus of black politics and, broader still, in any assessment of progressive coalition building among nonwhites in the United States. If the Rainbow Coalition means anything politically, it is the art of possibility, the specter of social change affected by a broad array of ethnic groups and working classes. Toure's comments offered no solutions or strategies, only rhetoric.

Yet Toure was the foil in this debate for another equally significant reason. He refused to negotiate his position, on the grounds that capitalism and U.S. imperialism were irredeemable systems of exploitation. Toure wants no part of "black capitalism" or protonationalist variants advocating economic self-help as a subset of national or global movements of capital. This is an implicit critique of a variety of projects, from the Nation of Islam's agenda for economic self-sufficiency, to John Johnson's labor-intensive entrepreneurship, to the new crop of would-be black Brahmins (the late

Reginald Lewis, et al.). In each, it remains unclear how the generation and reproduction of capital by a few will alter social structures and foster a more egalitarian
ethos in black communities plagued by underdevelopment. Had this been made
more explicit, it would have introduced a new tension to the debate.

The most lucid comments were, to my mind, those of Ramona Edelin. Despite her call for a "return to African values," which smacked of an indeterminate
culturalism (which Africa? which values?), her rationale for employing the term
"African-American" was most compelling. She linked the appellation to a "cultural
offensive," a transformation of educational curricula and programs in black communities across the United States in order to unpack an embedded history. While vague,
the suggestion of a revision of elementary school textbooks, children's games, and
other pedagogical devices represents one of the most significant challenges to organic intellectuals in the 1990s and points to a cultural sphere in which such
intellectuals have to become more actively engaged if the left is to appear relevant
to a generation of people raised on Pee Wee Herman, Jimmy Swaggart, Kool Moe
D., Sugar Ray Leonard, Eddie Murphy, and Ronald Reagan.

Another incident that highlights the complexities of this new union occurred in
the newsroom of WLIB, one of New York's most popular black radio stations.
A news report that referred to a dark-skinned woman with a Latino surname
brought confusion to the newsroom. "Everybody in the newsroom was struggling
with what to call her," said David Lampel, WLIB program director.[12] It was decided that "African-Latino" was the proper term. Suddenly we are confronted with
a fundamental quandary — should people of African descent who live in America,
but not in the United States, be known as something other than Americans? Are
blacks in the United States going to reproduce the same public/private, they/we dichotomies that nationally chauvinistic whites have mobilized in an effort to exclude
nonwhites from the national portrait? Is the quest for a more representative term
for U.S. blacks just a mimicry of all the other hyphenations of identity that have
preceded it?

Although these questions often elicit competing, essentialist responses, there are
no simple answers. In fact, these questions are replete with troubling juxtapositions
of their own. Yet they are questions to be grappled with, for if debate over the
hyphenation of black identity is considered just a matter of vocabulary, the term
"African-American" will become just one more element of black consciousness to
be appropriated by the state and civil society without any real modification of the
cultural and material conditions of U.S. blacks. Moreover, these questions will not be
dispelled by the canonical use of *any* single nomenclature, for these questions are
continuously present within the multifaceted constitution each individual represents.
"African" as prefix to "American" as it is colloquially understood seems to suggest
that the real meaning of black identity lies in the "American," and this may be closer
to the mark than the proponents of hyphenation would care to admit.

In no way do I want to suggest that either Jesse Jackson or other supporters of
the canonical adoption of "African-American" intended for their position to be implicated within the discursive categories of empire and imperialism. What is profoundly
important and — to my way of thinking, a fortunate confluence — is that it is Jackson
(via Ramona Edelin) who has placed the petals and seeds of black signification on

the table of public debate. The same person who, through his presidential candidacy and politics, has laid bare the increasingly conservative syllogism of Republican-Democratic debates, the first presidential candidate since Eugene Debs to suffuse a populist, progressive narrative into national politics, is now attempting to expand the contours of black ideology through a debate about naming.

The same political agent who has questioned the U.S. role in Latin and Meso-america and who pressed for a more vigilant response to the intransigence and genocidal practices of the South African state is also asking U.S. blacks to assume a generically African and decidedly non-American identity. This nexus of progressive cultural and political activism should not be rationalized as a logical extension of Jackson's political being but viewed as a possible feature of a yet-to-be formulated black radicalism, infused with narratives of class and gender, that will seek to construct a practical agenda for change on a national scale. In this sense it is Jackson as well as his more progressive rhetoric that must be pushed in the quest to expand radical voices and praxis in the United States.

It is imperative that progressive political and cultural movements by blacks in this country reject the idea of America as the United States. For to accept that definition, with its self-selected borders and dominions, is to impoverish a political and cultural heritage to which blacks from the Caribbean and Latin America have made important contributions. How could one, for example, recount the Harlem Renaissance as a historical moment without the contributions of Claude McKay and Marcus Garvey, two Jamaicans, or the tensions of nationalist, Pan-Africanist, and socialist tendencies without reference to the disputes between Garvey, W. E. B. Du Bois, and A. Philip Randolph? Could there be integrity to an account of black radicalism in the United States without the figure of the Trinidadian C. L. R. James, who organized black workers in Mississippi, wrote a still poignant analysis of race and class in the United States in 1948, and worked, along with W. E. B. Du Bois, George Padmore, and others, to formulate a Pan-Africanist agenda for the modern world?

The novels of three American writers provide examples of the need to reconsider the spatial and epistemological limitations that the United States as America poses. In addition to the structural and tonal similarities between Toni Morrison's *Song of Solomon* and Gabriel García Márquez's *One Hundred Years of Solitude,* there is the shared absence of an individual hero and an emphasis on the collective identity of two communities, Mercy and Macondo, as they struggle with communal antagonisms, racial hatred, and class conflict.

George Lamming, the Barbadian novelist, suggests that community is the predominant feature in much of Caribbean fiction, including his own. Note the following passage from a retrospective essay by Lamming about his own powerful novel *In the Castle of My Skin:*

> What I say now of *In the Castle of My Skin* is also true of other Caribbean writers. The book is crowded with names and people, and although each character is accorded a most vivid presence and force of personality, we are rarely concerned with the prolonged exploration of an individual consciousness. It is the collective human substance of the village itself which commands our attention. The village, you might say, is the central character.[13]

Lamming's village is largely constituted of black people struggling with national and communal identities in a postcolonial ethos. In this matter, we find similarities between Lamming's novel, *Song of Solomon,* and *One Hundred Years of Solitude* — between a Caribbean, a North American, and a Latin American novel. Each text stands in direct contrast to the conventional novel, with its highly individuated form.

On another level, these novels suggest the existence of alternative communities in various pockets of America, communities pressing onward in the face of cultural and material expropriation. It is the onward march of Lamming's, Morrison's, and Márquez's communities that distinguishes their narratives from much of American fiction. These three novelists have made the universal out of the particular (to paraphrase Wole Soyinka), and in doing so their tales have exposed the frailty and historically contingent construction of national boundaries.

The tale of the diaspora, like the three noted above, holds a subversive resonance when contrasted with that of the nation-state. At the same time that European powers constructed national dialogues, African slaves were being uprooted from communalist and other social systems in various parts of the African continent and scattered about the New World like fragments of a shaven gem. Africans and their distant relatives in the New World have abided by, and sometimes revolted against, the myth of national borders ever since.

Embedded in the tale of the diaspora is a symbolic revolt against the nation-state, and for this reason the diaspora holds a considerable significance. It suggests a transnational dimension to black identity: the African diaspora was a human necklace strung together by a thread known as the slave trade, a thread thrown across America with little regard for national boundaries.

As we witness the slow, grudging descent of the United States from its role as world policeman, we listen also to an increasingly chauvinistic national rhetoric that clamors for a return to "classic" or "traditional" values, values that the country has never, as a country, really known. We should recognize in the long term that such a contradiction must collapse under its own weight. As the internationalizing effects of capitalism are felt in the U.S. domestic economy, as they have been felt by countless nations and peoples before, and as U.S. citizens drive Korean-made cars to Japanese-owned workplaces in their own country, we should be made aware that the resurgence of this chauvinist rhetoric has no real basis. Yet we can abstract a valuable lesson from this contradiction if we realize that embedded within the concept of an African diaspora is the whole of America — North, Central, and South — and that the presence of African descendants in America is a symbolic counterpoint to the hegemonic equivalence of the United States as America.

Historically, blacks as human collectivities in the United States, Caribbean, and Latin America have been more suspicious of each other than of the nation-state system, capitalism, or bourgeois culture. In citing the significance of the concept of the diaspora, then, I am not glossing over the litany of contentious, often tragic encounters between and within black communities; rather, I mean to highlight the obverse of this conflict, the potential for a dissolution of the categories that separate these communities and an identification of the cultural and political features that link them. Du Bois, writing about the disputes between U.S., Caribbean, and other black activists in the United States during the 1920s, wrote:

My thoughts, the thoughts of Washington, . . . and others (Garvey, etc.) were the expression of social forces. . . . These forces or ideologies embraced more than our reasoned acts. They included physical, biological, and psychological force; habits, conventions, and enactments. . . . [T]he total result was the history of our day. That history may be epitomized in one word, Empire; the domination of white Europe over black Africa and yellow Asia, through political power built over the economic control of labor, income and ideas.[14]

This brilliant insight is the recognition of two histories at once related and distinct: the history of empire and the history of subordinate peoples. U.S. blacks lie at the vortex of conquest and decimation. And so does the hyphen between "African" and "American." I hope this essay has, among other things, made one thing clear: the debate about the term "African-American" is symptomatic of material and symbolic encounters between whites and nonwhites in both the Old World and the New. It is just one step in that awkward dance of reluctant partners known as "U.S. race relations," a dance of meanings, not pigmentations. The present debate over these meanings should be extended to encompass the colloquial understanding of America, with all of its complications.

NOTES

I would like to thank Henry Bienen, Danny Goldberg, Anders Stephanson, Paul Vogt, and Cornel West for their comments during the development of this essay.

1. *Webster's New International Dictionary,* 2d ed., s.v. "America."

2. Ralph Ellison, "What America Would Be Like without Blacks," in *Going to the Territory* (New York: Vintage Books, 1987), 108.

3. Ellen Rooney, "Who's Left Out? A Rose by Any Other Name Is Still Red; or, The Politics of Pluralism," *Critical Inquiry* 12 (spring 1986): 55.

4. Ellison, "What America Would Be Like," 109.

5. Rooney, "Who's Left Out?" 53.

6. Bayard Rustin, "Blacks? African-Americans? What's in a Name?" *New York Times,* February 1, 1989, A25.

7. Ibid.

8. Ibid. In an article on the debate over the term "African-American," Henry Louis Gates Jr. seems to make a similar claim with his distinction between "this undue concern with our name" and "economic and social equality" ("In Search of a Good Name," *Time,* March 6, 1989, 32).

9. Trey Ellis, "Remember My Name," *Village Voice,* June 13, 1989, 38.

10. Raymond Williams, *Marxism and Literature* (New York: Oxford University Press, 1977), 99.

11. Rustin, "Blacks?"

12. Quoted from David Lampel in an article entitled " 'African-American' Favored by Many of America's Blacks" (*New York Times,* January 31, 1989, A1, 14).

13. George Lamming, "*In the Castle of My Skin:* Thirty Years After," in *Anales del Caribe* (Havana: Centro de Estudios de Caribe/Casa de Las Américas, 1983), 3:279.

14. W. E. B. Du Bois, *Dusk of Dawn* (New York: Harcourt, Brace, 1940), 96.

Chapter 13
Just Looking for Trouble:
Robert Mapplethorpe and Fantasies of Race
Kobena Mercer

How does "race" feature in the politics of antipornography? Well, it does and it doesn't. Race is present as an emotive figure of speech in the rhetoric of certain feminist antipornography arguments; yet race is also markedly absent, since there appears to be no distinctly black perspective on the contentious issues of sexuality, censorship, and representation that underpin the volatile nature of the antiporn debate. Although Audre Lorde and Alice Walker made important contributions early on in the debate in the United States over a decade ago, the question of pornography has hardly been a top priority on the agenda of black feminist politics in Britain in the 1980s and 1990s.[1] If it is indeed the case that white and black women have not been equally involved in the antiporn movement, or have not made it a shared political priority, then we have to ask: What role does race play in the discourse of antipornography that has come mainly from white women?

Race as an Issue in Antipornography Feminism

When race is invoked to mobilize moral support for antipornography positions, it tends to function as a rhetorical trope enabling a gender and race analogy between violence against women and incitement to racial hatred. In their recent campaigns, Labour MPs Clare Short and Dawn Primarolo have frequently used this analogy to argue that just as black people are degraded by racist speech and hurt by racial violence, so women are harmed and victimized by sexist and misogynist representations that portray, and thus promote, the hatred and fear of women that erupt in all acts of male violence. It follows, so the argument goes, that just as the law is supposedly empowered to prohibit and punish incitement to racial hatred, new regulative legislation is needed to "protect" women from the harm and danger of male violence that pornography represents. Yet the 1965 Race Relations Act, which sought to prohibit racist speech, has never been particularly beneficial to black people — more often than not it has been used against black people to curtail our civil rights to representation and was proved to be notoriously useless and ineffective by the rise of new racist and fascist movements in the 1970s. Just as most black people know not to entrust our survival and protection to the state, one ought to question any argument, feminist or otherwise, that seeks to extend the intervention of the state in the form of prohibitionary legislation.

Indeed, from a black perspective, the problem lies with the very analogy between racial hatred and male violence because it is based on a prior equation between those sexually explicit words and images labeled "pornographic" and those acts of violence, brutality, and homicide that do indeed take place against women in "real life." This equation — that pornography is the theory, rape is the practice — is central to the radical feminist antipornography argument that gained considerable influence in the United States during the 1980s and is gaining ground in Britain now. One of the most worrying aspects of these developments is the strange alliance that has evolved between radical feminists demanding censorship in the name of women's freedom and the antiobscenity lobby of the new right, whose demands for the prohibition of sexual representations have always been part of the moral agenda of mainstream conservatism. For entirely different reasons, these two groups seek further state regulation of pornography, yet their convergence on this objective has created a wider constituency of support for a policy of cultural censorship. Where do black people stand in relation to this unhappy alliance?

While antiporn feminists are more likely than their neoconservative counterparts to observe that pornography itself is violently racist, one has to question the highly emotive way in which race is used only to simplify complex issues and polarize opinion, as if everything were a matter of black and white, as if everything depended on whether you are simply for or against pornography and, by implication, male violence. In a theoretical defense of the radical feminist view that pornography does not merely reflect male violence but is itself a form of violence even as representation, Susanne Kappeler uses race precisely in this way — not only to justify the unproven equation between images of sexual violence and actual violence experienced by women but to elicit a moral response of horror and outrage that lends further credence to the antiporn argument. At the beginning of her book *The Pornography of Representation,* by means of a graphic description of photographs depicting the mutilation, torture, and obliteration of a black African man — one Thomas Kasire of Namibia — for the gratification of his white, male, European captors, Kappeler hopes to persuade us that, essentially, all pornography entails that women experience the same kind of actual violence as the brutal, sadistic, and murderous violence of the colonial racism that resulted in the death of this black man.[2] Not only does this analogy reduce race to rhetoric — whereby the black/white polarity serves to symbolize an absolute morality based on an either-or choice between good and evil — but it offers no analysis of racial representation in pornography or of black people's experiences of it, as Kappeler nowhere acknowledges the relative absence of black women in defining the feminist antiporn agenda or the fact that black feminism, in all its varieties, has certainly not prioritized the issue as a touchstone of revolutionary morality.

Each of these issues concerning race, representation, and sexual politics has arisen in the very different context of Robert Mapplethorpe's avowedly homoerotic photography, which was at the center of a major controversy in the United States during 1989 and 1990. Paradoxically, as a result of the campaign led by Senator Jesse Helms to prevent the National Endowment for the Arts (NEA) from funding exhibitions of so-called indecent and obscene materials, Mapplethorpe's photographs have come to the attention of a far wider audience than at any point before his death, from AIDS, in 1989. Although Helms's proposed amendment to NEA funding criteria was eventually defeated, the virulent homophobia that characterized his campaign against Mapplethorpe's "immoral trash" has helped to create a climate of popular opinion favorable to cultural repression. Just as self-censorship has become routine among art-world decision makers, so the policing and prosecution of cultural practitioners — from feminist performance artist Karen Finley to the black rap group 2 Live Crew — have also become commonplace. What is truly disturbing about these trends is both the way in which the new right has successfully hijacked and appropriated elements of the feminist antipornography argument and the way in which some feminists have themselves joined ranks with the law-and-order state. An instance of this occurred in Cincinnati in 1990 when feminist campaigners aligned themselves with the city police department to close down the touring Mapplethorpe retrospective and prosecute the museum director responsible for the exhibition, Dennis Barrie, for the violation of "community standards."

Mapplethorpe's Black Male Nudes

In this context, I would like to offer a contribution to the debate on pornography that is based on my reading of Mapplethorpe's troublesome images of nude black men. Although the attack on Mapplethorpe focused mainly on his depictions of gay-male sadomasochism and portraits of naked children, his black male nudes are equally, if not more, problematic — not only because they explicitly resemble aspects of pornography but because his highly erotic treatment of the black male body seems to be supported by a whole range of racist myths about black sexuality.

"To shock" was always the key verb in the modernist vocabulary. Like other audiences and spectators confronted by the potent eroticism of Mapplethorpe's most shocking images, black audiences are not somehow exempt from the shock effect that Mapplethorpe's images so clearly intend to provoke. Indeed, it was this sense of outrage — not at the homoeroticism, but at the potential racism — that motivated my initial critique of the work, from a black gay-male perspective. I was shocked by what I saw: the profile of a black man whose head was cropped — or "decapitated," so to speak — holding his semitumescent penis through the Y-fronts of his underpants, which is the first image that confronts you in Mapplethorpe's 1982 publication *Black Males*. Given the relative silence of black voices at the time of Mapplethorpe's 1983 retrospective at the Institute of Contemporary Arts in London, when the art world celebrated his "transgressive" reputation, it was important to draw critical attention to the almost pornographic flamboyance with which Mapplethorpe, whose trademark is cool irony, seemed to perpetuate the racist stereotype that, essentially, the black man is nothing more than his penis.

Yet, as the context for the reception and interpretation of Mapplethorpe's work has changed, I have almost changed my mind about these photographs, primarily because I am much more aware of the danger of simply hurling about the accusation of "racism." It leads only to the closure of debate. Precisely because of the hitherto unthinkable alliance between the new right and radical feminism on the issue of pornography, there is now every possibility that a critique that stops only with this kind of moralistic closure inevitably plays into an antidemocratic politics of censorship and cultural closure sought by the ascendant forces of the new right. In what follows, I explain how and why I changed my mind.[3]

Picture this: two reasonably intelligent black gay men pore over Mapplethorpe's 1986 publication *The Black Book*. When a friend lent me his copy, this was exactly how it circulated between us: as an illicit and highly troublesome object of desire. We were fascinated by the beautiful bodies and seduced by the pleasure in looking as we perused the repertoire of images. We wanted to look, but we didn't always find what we wanted to see. This was because we were immediately disturbed by the racial dimension of the imagery and, above all, angered by the aesthetic objectification that reduced these individual black men to purely abstract visual "things," silenced in their own right as subjects and serving mainly as aesthetic trophies to enhance Mapplethorpe's privileged position as a white gay-male artist in the New York avant-garde. In short, we were stuck in a deeply ambivalent structure of feeling. In an attempt to make sense of this experience, I drew on elements of feminist cultural theory.

The first thing to notice about Mapplethorpe's black males — so obvious that it goes without saying — is that all the men are nude. Framed within the generic conventions of the fine-art nude, their bodies are aestheticized and eroticized as "objects" to be looked at. As such, they offer an erotic source of pleasure in the act of looking. But whose pleasure is being served? Regarding the depiction of women in dominant forms of visual representation, from painting to advertising or pornography, feminist cultural theory has shown that the female image functions predominantly as a mirror image of what men want to see. As a figment of heterosexual wish fulfillment, the female nude serves primarily to guarantee the stability of a phallocentric fantasy in which the omnipotent male gaze sees but is never itself seen. The binary opposition of seeing/being seen that informs visual representations of the female nude reveals that looking is never an innocent or neutral activity but is always powerfully loaded by the gendered character of the subject/object dichotomy in which, to put it crudely, men look and women are there to be looked at.

In Mapplethorpe's case, however, the fact that both artist and model are male sets up a tension of sameness that thereby transfers the frisson of "difference" from gender to racial polarity. In terms of the conventional dichotomy between masculinity as the active control of the gaze and femininity as its passive visual object, what we see in Mapplethorpe's case is the way in which the black/white duality of race overdetermines the power relations implicit in the gendered dichotomy between subject and object of representation.

In this sense, what is represented in Mapplethorpe's photographs is a "look," or a certain "way of looking," in which the pictures reveal more about the absent and invisible white male photographer who actively controls the gaze than about the black men whose beautiful bodies we see depicted in his photographs. Insofar as the pictorial space excludes any reference to a social, historical, cultural, or political context that might tell us something about the lives of the black models who posed for the camera, Mapplethorpe facilitates the projection of certain racial and sexual fantasies about the "difference" that black masculinity is assumed to embody. In this way, the photographs are very much about sexual investment in looking, because they disclose the tracing of desire on the part of the I/eye placed at the center of representation by the male gaze.

Through a combination of formal codes and conventions — the posing and posture of the body in the studio enclosure; the use of strong chiaroscuro lighting; the cropping, framing, and fragmentation of the whole body into parts — the "look" constructed not only structures the viewer's affective disposition toward the image but reveals something of the mise-en-scène of power, as well as desire, in the racial and sexual fantasies that inform Mapplethorpe's representation of black masculinity. Whereas the white gay-male sadomasochist pictures portray a subcultural sexuality that consists of "doing" something, the black men are defined and confined to "being" purely sexual and nothing but sexual — hence hypersexual. We look through a sequence of individually named African-American men, but we see only sexuality as the sum-total meaning of their black male identity. In pictures like "Man in a Polyester Suit" (1980), apart from the model's hands, it is the penis, and the penis alone, that identifies him as a black man.

Mapplethorpe's obsessive focus on this one little thing, the black man's genitals, and the way in which the glossy allure of the quality monochrome print becomes almost consubstantial with the shiny, sexy texture of black skin led me to argue that a certain racial fetishism is an important element in the pleasures (and displeasures) that the photographs bring into play. Such racial fetishism not only eroticizes the most visible aspect of racial difference — skin color — but also lubricates the ideological reproduction of "colonial fantasy," in which the white male subject is positioned at the center of representation by a desire for mastery, power, and control over the racialized and inferiorized black other. Hence, alongside the codes of the fine-art nude, Mapplethorpe seems to make use of the regulative function of the commonplace racist stereotype — the black man as athlete, mugger, or savage — in order to stabilize the invisible and all-seeing white subject at the center of the gaze, and thereby "fix" the black subject in its place not simply as the other but as the object in the field of vision that holds a mirror to the fears and fantasies of the supposedly omnipotent white male subject.

According to literary critic Homi Bhabha, "an important feature of colonial discourse is its dependence on the concept of 'fixity' in the ideological construction of otherness."[4] Just as Mapplethorpe's photographs of female bodybuilder Lady Lisa Lyon seem obsessively to pin her down by processing the image of her body through a thousand cultural stereotypes of femininity, so the obsessive undercurrent in his black male nudes would appear to confirm this emphasis on fixity as a sign that betrays anxiety as well as pleasure in the desire for mastery. Mapplethorpe's scopic fixation on the luxurious beauty of black skin thus implies a kind of "negrophilia," an aesthetic idealization of racial difference that merely inverts and reverses the binary axis of colonial discourse, in which all things black are equated with darkness, dirt, and danger, as manifest in the psychic representation of "negrophobia." Both positions, whether they overvalue or devalue the visible signs of racial difference, inhabit the shared space of colonial fantasy. These elements for a psychoanalytic reading of fetishism, as it is enacted in the theater of Mapplethorpe's sex-race fantasy, are forcefully brought together in a photograph such as "Man in a Polyester Suit."

The use of framing and scale emphasizes the sheer size of the big black penis revealed through the unzipped trouser fly. As Frantz Fanon said, when diagnosing the terrifying figure of "the Negro" in the fantasies of his white psychiatric patients, "one is no longer aware of the Negro, but only of a penis: the Negro is eclipsed. He is turned into a penis. He *is* a penis."[5] By virtue of the purely formal device of scale, Mapplethorpe summons up one of the deepest mythological fears in the supremacist imagination: namely, the belief that all black men have monstrously large willies. In the phantasmic space of the white male imaginary, the big black phallus is perceived as a threat not only to hegemonic white masculinity but to Western civilization itself, since the "bad object" represents a danger to white womanhood and therefore the threat of miscegenation, eugenic pollution, and racial degeneration. Historically, in nineteenth-century societies structured by race, white males eliminated the anxiety that their own fantastic images of black male sexuality excited through rituals of aggression in which the lynching of black men routinely involved the literal castration of the other's strange fruit.

The historical myth of penis size amounts to a "primal fantasy" in Western culture in that it is shared and collective in nature — and, moreover, a myth that is so pervasive and firmly held as a folk belief that modern sexology repeatedly embarked on the empirical task of actually measuring pricks to demonstrate its untruth. Now that the consensual management of liberal race relations no longer provides available legitimation for this popular belief, it is as if Mapplethorpe's picture performs a disavowal of the wish fulfillment inscribed in the myth: *I know* (it's not true that all black guys have big willies), *but* (nevertheless, in my photographs they do).

Within the picture, the binary character of everyday racial discourse is underlined by the jokey irony of the contrast between the black man's exposed private parts and the public display of social respectability signified by the three-piece business suit. The oppositions hidden and exposed, denuded and clothed, play upon the Manichaean dualism of nature and culture, savage and civilized, body and mind, inferior and superior, that informs the logic of dominant racial discourse. In this way, the construction of racial difference in the image suggests that sexuality, and nothing but sexuality, is the essential "nature" of the black man, because the cheap and tacky quality of the polyester suit confirms his failure to gain access to "culture." The camouflage of bourgeois respectability fails to conceal the fact that the black man, as the white man's racial other, originates, like his dick, from somewhere anterior to civilization.

Conflicting Readings of Mapplethorpe

Notwithstanding the problematic nature of Freud's pathologizing clinical vocabulary, his concept of fetishism can usefully be adapted, via feminist cultural theory, to help conceptualize issues of subjectivity and spectatorship in representations of race and ethnicity. Its account of the splitting of levels of belief may illuminate the prevalence of certain sexual fantasies and their role in the reproduction of racism in contemporary culture. The sexual fetish represents a substitute for something that was never there in the first place: the mother's penis, which the little boy expected to see. Despite conscious acknowledgment of sexual difference, the boy's castration anxiety forces the repression of his initial belief, such that it coexists on an unconscious level and finds manifestation, in adult sexuality, in the form of the erotic fetish.[6] One might say that, despite anatomical evidence, the belief symbolized in the fantasy of the big black willie — that black male sexuality is not only "different" but somehow "more" — is one many men and women, black and white, straight or gay, cling to because it retains currency and force as an element in the psychic reality of the social fantasies in which our racial and gendered identities have been historically constructed.

Yet because Freud's concept of fetishism is embedded in the patriarchal system of sexual difference that it describes, treating sexual perversion or deviation as a symptom that reveals the unconscious logic of the heterosexual norm, it is less useful as a tool for examining the perverse aestheticism of the modern homoerotic imagination that Mapplethorpe self-consciously employs. Moreover, there are limits to the race and gender analogy drawn from feminist cultural theory in the preceding analysis of visual fetishism: it ignores the obvious homoerotic specificity of the work. As a gay-male artist whose sexual identity locates him in a subordinate relation to heterosexual masculinity, Mapplethorpe is hardly representative of the hegemonic model of straight, white, bourgeois male identity traditionally privileged in art history as the centered subject and agent of representation. Above all, as the recent exhibition history of his work attests, far from demonstrating the stability of this supposedly centered white male subject, the vitriol and anxiety expressed in hostile attacks on Mapplethorpe's œuvre (such as those of the radical neoconservative art critic Hilton Kramer) would suggest that there is something profoundly troubling and disturbing about the emotional ambivalence experienced by different audiences through the salient shock effect of Mapplethorpe's work.

In light of the changed context of reception, the foremost question is how different audiences and readers produce different and conflicting readings of the same cultural text. The variety of conflicting interpretations of the value of Mapplethorpe's work would imply that the text does not bear one, singular, and unequivocal meaning but is open to a number of competing readings. Thus Mapplethorpe's photographic text has become the site for a range of antagonistic interpretations. Once we adopt this view, we need to reconsider the relationship between artist and audience, or author and reader, because although we habitually attempt to resolve the question of the ultimate "meaning" of a text by appealing to authorial intentions, poststructuralist theory has shown, by way of the "death of the author" argument, that individual intentions never have the last word in determining the meaning or value of a text. This is because readers themselves play an active role in interpreting a multivalent and open-ended modernist cultural text.

One might say, therefore, that the difficult and troublesome question raised by Mapplethorpe's black male nudes — do they reinforce or undermine racist myths about black sexuality? — is strictly unanswerable, since his aesthetic strategy makes an unequivocal yes/no response impossible. The question is left open by the author and is thus thrown back to the spectator. Our recognition of the unconscious sex-race fantasies that Mapplethorpe's images arouse with such perverse precision does not confirm a stable or centered subject-position but is experienced precisely as an emotional disturbance that troubles the viewer's sense of secure identity.

The recent actual death of the author entails a reconsideration of the issue of authorship and intentionality, and the reciprocal role of the reader, because the articulation of race and homosexuality in Mapplethorpe's art can also be seen as a subversive move that begins to unravel the violent ambiguity at the interface of the social and the emotional. To clarify my suggestion that his black male nudes are open to an alternative evaluation from that of my initial reading, I should come clean with regard to the specific character of my own subject-position as a black gay-male reader.

My angry emphasis on racial fetishism as a potentially exploitative process of objectification was based on the way in which I felt identified with the black men depicted in the photographs, simply by virtue of sharing the same "categorical" identity as a black man. As the source of this anger, the emotional identification can be best described again in Fanon's words as a feeling that "I am laid bare. I am over-determined from without. I am the slave not of the 'idea' that others have of me but of my own appearance. I am being dissected under white eyes. I am fixed. . . . Look, it's a Negro."[7] It was my anger at the aestheticizing effect of Mapplethorpe's coolly "ironic" appropriation of racist stereotypes that informed the description of visual fetishism as a process of reduction, or dehumanization. This argument has many similarities with the early feminist critique of images of women in pornography.[8] But the problem with this view is that it moralizes images in terms of a reductive dichotomy between good and bad, "positive" and "negative," and thus fails to recognize the ambivalence of the text. If, in contrast, we recognize that there is an important difference between saying that an image is racist and saying that it is "about" racism, then we need a more reflexive approach to the ambiguities set into motion in the destabilizing moment of Mapplethorpe's shock effect.

In this view, the strategic use of visual fetishism is not necessarily a bad thing, as it encourages the viewer to examine his or her own implication in the fantasies that the images arouse. Once I acknowledge my own location in the image reservoir as a gay subject — a desiring subject not only in terms of sharing a desire to look, but in terms of an identical object-choice already there in my own fantasies and wishes — then the articulation of meanings about eroticism, race, and homosexuality becomes a lot more complicated. Indeed, I am forced to confront the rather unwelcome fact that as a spectator I actually occupy the very position in the fantasy of mastery previously ascribed to the centered position of the white male subject! In other words, there was another axis of identification — between white gay-male author and black gay-male reader — that cut across the identification with the black men in the pictures. Could it not be the case that my anger was also mingled with feelings of jealousy, rivalry, or envy? If I shared the same desire to look, which would place me in the position of mastery attributed to the author, the anger in the initial critique might also have arisen from a shared, homosexual identification and thus a rivalry over the same unobtainable object of desire. Insofar as the anger and envy were effects of my identification with both the object and subject of the look, I would say that my specific identity as a black gay reader placed me in two contradictory positions at one and the same time. I am sure that emotions such as these are at issue in the rivalry of interpretations around Mapplethorpe's most contentious work. Black gay-male readers certainly do not have a monopoly on the conflicted and ambivalent structures of feeling they create. My point here is not confessional, but to use my own experience as a source of data about the complex operations of identification and desire that position us in antagonistic and contradictory relations of race, gender, and power, which are themselves partly constituted in representations. In revising my views, I have sought to reopen the question of ambivalence, because rather than simply project it on to the author (by asking whether he either perpetuates or challenges racism) one needs to take into account how different readers derive different meanings not only about race but about sexuality and desire in Mapplethorpe's work.

The Perverse Aesthetic

The whole point about the use of textual ambivalence in the modernist tradition is to foreground the uncertainty of any one, singular meaning — which, in the case of Mapplethorpe's double transgressions across race and homosexuality, is a risky business indeed. This is because the open-ended character of the images can provoke a racist reading as much as an antiracist one, elicit a homophobic reading as much as arouse a homoerotic one. A great deal depends on the reader and the social identity she or he brings to the text. The same statement — the black man is beautiful, say — retains the same denotative meaning but acquires different connotational values when enunciated by different groups of subjects: the same sentence, uttered by a white man, a black woman, a black man, or a white woman, would inevitably take on a qualitatively different "sound." Similarly, once we situate the network of relations between author, text, and reader, in the contingent, context-bound circumstances in which Mapplethorpe's work currently stands, then we can examine the way in which the open-ended structure of the text gives rise to antagonistic readings that are informed by the social identity of the audience.

Without returning to a naive belief in the author as a godlike figure of authority, it is necessary to argue that it really does matter who is speaking whenever artists, because of their sexual, gender, or racial identity, are assigned "minority" status in the arts and in culture at large. Once we take the biographical dimension of Mapplethorpe's work as a gay artist into account, it is possible to reinterpret the black male nudes as the beginning of an inquiry into the archive of race in Western culture and history, which has rendered black men into "invisible men," in Ralph Ellison's phrase. As Mapplethorpe put it in an interview shortly before his death, "At some point I started photographing black men. It was an area that hadn't been explored intensively. If you went through the history of nude male photography, there were very few black subjects. I found that I could take pictures of black men that were so subtle, and the form was so photographical." An awareness of the exclusion of the black subject from one of the most valued canonical genres of Western art — the nude — suggests that it is both possible and necessary to reread Mapplethorpe's work as part of an artistic inquiry into the hegemonic force of a Eurocentric aesthetics that historically rendered invisible not only black people but women, lesbians and gays, and others before the radical social transformations of the modern and postmodern period.

By virtue of a perverse aesthetic of promiscuous intertextuality, whereby the over-valued aura of the fine-art nude is contaminated by the filthy and degraded form of the commonplace stereotype, Mapplethorpe transgresses on several fronts to make visible that which is repressed and made invisible in the dominant, and dominating, tradition of the West against the rest. In the contemporary United States, for example, black males constitute one of the "lowest" social identities in the late-capitalist underclass: disenfranchised, disadvantaged, disempowered. Yet in Mapplethorpe's studio, some of the men who in all probability came from this class are elevated on to the pedestal of the transcendental aesthetic ideal of the male nude in Western culture, which had always excluded the black subject from such aesthetic idealization on account of its otherness. Mapplethorpe's achievement as a postmodern "society photographer" lies in the way he renders invisible men visible in a cultural system — art photography — that always historically denied or marginalized their existence. One can see in Mapplethorpe's use of homoeroticism a subversive strategy of perversion in which the liberal-humanist values inscribed in the idealized fine-art nude are led away from the higher aims of "civilization" and brought face-to-face with that part of itself repressed and devalued as "other" in the form of the banal, commonplace stereotype in everyday culture. What is experienced in the salient shock effect is the disruption of our normative expectations about distinctions that imply a rigid separation between fine art and popular culture or between art and pornography. Mapplethorpe's transgressive crossing of such boundaries has the effect of calling into question our psychic and social investment in these cultural separations.

Changing Political Climates

If I am now more prepared to offer a defense rather than a critique of Mapplethorpe's representations of race, because of the changed ideological context, it is because the stakes have also changed. I am convinced that it was not the death of the author so much as the cause of his death that was a major factor in the timing of the Helms campaign against the NEA. Almost all the discourse surrounding the furor noted that Mapplethorpe died of AIDS. The newfound legitimacy of political homophobia and the creation of new folk devils through the mismanagement of the AIDS crisis have proved fertile ground for the spread of popular authoritarian tendencies across the left/right spectrum. Yet the Mapplethorpe/NEA crisis in the United States was often perceived, like the Rushdie crisis in Britain, simply in terms of a straightforward opposition between censorship and freedom of artistic expression. This model of a crude binary frontier is unfeasible because what was at stake in the conflicting readings of Mapplethorpe was not a neat dichotomy between bigoted Philistines and enlightened cultured liberals but a new configuration of social actors, some of whom have engaged in unexpected alliances that have transformed the terrain of contestation.

In many ways the right's success in organizing a popular bloc of public opinion on issues like pornography derives from these new alliances. Just like the alliance formed between radical feminist antiporn activists and the local state legislature in the form of the Dworkin-MacKinnon-drafted Minneapolis Ordinance in 1984, or the appropriation of the feminist argument that pornography itself is violence in the official discourse of the Meese Commission in 1986, the Helms campaign has highlighted some significant developments in popular right-wing politics. In his original proposal to regulate public funding of art deemed "obscene and indecent," Jesse Helms went beyond the traditional stock of moral fundamentalism to add new grounds for legal intervention on the basis of discrimination against minorities. Helms wanted the state to intervene in instances where artistic and cultural materials "denigrate, debase or revile a person, group or class of citizens on the basis of race, creed, sex, handicap or national origin." By means of this rhetorical move, he sought to appropriate the language of liberal antidiscrimination legislation to promote a climate of opinion favorable to new forms of coercive intervention. In making such a move, the strategy is not simply to win support from black people and ethnic minorities, nor simply to modernize the traditional "moral" discourse against obscenity, but to broaden and extend the threshold of illegitimacy to a wider range of cultural texts. As the moral panic unfolds, more and more cultural forms transgress or come up against the symbolic boundary that such prohibitionary legislation seeks to impose. Consider the way in which parental warning labels on rap and rock albums have become commonplace: the Parents' Music Resource Centre that helped to initiate this trend in the 1980s has also inspired prosecutions of rock musicians on the grounds that their cultural texts do not simply "deprave and corrupt," as it were, but have actually caused violence, in the form of suicides.

Under these conditions — when, despite its initial emancipatory intentions, elements of the radical feminist antiporn movement of the 1980s have entered into alliance with neoconservative forces — it is not inconceivable that a reading of Robert Mapplethorpe's work as racist, however well intended, could serve the ends of the authoritarian trend supported by this new alliance of social actors. The AIDS crisis has also visibly brought to light the way in which homophobia can be used to draw upon conservative forces within minority cultures. In black British communities, the antilesbian and gay hostility expressed in the belief that homosexuality is a "white man's thing," and hence, because of the scapegoating of gay men, that AIDS is a "white man's disease," not only has helped to cement alliances between black people and the new right (for example, in the local campaign on "positive images" in Haringey, London, in 1987) but has had tragically self-defeating consequences in the black community itself. Men and women have been dying, but the psychic mechanism of denial and disavowal in such fear of homosexuality has been particularly apparent in many black responses to AIDS.

Yet these contradictory conditions have also shaped the emergence of a new generation of black lesbian and gay cultural activists in Britain and the United States. Their presence is seriously important not only because they contest the repressive precepts of authoritarian politics in both white society and in black communities but because their creativity points to new ways of making sense of the contemporary situation. Black lesbian and gay artists such as Isaac Julien, Pratibha Parmar, Michelle Parkerson, and Marlon Riggs in film and video; or Essex Hemphill,

Cheryl Clarke, Barbara Smith, and Joseph Beam in writing and criticism; or Sunil Gupta, Rotimi Fani-Kayode, or Lyle Harris in the medium of photography, have widened and pluralized the political and theoretical debates about eroticism, prohibition, transgression, and representation. In films such as Isaac Julien's *Looking for Langston* (1989) some of the difficult and troublesome questions about race and homosexuality that Mapplethorpe raised are taken on in a multifaceted dialogue on the lived experience of black gay desire. In his photographs, Rotimi Fani-Kayode also enters into this dialogue, not through a confrontational strategy but through an invitational mode of address that operates in and against the visual codes and conventions his work shares with Mapplethorpe's. But in this hybrid, Afrocentric, homoerotic image world, significant differences unfold as such artists critically "signify upon" the textual sources they draw from. In the hands of this new generation of black diaspora intellectuals rethinking sex, such "signifying" activity simultaneously critiques the exclusions and absences that previously rendered black lesbian and gay identities invisible and reconstructs new pluralistic forms of collective belonging and imagined community that broaden the public sphere of multicultural society.

Such radical changes in black queer visibility were unthinkable ten or fifteen years ago, and one would hope that their emergence now suggests new possibilities for an alternative set of popular alliances that seek to open up and democratize the politics of desire. In the event that the legislation sought by those opposed to whatever can be called "pornographic" is ever successful in Britain, it is far more likely that it will first be brought to bear on independent artists such as these rather than on the corporations and businessmen who own the porn industry, edit the tabloids, or sell advertising. To propose to outlaw something the definition of which no one seems to agree upon is hardly in the interests of anyone seeking not just the protection of our existing civil rights and liberties (few as they are in Britain) but the necessary changes that would further democratize and deepen new practices of freedom.

NOTES

1. Audre Lorde, "Uses of the Erotic: The Erotic as Power" (1978), and Alice Walker, "Coming Apart" (1979), both reprinted in Laura Lederer, ed., *Take Back the Night: Women on Pornography* (New York: William Morrow, 1980).

2. Susanne Kappeler, *The Pornography of Representation* (Cambridge: Polity Press, 1986), 5–10. One important alternative to the race and gender analogy is to open the debate to include racism both in pornography and in the women's movement. This is an important point, raised in the context of a historical overview of the mutual articulation of gender and sexuality in racial oppression, discussed by Tracey Gardner, "Racism in Pornography and the Women's Movement" (1978), in Lederer, ed., *Take Back the Night*.

3. See Kobena Mercer, "Imaging the Black Man's Sex," in Patricia Holland, Jo Spence, and Simon Watney, eds., *Photography/Politics,* vol. 2 (London: Comedia, 1986), and, for the revision of the initial analysis, "Skin Head Sex Thing: Racial Difference and the Homoerotic Imaginary," in Bad Object Choices, eds., *How Do I Look? Lesbian and Gay Film and Video* (Seattle: Bay Press, 1991). Related work on the cultural politics of black masculinity may be found in Isaac Julien and Kobena Mercer, "Race, Sexual Politics and Black Masculinity: A Dossier," in Rowena Chapman and Jonathan Rutherford, eds., *Male Order: Unwrapping Masculinity* (London: Lawrence and Wishart, 1988). The black male nude photographs referred to may be found in Robert Mapplethorpe, *Black Males* (Amsterdam: Gallerie Jurka, 1982); *The Black Book* (Munich: Schirme-Mosel, 1986); and Richard Marshall, ed., *Robert Mapplethorpe* (New York: Bullfinch Press, 1990).

4. Homi Bhabha, "The Other Question: Colonial Discourse and the Stereotype," *Screen* 24, no. 4 (1983): 18.

5. Frantz Fanon, *Black Skin, White Masks* (London: Pluto Press, 1952), 120.

6. Sigmund Freud, "Fetishism" (1923), in *The Pelican Freud Library,* vol. 7, *On Sexuality* (Harmondsworth, England: Penguin, 1977).

7. Fanon, *Black Skin, White Masks,* 82.

8. The humanist critique of objectification is taken up by Essex Hemphill in the introduction to Essex Hemphill, ed., *Brother to Brother: New Writings by Black Gay Men* (Boston: Alyson, 1991).

Part III

Gender and the Politics of Race

Chapter 14
Under Western Eyes: Feminist Scholarship and Colonial Discourses
Chandra Talpade Mohanty

Any discussion of the intellectual and political construction of "Third World feminisms" must address itself to two simultaneous projects: the internal critique of hegemonic "Western" feminisms and the formulation of autonomous feminist concerns and strategies that are geographically, historically, and culturally grounded. The first project is one of deconstructing and dismantling; the second is one of building and constructing. While these projects appear to be contradictory, the one working negatively and the other positively, unless these two tasks are addressed simultaneously, Third World feminisms run the risk of marginalization or ghettoization from both mainstream (right and left) and Western feminist discourses.

It is to the first project that I address myself. What I wish to analyze is specifically the production of the "Third World woman" as a singular, monolithic subject in some recent (Western) feminist texts. The definition of colonization I wish to invoke here is a predominantly *discursive* one, focusing on a certain mode of appropriation and codification of scholarship and knowledge about women in the Third World through the use of particular analytic categories employed in specific writings on the subject that take as their referent feminist interests as they have been articulated in the United States and Western Europe. If one of the tasks of formulating and understanding the locus of Third World feminisms is delineating the way in which they resist and *work against* what I am referring to as "Western feminist discourse," then an analysis of the discursive construction of Third World women in Western feminism is an important first step.

Clearly, neither Western feminist discourse nor Western feminist political practice is singular or homogeneous in its goals, interests, or analyses. However, it is possible to trace a coherence of *effects* resulting from the implicit assumption of "the West" (in all its complexities and contradictions) as the primary referent in theory and praxis. My reference to "Western feminism" is by no means intended to imply that it is a monolith. Rather, I am attempting to draw attention to the similar effects of various textual strategies used by writers that codify others as non-Western and hence themselves as (implicitly) Western. It is in this sense that I use the term "Western feminist." Similar arguments can be made about middle-class, urban African or Asian scholars who write about their rural or working-class sisters and assume their own middle-class cultures as the norm and codify working-class histories and

255

cultures as other. Thus, while this essay focuses specifically on what I refer to as "Western feminist" discourse on women in the Third World, the critiques I offer also pertain to Third World scholars who write about their own cultures and employ identical analytic strategies.

It ought to be of some political significance that the term "colonization" has come to denote a variety of phenomena in recent feminist and left writings in general. From its analytic value as a category of exploitative economic exchange in both traditional and contemporary Marxisms (see, in particular, Amin 1977; Baran 1962; and Gunder-Frank 1967) to its use by feminist women of color in the United States to describe the appropriation of their experiences and struggles by hegemonic white women's movements (see especially Joseph and Lewis 1981; and Moraga 1984; Moraga and Anzaldúa 1983; and Smith 1983), colonization has been used to characterize everything from the most evident economic and political hierarchies to the production of a particular cultural discourse about what is called the "Third World."[1] However sophisticated or problematical its use as an explanatory construct, colonization almost invariably implies a relation of structural domination and a suppression — often violent — of the heterogeneity of the subject(s) in question.

My concern about such writings derives from my own implication and investment in contemporary debates in feminist theory and the urgent political necessity of forming strategic coalitions across class, race, and national boundaries. The analytic principles discussed below serve to distort Western feminist political practices and limit the possibility of coalitions among (usually white) Western feminists, working-class feminists, and feminists of color around the world. These limitations are evident in the construction of the (implicitly consensual) priority of issues around which apparently *all* women are expected to organize. The necessary and integral connection between feminist scholarship and feminist political practice and organizing determines the significance and status of Western feminist writings on women in the Third World, for feminist scholarship, like most other kinds of scholarship, is not the mere production of knowledge about a certain subject. It is a directly political and discursive *practice* in that it is purposeful and ideological. It is best seen as a mode of intervention into particular hegemonic discourses (e.g., traditional anthropology, sociology, and literary criticism); it is a political praxis that counters and resists the totalizing imperative of age-old "legitimate" and "scientific" bodies of knowledge. Thus, feminist scholarly practices (reading, writing, critiquing, etc.) are inscribed in relations of power — relations that they counter, resist, or even perhaps implicitly support. There can, of course, be no apolitical scholarship.

The relationship between "Woman" (a cultural and ideological composite other constructed through diverse representational discourses — scientific, literary, juridical, linguistic, cinematic, etc.) and "women" (real, material subjects of their collective histories) is one of the central questions the practice of feminist scholarship seeks to address. This connection between women as historical subjects and the representation of Woman produced by hegemonic discourses is not a relation of direct identity or a relation of correspondence or simple implication.[2] It is an arbitrary relation set up by particular cultures. I would like to suggest that the feminist writings I analyze here discursively colonize the material and historical heterogeneities of the lives of women in the Third World, thereby producing/representing a composite, singular "Third World woman" — an image that appears arbitrarily constructed but nevertheless carries with it the authorizing signature of Western humanist discourse.[3]

I argue that assumptions of privilege and ethnocentric universality, on the one hand, and inadequate self-consciousness about the effect of Western scholarship on the Third World in the context of a world system dominated by the West, on the other, characterize a sizable extent of Western feminist work on women in the Third World. An analysis of "sexual difference" in the form of a cross-culturally singular, monolithic notion of patriarchy or male dominance leads to the construction of a similarly reductive and homogeneous notion of what I call the "Third World difference" — that stable, ahistorical something that apparently oppresses most if not all the women in these countries. And it is in the production of this Third World difference that Western feminisms appropriate and colonize the constitutive complexities that characterize the lives of women in these countries. It is in this process of discursive homogenization and systematization of the oppression of women in the Third World that power is exercised in much of recent Western feminist discourse, and this power needs to be defined and named.

In the context of the West's hegemonic position today — the context of what Anouar Abdel-Malek (1981) calls a struggle for "control over the orientation, regulation and decision of the process of world development on the basis of the advanced sector's monopoly of scientific knowledge and ideal creativity" — Western feminist scholarship on the Third World must be seen and examined precisely in terms of its inscription in these particular relations of power and struggle. There is, it should be evident, no universal patriarchal framework that this scholarship attempts to counter and resist — unless one posits an international male conspiracy or a monolithic, ahistorical power structure. There is, however, a particular world balance of power within which any analysis of culture, ideology, and socioeconomic conditions necessarily has to be situated. Abdel-Malek is useful here, again, in reminding us about the inherence of politics in the discourses of "culture":

> Contemporary imperialism is, in a real sense, a hegemonic imperialism, ex-excising to a maximum degree a rationalized violence taken to a higher level than ever before — through fire and sword, but also through the attempt to control hearts and minds. For its content is defined by the combined action of the military-industrial complex and the hegemonic cultural centers of the West, all of them founded on the advanced levels of development attained by monopoly and finance capital, and supported by the benefits of both the scientific and technological revolution and the second industrial revolution itself. (145–46)

Western feminist scholarship cannot avoid the challenge of situating itself and examining its role in such a global economic and political framework. To do any less would be to ignore the complex interconnections between First and Third World economies and the profound effect of this on the lives of women in all countries. I do not question the descriptive and informative value of most Western feminist writings on women in the Third World. I also do not question the existence of excellent work that does not fall into the analytic traps with which I am concerned. In fact I deal with an example of such work later on. In the context of an overwhelming silence about the experiences of women in these countries, as well as the need to forge international links between women's political struggles, such work is both pathbreaking and absolutely essential. However, I want to draw attention here both to the *explanatory potential* of particular analytic strategies employed by such writing and to their *political effect* in the context of the hegemony of Western scholarship. While feminist writing in the United States is still marginalized (except from the point of view of women of color addressing privileged white women), Western feminist writing on women in the Third World must be considered in the context of the global hegemony of Western scholarship — that is, the production, publication, distribution, and consumption of information and ideas. Marginal or not, this writing has political effects and implications beyond the immediate feminist or disciplinary audience. One such significant effect of the dominant "representations" of Western feminism is its conflation with imperialism in the eyes of particular Third World women.[4] Hence the urgent need to examine the *political* implications of our *analytic* strategies and principles.

My critique is directed at three basic analytic principles that are present in (Western) feminist discourse on women in the Third World. Since I focus primarily on the Zed Press Women in the Third World series, my comments on Western feminist discourse are circumscribed by my analysis of the texts in this series.[5] This is a way of focusing my critique. However, even though I am dealing with feminists who identify themselves as culturally or geographically from the West, as mentioned earlier, what I say about these presuppositions or implicit principles holds for anyone who uses these methods, whether Third World women in the West or Third World women in the Third World writing on these issues and publishing in the West. Thus, I am not making a culturalist argument about ethnocentrism; rather, I am trying to uncover how ethnocentric universalism is produced in certain analyses. As a matter of fact, my argument holds for any discourse that sets up its own authorial subjects as the implicit referent, that is, the yardstick by which to encode and represent cultural others. It is in this move that power is exercised in discourse.

The first analytic presupposition I focus on is involved in the strategic location of the category "women" vis-à-vis the context of analysis. The assumption of women as an already constituted, coherent group with identical interests and desires, regardless of class, ethnic or racial location, or contradictions, implies a notion of gender or sexual difference or even patriarchy that can be applied universally and cross-culturally. (The context of analysis can be anything from kinship structures and the organization of labor to media representations.) The second analytical presupposition is evident on the methodological level, in the uncritical way "proof" of universality and cross-cultural validity are provided. The third is a more specifically political presupposition underlying the methodologies and the analytic strategies, that is, the model of power and struggle they imply and suggest. I argue that as a result of the two modes — or, rather, frames — of analysis described above, a homogeneous notion of the oppression of women as a group is assumed, which, in turn, produces the image of an "average Third World woman." This average Third World woman leads an essentially truncated life based on her feminine gender (read: sexually constrained) and her being "Third World" (read: ignorant, poor, uneducated, tradition-bound, domestic, family-oriented, victimized, etc.). This, I suggest, is in contrast to the (implicit) self-representation of Western women as educated, as modern, as having control over their own bodies and sexualities, and the freedom to make their own decisions.

The distinction between Western feminist re-presentation of women in the Third World and Western feminist self-presentation is a distinction of the same order as that made by some Marxists between the "maintenance" function of the housewife and the real "productive" role of wage labor, or the characterization by developmentalists of the Third World as being engaged in the lesser production of "raw materials" in contrast to the "real" productive activity of the First World. These distinctions are made on the basis of the privileging of a particular group as the norm or referent. Men involved in wage labor, First World producers, and, I suggest, Western feminists who sometimes cast Third World women in terms of "ourselves undressed" (Rosaldo 1980), all construct themselves as the normative referent in such a binary analytic.

Women as a Category of Analysis; or, We Are All Sisters in Struggle

The phrase "women as a category of analysis" refers to the crucial assumption that all women, across classes and cultures, are somehow socially constituted as a homogeneous group identified prior to the process of analysis. This is an assumption that characterizes much feminist discourse. The homogeneity of women as a group is produced not on the basis of biological essentials but rather on the basis of secondary sociological and anthropological universals. Thus, for instance, in any given piece of feminist analysis, women are characterized as a singular group on the basis of a shared oppression. What binds women together is a sociological notion of the "sameness" of their oppression. It is at this point that an elision takes place between "women" as a discursively constructed group and "women" as material subject of their own history. Thus, the discursively consensual homogeneity of women as a group is mistaken for the historically specific material reality of groups of women. This results in an assumption of women as an always already constituted group, one that has been labeled powerless, exploited, sexually harassed, and so on, by feminist scientific, economic, legal, and sociological discourses. (Notice that this is quite similar to sexist discourse labeling women as weak, emotional, having math anxiety, etc.) This focus is not on uncovering the material and ideological specificities that constitute a particular group of women as "powerless" in a particular context. It is, rather, on finding a variety of cases of powerless groups of women to prove the general point that women as a group are powerless.

In this section I focus on six specific ways in which "women" as a category of analysis is used in Western feminist discourse on women in the Third World. Each of these examples illustrates the construction of "Third World women" as a homogeneous "powerless" group often located as implicit *victims* of particular socioeconomic systems. I have chosen to deal with a variety of writers — from Fran Hosken, who writes primarily about female genital mutilation, to writers from the Women in International Development (WID) school, who write about the effect of development policies on Third World women for both Western and Third World audiences. The similarity of assumptions about Third World women in all these texts forms the basis of my discussion. This is not to equate all the texts that I analyze, nor is it to equalize their strengths and weaknesses. The authors I deal with write with varying degrees of care and complexity; however, the *effect* of their representation of Third World women is a coherent one. In these texts women are defined as victims of male violence (Fran Hosken); victims as universal dependents (Beverly Lindsay and Maria Cutrufelli); victims of the colonial process (Maria Cutrufelli); victims of the Arab familial system (Juliette Minces); victims of *the* Islamic code (Patricia Jeffery); and, finally, victims of the economic development process (Beverley Lindsay and the [liberal] WID school). This mode of defining women primarily in terms of their *object status* (the way in which they are affected or not affected by certain institutions and systems) is what characterizes this particular form of the use of "women" as a category of analysis. In the context of Western women writing/ studying women in the Third World, such objectification (however benevolently motivated) needs to be both named and challenged. As Valerie Amos and Pratibha Parmar argue quite eloquently, "Feminist theories which examine our cultural practices as 'feudal residues' or label us 'traditional,' also portray us as politically immature women who need to be versed and schooled in the ethos of Western feminism. They need to be continually challenged" (1984, 7).[6]

Women as Victims of Male Violence

Fran Hosken, in writing about the relationship between human rights and female genital mutilation in Africa and the Middle East, bases her whole discussion/ condemnation of genital mutilation on one privileged premise: that the goal of this practice is to "mutilate the sexual pleasure and satisfaction of woman" (1981, 11). This, in turn, leads her to claim that woman's sexuality is controlled, as is her reproductive potential. According to Hosken, "male sexual politics" in Africa and around the world shares "the same political goal: to assure female dependence and subservience by any and all means" (14). Physical violence against women (rape, sexual assault, excision, infibulation, etc.) is thus carried out "with an astonishing consensus among men in the world" (14). Here, women are defined consistently as the *victims* of male control — as the "sexually oppressed."[7] Although it is true that the potential of male violence against women circumscribes and elucidates their social position to a certain extent, defining women as archetypal victims freezes them into "objects-who-defend-themselves," men into "subjects-who-perpetrate-violence," and (every) society into powerless (read: women) and powerful (read: men) groups of people. Male violence must be theorized and interpreted *within* specific societies in order both to understand it better and to organize effectively to change it.[8] Sisterhood cannot be assumed on the basis of gender; it must be forged in concrete historical and political practice and analysis.

Women as Universal Dependents

Beverly Lindsay's conclusion to the book *Comparative Perspectives of Third World Women: The Impact of Race, Sex, and Class* (1983, 298–306) states: "[D]ependency relationships, based upon race, sex, and class, are being perpetuated through social, educational, and economic institutions. These are the linkages among Third World Women." Here, as in other places, Lindsay implies that Third World women constitute an identifiable group purely on the basis of shared dependencies. If shared dependencies were all that was needed to bind Third World women together as a group, they would always be seen as an apolitical group with no subject status. Instead, if anything, it is the *common context* of political struggle against class, race, gender, and imperialist hierarchies that may constitute Third World women as a strategic group at this historical juncture. Lindsay also states that linguistic and cultural differences exist between Vietnamese and black American women, but "both groups are victims of race, sex, and class." Again, black and Vietnamese women are characterized by their victim status.

Similarly, examine statements such as, "My analysis will start by stating that all African women are politically and economically dependent" (Cutrufelli 1983, 13); "Nevertheless, either overtly or covertly, prostitution is still the main if not the only source of work for African women" (33). *All* African women are dependent. Prostitution is the only work option for African women as a *group*. Both statements are illustrative of generalizations sprinkled liberally through Maria Cutrufelli's book *Women of Africa: Roots of Oppression*. On the cover of the book, Cutrufelli is described as an Italian writer, sociologist, Marxist, and feminist. Today, is it possible to imagine writing a book entitled *Women of Europe: Roots of Oppression*? I am not objecting to the use of universal groupings for descriptive purposes. Women from the continent of Africa can be descriptively characterized as "women of Africa." It is when "women of Africa" becomes a homogeneous sociological grouping characterized by common dependencies or powerlessness (or even strengths) that problems arise — we say too little and too much at the same time.

This is because descriptive gender differences are transformed into the division between men and women. Women are constituted as a group via dependency relationships vis-à-vis men, who are implicitly held responsible for these relationships. When "women of Africa" as a group (versus "men of Africa" as a group?) are seen as a group precisely because they are generally dependent and oppressed, the analysis of specific historical differences becomes impossible, because reality is always apparently structured by divisions — two mutually exclusive and jointly exhaustive groups, the victims and the oppressors. Here the sociological is substituted for the biological, in order, however, to create the same — a unity of women. Thus, it is not the descriptive potential of gender difference but the privileged positioning and explanatory potential of gender difference as the *origin* of oppression that I question. In using "women of Africa" (as an already constituted group of oppressed peoples) as a category of analysis, Cutrufelli denies any historical specificity to the location of women as subordinate, powerful, marginal, central, or otherwise, vis-à-vis particular social and power networks. Women are taken as a unified "powerless" group prior to the analysis in question. Thus, it is then merely a matter of specifying the context *after the fact*. "Women" are now placed in the context of the family or in the workplace or within religious networks almost as if these systems existed outside the relations of women with other women, and women with men.

The problem with this analytic strategy, let me repeat, is that it assumes men and women are already constituted as sexual-political subjects prior to their entry into the arena of social relations. Only if we subscribe to this assumption is it possible to undertake analysis that looks at the "effects" of kinship structures, colonialism, organization of labor, and so on, on "women," defined in advance as a group. The crucial point that is forgotten is that women are produced through these very relations as well as being implicated in forming these relations. As Michelle Rosaldo argues, "[W]oman's place in human social life is not in any direct sense a product of the things she does (or even less, a function of what, biologically, she is) but the meaning her activities acquire through concrete social interactions" (1980, 400). That women mother in a variety of societies is not as significant as the value attached to mothering in these societies. The distinction between the act of mothering and the status attached to it is a very important one — one that needs to be stated and analyzed contextually.

Married Women as Victims of the Colonial Process

In Claude Lévi-Strauss's theory of kinship structure as a system of the exchange of women, what is significant is that exchange itself is not constitutive of the subordination of women; women are not subordinate because of the *fact* of exchange but because of the *modes* of exchange instituted and the values attached to these modes. However, in discussing the marriage ritual of the Bemba, a Zambian matrilocal, matrilineal people, Cutrufelli in *Women of Africa* focuses on the fact of the marital exchange of women before and after Western colonization, rather than the value attached to this exchange in this particular context. This leads to her definition of Bemba women as a coherent group affected in a particular way by colonization. Here again, Bemba women are constituted rather unilaterally as victims of the effects of Western colonization.

Cutrufelli cites the marriage ritual of the Bemba as a multistage event "whereby a young man becomes incorporated into his wife's family group as he takes up residence with them and gives his services in return for food and maintenance" (43). This ritual extends over many years, and the sexual relationship varies according to the degree of the girl's physical maturity. It is only after she undergoes an initiation ceremony at puberty that intercourse is sanctioned, and the man acquires legal rights over her. This initiation ceremony is the more important act of the consecration of women's reproductive power, so that the abduction of an uninitiated girl is of no consequence, while heavy penalty is levied for the seduction of an initiated girl. Cutrufelli asserts that European colonization has changed the whole marriage system. Now the young man is entitled to take his wife away from her people in return for money. The implication is that Bemba women have now lost the protection of tribal laws. The problem here is that while it is possible to see how the structure of the traditional marriage contract (versus the postcolonial marriage contract) offered women a certain amount of control over their marital relations, only an analysis of the political significance of the actual practice that privileges an initiated girl over an uninitiated one, indicating a shift in female power relations as a result of this ceremony, can provide an accurate account of whether Bemba women were indeed protected by tribal laws *at all times*.

It is not possible, however, to talk about Bemba women as a homogeneous group within the traditional marriage structure. Bemba women *before* the initiation are constituted within a different set of social relations compared to Bemba women *after* the initiation. To treat them as a unified group characterized by the fact of their "exchange" between male kin is to deny the sociohistorical and cultural specificities of their existence and the differential *value* attached to their exchange before and after their initiation. It is to treat the initiation ceremony as a ritual with no political implications or effects. It is also to assume that in merely describing the *structure* of the marriage contract, the situation of women is exposed. Women as a group are positioned within a given structure, but no attempt is made to trace the effect of the marriage practice in constituting women within an obviously changing network of power relations. Thus, women are assumed to be sexual-political subjects prior to entry into kinship structures.

Women and Familial Systems

Elizabeth Cowie (1978), in another context, points out the implications of this sort of analysis when she emphasizes the specifically political nature of kinship structures that must be analyzed as ideological practices that designate men and women as father, husband, wife, mother, sister, and so on. Thus, Cowie suggests, women as women are not *located* within the family. Rather, it is *in* the family, as an effect of kinship structures, that women as women are *constructed,* defined within and by the group. Thus, for instance, when Juliette Minces (1980) cites *the* patriarchal family as the basis for "an almost identical vision of women" that Arab and Muslim societies have, she falls into this very trap (see esp. 23). Not only is it problematical to speak of a vision of women shared by Arab and Muslim societies (i.e., over twenty different countries) without addressing the particular historical, material, and ideological power structures that construct such images, but to speak of the patriarchal family or the tribal kinship structure as the origin of the socioeconomic status of women is to assume again that women are sexual-political subjects prior to their entry into the family. So while, on the one hand, women attain value or status within the family, the assumption of a singular patriarchal kinship system (common to all Arab and Muslim societies) is what apparently structures women as an oppressed group in these societies! This singular, coherent kinship system presumably influences another separate and given entity, "women." Thus, all women, regardless of class and cultural differences, are affected by this system. Not only are *all* Arab and Muslim women seen to constitute a homogeneous oppressed group, but there is no discussion of the specific *practices* within the family that constitute women as mothers, wives, sisters, and so on. Arabs and Muslims, it appears, don't change at all. Their patriarchal family is carried over from the times of the prophet Muhammad. They exist, as it were, outside history.

Women and Religious Ideologies

A further example of the use of "women" as a category of analysis is found in cross-cultural analyses that subscribe to a certain economic reductionism in describing the relationship between the economy and factors such as politics and ideology. Here, in reducing the level of comparison to the economic relations between "developed and developing" countries, any specificity to the question of women is denied. Mina Modares (1981), in a careful analysis of women and Shiism in Iran, focuses on this very problem when she criticizes feminist writings that treat Islam as an ideology separate from and outside social relations and practices, rather than as a discourse that includes rules for economic, social, and power relations within society. Patricia Jeffery's (1979) otherwise informative work on Pirzada women in purdah considers Islamic ideology a partial explanation for the status of women in that it provides a justification for purdah. Here, Islamic ideology is reduced to a set of ideas whose internalization by Pirzada women contributes to the stability of the system. However, the primary explanation for purdah is located in the control that Pirzada men have over economic resources and the personal security purdah gives to Pirzada women.

By taking a specific version of Islam as *the* Islam, Jeffery attributes a singularity and coherence to it. Modares notes: "'Islamic Theology' then becomes imposed on a separate and given entity called 'women.' A further unification is reached: Women (meaning *all women*), regardless of their differing positions within societies, come to be affected or not affected by Islam. These conceptions provide the right ingredients for an unproblematic possibility of a cross-cultural study of women" (63). Marnia Lazreg makes a similar argument when she addresses the reductionism inherent in scholarship on women in the Middle East and North Africa:

> A ritual is established whereby the writer appeals to religion as the cause of gender inequality just as it is made the source of underdevelopment in much of modernization theory. In an uncanny way, feminist discourse on women from the Middle East and North Africa mirrors that of theologians' own interpretation of women in Islam. The overall effect of this paradigm is to deprive women of self-presence, of being. Because women are subsumed under religion presented in fundamental terms, they are inevitably seen as evolving in nonhistorical time. They virtually have no history. Any analysis of change is therefore foreclosed. (1988, 87)

While Jeffery's analysis does not quite succumb to this kind of unitary notion of religion (Islam), it does collapse all ideological specificities into economic relations and universalizes on the basis of this comparison.

Women and the Development Process

The best examples of universalization on the basis of economic reductionism can be found in the liberal Women in International Development literature. Proponents of this school seek to examine the effect of development on Third World women, sometimes from self-designated feminist perspectives. At the very least, there is an evident interest in and commitment to improving the lives of women in "developing" countries. Scholars such as Irene Tinker and Michelle Bo Bramsen (1972), Ester Boserup (1970), and Perdita Huston (1979) have all written about the effect of development policies on women in the Third World.[9] All four women assume "development" is synonymous with "economic development" or "economic progress." As in the case of Minces's patriarchal family, Hosken's male sexual control, and Cutrufelli's Western colonization, development here becomes the all-time equalizer. Women are affected positively or negatively by economic development policies, and this is the basis for cross-cultural comparison.

For instance, Huston (1979) states that the purpose of her study is to describe the effect of the development process on the "family unit and its individual members" in Egypt, Kenya, Sudan, Tunisia, Sri Lanka, and Mexico. She states that the "problems" and "needs" expressed by rural and urban women in these countries all center around education and training, work and wages, access to health and other services, political participation, and legal rights. Huston relates all these "needs" to insensitive development policies that exclude women as a group or category. For her, the solution is simple: implement improved development policies that emphasize training for women field-workers; use women trainees and women rural development officers; encourage women's cooperatives; and so on. Here again, women are assumed to be a coherent group or category prior to their entry into "the development process." Huston assumes that all Third World women have similar problems and needs. Thus, they must have similar interests and goals. However, the interests of urban, middle-class, educated Egyptian housewives, to take only one instance, could surely not be seen as being the same as those of their uneducated, poor maids. Development policies do not affect both groups of women in the same way. Practices that characterize women's status and roles vary according to class. Women are constituted as women through the complex interaction between class, culture, religion, and other ideological institutions and frameworks. They are not "women" — a coherent group — solely on the basis of a particular economic system or policy. Such reductive cross-cultural comparisons result in the colonization of the specifics of daily existence and the complexities of political interests that women of different social classes and cultures represent and mobilize.

Thus, it is revealing that for Huston, women in the Third World countries she writes about have "needs" and "problems" but few if any have "choices" or the freedom to act. This is an interesting representation of women in the Third World, one that is significant in suggesting a latent self-presentation of Western women that bears looking at. She writes, "What surprised and moved me most as I listened to women in such very different cultural settings was the striking commonality — whether they were educated or illiterate, urban or rural — of their most basic values: the importance they assign to family, dignity, and service to others" (115). Would Huston consider such values unusual for women in the West?

What is problematical about this kind of use of "women" as a group, as a stable category of analysis, is that it assumes an ahistorical, universal unity between women based on a generalized notion of their subordination. Instead of analytically *demonstrating* the production of women as socioeconomic political groups within particular local contexts, this analytical move limits the definition of the female subject to gender identity, completely bypassing social class and ethnic identities. What characterizes women as a group is their gender (sociologically, not necessarily biologically, defined) over and above everything else, indicating a monolithic notion of sexual difference. Because women are thus constituted as a coherent group, sexual difference becomes coterminous with female subordination, and power is automatically defined in binary terms: people who have it (read: men) and people who do not (read: women). Men exploit, women are exploited. Such simplistic formulations are historically reductive; they are also ineffectual in designing strategies to combat oppressions. All they do is reinforce binary divisions between men and women.

What would an analysis that did not do this look like? Maria Mies's work illustrates the strength of Western feminist work on women in the Third World that does not fall into the traps discussed above. Mies's study of the lace makers of Narsapur, India (1982), attempts to analyze carefully a substantial household industry in which "housewives" produce lace doilies for consumption in the world market. Through a detailed analysis of the structure of the lace industry, production and reproduction relations, the sexual division of labor, profits and exploitation, and the overall consequences of defining women as "nonworking housewives" and their work as "leisure-time activity," Mies demonstrates the levels of exploitation in this industry and the impact of this production system on the work and living conditions of the women involved in it. In addition, she is able to analyze the "ideology of the housewife," the notion of a woman sitting in the house, as providing the necessary subjective and sociocultural element for the creation and maintenance of a production system that contributes to the increasing pauperization of women and keeps them totally atomized and disorganized as workers. Mies's analysis shows the effect of a certain historically and culturally specific mode of patriarchal organization, an organization constructed on the basis of the definition of the lace-makers as "nonworking housewives" at familial, local, regional, statewide, and international levels. The intricacies and the effects of particular power networks not only are emphasized but form the basis of Mies's analysis of how this particular group of women is situated at the center of a hegemonic, exploitative world market.

This is a good example of what careful, politically focused, local analyses can accomplish. It illustrates how the category of women is constructed in a variety of political contexts that often exist simultaneously and overlaid on top of one another. There is no easy generalization in the direction of "women in India" or "women in the Third World"; nor is there a reduction of the political construction of the exploitation of the lace-makers to cultural explanations about the passivity or obedience that might characterize these women and their situation. Finally, this mode of local, political analysis, which generates theoretical categories from within the situation and context being analyzed, also suggests corresponding effective strategies for organizing against the exploitation faced by the lace-makers. Narsapur women are not mere victims of the production process, because they resist, challenge, and subvert the process at various junctures. Here is one instance of how Mies delineates the connections between the housewife ideology, the self-consciousness of the lace-makers, and their interrelationships as contributing to the latent resistances she perceives among the women:

> The persistence of the housewife ideology, the self-perception of the lace-makers as petty commodity producers rather than as workers, is not only upheld by the structure of the industry as such but also by the deliberate propagation and reinforcement of reactionary patriarchal norms and institutions. Thus, most of the lace-makers voiced the same opinion about the rules of *purdah* and seclusion in their communities which were also propagated by the lace exporters. In particular, the *Kapu* women said that they had never gone out of their houses, that women of their community could not do any other work than housework and lace work etc., but in spite of the fact that most of them still subscribed fully to the patriarchal norms of the *gosha* women, there were also contradictory elements in their consciousness. Thus, although they looked down with contempt upon women who were able to work outside the house — like the untouchable *Mala* and *Madiga* women or women of other lower castes — they could not ignore the fact that these women were earning more money precisely because they

were not respectable housewives but workers. At one discussion, they even admitted that it would be better if they could also go out and do coolie work. And when they were asked whether they would be ready to come out of their houses and work — in one place in some sort of a factory — they said they would do that. This shows that the *purdah* and housewife ideology, although still fully internalized, already had some cracks, because it has been confronted with several contradictory realities. (157)

It is only by understanding the *contradictions* inherent in women's location within various structures that effective political action and challenges can be devised. Mies's study goes a long way toward offering such analysis. While there are now an increasing number of Western feminist writings in this tradition,[10] there is also, unfortunately, a large block of writing that succumbs to the cultural reductionism discussed earlier.

Methodological Universalisms; or, Women's Oppression Is a Global Phenomenon

Western feminist writings on women in the Third World subscribe to a variety of methodologies to demonstrate the universal cross-cultural operation of male dominance and female exploitation. I summarize and critique three such methods below, moving from the simplest to the most complex.

First, proof of universalism is provided through the use of an arithmetic method. The argument goes like this: the greater the number of women who wear the veil, the more universal is the sexual segregation and control of women (Deardon 1975, 4–5). Similarly, a large number of different, fragmented examples from a variety of countries also apparently add up to a universal fact. For instance, Muslim women in Saudi Arabia, Iran, Pakistan, India, and Egypt all wear some sort of a veil. Hence, the argument goes, sexual control of women is a universal fact in those countries (Deardon 1975, 7, 10). Fran Hosken writes, "Rape, forced prostitution, polygamy, genital mutilation, pornography, the beating of girls and women, purdah (segregation of women) are all violations of basic human rights" (1981, 15). By equating purdah with rape, domestic violence, and forced prostitution, Hosken asserts that purdah's "sexual control" function is the primary explanation for its existence, whatever the context. Institutions of purdah are thus denied any cultural and historical specificity, and contradictions and potentially subversive aspects are totally ruled out.

In both these examples, the problem is not in asserting that the practice of wearing a veil is widespread. This assertion can be made on the basis of numbers. It is a descriptive generalization. However, it is the analytic leap from the practice of veiling to an assertion of its general significance in controlling women that must be questioned. While there may be a physical similarity in the veils worn by women in Saudi Arabia and Iran, the specific meaning attached to this practice varies according to the cultural and ideological context. In addition, the symbolic space occupied by the practice of purdah may be similar in certain contexts, but this does not automatically indicate that the practices themselves have identical significance in the social realm. For example, as is well known, Iranian middle-class women veiled themselves during the 1979 revolution to indicate solidarity with their veiled, working-class sisters, while in contemporary Iran, mandatory Islamic laws dictate that all Iranian women wear veils. While in both these instances, similar reasons might be offered for the veil (opposition to the Shah and Western cultural colonization in the first case and the true Islamization of Iran in the second), the concrete *meanings* attached to Iranian women wearing the veil are clearly different in both historical contexts. In the first case, wearing the veil is both an oppositional and a revolutionary gesture on the part of Iranian middle-class women; in the second case, it is a coercive, institutional mandate (see Tabari 1980 for detailed discussion). It is on the basis of such context-specific differentiated analysis that effective political strategies can be generated. To assume that the mere practice of veiling women in a number of Muslim countries indicates the universal oppression of women through sexual segregation not only is analytically reductive but also proves quite useless when it comes to the elaboration of oppositional political strategy.

Second, concepts such as reproduction, the sexual division of labor, the family, marriage, household, patriarchy, and so on are often used without their specification in local cultural and historical contexts. Feminists use these concepts in providing explanations for women's subordination, apparently assuming their universal applicability. For instance, how is it possible to refer to "the" sexual division of labor when the *content* of this division changes radically from one environment to the next and from one historical juncture to another? At its most abstract level, it is the fact of the differential assignation of tasks according to sex that is significant; however, this is quite different from the *meaning* or *value* that the content of this sexual division of labor assumes in different contexts. In most cases the assigning of tasks on the basis of sex has an ideological origin. There is no question that a claim such as "women are concentrated in service-oriented occupations in a large number of countries around the world" is descriptively valid. Descriptively, then, perhaps the existence of a similar sexual division of labor (where women work in service occupations such as nursing, social work, etc., and men in other kinds of occupations) in a variety of different countries can be asserted. However, the concept of the "sexual division of labor" is more than just a descriptive category. It indicates the differential *value* placed on men's work versus women's work.

Often the mere existence of a sexual division of labor is taken to be proof of the oppression of women in various societies. This results from a confusion between and collapsing together of the descriptive and explanatory potential of the concept of the sexual division of labor. Superficially similar situations may have radically different, historically specific explanations and cannot be treated as identical. For instance, the rise of female-headed households in middle-class America might be construed as a sign of great independence and feminist progress, the assumption being that this increase has to do with women choosing to be single parents, with an increasing number of lesbian mothers, and so on. However, the recent increase in female-headed households in Latin America,[11] which might at first be seen as indicating that women are acquiring more decision-making power, is concentrated among the poorest strata, where life choices are the most constrained economically. A similar argument can be made for the rise of female-headed families among black and Chicana women in the United States. The positive correlation between this and the level of poverty among women of color and white working-class women in the

United States has now even acquired a name: the feminization of poverty. Thus, while it is possible to state that there is a rise in female-headed households in the United States and in Latin America, this rise cannot be discussed as a universal indicator of women's independence, nor can it be discussed as a universal indicator of women's impoverishment. The *meaning* of and *explanation* for the rise obviously vary according to the sociohistorical context.

Similarly, the existence of a sexual division of labor in most contexts cannot be sufficient explanation for the universal subjugation of women in the workforce. That the sexual division of labor does indicate a devaluation of women's work must be shown through analysis of particular local contexts. In addition, devaluation of *women* must also be shown through careful analysis. In other words, the "sexual division of labor" and "women" are not commensurate analytical categories. Concepts such as the sexual division of labor can be useful only if they are generated through local, contextual analyses (see Eldhom, Harris, and Young 1977). If such concepts are assumed to be universally applicable, the resultant homogenization of class, race, religion, and daily material practices of women in the Third World can create a false sense of the commonality of oppressions, interests, and struggles between and among women globally. Beyond sisterhood there are still racism, colonialism, and imperialism!

Finally, some writers confuse the use of gender as a superordinate category of analysis with the universalistic proof and instantiation of this category. In other words, empirical studies of gender differences are confused with the analytical organization of cross-cultural work. Beverly Brown's (1983) review of the book *Nature, Culture and Gender* (Strathern and McCormack 1980) best illustrates this point. Brown suggests that nature:culture and female:male are superordinate categories that organize and locate lesser categories (such as wild/domestic and biology/technology) within their logic. These categories are universal in the sense that they organize the universe of a system of representations. This relation is totally independent of the universal substantiation of any particular category. Brown's critique hinges on the fact that rather than clarify the generalizability of nature:culture :: female:male as subordinate organization categories, *Nature, Culture and Gender* construes the universality of this equation to lie at the level of empirical truth, which can be investigated through fieldwork. Thus, the usefulness of the nature:culture :: female:male paradigm as a universal mode of the organization of representation within any particular sociohistorical system is lost. Here, methodological universalism is assumed on the basis of the reduction of the nature:culture :: female:male analytic categories to a demand for empirical proof of its existence in different cultures. Discourses of representation are confused with material realities, and the distinction made earlier between "Woman" and "women" is lost. Feminist work that blurs this distinction (which is, interestingly enough, often present in certain Western feminists' self-representation) eventually ends up constructing monolithic images of "Third World women" by ignoring the complex and mobile relationships between their historical materiality on the level of specific oppressions and political choices, on the one hand, and their general discursive representations, on the other.

To summarize: I have discussed three methodological moves identifiable in feminist (and other academic) cross-cultural work that seeks to uncover a universality in women's subordinate position in society. The next and final section pulls together the previous sections, attempting to outline the political effects of the analytical strategies in the context of Western feminist writing on women in the Third World. These arguments are not against generalization as much as they are for careful, historically specific generalizations responsive to complex realities. Nor do these arguments deny the necessity of forming strategic political identities and affinities. Thus, while Indian women of different religions, castes, and classes might forge a political unity on the basis of organizing against police brutality toward women (see Kishwar and Vanita 1984), an *analysis* of police brutality must be contextual. Strategic coalitions that construct oppositional political identities for themselves are based on generalization and provisional unities, but the analysis of these group identities cannot be based on universalistic, ahistorical categories.

The Subject(s) of Power

This last section returns to an earlier point about the inherently political nature of feminist scholarship and attempts to clarify my point about the possibility of detecting a colonialist move in the case of a hegemonic connection between the First and Third Worlds in scholarship. The nine texts in Zed Press's Women in the Third World series that I have discussed[12] focused on the following common areas in examining women's "status" within various societies: religion, family/kinship structures, the legal system, the sexual division of labor, education, and, finally, political resistance. A large number of Western feminist writings on women in the Third World focus on these themes. Of course the Zed texts have varying emphases. For instance, two of the studies, *We Shall Return: Women of Palestine* (Bendt and Downing 1982) and *We Will Smash This Prison: Indian Women in Struggle* (Omvedt 1980), focus explicitly on female militancy and political involvement, while *The House of Obedience: Women in Arab Society* (Minces 1980) deals with Arab women's legal, religious, and familial status. In addition, each text evidences a variety of methodologies and degrees of care in making generalizations. Interestingly enough, however, almost all the texts assume "women" as a category of analysis in the manner designated above.

Clearly this is an analytical strategy that is neither limited to these Zed Press publications nor symptomatic of Zed Press publications in general. However, each of the particular texts in question assumes "women" have a coherent group identity within the different cultures discussed, prior to their entry into social relations. Thus, Gail Omvedt can talk about "Indian women" while referring to a particular group of women in the state of Maharashtra; Cutrufelli can discuss "women of Africa"; and Minces can talk about "Arab women" — all as if these groups of women have some sort of obvious cultural coherence, distinct from men in these societies. The "status" or "position" of women is assumed to be self-evident because women as an already constituted group are *placed* within religious, economic, familial, and legal structures. However, this focus whereby women are seen as a coherent group across contexts, regardless of class or ethnicity, structures the world in ultimately binary, dichotomous terms, where women are always seen in opposition to men, patriarchy is always necessarily male dominance, and the religious, legal, economic, and familial systems are implicitly assumed to be constructed by men. Thus, both men and women are always apparently constituted whole populations, and relations of dominance and exploitation are also posited in terms of whole peoples — wholes coming into exploitative relations. It is only when men and women are seen as different categories or groups possessing different *already constituted* categories of experience, cognition, and interests *as groups* that such a simplistic dichotomy is possible.

What does this imply about the structure and functioning of power relations? The setting up of the commonality of Third World women's struggles across classes and cultures against a general notion of oppression (rooted primarily in the group in power — i.e., men) necessitates the assumption of what Michel Foucault (1980, 135–45) calls the "juridico-discursive" model of power, the principal features of which are "a negative relation" (limit and lack), an "insistence on the rule" (which forms a binary system), a "cycle of prohibition," the "logic of censorship," and a "uniformity" of the apparatus functioning at different levels. Feminist discourse on the Third World that assumes a homogeneous category — or group — called women necessarily operates through the setting up of originary power divisions. Power relations are structured in terms of a unilateral and undifferentiated source of power and a cumulative reaction to power. Opposition is a generalized phenomenon created as a response to power — which, in turn, is possessed by certain groups of people.

The major problem with such a definition of power is that it locks all revolutionary struggles into binary structures — possessing power versus being powerless. Women are powerless, unified groups. If the struggle for a just society is seen in terms of the move from powerlessness to power for women as a *group,* and this is the implication in feminist discourse that structures sexual difference in terms of the division between the sexes, then the new society would be structurally identical to the existing organization of power relations, constituting itself as a simple *inversion* of what exists. If relations of domination and exploitation are defined in terms of binary divisions — groups that dominate and groups that are dominated — then surely the implication is that the accession to power of women as a group is sufficient to dismantle the existing organization of relations. But women as a group are not in some sense essentially superior or infallible. The crux of the problem lies in that initial assumption of women as a homogeneous group or category ("the oppressed"), a familiar assumption in Western radical and liberal feminisms.[13]

What happens when this assumption of "women as an oppressed group" is situated in the context of Western feminist writing about Third World women? It is here that I locate the colonialist move. By contrasting the representation of women in the Third World with what I referred to earlier as Western feminisms' self-presentation in the same context, we see how Western feminists alone become the true "subjects" of this counterhistory. Third world women, in contrast, never rise above the debilitating generality of their "object" status.

While radical and liberal feminist assumptions of women as a sex class might elucidate (however inadequately) the autonomy of particular women's struggles in the West, the application of the notion of women as a homogeneous category to women in the Third World colonizes and appropriates the pluralities of the simultaneous location of different groups of women in social class and ethnic frameworks; in doing so it ultimately robs them of their historical and political *agency.* Similarly, many Zed

Press authors who ground themselves in the basic analytic strategies of traditional Marxism also implicitly create a "unity" of women by substituting "women's activity" for "labor" as the primary theoretical determinant of women's situation. Here again, women are constituted as a coherent group not on the basis of "natural" qualities or needs but on the basis of the sociological "unity" of their role in domestic production and wage labor (see Haraway 1985, esp. 76). In other words, Western feminist discourse, by assuming women as a coherent, already constituted group that is placed in kinship, legal, and other structures, defines Third World women as subjects *outside* social relations, instead of looking at the way women are constituted *through* these very structures.

Legal, economic, religious, and familial structures are treated as phenomena to be judged by Western standards. It is here that ethnocentric universality comes into play. When these structures are defined as "underdeveloped" or "developing" and women are placed within them, an implicit image of the "average Third World woman" is produced. This is the transformation of the (implicitly Western) "oppressed woman" into the "oppressed Third World woman." While the category of "oppressed woman" is generated through an exclusive focus on gender difference, "the oppressed Third World woman" category has an additional attribute — the "Third World difference"! The Third World difference includes a paternalistic attitude toward women in the Third World.[14] Since discussions of the various themes I identified earlier (kinship, education, religion, etc.) are conducted in the context of the relative "underdevelopment" of the Third World (a move that constitutes nothing less than unjustifiably confusing development with the separate path taken by the West in its development, as well as ignoring the directionality of the power relationship between the First and Third Worlds), Third World women as a group or category are automatically and necessarily defined as religious (read: not progressive), family-oriented (read: traditional), legally unsophisticated (read: they are still not conscious of their rights), illiterate (read: ignorant), domestic (read: backward), and sometimes revolutionary (read: their country is in a state of war; they must fight!). This is how the "Third World difference" is produced.

When the category of "sexually oppressed women" is located within particular systems in the Third World that are defined on a scale that is normed through Eurocentric assumptions, not only are Third World women defined in a particular way prior to their entry into social relations, but since no connections are made between first and Third World power shifts, the assumption is reinforced that the Third World just has not evolved to the extent that the West has. This mode of feminist analysis, by homogenizing and systematizing the experiences of different groups of women in these countries, erases all marginal and resistant modes and experiences.[15] It is significant that none of the texts I reviewed in the Zed Press series focuses on lesbian politics or the politics of ethnic and religious marginal organizations in Third World women's groups. Resistance can thus be defined only as cumulatively reactive, not as something inherent in the operation of power. If power, as Michel Foucault has argued, can be understood only in the context of resistance,[16] this misconceptualization is both analytically and strategically problematical. It limits theoretical analysis as well as reinforces Western cultural imperialism. For in the context of a First/Third World balance of power, feminist analyses that perpetrate and sustain the hegemony of the idea of the superiority of the West produce a corresponding set of universal images of the Third World woman, images such as the veiled woman, the powerful mother, the chaste virgin, the obedient wife, and so on. These images exist in universal, ahistorical splendor, setting in motion a colonialist discourse that exercises a very specific power in defining, coding, and maintaining existing First/Third World connections.

To conclude, let me suggest some disconcerting similarities between the typically authorizing signature of such Western feminist writings on women in the Third World and the authorizing signature of the project of humanism in general — humanism as a Western ideological and political project that involves the necessary recuperation of the "East" and "Woman" as others. Many contemporary thinkers, including Michel Foucault (1978, 1980), Jacques Derrida (1974), Julia Kristeva (1980), Gilles Deleuze and Félix Guattari (1977), and Edward Said (1978), have written at length about the underlying anthropomorphism and ethnocentrism that constitute a hegemonic humanistic problematic that repeatedly confirms and legitimates (Western) man's centrality. Feminist theorists such as Luce Irigaray (1981), Sarah Kofman (see Berg 1982), and Hélène Cixous (1981) have also written about the recuperation and absence of woman/women within Western humanism. The focus of the work of all these thinkers can be stated simply as an uncovering of the political *interests* that underlie the binary logic of humanistic discourse and ideology, whereby, as a valuable essay puts it, "the first (majority) term (Identity, Universality, Culture, Disinterestedness, Truth, Sanity, Justice, etc.), which is, in fact, secondary and derivative (a construction), is privileged over and colonizes the second (minority) term (difference, temporality, anarchy, error, interestedness, insanity, deviance, etc.), which is, in fact, primary and originative" (Spanos 1984). In other words, it is only insofar as "woman/women" and "the East" are defined as *others,* or as peripheral, that (Western) man/humanism can represent him/itself as the center. It is not the center that determines the periphery, but the periphery that, in its boundedness, determines the center. Just as feminists such as Kristeva and Cixous deconstruct the latent anthropomorphism in Western discourse, I have suggested a parallel strategy in this essay in uncovering a latent ethnocentrism in particular feminist writings on women in the Third World.[17]

As discussed earlier, a comparison between Western feminist self-presentation and Western feminist representation of women in the Third World yields significant results. Universal images of the Third World woman (the veiled woman, chaste virgin, etc.), images constructed from adding the "Third World difference" to "sexual difference," are predicated upon (and hence obviously bring into sharper focus) assumptions about Western women as secular, liberated, and having control over their own lives. This is not to suggest that Western women *are* secular, liberated, and in control of their own lives. I am referring to a *discursive* self-presentation, not necessarily to material reality. If this were material reality, there would be no need for political movements in the West. Similarly, only from the vantage point of the West is it possible to define the Third World as underdeveloped and economically dependent. Without the overdetermined discourse that creates the *third* world, there would be no (singular and privileged) First World. Without the "Third World woman," the particular self-presentation of Western women mentioned above would be problematical. I am suggesting, then, that the one enables and sustains the other. This is not to say that the signature of Western feminist writings on the Third World has the same authority as the project of Western humanism. However, in the context of the hegemony of the Western scholarly establishment in the production and dissemination of texts, and in the context of the legitimating imperative of humanistic and scientific discourse, the definition of "the Third World woman" as a monolith might well tie into the larger economic and ideological praxis of "disinterested" scientific inquiry and pluralism that are the surface manifestations of a latent economic and cultural colonization of the "non-Western" world. It is time to move beyond the Marx who found it possible to say: they cannot represent themselves; they must be represented.

NOTES

This essay would not have been possible without S. P. Mohanty's challenging and careful reading. I would also like to thank Biddy Martin for our numerous discussions about feminist theory and politics. They both helped me think through some of the arguments herein.

1. Terms such as "Third World" and "First World" are very problematical both in suggesting oversimplified similarities between and among countries labeled thus and in implicitly reinforcing existing economic, cultural, and ideological hierarchies that are conjured up in using such terminology. I use the term "Third World" with full awareness of its problems, only because this is the terminology available to us at the moment. Throughout this essay, then, I use the term critically.

2. I am indebted to Teresa de Lauretis for this particular formulation of the project of feminist theorizing. See especially her introduction to de Lauretis (1984); see also Sylvia Wynter, "The Politics of Domination," unpublished manuscript.

3. This argument is similar to Homi Bhabha's definition of colonial discourse as strategically creating a space for a subject people through the production of knowledge and the exercise of power. The full quote reads: "[C]olonial discourse is an apparatus of power,... an apparatus that turns on the recognition and disavowal of racial/cultural/historical differences. Its predominant strategic function is the creation of a space for a subject people through the production of knowledge in terms of which surveillance is exercised and a complex form of pleasure/unpleasure is incited. It (i.e., colonial discourse) seeks authorization for its strategies by the production of knowledge by coloniser and colonised which are stereotypical but antithetically evaluated" (1983, 23).

4. A number of documents and reports on the UN International Conferences on Women, Mexico City, 1975, and Copenhagen, 1980, as well as the 1976 Wellesley Conference on Women and Development attest to this. Nawal el Saadawi, Fatima Mernissi, and Mallica Vajarathon (1978) characterize this conference as "American-planned and organized," situating Third World participants as passive audiences. They focus especially on Western women's lack of self-consciousness about their implication in the effects of imperialism and racism, a lack revealed in their assumption of an "international sisterhood." Euro-American feminism that seeks to establish itself as the only legitimate feminism has been characterized as "imperial" by Valerie Amos and Pratibha Parmar (1984).

5. The Zed Press Women in the Third World series is unique in its conception. I choose to focus on it because it is the only contemporary series I have found that assumes that women in the Third World are a legitimate and separate subject of study and research. Since 1985, when the present essay was first written, numerous new titles have appeared in the Women in the Third World series. Thus, I suspect that Zed has come to occupy a rather privileged position in the dissemination and construction of discourses by and about Third World women. A number of the books in this series are excellent, especially those that deal directly with women's resistance struggles. In addition, Zed Press consistently publishes progressive feminist, antiracist, and anti-imperialist texts. However, a number of the texts written by feminist sociologists, anthropologists, and journalists are symptomatic of the kind of Western feminist work on women in the Third World that concerns me. Thus, an analysis of a few of these particular works in this series can serve as a representative point of entry into the discourse I am attempting to locate and define. My focus on these texts is therefore an attempt at an internal critique:

I simply expect and demand more from this series. Needless to say, progressive publishing houses also carry their own authorizing signatures.

6. Elsewhere I have discussed this particular point in detail in a critique of Robin Morgan's construction of "women's herstory" in her introduction to Morgan 1984 (see C. T. Mohanty [1987], esp. 35–37).

7. Another example of this kind of analysis is Mary Daly's (1978) *Gyn/Ecology*. Daly's assumption in this text, that women as a group are sexually victimized, leads to her very problematic comparison between the attitude toward women witches and healers in the West, Chinese foot-binding, and the genital mutilation of women in Africa. According to Daly, women in Europe, China, and Africa constitute a homogeneous group as victims of male power. Not only does this label (i.e., sexual victims) eradicate the specific historical and material realities and contradictions that lead to and perpetuate practices such as witch-hunting and genital mutilation, but it also obliterates the differences, complexities, and heterogeneities of the lives of, for example, women of different classes, religions, and nations in Africa. As Audre Lorde (1983) has pointed out, women in Africa share a long tradition of healers and goddesses that perhaps binds them together more appropriately than their victim status. However, both Daly and Lorde fall prey to universalistic assumptions about "African women" (both negative and positive). What matters is the complex, historical range of power differences, commonalities, and resistances that exist among women in Africa and that construct African women as subjects of their own politics.

8. See Eldhom, Harris, and Young (1977) for a good discussion of the necessity to theorize male violence within specific societal frameworks, rather than assume it as a universal.

9. These views can also be found in differing degrees in collections such as Wellesley Editorial committee (1977) and *Signs* (1981). For an excellent introduction to WID issues, see ISIS (1984). For a politically focused discussion of feminism and development and the stakes for poor Third World women, see Sen and Grown (1987).

10. See essays by Vanessa Maher, Diane Elson and Ruth Pearson, and Maila Stevens in Young, Walkowitz, and McCullagh (1981); and essays by Vivian Mob and Michèle Mattelart in Nash and Safa (1980). For examples of excellent, self-conscious work by feminists writing about women in their own historical and geographical locations, see Lazreg (1988) on Algerian women, Spivak's "A Literary Representation of the Subaltern: A Woman's Text from the Third World" (in Spivak [1987], 241–68), and Mani (1987).

11. Harris (1983b). Other MRG reports include Deardon (1975) and Jahan (1980).

12. List of Zed Press publications: Jeffery (1979); Latin American and Caribbean Women's Collective, *Slaves of Slaves: The Challenge of Latin American Women* (1980); Omvedt (1980); Minces (1980); Bobby Siu, *Women of China: Imperialism and Women's Resistance, 1900–1949* (1981); Bendt and Downing (1982); Cutrufelli (1983); Maria Mies, *The Lace Makers of Narsapur: Indian House-wives Produce for the World Market* (1982); Miranda Davis, ed., *Third World/Second Sex: Women's Struggles and National Liberation* (1983).

13. For succinct discussions of Western radical and liberal feminisms, see H. Eisenstein (1983) and Z. Eisenstein (1981).

14. Amos and Parmar (1984) describe the cultural stereotypes present in Euro-American feminist thought: "The image is of the passive Asian woman subject to oppressive practices within the Asian family with an emphasis on wanting to 'help' Asian women liberate themselves from their role. Or there is the strong, dominant Afro-Caribbean woman, who despite her 'strength' is exploited by the 'sexism' which is seen as being a strong feature in relationships between Afro-Caribbean men and women" (9). These images illustrate the extent to which paternalism is an essential element of feminist thinking that incorporates the above stereotypes, a paternalism that can lead to the definition of priorities for women of color by Euro-American feminists.

15. I discuss the question of theorizing experience in C. T. Mohanty (1987) and Mohanty and Martin (1986).

16. This is one of Foucault's (1978, 1980) central points in his reconceptualization of the strategies and workings of power networks.

17. For an argument that demands a new conception of humanism in work on Third World women, see Lazreg (1988). While Lazreg's position might appear to be diametrically opposed to mine, I see it as a provocative and potentially positive extension of some of the implications that follow from my arguments. In criticizing the feminist rejection of humanism in the name of "essential Man," Lazreg points to what she calls an "essentialism of difference" within these very feminist projects. She asks:

"To what extent can Western feminism dispense with an ethics of responsibility when writing about different women? The point is neither to subsume other women under one's own experience nor to uphold a separate truth for them. Rather, it is to allow them to be while recognizing that what they are is just as meaningful, valid, and comprehensible as what we are....Indeed, when feminists essentially deny other women the humanity they claim for themselves, they dispense with any ethical constraint. They engage in the act of splitting the social universe into us and them, subject and objects" (99–100). This essay by Lazreg and an essay by S. P. Mohanty (1989) suggest positive directions for self-conscious cross-cultural analyses, analyses that move beyond the deconstructive to a fundamentally productive mode in designating overlapping areas for cross-cultural comparison. The latter essay calls not for a "humanism" but for a reconsideration of the question of the "human" in a posthumanist context. It argues (1) that there is no necessary "incompatibility between the deconstruction of Western humanism" and such "a positive elaboration" of the human, and (2) that such an elaboration is essential if contemporary political-critical discourse is to avoid the incoherencies and weaknesses of a relativist position.

REFERENCE LIST

Abdel-Malek, Anouar. 1981. *Social Dialectics: Nation and Revolution*. Albany: State University of New York Press.

Amin, Samir. 1977. *Imperialism and Unequal Development*. New York: Monthly Review Press.

Amos, Valeri, and Pratibha Parmar. 1984 "Challenging Imperial Feminism." *Feminist Review* 17:3–19.

Baran, Paul A. 1962. *The Political Economy of Growth*. New York: Monthly Review Press.

Bendt, Ingela, and James Downing. 1982. *We Shall Return: Women in Palestine*. London: Zed Press.

Berg, Elizabeth. 1982. "The Third Woman." *Diacritics* (summer): 11–20.

Bhabha, Homi. 1983. "The Other Question — The Stereotype and Colonial Discourse." *Screen* 24, no. 6:23

Boserup, Ester. 1970. *Women's Role in Economic Development*. New York: St. Martin's Press; London: Allen and Unwin.

Brown, Beverly. 1983. "Displacing the Difference – Review, *Nature, Culture and Gender*." *m/f* 8:79–89.

Cixous, Hélène. 1981. "The Laugh of the Medusa." In Marks and De Courtivron (1981).

Cowie, Elizabeth. 1978. "Woman as Sign." *m/f* 1:49–63.

Cutrufelli, Maria Rosa. 1983. *Women of Africa: Roots of Oppression*. London: Zed Press.

Daly, Mary. 1978. *Gyn/Ecology: The Metaethics of Radical Feminism*. Boston: Beacon Press.

Deardon, Ann, ed. 1975. *Arab Women*. London: Minority Rights Group Report, no. 27.

de Lauretis, Teresa. 1984. *Alice Doesn't: Feminism, Semiotics, Cinema*. Bloomington: Indiana University Press.

———. 1986. *Feminist Studies/Critical Studies*. Bloomington: Indiana University Press.

Deleuze, Gilles, and Félix Guattari. 1977. *Anti-Oedipus: Capitalism and Schizophrenia*. New York: Viking.

Derrida, Jacques. 1974. *Of Grammatology*. Baltimore: Johns Hopkins University Press.

Eisenstein, Hester. 1983. *Contemporary Feminist Thought*. Boston: G. K. Hall.

Eisenstein, Zillah. 1981. *The Radical Future of Liberal Feminism*. New York: Longman.

Eldhom, Felicity, Olivia Harris, and Kate Young. 1977. "Conceptualising Women." *Critique of Anthropology "Women's Issue,"* no. 3.

el Saadawi, Nawal, Fatima Mernissi, and Mallica Vajarathon. 1978. "A Critical Look at the Wellesley Conference." *Quest* 4, no. 2 (winter): 101–7.

Foucault, Michel. 1978. *History of Sexuality*. Volume 1. New York: Random House.

———. 1980. *Power/Knowledge*. New York: Pantheon.

Gunder-Frank, Audre. 1967. *Capitalism and Underdevelopment in Latin America*. New York: Monthly Review Press.

Haraway, Donna. 1985. "A Manifesto for Cyborgs: Science, Technology and Socialist Feminism in the 1980s." *Socialist Review* 80 (March/April): 65–108.

Harris, Olivia. 1983a. *Latin American Women*. London: Minority Rights Group Report, no. 57.

———. 1983b. "Latin American Women — An Overview." In Harris (1983a).

Hosken, Fran. 1981. "Female Genital Mutilation and Human Rights." *Feminist Issues* 1, no. 3.

Huston, Perdita. 1979. *Third World Women Speak Out*. New York: Praeger.

Irigaray, Luce. 1981. "This Sex Which Is Not One" and "When the Goods Get Together." In Marks and De Courtivron (1981).

ISIS. 1984. *Women in Development: A Resource Guide for Organization and Action*. Philadelphia: New Society Publishers.

Jahan, Rounaq, ed. 1980. *Women in Asia*. London: Minority Rights Group.

Jeffery, Patricia. 1979. *Frogs in a Well: Indian Women in Purdah*. London: Zed Press.

Joseph, Gloria, and Jill Lewis. 1981. *Common Differences: Conflicts in Black and White Feminist Perspectives*. Boston: Beacon Press.

Kishwar, Madhu, and Ruth Vanita. 1984. *In Search of Answers: Indian Women's Voices from Manushi*. London: Zed Press.

Kristeva, Julia. 1980. *Desire in Language*. New York: Columbia University Press.

Lazreg, Marnia. 1988. "Feminism and Difference: The Perils of Writing as a Woman on Women in Algeria." *Feminist Issues* 14, no. 1 (spring): 81–107.

Lindsay, Beverley, ed. 1983. *Comparative Perspectives of Third World Women: The Impact of Race, Sex, and Class*. New York: Praeger.

Lorde, Audre. 1983. "An Open Letter to Mary Daly." In Moraga and Anzaldúa (1983), 94–97.

Mani, Lab. 1987. "Contentious Traditions: The Debate on SATI in Colonial India." *Cultural Critique* 7 (fall): 119–56.

Marks, Elaine, and Isabel De Courtivron. 1981. *New French Feminisms*. New York: Schocken.

Mies, Maria. 1982. *The Lace Makers of Narsapur: Indian Housewives Produce for the World Market*. London: Zed Press.

Minces, Juliette. 1980. *The House of Obedience: Women in Arab Society*. London: Zed Press.

Modares, Mina. 1981. "Women and Shi'ism in Iran." *m/f* 5/6, 6:61–82.

Mohanty, Chandra Talpade. 1987. "Feminist Encounters: Locating the Politics of Experience." *Copyright* 1, *Fin de Siècle 2000*: 30–44.

Mohanty, Chandra Talpade, and Biddy Martin. 1986. "Feminist Politics: What's Home Got to Do with It?" In de Lauretis (1986)

Mohanty, S. P. 1989. "Us and Them: On the Philosophical Bases of Political Criticism." *Yale Journal of Criticism* 2 (March): 1–31.

Moraga, Cherríe. 1984. *Loving in the War Years*. Boston: South End Press

Moraga, Cherríe, and Gloria Anzaldúa, eds. 1983. *This Bridge Called My Back: Writings by Radical Women of Color*. New York: Kitchen Table Press.

Morgan, Robin, ed. 1984. *Sisterhood Is Global: The International Women's Movement Anthology*. New York: Anchor Press/Doubleday; Harmondsworth, England: Penguin.

Nash, June, and Helen I. Safa, eds. 1980. *Sex and Class in Latin America: Women's Perspectives on Politics, Economics and the Family in the Third World*. South Hadley, Mass.: Bergin and Garvey.

Omvedt, Gail. 1980. *We Will Smash This Prison: Indian Women in Struggle*. London: Zed Press.

Rosaldo, M. A. 1980. "The Use and Abuse of Anthropology: Reflections on Feminism and Cross-Cultural Understanding." *Signs* 53:389–417.

Said, Edward. 1978. *Orientalism*. New York: Random House.

Sen, Gib, and Caren Grown. 1987. *Development Crises and Alternative Visions: Third World Women's Perspectives*. New York: Monthly Review Press.

Signs. 1981. Special Issue, *Development and the Sexual Division of Labor* 7, no. 2 (winter).

Smith, Barbara, ed. 1983. *Home Girls: A Black Feminist Anthology*. New York: Kitchen Table Press.

Spanos, William V. 1984. "Boundary 2 and the Polity of Interest: Humanism, the 'Center Elsewhere' and Power." *Boundary 2* 12, 3/13, no. 1 (spring/fall).

Spivak, Gayatri Chakravorty. 1987. *In Other Worlds: Essays in Cultural Politics*. New York: Methuen.

Strathern, Marilyn, and Carol McCormack, eds. 1980. *Nature, Culture and Gender*. Cambridge: Cambridge University Press.

Tabari, Azar. 1980. "The Enigma of the Veiled Iranian Women." *Feminist Review* 5:19–32.

Tinker, Irene, and Michelle Bo Bramsen, eds. 1972. *Women and World Development*. Washington, D.C.: Overseas Development Council.

Wellesley Editorial committee, ed. 1977. *Women and National Development: The Complexities of Change*. Chicago: University of Chicago Press.

Young, Kate, Carol Walkowitz, and Roslyn McCullagh, eds. 1981. *Of Marriage and the Market: Women's Subordination in International Perspective*. London: CSE Books.

Chapter 15
Traddutora, Traditora:
A Paradigmatic Figure of Chicana Feminism
Norma Alarcón

> *When the Spanish conquistador appears, this woman [a Mayan] is no more than the site where the desire and wills of two men meet. To kill men to rape women: these are at once proof that a man wields power and his reward. The wife chooses[!] to obey her husband and the rules of her own society, she puts all that remains of her personal will into defending the violence [of her own society] of which she has been the object....Her husband of whom she is the "internal other,"...leaves her no possibility of asserting herself as a free subject.*
>
> Tzvetan Todorov, *The Conquest of America*

In his splendid book *Quetzalcóatl and Guadalupe,* Jacques Lafaye gives a fascinating account of the roles those two divine and mythic figures played in the formation of the Mexican national consciousness.[1] Quetzalcóatl, on the one hand, was an Aztec god whose name, so the missionaries argued, was the natives' own name for the true Messiah. Guadalupe, on the other hand, was the emerging Mexican people's native version of the Virgin Mary and, in a sense, substituted for the Aztec goddess Tonantzin. By the time of Mexican independence from Spain in 1821, Guadalupe had emerged triumphant as the national patroness of Mexico, and her banner was often carried into battle. In a well-known article, which may have inspired Lafaye, Eric R. Wolf comments that

> the Mexican War of Independence marks the final realization of the apocalyptic promise....[T]he promise of life held out by the supernatural mother has become the promise of an independent Mexico, liberated from the irrational authority of the Spanish father-oppressors, and restored to the chosen nation whose election had been manifest in the apparition of the Virgin at Tepeyac....Mother, food, hope, health, life; supernatural salvation from oppression; chosen people and national independence — all find expression in a single symbol.[2]

There is sufficient folklore, as well as documentary evidence of a historical and literary nature, to suggest that the indigenous female slave Malintzin Tenepal was transformed into Guadalupe's monstrous double and that her "banner" also aided and abetted in the nation-making process or, at least, in the creation of nationalistic perspectives. On Independence Day of 1861, for example, Ignacio (El Nigromante) Ramírez, politician and man of letters, reminded the celebrants that Mexicans owed their defeat by Cortés to Malintzin — Cortés's whore.[3] Moreover, Malintzin may be compared to Eve, especially when she is viewed as the originator of the Mexican people's fall from grace and the procreator of a "fallen" people. Thus, Mexico's own binary pair, Guadalupe and Malintzin, reenact within this dualistic system of thought the biblical stories of human creation and the human condition. In effect, as a political compromise between conquerors and conquered, Guadalupe is the neo-representative of the Virgin Mary and the native goddess Tonantzin, while Malintzin stands in the periphery of the new patriarchal order and its sociosymbolic contract.[4]

Indeed, the "false god" and conqueror Hernán Cortés and Malintzin are the countercouple, the monstrous doubles, to Lafaye's Quetzalcóatl and Guadalupe. These two monstrous figures become, in the eyes of the later generations of "natives," symbols of unbridled conquering power and treachery, respectively.[5] Malintzin comes to be known as La Lengua, literally meaning "the tongue." La Lengua was the metaphor used by Cortés and the chroniclers of the conquest to refer to Malintzin the translator. However, she not only translated for Cortés and his men — she also bore Cortés's children. Thus, a combination of Malintzin-translator and Malintzin-procreator becomes the main feature of her subsequently ascribed treacherous nature.

In the eyes of the conquered (oppressed), anyone who approximates La Lengua or Cortés (oppressor), in word or deed, is held suspect and liable to become a sacrificial monstrous double. Those who use the oppressor's language are viewed as outside of the community, thus rationalizing their expulsion, but, paradoxically, they also help to constitute the community. In *Violence and the Sacred*, René Girard has observed that the religious mind "strives to procure, and if need be to invent, a sacrificial victim as similar as possible to its ambiguous vision of the original victim. The model it imitates is not the true double, but a model transfigured by the mechanism of the 'monstrous double.' "[6] If in the beginning Cortés and Malintzin are welcomed as saviors from, and avengers of, Aztec imperialism, soon each is unmasked and "sacrificed," that is, expelled so that the authentic gods may be recovered, awaited, and/or invented. While Quetzalcóatl could continue to be awaited, Guadalupe was envisioned, and her invention was under way as the national Virgin Mother and goddess only twelve years after Cortés's arrival. Guadalupe, as Lafaye himself suggests, is a metaphor that has never wholly taken the place of Tonantzin. As such, Guadalupe is capable of alternately evoking the Catholic and meek Virgin Mother and the prepatriarchal and powerful earth goddess. In any case, within a decade of the invasion, both Cortés and Malintzin began to accrue their dimensions as scapegoats who became the receptacle of human rage and passion, of the very real hostilities that "all the members of the community feel for one another."[7] In the context of a religiously organized society, one can observe in the scapegoating of Cortés and Malintzin "the very real metamorphosis of reciprocal violence into restraining violence through the agency of unanimity."[8] The unanimity is elicited by the chosen scapegoats, and violence is displaced onto them. That mechanism then structures many cultural values, rituals, customs, and myths. Among people of Mexican descent, from this perspective, anyone who has transgressed the boundaries of perceived group interests and values often has been called a *malinche* or *malinchista*. Thus, the contemporary recuperation and positive redefinitions of Malintzin's name bespeak an effort to go beyond religiously organized Manichaean thought. There is nothing more fascinating or intriguing, as Lafaye demonstrates, than to trace the transformation of legends into myths that contribute to the formation of national consciousness. However, by tracing only the figures of transcendence — the recovered or displaced victims of the impersonators — we are left without a knowledge of the creation process of the scapegoats, whether it be through folklore, polemics, or literature. An exploration of Cortés's role as monstrous double shall be left for another occasion. It is clear that often his role is that of the conqueror, usurper, foreigner, and/or invader.[9] In the course of almost five centuries Malintzin has alternately retained one of her three names — Malintzin (the name given her by her parents), Marina (the name given her by the Spaniards), or Malinche (the name given her by the natives in the midst of the conquest). The epithet La Chingada has surfaced most emphatically in our century to refer to her alleged ill-fated experience at the hands of the Spaniards.[10] The epithet also emphasizes the sexual implications of having been conquered — the rape of women and the emasculation of men.

Guadalupe and Malintzin almost always have been viewed as oppositional mediating figures, though the precise moment of inception may well elude us. On the one hand, Guadalupe has come to symbolize transformative powers and sublime transcendence and is the standard carried into battle in utopically inspired movements. Always viewed by believers as capable of transforming the petitioner's status and promising sublime deliverance, she transports us beyond or before time. On the other hand, Malintzin represents feminine subversion and treacherous victimization of her people because she was a translator in Cortés's army. Guadalupe and Malintzin have become a function of each other. Be that as it may, quite often one or the other figure is recalled as being present at the "origins" of the Mexican community, thereby emphasizing its divine and sacred constitution or, alternately, its damned and secular fall. The religiously rooted community, as Girard notes, "is both attracted and repelled by its own origins. It feels the constant need to reexperience them, albeit in veiled and transfigured form, . . . by exercising its memory of the collective expulsion or carefully designated objects."[11] Although Guadalupe is thought to assuage the community's pain because of its fall from grace, Malintzin elicits a fascination entangled with loathing, suspicion, and sorrow. As translator she mediates between antagonistic cultural and historical domains. If we assume that language is always in some sense metaphoric, then any discourse, oral or written, is liable to be implicated in treachery when perceived to be going beyond repetition of what the community perceives as the true and/or authentic concept, image, or narrative. The act of translating, which often introduces different concepts and perceptions, displaces and may even do violence to local knowledge through language. In the process, these concepts and perceptions may be assessed as false or inauthentic.

Traditional nonsecular societies, be they oral or print cultures, tend to be very orthodox and conservative, interpreting the life-world in highly Manichaean terms. It is common in largely oral cultures to organize knowledge, values, and beliefs around symbolic icons, figures, or even persons, a process that was characteristic of both the Spanish and the natives at the time of the conquest and that is surprisingly widespread in Mexican/Chicano culture today.[12] In such a binary, Manichaean system of thought, Guadalupe's transcendentalizing power, silence, and maternal self-sacrifice are the positive, contrasting attributes to those of a woman who speaks as a sexual being and independently of the maternal role. To speak independently of her maternal role, as Malintzin did, is viewed in such a society as a sign of catastrophe, for the mother is meant to articulate not her own needs and desires but only those of her children. Because Malintzin the translator is perceived as speaking for herself and not the community, however it defines itself, she is a woman who has betrayed her primary cultural function — maternity. The figure of the mother is bound to a double reproduction, *strictu sensu* — that of her people and her culture. In a traditional society organized along metaphysical or cosmological figurations of good and evil, cultural deviation from the norm is not easily tolerated or valued in the name of inventiveness or originality. In such a setting, to speak or translate in one's behalf rather than in behalf of the group's perceived interests and values is tantamount to betrayal. Thus, the assumption of an individualized nonmaternal voice, such as that of Chicanas during and after the Chicano movement (1965–75),[13] has been cause to label them *malinches* or *vendidas* (sellouts) by some, consequently prompting Chicanas to vindicate Malinche in a variety of ways, as we shall see. Thus, within a culture such as the Mexican/Chicano culture, if one should want to do more than merely break with it, should want to acquire a voice of one's own, then that will require revision and appropriation of cherished metaphysical beliefs.

The Mexican poet and cultural critic Octavio Paz was one of the first to note — in his book *The Labyrinth of Solitude*[14] — a metonymic link between Malintzin and the epithet La Chingada, which is derived from the Hispanicized Nahuá verb *chingar*. Today La Chingada is often used as a synonym for Malintzin. Paz himself reiterates the latter in his foreword to Lafaye's book by remarking that "the secret life of the mestizo oscillates between La Chingada and Tonantzin/Guadalupe."[15]

Although Paz's views are often the contemporary point of departure for current revisions of the legend and myth of Malintzin, there are two previous stages in its almost five-hundred-year trajectory. The first corresponds to the chroniclers and inventors of the legends; the second corresponds to the development of the traitor myth and scapegoat mechanism, which apparently came to fruition in the nineteenth century during the Mexican independence movement.[16] In this essay I would like to focus on the third, modernistic stage, which some twentieth-century women and men of letters have felt compelled to initiate in order to revise and vindicate Malintzin.

In writing *The Labyrinth of Solitude* to explicate Mexican people and culture, Octavio Paz was also paying homage to Alfonso Reyes's call to explore and discover the Mexican people's links to the past, a call Reyes put forth in his *Visión de Anáhuac* (1915).[17] In that work Reyes suggested that Doña Marina, as he calls her, was the metaphor par excellence of Mexico and its conquest, oppression, and victimization, all of which are very much a part of Mexican life and "historical emotion."[18] Although Reyes's vision was somewhat muted by the decorous language of the beginning of the century, Paz exploits the modernistic break with the sacred in order to expand and clarify Reyes's Doña Marina by transfiguring her into La Chingada. In his chapter "The Sons of La Malinche," Paz argues, as Reyes did before him, that "our living attitude . . . is history also"[19] and concludes that La Malinche is the key to the Mexican people's origins. In his view, Malintzin is more properly our historically grounded originator and accounts for our contemporary "living attitude." However, Paz is not interested in history per se but in the affective and imaginary ways in which that history is/has been experienced and the ways in which Mexicans have responded to it. Paz explores the connections between Malintzin and La Chingada, that is, the sexual victim, the raped mother. He argues that as a taboo verb (and noun), *chingar* lacks etymological documentation, yet it is part of contemporary speech. Independent of any historical record, the word's existence and significance seem phantasmagoric, illusory. In Terry Eagleton's terms, then, Paz goes to work on the apparently illusory, "the ordinary ideological experience of men,"[20] and tries to demonstrate its connection to historical events and, by implication, men's attitudes toward the feminine. In doing so, however, he transforms Malintzin into the Mexican people's primeval mother, albeit the raped one. To repudiate her, he argues, is to break with the past, to renounce the "origins."

Paz believes that he is struggling against "a will to eradicate all that has gone before."[21] He concludes by saying that Cortés's and Malintzin's permanence in the Mexican's imagination and sensibilities reveals that they are more than historical figures — they are symbols of a secret conflict that Mexicans have still not resolved. Through the examination of taboo phrases, Paz makes Malintzin the muse/mother, albeit raped and vilified — hence, also La Chingada. In calling attention to the fact that Malintzin and Cortés are more than historical figures, Paz in effect is implying that they are part and parcel of Mexican ideology — Mexicans' living attitude; thus they have been abducted from their historical moment and are continuing to haunt the Mexican through the workings of that ideology. In a sense, by making Malintzin the founding mother of Mexicans, Paz has unwittingly strengthened the ideological ground that was there before him while simultaneously desacralizing Mexicans' supposed origins by shifting the founding moment from Guadalupe to Malintzin. Paradoxically, Paz has displaced the myth of Guadalupe, not with history, but with a neomyth, a reversal properly secularized yet unaware of its misogynist residue. Indeed, Paz's implied audience is male — the so-called illegitimate mestizo who may well bristle at the thought that he is outside the legitimate patriarchal order, like women! In Paz's figurations, illegitimacy predicated the Mexican founding order. It is a countersuggestion to the belief that Guadalupe legitimized the Mexican founding order. The primary strategy in Paz's modern (secular) position is to wrest contemporary consciousness away from religious cosmologies.

Unlike Reyes, Paz mentions that "the Mexican people have not forgiven Malinche for her betrayal."[22] As such, he emphasizes the ambivalent attitude toward the origins despite the need for acceptance and a change of consciousness. In *Todos los gatos son pardos,* Carlos Fuentes also pleads for acceptance of the "murky" and knotted beginnings of the Mexican people.[23] However, if Paz implicitly acknowledges the asymmetrical relationship between slave (Malintzin) and master (Cortés) by saying that Mexicans' neosymbolic mother was raped, Fuentes privileges Malintzin's attributed desire for vengeance against her people — hence her alliance with Cortés. Subsequently, Fuentes has Malintzin reveal herself as a misguided fool, thus becoming the ill-fated mother-goddess/muse/whore, a tripartite figure who possesses the gift of speech. The gift, in the end, makes her a traitor. She self-consciously declares herself La Lengua, "Yo solo soy la lengua," adding that objects ultimately act out the destiny that the logos proposes.[24] In this instance, Fuentes, along with such contemporaries as Rosario Castellanos, Elena Poniatowska, José Emilio Pacheco, and Octavio Paz, is portraying through Malintzin the belief that literature is the intention, through the power of language, to recover memory by recovering the word and to project a future by possessing the word.[25] The underlying assumption is that history, insofar as it obeys ideological and metaphysical constraints, does not truly recover human events and experience, nor is it capable of projecting change — thus literature is allocated those functions. Simultaneously, however, and perhaps unknowingly, this point of view ironically suggests that literature (language) also narrates ideological positions that construct readers. In suggesting that their literary production is a theory of history, these Mexican writers also appear to suggest that it is capable of effecting historical changes. It is clear that both Paz and Fuentes view themselves as catalysts, as movers and shakers of the "academic" historians of their time and country. From a secular perspective, Paz and Fuentes see themselves as more radical and as providing a cultural critique. They explode myths with countermyths, or narrative with counternarrative.[26]

In Fuentes's *Todos los gatos son pardos,* Malintzin is the narrator who is in possession of speech. She is, as a result, given the task of recovering the experience of the conquest by spanning the confrontation between powers — that of Cortés and Montezuma. Thus, for Fuentes, narration is a feminine art in opposition to the masculine "arts of power," a bridge for disparate power brokers, who thus make use of Malintzin's mediating image. One can observe here a romantic artifice — woman the mother-goddess/muse/whore who is knowledge itself, if only the male artists can decipher it; in this Fuentes falls in line with many other writers from Goethe to Paz. It is, of course, ironic that narrative should be viewed even symbolically as a feminine art, or an art embedded in the feminine, since few women have practiced it throughout history. But as the fallen goddess in Fuentes, Malintzin recalls patriarchy's Eve, the first linguistic mediator and the primeval biblical mother and traitor, who, of course, is later replaced by the Virgin Mary, alias Guadalupe — the go-between mediating two cultural spaces that are viewed as antithetical to each other.

To suggest that language itself, as mediator, is our first betrayal, the Mexican novelist and poet José Emilio Pacheco writes a deceptively simple yet significant poem entitled "Traddutore, traditori" (Translator, traitor). In the poem, Pacheco names the three known translators during the time of the conquest — Jerónimo Aguilar, Gonzalo Guerrero, and Malintzin. Pacheco claims that we are indebted to this trio for the knot called Mexico ("el enredo llamado Mexico").[27] For Pacheco, what might have been "authentic" to each cultural discourse before the collision has now been transformed by language's creative and transformative powers. The translators, who use language as their mediating agent, have the ability, consciously or unconsciously, to distort or to convert the "original" event, utterance, text, or experience, thus rendering them false, "impure." The Mexican cultural and biological entanglement is due to the metaphoric property of language and the language traders. By translating, by converting, by transforming one thing into another, by interpreting (in all senses suggested by the dictionary), the "original," supposedly clear connection between words and objects is disrupted and corrupted. The "corruption" that takes place through linguistic mediation may make the speaker a traitor in the view of others — not just simply a traitor, but a traitor to tradition that is represented and expressed in the "original" event, utterance, text, or experience. In Pacheco's poem the treacherous acts are rooted in language as mediator, language as substitution, that is, as metaphor.

It is through metaphor and metonymy that Reyes, Paz, Fuentes, and Pacheco have been working to revise, reinterpret, or reverse Malintzin's significations. In the twentieth century, they are the first appropriators "rescuing" her from "living attitudes." To cast her in the role of scapegoat, monstrous double, and traitor, as other men have done, is to deny Mexicans' own monstrous beginnings, that is, the monstrous beginnings of the mestizo (mixed-blood) people in the face of an ethic of purity and authenticity as absolute value. By recalling the initial translators and stressing the role of linguistic mediation, Pacheco's revisions are the most novel and diffuse the emphasis on gender and sexuality that the others rely on for their interpretive visions. Paz and Fuentes have patently sexualized Malintzin more than any other writers before them. In so doing they lay claim to a recovery of the (maternal) female body as a secular, sexual, and signifying entity. Sometimes, however, their perspective hovers between attraction and repulsion, revealing their attitudes toward the feminine and their "origins." For Fuentes, Malintzin's sexuality is devouring, certainly the monstrous double of Guadalupe, the asexual and virginal feminine.

Chicano writers have been particularly influenced by Paz's and Fuentes's revisions of Malintzin. The overall influence can be traced not only to the fascination that their writings exert but to the fact that their work was included in early texts used for Chicano studies. Two such texts were *Introduction to Chicano Studies* and *Literatura Chicana: Texto y contexto.*[28] The Chicanos, like the Mexicans, wanted to recover their origins. However, many Chicanos emphasized the earlier nationalistic interpretations of Malintzin as the traitorous mediator who should be expelled from the community rather than accepted, as Paz and Fuentes had suggested. In their quest for "authenticity," Chicanos often desired the silent mediator — Guadalupe, the unquestioning transmitter of tradition and deliverer from oppression. Thus, it should not have come as a surprise that the banner of Guadalupe was one of those carried by the Chicano farmworkers in their strike march of 1965.[29]

In discussing woman's role in traditional cultures, anthropologist Sherry Ortner has stated:

> Insofar as woman is universally the primary agent of early socialization and is seen as virtually the embodiment of the functions of the domestic group, she will tend to come under the heavier restrictions, and circumscriptions surrounding the unit. Her (culturally defined) intermediate position between nature and culture, here having the significance of her mediation (i.e. performing conversion functions) between nature and culture, would account not only for her lower status but for the greater restrictions placed upon her activities.... [S]ocially engendered conservatism and traditionalism of woman's thinking is another — perhaps the worst, certainly the most insidious — mode of social restriction, and would clearly be related to her traditional function of producing well-socialized members of the group.[30]

The woman who fulfills this expectation is more akin to the feminine figure of transcendence, that is, Guadalupe. In a binary, Manichaean society, which a religious society is almost by definition, the one who does not fulfill this expectation is viewed as subversive or evil and is vilified through epithets the community understands. If one agrees with Adrienne Rich, not to speak of others since Coleridge, that the imagination's power is potentially subversive, then for many Chicanas, "to be a female human being trying to fulfill traditional female functions in a traditional way [is] in direct conflict"[31] with their creativity and inventiveness, as well as with their desire to transform their cultural roles and redefine themselves in accordance with their experience and vision. If literature's intention is, in some sense, the recovery or projection of human experience, as the Mexican writers discussed above also suggest, then linguistic representation of it could well imply a "betrayal" of tradition, of family, of what is ethically viewed as "pure and authentic," since literature involves a conversion into interpretive language rather than ritualized repetition. It is not surprising, then, that some of the most talented writers and intellectuals of contemporary Chicana culture should be fascinated with the figure most perceived as the transgressor of a previous culture believed to be "authentic." It is through a revision of tradition that self and culture can be radically reenvisioned and reinvented. Thus, in order to break with tradition, Chicanas, as writers and political activists, simultaneously legitimate their discourse by grounding it in the Mexican/Chicano community and by creating a "speaking subject" in their reappropriation of Malintzin from Mexican writers and Chicano oral tradition — through her they begin a recovery of aspects of their experience as well as of their language. In this way, the traditional view of femininity invested in Guadalupe is avoided and indirectly denied and reinvested in a less intractable object. Guadalupe's political history represents a community's expectations and utopic desires through divine mediation. Malintzin, however, as a secularly established "speaking subject," unconstrained by religious beliefs, lends herself more readily to articulation and representation, both as subject and object.[32] In a sense, Malintzin must be led to represent herself, to become the subject of representation, and the closest she can come to this is by sympathizing with latter-day speaking female subjects. Language, as Mikhail Bakhtin has noted,

> becomes "one's own" only when the speaker populates it with her own intention, her own accent, when she appropriates the word, adapting it to her own semantic and expressive intention. Prior to this moment of appropriation, the word does not exist in a neutral and impersonal language (it is not, after all, out of a dictionary that the speaker gets her words!), but rather it exists in other people's mouths, in other people's contexts, serving other people's intentions: it is from there that one must take the word, and make it one's own. . . . Language is not a neutral medium that passes freely and easily into the private property of the speaker's intentions; it is populated — over populated with the intentions of others. Expropriating, forcing it to submit to one's own intentions and accents, is a difficult and complicated process.[33]

Expropriating Malintzin from the texts of others and filling her with the intentions, significances, and desires of Chicanas have taken years. Mexican men had already effected the operation for their own ends; it was now women's turn. (Although in this essay I deal only with the efforts of Chicanas, some Mexican women writers such as Juana Alegría and Rosario Castellanos have also worked with this figure and have contested male representations.)

One of the first to feel the blow of the masculine denigration of Malintzin was Adelaida R. del Castillo. It was a blow that she apparently felt personally on behalf of all Chicanas, thus provoking her to say that the denigration of Malintzin was tantamount to a defamation of "the character of the Mexicana/Chicana female."[34] For Chicanas, as del Castillo implies, Malintzin was more than a metaphor or foundation/neomyth, as Paz would have it; she represented a specific female experience that was being misrepresented and trivialized. By extension, Chicanas/Mexicanas were implicated; del Castillo's attempt to appropriate Malintzin for herself and Chicanas in general involved her in vindication and revision. It is not only Malintzin's appropriation and revision that is at stake, but Chicanas' own cultural self-exploration, self-definition, and self-invention through and beyond the community's sociosymbolic system and contract. The process, however, is complicated by Chicanas' awareness that underlying their words there is also a second (if not secondary) sociosymbolic order — the Anglo-American. The Chicana leaves herself open to the accusation of Anglicizing the community, just as Malinche Hispanicized it, because her attempts at self-invention are "inappropriate" to her culture and her efforts are viewed as alien to the tradition. In other words, changes wreak havoc with the perceived "authenticity." Each writer, as we shall see, privileges a different aspect of Malintzin's "lives" — that is, the alleged historical experience and/or the inherited imaginary or ideological one.

Adaljiza Sosa Riddell, in "Chicanas in El Movimiento," an essay written in the heat of the Chicano movement of the early 1970s, views Malintzin as a cultural paradigm of the situation of contemporary Chicanas.[35] She thinks the relationship of Chicanas to Chicanos in the United States has paralleled Malintzin's relationship to the indigenous people in the light of the Spanish conquest. Riddell concludes that Chicanas, like Malintzin before them, have been doubly victimized — by dominant Anglo society and by Mexican/Chicano communities. In turn, these factors account for some Chicanas' ambiguous and ambivalent position in the face of an unexamined nationalism. Riddell's passionate attempt at revision and appropriation is both a plea for understanding some women's "mediating" position and an apology — an apologia full of irony, for it is the victim's apologia!

Victimization in the context of colonization and of patriarchal suppression of women is a theme shared by Carmen Tafolla in her poem "La Malinche."[36] Tafolla's Malintzin claims that she has been misnamed and misjudged by men who had ulterior motives. In Tafolla's poem, Malintzin goes on to assert that she submitted to the Spaniard Cortés because she envisioned a new race; she wanted to be the founder of a people. There are echoes of Paz and Fuentes in Tafolla's view, yet she differs by making Malintzin a woman possessed of clear-sighted intentionality, thus avoiding attributions of vengeance.

As Tafolla transforms Malintzin into the founder of a new race through visionary poetry, Adelaida R. del Castillo effects a similar result through a biography that is reconstructed with the few "facts" left us by the chroniclers. In her essay, del Castillo claims that Malintzin "embodies effective, decisive action. . . . Her actions syncretized two conflicting worlds causing the emergence of a new one, our own. . . . [W]oman acts not as a goddess in some mythology"[37] but as a producer of history. Del Castillo goes on to say that Malintzin should be "perceived as a woman who was able to act beyond her prescribed societal function (i.e., servant and concubine) and perform as one who was willing to make great sacrifices for what she believed to be a philanthropic conviction."[38] Del Castillo wants to avoid the mythmaking trap by evading "poetic language" and by appealing to "historical facts." In a sense, unlike the male Mexican writers reviewed, she privileges history as a more truthful account than literature. (This may spell the difference between del Castillo's Anglo-American education and experience and that of Mexican nationals for whom history often is reconstructed anew with each new regime, thereby encouraging a cynical attitude. Perspectives on the disciplines of history and literature differ according to one's location, experience, and education.) However, notwithstanding her famed translating abilities, Malintzin has left us no recorded voice because she was illiterate; that is, she could not leave us a sense of herself and of her experience. Thus our disquisitions truly take place over her corpse and have no clue as to her own words, but instead refer to the words of the chroniclers who themselves were not free of self-interest, motive, and intention. Thus, all interpreters of her figure are prey to subjectivized mythmaking once they begin to attribute motives, qualities, and desires to her regardless of the fact that they have recourse to historical motifs regarding her role, a role seen through the eyes of Cortés, Bernal Díaz del Castillo, Tlaxcaltecas, and many others present at the time.

For Adelaida R. del Castillo, then, Malintzin should be viewed as a woman who made a variety of *choices* because of a "philanthropic conviction," that is, her conviction that Cortés was Quetzalcóatl and, subsequently, that Christ was the true Quetzalcóatl, or that the true Quetzalcóatl was Christ — hence Malintzin's role in converting the indigenous population and her "sense of deliverance when she recognized that the Spaniards resembled Quetzalcóatl."[39] In other words, Malintzin initially fell victim to a mistaken identity but subsequently recognized Quetzalcóatl in Christ and displaced her devotion onto Cortés, onto Christ, and, subsequently, onto the child who would represent the new race. I think there is as much a revision of Paz and Fuentes as of history (i.e., the chroniclers) in del Castillo's interpretation, as well as a repudiation of Paz's views of woman's passive sexuality. In short, as del Castillo revises a "mythology" (as she names it in opposition to history) with which she feels implicated, she appears to be reading two texts at once, the purported "original" one (the chroniclers) and the "mythology of the original" (Paz and Fuentes). These texts are separated by almost five centuries; however, del Castillo wants to appropriate Malintzin for herself, as one whose face reflects her vision — Malintzin as agent, choice-maker, and producer of history. Actually, the whole notion of choice, an existentialist notion of twentieth-century Anglo-European philosophy, needs to be problematized in order to understand the constraints under which women of other cultures, times, and places live. In trying to make Malintzin a motivated "producer of history," del Castillo is not so much reconstructing Malintzin's own historical moment as she is using her both to counter contemporary masculine discourse and to project a newer sense of a female self, a speaking subject with a thoroughly modern view of historical consciousness.

A similar strategy is used by Cordelia Candelaria in the essay "La Malinche, Feminist Prototype."[40] For Candelaria, Malintzin is the feminist prototype because she "defied traditional social expectations of woman's role."[41] Candelaria enumerates a variety of roles that Malintzin enacted: "liaison, guide to [the] region, advisor on native customs and beliefs, and strategist.... [T]he least significant role was that of mistress."[42] Although such a description may fit with the roles described by the chroniclers, the verb "defied" does not harmonize with the chroniclers' portrayals. It is difficult to know to what extent it was possible to defy either native or Spanish cultures since both adhered to the trinitarian worldview of authority, religion, and tradition. The defiance Candelaria speaks of is rooted in contemporary existentialist philosophy, which has been as yet an unfinished revolt against the former worldview.[43] In revising the image of Malintzin, Candelaria privileges a self capable of making choices and of intellectual acumen over a self-manifesting sexuality and polyglotism, thus avoiding in effect the two most significant charges against her. Since sexuality, especially as ascribed to the maternal, and language are such powerful aspects of culture, it is in my opinion inadvisable to avoid them; they must be kept in view by the newer sense of a self who challenges traditions.

In her poem "Chicana Evolution," Sylvia Gonzáles awaits Malintzin's return as a redeeming mother/goddess.[44] In this poem Gonzáles views the self as a "Chicana/ Daughter of Malinche."[45] Gonzáles claims to await Malinche's return so that Malinche may deny her traitorous guilt, cleanse her flesh, and "sacrifice herself" in "redemption of all her forsaken daughters"[46] — the New World's Demeter, perhaps, who shall rescue all Chicana Persephones. Whereas Fuentes will have Malintzin redeem the latter-day sons/Quetzalcóatl, Gonzáles will have her redeem the daughters. This redemptory return will empower Gonzáles's creativity; she admires those women who have stripped themselves of passivity with their "pens."[47] At present, however, she feels overwhelmed by her definitions — "a creation of actions/as well as words."[48] For Gonzáles, writing itself is empowering, yet she postpones the daughter's actual enablement, as if the appropriation of language were still to take place. As a result, her revision is gloomy — we still await. Our deliverance is viewed in apocalyptic terms, but Malinche has been substituted for Guadalupe.

The intertextual debate between women and men raises the following question implicitly: Does Malintzin belong to the sons or the daughters? Each answers for himself or herself, narrowing the quarrel to a struggle for the possession of the neomaternal figure. Malintzin's procreative role is privileged in one way or another by most of these rites. Who shall speak for her, represent her? Is she now the procreator of the new founding order? Who will define that order?

In the face of patriarchal tradition, Malintzin as mother-goddess/muse/whore is viewed by some as the daughters' own redemptress. In a three-part poem called "La Chingada," Alma Villanueva envisions Malintzin as the displaced and desecrated prepatriarchal goddess who has returned to redeem and empower her daughters and to transform the sons. Villanueva states in a short preface to the poem: "This poem is a furious response centuries later to masculine culture, that is, a patriarchal destructive power that threatens all existence"; the destructiveness emanates from "a strange, disembodied, masculine God" through whom men first "discredited the first raped woman, when the feminine was forced to abdicate its sacred power."[49] In the pre-visionary section, Villanueva suggests that the Mexican/Chicana Malintzin, also known as La Chingada, is a recent reenactment and parody of the more ancient routing of the goddess, one of whose names was Demeter.

Within the poem itself, the goddess Malintzin/Demeter calls upon the sons to transform themselves into "loving men capable of reinventing love." That feat can be achieved only by evoking the "girlchild inside" of them, by healing all the nameless wild animals that they killed and watched die because of some masculine quest or ritual.[50] In part 11, titled "The Dead," in opposition to part 1, which was titled "The Living," the goddess, who is now conflated with La Llorona/Mater Dolorosa, mourns her dead daughters.[51] The daughters were prepared for their defeat through socialization. The malediction "Hijos de La Chingada" is reserved for the sons, who in profound irony have been birthed to kill the mourned daughters. Subsequently, the goddess calls upon the daughters to give birth to themselves, to renew their being. Both sons and daughters are forbidden to look back to old religious models and are urged to re-create themselves with the goddess's help. She is willing to sacrifice herself so that "You are born, at last, unto / yourself!"[52] In her representation of Malintzin, Villanueva tries to fulfill Adrienne Rich's view of a daughter's desire for a mother "whose love and whose power were so great as to undo rape and bring her back from death."[53]

Villanueva's interpretation of Malintzin draws on elements from Paz, who, along with Rich in *Of Woman Born: Motherhood as Experience and Institution,* is one of the epigrammatic voices preceding the poem.[54] Villanueva also borrows elements from Fuentes; however, she replaces his view of a vengeful Malintzin with a redeeming figure, one who will not be still until she is recognized as patriarchy's suppressed woman, the one upon whose body Western civilization has been built — hence, the call for erasing religious models that hold daughters and sons back from newer senses of self. In her feminist revision, Villanueva differs from Paz and Fuentes in that she does not "plead" for acceptance of Malintzin as goddess/raped mother. On the contrary, Malintzin speaks on her own behalf and is enraged over her suppression, desecration, and rape, all of which have disenabled the female line. A crime has been committed against the mother-goddess, and she demands retribution and justice. Villanueva addresses directly the sexual and linguistic aspects of Malintzin's so-called betrayal, precisely what Candelaria avoids in her representation. In reading Villanueva's poem, one is made aware of the powerful charge effected when the speaking subject appropriates language and expresses her rage at the suppression of maternal self-representation.

Lucha Corpi refers to Malintzin by her Spanish name, Marina. This factor is significant because Corpi inscribes Marina into biblical discourses rather than prepatriarchal ones. Thus, it follows that she should be called Marina, as the Spaniards baptized her. For Corpi, Marina is a parody and reenactment of Eve and Mary, a woman who has sacrificed herself for the latter-day daughter and who, because of her experience, presages a renewing and enabling cycle. In four poems, or one poem consisting of four parts, which are in turn titled "Marina Mother," "Marina Virgin," "The Devil's Daughter," and "She (Distant Marina)," Corpi revises the story of Marina/Malintzin.[55] Marta Sánchez, in *Contemporary Chicana Poetry: A Critical Approach to an Emerging Literature,* views Corpi's cycle of poems accurately, I think, when she observes that "Corpi's cultural paradigm leaves readers no alternative but to accept a passive Marina who can do nothing about her situation."[56] "Marina Madre" is perceived as a victim of her own feminine condition. That is, insofar as women are women and mothers, they are incommensurably vulnerable. Using images that allude to the Old and New Testaments, Corpi imagines a Marina made of the "softest clay" by the Patriarchs ("los viejos"); she envisions her as one who was like either Eve ("her name written on the patriarchal tree") or Mary ("the fruit of her womb stolen"); moving nearer to us in time, she sees Marina as one abandoned and vilified by father, husband, and son. The reference to father, husband, and son may be seen as an allusion to the male triad in one God–Father, Son, and Holy Ghost — as the Catholic tradition holds. By planting the soul in the earth, Corpi's latter-day Marina reinscribes herself and awaits her own renewal. The "she" in the fourth poem — "She (Distant Marina)" — is that contemporary daughter who is imagined as a "mourning shadow of an ancestral figure" crossing a bridge leading to a new time and space, a reconstructed self. The passive, victimized Marina of the first two poems is left behind. Marta Sánchez has also suggested that the bridge is the boundary crossed "between Mexico and the United States."[57] Both Corpi's reinscription and Sánchez's interpretation of it continue to emphasize the mediating function assigned to Marina, though from a Chicano point of view in which the Spaniards, harbingers of a different existence, are now replaced by Anglo-Americans. It is important to reiterate the value placed by many Chicanas on a primary identification with the indigenous people or recuperations of that identity and the rejection of a Spanish one, despite the use of the Spanish language. However, these rhetorical strategies are now often undertaken to underscore our differences from Anglo-Americans.

For Gonzáles, Villanueva, and Corpi, the forced disappearance of the mother/goddess leads to the daughters' own abjection. The daughters are doomed to repeat the cycle until the ancient powers of the goddess are restored. Of the three, however, Villanueva is the only one who, in appropriating Malintzin, makes her a speaking subject on her own behalf and on behalf of the daughters in a truly powerful way. Gonzáles and Corpi objectify her and leave us with a promise of vindication.

Cherríe Moraga also explores the significations of Malintzin in her book *Loving in the War Years: Lo que nunca pasó por sus labios*.[58] Moraga feels, on the one hand, a need to recover the race of the biographical mother so that she may recover her ethnosexual identity and, on the other, a need to appropriate her political and literary voice.[59] Simultaneously, however, a search for the identity of, and relation between, self and mother also requires an exploration of the myth of Malintzin, who is our "sexual legacy."[60] That legacy is inscribed in cruel epithets such as La Chingada and La Vendida (The Traitor). These epithets are in turn used on women to stigmatize, to limit the quest for autonomy, and to limit "the Chicana imagination . . . before it has a chance to consider some of the most difficult questions."[61] Moraga points to the double bind of the Chicana who defies tradition: she is viewed as either a traitor to her race or a lesbian. As such, not only is the lesbian in the Chicano imagination *una Malinchista,* but the latter is also seen as a lesbian. Feminism, which questions patriarchal tradition by representing women's subjectivity and/or interjecting it into extant discursive modes, thereby revising them, may be equated with *malinchismo* or lesbianism. Even as she recognizes the double bind, Moraga proceeds to identify herself as a lesbian who, as such, represents the "most visible manifestation of a woman taking control of her own sexual identity and destiny, who severely challenges the anti-feminist Chicano/a."[62] Moraga thinks that if she were not a lesbian she would still be viewed as one by a culture that does not understand the pursuit of a sexual identity beyond heterosexism.[63] In a sense, for Moraga, lesbianism in Chicano culture is the ultimate trope for the pursuit of newer gender identities, for anything that smacks of difference in the face of traditional gender values. Rather than try to revise the myths of Malintzin, Moraga has no choice but to declare that, indeed, she comes "from a long line of vendidas."[64] One could, however, opt for Lorna D. Cervantes's sarcastic view of the usual male perception of Malintzin's figure by stating ambiguously, as does the title of her poem, "Baby, You Cramp My Style."[65] Baby is, of course, a double allusion — to him who would impose his notions on her and to Malinche, whose historical existence and subsequent interpretations are a burden.

Moraga and Cervantes, in a sense, become the heroines of their own individualized vision and revision, for it is through their appropriations that we proceed beyond Malinche. However, have they truly integrated the "treacherous" Malintzin whose ascribed attributes are the source of contention — the speaking subject and procreator? On the one hand, Cervantes's sarcasm is a dismissal of the subject in favor of her own future self-creation. On the other hand, if one follows Moraga's reasoning and takes it one step further, then one would have to say that the ultimate trope for the pursuit of new gender identities is not so much lesbianism as it is the speaking subject who is also a lesbian mother or perhaps one who articulates and visualizes herself and procreation beyond heterosexism. If newer racial and gendered identities are to be forged, the insight arrived at in writing needs to be communicated to millions of women who still live under such metaphoric controls. How are they to be persuaded to accept these insights if they still exist under the ideology that incorporates Guadalupe and Malintzin?

If, for Mexican male writers, the originating rape is of paramount importance because it places in question their legitimacy as sons, Chicanas — with the exception of Villanueva, who accepts Paz's view — do not even mention rape in connection with Malintzin. Paz, as far as I can discern, was the first writer to advance forcefully the metonymic relations between three terms — Malintzin, La Chingada, and rape. Although pillage and rape are almost by definition factors of conquest and colonization, there is no trace of evidence that Malintzin suffered the violent fate of other indigenous women, strictly speaking — though her disappearance from the record is troublesome and puzzling. One may even argue that she performed as she did to avoid rape and violence upon her body, to "choose" negatively between lesser evils. Clearly, in patriarchal and patrilineal societies — which these were — sons stand to lose a great deal more if they are illegitimate offspring of rapes. Daughters, like their mothers, would still have to struggle to protect themselves from rapists. "Legitimacy" under these circumstances at best grants a female protection from rape; it does not make a woman her father's heir nor even give her a sure claim to her offspring. For the men, the so-called rape is largely figurative, a sign of their "emasculating" loss; for the women, it is literal. There is irony in Paz's insistence that Malintzin should also serve as the figure for "our" rape since it may well be that she saved herself from such a fate through diligent service. There are no choices for slaves, only options between lesser evils.

Because Malintzin's neosymbolic existence in the masculine imagination has affected the actual experience of so many Mexicanas and Chicanas, it became necessary for "her daughters" to revise her scanty biography. Through revisions, many undertaken in isolation, contemporary Chicana writers have helped to lay bare Malintzin's double etymology, which until recently appeared illusory and hallucinatory: one privileges the sociosymbolic possibilities for signification; the second, the existential and historical implications. Some of the writers discussed have actually, as speaking subjects, reemphasized the patriarchal view of the maternal/feminine as mediator, even though they wish to represent her themselves. Others have transformed her into the neomyth of the goddess. Still others have foregrounded roles such as "choice-maker," "history-producer," and "self-aware speaking subject," all of which are part of modern and contemporary experience and desire. In a sense, they sidestep the image of Malintzin as raped mother and part of the feminine condition. Except for Villanueva, who follows Paz in this respect, no one has explored the full impact — imaginary or not — that such an image may have for us. It emphasizes that Mexicans' beginnings, which took place barely half a millennium ago, are drenched in violence, not simply symbolic but historically coinciding with European expansionist adventures. It implies that the object of that violence was/has been feminine (or feminized) and that it barely begins to be recovered as subject or even object of Mexicans' history. Because the European expansionists of the time were Christians, it implies that indeed the ancient putative suppression of the goddess was reenacted; the missionaries did not have a problem assimilating Quetzalcóatl into their discourse but suppressed Tonantzin. However, because Chicanas have begun the appropriation of history, sexuality, and language for themselves, they find themselves situated at the cutting edge of a new historical moment involving a radical though fragile change in consciousness. It is an era in which we live in simultaneous time zones from the pre-Colombian to the ultramodern, from the cyclical to the linear. The latter is certainly a theme in the work of Carlos Fuentes, Rosario Castellanos, Octavio Paz, and other contemporary Mexican writers. However, I think that the objectified thematics have now passed onto a more consciously claimed subjectivity in the work of Chicanas such as Gloria Anzaldúa.[66] Moreover, such subjectivity is capable of shedding light on Chicanas' present historical situation without necessarily, in this newer key, falling prey to a mediating role; it can foster stunning insights into Chicanas' complex culture by taking hold of the variegated imaginative and historical discourses that have informed the constructions of race, gender, and ethnicities in the last five hundred years and that still reverberate in our time. Issues of class and color (i.e., race and ethnicity) per se have not entered the appropriation because, I think, the historical person and textual figure of Malintzin (indigenous female slave in her own society as well as in the one taking shape under the Spaniards) implicitly subsume those as part of her condition, hence the possibility of her suppression as feminine/maternal speaking subject. This could very well signify that anyone *completely* deprived of voice within the Anglo-European and Spanish imperialist projects has by definition been an impoverished and/or enslaved woman of color.

Here, then, is a powerful reason why the notion of the "literature of women of color" in the United States is one of the most novel ideas to have arisen in the Anglo-European imperialist context. Such a notion is yet to be part of Mexican or Latin American criticism; we have yet to see how women in Mexico and Latin America begin to resolve their struggle for self-representation. Mexican writers Elena Poniatowska and Rosario Castellanos have many a heroine who is a woman of color. Consciously or unconsciously, they have tried, as upper-class Mexican writers, to understand the complexity of the relationship between a woman of color (or a native one) and Anglo-European patriarchal history and thought. It is in the vibrations of that distance between them that the appropriation of the many transformations of a woman of color lies.

In a more recent appropriation of Malintzin, Tzvetan Todorov appears to agree with some of the Chicanas discussed, which is an interesting phenomenon because for each the work of the other was unavailable at the time of writing. The agreement appears coincidental for those of us who have been forced for historical, political, and economic reasons to become perennial migrants in search of "home." For Todorov, Malintzin is the

> first example, and thereby the symbol, of the cross-breeding of cultures; she thereby heralds the modern state of Mexico and beyond that, the present state of us all, since if we are not invariably bilingual, we are inevitably bi- or tri-cultural. La Malinche glorifies mixture to the detriment of purity... and the role of the intermediary. She does not simply submit to the other...; she adopts the other's ideology and serves it in order to understand her own culture better, as is evidenced by the effectiveness of her conduct (even if "understanding" here means destroying).[67]

The reconstruction of Chicanas as women or as exiles from "home" due to subjugations is fraught with paradox, contradiction, and unlikely partners, such as Mexican male writers and Todorov. Although Todorov does not mention the role of gender and sexuality in his interpretation, he readily finds a point of identification for himself.

As historical subject, Malintzin remains shrouded in preternatural silence, and as object, she continues to be on trial for speaking and bearing the enemy's children and continues to be a constant source of revision and appropriation — indeed, for articulating our modern and postmodern condition. The "discovery" and colonization of what is presently called the Third World could just as well be said to have started when the Spaniards conquered Mexico as at any other moment — it was also a time when a significant portion of Europe was about to inaugurate the modern epoch, that is, the Reformation, Copernicus, Galileo, Cartesian philosophy, and so on. Thus the quarrel over the interpretation of Malintzin serves not only as a heuristic device for the assumption of feminism in a traditionalist and essentialist setting where men refuse to let women speak for themselves, or women feel constrained from speaking, but also as the measurement of discursive maneuvers in the effort to secularize or appropriate thought for oneself. It is noteworthy that these maneuvers have to be undertaken under the auspices of a woman — the one who did not remain the "internalized other" of the European's other. And what about the women who remain the "internalized others," that is, the ones who submit or are "offerings" to the colonizers? What can we make of such gifts? Do they become, like the Mayan woman in the epigraph at the beginning of this essay, a woman in the service of violence against herself?

Much of the Chicana feminist work of the 1970s, like Anglo-American feminist work, was launched around the assumption of a unified subject organized oppositionally to men from a perspective of gender differences. The assumption that the subject is autonomous, self-determining, and self-defining has been a critical space shared by many feminists because it opens up vistas of agency for the subject. Often that critical space has generated the notion, especially among Anglo-Americans, that women's oppression can be described universally from the perspective of gender differences, as if boundaries of race, ethnicities, and class had not existed. The fact that Todorov also shares that critical space makes it possible for him to project onto La Malinche observations similar to those of some Chicanas, ironically even more similar than those of Mexican men. Mexican men do not forget that she is an Indian and a woman, thus making it possible for them to understand the "betrayal" on the grounds that she would not want to remain "in the service of violence against herself." However, to the extent that we know it, the story of La Malinche demonstrates that crossing ethnic and racial boundaries does not necessarily free her from violence against herself; moreover, once her usefulness is over, she is an Indian and a woman. She crosses over to a site where there is no "legitimated" place for her in the conqueror's new order. Crossings over by "choice" or by force become sporadic individual arrangements that do not necessarily change the status of Indian women or women of color, for example. The realization that the "invitation" to cross over, when it is extended, does not ameliorate the lot of women of color in general led, in the 1980s, to a feminist literature by Chicanas and women of color that demonstrates that, despite some shared critical perspectives, boundaries exist and continue to exist, thus accounting for differential experiences that cannot be contained under the sign of a universal woman or women. Yet for Mexicans, Guadalupe is a symbol that continues to exist for the purpose of "universalizing" and containing women's lives within a discrete cultural banner, which may be similar to those of other cultures. In contrast, the diverse twentieth-century interpretations of La Malinche rupture the stranglehold of religion by introducing the notion of historical, sexual, and linguistic agency, though it was not necessarily available to La Malinche herself at the beginning of the Mexican colonial period.

Postmodern feminist theories have arisen to supplant gender-standpoint epistemology and to diffuse explanatory binarisms. However, a critical question arises: Do they free women of color from the "service of violence against themselves," or do they only rationalize it well? For those of us who simultaneously assume a critical position and a kinship with "native women" and women of color, the "philosophical bases of political criticism"[68] and cognitive practices are as important as the deployment of critical theories. Do they also function to help keep women from doing service against themselves — if not, why not?

NOTES

1. Jacques Lafaye, *Quetzalcóatl y Guadalupe: La formación de la conciencia en Mexico (1531–1813)*, trans. Ida Vitale (Mexico City: Fondo de Cultura Economica, 1983); Eng. trans., *Quetzalcóatl y Guadalupe: The Formation of Mexican National Consciousness 1531–1813,* trans. Benjamin Keen (Chicago: University of Chicago Press, 1987).

2. Eric R. Wolf, "The Virgen de Guadalupe: A Mexican National Symbol," *Journal of American Folklore* 71, no. 279 (January–March 1958): 38.

3. Cited in Gustavo A. Rodríguez, *Doña Marina* (Mexico City: Imprenta de la Secretaria de Relaciones Exteriores, 1935), 48.

4. I borrow the notion of "sociosymbolic contract" from Julia Kristeva. She uses the notion in the essay "Women's Time," trans. Alice Jardine and Harry Blake, *Signs* 7, no. 1 (autumn 1981): 13–35. I take it to mean a kind of contract within which the social life of women (and some men) is expected

to conform or live up to a metaphysical (essential) configuration of who they ought to become in the socialization process. These metaphysical configurations are accompanied by culture-specific "semantic charters." Pierre Maranda suggests that "semantic characters condition our thought and emotions. They are culture specific networks that we internalize as we undergo the process of socialization." Moreover, these charters or signifying systems "have an inertia and momentum of their own. There are semantic domains whose inertia is high: kinship terminologies, the dogmas of authoritarian churches, the conception of sex roles." See his essay "The Dialectic of Metaphor: An Anthropological Essay on Hermeneutics," in *The Reader in the Text: Essays on Audience and Interpretation,* ed. Susan R. Suleiman and Inge Crosman (Princeton, N.J.: Princeton University Press, 1980), 184–85.

5. The "natives" who come to hate Cortés and Malintzin are the mestizos — the mixed-blood offspring — because the indigenous people at the time of the conquest often welcomed them as liberators. It is of interest to note that throughout the Mexican colonial period the missionaries staged secular plays for the indigenous population in which Cortés and Malintzin were represented as their liberators. Some parishes, even today, continue to reenact these plays in dispersed communities. I draw the preceding comments from Norma Contu's work in progress, "Secular and Liturgical Folk Drama," presented at the National Association of Chicano Studies, Los Angeles, March 29–April 1, 1989.

6. René Girard, *Violence and the Sacred,* trans. Patrick Gregory (Baltimore: Johns Hopkins University Press, 1977), 273.

7. Ibid., 99.

8. Ibid., 96.

9. Cortés's misfortunes with the Spanish Crown may be linked to the need of the successor colonizers and the colonized to extirpate him from their relations with Spain. Certainly, he has been expelled from public life in Mexico, where no monuments or mementos to his role in the conquest may be seen. Ironically, he is very much in everyone's mind.

10. The term *la chingada* is used to refer, literally, to a woman who is "fucked" or "fucked over." Thus, Paz and others suggest a metonymic relation to rape. When used in the past participle, passivity is implied. The verb and its derivatives imply violent action, and much depends on context and the speaker's inflection. To refer to a masculine actor, the term *chingon* is used.

11. Girard, *Violence and the Sacred,* 99.

12. I draw on the work of Walter J. Ong for parts of this discussion, especially *The Presence of the Word: Some Prolegomena for Cultural and Religious History* (New Haven: Yale University Press, 1967), and *Orality and Literacy: The Technologizing of the Word* (New York: Methuen, 1982).

13. These dates are highly arbitrary, especially the closing date. There is consensus among Chicano critics that the production of contemporary Chicano literature began in conjunction with César Chávez's National Farm Workers' Association strike of 1965, noting the fact that Luis Valdez's Teatro Campesino was inaugurated on the picket lines. See Marta Sánchez's *Contemporary Chicana Poetry: A Critical Approach to an Emerging Literature* (Berkeley: University of California Press, 1985), 2–6. For the recuperation of the term *vendida* (sellout), see Cherríe Moraga's essay "A Long Line of Vendidas," in her *Loving in the War Years: Lo que nunca pasó por sus labios* (Boston: South End Press, 1983), 90–117.

14. Although the Spanish original was published in 1950, I use the Lysander Kemp translation of Octavio Paz, *The Labyrinth of Solitude: Life and Thought in Mexico* (New York: Grove Press, 1961).

15. Octavio Paz, foreword to Lafaye, *Quetzalcóatl y Guadalupe,* 22.

16. These stages suggested themselves to me while I was reading Rachel Phillips's essay "Marina/Malinche: Masks and Shadows," in *Women in Hispanic Literature: Icons and Fallen Idols,* ed. Beth Miller (Berkeley: University of California Press, 1983), 97–114. See also Rodríguez, *Doña Marina,* and Cantú, "Secular and Liturgical Folk Drama."

17. I use Alfonso Reyes, *Visión de Anáhuac* (Mexico City: El Colegio de Mexico, 1953); the work was originally published in 1915.

18. Ibid., 61–62.

19. Paz, *Labyrinth of Solitude,* 87.

20. Terry Eagleton, *Marxism and Literary Criticism* (Berkeley: University of California Press, 1976), 19.

21. Paz, *Labyrinth of Solitude,* 87.

22. Ibid., 86.

23. Carlos Fuentes, *Todos los gatos son pardos* (Mexico City: Siglo XXI, 1984 [1970]).

24. Ibid., 64, 99.

25. Ibid., 5–6.

26. An interesting study of Paz's and Fuentes's work is presented by Edmond Cros, *Theory and Practice of Sociocriticism,* trans. Jerome Schwartz (Minneapolis: University of Minnesota Press, 1988), 153–89.

27. José Emilio Pacheco, *Islas a la deriva* (Mexico City: Siglo XXI, 1976), 27–28.

28. For example, Octavio Paz's "The Sons of La Malinche" may be found in *Introduction to Chicano Studies: A Reader,* ed. Livie Isauro Duran and H. Russell Bernard (New York: Macmillan, 1973), 17–27, and Carlos Fuentes's "The Legacy of La Malinche," in *Literatura Chicana: Texto y contexto,* ed. Antonia Castaneda Shular, Tomás Ybarra-Frausto, and Joseph Sommers (New York: Prentice-Hall, 1972), 304–6.

29. For a perspective on men's implicit or explicit use of oppositional female figures whose outlines may be rooted in Guadalupe-Malintzin, see Juan Bruce-Novoa, "One More Rosary for Doña Marina," *Confluencia* 1, no. 22 (spring 1986): 73–84. In the 1980s some Chicana visual artists began experimenting with the image of Guadalupe. Ester Hernández, for example, depicts the Virgin executing a karate kick. Santa Barraza depicts a newly unearthed Coatlicue (Mesoamerican fertility goddess) pushing Guadalupe upward and overpowering her. The contrastive images tell the story of the difference between them — the one small, the other huge. See reproductions of these works in *Third Woman* 4 (1989): 42, 153, respectively. Yolanda M. López has portrayed Guadalupe walking in high-heel sandals. The reproduction that *Fem* 8, no. 34 (June–July 1984) carried on its cover provoked a large amount of hate mail, accusing the editors of being "Zionists." According to Hernández's personal communication, the exhibit of her Guadalupe ink drawing caused a minor scandal in a small California town. She had to leave the exhibit to avoid violent attack. Community leaders had to schedule workshops to discuss the work and the artist's rights. Modern revisions of Guadalupe are fraught with difficulty and may well be the reason why Chicana writers have bypassed her. She still retains a large, devoted following.

30. Sherry B. Ortner, "Is Female to Male as Nature Is to Culture?" in *Woman, Culture, and Society,* ed. Michelle Zimbalist Rosaldo and Louise Lamphere (Stanford, Calif.: Stanford University Press, 1974), 85.

31. Adrienne Rich, *On Lies, Secrets, and Silence: Selected Prose, 1966–1978* (New York: W. W. Norton, 1979), 43.

32. For the notion of the "speaking subject" I am guided by Julia Kristeva's work, especially "The Ethics of Linguistics," in *Desire in Language: A Semiotic Approach to Literature and Art,* trans. Thomas Gora, Alice Jardine, and Leon S. Roudiez (New York: Columbia University Press, 1980), 23–25.

33. I have taken the liberty of changing all of the "he's" in Bakhtin's text to "she's." See Mikhail M. Bakhtin, *The Dialogic Imagination: Four Essays,* trans. Caryl Emerson and Michael Holquist, ed. Michael Holquist (Austin: University of Texas Press, 1981), 293–94.

34. Adelaida R. del Castillo, "Malintzin Tenepal: A Preliminary Look into a New Perspective," in *Essays on La Mujer,* ed. Rosaura Sánchez and Rosa Martínez Cruz (Los Angeles: Chicano Studies Center Publications, University of California–Los Angeles, 1977), 141.

35. Adaljiza Sosa Riddell, "Chicanas in El Movimiento," *Aztlán* 5, nos. 1–2 (1974): 155–65.

36. Carmen Tafolla, "La Malinche," in *Five Poets of Aztlán,* ed. Santiago Daydi-Tolson (Binghamton, N.Y.: Bilingual Press, 1985), 193–95.

37. Del Castillo, "Malintzin Tenepal," 125.

38. Ibid., 126.

39. Ibid., 130.

40. Cordelia Candelaria, "La Malinche, Feminist Prototype," *Frontiers* 5, no. 2 (1980): 1–6.

41. Ibid., 6.

42. Ibid., 3.

43. The unfinished revolt is discussed by Hannah Arendt, *Between Past and Future: Eight Exercises in Political Thought* (London: Penguin Books, 1978).

44. Sylvia Gonzáles, "Chicana Evolution," in *The Third Woman: Minority Women Writers of the United States,* ed. Dexter Fisher (Boston: Houghton Mifflin, 1980), 418–22.

45. Ibid., 420.

46. Ibid.

47. Ibid.

48. Ibid., 419.

49. Alma Villanueva, "La Chingada," in *Five Poets of Aztlán,* 140.

50. Ibid., 153.

51. In "La Llorona, the Third Legend of Greater Mexico: Cultural Symbols, Women, and the Political Unconscious," *Renato Rosaldo Lecture Series Monograph* 2 (1984–85) (Tucson: Mexican American Studies and Research Center, University of Arizona, spring 1986): 59–93, José Limón has argued that La Llorona (The Weeping Woman) would make a more effective feminist cultural symbol for women of Mexican descent. In fact, he argues that Chicana have failed to recognize her potential feminist political importance. In my view, La Llorona fails to meet some of the modern and secularizing factors that Chicanas have felt they have needed in order to speak for themselves. The so-called second wave of global feminism forces contemporary women to deal with the notion of the self and subjectivity that previous feminisms have often bypassed in favor of women's rights on the basis of being wives and mothers. The current debate on La Malinche goes beyond that.

52. Villanueva, "La Chingada," 163.

53. Cited in ibid., 142.

54. Adrienne Rich, *Of Woman Born: Motherhood as Experience and Institution* (New York: W. W. Norton, 1976).

55. Lucha Corpi, "Marina Mother," "Marina Virgin," "The Devil's Daughter," and "She (Distant Marina)," in *Palabras de Mediodía/Noon Words: Poems,* trans. Catherine Rodríguez-Nieto (Berkeley: El Fuego de Aztlán Publications, 1980), 118–25.

56. Sánchez, *Contemporary Chicana Poetry,* 190.

57. Ibid., 194.

58. Cherríe Moraga, *Loving in the War Years.*

59. For a complementary essay on the way Chicana writers have reconstructed the relationship between the self and the mother in order to redefine their feminine/feminist identity, see Norma Alarcón, "What Kind of Lover Have You Made Me Mother?" in *Women of Color: Perspectives on Feminism and Identity,* ed. Audrey T. McCluskey, Women's Studies Monograph Series, no. 1 (Bloomington: Indiana University Press, 1985), 85–110.

60. Moraga, *Loving in the Wars Years,* 99.

61. Ibid., 112.

62. Ibid., 113.

63. In charging the Chicano community with heterosexism, Moraga relies on Adrienne Rich's sense of the term in "Compulsory Heterosexuality and Lesbian Existence," in *Women— Sex and Sexuality,* ed. Catharine R. Stimpson and Ethel Spector Person (Chicago: University of Chicago Press, 1980), 62–91.

64. Moraga, *Loving in the War Years,* 117.

65. Lorna D. Cervantes, "Baby, You Cramp My Style," *El Fuego de Aztlán* 1, no. 4 (1977): 39.

66. Gloria Anzaldúa, *Borderlands/La Frontera: The New Mestiza* (San Francisco: Aunt Lute, 1987).

67. Tzvetan Todorov, *The Conquest of America: The Conquest of the Other,* trans. Richard Howard (New York: Harper and Row, 1985), 101.

68. The gulf between criticism and politics or criticism and cognitive practices is examined by S. P. Mohanty, "Us and Them: On the Philosophical Bases of Political Criticism," *Yale Journal of Criticism* 2, no. 2 (1989): 1–31; Mary E. Hawkesworth, "Knowers, Knowing, Known: Feminist Theory and Claims of Truth," Signs 14, no. 3 (spring 1989): 533–57; Edward W. Said, *The World, the Text, and the Critic* (Cambridge, Mass.: Harvard University Press, 1983); and Chandra T. Mohanty, "Under Western Eyes: Feminist Scholarship and Colonial Discourse," above.

Chapter 16
American Indian Women: At the Center
of Indigenous Resistance in Contemporary
North America
M. Annette Jaimes with Theresa Halsey

> *A people is not defeated until the hearts of its women are on the ground.*
> Traditional Cheyenne Saying

> *The United States has not shown me the terms of my surrender.*
> Marie Lego — Pit River Nation, 1970

The two brief quotations forming the epigraph of this essay were selected to represent a constant reality within Native American life from the earliest times. This reality is that women have always formed the backbone of indigenous nations on the North American continent. It is we — contrary to those images of meekness, docility, and subordination to males with which we have been typically portrayed by the dominant culture's books and movies, by anthropology, and by political ideologues of both rightist and leftist persuasions — who have formed the very core of indigenous resistance to genocide and colonization since the first moment of conflict between Indians and invaders. In contemporary terms, this heritage has informed and guided generations of native women such as the elder Marie Lego, who provided crucial leadership to the Pit River Nation's land-claims struggle in northern California during the 1970s.[1]

In Washington State, women such as Janet McCloud (Tulalip) and Ramona Bennett (Puyallup) had already assumed leading roles in the fishing-rights struggles of the 1960s, efforts that, probably more than any other phenomenon, set in motion the "hard-line" Indian liberation movements of the modern day. These were not political organizing campaigns of the ballot and petition sort. Rather, they were, and continue to be, conflicts involving the disappearance of entire peoples. Bennett has explained the nature of the fishing-rights confrontations in these terms:

> At this time, our people were fighting to preserve their last treaty right — the right to fish. We lost our land base. There was no game in the area. We're dependent not just economically but culturally on the right to fish. Fishing is part of our art forms and religion and diet, and the entire culture is based around it. And so when we talk about [Euroamerica's] ripping off the right to fish, we're talking about cultural genocide.[2]

The Indians' "fish-ins" were initially pursued within a framework of civil disobedience and principled nonviolence, which went nowhere other than to incur massive official and quasi-official violence in response. Bennett recounts:

They [the police] came right on the reservation with a force of three hundred people. They gassed us, they clubbed people around, they laid $125,000 bail on us. At that time I was a member of the Puyallup Tribal Council, and I was spokesman for the camp [of local fishing-rights activists]. And I told them what our policy was: that we were there to protect our Indian fishermen. And because I used a voice-gun, I'm being charged with inciting a riot. I'm faced with an eight year sentence.[3]

An elder Nisqually woman pushed the fishing-rights movement in western Washington to adopt the policy of armed self-defense that ultimately proved successful (the struggle in eastern Washington took a somewhat different course to the same position and results):

Finally, one of the boys went down to the river to fish, and his mother went up on the bank. And she said: "This boy is nineteen years old and we've been fighting on this river for as many years as he's been alive. And no one is going to pound my son around, no one is going to arrest him. No one is going to touch my son or I'm going to shoot them." And she had a rifle.... Then we had an armed camp in the city of Tacoma.[4]

The same sort of dynamic was involved in South Dakota during the early 1970s, when elder Oglala Lakota women such as Ellen Moves Camp and Gladys Bissonette assumed the leadership in establishing what was called the Oglala Sioux Civil Rights Organization (OSCRO) on the Pine Ridge Reservation. According to Bissonette, "Every time us women gathered to protest or demonstrate, they [federal authorities] always aimed machine guns at us women and children."[5] In response, she became a major advocate of adopting a posture of armed self-defense at the reservation hamlet of Wounded Knee in 1973, remained within the defensive perimeter for the entire seventy-one days the U.S. government besieged the Indians inside, and became a primary negotiator for what was called the "Independent Oglala Nation."[6] Both women remained quite visible in the Oglala resistance to U.S. domination despite a virtual counterinsurgency war waged by the government on Pine Ridge during the three years following Wounded Knee.[7]

At Big Mountain, in the former "Navajo-Hopi Joint Use Area" in Arizona, where the federal government is even now attempting to forcibly relocate more than ten thousand traditional Diné (Navajos) in order to open the way for corporate exploitation of the rich coal reserves underlying their land, it is again elder women who have stood at the forefront of resistance, refusing to leave the homes of their ancestors. One of them, Pauline Whitesinger, was the first to physically confront government personnel attempting to fence off her land. Another, Katherine Smith, was the first to do so with a rifle.[8] Such women have constituted a literal physical barrier blocking consummation of the government's relocation/mining efforts for more than a decade.[9] Many similar stories, all of them from the past quarter-century, might be told in order to demonstrate the extent to which women have galvanized and centered contemporary native resistance.

The costs of such uncompromising (and uncompromised) activism have often been high. To quote Ada Deer, who, along with Lucille Chapman, became an essential spokesperson for the Menominee restoration movement in Wisconsin during the late 1960s and early 1970s: "I wanted to get involved. People said I was too young, too naïve — you can't fight the system. I dropped out of law school. That was the price I had to pay to be involved."[10] Gladys Bissonette lost a son, Pedro, and a daughter, Jeanette, murdered by federal surrogates on Pine Ridge in the aftermath of Wounded Knee.[11] Other native women, such as American Indian Movement (AIM) members Tina Trudell and Anna Mae Pictou Aquash, have paid with their own and sometimes their children's lives for their prominent defiance of their colonizers.[12] Yet it stands as a testament to the strength of American Indian women that such grim sacrifices have served not to deter them from standing up for the rights of native people but as an inspiration to do so. Mohawk activist/scholar Shirley Hill Witt recalls the burial of Aquash after her execution-style murder on Pine Ridge:

> Some women had driven from Pine Ridge the night before — a very dangerous act — "to do what needed to be done." Young women dug the grave. A ceremonial tipi was set up.... A woman seven months pregnant gathered sage and cedar to be burned in the tipi. Young AIM members were pallbearers: they laid her on pine boughs while spiritual leaders spoke the sacred words and performed the ancient duties. People brought presents for Anna Mae [Pictou Aquash] to take with her to the spirit world. They also brought presents for her two sisters to carry back to Nova Scotia with them to give to her orphaned daughters.... The executioners of Anna Mae did not snuff out a meddlesome woman. They exalted a Brave-Hearted Woman for all time.[13]

The motivations of indigenous women in undertaking such risks are unequivocal. As María Sánchez, a leading member of the Northern Cheyennes' resistance to corporate "development" of their reservation, puts it: "I am the mother of nine children. My concern is for their future, for their children, and for future generations. As a woman, I draw strength from the traditional spiritual people,...from my nation. The oil and gas companies are building a huge gas chamber for the Northern Cheyennes."[14] Pauline Whitesinger has stated, "I think there is no way we can survive if we get moved to some other land away from ours. We are just going to waste away. People tell me to move, but I've got no place to go. I am not moving anywhere, that is certain."[15] Roberta Blackgoat, another leader of the Big Mountain resistance, concurs: "If this land dies, the people die with it. We are a nation. We will fight anyone who tries to push us off our land."[16] All across North America, the message from native women is the same.[17] The explicitly nationalist content of indigenous women's activism has been addressed by Lorelei DeCora Means, a Minneconjou Lakota AIM member and one of the founders of Women of All Red Nations (WARN):

> We are *American Indian* women, in that order. We are oppressed, first and foremost, as American Indians, as peoples colonized by the United States of America, *not* as women. As Indians, we can never forget that. Our survival, the survival of every one of us — man, woman and child — *as Indians* depends on it. Decolonization is the agenda, the whole agenda, and until it is accomplished, it is the *only* agenda that counts for American Indians. It will take every one of us — every single one of us — to get the job done. We haven't got the time, energy or resources for anything else while our lands are being destroyed and our children are dying of avoidable diseases and malnutrition.

So we tend to view those who come to us wanting to form alliances on the basis of "new" and "different" or "broader" and "more important" issues to be a little less than friends, especially since most of them come from the Euro-American population which benefits most directly from our ongoing colonization.[18]

Janet McCloud has stated:

Most of these "progressive" non-Indian ideas, like "class struggle" would at the present time divert us into participating as "equals" in our own colonization. Or, like "women's liberation," would divide us among ourselves in such a way as to leave us colonized in the name of "gender equity." Some of us can't help but think maybe a lot of these "better ideas" offered by non-Indians claiming to be our "allies" are intended to accomplish exactly these sorts of diversion and disunity within our movement. So, let me toss out a different sort of "progression" to all you marxists and socialists and feminists out there. *You* join *us* in liberating *our* land and lives. Lose the privilege *you* acquire at *our* expense by occupying *our* land. Make *that* your first priority for as long as it takes to make it happen. *Then* we'll join you in fixing up whatever's left of the class and gender problems in your society, and our own, if need be. *But,* if you're not willing to do *that,* then don't presume to tell *us* how we should go about our liberation, what priorities and values we should have. Since you're standing on our land, we've got to view you as just another oppressor trying to hang on to what's ours. And that doesn't leave us a whole lot to talk about, now does it?[19]

Myths of Male Dominance

A significant factor militating against fruitful alliances — or even dialogue — between Indians and non-Indians is the vast complex of myths imposed and stubbornly defended by the dominant culture as a means of "understanding" Native America both historically and topically. As concerns indigenous women in particular, this fantastical lexicon includes what anthropologist Eleanor Burke Leacock has termed the "myths of male dominance."[20] Adherence to the main stereotypes of these myths seems to be entirely transideological within the mainstream of American life, a matter readily witnessed by offerings in the mass media by Paul Valentine, a remarkably reactionary critic for the *Washington Post,* and Barbara Ehrenreich, an ostensibly socialist-feminist columnist for *Time* magazine and several more progressive publications.

In a hostile review of the film *Dances with Wolves* published in April 1991, Valentine denounces producer-director Kevin Costner for having "romanticized" American Indians.[21] He then sets forth a series of outlandish contentions designed to show how nasty things really were in North America before Europeans came along to set things right. An example of the sheer absurdity with which his polemic is laced is a passage in which he has "the Arapaho of eastern Colorado . . . igniting uncontrolled grass fires on the prairies," which remained barren of grass "for many years afterward," causing mass starvation among the buffalo (as any high school botany student might have pointed out, a fall burn-off actually stimulates spring growth of most grasses, prairie grasses included). He then proceeds to explain the lot of native women in precontact times — they were haulers of "the clumsy two stick travois used to transport a family's belongings on the nomadic seasonal treks" (there were virtually no precontact "nomads" in North America, and dogs were used to drag travois prior to the advent of horses).[22]

Ehrenreich, for her part, had earlier adopted a similar posture in a *Time* magazine column arguing against the rampant militarism engulfing the U.S. during the fall of 1990. In her first paragraph, while taking a couple of gratuitous and utterly uninformed shots at the culture of the southeast African Masai and indigenous Solomon Islanders, she implies America's jingoist policies in the Persian Gulf had "descended" to the level of such "primitive" — and male-dominated — "warrior cultures" as "the Plains Indian societies," where "the passage to manhood requires the blooding of the spear, the taking of a scalp or head."[23] Ehrenreich's thoroughly arrogant use of indigenous cultures as a springboard from which to launch into the imagined superiority of her own culture and views is no more factually supportable than Valentine's and is every bit as degrading to native people of *both* genders. Worse, she extends her "analysis" as a self-proclaimed "friend of the oppressed" rather than as an unabashed apologist for the status quo.

The truth of things was, of course, rather different. To take Ehrenreich's thesis first, the Salish/Kootenai scholar D'Arcy McNickle long ago published the results of lengthy and painstaking research that showed that 70 percent or more of all precontact societies in North America practiced no form of warfare at all.[24] This may have been due in part to the fact that, as Laguna researcher Paula Gunn Allen has compellingly demonstrated in her book *The Sacred Hoop,* traditional native societies were never male-dominated and there were likely no "warrior cultures" worthy of the name before the European invasion.[25] There is no record of *any* American Indian society, even after the invasion, requiring a man to kill in war before he could marry. To the contrary, military activity — including being a literal warrior — was never an exclusively male sphere of endeavor.

Although it is true that women were typically accorded a greater social value in indigenous tradition — both because of their biological ability to bear children and for reasons that will be discussed below — and therefore tended to be noncombatant to a much greater degree than men, female fighters were never uncommon once the necessity of real warfare was imposed by Euro-Americans.[26] These included military commanders like Cousaponakeesa — Mary Matthews Musgrove Bosomworth, the "Creek Mary" of Dee Brown's 1981 novel — who led her people in a successful campaign against the British at Savannah during the 1750s.[27] Lakota women traditionally maintained at least four warrior societies of their own, entities that are presently being resurrected.[28] Among the Cherokees, there was Da'nawagasta, or "Sharp War," an especially tough warrior and head of a women's military society.[29] The Piegans maintained what has been mistranslated as "Manly-Hearted Women," more accurately understood as being "Strong-Hearted Women," a permanent warrior society.[30] The Cheyennes in particular fielded a number of strong women fighters, such as Buffalo Calf Road (who distinguished herself both at the Battle of the Rosebud in 1876 and during the 1878 "Cheyenne Breakout"), amid the worst period of the wars of annihilation waged against them by the United States.[31] Many other native cultures produced comparable figures, a tradition into which the women named in the preceding section fit well. This serves to debunk the tidy (if grossly misleading and divisive) male/female, warlike/peaceful dichotomies deployed by such Euro-American feminist thinkers as Ehrenreich and Robin Morgan.[32]

More important than their direct participation in military activities was native women's role in making key decisions, not only about matters of peace and war but in all other aspects of socioeconomic existence. Although Gunn Allen's conclusion that traditional indigenous societies added up to "gynocracies" is undoubtedly overstated and misleading, this is not to say that Native American women were not politically powerful. Creek Mary was not a general per se but essentially head of state within the Creek Confederacy. Her status was that of "Beloved Woman," a position better recorded with regard to the system of governance developed among the Cherokees slightly to the north of Creek domain:

> Cherokee women had the right to decide the fate of captives, decisions that were made by vote of the Women's Council and relayed to the district at large by the War Woman or Pretty Woman. The decisions had to be made by female clan heads because a captive who was to live would be adopted into one of the families whose affairs were directed by the clan-mothers. The clan-mothers also had the right to wage war, and as Henry Timberlake wrote, the stories about Amazon women warriors were not so farfetched considering how many Indian women were famous warriors and powerful voices in the councils.... The war women carried the titled Beloved Women, and their power was great.... The Women's Council, as distinguished from the District, village, or Confederacy councils, was powerful in a number of political and socio-spiritual ways, and may have had the deciding voice on which males would serve on the Councils.... Certainly the Women's Council was influential in tribal decisions, and its spokeswomen served as War Women and Peace Women, presumably holding offices in the towns designated as red towns and white towns, respectively. Their other powers included the right to speak in the Men's Council [although men lacked a reciprocal right, under most circumstances], the right to choose whom and whether to marry, the right to bear arms, and the right to choose their extramarital occupations.[33]

While Creek and Cherokee women "may" have held the right to select which males assumed positions of political responsibility, this was unquestionably the case within the Haudenosaunee (Six Nations Iroquois Confederacy) of New York State. Among the "Sixers," each of the fifty extended families (clans) was headed by a clan mother. These women formed a council within the confederacy that selected the males who would hold positions on a second council, composed of men, representing the confederacy's interests, both in formulation of internal policies and in conduct of external relations. Any time certain male council members adopted positions or undertook policies perceived by the women's council as being contrary to the people's interests, their respective clan mothers retained the right to replace them. Although much diminished after two centuries of U.S. colonial domination, this "longhouse" form of government is ongoing today.[34]

The Haudenosaunee were hardly alone among northeastern peoples in according women such a measure of power. At the time of the European arrival in North America, the Narragansett of what is now Rhode Island were headed by a *sunksquaw,* or female chief. The last of these, a woman named Magnus, was executed along with ninety other members of the Narragansett government after their defeat by the English Major, James Talcot, in 1675.[35] During the same period, the Esopus Confederacy was led, at least in part, by a woman named Mamanuchqua (also known as Mamareoktwe, Mamaroch, and Mamaprocht).[36] The Delawares *generically* referred to themselves as "women," considering the term to be supremely complementary.[37] Among other Algonquin peoples of the Atlantic Coast region — for example, the Wampanoag and Massachusetts Confederacies, and the Niaticks, Scaticooks, Niantics, Pictaways, Powhatans, and Caconnets — much the same pattern prevailed:

> From before 1620 until her death in 1617, a squaw-sachem known as the "Massachusetts Queen" by the Virginia colonizers governed the Massachusetts Confederacy. It was her fortune to preside over the Confederacy's destruction as the people were decimated by disease, war, and colonial manipulations.... Others include the Pocasett sunksquaw Weetamoo, who was King Philip's ally and "served as a war chief commanding over 300 warriors" during his war with the British.... Awashonks, another [woman head of state] of the Mid-Atlantic region, was squaw-sachem of the Sakonnet, a [nation] allied with the Wampanoag Confederacy. She [held her office] in the latter part of the seventeenth century. After fighting for a time against the British during King Philip's War, she was forced to surrender. Because she then convinced her warriors to fight with the British, she was able to save them from enslavement in the West Indies.[38]

Women's power within traditional Indian societies was also grounded in other ways. While patrilineal/patrilocal cultures did exist, most precontact North American civilizations functioned on the basis of matrilineage and matrilocality. Insofar as family structures centered upon the identities of wives rather than husbands — men joined women's families, not the other way around — and because men were usually expected to relocate to join the women they married, the context of native social life was radically different from that which prevailed (and prevails) in European and Euro-derived cultures:[39]

> Many of the largest and most important Indian peoples were matrilineal....Among these were: in the East, the Iroquois, the Siouan [nations] of the Piedmont and Atlantic coastal plain, the Mohegan, the Delaware, various other [nations] of southern New England, and the divisions of the Powhatan Confederacy in Virginia; in the South, the Creek, the Choctaw, the Chickasaw, the Seminole, and the [nations] of the Caddoan linguistic family; in the Great Plains, the Pawnee, the Hidatsa, the Mandan, the Oto, the Missouri, and the Crow and other Siouan [nations]; in the Southwest, the Navajo, and the numerous so-called Pueblo [nations], including the well known Hopi, Laguna, Acoma, and Zuni.[40]

In many indigenous societies, the position of women was further strengthened economically, by virtue of their owning all or most property. Haudenosaunee women, for example, owned the fields that produced about two-thirds of their people's diet.[41] Among the Lakota, men owned nothing but their clothing, a horse for hunting, weapons, and spiritual items; homes, furnishings, and the like were the property of their wives. All a Lakota woman needed to do in order to divorce her husband was to set his meager personal possessions outside the door of their lodge, an action against which he had no appeal under traditional law.[42] Much the same system prevailed among the Anishinabe and numerous other native cultures. As Mary Oshana, an Anishinabe activist, has explained:

Matrilineal [nations] provided the greatest opportunities for women: women in these [nations] owned houses, furnishings, fields, gardens, agricultural tools, art objects, livestock and horses. Furthermore, these items were passed down through female lines. Regardless of their marital status, women had the right to own and control property. The woman had control of the children and if marital problems developed the man would leave the home.[43]

Additional reinforcement of native women's status accrues from the spiritual traditions of most of North America's indigenous cultures. First, contrary to the Euro-American myth that American Indian spiritual leaders are invariably something called "medicine men," women have always held important positions in this regard. Prime examples include Coocoochee of the Mohawks, Sanapia of the Comanches, and Pretty Shield of the Crows.[44] Among the Zuni and other Puebloan cultures, women were members of the Rain Priesthood, the most important of that society's religious entities.[45] Women are also known to have played crucial leadership roles within Anishinabe, Blackfeet, Chilula, and Diné spiritual practices, as well as those of many other native societies.[46]

Second, and more important in some ways, virtually all indigenous religions on the North American continent exhibit an abundant presence of feminine elements within their cosmologies.[47] When contrasted to the hegemonic masculinity of the deities embraced by such "world religions" as Judeo-Christianity and Islam — and the corresponding male supremacism marking those societies that adhere to them — the real significance of concepts like Mother Earth (universal), Spider Woman (Hopi and Diné), White Buffalo Calf Woman (Lakota), Grandmother Turtle (Iroquois), Sky Woman (Iroquois), Hard Beings Woman (Hopi), Sand Altar Woman (Hopi), First Woman (Abanaki), Thought Woman (Laguna), Corn Woman (Cherokee), and Changing Woman (Diné) becomes rather obvious.[48] So too does the real rather than mythical status of women in traditional Native American life. Indeed, as Diné artist Mary Morez has put it, "In [our] society, the woman is the dominant figure who becomes the wise one with old age. It's a [matrilineal/matrilocal] society, you know. But the Navajo woman never demands her status. She achieves, earns, accomplishes it through maturity. That maturing process is psychological. It has to do with one's feelings for the land and being part of the whole cycle of nature. It's difficult to describe to a non-Indian."[49]

Bea Medicine, a Hunkpapa Lakota scholar, concurs, noting that "our power is obvious. [Women] are primary socializers of our children. Culture is transmitted primarily through the mother. The mother teaches languages, attitudes, beliefs, behavior patterns, etc."[50] Anishinabe writer-activist Winona LaDuke concludes,

> Traditionally, American Indian women were never subordinate to men. Or vice versa, for that matter. What native societies have always been about is achieving balance in all things, gender relations no less than any other. Nobody needs to tell us how to do it. We've had that all worked out for thousands of years. And, left to our own devices, that's exactly how we'd be living right now.[51]

Or, as Priscilla K. Buffalohead, another Anishinabe scholar, has put it, "[We] stem from egalitarian cultural traditions. These traditions are concerned less with equality of the sexes and more with the dignity of the individual and their inherent right — whether they be women, men or children — to make their own choices and decisions."[52]

Disempowerment

The reduction of the status held by women within indigenous nations was a first priority for European colonizers eager to weaken and destabilize target societies. With regard to the Montagnais and Naskapi of the St. Lawrence River Valley, for example, the French, who first entered the area in the 1550s, encountered a people among whom "women have great power.... A man may promise you something and if he does not keep his promise, he thinks he is sufficiently excused when he tells you that his wife did not wish him to do it."[53] The French responded, beginning in 1633, by sending Jesuit missionaries to show the natives a "better and more enlightened way" of comporting themselves, a matter well chronicled by the priest Paul Le Jeune. About the priest, Eleanor Burke Leacock has written:

> Though some observers saw women as drudges, Le Jeune saw women as holding "great power" and having "in every instance . . . the choice of plans, of undertakings, of journeys, of winterings." Indeed, independence of women was considered a problem by the Jesuits, who lectured the men about "allowing" their wives sexual and other freedom and sought to introduce European principles of obedience.[54]

Likely, the Jesuit program would have gone nowhere had the sharp end of colonization not undercut the Montagnais-Naskapi traditional economy, replacing it with a system far more reliant upon fur trapping and traders by the latter part of the seventeenth century.[55] As their dependence upon their colonizers increased, the Indians were compelled to accept more and more of the European brand of "morality." The Jesuits imposed a form of monogamy in which divorce was forbidden, implemented a system of compulsory Catholic education, and refused to deal with anyone other than selected male "representatives" of the Montagnais and Naskapi in political or economic affairs (thus deforming the Indian structure of governance beyond recognition).[56] Gunn Allen writes:

> Positions of formal power such as political leadership, [spiritual leadership], and matrilocality, which placed the economic dependence of a woman with children in the hands of her mother's family, . . . shifted. [Spiritual and political] leadership were male [by 1750], and matrilocality had become patrilocality. This is not so strange given the economics of the situation and the fact that over the years the Montagnais became entirely Catholicized.[57]

Among the Haudenosaunee, who were not militarily defeated until after the American Revolution, such changes took much longer. It was not until the early nineteenth century — in an attempt to adjust to the new circumstances of subordination to the United States — that the Seneca prophet Handsome Lake promulgated a new code of law and social organization that replaced their old "petticoat government" with a male-centered model more acceptable to the colonizers.[58] In attempting to shift power from "the meddling old women" of Iroquois society,

> Handsome Lake advocated that young women cleave to their husbands rather than to their mothers and abandon the clan-mother-controlled Longhouse in favor of a patriarchal, nuclear family arrangement.... While the shift was never complete, it was sufficient. Under the Code of Handsome Lake, which was the tribal version of the white man's way, the Longhouse declined in importance, and eventually Iroquois women were firmly under the thumb of Christian patriarchy.[59]

To the south, "[T]he British worked hard to lessen the power of women in Cherokee affairs. They took Cherokee men to England and educated them in European ways. These men returned to Cherokee country and exerted great influence in behalf of the British in the region."[60] Intermarriage was also encouraged, with markedly privileged treatment accorded mixed-blood offspring of such unions by English colonialists. In time, when combined with increasing Cherokee dependence on the British trade economy, these advantages resulted in a situation where "men with little Cherokee blood [and even less loyalty] wielded considerable power over the nation's policies."[61] Aping the English, this new male leadership set out to establish a plantation economy devoted to the growing of cotton and tobacco:

> The male leadership bought and sold not only black men and women but men and women from neighboring tribes, the women of the leadership retreated to Bible classes, sewing circles, and petticoats that rivaled those of their white sisters. Many of these upper-strata Cherokee women married white ministers and other opportunists, as the men of their class married white women, often the daughters of white ministers.... Cherokee society became rigid and modeled on Christian white social organization of upper, middle, and impoverished classes usually composed of very traditional clans.[62]

This situation, of course, greatly weakened the Cherokee Nation, creating sharp divisions within it that have not completely healed even to the present day. Moreover, it caused Euro-Americans in surrounding areas to covet not only Cherokee land per se but the lucrative farming enterprises built up by the mixed-blood male caste. This was a powerful incentive for the United States to undertake the compulsory removal of the Cherokees and other indigenous nations from east of the Mississippi River to points west during the first half of the nineteenth century.[63] The reaction of assimilated Cherokees was an attempt to show their "worth" by becoming even more ostentatiously Europeanized:

> In an effort to stave off removal, the Cherokee in the early 1800s, under the leadership of men such as Elias Boudinot, Major Ridge, and John Ross (later Principal Chief of the Cherokee in Oklahoma Territory), and others, drafted a constitution that disenfranchised women and blacks. Modeled after the Constitution of the United States, whose favor they were attempting to curry, and in conjunction with Christian sympathizers to the Cherokee cause, the new Cherokee constitution relegated women to the position of chattel.... [Under such conditions], the last Beloved Woman, Nancy Ward, resigned her office in 1817, sending her cane and her vote on important questions to the Cherokee Council.[64]

Despite much groveling by the "sellouts," Andrew Jackson ordered removal of the Cherokees — as well as the Creeks, Choctaws, Chickasaws, and Seminoles — to begin in 1832.[65] By 1839, the "Trail of Tears" was complete, with catastrophic population loss for each of the indigenous nations involved.[66] By the latter stage, traditionalist Cherokees had overcome sanctions against killing other tribal members in a desperate attempt to restore some semblance of order within their nation: Major Ridge, his eldest son, John, and Elias Boudinot were assassinated on June 22, 1839.[67] Attempts were made to eliminate other members of the "Ridge Faction," such as Stand Watie, John A. Bell, James Starr, and George W. Adair, but these failed and the assimilationist faction continued to do substantial damage to Cherokee sovereignty.[68] Although John Rollin Ridge, the major's grandson, was forced to flee to California in 1850 and was unable to return to Cherokee country until after the Civil War,[69] Stand Watie (Boudinot's younger brother) managed to lead a portion of the Cherokees into a disastrous alliance with the confederacy, an alliance from which the nation never recovered.[70]

Across the continent, the story was the same in every case. In *not one* of the more than 370 ratified and perhaps 300 unratified treaties negotiated by the United States with indigenous nations was the federal government willing to allow participation by native women. In *none* of the several thousand nontreaty agreements reached between the United States and these same nations were federal representatives prepared to discuss anything at all with women. In *no* instance was the United States open to recognizing a female as representing her people's interests when it came to administering the reservations onto which American Indians were ultimately forced; always, men were required to do what was necessary to secure delivery of rations, argue for water rights, and all the rest.[71] Meanwhile, as Rebecca Robbins points out, the best and most patriotic of the indigenous male leadership — men like Tecumseh, Osceola, Crazy Horse, and Sitting Bull — were systematically assassinated or sent to faraway prisons for extended periods. The male leadership of the native resistance was then replaced with men selected on the basis of their willingness to cooperate with their oppressors. Exactly how native women coped with this vast alteration of their circumstances, and those of their people more generally, is a bit mysterious:

> If a generalization may be made, it is that female roles of mother, sister, and wife were ongoing because of the continued care they were supposed to provide for the family. But what of the role of women in relationship to agents, to soldiers guarding the "hostiles," and to their general physical deprivation in societies whose livelihood and way of life had been destroyed along with the bison? We are very nearly bereft of data and statements which could clarify the transitional status of women during this period. The strategies adopted for cultural survival and the means of transmitting these to daughters and nieces are valuable adaptive mechanisms which cannot be even partially reconstructed.[72]

These practical realities, imposed quite uniformly by the conquerors, were steadily reinforced by officially sponsored missionizing and mandatory education in boarding schools, processes designed to inculcate the notion that such disempowerment of Indian women and liquidation of "recalcitrant" males was "natural, right, and inevitable."[73] As Jorge Noriega notes, the purpose of the schools in particular was never to "educate" American Indian children, but rather to indoctrinate them into accepting the dissolution of their cultures and the intrinsic "superiority" of the Euro-American cultural values for which they were to abandon their own.[74] In certain instances, further instruction was provided to individuals selected to form a permanent "broker class" administering native societies in behalf of the United States.[75] The Manifest Destiny that Euro-America believed entitled it to undertake such culturally genocidal actions was unequivocal. As George Ellis, a well-known Euro-American clergyman and author put it in 1882, at the very point the United States had completed its wars of conquest against Native America and was setting out to consolidate the manner of its colonial rule:

> We [whites] have a full right, by our own best wisdom, and then even by compulsion, to dictate terms and conditions to them [Indians]; to use constraint and force; to say what we intend to do, and what we must and shall do.... This rightful power of ours will relieve us from conforming to, or even consulting to any troublesome extent, the views and inclinations of the Indians whom we are to manage.... The Indian must be made to feel he is in the grasp of a superior.[76]

Contemporary Conditions

The disempowerment of native women corresponded precisely with the extension of colonial domination of each indigenous nation. During the first half of the twentieth century, federal authorities developed and perfected the mechanisms of control over Indian land, lives, and resources through such legislation as the General Allotment Act (passed in 1887, but very much ongoing through the 1920s), the 1924 Indian Citizenship Act, and the Indian Reorganization Act of 1934. All of this was done under the premises of the "trust" and "plenary power" doctrines, and all of it was done for profits taken at the direct expense of native people. As Cheyenne historian Roxanne Dunbar Ortiz has observed: "Throughout this century, the United States government has promoted the corporate exploitation of Indian lands and resources by making unequal agreements on behalf of Indian peoples and cooperating closely with transnational corporations in identifying strategic resources and land areas."[77]

Hence, indigenous nations were systematically denied use of and benefits from even those residual lands they nominally retained. Denied their traditional economies, they were compelled to become absolutely dependent upon government subsidies to survive or — where possible — to join the lowest paid sector of the U.S. workforce. Peoples that had been entirely self-sufficient for thousands of years — indeed, many of them had historically been quite wealthy — were reduced to abject poverty.[78] The capstone of this drive to utilize law as "the perfect instrument of empire" came during the 1950s, when the government set out to drive native people from the land altogether. Beginning in 1954, Congress effected statutes unilaterally "terminating" (dissolving, for purposes of federal recognition) entire indigenous peoples such as the Klamath and Menominee and coercing thousands of others to relocate from their reservations to non-Indian urban centers. In this way, Indian reservations were systematically opened up for greater corporate utilization.[79]

Once "urbanized," those Indians who had been able to find subsistence employment on farms or ranches and/or engage in gardening and limited livestock rearing
of their own were forced into the most marginal occupations or left unemployed
altogether.[80]

As concerns native women in the workforce, whereas 47.2 percent of them had
been employed in agriculture in 1900, only 2.1 percent remained so by 1970. Meanwhile, whereas only 0.1 percent of them had been in low-paying clerical positions in
high-cost urban economies at the turn of the century, 25.9 percent held such jobs by
1970. For "service occupations" such as waiting tables, the figures were 12.1 percent
in 1900, 25.9 percent as of 1970.[81] The data for native men were even more dismal,
with nearly 65 percent being completely unemployed nationally.[82] By 1969, even
the most conservative statistics revealed that more than 40 percent of all American
Indians, as compared to 14 percent of the total population, lived below the poverty
line.[83] In an effort to compensate,

> Native American women's labor force participation rates rose sharply between 1970 and
> 1980, from 35 percent to 48 percent. Those who held full-time, year-round jobs earned
> nearly 89 percent as much as white women. . . . Despite these gains, nearly three-quarters
> of American Indian women were employed in the secondary labor market in 1980,
> compared to two-thirds of European American women and one-third of European
> American men. Repressive, inaccessible, and inadequate education bears much of the
> blame for this low occupation status, along with discrimination by employers and
> fellow employees and stagnation of the reservation economy. Almost one-quarter of
> all American Indian women had not completed high school in 1980, compared to
> 16 percent of white women.[84]

For Native American males, the situation was nearly as bad:

> Those men who managed to find full-time jobs earned . . . only three-fourths as much
> as white men. Moreover, American Indian men have suffered the highest rate of
> unemployment (17 percent in 1980), the highest rate of part-time work (58 percent),
> and a high rate of non-participation in the formal labor force (31 percent). . . . A [heavily
> male-skewed] BIA [Bureau of Indian Affairs] study of the labor force status of the
> 635,000 American Indians living on and adjacent to reservations in January 1989 showed
> that one-third were unemployed and one-third earned less than $7,000.[85]

In 1976, the federal government itself officially acknowledged that American Indians were far and away the most impoverished ethnic group in North America,
living as a whole in conditions virtually identical to those prevailing in many of
the poorer Third World locales.[86] In Canada, circumstances were much the same,
with "unemployment, suicide, school drop-out rates, health problems and housing
shortages at epidemic levels on most reserves."[87] With regard to native women in
particular, as the Canadian government admitted in 1979: "Indian women likely rank
among the most severely disadvantaged in Canadian society. They are worse off
economically than both Indian men and Canadian women and although they live
longer than Indian men, their life-expectancy does not approach that of Canadian
women generally."[88]

Such poverty indeed breeds short life-spans. In 1980, a reservation-based American Indian man in the United States could expect to live only slightly over forty-five

years, a woman barely two years longer on the average — as North America's highest rates of death from malnutrition, exposure, diabetes, tuberculosis, typhoid, diphtheria, measles, and even bubonic plague took their toll. Infant mortality among reservation-based American Indians was also seven times the national average.[89] Under these conditions, the despair experienced by American Indians of both genders has manifested itself in the most pronounced incidence of alcoholism (and other substance abuse) of any ethnic group in the United States. In turn, the cycle of drunkenness results in vastly increased rates of death, not only from ailments like cirrhosis of the liver but from accidents, often but not always involving automobiles.[90] Alcohol causes other forms of extreme social disruption — children born with fetal alcohol syndrome, children born out of wedlock, child abuse and abandonment — unknown in traditional native societies.[91] The intensity of colonially induced despair also led Native North America as a whole to experience a wave of teen suicide during the 1980s that ran several times the national average.[92] Further, "In 1980, nearly one in four American Indian families was maintained by a woman (over twice the rate for whites and Asians), and 47 percent of these single-mother families were considered poor by federal guidelines. Among women with children under six, the poverty rate stood at a shocking 82 percent."[93]

On balance, the situation breeds frustration and rage of the most volatile sort, especially among native males, who have been at once heaped with a range of responsibilities utterly alien to their tradition — "head of the household," sole "breadwinner," and so forth — while being structurally denied any viable opportunity to act upon them.[94] In perfect Fanonesque fashion, this has led to a perpetual spiral of internalized violence in which Indian men engage in brutal (and all too often lethal) bar fights with one another and/or turn their angry attentions on their wives and children.[95] Battering has become endemic on some reservations, as well as in the Indian ghettos that exist in most U.S. cities, with the result that at least a few Indian women have been forced to kill their spouses in self-defense:[96]

A headline in the *Navajo Times* in the fall of 1979 reported that rape was the number one crime on the Navajo reservation. In a professional mental health journal of the Indian Health Services, Phyllis Old Dog Cross reported that incest and rape are common among the Indian women seeking services and that their incidence [was] increasing. "It is believed that at least 80 percent of the Native Women seen at the psychiatric service center (5 state area) have experienced some sort of sexual assault."[97]

As Paula Gunn Allen has observed,

Often it is said [correctly] that the increase of violence against women is the result of various sociological factors such as oppression, racism, poverty, hopelessness, emasculation of men, and loss of male self-esteem as their place within traditional society has been systematically destroyed by increasing urbanization, industrialization, and institutionalization, but seldom do we notice that for the past forty to fifty years, American popular media have depicted American Indian men as bloodthirsty savages treating women cruelly. While traditional Indian men seldom did any such thing — and in fact amongst most [nations] abuse of women was simply unthinkable, as was abuse of children or the aged — the lie about "usual" male Indian behavior seems to have taken root and now bears its brutal and bitter fruit.[98]

Gunn Allen goes on to note, "It is true that colonization destroyed roles that had given men their sense of self-esteem and identity, but the significant roles lost were not those of hunter and warrior. Rather, colonization took away the security of office men once derived from their ritual and political relationship to women."[99]

Throughout the twentieth century, new federal policies have been formulated to target the power of American Indian women specifically, most usually within their traditional capacity as familial anchors. One evidence of this has been the systematic and persistent forced transfer of Indian children into non-Indian custody, a patent violation of the 1948 UN Convention on Punishment and Prevention of the Crime of Genocide.[100] As of 1974, the Association of American Indian Affairs estimated that between 25 and 35 percent of all native youth were either adopted by Euro-Americans, placed in non-Indian foster homes, or permanently housed in institutional settings, while another 25 percent were "temporarily" placed in government or church-run boarding schools each year.[101] Although strong agitation, primarily by Indian women and their supporters, forced Congress to partially correct the situation through passage of the Indian Child Welfare Act (PL 95–608, 25 U.S.C., §1901 et seq.) in 1978, the issue remains a very real one.

Even more grotesque was a policy of involuntary surgical sterilization — another blatant breach of the UN convention on genocide — imposed upon native women, usually without their knowledge, by the Bureau of Indian Affairs's so-called Indian Health Service (IHS) during the late 1960s and first half of the 1970s.[102] Existence of the sterilization program was revealed through analysis of secret documents removed by AIM members from BIA's Washington, D.C., headquarters during its occupation by those participating in the Trail of Broken Treaties in November 1972. A resulting 1974 study by WARN concluded that as many as 42 percent of all Indian women of child-bearing age had by that point been sterilized without their consent.[103] The WARN estimates were probably accurate, as is revealed in a subsequent General Accounting Office (GAO) investigation, restricted to examining only the years 1973–76 and a mere four of the many IHS facilities. The GAO study showed that during the three-year sample period, 3,406 involuntary sterilizations (the equivalent of over a half-million among the general population) had been performed in just these four hospitals.[104] As a result of strong agitation by native women and their supporters, the IHS was transferred to the Department of Health and Human Services in 1978.

As Gunn Allen has aptly put it,

Currently our struggles are on two fronts: physical survival and cultural survival. For women this means fighting alcoholism and drug abuse (our own and that of our husbands, lovers, parents, children); poverty,... rape, incest, battering by Indian [and non-Indian] men; assaults on fertility and other health matters by the Indian Health Service and Public Health Service; high infant mortality due to substandard medical care, nutrition, and health information; poor educational opportunities or education that takes us away from our traditions, language, and communities; suicide, homicide, or similar expressions of self-hatred; lack of economic opportunities; substandard housing; sometimes violent and often virulent racist attitudes and behaviors directed against us by an entertainment and educational system that wants only one thing from Indians: our silence, our invisibility, and our collective death.... To survive culturally, American Indian women must often fight the United States government, the tribal [puppet] governments, women and men of their [nation] who are...threatened by attempts to change...the colonizers' revisions of our lives, values, and histories.[105]

Fighting Back

The patterns of resistance by which American Indians have fought back against the overwhelming oppression of their colonization are actually as old as the colonization itself, occurring in an uninterrupted flow from the early 1500s onward. As with any struggle, however, native resistance has been cyclical in terms of its intensity and varied in its expression over time. The "modern era" in this regard was perhaps ushered in with the adoption by Indians of written articulation as a mode of political action. Women, beginning with the Northern Paiute writer-activist Sarah Winnemucca Hopkins, have played a decisive role in developing this new tool for indigenous utilization.[106] Winnemucca's autobiographical *Life among the Piutes: Their Wrongs and Claims,* first published in 1883,[107] laid the groundwork for the subsequent efforts of the Santee Dakota writer Ohiyesa (Charles Eastman), whose early twentieth-century books and articles yielded a significant effect in terms of altering the assimilationist policies of the federal government.[108]

Winnemucca was hardly alone in her endeavor. Contemporaneous with Ohiyesa — and carrying a much sharper edge in both her writing and her activism — was Zitkala-sa (Gertrude Bonnin), a Lakota who was the first to announce proudly and in print that she considered her own traditions not simply the equal of anything Euro-America had to offer but "superior to white ways and values."[109] She was followed by Ella Deloria, another Lakota author relatively unequivocal in her affirmation of "Indianness."[110] Together, these early Indian women writers set in motion a dynamic wherein native women reasserted their traditional role as "voice of the people," albeit through a much different medium than had historically prevailed. By the late 1970s, Native American literature had assumed a critical galvanizing role within indigenous liberation struggles in North America, and women such as Leslie Marmon Silko (Laguna), Wendy Rose (Hopi), Joy Harjo (Creek), Linda Hogan (Chickasaw), and Mary TallMountain (Athabascan) were providing the muscle and sinew of the effort.[111] The female presence in native literature continued to increase in importance during the latter 1980s, with the emergence of work by Louise Erdrich (Turtle Mountain Anishinabe), Chrystos (Menominee), and others.[112]

As was noted in the first section, translation of these literary sentiments into serious confrontations began to occur in noticeable fashion with the fish-in movement in the Pacific Northwest during the 1960s. This began to happen, in the words of Bobbi Lee, a Canadian *métis* active in the fishing-rights struggle, "when the women just became fed up. They ran out of patience with what was going on and decided it was time to change things."[113] She describes her first demonstration at the Washington State capitol building:

> Most of the militants there at [the] demonstration in Olympia...were women and three of them did most of the speaking....They were traditionalists so there was nothing unusual about women acting as spokes[people] for the group. In fact, they told me they

were having trouble getting the men involved. The only man who spoke was Hank Adams, who's been to a university and wasn't traditional.[114]

The same sort of thing happened with AIM, an entity that received much of its early impetus from the fishing-rights movement and the examples set by Marie Lego and others engaged in the Pit River land struggle. Mary Jane Wilson, an Anishinabe activist, was — along with Dennis Banks and George Mitchell — a founder of the organization in 1968.[115] As AIM began to grow, much of the grassroots membership that made it successful was comprised of women.[116] As was mentioned above, on the Pine Ridge Lakota Reservation, which became the focal point of the movement's pitched battles with federal forces during the mid-1970s, the staunchest and most active traditionalist support came from elder Oglala women.[117] Again, it was almost exclusively women who established and maintained the AIM survival schools during the latter part of that decade.[118]

When it came to repression, however, males bore the brunt. Although female leadership had been readily apparent throughout the confrontation at Wounded Knee, the government simply repeated its historical pattern, targeting six Indian men — Russell Means (Oglala), Pedro Bissonette (Oglala), Leonard Crow Dog (Sicangu Lakota), Dennis Banks (Anishinabe), Carter Camp (Ponca), and Stan Holder (Wichita) — to face up to triple sentences of life plus eighty-eight years in the so-called "Wounded Knee Leadership Trials."[119] To be sure, AIM women *were* charged, brought to trial, and sometimes convicted — Kamook Nichols Banks (Oglala), Joanna LeDeaux (Oglala), and Nilak Butler (Inuit), to name but three examples, served appreciable sentences — but for every woman locked up, there were a dozen or more men.[120] Twenty-one women and two children were also among the minimum of sixty-nine AIM members and supporters killed by government surrogates on Pine Ridge between mid-1973 and mid-1976, the peak period of the U.S. counterinsurgency warfare directed at the organization. The disproportionate emphasis placed by federal authorities upon "neutralizing" AIM men is apparent in the fact that the remaining forty-six fatalities were adult males.[121] As Madonna (Gilbert) Thunderhawk, a Hunkpapa Lakota AIM member and a founder of WARN, was to put it in 1980: "Indian women have *had* to be strong because of what this colonialist system has done to our men ... alcohol, suicides, car wrecks, the whole thing. And after Wounded Knee, while all that persecution of the men was going on, we women had to keep things going."[122]

Carrying the weight in this fashion instilled in a whole generation of hard-line native women activists not only a strong sense of confidence in their own ability to get things done (as opposed to simply getting them started) but a deep sensitivity to the unequal degree of risk incurred by Indian men fighting to throw off the shackles — both physical and psychological — of colonization.[123] As veteran fishing-rights activist Janet McCloud asserted after a 1980 meeting in which AIM was harshly criticized for its "male dominance" and the alleged "opportunism" of its more celebrated men:

The tribal leaders and others who denounce AIM justify their actions by pointing out the human weaknesses of individual AIM people, with never a glance to their own.... Indian people can disagree till doomsday about which defensive strategy is best, or whether we should even resist. If we continue to disagree on politics, policy, philosophy, and enter into destructive personality clashes, we will lose all. . . . Few acknowledge that real change began to take place only after the tremendous sacrifices of the young [male] warriors of the American Indian Movement. The beneficiaries of the Movement [accept the gains] while the real warriors lie unrecognized in their graves or in prison cells. . . . We need our warriors, and where are they? In prisons, in hiding, pursued relentlessly by the FBI. . . . How many [of us] will take the time to send a card or a letter to the warriors rotting in prisons? It is time Indian people, those who have received most from the American Indian Movement, took some time to count their blessings, to give credit where credit is due. Don't forget the warriors, we may never see their like again.[124]

The AIM women's response to the sexism internalized by their male counterparts as part of the colonizing process was to resume the time-honored practice of establishing the political equivalent of traditional women's societies. WARN was first, initiated in 1974. It was followed by McCloud's Northwest Indian Women's Circle in 1981 and, more recently, the Indigenous Women's Network (IWN). Formed by Winona LaDuke and Ingrid Wasinawatok-El Issa (Oneida), a long-time AIM member and mainstay of the International Indian Treaty Council, IWN has begun to publish a journal entitled *Indigenous Woman*. The purpose of such organizations has been explained by WARN founder Phyllis Young (Hunkpapa Lakota):

What we are about is drawing on our traditions, regaining our strength as women in the ways handed down to us by our grandmothers, and their grandmothers before them. Our creation of an Indian women's organization is not a criticism or division from our men. In fact, it's the exact opposite. Only in this way can we organize ourselves as Indian women to meet our responsibilities, to be fully supportive of the men, to work in tandem with them as partners in a common struggle for the liberation of our people and our land. . . . The men understand this, and they support our effort. So, instead of dividing away from the men, what we are doing is building strength and unity in the traditional way.[125]

Correspondingly, the power and presence of women within the Indian liberation movement, already strong, have if anything increased since the 1960s and 1970s. During the 1980s, aside from the earlier-mentioned leadership of elder Diné women in the sustained resistance to forced relocation at Big Mountain, a comparable function was assumed by the Western Shoshone sisters Mary and Carrie Dann in Nevada vis-à-vis a federal drive to take their people's homeland.[126] In northern California, it was Abby Abinanti, a Yurok attorney, who led the legal defense against a government/corporate plan to desecrate a site sacred to her own and several other peoples in the area. Anywhere confrontations over Indian rights are occurring in the United States, native women are playing crucial roles. Moreover, by the early 1980s, women had (re)assumed the primary leadership position in 67 of the 304 remaining reservation-based indigenous nations within the forty-eight contiguous states, and the number is growing steadily.[127]

The struggle has also been sharp in Canada, where, under provision of section 12.1.b of the 1876 Indian Act (amended in 1951), a particularly virulent form of patrilineage was built into the definition of "Indianness." Under the act, an Indian woman who married a non-Indian or anyone outside her "tribe" was herself (along with her children) legally and automatically deprived of her "Indian Status."[128] Such reversal of traditional matrilineage principles — not to mention the overt racism and sexism involved — had been challenged from 1952 onward, notably by Mohawk leader Mary Two-Axe Early of the Caughnawaga Reserve in Quebec.[129] After losing several cases on the issue in Canadian courts during the early 1970s, a group of Maliseet women from the Tobique Reserve in New Brunswick decided to place the situation of one of their number, Sandra Lovelace Sappier, before the United Nations:

> The Tobique women's strategy of going to the United Nations did exert tremendous pressure on the [Ottawa] government to change the Indian Act. On December 29, 1977, the complaint of Sandra Lovelace against the Canadian government was communicated to the United Nations Human Rights Committee in Geneva, Switzerland. Because of delays by the Canadian government in responding to the Human Rights Committee's requests for information, the final verdict was not made until July 30, 1981. The decision found that Canada was in violation of the International Covenant on Civil and Political Rights. Canada was in breach of the Covenant because the Indian Act denied Sandra Lovelace the *legal* right to live in the community of her birth.[130]

As a result of the Lovelace case, the Canadian government was forced to make a further revision to the Indian Act in 1985 that eliminated discrimination against women, opening the way for resumption of traditional matrilineal/matrilocal expression among indigenous societies across the country. Along the way, the Tobique Women's Political Action Group was forced to confront the broker class of their own male population, who had been placed in positions of "leadership" by the Canadian rather than their own governing system and who were thus threatened by the women's actions; the women physically occupied tribal office buildings and effectively evicted the men, beginning in September 1977.[131] Their actions had considerable ramifications, as is witnessed by the fact that native women in Canada now often serve as chief spokespersons for their peoples. One example is Sharon Venne, a Cree attorney selected during the 1980s to represent the Treaty Six Nations of Alberta in international forums.[132] Another example is Norma Kassi, official spokesperson for the Swich'in Nation, elected member of the Yukon Legislative Assembly, and organizer of a broad coalition to oppose oil and gas development on the North Slope of Alaska.[133]

Thus, both north and south of the Euro-American border separating the United States and Canada, intense struggles have been waged by indigenous people over the past three decades against the sorts of conditions depicted in the preceding section. While it is obvious that the problems confronted have not been solved, it is equally plain that substantial gains have been made in terms of positioning Native North America to change these circumstances through decolonization and reassertion of its self-determining, self-defining, and self-sufficient existence. In each instance, native women — as *Indians,* first, last, and always — have asserted their traditional right and assumed their traditional responsibility of standing at the very center of the fray.

Native American Women and Feminism

Given the reality that Native Americans today comprise only about 0.6 percent of the North American population, and the magnitude of the problems we face, it would seem imperative that we attract support from non-Indian groups, forming alliances and coalitions where possible on the basis of some mutually recognized common ground. Many efforts in this regard have been attempted by native activists with varying degrees of success. On the face of it, both the "matriarchal" aspects of indigenous traditions and the nature of many of the struggles engaged in by contemporary native women appear to lend themselves to such a union with what the broader population has come to describe as "feminism." Accordingly, a number of prominent native women activists such as Shirley Hill Witt, Rayna Green (Cherokee), Annie Wauneka (Diné), and Susanne Shown Harjo (Lakota/Creek) have, at least at times, adopted the feminist descriptor to define their own perspectives.[134] American Indian women's organizations of this persuasion, such as OHOYO, have also made appearances.[135] Paula Gunn Allen has gone further in her attempts to make the link, arguing that indigenous tradition represents the "red roots" of the feminist impulse among all people in North America, whether its various adherents and opponents realize it or not.[136]

It should be noted, however, that those who have most openly identified themselves in this fashion have tended to be among the more assimilated of Indian women activists, generally accepting the colonialist ideology that indigenous nations are now legitimate subparts of the U.S. geopolitical corpus rather than separate nations and that Indian people are now a minority within the overall population rather than the citizenry of their own distinct nations. These women are therefore devoted to "civil rights" rather than liberation per se. Native American women who are more genuinely sovereigntist in their outlook have proved far more dubious about the potentials offered by feminist politics and alliances: "At the present time, American Indians in general are not comfortable with feminist analysis or action within reservation or urban Indian enclaves. Many Indian women are uncomfortable because they perceive it (correctly) as white-dominated."[137] In practice, as Lorelei Means has put it, this means the following:

> White women, most of them very middle class and, for whatever they think their personal oppression is, as a group they're obviously the material beneficiaries of the colonial exploitation their society has imposed upon ours . . . they come and they look at the deformity of our societies produced by colonization, and then they criticize the deformity. They tell us we have to move "beyond" our culture in order to be "liberated" like them. It's just amazing. . . . They virtually demand that we give up our own traditions in favor of what they imagine their own to be, just like the missionaries and the government and all the rest of the colonizers. It was being forced *away* from our own traditions that deformed us — that made the men sexists and things like that — in the first place. What we need to be is *more*, not less Indian. But every time we try to explain this to our self-proclaimed "white sisters," we either get told we're missing the point — we're just dumb Indians, after all — or we're accused of "self-hatred" as women. A few experiences with this sort of arrogance and you start to get the idea maybe all this feminism business is just another extension of the same old racist, colonialist mentality.[138]

Janet McCloud explains that "many Anglo women try, I expect in all sincerity, to tell us that our most pressing problem is male supremacy. To this, I have to say, with all due respect, *bullshit.* Our problems are what they've been for the past several hundred years: white supremacism and colonialism. And that's a supremacism and a colonialism of which white feminists are still very much a part."[139] Pam Colorado, an Oneida scholar working in Canada, observes:

> It seems to me the feminist agenda is basically one of rearranging social relations within the society which is occupying our land and utilizing our resources for its own benefit. Nothing I've encountered in feminist theory addresses the fact of our colonization, or the wrongness of white women's stake in it. To the contrary, there seems to be a presumption among feminist writers that the colonization of Native America will, even *should,* continue permanently. At least there's no indication any feminist theorist has actively advocated pulling out of Indian Country, should a "transformation of social relations" actually occur. Instead, feminists appear to share a presumption in common with the patriarches they oppose, that they have some sort of inalienable right to simply go on occupying our land and exploiting our resources for as long as they like. Hence, I can only conclude that, like marxism, which arrives at the same outcome through class rather than gender theory, feminism is essentially a Euro-supremacist ideology and is therefore quite imperialist in its implications.[140]

Evidence of the colonialist content of much Euro-American feminist practice has been advanced, not just at the material level, but in terms of cultural imperialism. Andrea Smith, a Makah writing in *Indigenous Woman,* has denounced feminists of the New Age persuasion for "ripping off" native ceremonies for their own purposes, putting them on notice that "as long as they take part in Indian spiritual abuse, either by being consumers of it, or by refusing to take a stand on [the matter], Indian women will consider white 'feminists' to be nothing more than agents in the genocide of [native] people."[141] Another increasingly volatile issue in this connection has been the appropriation and distortion of indigenous traditions concerning homosexuality by both "radical" or lesbian feminists and gay male activists.[142] Particularly offensive have been non-Indian efforts to convert the indigenous custom of treating homosexuals (often termed *berdache* by anthropologists) as persons endowed with special spiritual powers into a polemic for mass organizing within the dominant society.[143]

Although the special and deeply revered status accorded homosexuals by native societies derived precisely from their being relatively rare, the desire of non-Indian gays and lesbians to legitimate their preferences within the context of their own much more repressive society, and to do so in ways that reinforce an imagined superiority of these preferences, has led many of them to insist upon the reality of a traditional Native North America in which nearly *everyone* was homosexual. Unfortunately, Paula Gunn Allen, in pandering to the needs and tastes of non-Indian gay and lesbian organizers, has done much to reinforce their willful misimpressions of indigenous tradition: "[L]esbianism and homosexuality were probably commonplace. Indeed, same-sex relationships may have been the norm for primary pair-bonding. There were clans and bands or villages, but the primary personal unit tended to include members of one's own sex rather than members of the opposite sex."[144]

Although Gunn Allen hurriedly goes on to note that it "is questionable whether these practices would be recognized as lesbian by the politically radical lesbian community of today,"[145] her sweeping exaggeration has been seized upon by those seeking to deploy their own version of "noble savage" mythology for political purposes. To paraphrase an Inuit lesbian poet who wishes not to be further identified:

> I've always been very well accepted and supported within my community for who I am. But now comes this idea, brought in from the outside for reasons that really have nothing to do with us, that Indianness and homosexuality are somehow fused, that you can't "really" be Indian unless you're gay or lesbian, or at least bisexual. The implication is that I'm assessed as being more traditional, and my heterosexual friends less traditional, on the basis of sexual preference. This is not an Indian idea. It's absurd, and it's deeply resented by all of us. But the danger is that it could eventually cause divisions among us Indians that never existed before, and right at the point when we're most in need of unity.

Or, as Chrystos, also a lesbian, has put it:

> This is just another myth imposed by white people for their own purposes, at our expense. And while I may consider it to be more pleasant, it's really no better than the myth of us being savage scalpers and torturers, stone age hunter-gatherers, and all the rest. We have *all* come to the point where we must pull ourselves together in our common humanity if we are to survive. That can only happen on the basis of *truth,* not the projection of still another white fantasy.[146]

For their efforts at lending a native voice to discussions of homosexuality in indigenous tradition, and leading things in a positive contemporary direction, both women have often been called "homophobic." Nonlesbian Indian women who have attempted to make the same points have often been labeled "heterosexist," a designation that prompted at least one of them to respond that "a very vocal part of the white women's movement seems to be afflicted with what you could call homosexism."[147] Janet McCloud has concluded that, under such circumstances, there is little, if anything, to be gained by Indian women making a direct linkup with feminism.[148]

Other, less "radical," native women have arrived at essentially the same conclusion. Laura Waterman Wittstock, a Seneca leader, went on record early with the message that "tribalism, not feminism, is the correct route" for native women to follow.[149] Similarly, Blackfeet traditionalist Beverly Hungry Wolf, in her autobiography, is quite clear that only adherence to "the ways of [her] grandmothers" allowed her to remain unconfused in her cultural-sexual identity throughout her life.[150] They are joined by younger women like the Anishinabe-Choctaw scholar Clara Sue Kidwell, who has explored the problems of communicating a coherent indigenous female cultural-sexual identity in the colonial context and determined that recovery of traditional forms is more than ever called for.[151] Even some Euro-American feminist researchers who have applied analysis rather than "sisterhood is powerful" sloganeering to their understanding of Native North America concede that the "social and economic positions of Indian women make them more like Indian men" than like white women (conversely, of course, this makes Euro-American women more like white men than like Indian women, a factor left conspicuously unremarked).[152]

The Road Ahead

Interestingly, women of other nonwhite sectors of the North American population have shared many native women's criticisms of the Euro-American feminist phenomenon. African-American women in particular have been outspoken in this regard. As Gloria Joseph argues:

> The White women's movement has had its own explicit forms of racism in the way it has given high priority to certain aspects of struggles and neglected others...because of the inherently racist assumptions and perspectives brought to bear in the first articulations by the White women's movement....The Black movement scorns feminism partially on the basis of misinformation, and partially due to a valid perception of the White middle class nature of the movement. An additional reason is due to the myopic ways that White feminists have generalized their sexual-political analysis and have confirmed their racism in the forms their feminism has assumed.[153]

The "self-righteous indignation" and defensiveness Joseph discerns on the part of most Euro-American feminists when confronted with such critiques are elsewhere explained by bell hooks as a response resting in the vested interest of those who feel it:

> [F]eminist emphasis on "common oppression" in the United States was less a strategy for politicization than an appropriation by conservative and liberal women of a radical political vocabulary that masked the extent to which they shaped the movement so that it addressed and promoted their class interests....White women who dominate feminist discourse, who for the most part make and articulate feminist theory, have little or no understanding of white supremacy as a racial politic, of the psychological impact of class, of their [own] political status within a racist, sexist, capitalist state.[154]

"I was struck," hooks says in her first book, *Ain't I a Woman,* "by the fact that the ideology of feminism, with its emphasis on transforming and changing the social structure of the U.S., in no way resembled the reality of American feminism. Largely because [white] feminists themselves, as they attempted to take feminism beyond the realm of radical rhetoric into the sphere of American life, revealed that they remained imprisoned in the very structures they hoped to change. Consequently, the sisterhood we all talked about has not become a reality."[155] It is time to "talk back" to white feminists, hooks argues, "spoiling their celebration, their 'sisterhood,' their 'togetherness.' "[156] This must be done because in adhering to feminism in its present form,

> we learn to look to those empowered by the very systems of domination that wound and hurt us for some understanding of who we are that will be liberating and we never find that. It is necessary for [women of color] to do the work ourselves if we want to know more about our experience, if we want to see that experience from perspectives not shaped by domination.[157]

Asian-American women, Chicanas, and Latinas have agreed in substantial part with such assessments.[158] Women of color in general tend not to favor the notion of a "politics" that would divide and weaken their communities by defining men as the enemy. It is not for nothing that no community of color in North America has ever produced a counterpart to white feminism's SCUM (Society for Cutting Up Men).

Women's liberation, in the view of most "minority" women in the United States and Canada, cannot occur in any context other than the wider liberation — from Euro-American colonial domination — of the peoples of which women of color are a part. Our sense of priorities is therefore radically — and irrevocably — different from those espoused by the "mainstream" women's movement.

Within this alienation from feminism lies the potential for the sorts of alliances that may in the end prove most truly beneficial to American Indian people. By forging links to organizations composed of other women of color, based not merely in gender oppression but in racial and cultural oppression, native women can prove instrumental in creating an alternative movement of women in North America, one that is mutually respectful of the rights, needs, cultural particularities, and historical divergences of each sector of its membership and that is therefore free of the adherence to white supremacist hegemony previously marring feminist thinking and practice. Any such movement of women — including those Euro-American women who see its thrust as corresponding to their own values and interests as human beings — cannot help but be of crucial importance within the liberation struggles waged by peoples of color to dismantle the apparatus of Eurocentric power in every area of the continent. The greater the extent to which these struggles succeed, the closer the core agenda of Native North America — recovery of land and resources, reassertion of self-determining forms of government, and reconstitution of traditional social relations within our nations — comes to realization.

NOTES

1. For further information on Marie Lego and the context of her struggle, see M. Annette Jaimes, "The Pit River Indian Land Claims Dispute in Northern California," *Journal of Ethnic Studies* 4, no. 4 (winter 1987).

2. Quoted in Jane B. Katz, *I Am the Fire of Time: The Voices of Native American Women* (New York: E. P. Dutton, 1977), 146.

3. Quoted in ibid., 147. Bennett was eventually acquitted after being shot, while seven-months pregnant, and wounded by white "vigilantes."

4. Ibid.

5. Quoted in ibid., 141.

6. The best account of the roles of Gladys Bissonette and Ellen Moves Camp during the siege may be found in *Voices from Wounded Knee, 1973* (Mohawk Nation via Rooseveltown, N.Y.: Akwesasne Notes, 1974).

7. See Ward Churchill and Jim Vander Wall, *The COINTELPRO Papers: Documents on the FBI's Secret Wars against Dissent in the United States* (Boston: South End Press, 1990), 231–302. Also see Peter Matthiessen, *In the Spirit of Crazy Horse,* 2d ed. (New York: Viking, 1991).

8. See Jerry Kammer, *The Second Long Walk: The Navajo-Hopi Land Dispute* (Albuquerque: University of New Mexico Press, 1980), 1–2, 209.

9. For further information on Big Mountain, see Anita Parlow, *Cry, Sacred Land: Big Mountain, USA* (Washington, D.C.: Christic Institute, 1988).

10. Quoted in Katz, *I Am the Fire,* 151. For further background on Ada Deer, see her autobiography, Ada Deer with R. E. Simon Jr., *Speaking Out* (Chicago: Children's Press, 1970).

11. On the murders of Pedro and Jeanette Bissonette, see Ward Churchill and Jim Vander Wall, *Agents of Repression: The FBI's Secret Wars against the Black Panther Party and the American Indian Movement* (Boston: South End Press, 1988), 187, 200–203.

12. Concerning the murders of Tina Manning Trudell, her three children (Ricarda Star, age five; Sunshine Karma, three; and Eli Changing Sun, one), and her mother, Leah Hicks Manning, see ibid., 361–64. On Aquash, see Johanna Brand, *The Life and Death of Anna Mae Aquash* (Toronto: James Lorimar, 1978).

13. Shirley Hill Witt, "The Brave-Hearted Women: The Struggle at Wounded Knee," *Akwesasne Notes* 8, no. 2 (1976): 16.

14. Quoted in Katz, *I Am the Fire,* 145–46.

15. Quoted in Kammer, *Second Long Walk,* 18.

16. From a talk delivered during International Women's Week, the University of Colorado at Boulder, April 1984 (tape on file).

17. Such sentiments are hardly unique to the United States. For articulations by Canadian Indian women, see Janet Silman, *Enough Is Enough: Aboriginal Women Speak Out* (Toronto: Women's Press, 1987).

18. From a talk delivered during International Women's Week, the University of Colorado at Boulder, April 1985 (tape on file).

19. From a talk delivered during International Women's Week, University of Colorado at Boulder, April 1984 (tape on file).

20. Eleanor Burke Leacock, *Myths of Male Dominance: Collected Articles* (New York: Monthly Review Press, 1981).

21. Paul Valentine, "Dances with Myths," *Washington Post,* reprinted in the *Boulder Daily Camera,* April 7, 1991.

22. Valentine also informs us that these "nomadic hunters and gatherers moved from spot to spot, strewing refuse in their wake." (What *sort* of "refuse"? Plastic? Aluminum cans? Polyvinyl chlorides?) He then runs down the usual litany of imagined native defects: "[Indians] were totalitarian, warlike and extremely brutal. Some practiced slavery, torture, human sacrifice and cannibalism, and imposed rigid social dictatorships." That there is not one shred of solid evidence supporting any of this is no bother. Valentine and his ilk simply condemn anyone bothering with the facts as a "politically correct . . . revisionist." Left unexplained is why anyone might deliberately seek to be politically *in*correct or why blatant inaccuracies or lies — such as those in which they trade — shouldn't be revised and corrected.

23. Barbara Ehrenreich, "The Warrior Culture," *Time,* October 15, 1990. It should be noted that the practice of scalping, derived from the taking of heads, was introduced to North America by the British, who had earlier developed the technique during the conquest and colonization of Ireland (see Nicholas P. Canny, "The Ideology of English Colonization: From Ireland to America," *William and Mary Quarterly,* 3d ser., no. 30 [1973]: 575–98). For a more detailed response, see Ward Churchill's letter on the article (frozen out of *Time*) in *Z* (magazine), November 1990.

24. D'Arcy McNickle, *The Surrounded,* 2d ed. (Albuquerque: University of New Mexico Press, 1978). For a description of the sort of "war" practiced by the other societies, see Tom Holmes's essay in *The State of Native America: Genocide, Colonization, and Resistance,* ed. M. Annette Jaimes (Boston: South End Press, 1992).

25. Paula Gunn Allen, *The Sacred Hoop: Recovering the Feminine in American Indian Traditions* (Boston: Beacon Press, 1986), 266.

26. Indication of the relatively higher valuation placed upon women may be found in the fact that among the Iroquois, Susquehannahs, and Abenakis ("Hurons"), for example, the penalty for killing a woman was double that for killing a man (see Caroline Thomas Foreman, *American Indian Women Chiefs* [Muskogee, Okla.: Hoffman, 1954], 9). On the diversity of native women's social functions and activities, see Valerie Shirer Mathes, "A New Look at the Role of Women in Indian Societies," *American Indian Quarterly* 2, no. 2 (1975): 131–39.

27. See Foreman, *American Indian Women Chiefs,* 85–87. See also E. Merton Coulter, "Mary Musgrove, Queen of the Creeks: A Chapter of the Early Georgia Troubles," *Georgia Historical Quarterly* 11, no. 1 (1927): 1–30, and John Pitts Corry, "Some New Light on the Bosworth Claims," *Georgia Historical Quarterly* 25 (1941): 195–224. The novel in question is Dee Brown, *Creek Mary's Blood* (New York: Simon and Schuster, 1981).

28. Discussion with Madonna Thunderhawk (Hunkpapa Lakota), April 1985; discussion with Robert Grey Eagle (Oglala Lakota), July 1991.

29. Foreman, *American Indian Women Chiefs,* 85.

30. See Oscar Lewis, "Manly-Hearted Women among the Northern Piegan," *American Anthropologist* 43 (1941): 173–87.

31. On Buffalo Calf Road, see Rosemary Agonito and Joseph Agonito, "Resurrecting History's Forgotten Women: A Case Study from the Cheyenne Indians," *Frontiers: A Journal of Women's Studies* 6 (fall 1981): 8–9, and Mari Sandoz, *Cheyenne Autumn* (New York: Avon Books, 1964). Information

on four other nineteenth-century warrior women may be found in John C. Ewers, "Deadlier Than the Male," *American Heritage* 16 (1965): 10–13. More generally, see Bea Medicine, " 'Warrior Women': Sex Role Alternatives for Plains Indian Women," in Patricia Albers and Beatrice Medicine, eds., *The Hidden Half: Studies of Plains Indian Women* (Lanham, Md.: University Press of America, 1983), 267–80.

32. Robin Morgan's *The Demon Lover: On the Sexuality of Terrorism* (New York: W. W. Norton, 1989), in which any female engaged in physical combat is found to be the mere pawn of some man (or at least "male energy"), is the most extraordinarily insulting and demeaning treatise possible, not only for Native American women but for African-Americans like Assata Shakur, Latinas like Lolita Labrón and Alejandrina Torres, Europeans like Ingrid Barabass and Monica Helbing, Euro-Americans like Susan Rosenberg and Linda Evans, and perhaps a quarter of the female populations of Africa, Asia, and Palestine.

33. Gunn Allen, *Sacred Hoop,* 36–37. She is drawing on Lt. Henry Timberlake, *Lieutenant Henry Timberlake's Memoirs* (Marietta, Ga., 1948), 94.

34. Concerning the ongoing nature of the longhouse government and women's role in it, see "A Woman's Ways: An Interview with Judy Swamp," *Parabola* 5, no. 4 (1980): 52–61. See also Katsi Cook, "The Women's Dance: Reclaiming Our Powers on the Women's Side of Life," *Native Self-Sufficiency* 6 (1981): 17–19.

35. See Robert Steven Grumet, "Sunksquaws, Shamans, and Tradeswomen: Middle-Atlantic Coastal Algonkian Women during the 17th and 18th Centuries," in Mona Etienne and Eleanor Burke Leacock, eds., *Women and Colonization: Anthropological Perspectives* (New York: Praeger, New York, 1980).

36. Ibid., 51–52.

37. See Anthony F. C. Wallace, "Women, Land, and Society: Three Aspects of Aboriginal Delaware Life," *Pennsylvania Archaeologist* 17 (1947): 1–35, and C. S. Weslager, "The Delaware Indians as Women," *Journal of the Washington Academy of Science* 37 (September 15, 1947): 298–304.

38. Gunn Allen, *Sacred Hoop,* 35. She relies heavily on Grumet, "Sunksquaws."

39. For further information on these customs, see Carolyn Niethammer, *Daughters of the Earth: The Lives and Legends of Native American Women* (New York: Macmillan, 1977). See also Clara Sue Kidwell, "The Power of Women in Three American Indian Societies," *Journal of Ethnic Studies* 6, No. 3 (1979): 113–21. For an overview of the extent to which matrilineal/matrilocal societies predominated in precontact Native North America, see Robert H. Lowie, "The Matrilineal Complex," *University of California Publications in Archaeology and Ethnology* 16 (1919–20): 29–45.

40. John Upton Terrell, and Donna M. Terrell, *Indian Women of the Western Morning: Their Life in Early America* (New York: Anchor Books, 1974), 24.

41. See Judith K. Brown, "Economic Organization and the Position of Women among the Iroquois," *Ethnohistory* 17, nos. 3–4 (summer–fall 1970): 151–67. See also Bruce G. Trigger, "Iroquoian Matriliny," *Pennsylvania Archaeologist* 48 (1978): 55–65.

42. See Marla N. Powers, *Oglala Women: Myth, Ritual, and Reality* (Chicago: University of Chicago Press, 1986), 89.

43. Mary Oshana, "Native American Women in Westerns: Reality and Myth," *Frontiers: A Journal of Women's Studies* 6 (fall 1981): 46.

44. See Helen Hornbeck Tanner, "Coocoochee: Mohawk Medicine Woman," *American Indian Culture and Research Journal* 3, no. 3 (1979): 23–42; David Jones, *Sanapia: A Comanche Medicine Woman* (New York: Holt, Rinehart and Winston, 1968); and Frank Linderman, *Pretty Shield: Medicine Woman of the Crows* (1932; reprint, New York: John Day, 1974).

45. Terrell and Terrell, *Indian Women,* 25.

46. See Ruth Landes, *The Ojibwa Religion and the Midewiwin* (Madison: University of Wisconsin Press, 1968); Susan Kent, "Hogans, Sacred Circles and Symbols: The Navajo Use of Space," in David Brugge and Charlotte J. Frisbie, eds., *Essays in Honor of Leland Wyman* (Santa Fé: Museum of New Mexico Press, 1982); Robert G. Lake, "Chilula Religion and Ideology: A Discussion of Native American Humanistic Concepts and Processes," *Humbolt Journal of Social Relations* 7, no. 2 (1980): 113–34; and Alice Kehoe, "Old Woman Had Great Power," *Western Canadian Journal of Anthropology* 6, no. 3 (1976): 68–76. See also Ann Thrift Nelson, "Native American Women's Ritual Soldalities in Native North America," *Western Canadian Journal of Anthropology* 6, no. 3 (1976): 29–67.

47. For a thorough analysis of the metatheological precepts embodied in indigenous American spirituality, see Vine Deloria Jr., *God Is Red* (New York: Grossett and Dunlap, 1973; reprint, New York: Dell Books, 1983). Further elaboration is provided in Deloria's *Metaphysics of Modern Existence* (New York: Harper and Row, 1979).

48. Contrary to the contentions of University of Colorado professor of religious studies Sam Gill, the idea of Mother Earth — which is quite universal among Native North Americans — was *not* imported from Europe (Sam D. Gill, *Mother Earth: An American Story* [Chicago: University of Chicago Press, 1987]). For detailed refutation, see the special section of *Bloomsbury Review* 8, no. 5 (September–October 1988), edited by M. Annette Jaimes and devoted to critique of Gill's thesis and methods.

49. Quoted in Katz, *I Am the Fire*, 126. For further background on the status of Diné women, see Irene Stewart, *A Voice in Her Tribe: A Navajo Woman's Own Story* (Socorro, N.M.: Ballena Press, 1980), and Ruth Roessel, *Women in Navajo Society* (Rough Rock, Ariz.: Navajo Resource Center, 1981).

50. Quoted in Katz, *I Am the Fire,* 123.

51. From a talk delivered during International Women's Week, University of Colorado at Boulder, April 1985 (tape on file).

52. Priscilla K. Buffalohead, "Farmers, Warriors, Traders: A Fresh Look at Ojibway Women," *Minnesota History* 48 (summer 1983): 236.

53. Rubin Gold Thwaites, ed., *The Jesuit Relations and Allied Documents*, 71 vols. (Cleveland: Burrow Brothers, 1906), 5:179.

54. Leacock, *Myths of Male Dominance,* 35.

55. For a broader examination of the impact of the fur trade upon the internal structures of indigenous societies, see Sylvia Van Kirk, ed., *Many Tender Ties: Women in Fur-Trade Society, 1670– 1870* (Norman: University of Oklahoma Press, 1980).

56. Eleanor Burke Leacock, "Montagnais Women and the Jesuit Program for Colonization," in ibid., 43–62.

57. Gunn Allen, *Sacred Hoop,* 40.

58. The expression "petticoat government" comes from the British colonialist John Adair in regard to the Cherokee Nation. See John P. Brown, *Old Frontiers* (Madison: State Historical Society of Wisconsin, 1938), 20.

59. Gunn Allen, *Sacred Hoop,* 33. She relies upon William Brandon, *The Last Americans: The Indian in American Culture* (New York: McGraw-Hill, 1974), 214.

60. Gunn Allen, *Sacred Hoop,* 37.

61. Ibid. It should be noted that this calculated and vicious colonialist use of mixed-bloods as a means to undercut traditional societies, a tactic that is ongoing in the present day, is a primary cause of the sort of racially oriented infighting among Indians that continues to confuse the questions of Indian identity.

62. Ibid.

63. For a solid sample of the avaricious sentiments involved in this federal policy, see U.S. Congress, *Speeches on the Passage of the Bill for Removal of the Indians, Delivered in the Congress of the United States, April and May, 1830* (Boston: Perkins and Marvin, 1830; Millwood, N.Y.: Kraus Reprint Co., 1973).

64. Gunn Allen, *Sacred Hoop,* 37–38. It should be noted that the three men named did not share the same position on Cherokee removal. John Ross, "despite his large degree of white blood," was an ardent Cherokee patriot and fought mightily against U.S. policy (see Rachel E. Eaton, *John Ross and the Cherokee People* [Muskogee, Okla.: Cherokee National Museum, 1921]). Boudinot and Major Ridge (or "The Ridge") were devout assimilationists who worked — for a fee — to further U.S. interests by engineering an appearance of acceptance of removal among their own people (see Thurman Wilkins, *Cherokee Tragedy: The Ridge Family and the Decimation of a People* [Norman: University of Oklahoma Press, 1986]). On Nancy Ward, see Norma Tucker, "Nancy Ward: Gighau of the Cherokees," *Georgia Historical Quarterly* 53 (June 1969): 192–200.

65. On the forced relocation, see Caleb Pirtle III, *The Trail of Broken Promises: Removal of the Five Civilized Tribes to Oklahoma* (Austin, Tex.: Eakin Press, 1987).

66. Cherokee demographer Russell Thornton estimates that about ten thousand Cherokees — approximately half the nation's population — perished as a result of the Trail of Tears. See Russell Thornton, *The Cherokees: A Population History* (Lincoln: University of Nebraska Press, 1990), 73–77.

67. See Emmet McDonald Starr, *Starr's History of the Cherokee Indians* (1922; reprint, Fayetteville, Ark.: Indian Heritage Association, 1967), 113.

68. Morris L. Wardell, *A Political History of the Cherokee Nation, 1838–1907* (1938; reprint, Norman: University of Oklahoma Press, 1977), 17.

69. See James W. Parins, *John Rollin Ridge: His Life and Works* (Lincoln: University of Nebraska Press, 1991).

70. See Kenny A. Franks, *Stand Watie and the Agony of the Cherokee Nation* (Memphis: Memphis State University Press, 1979).

71. I have been through hundreds of the relevant documents — all of them engineered in Washington, D.C. — without ever coming across a single reference to federal negotiators dealing with a native woman responsibly. Instead, they appear to have been quite uniformly barred from meetings and other proceedings, these being "men's work" in the Euro-American view. Early reservation records are replete with the same attitude.

72. Bea Medicine, "The Interaction of Culture and Sex Roles in Schools," in U.S. Department of Education, Office of Educational Research and Development, National Institute of Education, *Conference on Educational and Occupational Needs of American Indian Women, October 1976* (Washington, D.C.: U.S. Government Printing Office, 1980), 149.

73. For an excellent firsthand recounting of the process, see Lilah Denton Lindsey, "Memories of the Indian Territory Mission Field," *Chronicles of Oklahoma* 36 (summer 1958): 181–98.

74. The extent to which Indians were provided just enough "education" to disorient them in their traditional ways, and condition them to accept subordination to Euro-America, is revealed in the federal government's own data from the third quarter of the twentieth century. In an official study, it was shown that — despite a century of governmentally imposed "schooling" — Native Americans still exhibited the lowest level of educational attainment of any U.S. population group. See U.S. Department of Health, Education, and Welfare, *A Statistical Portrait of the American Indian* (Washington, D.C.: U.S. Government Printing Office, 1976).

75. The term "broker class" is from Rodolfo Acuña, *Occupied America: A History of Chicanos,* 3d ed. (New York: Harper and Row, 1988).

76. Quoted in Angie Debo, *A History of the Indians of the United States* (Norman: University of Oklahoma Press, 1970), 238.

77. Roxanne Dunbar Ortiz, "Land and Nationhood: The American Indian Struggle for Self-Determination and Survival," *Socialist Review* 63–64 (May–August 1982): 107.

78. A good survey of the extent of indigenous wealth may be found in Jack Weatherford, *Indian Givers: How the Indians of the Americas Transformed the World* (New York: Crown, 1989).

79. For a detailed examination of the surge in corporate activity in the West that accompanied termination and relocation in the 1950s and that has continued thereafter, see Peter Wiley and Robert Gottlieb, *Empires in the Sun: The Rise of the American West* (New York: G. P. Putnam's, 1982).

80. A useful reading on the effects of relocation upon native women is Wynne Hanson, "The Urban Indian Woman and Her Family," *Social Casework: The Journal of Contemporary Social Work* (October 1980): 476–83.

81. These data are from a table provided in Teresa L. Amott and Julie A. Matthaei, *Race, Gender, and Work: A Multicultural Economic History of Women in the United States* (Boston: South End Press, 1991), 48.

82. U.S. Bureau of the Census, *1970 Census of the Population,* vol. 1, *Characteristics of the Population, Part I, United States Summary* (Washington, D.C.: U.S. Government Printing Office, 1971), sec. 1, table 90, p. 390.

83. U.S. Department of Education, *Conference on Educational and Occupational Needs,* 304.

84. Amott and Matthaei, *Race, Gender, and Work,* 58–59.

85. Ibid., 57, 59–60.

86. See *Statistical Portrait of the American Indian.* A good reading to accompany these data is LaDonna Hart, "Enlarging the American Dream: American Indian Women," *American Education* 13, no. 4 (1977).

87. Silman, *Enough Is Enough,* 11.

88. Research Branch, P. R. E., Indian and Inuit Affairs Program, *A Demographic Profile of Registered Indian Women* (Ottawa, Canada, October 1979), 31.

89. U.S. Department of Health and Human Services, *Chart Series Book* (Washington, D.C.: Public Health Service, 1988 [HE20.9409.988]). For perspectives on how these data apply to native women specifically, see Rosemary Wood, "Health Problems Facing American Indian Women," in U.S. Department of Education, *Conference on Educational and Occupational Needs.*

90. On the Pine Ridge Reservation in South Dakota, for example, a stretch of road — about one mile long — between the off-reservation hamlet of White Clay (Nebraska) and the village of Pine Ridge is marked by a billboard displaying a skull wearing a war bonnet and captioned with a warning not to

drink and drive. Over the past twenty years, more than a hundred Indians have died on this tiny strip of asphalt after having gotten drunk in White Clay and then attempted to drive home.

91. See Charon Asetoyer, "Fetal Alcohol Syndrome — 'Chemical Genocide,' " in *Indigenous Women on the Move*, IWGIA Document 66 (Copenhagen: International Work Group on Indigenous Affairs, 1990), 87–92.

92. The worst case seems to have occurred on the Wind River Reservation in Wyoming, where an estimated fourteen Shoshone and Arapaho youths between fourteen and eighteen years of age took their own lives in 1985.

93. Amott and Matthaei, *Race, Gender, and Work*, 59.

94. For an analysis of at least some of the causative factors in one major indigenous society, see Bea Medicine, "The Dakota Family and the Stresses Thereon," *Pine Ridge Research Bulletin* 9 (1969): 1–20.

95. For a survey on current conditions in both the United States and Canada, see Winona LaDuke, "Domestic Violence in a Native Community: The Ontario Native Women's Association Report and Response," *Indigenous Woman* 1, no. 1 (spring 1991): 38–41. For the most lucid articulation of why the colonized tend to turn such rage upon one another rather than upon the colonizers who generate it, see Frantz Fanon, *The Wretched of the Earth* (New York: Grove Press, 1966).

96. A celebrated case is that of Rita Silk Nauni, a Lakota woman who killed her abusive husband, only to be arrested and brutalized by police in Oklahoma, tried, convicted of murder, and sentenced to life imprisonment (see Pelican Lee and Jane Wing, "Rita Silk Nauni vs. the State," *Off Our Backs* 11 (February 1981).

97. Gunn Allen, *Sacred Hoop*, 191. She is quoting from Phyllis Old Dog Cross, "Sexual Abuse, a New Threat to Native American Women: An Overview," *Listening Post: A Periodical of the Mental Health Programs of the Indian Health Services* 6, no. 2 (April 1982): 18.

98. Gunn Allen, *Sacred Hoop*, 192.

99. Ibid., 202.

100. See Tillie Blackbear Walker, "American Indian Children: Foster Care and Adoptions," in U.S. Department of Education, *Conference on the Educational and Occupational Needs*, 185–210.

101. Gail Marks-Jarvis, "The Fate of the Indian," *National Catholic Reporter* (May 27, 1977): 4. Another means undertaken to undermine women's familial role may be found in the 1978 Supreme Court ruling *Santa Clara Pueblo v. Martinez* (436 U.S. 49), in which it was concluded that an all-male tribal council had the prerogative of excluding the children of a woman who married a nontribal member from membership in the tribe while including the children of men who married nontribal members. While the action of the Santa Clara tribal council and the Supreme Court's ruling were consistent with a supposedly traditional Santa Clara system of patrilineage, both groups left unaddressed the fact that the father of the children in question is a member of the matrilineal society. Hence, the children were left with no recognition or rights as Indians at all. Further, there are strong indications that Santa Clara is a traditionally matrilineal rather than patrilineal culture (see W. W. Hill, *An Ethnography of the Santa Clara Pueblo* [Albuquerque: University of New Mexico Press, 1982]). Regardless of the correct interpretation of Santa Clara tradition, the outcome of this case obviously holds broad potential ramifications for all of Indian Country.

102. See Brint Dillingham, "Indian Women and IHS Sterilization Practices," *American Indian Journal* 3, no. 1 (January 1977): 27–28. During this same and earlier periods, similar involuntary sterilization programs were being implemented on other women of color, as with Chicanas of the Los Angeles area (see Acuña, *Occupied America*, 395). It is estimated that by 1966, one-third of the women of child-bearing age on the U.S. controlled island of Puerto Rico had been sterilized without their informed consent (see Margarita Ostalaza, *Política sexual y socialización política de la mujer Puertorriqueña: La consolidación del bloque histórico colonial de Puerto Rico* [Río Piedras, P.R.: Ediciones Huracán, 1989]). On the mainland, the Puerto Rican women's organization MULANEH discovered that, by 1979, 44 percent of Puertorriqueñas in New Haven, Connecticut, had been sterilized. In Hartford, Connecticut, the figure stood at 51 percent (see "Committee for Abortion Rights and against Sterilization Abuse," in *Women under Attack: Abortion, Sterilization Abuse, and Reproductive Freedom* [New York: CASARA, 1979).

103. An extract of the WARN study may be found in WARN, *Native American Women* (New York: International Indian Treaty Council, 1975). A summary is also contained in WARN, *Women of All Red Nations* (Porcupine, S.D.: We Will Remember Group, 1978).

104. Cited in Janet Larson, "And Then There Were None: IHS Sterilization Practice," *Christian Century* 94 (January 26, 1976). See also Bill Wagner, "Lo, the Poor and Sterilized Indian," *America* 136 (January 29, 1977).

105. Gunn Allen, *Sacred Hoop*, 191, 193.

106. For the most comprehensive biography, see Gae Whitney Canfield, *Sarah Winnemucca of the Northern Paiutes* (Norman: University of Oklahoma Press, 1983).

107. Sarah Winnemucca Hopkins, *Life among the Piutes: Their Wrongs and Claims* (1883; reprint, Bishop, Calif.: Chalfant Press, 1969).

108. See Raymond Wilson, *Ohiyesa: Charles Eastman, Santee Sioux* (Urbana: University of Illinois Press, 1983).

109. See particularly Gertrude (Zitkala-sa) Bonnin, "Why I Am a Pagan," *Atlantic Monthly* 90 (1902): 801–3. Bonnin's major works were *Old Indian Legends* (1901; reprint, Lincoln: University of Nebraska Press, 1985) and *American Indian Stories* (1921; reprint, Lincoln: University of Nebraska Press, 1979). For biographical and critical analysis, see Mary Stout, "Zitkala-sa: The Literature of Politics," in Bo Schöler, ed., *Coyote Was Here: Essays on Contemporary Native American Literary and Political Mobilization* (Aarhus, Denmark: University of Aarhus, 1984), 70–78.

110. Ella Cara Deloria's most important book in terms of political content was probably *Speaking of Indians* (1944; reprint, Vermillion, S.D.: Dakota Press, 1979). For biographical and critical analysis, see Bea Medicine, "Ella C. Deloria: The Emic Voice," *Melus* 7, no. 4 (winter 1980): 23–30.

111. Interesting insights into the position of women within the American Indian literary movement of the 1970s and 1980s may be found in Brian Swann and Arnold Krupat, eds., *Recovering the World: Essays on Native American Literature* (Berkeley: University of California Press, 1987). For a broad sample of the writing involved, see Paula Gunn Allen, *Spider Woman's Granddaughters: Traditional Tales and Contemporary Writing by American Indian Women* (Boston: Beacon Press, 1989).

112. See, for example, Louise Erdrich, *Love Medicine* (New York: Holt, Rinehart, and Winston, 1984), and idem, *Tracks* (New York: Holt, Rinehart, and Winston, 1989); Chrystos, *Not Vanishing* (Vancouver, B.C.: Press Gang Publishers, 1988), and idem, *Dream On* (Vancouver, B.C.: Press Gang Publishers, 1991).

113. Bobbi Lee, *Bobbi Lee: Indian Rebel* (Richmond, B.C., Canada: LSM Information Center, 1975), 89.

114. Ibid., 91–92.

115. Conversation with Dennis J. Banks, March 1988 (notes on file).

116. Probably the best account to date of rank-and-file female participation in AIM may be found in Mary Crow Dog, with Richard Erdoes, *Lakota Woman* (New York: Grove, Weidenfeld, 1990).

117. See *Voices from Wounded Knee*.

118. On AIM's educational efforts, see Susan Braudy, "We Will Remember Survival School: The Women and Children of the American Indian Movement," *Ms.* 5 (July 1976): 94–120.

119. On the gender disparity in targeting, and the "leadership trials" themselves, see Churchill and Vander Wall, *Agents of Repression*. The maximal jeopardy was faced by Russell Means, who walked out of Wounded Knee charged with forty-seven felonies and three misdemeanors.

120. On the three women mentioned, see ibid. Traditional Oglala women who were AIM supporters were also sometimes targeted for politically motivated prosecution. See Paula Giese, "Free Sarah Bad Heart Bull," *North Country Anvil* 13 (October–November 1974): 64–71.

121. The women and children were Priscilla White Plume (July 14, 1973), Lorinda Red Paint (February 27, 1974), Roxeine Roark (April 19, 1974), Delphine Crow Dog (November 9, 1974), Elaine Wagner (November 30, 1974), Yvette Lorraine Lone Hill (December 28, 1974), Edith Eagle Hawk and her two children (March 21, 1975), Jeanette Bissonette (March 27, 1975), Hilda R. Good Buffalo (April 4, 1975), Jancita Eagle Deer (April 4, 1975), Leah Spotted Eagle (June 15, 1975), Olivia Binias (October 26, 1975), Janice Black Bear (October 26, 1975), Michelle Tobacco (October 27, 1975), Lydia Cut Grass (January 5, 1976), Lena R. Slow Bear (February 6, 1976), Anna Mae Pictou Aquash (ca. February 14, 1976), Betty Jo Dubray (April 28, 1976), Julia Pretty Hips (May 9, 1976), Betty Means (July 3, 1976), and Sandra Wounded Foot (July 19, 1976). For a complete list of AIM casualties on Pine Ridge during this period, see Churchill and Vander Wall, *COINTELPRO Papers*, 393–94.

122. Quoted in Peter Matthiessen, *In the Spirit of Crazy Horse*, 2d ed. (New York: Viking Press, 1991), 417.

123. For additional information on this period, see Winona LaDuke, "In Honor of Women Warriors," *Off Our Backs* 11 (February 1981).

124. Janet McCloud, "Open Letter," *Oyate Wicaho* (January 1981).

125. Statement at Manderson, S.D., November 1978 (tape on file).

126. See Dagmar Thorpe, "Native Political Organizing in Nevada: A Woman's Perspective," *Native Self-Sufficiency* 6 (1981).

127. Gunn Allen, *Sacred Hoop*, 31. It should be noted that the federal government currently recognizes the formal existence of 482 "tribes," but not all have reservation land bases.

128. This is referred to as the "status question" in Canada. See Kathleen Jamieson, *Indian Women and the Law in Canada: Citizens Minus* (Ottawa: Advisory Council on the Status of Women/Indian Rights for Indian Women, 1978).

129. Ibid.

130. Silman, *Enough Is Enough,* 176.

131. Ibid. Aside from Sandra Lovelace Sappier, other members of the Action Group are Glenna Perley, Caroline Ennis, Lilly Harris, Ida Paul, Eva Saulis, Juanita Perley, Shirley Bear, Karen Perley, Mavis Goerers, Joyce Sappier, Bet-te Paul, and Cheryl Bear.

132. For a sample of Sharon Venne's work in this regard, see her "Treaty and Constitution in Canada: A View from Treaty Six," in Ward Churchill, ed., *Critical Issues in Native North America,* IWGIA document 62 (Copenhagen: International Work Group on Indigenous Affairs, 1989), 96–115.

133. On Norma Kassi, see Ismaellillo and Robin Wright, eds., *Native Peoples in Struggle: Cases from the Fourth Russell Tribunal and Other International Forums* (Bombay, N.Y.: Anthropology Resource Center and ERIN Publications, 1982).

134. See, for example, Rayna Green, "Diary of a Native American Feminist," *Ms.* 10 (July 1982). See also Shirley Hill Witt, "Native Women Today: Sexism and the Indian Woman," *Civil Rights Digest* 6 (spring 1974): 29–35, and Annie D. Wauneka, "The Dilemma for Indian Women," *Wassaja* 4 (September 1976).

135. OHOYO was established on the basis of a federal grant under the Women's Educational Equity Act (WEEA) in 1974. It was to create "an Indian brand of feminism," according to the director of WEEA, a non-Indian woman. There was always a serious tension between its "leadership," which was based in Washington, D.C., and was preoccupied with gender issues, and its grassroots membership, which sought to focus on matters such as land and treaty rights. The national office of OHOYO was strongly criticized by WARN in 1981 for "dividing the Indian community, and diverting attention away from the real struggles of Indian people." The organization was defunded and dissolved in 1985.

136. See Gunn Allen, "Who Is Your Mother? Red Roots of White Feminism," in *Sacred Hoop,* 209–21.

137. Ibid., 224.

138. Lorelei Means talk.

139. Janet McCloud talk.

140. Letter to Ward Churchill, October 1985 (copy provided to author).

141. Andrea Smith, "The New Age Movement and Native Spirituality," *Indigenous Woman* 1, no. 1 (spring 1991): 18–19.

142. One of the more glaring examples of this phenomenon within the gay-male community has been Walter Williams's book, *The Spirit and the Flesh: Sexual Diversity in American Indian Culture* (Boston: Beacon Press, 1986).

143. *Berdache* is an utterly inappropriate term by which to describe American Indian homosexuality insofar as it refers to the practice of certain sectors of the Arab male population of keeping slave boys for sexual purposes.

144. Gunn Allen, *Sacred Hoop,* 256.

145. Ibid.

146. Talk given during International Women's Week, University of Colorado at Boulder, April 1991 (tape on file).

147. Conversation with Vivian Locust (Oglala Lakota), June 1990 (notes on file).

148. Dan Bomberry, ed., "Sage Advice from a Long Time Activist: Janet McCloud," *Native Self-Sufficiency* 6 (1981).

149. See Laura Waterman Wittstock, "Native American Women in the Feminist Milieu," in John Maestas, ed., *Contemporary Native American Addresses* (Salt Lake City: Brigham Young University Press, 1976).

150. Beverly Hungry Wolf, *The Ways of My Grandmothers* (New York: William Morrow, 1980).

151. See Clara Sue Kidwell, "American Indian Women: Problems of Communicating a Cultural/Sexual Identity," *Creative Woman* 2, no. 3 (1979): 33–38.

152. See, for example, Kathleen Jamieson, "Sisters under the Skin: An Exploration of the Implications of Feminist Materialist Perspective Research," *Canadian Ethnic Studies* 13, no. 1 (1981): 130–43.

153. Gloria I. Joseph and Jill Lewis, *Common Differences: Conflicts in Black and White Feminist Perspectives* (Boston: South End Press, 1981), 4–6.

154. bell hooks, *Feminist Theory: From Margin to Center* (Boston: South End Press, 1984), 4–6.

155. bell hooks, *Ain't I a Woman: Black Women and Feminism* (Boston: South End Press, 1981), 190.

156. bell hooks, *Talking Back: Thinking Feminist, Thinking Black* (Boston: South End Press, 1989), 149.

157. Ibid., 150–51.

158. For a sample of these perspectives, see Cherríe Moraga and Gloria Anzaldúa, eds., *This Bridge Called My Back: Writings by Radical Women of Color* (New York: Kitchen Table Press, 1983).

Chapter 17
"On the Threshold of Woman's Era": Lynching, Empire, and Sexuality in Black Feminist Theory

Hazel V. Carby

> *If the fifteenth century discovered America to the Old World, the nineteenth is discovering woman to herself....*
>
> *Not the opportunity of discovering new worlds, but that of filling this old world with fairer and higher aims than the greed of gold and the lust of power, is hers. Through weary, wasting years men have destroyed, dashed in pieces, and overthrown, but to-day we stand on the threshold of woman's era, and woman's work is grandly constructive. In her hand are possibilities whose use or abuse must tell upon the political life of the nation, and send their influence for good or evil across the track of unborn ages.*
>
> Frances E. W. Harper, "Woman's Political Future"

> *The world of thought under the predominant man-influence, unmollified and unrestrained by its complementary force, would become like Daniel's fourth beast: "dreadful and terrible, and strong exceedingly;" "it had great iron teeth; it devoured and brake in pieces, and stamped the residue with the feet of it;" and the most independent of us find ourselves ready at times to fall down and worship this incarnation of power.*
>
> Anna Julia Cooper, *A Voice from the South*

My purpose in this essay is to describe and define the ways in which Afro-American women intellectuals, in the last decade of the nineteenth century, theorized about the possibilities and limits of patriarchal power through its manipulation of racialized and gendered social categories and practices. The essay is especially directed toward two academic constituencies: the practitioners of Afro-American cultural analysis and of feminist historiography and theory. The dialogue with each has its own peculiar form, characterized by its own specific history; yet both groups are addressed in an assertion of difference, of alterity, and in a voice characterized by an anger dangerously self-restrained. For it is not in the nature of Caliban to curse; rather, like Caliban, the black woman has learned from the behavior of her master and mistress that if accommodation results in a patronizing loosening of her bonds, liberation will be more painful.

On the one hand, Afro-American cultural analysis and criticism have traditionally characterized the turn of the century as the age of Booker T. Washington and W. E. B. Du Bois. Afro-American studies frame our response to that period within a conceptual apparatus limiting historical interpretation to theories of exceptional male intellectual genius as exemplified in the texts *Up from Slavery* and *The Souls of Black Folk.* I wish to reconsider the decade of the 1890s as the "woman's era" not merely in order to insert women into the gaps in our cultural history (to compete for intellectual dominance with men) but also in order to shift the object of interpretation from examples of individual intellectual genius to the collective production and interrelation of forms of knowledge among black women intellectuals. The intellectual discourse of black women during the 1890s includes a wide variety of cultural practices. This essay, however, will concentrate on the theoretical analyses of race, gender, and patriarchal power found in the essays of Anna Julia Cooper, the journalism of Ida B. Wells, and the first novel of Pauline Hopkins.

On the other hand, feminist theory and its academic practice, "women's studies," appear if not content with, then at least consistent in, their limited concern with a small minority of the women of the planet: those white, middle-class inhabitants of the metropolises. Although feminist scholarship has made the histories of these women visible, it has done so by reconstituting patriarchal power on another terrain rather than by promising a strategy for its abolition. This leaves us with the same complaint as our nineteenth-century black foremothers: feminist theory supports and reproduces a racist hierarchy. Feminist investigations of nineteenth-century women writers actively ignore nonwhite women; some of the most recent, exciting, and innovative thinking on sexuality relegates black women to a paragraph and secondary sources. Ellen DuBois and Linda Gordon, in their essay "Seeking Ecstasy on the Battlefield: Danger and Pleasure in Nineteenth-Century Feminist Sexual Thought," argue that "the black women's movement conducted a particularly militant campaign for respectability, often making black feminists spokespeople for prudery in their communities," without direct reference to one of these black feminists or their work. Their subject is "how feminists conceptualized different sexual dangers, as a means of organizing *resistance* to sexual oppression"; their motivation is to examine how these strategies changed and to learn what historical understanding can be brought to contemporary feminist campaigns.[1] I hope that a discussion of Cooper, Wells, and Hopkins in the context of the black women's movement will direct readers to move beyond the dismissal implied in the term "prudery" and to consider more seriously how black feminists conceptualized the possibilities for resisting sexual oppression.

The 1890s were a time of intense activity and productivity for Afro-American women intellectuals. The decade opened with the publication of Frances Harper's *Iola Leroy,* Cooper's *A Voice from the South,* and Wells's *Southern Horrors: Lynch Law in All Its Phases.*[2] In 1893, as part of the World's Columbian Exposition, the World's Congress of Representative Women met in Chicago. Among others, Hallie Q. Brown, Anna Julia Cooper, Fannie Jackson Coppin, Sarah J. Early, Frances Harper, Fannie Barrier Williams, and Frederick Douglass — six black women and one black man — addressed the gathering. Harper told her audience that she felt they were standing "on the threshold of woman's era"; in 1894, *Woman's Era* was the name chosen for the journal run by the Woman's Era Club in Boston.[3] The club movement grew rapidly among Afro-American women and culminated in the first Congress of Colored Women of the United States, which convened in Boston in 1895. In 1896, the National Federation of Colored Women and the National League of Colored Women united in Washington, D.C., to form the National Association of Colored Women

(NACW). For the first time, black women were nationally organized to confront the various modes of their oppression.[4]

The decade opened and closed with the publication of novels by black women: Harper's *Iola Leroy* and the first of Hopkins's four novels, *Contending Forces* (1900). Both authors intended that their texts contribute to the struggle for social change in a period of crisis for the Afro-American community. Their novels were meant to be read as actively attempting to change the structure of the Afro-American culture of which they were a part. As an integral part of a wider movement among black women intellectuals, these books both shaped and were shaped by strategies for resisting and defeating oppression. Organizing to fight included writing to organize. The novels do not merely reflect constituencies but attempt to structure Afro-American struggles in particular directions; both are loci of political and social interests that try to form, not just reveal, their constituencies. Afro-American women were attempting to define the political parameters of gender, race, and patriarchal authority and were constantly engaged with these issues in both fiction and nonfiction. The formation of the NACW provided a forum for the exchange of ideas among Afro-American women intellectuals, within a structure that disseminated information nationally. Black women's clubs provided a support for, but were also influenced by, the work of their individual members. Hopkins, for example, read from the manuscript of *Contending Forces* to the members of the Woman's Era Club in Boston; in turn, those members were part of the constituency that Hopkins tried to mobilize to agitate against Jim Crow segregation and the terrorizing practices of lynching and rape.

As intellectuals, these women organized around issues that addressed all aspects of the social organization of oppression. Arrival at the threshold of the woman's era did not lead to concentration on what could be narrowly construed as women's issues — whether domestic concerns or female suffrage. Cooper characterized the opportunity this way: "To be a woman of the Negro race in America, and to be able to grasp the deep significance of the possibilities of the crisis, is to have a heritage . . . unique in the ages" (*VS*, 144). Cooper saw the responsibility of the black woman to be the reshaping of society: "Such is the colored woman's office. She must stamp weal or woe on the coming history of this people" (*VS*, 145). To illustrate the process of exchange of ideas within the discourse of the woman's era, I will concentrate on one object of analysis: a theory of internal and external colonization developed in the works of Cooper and Wells and finally figured in the fiction of Hopkins.

As indicated in the epigraphs to this essay, both Harper and Cooper associated imperialism with unrestrained patriarchal power. Prefiguring Hopkins, Harper and Cooper reassessed the mythology of the founding fathers in terms of rampant lust, greed, and destruction: they portray white male rule as bestial in its actual and potential power to devour lands and peoples. Cooper developed a complex analysis of social, political, and economic forces as being either distinctly masculine or feminine in their orientation and consequences. She saw an intimate link between internal and external colonization, between domestic racial oppression and imperialism. While her critique of imperialism and institutionalized domestic racism is a particularly good example of her larger theories of masculine and feminine practices and spheres of influence, it is important to stress that her categories were not dependent on biological distinction. Cooper made it clear in her application of such analyses that women could conform to masculinist attitudes and practices and men could display womanly virtues.

Cooper saw the imperialist or expansionist impulse, with its ideology of racial categorization, as a supreme manifestation of patriarchal power. She argued that the source of such flagrant abuse had to be questioned, challenged, and opposed:

> Whence came this apotheosis of greed and cruelty? Whence this sneaking admiration we all have for bullies and prize-fighters? Whence the self-congratulation of "dominant" races, as if "dominant" meant "righteous" and carried with it a title to inherit the earth? Whence the scorn of so-called weak or unwarlike races and individuals, and the very comfortable assurance that it is their manifest destiny to be wiped out as vermin before this advancing civilization? [*VS*, 51]

Cooper refers to P. Lowell's *Soul of the Far East,* an imperialist treatise that predicted the death of all Asian peoples and cultures "before the advancing nations of the West." She indicts the author as a "scion of an upstart race" who felt confident that, with the stroke of a pen, he could consign "to annihilation one-third the inhabitants of the globe — a people whose civilization was hoary headed before the parent elements that begot his race had advanced beyond nebulosity" (*VS*, 52). The world under a dominant male influence is compared to the beast from the Book of Daniel, devouring all before it and demanding that it be worshiped as an incarnation of power. The complementary force, the female influence, is unable to restrain "the beast"; the rampant will to dominate and despise the weak is also present in the racist attitudes of white women. Cooper saw patriarchal power revealed in the imperialist impulse, but she also saw that that power was nurtured and sustained at home by an elite of white women preoccupied with maintaining their caste status (see *VS*, 86–87).

Cooper felt strongly that the only effective counter to patriarchal abuse of power — the feminine — had to be developed through the education of women. Education held possibilities for the empowerment of women, who could then shape the course of a future society that would exercise sensitivity and sympathy toward all who were poor and oppressed. White women, however, rarely exercised their power in sympathy with their black sisters. Cooper was well aware of this, and some of her most vituperative work attacks the exclusionary practices and discourse of white women's organizations that presumed to exist for and address the experiences of "women." Cooper challenged white women, as would-be leaders of reform, to revolutionize their thinking and practices. She challenged them to transform their provincial determination to secure gender and class interests at the expense of the rights of the oppressed (see *VS*, 123–24).

These gender and class interests were disguised when the issue of justice began to be displaced by debates about the dangers of social equality — debates that concerned the possible status of subject peoples abroad as well as the position of blacks in the United States. Cooper recognized — and condemned as fallacious — the concept of social equality with its implications of forced association between the races. This was not the social justice that blacks demanded. On the contrary, Cooper asserted, forced association was the manacled black male and the raped black woman, both internally colonized. Social equality masked the real issue: autonomy and the right to self-determination.

Cooper understood that the smoke screen of social equality obscured questions of heritage and inheritance that appeared in the figure of "blood" and gained consensual dominance in both the North and the South (see *VS,* 103–4). She became convinced that the key to understanding the unwritten history of the United States was the dominance of southern "influence, ideals, and ideas" over the whole nation. Cooper saw that the manipulative power of the South was embodied in the southern patriarch, but she described its concern with "blood," inheritance, and heritage in entirely female terms and as a preoccupation that was transmitted from the South to the North and perpetuated by white women. The South represented not red blood but blue:

> If your own father was a pirate, a robber, a murderer, his hands are dyed in red blood, and you don't say very much about it. But if your great great great grandfather's grandfather stole and pillaged and slew, and you can prove it, your blood has become blue and you are at great pains to establish the relationship.... [The South] had blood; and she paraded it with so much gusto that the substantial little Puritan maidens of the North, who had been making bread and canning currants and not thinking of blood the least bit, began to hunt up the records of the Mayflower to see if some of the passengers thereon could not claim the honor of having been one of William the Conqueror's brigands, when he killed the last of the Saxon Kings and, red-handed, stole his crown and his lands. (VS, 103–4)

Ridicule effectively belittles and undermines the search for an aristocratic heritage and proof of biological racial superiority; it also masks a very serious critique of these ideologies that Hopkins was to develop in her fiction. The juxtaposition of "red" with "blue" blood reveals the hidden history of national and nationalist heritage to be based on the principles of murder and theft — piracy. Hopkins drew from this analysis of the methods of expansionism, as it applied to the colonization of the Americas and to the imperialist ventures of the United States, as she demystified the mythological pretensions of the American story of origins in her fiction.

By linking imperialism to internal colonization, Cooper thus provided black women intellectuals with the basis for an analysis of how patriarchal power establishes and sustains gendered and racialized social formations. White women were implicated in the maintenance of this wider system of oppression because they challenged only the parameters of their domestic confinement; by failing to reconstitute their class and caste interests, they reinforced the provincialism of their movement. Ultimately, however, Cooper placed her hopes for change on the possibility of a transformed woman's movement. She wanted to expand the rubric defining the concerns of women to encompass an ideal and practice that could inspire a movement for the liberation of all oppressed peoples, not just a movement for the defense of parochial and sectional interests in the name of "woman" (see *VS,* 125).

The pen of Ida B. Wells was aimed at a different target — lynching, as a practice of political and economic repression. Wells's analysis of the relation between political terrorism, economic oppression, and conventional codes of sexuality and morality has still to be surpassed in its incisive condemnation of the patriarchal manipulation of race and gender.[5] Her achievement drew upon the support of club women but also provided the impetus for the formation of antilynching societies. *Southern Horrors*, on the one hand, was dedicated to the Afro-American women of New York and Brooklyn, whose contributions had made publication of the pamphlet possible. On the other hand, Wells claimed in her autobiography that the meetings to organize her first antilynching lecture and the forum itself were "the real beginning of the club movement among the colored women" in the United States.[6] The gathering of black women from Philadelphia, New York, Boston, and other cities indicated that organization was already embryonic. The meeting on one particular issue, lynching, was a catalyst for the establishment of numerous clubs and a general movement that would extend beyond any one issue.

Wells established in *Southern Horrors* that the association between lynching and rape was strictly a contemporary phenomenon; she argued that there was no historical foundation for that association, since "the crime of rape was unknown during four years of civil war, when the white women of the South were at the mercy of the race which is all at once charged with being a bestial one" (*SH*, 5). She indicted the miscegenation laws, which, in practice, were directed at preventing sexual relations between white women and black men. The miscegenation laws thus pretended to offer "protection" to white women but left black women the victims of rape by white men and simultaneously granted to these same men the power to vilify black men as a potential threat to the virtue of white womanhood. Wells asserted that "there are many white women in the South who would marry colored men if such an act would not place them at once beyond the pale of society and within the clutches of the law." The miscegenation laws, in her opinion, only operated against "the legitimate union of the races" (*SH*, 6). In her publications and speeches, Wells increasingly used evidence from the white press — statistics on lynchings and reports that substantiated her claims that black male/white female sexual relationships were encouraged by white women. Wells used the white press in this way not only to avoid accusations of falsification or exaggeration but also because she wanted to reveal the contradictions implicit in the association of lynching with the rape of white women. She wanted to condemn the murderers out of their own mouths (see *RR*, 15).

Wells recognized that the Southerners' appeal to Northerners for sympathy on the "necessity" of lynching was very successful. It worked, she thought, through the claim that any condemnation of lynching constituted a public display of indifference to the "plight" of white womanhood. Wells demonstrated that, while accusations of rape were made in only one-third of all lynchings, the cry of rape was an extremely effective way to create panic and fear. Lynching, she argued, was an institutionalized practice supported and encouraged by the established leaders of a community and the press they influenced. The North conceded to the South's argument that rape was the cause of lynching; the concession to lynching for a specific crime in turn conceded the right to lynch any black male for any crime: the charge of rape became the excuse for murder. The press acted as accomplices in the ideological work that disguised the lesson of political and economic subordination that the black community was being taught. Black disenfranchisement and Jim Crow segregation had been achieved; now, the annihilation of a black political presence was shielded behind a "screen of defending the honor of [white] women" (*SH*, 14). Those who remained silent while disapproving of lynching were condemned by Wells for being as guilty as the actual perpetrators of lynching.

The lesson the black community should learn, Wells argued, was to recognize its economic power. The South owed its rehabilitation to northern capital, on the one hand, and to Afro-American labor, on the other: "By the right exercise of his power as the industrial factor of the South, the Afro-American can demand and secure his rights." But economic power was only one force among the possible forms of resistance; she concluded: "[A] Winchester rifle should have a place of honor in every black home" (*SH,* 23). Wells knew that emancipation meant that white men lost their vested interests in the body of the Negro and that lynching and the rape of black women were attempts to regain control. The terrorizing of black communities was a political weapon that manipulated ideologies of sexuality. Wells analyzed how ideologies of manhood — as well as of citizenship — were embodied in the right to vote. The murder of blacks was so easily accomplished because they had been granted the right to vote but not the means to protect or maintain that right. Thus, Wells was able to assert that the loss of the vote was both a political silencing and an emasculation that placed black men outside the boundaries of contemporary patriarchal power. The cry of rape, which pleaded the necessity of revenge for assaulted white womanhood, attempted to place black males "beyond the pale of human sympathy" (*RR,* 12). Black women were relegated to a place outside the ideological construction of "womanhood." That term included only white women; therefore the rape of black women was of no consequence outside the black community.

Wells's analysis of lynching and her demystification of the political motivations behind the manipulation of both black male and female and white female sexuality led her into direct confrontation with women like Frances Willard, president of the Woman's Christian Temperance Union (WCTU), who considered themselves progressive but refused to see lynching as an institutionalized practice. Willard's attitude and Wells's conclusion that Willard was "no better or worse than the great bulk of white Americans on the Negro questions" (*RR,* 85) are indicative of the racism that Cooper condemned in white women's organizations. As Harper also pointed out, there was not a single black woman admitted to the southern WCTU. What Cooper called the white woman's concern with caste was evident in the assumption of many "progressive" white women that rape actually *was* the crime to which lynching was the response.[7]

For Cooper, imperialism linked all those oppressed under the domination of the United States. Patriarchy, for her, was embodied in these acts of violence; therefore she ultimately placed her focus and hopes for the future on a transformed woman's movement. Wells, in her analysis of lynching, provided for a more detailed dissection of patriarchal power, showing how it could manipulate sexual ideologies to justify political and economic subordination. Cooper had failed to address what proved central to the thesis of Wells — that white men used their ownership of the body of the white female as a terrain on which to lynch the black male. White women felt that their caste was their protection and that their interests lay with the power that ultimately confined them. Although Cooper identified the relation between patriarchal power and white women's practice of racial exclusion, she did not examine and analyze what forged that relation. She preferred to believe that what men taught women could be unlearned if women's education were expanded. Wells was able to demonstrate how a patriarchal system, which had lost its total ownership over black male bodies, used its control over women to attempt to completely circumscribe the actions of black males. As black women positioned outside the "protection" of the ideology of womanhood, both Cooper and Wells felt that they could see clearly the compromised role of white women in the maintenance of a system of oppression.

Black women listened, organized, and acted on the theses of both Wells and Cooper, but very few white women responded to their social critiques. Cooper was right to argue that a transformed woman's movement, purged of racism, would have provided a liberating experience for white women themselves. But racism led to concession, to segregated organizations, and, outside the antilynching movement, to a resounding silence about — and therefore complicity in — the attempt to eliminate black people politically, economically, and, indeed, physically.

Pauline Hopkins shared this very real fear that black people were threatened with annihilation. She addressed her plea to "all Negroes, whether Frenchmen, Spaniards, Americans or Africans to rediscover their history as one weapon in the struggle against oppression."[8] Hopkins challenged the readers of her work to bear witness to her testimony concerning the international dimensions of the crisis:

> The dawn of the Twentieth century finds the Black race fighting for existence in every quarter of the globe. From over the sea Africa stretches her hands to the American Negro and cries aloud for sympathy in her hour of trial.... In America, caste prejudice has received fresh impetus as the "Southern brother" of the Anglo-Saxon family has arisen from the ashes of secession, and like the prodigal of old, has been gorged with fatted calf and "fixin's."[9]

As a black intellectual, Hopkins conceived of her writing as an inspiration to political action, as establishing a pattern for encouraging forms of resistance and agitation, and as an integral part of the refutation of the politics of oppression.

Hopkins regarded fiction in particular as a cultural form of great historical and political significance. In the preface to her first novel, *Contending Forces* (1900), she asserted its "religious, political and social" value and urged other black writers to "*faithfully portray the inmost thoughts and feelings of the Negro with all the fire and romance which lie dormant in our history*."[10] History is the crucial element in Hopkins's fiction: current oppressive forces, she argued, must be understood in the context of past oppression. "Mob-law is nothing new.... The atrocity of the acts committed one hundred years ago are duplicated today, when slavery is supposed no longer to exist" (*CF*, 14, 15). This thesis is a cornerstone of *Contending Forces*. Drawing upon the theoretical perspectives of women like Cooper and Wells as well as the central concerns of the black woman's movement as a whole, Hopkins figures lynching and rape as the two political weapons of terror wielded by the powers behind internal colonization.

Contending Forces opens with a brief recounting of family history. Charles Montfort, a West Indian planter, decides to move his family and estate of slaves from Bermuda to North Carolina in response to the increasing agitation in the British Parliament for the abolition of slavery. Montfort acts to protect his commercial interests and profits. Hopkins is careful to remove any motivation or intention on his part that could be attributed to cruelty or personal avariciousness. Thus she establishes the economic basis of slavery as the primary factor in this decision that precipitates all the events and conditions in the rest of the text. Once the Montfort estate has been established in North Carolina, the focus of the novel gravitates toward Grace Montfort and the suspicion, which becomes rumor, that her blood is "polluted" by an African strain. Hopkins utilizes what Cooper had identified as the American obsession with "pure blood" and reveals its mythological proportions. It is actually irrelevant whether Grace Montfort is a black or a white woman. Her behavior is classically that of "true womanhood" — but her skin is a little too "creamy." The reader is not apprised of her actual heritage; what is important is the mere suspicion of black blood. This results in the social ostracism of her whole family, while Grace herself, denied her station on the pedestal of virtue, becomes the object of the illicit sexual desire of a local landowner, Anson Pollock. The possibility that Grace might be black leads directly to the murder of Charles Montfort, the rapes of Grace and her black foster sister Lucy, and the enslavement of the two Montfort sons, Jesse and Charles.

Grace Montfort rejects the advances of Pollock, who then plots to avenge his wounded pride and satisfy his sexual obsession. Under the pretense of quelling an imminent rebellion by Montfort's slaves, Pollock uses the "committee on public safety" — in fact, a vigilante group — to raid the Montfort plantation. Montfort himself is quickly dispatched by a bullet in the brain, leaving Grace prey to Pollock. In a graphic and tortured two-page scene, Hopkins represents a brutal rape in a displaced form: Grace is whipped by two members of the "committee." Her clothes are ripped from her, and she is "whipped" alternately "by the two strong, savage men." Hopkins's replacement of the phallus by the "snaky leather thong" is crude but effective, and the reader is left in no doubt about the kind of outrage that has occurred when "the blood stood in a pool about her feet" (*CF,* 69).

Grace commits suicide, in the tradition of outraged virtue, and Pollock takes Lucy, Grace's black maid and slave, as his mistress instead. But the actual and figurative ravishing of "grace" at the hand of southern brutality establishes the link that Hopkins is drawing between rape and its political motivation as a device of terrorism. Both Charles and Grace Montfort are punished because they threatened to break the acceptable codes that bound the slave system. The possibility of miscegenation represented the ultimate violation of the white woman's social position and required the degradation of the transgressor and the relegation of her offspring to the status of chattel. The two sons represent two possible histories. Charles Jr. is bought and eventually grows up "white" in Britain. Jesse escapes into the black communities of Boston and, later, New Hampshire; he is the ancestor of the black family that is the main subject of the novel.

This preliminary tale acts as an overture to the main body of *Contending Forces,* containing the clues and themes that will eventually provide the resolutions to the crises of relations between the main characters. Living in Boston at the turn of the century, the Smith family inherits this tale of its ancestors: the tale appears remote from their everyday lives but is retained in the naming of their children. Ma Smith, her husband dead, runs a lodging house with her son, William Jesse Montfort, and her daughter, Dora Grace Montfort. The two other main characters are both lodgers, John P. Langley, engaged to Dora, and Sappho Clark, a woman who is mysteriously hiding her personal history. All these characters cannot move forward into the future until their relation to the past is revealed. Hopkins displaces a direct attack on the increasing separation of the races onto issues of inheritance, heritage, and culture — issues where bloodlines between the races are so entangled that race as a biological category is subordinated to race as a political category. The historical importance of rape is crucial to the construction of Hopkins's fictionalized history: it is through the rapes of Grace and Lucy that the two races share an intertwined destiny.

Shifting contemporary debates about race from the biological to the political level was a crucial move for Hopkins to make in her fiction. At the height of debate about the consequences of colonizing overseas territories, Hopkins attempted to disrupt imperialist discourse concerning empires composed primarily of nonwhite peoples. The grounds of imperialist argument derived their problematic from the experience of the internal colonization of American Indians and black Americans. At the moment when black Americans were again being systematically excluded from participation in social institutions, the status of people who lived in what the United States now deemed its "possessions" was an integral component of the contemporary discourse on race. "Mixing blood" was seen as a threat to the foundations of North American civilization.[11]

Hopkins intended to disrupt this imperialist discourse through the figuration of an alternative set of historical consequences. The degradation of a race is represented as being the result not of amalgamation but of an abuse of power — the use of brutality against an oppressed group equates with savagery, in Hopkins's terms. She quotes Ralph Waldo Emerson on her title page and again in the body of the text: "The civility of no race can be perfect whilst another race is degraded." The link that Hopkins establishes between Britain and the West Indies makes visible a colonial relationship that enables her to direct a critique of imperial relations to an American readership. Hopkins carefully demonstrates that blacks are a colonized people for whom it is a necessity that history be rewritten. The histories of the externally colonized and the internally colonized are interwoven in many ways but primarily through questions of rightful inheritance. In Hopkins's fictional world, one consequence of external colonization is that a debt must be paid from the profits of the slave trade and Charles Montfort's plantation. For the purposes of this essay, however, I want to concentrate on Hopkins's presentation of the two main weapons of terror of internal colonization: lynching and rape.

At the heart of the text are two tales told at a public gathering by Luke Sawyer, who is black. In the first, a lynching is the central focus of concern; in the second, a rape. Both tales confirm the privileging of these two acts in Hopkins's thesis of "contending forces." The first history that Luke tells is of his father, whose success in trade resulted in competition with white traders, threats on his life, and, ultimately, a mob attack on his home and family. His act of self-defense — firing into the mob — is punished by lynching; the women are whipped and raped to death, the two babies slaughtered.

The second tale follows from the first. Luke escapes into the woods and is found by a black planter, Beaubean, who rescues him and takes him into his home to raise as a son. Beaubean has a wealthy and politically influential white half-brother, who assumes a stance of friendship toward the whole family but particularly toward

Beaubean's daughter, Mabelle. At the age of fourteen, Mabelle is kidnapped by this uncle, raped, and left a prisoner in a brothel. After weeks of searching, Beaubean finds Mabelle and confronts his brother with the crime — only to be asked "What does a woman of mixed blood, or any Negress, for that matter, know of virtue?" (*CF*, 261). Beaubean is offered a thousand dollars by his brother, which he rejects with a threat to seek justice in a federal court. Beaubean's threat is promptly met with mob action: his house is set on fire and its occupants shot. Luke escapes with Mabelle and places her in a convent.

Hopkins concentrates on the practices of oppression — the consequences of white supremacy — in reconstructing the history of her characters. The predominance of mulattos and octoroons in the novel is not intended to glorify the possibilities of the black race if only it would integrate with (and eventually lose itself within) the white race.[12] On the contrary, Hopkins states categorically in this novel and through-out her work that "miscegenation, either *lawful* or *unlawful,* we *do not want*" (*CF*, 264). The presence of racially mixed characters throughout the text empha-sizes particular social relations and practices and must be understood historically. Such characters are often the physical consequences of a social system that exer-cised white supremacy through rape. Use of the mulatto figure, as a literary device, has two primary functions: it enables an exploration of the relation between the races while, at the same time, it expresses the relation between the races. It is a narrative mechanism of mediation frequently used in a period when social conven-tion dictated an increased and more absolute distance between black and white. The figure of the mulatto allows for a fictional representation and reconstruction of the socially proscribed. Hopkins's particular use of such figuration is intended, in part, to demythologize concepts of "pure blood" and "pure race." More important, how-ever, it is an attempt to demonstrate the crucial role of social, political, and economic interests in determining human behavior by negating any proposition of degeneracy through amalgamation. Hopkins transposes contemporary accusations that misce-genation is the inmost desire of the nonwhite peoples of the earth by reconstructing miscegenation as the result of white rape.

Hopkins saw clearly that the threat to white supremacy was not black sexuality but the potential of the black vote. Rape, she argued, should be totally separated from the issue of violated white womanhood and then recast as part of the social, political, and economic oppression of blacks:

> Lynching was instituted to crush the manhood of the enfranchised black. Rape is the crime which appeals most strongly to the heart of the home life. . . . *The men who created the mulatto race, who recruit its ranks year after year by the very means which they invoked lynch law to suppress,* bewailing the sorrows of violated womanhood!
>
> No; it is not rape. If the Negro votes, he is shot; if he marries a white woman, he is shot . . . or lynched — he is a pariah whom the National Government cannot defend. But if he defends himself and his home, then is heard the tread of marching feet as the Federal troops move southward to quell a "race riot." (*CF*, 270–71)

The analysis of rape and its links to lynching as a weapon of political terror is, ob-viously, shaped by the arguments and indictments of Wells. In Hopkins's fictional reconstruction of the social relations between white and black, the two parts of the text move across generations and thus, through historical knowledge, invalidate the understanding of cause and effect then being reasserted through white patriarchal supremacy. Hopkins offers her readers an alternative story of origins where the characters are not holistic creations but the terrain on which the consequences of the authorial assertion of history are worked through. This can be clearly seen in the creation of Sappho Clark, the dominant female figure in the text, who has two identities.

The disguise — that which hides true history — is Sappho, the poet of Lesbos, who was admired and loved by both men and women, though her erotic poetry was addressed to women. The Sappho of *Contending Forces* embodies the potential for utopian relationships between women and between women and men; she represents a challenge to a patriarchal order. To Dora, whose duties running the boardinghouse confine her to a domestic existence, Sappho is the independent woman who, in their intimate moments together, talks of the need for suffrage and the political activity of women (see *CF,* 125). Sappho disrupts Dora's complacency — Dora will "generally accept whatever the men tell me as right" — and leads her to reassess the importance of friendships with women. But Sappho as an ideal of womanhood does not exist except as a set of fictional possibilities. In order to function, to work and survive, Sappho's younger self, Mabelle Beaubean, a product of miscegenation and the subject of rape, has had to bury her violated womanhood and deny her progeny. Like Sappho of Lesbos, Sappho Clark has a child, "whose form is like / gold flowers."[13] But unlike Sappho of Lesbos, Mabelle exists in a patriarchal order; her body is colonized, her child the fruit of rape. Sappho Clark journeys toward the retrieval of a whole identity, one that will encompass a combination of the elements of Sappho and Mabelle. Such an identity leads to an acceptance of a motherhood that, like that of Sappho of Lesbos, does not require that a male occupy the space of father.

The most significant absence in the network of social forces is the black father. In narrative, the father is a figure that mediates patriarchal control over women; in most texts by nineteenth-century black women, this control is exercised by white men who politically, socially, and economically attempt to deny patriarchal power to black men. This absent space in fiction by black women confirms this denial of patriarchal power to black men, but Hopkins uses that space to explore the possibilities of alternative black male figures. Black men are depicted in peer relations, as brothers, or as potential partners/lovers. Women are not seen as the subject of exchange between father and husband; neither are their journeys limited to the distance between daughter and wife. The narrative impulse is toward utopian relations between black men and black women as partners, sexual or nonsexual.

Nineteenth-century black feminists cannot be dismissed simply as "spokespeople for prudery in their communities." Their legacy to us is theories that expose the colonization of the black female body by white male power and the destruction of black males who attempted to exercise any oppositional patriarchal control. When accused of threatening the white female body, the repository of heirs to property and power, the black male, and his economic, political, and social advancement, is lynched out of existence. Cooper, Wells, and Hopkins assert the necessity of seeing the relation between histories: the rape of black women in the 1890s is directly linked to the rape of the female slave. Their analyses are dynamic and not limited to a parochial understanding of "women's issues"; they have firmly established the dialectical relation between economic/political power and economic/sexual power in the battle for control of women's bodies.

A desire for the possibilities of the uncolonized black female body occupies a utopian space; it is the false hope of Sappho Clark's pretend history. Black feminists understood that the struggle would have to take place on the terrain of the previously colonized: the struggle was to be characterized by redemption, retrieval, and reclamation — not, ultimately, by an unrestrained utopian vision. Sappho could not deny the existence of the raped Mabelle but, instead, had to reunite with the colonized self. Thus, these black feminists expanded the limits of conventional ideologies of womanhood to consider subversive relationships between women, motherhood without wifehood, wifehood as a partnership outside of an economic exchange between men, and men as partners and not patriarchal fathers. As DuBois and Gordon have argued so cogently, we have "150 years of feminist theory and praxis in the area of sexuality. This is a resource too precious to squander by not learning it, in all its complexity."[14] But let us learn *all* of it, not only in its complexity but also in its difference, and so stand again on the "threshold of woman's era" — an era that can encompass all women.

NOTES

1. Ellen Carol DuBois and Linda Gordon, "Seeking Ecstasy on the Battlefield: Danger and Pleasure in Nineteenth-Century Feminist Sexual Thought," in *Pleasure and Danger: Exploring Female Sexuality,* ed. Carole S. Vance (Boston, 1984), 34, 33.

2. See Frances E. W. Harper, *Iola Leroy; or, Shadows Uplifted* (Philadelphia, 1892), and Anna Julia Cooper, *A Voice from the South; By a Black Woman of the South* (Xenia, Ohio, 1892); all further references to the latter work, abbreviated *VS,* will be included in the text; see also Ida B. Wells-Barnett, *On Lynchings: Southern Horrors; A Red Record; Mob Rule in New Orleans* (New York, 1969); all further references to *Southern Horrors* and *A Red Record,* respectively abbreviated *SH* and *RR,* are to this collection and will be included in the text. These were preceded by a novel by "Forget-Me-Not" [Emma Dunham Kelley], *Megda* (Boston, 1891) and followed by the publication of a story by Victoria Earle Matthews, *Aunt Lindy: A Story Founded on Real Life* (New York, 1893) and a survey by N. F. [Gertrude] Mossell, *The Work of the Afro-American Woman* (Philadelphia, 1894).

3. Frances E. W. Harper, "Woman's Political Future," in *World's Congress of Representative Women,* ed. May Wright Sewell, 2 vols. (Chicago, 1894), 1:433–34.

4. This paragraph draws upon material from Hazel V. Carby, *Reconstructing Womanhood: The Emergence of the Afro-American Woman Novelist* (New York, 1989).

5. Wells's pamphlet *Southern Horrors: Lynch Law in All Its Phases* was published in 1892; *A Red Record: Tabulated Statistics and Alleged Causes of Lynchings in the United States, 1892–1893–1894* was published in 1895; and *Mob Rule in New Orleans* was published in 1900. All three have been reprinted in Wells-Barnett, *On Lynchings.* My account of some of her arguments is oversimplified and extremely adumbrated.

6. Wells, quoted in Alfreda M. Duster, ed., *Crusade for Justice: The Autobiography of Ida B. Wells* (Chicago, 1970), 81.

7. See Bettina Aptheker, ed., *Lynching and Rape: An Exchange of Views,* American Institute for Marxist Studies Occasional Paper 25 (San José, Calif., 1977), 29.

8. Pauline Hopkins, "Toussaint L'Overture," *Colored American Magazine* 2 (November 1900): 10, 24.

9. Pauline Hopkins, "Heroes and Heroines in Black," *Colored American Magazine* 3 (January 1903): 211.

10. Pauline Hopkins, *Contending Forces: A Romance Illustrative of Negro Life North and South*

(1900; Carbondale, Ill., 1978), 13, 14; all further references to this work, abbreviated *CF,* will be included in the text.

11. See Robert L. Allen, *Reluctant Reformers: Racism and Social Reform Movements in the United States* (Garden City, N.Y., 1975), and Christopher Lasch, *The World of Nations: Reflections on American History, Politics, and Culture* (New York, 1973), 70–79.

12. Gwendolyn Brooks misunderstands Hopkins to be arguing for integration; see Brooks, afterword to Hopkins, *Contending Forces,* 403–9.

13. Sappho, fragment 132, quoted in Sarah B. Pomeroy, *Goddesses, Whores, Wives, and Slaves: Women in Classical Antiquity* (New York, 1975), 54.

14. DuBois and Gordon, "Seeking Ecstasy on the Battlefield," 43.

Chapter 18
Making Empire Respectable:
The Politics of Race and Sexual Morality
in Twentieth-Century Colonial Cultures
Ann Laura Stoler

The shift away from viewing colonial elites as homogeneous communities of common interest marks an important trajectory in the anthropology of empire, signaling a major rethinking of gender relations within it. More recent attention to the internal tensions of colonial enterprises has placed new emphasis on the quotidian assertion of European dominance in the colonies, on imperial interventions in domestic life, and thus on the cultural prescriptions by which European women and men lived (Callan and Ardener 1984; Knibiehler and Goutalier 1985; Reijs et al. 1986; Callaway 1987; Strobel 1987). Having focused on how colonizers have viewed the indigenous other, we are beginning to sort out how Europeans in the colonies imagined themselves and constructed communities built on asymmetries of race, class, and gender — entities significantly at odds with the European models on which they were drawn.

These feminist attempts to engage the gender politics of Dutch, French, and British imperial cultures converge on some strikingly similar observations: namely, that European women in these colonies experienced the cleavages of racial dominance and internal social distinctions very differently than men precisely because of their ambiguous positions, as both subordinates in colonial hierarchies and as active agents of imperial culture in their own right. Concomitantly, the majority of European women who left for the colonies in the late nineteenth and early twentieth centuries confronted profoundly rigid restrictions on their domestic, economic, and political options, more limiting than those of metropolitan Europe at the time and sharply contrasting with the opportunities open to colonial men.

In one form or another these studies raise a basic question: In what ways were gender inequalities essential to the structure of colonial racism and imperial authority? Was the strident misogyny of imperial thinkers and colonial agents a byproduct of received metropolitan values ("they just brought it with them"), a reaction to contemporary feminist demands in Europe ("women need to be put back in their breeding place"), or a novel and pragmatic response to the conditions of conquest? Was the assertion of European supremacy in terms of patriotic manhood and racial virility an expression of imperial domination or a defining feature of it?

In this essay I examine some of the ways in which colonial authority and racial distinctions were fundamentally structured in gendered terms. I look specifically at how the administrative and medical discourse and management of European sexual activity, reproduction, and marriage related to the racial politics of colonial rule. Focusing on French Indochina and the Dutch East Indies in the early twentieth century, but drawing on other contexts, I suggest that the very categories of "colonizer" and "colonized" were secured through forms of sexual control that defined the domestic arrangements of Europeans and the cultural investments by which they identified themselves.[1] Gender-specific sexual sanctions demarcated positions of power by refashioning middle-class conventions of respectability, which, in turn, prescribed the personal and public boundaries of race.

Colonial authority was constructed on two powerful, but false, premises. The first was the notion that Europeans in the colonies made up an easily identifiable and discrete biological and social entity — a "natural" community of common class interests, racial attributes, political affinities, and superior culture. The second was the related notion that the boundaries separating colonizer from colonized were thus self-evident and easily drawn (Stoler 1989). Neither premise reflected colonial realities (see, e.g., Cooper 1980; Drooglever 1980; Ridley 1983; Prochaska 1989). Internal divisions developed out of conflicting economic and political agendas, frictions over appropriate methods for safeguarding European privilege and power, and competing criteria for reproducing a colonial elite and for restricting its membership.

The latter, the colonial politics of exclusion, was contingent on constructing categories: legal and social classifications designating who was "white," who was "native," who could become a citizen rather than a subject, which children were legitimate progeny and which were not. What mattered were not only one's physical properties but who counted as "European" and by what measure.[2] Skin shade was too ambiguous; bank accounts were mercurial; religious belief and education were crucial but never enough. Social and legal standing derived not only from color but from the silences, acknowledgments, and denials of the social circumstances in which one's parents had sex (Martínez-Alier 1974; Ming 1983; Taylor 1983). Sexual unions in the context of concubinage, domestic service, prostitution, or church marriage derived from the hierarchies of rule; but these were negotiated and contested arrangements, bearing on individual fates and the very structure of colonial society. Ultimately inclusion or exclusion required regulating the sexual, conjugal, and domestic life of *both* Europeans in the colonies and their colonized subjects.

Colonial observers and participants in the imperial enterprise appear to have had unlimited interest in the sexual interface of the colonial encounter (Malleret 1934:216; Pujarniscle 1931:106; Loutfi 1971:36). Probably no subject is discussed more than sex in colonial literature and no subject more frequently invoked to foster the racist stereotypes of European society. The tropics provided a site of European pornographic fantasies long before conquest was underway, but with a sustained European presence in colonized territories, sexual prescriptions by class, race, and gender became increasingly central to the politics of rule and subject to new forms of scrutiny by colonial states (Loutfi 1971; Gilman 1985:79).[3]

While anthropologists have attended to how European, and particularly Victorian, sexual mores affected *indigenous* gendered patterns of economic activity, political participation, and social knowledge, less attention has been paid to the ways in which sexual control affected the very nature of colonial relations themselves

(Tiffany and Adams 1985). In colonial scholarship more generally, sexual domination has figured as a social metaphor of European supremacy. Thus, in Edward Said's treatment of Orientalist discourse, the sexual submission and possession of Oriental women by European men *"stands for* the pattern of relative strength between East and West" (1979:6). In this "male power-fantasy," the Orient is penetrated, silenced, and possessed (ibid.:207). Sexuality illustrates the iconography of rule, not its pragmatics; sexual asymmetries are tropes to depict other centers of power.

Such a treatment begs some basic questions. Was sexuality merely a graphic substantiation of who was, so to speak, on the top? Was the medium the message, or did sexual relations always "mean" something else, stand in for other relations, evoke the sense of *other* (pecuniary, political, or some possibly more subliminal) desires? This analytic slippage between the sexual symbols of power and the politics of sex runs throughout the colonial record and contemporary commentaries upon it. Certainly some of this is due to the polyvalent quality of sexuality, which is symbolically rich and socially salient at the same time. But sexual control was more than a "social enactment" — much less a convenient metaphor — for colonial domination (Jordan 1968:141); it was, as I argue here, a fundamental class and racial marker implicated in a wider set of relations of power (Ballhatchet 1980).

The relationship between gender prescriptions and racial boundaries still remains unevenly unexplored. While we know that European women of different classes experienced the colonial venture very differently from one another and from men, we still know relatively little about the distinct investments they had in a racism they shared (Van Helten and Williams 1983; Knibiehler and Goutalier 1985; Callaway 1987). New feminist scholarship has begun to sort out the unique colonial experience of European women as they were incorporated into and resisted and affected the politics of their men. But the emphasis has tended to be on the broader issue of gender subordination and colonial authority, not more specifically on how sexual control figured in the construction of racial boundaries per se.[4]

The linkage between sexual control and racial tensions is both obvious and elusive at the same time. While sexual fear may at base be a racial anxiety, we are still left to understand why such anxieties are expressed through sexuality (Takaki 1977). If, as Sander Gilman (1985) claims, sexuality is the most salient marker of otherness, organically representing racial difference, then we should not be surprised that colonial agents and colonized subjects expressed their contests — and vulnerabilities — in these terms.

An overlapping set of discourses has provided the psychological and economic underpinnings for colonial distinctions of difference, linking fears of sexual contamination, physical danger, climatic incompatibility, and moral breakdown to a European colonial identity with a racist and class-specific core. Colonial scientific reports and the popular press are laced with statements and queries varying on a common theme: "native women bear contagions"; "white women become sterile in the tropics"; "colonial men are susceptible to physical, mental and moral degeneration when they remain in their colonial posts too long." To what degree are these statements medically or politically grounded? We need to unpack what is metaphor, what is perceived as dangerous (is it disease, culture, climate, or sex?), and what is not.

In the sections that follow I look at the relationship between the domestic arrangements of colonial communities and their wider political structures. The first part examines the colonial debates over European family formation and over the relationship between subversion and sex in an effort to trace how evaluations of concubinage, morality, and white prestige more generally were altered by new tensions within colonial cultures and by new challenges to imperial rule.

The second part examines what I call the "cultural hygiene" of colonialism. Focusing on the early twentieth century as a break point, I take up the convergent metropolitan and colonial discourses on health hazards in the tropics, race-thinking, and social reform as they related to shifts in the rationalization of colonial management. In tracing how fears of "racial degeneracy" were grounded in class-specific sexual norms, I return to how and why biological and cultural distinctions were defined in gender terms.

The Domestic Politics of Colonialism: Concubinage and the Restricted Entry of European Women

The regulation of sexual relations was central to the development of particular kinds of colonial settlements and to the allocation of economic activity within them. Who bedded and wedded with whom in the colonies of France, England, Holland, and Iberia was never left to chance. Unions between Annamite women and French men, between Javanese women and Dutch men, between Spanish men and Inca women produced offspring with claims to privilege, whose rights and status had to be determined and prescribed. From the early seventeenth century through the twentieth century, the sexual sanctions and conjugal prohibitions of colonial agents were rigorously debated and carefully codified. In these debates over matrimony and morality, trading and plantation company officials, missionaries, investment bankers, military high commands, and agents of the colonial state confronted one another's visions of empire and the settlement patterns on which it would rest.

In 1622 the Dutch East Indies Company arranged for the transport of six poor but marriageable young Dutch women to Java, providing them with clothing, a dowry upon marriage, and a contract binding them to five years in the Indies (Taylor 1983:12). Aside from this and one other short-lived experiment, immigration of European women to the East Indies was consciously restricted for the next two hundred years. Enforcing the restriction by selecting bachelors as their European recruits, the company legally and financially made concubinage the most attractive domestic option for its employees (Blussé 1986:173; Ming 1983:69; Taylor 1983:16).

It was not only the Dutch East Indies Company that had profited from such arrangements. In the nineteenth and early twentieth centuries, salaries of European recruits to the colonial armies, bureaucracies, plantation companies, and trading enterprises were kept artificially low because local women provided domestic services for which new European recruits would otherwise have had to pay. In the mid-1800s, such arrangements were de rigueur for young civil servants intent on setting up households on their own (Ritter 1856:21). Despite some clerical opposition, at the end of the century concubinage was the most prevalent living arrangement for European colonials in the Indies (Ming 1983:70; Taylor 1983:16; van Marle 1952:486).

Referred to as *nyai* in Java and Sumatra, *congai* in Indochina, and *petite épouse* throughout the French empire, the colonized woman living as a concubine to a European man formed the dominant domestic arrangement in colonial cultures through the early twentieth century. Unlike prostitution, which could and often did result in a population of syphilitic and therefore nonproductive European men, concubinage was considered to have a stabilizing effect on political order and colonial health — a relationship that kept men in their barracks and bungalows, out of brothels and less inclined to perverse liaisons with one another.

In Asia and Africa, corporate and government decision makers invoked the social services that local women supplied as "useful guides to the language and other mysteries of the local societies" (Malleret 1934:216; Cohen 1971:122). Handbooks for incoming plantation employees bound for Tonkin, Sumatra, and Malaya urged men to find local "companions" as a prerequisite for quick acclimatization, as insulation from the ill-health that sexual abstention, isolation, and boredom were thought to bring (Butcher 1979:200, 202; Hesselink 1987:208; Braconier 1933:922; Dixon 1913:77). Although British and Dutch colonial governments officially banned concubinage in the early twentieth century, such measures were only selectively enforced. It remained tacitly condoned and practiced long after (Hyam 1986a; Callaway 1987:49). In Sumatra's plantation belt, newly opened in the late nineteenth century, for example, Javanese and Japanese *huishoudsters* (householders) remained the rule rather than the exception through the 1920s (Clerkx 1961:87–93; Stoler 1985a:31–34; Lucas 1986:84).

"Concubinage" was a contemporary term that referred to the cohabitation outside of marriage between European men and Asian women; in fact, it glossed a wide range of arrangements that included sexual access to a non-European woman as well as demands on her labor and legal rights to the children she bore (Pollmann 1986:100; Lucas 1986:86).[5] Native women (like European women in a later period) were to keep men physically and psychologically fit for work and marginally content, not distracting or urging them out of line, imposing neither the time-consuming nor the financial responsibilities that European family life was thought to demand (Chivas-Baron 1929:103).[6]

To say that concubinage reinforced the hierarchies on which colonial societies were based is not to say that it did not make those distinctions more problematic at the same time. Grossly uneven sex ratios on North Sumatran estates made for intense competition among male workers and their European supervisors, with *vrouwen perkara* (disputes over women) resulting in assaults on whites, new labor tensions, and dangerous incursions into the standards deemed essential for white prestige (Stoler 1985a:33; Lucas 1986:90–91). In the Netherlands Indies more generally, an unaccounted number of impoverished Indo-European women moving between prostitution and concubinage further disturbed the racial sensibilities of the Dutch-born elite (Hesselink 1987:216). Metropolitan critics were particularly disdainful of such domestic arrangements on moral grounds — all the more so when these unions *were* sustained and personally significant relationships, thereby contradicting the racial premise of concubinage as an emotionally unfettered convenience.[7] But perhaps most important, the tension between concubinage as a confirmation and compromise of racial hierarchy was realized in the progeny that it produced: "mixed-bloods," poor "indos," and abandoned *métis* children who straddled the divisions of ruler and ruled threatened to blur the colonial divide.

Nevertheless, colonial governments and private business tolerated concubinage and actively encouraged it — principally by restricting the emigration of European women to the colonies and by refusing employment to married male European recruits. Although many accounts suggest that European women chose to avoid early pioneering ventures, and this must have been true in some cases, the choice was more often not their own (see Fredrickson 1981:109). Nor were the restrictions on marriage and women's emigration lifted as each colony became politically stable, medically upgraded, and economically secure, as it is often claimed. Conjugal constraints lasted well into the twentieth century, long after rough living and a scarcity of amenities had become conditions of the past. In the Indies army, marriage was a privilege of the officer corps while barrack concubinage was instituted and regulated for the rank and file. In the twentieth century, formal and informal prohibitions set by banks, estates, and government services operating in Africa, India, and Southeast Asia restricted marriage during the first three to five years of service, while some prohibited it altogether (Moore-Gilbert 1986:48; Woodcock 1969:164; Tirefort 1979:134; Gann and Duignan 1978:240).

European demographics in the colonies were shaped by these economic and political exigencies and thus were sharply skewed by sex. Among the laboring immigrant and native populations as well as among Europeans, the number of men exceeded that of women by two to twenty-five times. While in the Netherlands Indies, the overall ratio of European women to men rose from forty-seven per one hundred to eighty-eight per one hundred between 1900 and 1930, on Sumatra's plantation belt in 1920 there were still only sixty-one European women per one hundred European men (Taylor 1983:128; *Koloniale Verslag,* quoted in Lucas 1986:82). In Tonkin, European men (totaling more than fourteen thousand) sharply outnumbered European women (just over three thousand) as late as 1931 (Gantes 1981:138). What is important here is that by controlling the availability of European women and the sorts of sexual access condoned, state and corporate authorities controlled the very social geography of the colonies, fixing the conditions under which European populations and privileges could be reproduced.

The marriage prohibition was both a political and an economic issue, defining the social contours of colonial communities and the standards of living within them. But, as significantly, it revealed how deeply the conduct of private life and the sexual proclivities that individuals expressed were tied to corporate profits and to the security of the colonial state. Nowhere were the incursions on domestic life more openly contested than in North Sumatra in the early 1900s. It was thought that unseemly domestic arrangements could encourage subversion as strongly as acceptable unions could avert it. Family stability and sexual "normalcy" were thus linked to political agitation or quiescence in very concrete ways.

Since the late nineteenth century, the major North Sumatran tobacco and rubber companies had neither accepted married applicants nor allowed them to take wives while in service (Schoevers 1913:38; Clerkx 1961:31–34). Company authorities argued that new employees with families in tow would be a financial burden, risking the emergence of a "European proletariat" and thus a major threat to white prestige (Kroniek 1917:50; *Sumatra Post* 1913). Low-ranking plantation employees protested against these company marriage restrictions, an issue that mobilized their ranks behind a broad set of demands (Stoler 1989:144). Under employee pressure, the prohibition was relaxed to a marriage ban for the first five years of service. This restriction, however, was never placed on everyone; it was pegged to salaries and dependent on the services of local women, which kept the living costs and wages of subordinate and incoming staff artificially low.

Domestic arrangements thus varied as government officials and private businesses weighed the economic versus political costs of one arrangement over another, but such calculations were invariably meshed. Europeans in high office saw white prestige and profits as inextricably linked, and attitudes toward concubinage reflected that concern (Brownfoot 1984:191). Thus in Malaya through the 1920s, concubinage was tolerated precisely because "poor whites" were not. Government and estate administrators argued that white prestige would be imperiled if European men became impoverished in attempting to maintain middle-class lifestyles and European wives (Butcher 1979:26). In late nineteenth-century Java, in contrast, concubinage itself was considered to be a major source of white pauperism; in the early 1900s it was vigorously condemned at precisely the same time that a new colonial morality passively condoned illegal brothels (Het Pauperisme Commissie 1901; Nieuwenhuys 1959:20–23; Hesselink 1987:208).

What explains such a difference? At least part of the answer must be sought in the effects concubinage was seen to have on European cultural identity and on the concerns for the community consensus on which it rests. Concubinage "worked" as long as the supremacy of *Homo Europeaus* was clear. When it was thought to be in jeopardy, vulnerable, or less than convincing, as in the 1920s in Sumatra, colonial elites responded by clarifying the cultural criteria of privilege and the moral premises of their unity. Concubinage was replaced by more restricted sexual access in the politically safe (but medically unsatisfactory) context of prostitution and, where possible, in the more desirable setting of marriage between "full-blooded" Europeans (Taylor 1977:29). As we shall see in other colonial contexts, such shifts in policy and practice often coincided with an affirmation of social hierarchies and racial divisions in less ambiguous terms.[8] Thus, it was not only morality that vacillated but the very definition of white prestige — and what its defense should entail. What upheld that prestige was not a constant; concubinage was socially lauded at one time and seen as a political menace at another. Appeals to white prestige were a gloss for different intensities of racist practice, were gender-specific and culturally coded.

Thus far I have treated colonial communities as a generic category despite the sharp demographic, social, and political distinctions *among* them. North Sumatra's European-oriented, overwhelmingly male colonial population, for example, contrasted sharply with the more sexually balanced mestizo culture that emerged in seventeenth- and eighteenth-century colonial Java.[9] Such demographic variation, however, was not the "bedrock" of social relations (Jordan 1968:141); sex ratios derived from specific strategies of social engineering and were thus political responses in themselves. While recognizing that these demographic differences and the social configurations to which they gave rise still need to be explained, I have chosen here to trace some of the common politically gendered issues that a range of colonial societies shared — that is, some of the similar (and counterintuitive) ways in which the positioning of European women facilitated racial distinctions and new efforts to modernize colonial control.[10]

Racist but Moral Women: Innocent but Immoral Men

Perhaps nothing is as striking in the sociological accounts of colonial communities as the extraordinary changes that are said to accompany the entry of European-born women. These adjustments shifted in one direction: toward European lifestyles accentuating the refinements of privilege and the etiquettes of racial difference. Most accounts agree that the presence of these women put new demands on the white communities to tighten their ranks, clarify their boundaries, and mark out their social space. The material culture of French settlements in Saigon, outposts in New Guinea, and estate complexes in Sumatra was retailored to accommodate the physical and moral requirements of a middle-class and respectable feminine contingent (Malleret 1934; Gordon and Meggitt 1985; Stoler 1989). Housing structures in Indochina were partitioned; residential compounds in the Solomon Islands were enclosed; servant relations in Hawaii were formalized; dress codes in Java were altered; food and social taboos in Rhodesia and the Ivory Coast became more strict. Taken together, the changes encouraged new kinds of consumption and new social services catering to these new demands (Boutilier 1984; Spear 1963; Woodcock 1969; Cohen 1971).

The arrival of large numbers of European women thus coincided with an embourgeoisement of colonial communities and with a significant sharpening of racial lines. European women supposedly required more metropolitan amenities than men and more spacious surroundings to allow it; their more delicate sensibilities required more servants and thus suitable quarters — discrete and enclosed. In short, white women needed to be maintained at elevated standards of living, in insulated social spaces cushioned with the cultural artifacts of "being European." Whether women or men set these new standards is left unclear. Who exhibited "overconcern" and a "need for" segregation (Beidelman 1982:13)? Male doctors advised French women in Indochina to have their homes built with separate domestic and kitchen quarters (Grall 1908:74). Segregationist standards were what women "deserved" and more importantly were what white male prestige required that they maintain.

Colonial rhetoric on white women was riddled with contradictions. At the same time that new female immigrants were chided for not respecting the racial distance of local convention, an equal number of colonial observers accused these women of being more avid racists in their own right (Spear 1963; Nora 1961). Allegedly insecure and jealous of the sexual liaisons of European men with native women, bound to their provincial visions and cultural norms, European women in Algeria, the Indies, Madagascar, India, and West Africa were uniformly charged with constructing the major cleavages on which colonial stratification rested (Spear 1963:140; Nora 1961:174; Mannoni 1964:115; Gann and Duignan 1978:242; Kennedy 1947:164; Nandy 1983:9).

What is most startling here is that women, otherwise marginal actors on the colonial stage, are charged with dramatically reshaping the face of colonial society, imposing their racial will on African and Asian colonies where "an iron curtain of ignorance" replaced "relatively unrestrained social intermingling" in earlier years (Vere Allen 1970:169; Cohen 1971:122). European women were not only the bearers of racist beliefs but hard-line operatives who put them into practice, encouraging class distinctions among whites while fostering new racial antagonisms, no longer muted by sexual access (Vere Allen 1970:168).[11] Are we to believe that sexual intimacy with European men yielded social mobility and political rights for colonized women? Or, even less likely, that because British civil servants bedded with Indian women, somehow Indian men had more "in common" with British men and enjoyed more parity? Colonized women could sometimes parlay their positions into personal profit and small rewards, but these were *individual* negotiations with no social, legal, or cumulative claims.

Male colonizers positioned European women as the bearers of a redefined colonial morality. But to suggest that women fashioned this racism out of whole cloth is to miss the political chronology in which new intensities of racist practice arose. In the African and Asian contexts already mentioned, the arrival of large numbers of European wives, and particularly the fear for their protection, followed from new terms and tensions in the colonial encounter. The presence and protection of European women were repeatedly invoked to clarify racial lines. Their presence coincided with perceived threats to European prestige (Brownfoot 1984:191), increased racial conflict (Strobel 1987:378), covert challenges to the colonial order, outright expressions of nationalist resistance, and internal dissension among whites themselves (Stoler 1989:147).

If white women were the primary force behind the decline of concubinage, as is often claimed, then they played this role as participants in a broader racial realignment and political plan (Knibiehler and Goutalier 1985:76). This is not to suggest that European women were passive in this process, as the dominant themes in their novels attest (Taylor 1977:27). Many European women did oppose concubinage not because of their inherent jealousy of native women but, as they argued, because of the double standard it condoned for European men (Clerkx 1961; Lucas 1986:94–95).[12] The voices of European women, however, had little resonance until their objections coincided with a realignment in racial and class politics.

Dealing with Transgressions: Policing the Peril

The gender-specific requirements for colonial living, referred to above, were constructed on heavily racist evaluations that pivoted on the heightened sexuality of colonized men (Tiffany and Adams 1985). Although European women were absent from men's sexual reveries in colonial literature, men of color were considered to see them as desired and seductive figures. European women needed protection because men of color had "primitive" sexual urges and uncontrollable lust, aroused by the sight of white women (Strobel 1987:379; Schmidt 1987:411). In some colonies, that sexual threat was latent; in others, it was given a specific name.

In southern Rhodesia and Kenya in the 1920s and 1930s, preoccupations with the "black peril" (referring to the professed dangers of sexual assault on white women by black men) gave rise to the creation of citizens' militias, ladies' riflery clubs, and investigations as to whether African female domestic servants would not be safer to employ than men (Kirkwood 1984:158; Schmidt 1987:412; D. Kennedy 1987:128–147). In New Guinea, the White Women's Protection Ordinance of 1926 provided "the death penalty for any person convicted for the crime of rape or attempted rape upon a European woman or girl" (Inglis 1975:vi). And as late as 1934, Solomon Islands authorities introduced public flogging as punishment for "criminal assaults on [white] females" (Boutilier 1984:197).

What do these cases have in common? First, the rhetoric of sexual assault and the measures used to prevent it had virtually no correlation with the incidence of rape of European women by men of color. Just the contrary: there was often no evidence, ex post facto or at the time, that rapes were committed or that rape attempts were made (Schmidt 1987; Inglis 1975; Kirkwood 1984; D. Kennedy 1987; Boutilier 1984). This is not to suggest that sexual assaults never occurred, but that their incidence had little to do with the fluctuations in anxiety about them. Second, the rape laws were race-specific; sexual abuse of black women was not classified as rape and therefore was not legally actionable, nor did rapes committed by white men lead to prosecution (Mason 1958:246–47). If these accusations of sexual threat were not prompted by the fact of rape, what did they signal and to what were they tied?

Allusions to political and sexual subversion of the colonial system went hand in hand. Concern over protection of white women intensified during real and perceived crises of control — provoked by threats to the internal cohesion of the European communities or by infringements on their borders. While the chronologies differ, we can identify a patterned *sequence* of events in which Papuan, Algerian, and South African men heightened their demands for civil rights and refused the constraints imposed upon their education, movements, or dress (Inglis 1975:8, 11; Sivan 1983:178). Rape charges were thus based on perceived transgressions of political and social space. "Attempted rapes" turned out to be "incidents" of a Papuan man "discovered" in the vicinity of a white residence, a Fijian man who entered a European patient's room, a male servant poised at the bedroom door of a European woman asleep or in half-dress (Boutilier 1984:197; Inglis 1975:11; Schmidt 1987:413). With such a broad definition of danger, all colonized men of color were potential aggressors.

Accusations of sexual assault frequently followed upon heightened tensions within European communities — and renewed efforts to find consensus within them. In South Africa and Rhodesia, the relationship between reports of sexual assault and strikes among white miners and railway workers is well documented (van Onselen 1982:51; D. Kennedy 1987:138). Similarly, in the late 1920s, when labor protests by Indonesian workers and European employees were most intense, Sumatra's corporate elite expanded their vigilante organizations, intelligence networks, and demands for police protection to ensure their women were safe and their workers "in hand" (Stoler 1985b). In this particular context where the European community had been blatantly divided between low-ranking estate employees and the company elite, common interests were emphasized and domestic situations were rearranged.

In Sumatra's plantation belt, subsidized sponsorship of married couples replaced the recruitment of single Indonesian workers and European staff, with new incentives provided for family formation in both groups. This recomposed labor force of family men in "stable households" explicitly weeded out the politically malcontent. With the marriage restriction finally lifted for European staff in the 1920s, young men sought marriages with Dutch women. Higher salaries, upgraded housing, elevated bonuses, and a more mediated chain of command between colonized fieldworker and colonial managers clarified economic and political interests. With this shift, the vocal opposition to corporate and government directives, sustained by an independent union of European subordinates for nearly two decades, was effectively dissolved (Stoler 1989:152–153).

The remedies intended to alleviate sexual danger embraced a common set of prescriptions for securing white control: increased surveillance of native men, new laws stipulating severe corporal punishment for the transgression of sexual and social boundaries, and the creation of areas made racially off limits. This moral rearmament of the European community and reassertion of its cultural identity charged European women with guarding new norms. While instrumental in promoting white solidarity, it was partly at their own expense. As we shall see, they were nearly as closely surveilled as colonized men (Strobel 1987).

While native men were legally punished for alleged sexual assaults, European women were frequently blamed for provoking those desires. New arrivals from Europe were accused of being too familiar with their servants, lax in their commands, indecorous in speech and dress (Vellut 1982:100; D. Kennedy 1987:141; Schmidt 1987:413). The Rhodesian Immorality Act of 1916 "made it an offence for a white woman to make an indecent suggestion to a male native" (Mason 1958:247). In Papua New Guinea, "everyone" in the Australian community agreed that rape assaults were caused by a "younger generation of white women" who simply did not know how to treat servants (Inglis 1975:80). In Rhodesia as in Uganda, women were restricted to activities within the European enclaves and dissuaded from taking up farming on their own (Gartrell 1984:169; D. Kennedy 1987:141). As in the American South, "etiquettes of chivalry controlled white women's behavior even as [it] guarded caste lines" (Dowd Hall 1984:64). A defense of community, morality, and white male power affirmed the vulnerability of white women and the sexual threat posed by native men and created new sanctions to limit the liberties of both.

Although European colonial communities in the early twentieth century assiduously monitored the movements of European women, some European women did work. French women in the settler communities of Algeria and Senegal ran farms, rooming houses, and shops along with their men (Baroli 1967:159; O'Brien 1972). Elsewhere, married European women "supplemented" their husbands' incomes, helping to maintain the "white standard" (Tirefort 1979; Mercier 1965:292). Women were posted throughout the colonial empires as missionaries, nurses, and teachers; while some women openly questioned the sexist policies of their male superiors, by and large their tasks buttressed rather than contested the established cultural order (Knibiehler and Goutalier 1985; Callaway 1987:111).

French feminists urged women with skills (and a desire for marriage) to settle in Indochina at the turn of the century, but colonial administrators were adamantly against their immigration. Not only was there a surfeit of widows without resources, but European seamstresses, florists, and children's outfitters could not compete with the cheap and skilled labor provided by well-established Chinese firms (Corneau 1900:10, 12). In Tonkin in the 1930s there was still "little room for single women, be they unmarried, widowed or divorced"; most were shipped out of the colony at the government's charge (Gantes 1981:45).[13] Firmly rejecting expansion based on "poor white" (*petit blanc*) settlement as in Algeria, French officials in Indochina dissuaded *colons* with insufficient capital from entry and promptly repatriated those who tried to remain.[14] Single women were seen as the quintessential *petit blanc*, with limited resources and shopkeeper aspirations. Moreover, they presented the dangerous possibility that straitened circumstances would lead them to prostitution, thereby degrading European prestige at large.

In the Dutch East Indies, state officials identified European widows as one of the most economically vulnerable and impoverished segments of the European community (Het Pauperisme Commissie 1901:28). Professional competence did not leave European women immune from marginalization. Single professional women were held in contempt as were European prostitutes, with surprisingly similar objections.[15] The important point is that numerous categories of women fell outside the social space to which European colonial women were assigned — namely, as custodians of family welfare and respectability and as dedicated and willing subordinates to, and supporters of, colonial men. The rigor with which these norms were applied becomes more comprehensible when we see how a European family life and bourgeois respectability became increasingly tied to notions of racial survival, imperial patriotism, and the political strategies of the colonial state.

White Degeneracy, Motherhood, and the Eugenics of Empire

de-gen-er-ate adj. [*L.* degeneratus, *pp. of* degenerare, *to become unlike one's race*, degenerate < degener, *not genuine, base* < de-, *from* + genus, *race, kind: see* genus]. *1. having sunk below a former or normal condition, character, etc.; deteriorated 2. morally corrupt; depraved* — n. *a degenerate person, esp. one who is morally depraved or sexually perverted* — vi -at' ed, -at' ing . . . *2. to decline or become debased morally, culturally, etc.* . . . *3.* Biol. *to undergo degeneration; deteriorate*

Webster's New World Dictionary

European women were essential to the colonial enterprise and the solidification of racial boundaries in ways that repeatedly tied their supportive and subordinate posture to community cohesion and colonial peace. These features of their positioning within imperial politics were powerfully reinforced at the turn of the century by a metropolitan bourgeois discourse (and an eminently anthropological one) intensely concerned with notions of "degeneracy" (Le Bras 1981:77). Middle-class morality, manliness, and motherhood were seen as endangered by the intimately linked fears of "degeneration" and miscegenation in scientifically construed racist beliefs (Mosse 1978:82).[16] Due to environmental and/or inherited factors, degeneracy could be averted positively by eugenic selection or negatively by eliminating the "unfit" (Mosse 1978:87; Kevles 1985:70–84). Eugenic arguments used to explain the social malaise of industrialization, immigration, and urbanization in the early twentieth century derived from the notion that acquired characteristics were inheritable and thus that poverty, vagrancy, and promiscuity were class-linked biological traits, tied to genetic material as directly as night blindness and blond hair.

Appealing to a broad political and scientific constituency at the turn of the century, eugenic societies included advocates of infant welfare programs, liberal intellectuals, conservative businessmen, Fabians, and physicians with social concerns. By the 1920s, however, these societies contained an increasingly vocal number of those who called for and put into law, if not practice, the sterilization of significant numbers in the British, German, and American working-class populations (Mosse 1978:87; 1985:122).[17] Negative eugenics never gained the same currency in Holland as it did elsewhere; nevertheless, it seems clear from the Dutch and Dutch Indies scientific and popular press that concerns with hereditary endowment and with "Indo degeneracy" were grounded in a cultural racism that rivaled its French variant, if in a somewhat more muted form.[18]

Feminists attempted to appropriate this rhetoric for their own birth control programs, but eugenics was essentially elitist, racist, and misogynist in principle and practice (Gordon 1976:395; Davin 1978; Hammerton 1979). Its proponents advocated a pronatalist policy toward the white middle and upper classes, a rejection of work roles for women that might compete with motherhood, and "an assumption that reproduction was not just a function but the purpose . . . of a woman's life" (Gordon 1976:134). In France, England, Germany, and the United States, positive eugenics placed European women of "good stock" as "the fountainhead of racial strength" (Ridley 1983:91), exalting the cult of motherhood while subjecting it to more thorough scientific scrutiny (Davin 1978:12).

As part of metropolitan class politics, eugenics reverberated in the colonies in predictable as well as unexpected forms. The moral, biological, and sexual referents of the notion of degeneracy (distinct in the dictionary citation above) came together in how the concept was actually deployed. The "colonial branch" of eugenics embraced a theory and practice concerned with the vulnerabilities of white rule and new measures to safeguard European superiority. Designed to control the procreation of the "unfit" lower orders, eugenics targeted "the poor, the colonized, or unpopular strangers" (Hobsbawm 1987:253). It was, however, also used by metropolitan observers against colonials and by colonial elites against "degenerate" members among themselves (Koks 1931:179–89). While studies in Europe and the United States focused on the inherent propensity of the poor for criminality, in the Indies delinquency among poor Indo-European children was biologically linked to the amount of "*native blood*" they had (Braconier 1918:11). Eugenics provided not so much a new vocabulary as a medical and moral basis for anxiety over white prestige, an anxiety that reopened debates over segregated residence and education, new standards of morality, sexual vigilance, and the rights of certain Europeans to rule.

Eugenic influence manifested itself, not in the direct importation of metropolitan practices such as sterilization, but in a translation of the political *principles* and the social values that eugenics implied. In defining what was unacceptable, eugenics also identified what constituted a "valuable life": "a gender-specific work and productivity, described in social, medical and psychiatric terms" (Bock 1984:274). Applied to European colonials, eugenic statements pronounced what kind of people should represent Dutch or French rule, how they should bring up their children, and with whom they should socialize. Those concerned with issues of racial survival and racial purity invoked moral arguments about the national duty of French, Dutch, British, and Belgian colonial women to stay at home.

If in Britain racial deterioration was conceived to be a result of the moral turpitude and the ignorance of working-class mothers, in the colonies, the dangers were more pervasive, the possibilities of contamination worse. Formulations to secure European rule pushed in two directions: on the one hand, away from ambiguous racial genres and open domestic arrangements, and, on the other hand, toward an upgrading, homogenization, and a clearer delineation of European standards; away from miscegenation toward white endogamy; away from concubinage toward family formation and legal marriage; away from, as in the case of the Indies, mestizo customs and toward metropolitan norms (Taylor 1983; van Doorn 1985). As stated in the bulletin of the Netherlands Indies' Eugenic Society, "[E]ugenics is nothing other than belief in the possibility of preventing degenerative symptoms in the body of our beloved *moedervolken,* or in cases where they may already be present, of counteracting them" (Rodenwalt 1928:1).

Like the modernization of colonialism itself, with its scientific management and educated technocrats with limited local knowledge, colonial communities of the early twentieth century were rethinking the ways in which their authority should be expressed. This rethinking took the form of asserting a distinct colonial morality, explicit in its reorientation toward the racial and class markers of "Europeanness," emphasizing transnational racial commonalities despite national differences — distilling a *Homo Europeaus* of superior health, wealth, and intelligence as a white man's norm. As one celebrated commentator on France's colonial venture wrote: "[O]ne might be surprised that my pen always returns to the words *blanc* [white] or 'European' and never to *'Français.'* . . . [I]n effect colonial solidarity and the obligations that it entails ally all the peoples of the white races" (Pujarniscle 1931:72; also see Delavignette 1946:41).

Such sensibilities colored imperial policy in nearly all domains, with fears of physical contamination merging with those of political vulnerability. To guard their ranks, whites had to increase their numbers and to ensure that their members blurred neither the biological nor the political boundaries on which their power rested.[19] In the metropole, the socially and physically "unfit," the poor, the indigent, and the insane were to be either sterilized or prevented from marriage. In the British and Belgian colonies, among others, it was these very groups among Europeans who were either excluded from entry or institutionalized while they were there and when possible sent home (Arnold 1979; see also Vellut 1987:97).

Thus, whites in the colonies adhered to a politics of exclusion that policed their members as well as the colonized. Such concerns were not new to the 1920s (Taylor 1983; Sutherland 1982). As early as the mid–eighteenth century, the Dutch East Indies Company had already taken "draconian measures" to control pauperism among "Dutchmen of mixed blood" (*Encyclopedie van Nederland-Indie* 1919:367). In the same period, the British East Indies Company legally and administratively dissuaded lower-class European migration and settlement, with the argument that they might destroy Indian respect for "the superiority of the European character" (quoted in Arnold 1983:139). Patriotic calls to populate Java in the mid-1800s with poor Dutch farmers were also condemned, but it was with new urgency that these possibilities were rejected in the following century as challenges to European rule were more profoundly felt.

Measures were taken both to avoid the migration of poor whites and to produce a colonial profile that highlighted the vitality, colonial patriotism, and racial superiority of European men (Loutfi 1971:112–13; Ridley 1983:104).[20] Thus, British colonial administrators were retired by the age of fifty-five, ensuring that "no Oriental was ever allowed to see a Westerner as he aged and degenerated, just as no Westerner needed ever to see himself . . . as anything but a vigorous, rational, ever-alert young Raj" (Said 1979:42). In the twentieth century, these "men of class" and "men of character" embodied a modernized and renovated colonial rule; they were to safeguard the colonies against physical weakness, moral decay, and the inevitable degeneration that long residence in the colonies encouraged and the temptations that interracial domestic situations had allowed.

Given this ideal, it is not surprising that colonial communities strongly discouraged the presence of nonproductive men. Dutch and French colonial administrators expressed a constant concern with the dangers of unemployed or impoverished Europeans. During the succession of economic crises in the early twentieth century, relief agencies in Sumatra, for example, organized fund-raisers, hill-station retreats, and small-scale agricultural schemes to keep "unfit" Europeans "from roaming around" (Kroniek 1917:49). The colonies were neither open for retirement nor tolerant of the public presence of poor whites. During the 1930s depression, when tens of thousands of Europeans in the Indies found themselves without jobs, government and private resources were quickly mobilized to ensure that they were not "reduced" to native living standards (Veerde 1931; Kantoor van Arbeid 1935). Subsidized health care, housing, and education complemented a rigorous affirmation of European cultural standards in which European womanhood played a central role in keeping men *civilisé*.

On Cultural Hygiene: The Dynamics of Degeneration

The shift in imperial thinking that we can identify in the early twentieth century focuses not only on the otherness of the colonized but on the otherness of colonials themselves. In metropolitan France, a profusion of medical and sociological tracts pinpointed the colonial as a distinct and degenerate social type, with specific psychological and even physical characteristics (Maunier 1932; Pujarniscle 1931).[21] Some of that difference was attributed to the debilitating effects of climate and social milieu, "such that after a certain time, he [the colonial] has become both physically and morally a completely different man" (Maunier 1932:169).

Medical manuals warned that people who stayed "too long" were in grave danger of overfatigue, of individual and racial degeneration, of physical breakdown (not just illness), of cultural contamination, and of neglect of the conventions of supremacy and *agreement* about what they were (Dupuy 1955:184–85). What were identified as the degraded and unique characteristics of French colonials — "ostentation," "speculation," "inaction," and a general "demoralization" — were "faults" contracted from native culture, which now marked them as *décivilisé* (Maunier 1932:174; Jaurequiberry 1924:25).

Colonial medicine reflected and affirmed this slippage between physical, moral, and cultural degeneracy in numerous ways. The climatic, social, and work conditions of colonial life gave rise to a specific set of psychotic disorders affecting *l'equilibre cerebral,* predisposing Europeans in the tropics to mental breakdown (Hartenberg 1910; Abatucci 1910). Neurasthenia was a major problem in the French empire and supposedly accounted for more than half the Dutch repatriations from the Indies to Holland (Winckel 1938:352). In Europe and America, it was "the phantom disease, . . . the classic illness of the late 19th century," intimately linked to sexual deviation and to the destruction of the social order itself (Gilman 1985: 199, 202).

While in Europe neurasthenia was considered to signal a decadent overload of "modern civilization" and its high-pitched pace, in the colonies its etiology took the *reverse* form. Colonial neurasthenia was allegedly caused by a *distance* from civilization and European community and by proximity to the colonized. The susceptibility of a colonial male was increased by an existence "outside of the social framework to which he was adapted in France, isolation in outposts, physical and moral fatigue, and modified food regimes" (Joyeux 1937:335).[22]

The proliferation of hill stations in the twentieth century reflected these political and physical concerns. Invented in the early nineteenth century as sites for military posts and sanitariums, hill stations provided "European-like environments" in which colonials could recoup their physical and mental well-being by simulating the conditions "at home" (King 1976:165). Isolated at relatively high altitudes, they took on new importance with the arrival of increasing numbers of European women and children, considered particularly susceptible to anemia, depression, and ill-health.[23] Vacation bungalows and schools built in these "naturally" segregated surroundings provided cultural refuge and regeneration (Price 1939).

Some doctors considered the only treatment to be "le retour en Europe" (return to Europe) (Joyeux 1937:335; Pujarniscle 1931:28). Others encouraged a local set of remedies, prescribing a bourgeois ethic of morality and work. This included sexual moderation, a "regularity and regimentation" of work, abstemious diet, physical exercise, and *European* camaraderie, buttressed by a solid family life with European children, raised and nurtured by a European wife (Grall 1908:51; Price 1939: also see D. Kennedy 1987:123). Guides to colonial living in the 1920s and 1930s reveal this marked shift in outlook; Dutch, French, and British doctors now denounced the unhealthy, indolent lifestyles of "old colonials," extolling the active, engaged, and ever-busy activities of the new breed of colonial husband and wife (Raptschinsky 1941:46). Women were exhorted to actively participate in household management and child-care and otherwise to divert themselves with botanical collections and "good works" (Chivas-Baron 1929; Favre 1938).

Cultural Contamination, Children, and the Dangers of Métissage

> [*Young colonial men*] *are often driven to seek a temporary companion among women of color; this is the path by which, as I shall presently show, contagion travels back and forth, contagion in all senses of the word.*
>
> Maunier 1932:171

Racial degeneracy was thought to have social causes and political consequences, both tied to the domestic arrangements of colonialism in specific ways. *Métissage* (interracial unions) generally, and concubinage in particular, represented the paramount danger to racial purity and cultural identity in all its forms. It was through sexual contact with women of color that French men "contracted" not only disease but debased sentiments, immoral proclivities, and extreme susceptibility to decivilized states (Dupuy 1955:198).

By the early twentieth century, concubinage was denounced for undermining precisely those things that it was charged with fortifying decades earlier. Local women, who had been considered protectors of men's well-being, were now seen as the bearers of ill-health and sinister influences; adaptation to local food, language, and dress, once prescribed as healthy signs of acclimatization, were now sources of contagion and loss of the (white) self. The benefits of local knowledge and sexual release gave way to the more pressing demands of respectability, the community's solidarity, and its mental health. Increasingly, French men in Indochina who kept native women were viewed as passing into "the enemy camp" (Pujarniscle 1931:107). Concubinage became not only the source of individual breakdown and ill-health but the biological and social root of racial degeneration and political unrest. Children born of these unions were "the fruits of a regrettable weakness" (Mazet 1932:8), physically marked and morally marred with "the defaults and mediocre qualities of their [native] mothers" (Douchet 1928:10).

Concubinage was not as economically tidy and politically neat as colonial policy-makers had hoped. It concerned more than sexual exploitation and unpaid domestic work; it was about children — many more than official statistics often revealed — and who was to be acknowledged as a European and who was not. Concubines' children posed a classificatory problem, impinging on political security and white prestige. The majority of such children were not recognized by their fathers, nor were they reabsorbed into local communities as authorities often claimed. Although some European men legally acknowledged their progeny, many repatriated to Holland, Britain, or France and cut off ties and support to mother and children (Brou 1907; Ming 1983:75). Native women had responsibility for, but attenuated rights over, their own offspring. They could neither prevent their children from being taken from them nor contest paternal suitability for custody. While the legal system favored a European upbringing, it made no demands on European men to provide it; many children became wards of the state, subject to the scrutiny and imposed charity of the European-born community at large.

Concubines' children were invariably counted among the ranks of the European colonial poor, but European paupers in the Netherlands Indies in the late nineteenth century came from a far wider strata of colonial society than that of concubines alone (Het Pauperisme Commissie 1903). Many Indo-Europeans had become increasingly marginalized from strategic political and economic positions in the early twentieth century, despite new educational opportunities encouraged at the turn of the century. In the 1920s and 1930s, youths born and educated in the Indies were uncomfortably squeezed between an influx of new colonial recruits from Holland and the educated *inlander* (native) population with whom they were in direct competition for jobs (Mansvelt 1932:295).[24] At the turn of the century, volumes of official reports were devoted to documenting and alleviating the proliferation on Java of a "rough" and "dangerous pauper element" among Indo-European clerks, low-level officials, and vagrants (*Encyclopedie van Nederland-Indie* 1919:367).

European pauperism in the Indies reflected broad inequalities in colonial society, underscoring the social heterogeneity of the category "European" itself. Nonetheless, as late as 1917, concubinage was still seen by some as its major cause and as the principal source of *blanken-haters* (white-haters) (Braconier 1917:298). Concubinage became equated with a progeny of "malcontents," of "parasitic" whites, idle and therefore dangerous. The fear of concubinage was carried yet a step further and tied to the political fear that such Eurasians would demand economic access and political rights and would express their own interests through alliance with (and leadership of) organized opposition to Dutch rule (Mansvelt 1932; Blumberger 1939).[25]

Racial prejudice against *métis* was often, as in the Belgian Congo, "camouflaged under protestations of 'pity' for their fate, as if they were *'malheureux'* [unhappy] beings by definition" (Vellut 1982:103). They were objects of charity, and their protection in Indochina was a cause célèbre of European women — feminists and staunch colonial supporters — at home and abroad (Knibiehler and Goutalier 1985:37). European colonial women were urged to oversee their "moral protection," to develop their "natural" inclination toward French society, to turn them into "partisans of French ideas and influence" instead of revolutionaries (Chenet 1936:8; Sambuc 1931:261). The gender breakdown is clear: moral instruction reflected fears of sexual promiscuity in *métisse* girls and the political threat of *métis* boys turned militant men.

Orphanages for abandoned European and Indo-European children were not new features of twentieth-century colonial cultures; however, their importance increased vastly as an ever larger number of illegitimate children of mixed parentage populated gray zones along colonial divides. In the Netherlands Indies by the mid–eighteenth century, state orphanages for Europeans were established to prevent "neglect and degeneracy of the many free-roaming poor bastards and orphans of Europeans" (quoted in Braconier 1917:293). By the nineteenth century, church, state, and private organizations had become zealous backers of orphanages, providing some education but stronger doses of moral instruction. In India, civil asylums and charity schools cared for European and Anglo-Indian children in "almost every town, cantonment and hill-station" (Arnold 1979:108). In French Indochina in the 1930s, virtually every colonial city had a home and society for the protection of abandoned *métis* youth (Chenet 1936; Sambuc 1931:256–72; Malleret 1934:220).

Whether these children were in fact "abandoned" by their Asian mothers is difficult to establish; the fact that *métis* children living in native homes were often *sought out* by state and private organizations and placed in these institutions to protect them against the "demoralised and sinister" influences of native *kampong* life suggests another interpretation (Taylor 1983). Public assistance in India, Indochina, and the Netherlands Indies was designed not only to keep fair-skinned children from running barefoot in native villages but to ensure that the proliferation of European pauper settlements was curtailed and controlled.[26] The preoccupation with creating a patriotic loyalty to French and Dutch culture among children was symptomatic of a more general fear — namely, that there were *already* patricides of the colonial fatherland in the making; that the girls would grow up to fall into prostitution; that the boys — with emotional ties to native women and indigenous society — would grow up to join the *verbasterd* (degenerate) and *décivilisé* enemies of the state (Braconier 1917:293; Pouvourville 1926; Sambuc 1931:261; Malleret 1934).

European Motherhood and Middle-Class Morality

A man remains a man as long as he is under the watch of a woman of his race.
George Hardy, quoted in Chivas-Baron 1929:103

Rationalization of imperial rule and safeguards against racial degeneracy in European colonies merged in the emphasis on particular moral themes. Both entailed a reassertion of European conventions, middle-class respectability, more frequent ties with the metropole, and a restatement of what was culturally distinct and superior about how colonials ruled and lived. For those women who came to join their spouses or to find husbands, the prescriptions were clear. Just as new plantation employees were taught to manage the natives, women were schooled in colonial propriety and domestic management. French manuals, such as those on colonial hygiene in Indochina, outlined the duties of colonial wives in no uncertain terms. As "auxiliary forces" in the imperial effort they were to "conserve the fitness and sometimes the life of all around them" by ensuring that "the home be happy and gay and that all take pleasure in clustering there" (Grall 1908:66; Chailley-Bert 1897). Practical guides to life in the Belgian Congo instructed (and indeed warned) *la femme blanche* that she was to keep "order, peace, hygiene, and economy" (Favre 1938:217) and to "perpetuate a vigorous race" while preventing any "laxity in our administrative mores" (Favre 1938:256; Travaux du Groupe d'Études Coloniales 1910:10).

This "division of labor" contained obvious asymmetries. Men were considered more susceptible to moral turpitude than women, who were thus held responsible for the immoral states of men. European women were to create and protect colonial prestige, insulating their men from cultural and sexual contact with the colonized (Travaux du Groupe d'Études Coloniales 1910:7). Racial degeneracy would be curtailed by European women, who were charged with regenerating the physical health, the metropolitan affinities, and the imperial purpose of their men (Hardy 1929:78).

At the heart of these attitudes was a reassertion of racial difference that harnessed nationalistic rhetoric and markers of middle-class morality to its cause (Delavignette 1946:47; Loutfi 1971:112; Mosse 1978:86). George Mosse describes European racism in the early twentieth century as a "scavenger ideology," annexing nationalism and bourgeois respectability such that control over sexuality was central to all three (1985:10, 133–52). If the European middle class sought respectability "to maintain their status and self-respect against the lower-classes, and the aristocracy," then in the colonies, respectability was a defense against the colonized and a way for the colonizers to more clearly define themselves (Mosse 1985:5). Good colonial living now meant hard work, no sloth, and physical exercise rather than sexual release, which had been one rationale for condoning concubinage and prostitution in an earlier period. The debilitating influences of climate could be surmounted by regular diet and meticulous personal hygiene, over which European women were to take full charge. Manuals on how to run a European household in the tropics provided detailed instructions in domestic science, moral upbringing, and employer-servant relations. Adherence to strict conventions of cleanliness and cooking occupied an inordinate amount of women's time (Hermans 1925; Ridley 1983:77). Both activities entailed a constant surveillance of native nursemaids, laundrymen, and live-in servants, while reinforcing the domestication of European women themselves (Brink 1920:43).

Leisure, good spirit, and creature comforts became the obligation of women to provide, the racial duty of women to maintain. Sexual temptations with women of color would be curtailed by a happy family life, much as "extremist agitation" on Sumatra's estates was to be averted by selecting married recruits and by providing family housing to permanent workers (Stoler 1985a). Moral laxity would be eliminated through the example and vigilance of women whose status was defined by their sexual restraint and dedication to their homes and to their men.

The perceptions and practice that bound women's domesticity to national welfare and racial purity were not applied to colonial women alone. Child-rearing in late nineteenth-century Britain was hailed as a national, imperial, and racial duty, as it was in Holland, the United States, and Germany at the same time (Davin 1978:13; Smith-Rosenberg and Rosenberg 1973:35; Bock 1984:274; Stuurman 1985). In France, where declining birthrates were of grave concern, popular colonial authors such as Pierre Mille pushed mothering as women's "essential contribution to the imperial mission of France" (Ridley 1983:90). With motherhood at the center of empire-building, pronatalist policies in Europe forced some improvement in colonial medical facilities, the addition of maternity wards, and increased information about and control over the reproductive conditions of European and colonized women alike. Maternal and infant health programs instructed European women in the use of milk substitutes, wet nurses, and breast-feeding practices in an effort to encourage more women to stay in the colonies and in response to the many more that came (Hunt 1988). But the belief that the colonies were medically hazardous for white women meant that motherhood in the tropics was not only a precarious but a conflicted endeavor. French women bound for Indochina were warned that they would only be able to fulfill their maternal duty "with great hardship and damage to [their] health" (Grall 1908:65).

Real and imagined concern over individual reproduction and racial survival contained and compromised white colonial women in a number of ways. Tropical climates were said to cause low fertility, prolonged amenorrhea, and permanent sterility (Rodenwalt 1928:3; Hermans 1925:123). Belgian doctors confirmed that "the woman who goes to live in a tropical climate is often lost for the reproduction of the race" (Knibiehler and Goutalier 1985:92; Vellut 1982:100). The climatic and medical conditions of colonial life were associated with high infant mortality, such that "the life of a European child was nearly condemned in advance" (Grall 1908:65; Price 1939:204).

These perceived medical perils called into question whether white women and thus "white races" could actually reproduce if they remained in the tropics for extended periods of time. An international colonial medical community cross-referenced one another in citing evidence of racial sterility by the second or third generation (Harwood 1938:132; Cranworth, quoted in D. Kennedy 1987:115). While such a dark view of climate was not prevalent in the Indies, psychological and physical adaptation was never a given. Dutch doctors repeatedly quoted German physicians, if not to affirm the inevitable infertility among whites in the tropics, at least to support their contention that European-born women and men (*totoks*) should never stay in the colonies too long (Hermans 1925:123). Medical studies in the 1930s, such as that supported by the Netherlands Indies Eugenic Society, were designed to test whether fertility rates differed by "racial type" between Indo-European and European-born women and whether children of certain Europeans born in the Indies displayed different "racial markers" than their parents (Rodenwalt 1928:4).

Like the discourse on degeneracy, the fear of sterility was less about the biological survival of whites than about their political viability and cultural reproduction. These concerns were evident in the early 1900s, coming to a crescendo in the 1930s when white unemployment hit the colonies and the metropole at the same time. The depression made repatriation of impoverished French and Dutch colonial agents unrealistic, prompting speculation as to whether European working classes could be relocated in the tropics without causing further racial degeneration (Winckel 1938; Price 1939). Although white migration to the tropics was reconsidered, poor white settlements were rejected on economic, medical, and psychological grounds (Feuilletau de Bruyn 1938:27). Whatever the solution, such issues hinged on the reproductive potential of European women, invasive questionnaires (which many women refused to answer) concerning their "acclimatization," and detailed descriptions of their sexual lives.

Imperial perceptions and policies fixed European women in the colonies as "instruments of race-culture" in what proved to be personally difficult and contradictory ways (Hammerton 1979). Child-rearing manuals faithfully followed the sorts of racist principles that constrained the activities of women charged with child-care (Grimshaw 1983:507). Medical experts and women's organizations recommended strict surveillance of children's activities (Mackinnon 1920:944) and careful attention to those with whom they played. Virtually every medical and household handbook in the Dutch, French, and British colonies in the early twentieth century warned against leaving small children in the unsupervised care of local servants. In the Netherlands Indies, it was the "duty" of the *hedendaagsche blanke moeder* (modern white mother) to take the physical and spiritual upbringing of her offspring away from the *babu* (native nursemaid) and into her own hands (Wanderken 1943:173). Precautions had to be taken against "sexual danger," against unclean habits of domestics, and against a "stupid negress" who might leave a child exposed to the sun (Bauduin 1941; Bérenger-Féraud 1875:491). Even in colonies where the climate was not considered unhealthy, European children supposedly thrived well "only up to the age of six" when native cultural influences came into stronger play (Price 1939:204; Grimshaw 1983:507). In the Dutch East Indies, where educational facilities for European children were considered excellent, some still deemed it imperative to send them back to Holland to avoid the "precocity" associated with the tropics and the "danger" of contact with *indiscne* youths not from "full-blooded European elements" (Bauduin 1941:63):

> We Dutch in the Indies live in a country which is not our own. . . . [W]e feel instinctively that our blonde, white children belong to the blonde, white dunes, the forests, the moors, the lakes, the snow. . . . A Dutch child should grow up in Holland. There they will acquire the characteristics of their race, not only from mother's milk but also from the influence of the light, sun and water, of playmates, of life, in a word, in the sphere of the fatherland. This is not racism. (Bauduin 1941:63–64)

But even in the absence of such firm convictions, how to assure the "moral upbringing" of European children in the colonies remained a primary focus of women's organizations in the Indies and elsewhere right through decolonization.[27] In many colonial communities, school-age children were packed off to Europe for education and socialization. In those cases European women were confronted with a difficult set of choices that entailed separation from either their children or their husbands. Frequent trips between colony and metropole not only separated families but also broke up marriages and homes (Malleret 1934:164; Grimshaw 1983:507; Callaway 1987:183–84). The important point is that the imperial duty of women to closely surveil husbands, servants, and children profoundly affected the social space they occupied and the economic activities in which they could feasibly engage.

Shifting Strategies of Rule and Sexual Morality

> *Though sex cannot of itself enable men to transcend racial barriers, it generates some admiration and affection across them, which is healthy, and which cannot always be dismissed as merely self-interested and prudential. On the whole, sexual interaction between Europeans and non-Europeans probably did more good than harm to race relations; at any rate, I cannot accept the feminist contention that it was fundamentally undesirable.*
>
> Hyam 1986b:75

The political etymology of colonizer and colonized was gender- and class-specific. The exclusionary politics of colonialism demarcated not just external boundaries but interior frontiers, specifying internal conformity and order among Europeans themselves. I have tried to show that the categories of colonizer and colonized were secured through notions of racial difference constructed in gender terms. Redefinitions of sexual protocol and morality emerged during crises of colonial control precisely because they called into question the tenuous artifices of rule *within* European communities and what marked their borders. Even from the limited cases we have reviewed, several patterns emerge. First and most obviously, colonial sexual prohibitions were racially asymmetric and gender-specific. Thus racial attributes were rarely discussed in nongendered terms; one was always a black *man,* an Asian *woman.* Second, interdictions against interracial unions were rarely a primary impulse in the strategies of rule. Interracial unions (as opposed to marriage) between European men and colonized women aided the long-term settlement of European men in the colonies while ensuring that colonial patrimony stayed in limited and selective hands. In India, Indochina, and South Africa in the early centuries — colonial contexts usually associated with sharp social sanctions against interracial unions — "mixing" was systematically tolerated and even condoned.[28]

Changes in sexual access and domestic arrangements have invariably accompanied major efforts to reassert the internal coherence of European communities and to redefine the boundaries of privilege between the colonizer and the colonized. Sexual union in itself, however, did not automatically produce a larger population legally classified as "European." On the contrary, miscegenation signaled neither the absence nor the presence of racial prejudice in itself; hierarchies of privilege and power were written into the *condoning* of interracial unions, as well as into their condemnation.

While the chronologies vary from one colonial context to another, we can identify some parallel shifts in the strategies of rule and in sexual morality. Concubinage fell into moral disfavor at the same time that new emphasis was placed on the standardization of European administration. While this occurred in some colonies by the early twentieth century and in others later on, the correspondence between rationalized rule, bourgeois respectability, and the custodial power of European women to protect their men seems strongest during the interwar years when Western scientific and technological achievements were then in question and native nationalist and labor movements were energetically pressing their demands.[29] Debates concerning the need to systematize colonial management and dissolve the provincial and personalized satraps of "the old-time *colon*" in the French empire invariably targeted and condemned the unseemly domestic arrangements in which they lived. British high colonial officials in Africa imposed new "character" requirements on their subordinates, designating specific class attributes and conjugal ties that such a selection implied (Kuklick 1979). Critical to this restructuring was a new disdain for colonials too adapted to local custom, too removed from the local European community, and too encumbered with intimate native ties. As in Sumatra, this hands-off policy distanced Europeans in more than one sense: it forbade European staff both from personal confrontations with their Asian fieldhands and from the limited local knowledge they gained through sexual ties.

At the same time, medical expertise confirmed the salubrious benefits of European camaraderie and frequent home leaves, of a cordon sanitaire, not only around European enclaves but around each home. White prestige became defined by this rationalized management and by the moral respectability and physical well-being of its agents, with which European women were charged. Colonial politics locked European men and women into a routinized protection of their physical health and social space in ways that bound gender prescriptions to class conventions, thereby fixing the racial cleavages between "us" and "them."

I have focused here on the multiple levels at which sexual control figured in the substance, as well as the iconography, of racial policy and imperial rule. But colonial politics was obviously not just about sex; nor did sexual relations reduce to colonial politics. On the contrary, sex in the colonies was about sexual access and reproduction, class distinctions and racial privileges, nationalism and European identity in different measure and not all at the same time. These major shifts in the positioning of women were signaled not by the penetration of capitalism per se but by more subtle changes in class politics and imperial morality and were responses to the vulnerabilities of colonial control. As we attempt broader ethnographies of empire, we may begin to capture how European culture and class politics resonated in colonial settings, how class and gender discriminations not only were translated into racial attitudes but themselves reverberated in the metropole as they were fortified on colonial ground. Such investigations should help show that sexual control was both an instrumental image for the body politic, a salient part standing for the whole, and itself fundamental to how racial policies were secured and how colonial projects were carried out.

NOTES

1. Here I focus primarily on the dominant male discourse (and less on women's perceptions of social and legal constraints) since it was the structural positioning of European women in colonial society and how their needs were defined *for,* not *by,* them that most directly accounted for specific policies.

2. See Verena Martínez-Alier (1974) on the subtle and changing criteria by which color was assigned in nineteenth-century Cuba. Also see A. van Marle (1952) on shifting cultural markers of European membership in the nineteenth- and early twentieth-century Netherlands Indies.

3. See Malleret (1934:216–41). See also Tiffany and Adams, who argue that "the Romance of the Wild Woman" expressed critical distinctions between civilization and the primitive, culture and nature, and the class differences between the repressed middle-class woman and "her regressively primitive antithesis, the working-class girl" (Tiffany and Adams 1985:13).

4. Many of these studies focus on South Africa and tend to provide more insight into the composition of the black labor force than into the restrictions on European women themselves (Cock 1980; Gaitskell 1983; Hansen 1986). Important exceptions are those that have traced historical changes in colonial prostitution and domestic service where restrictions were explicitly class-specific and directly tied racial policy to sexual control (Ming 1983; Van Heyningen 1984; Hesselink 1987; Schmidt 1987).

5. As Tessel Pollman suggests, the term *nyai* glossed several functions: household manager, servant, housewife, wife, and prostitute. Which of these was most prominent depended on the character of both partners and on the prosperity of the European man (1986:100). Most colonized women, however, combining sexual and domestic service within the abjectly subordinate contexts of slave or "coolie," lived in separate quarters and exercised very few legal rights; they could be dismissed without reason or notice, were exchanged among European employers, and, most significantly, as stipulated in the Indies Civil Code of 1848, "had no rights over children recognized by a white man" (Taylor 1977:30). On Java, however, some *nyai* achieved some degree of limited authority, managing the businesses as well as the servants and household affairs of better-off European men (Nieuwenhuys 1959:17; Lucas 1986:86; Taylor 1983).

6. While prostitution served some of the colonies for some of the time, it was economically costly, medically unwieldy, and socially problematic. Venereal disease was difficult to check even with the elaborate system of lock-hospitals and contagious disease acts of the British empire and was of little interest to those administrations bent on promoting permanent settlement (Ballhatchet 1980; Ming 1983). When concubinage was condemned in the 1920s in India, Malaya, and Indonesia, venereal disease spread rapidly, giving rise to new efforts to reorder the domestic arrangements of European men (Butcher 1979:217; Ming 1983; Braconier 1933; Ballhatchet 1980).

7. See Ritter, who describes these arrangements in the mid–nineteenth century as a "necessary

evil" with no emotional attachments, because for the native woman, "the meaning of our word 'love' is entirely unknown" (1856:21).

8. In the case of the Indies, interracial marriages increased at the same time that concubinage fell into sharp decline (van Marle 1952). This rise was undoubtedly restricted to *Indisch* Europeans (those born in the Indies), who may have been eager to legalize preexisting unions in response to the moral shifts accompanying a more European cultural climate of the 1920s (van Doorn 1985). It undoubtedly should not be taken as an indication of less closure among the highly endogamous European-born population of that period (I owe this distinction in conjugal patterns to Wim Hendrik).

9. On the differences between Java's European community, which was sharply divided between the *totoks* (full-blooded Dutch born in Holland) and the *Indisch* majority (Europeans of mixed parentage and/or those Dutch born in the Indies), and Sumatra's European-oriented and non-*Indisch* colonial community, see Muller (1912), Wertheim (1959), van Doorn (1985), and Stoler (1985b).

10. Similarly, one might draw the conventional contrast between the different racial policies in French, British, and Dutch colonies. However, despite French assimilationist rhetoric, Dutch tolerance of intermarriage, and Britain's overtly segregationist stance, the similarities in the actual maintenance of racial distinctions through sexual control in these varied contexts are perhaps more striking than the differences. For the moment, it is these similarities with which I am concerned. See, for example, Simon (1981:46–48), who argues that although French colonial rule was generally thought to be more racially tolerant than that of Britain, racial distinctions in French Indochina were *in practice* vigorously maintained.

11. Cf. Degler, who also attributes the tenor of race relations to the attitudes of European women — not, however, because they were inherently more racist but because in some colonial contexts they were able to exert more influence over the extramarital affairs of their men (1971:238).

12. Although some Dutch women in fact championed the cause of the wronged *nyai,* urging improved protection for nonprovisioned women and children, they rarely went so far as to advocate for the legitimation of these unions in legal marriage (Taylor 1977:31–32; Lucas 1986:95).

13. Archive d'Outre Mer, "Emigration des femmes aux colonies," GG9903, 1897–1904; GG7663, 1893–94.

14. See Archive d'Outre Mer, series S.65, "Free Passage accorded to Europeans," including dossiers on "free passage for impoverished Europeans," for example, GG9925, 1897; GG2269, 1899–1903.

15. See Van Onselen (1982:103–162), who argues that the presence of European prostitutes and domestics-turned-prostitutes in South Africa was secured by a large, white working-class population and a highly unstable labor market for white working-class women (1982:103–162). See also Van Heyningen, who ties changes in the history of prostitution among continental women in the Cape Colony to new notions of racial purity and the large-scale urbanization of blacks after the turn of the century (1984:192–95).

16. As George Mosse notes, the concept of racial degeneration had been tied to miscegenation by Gobineau and others in the early 1800s but gained common currency in the decades that followed, entering European medical and popular vocabulary at the turn of the century (1978:82–88).

17. British eugenicists petitioned to refuse marriage licenses to the mentally ill, vagrants, and the chronically unemployed (Davin 1978:16; Stepan 1982:123). In the United States, a model eugenic sterilization law from 1922 targeted, among others, "orphans, homeless and paupers," while in Germany during the same period, "sterilization was widely and passionately recommended as a solution to shiftlessness, . . . illegitimate birth, . . . poverty, and the rising costs of social services" (Bajema 1976:138; Bock 1984:274).

18. The active interest of French anthropologists in the relationship between eugenics and immigration (and therefore in the U.S. sterilization laws, in particular) was not shared in the Netherlands (see Schneider [1982] on the particularities of eugenics in France). For some examples of eugenically informed race studies in the Dutch colonial context, see *Ons Nageslacht,* the *Geneeskundig Tijdschrift voor Nederlandsch-Indie,* as well as the numerous articles relating to "the Indo problem" that appeared in the Indies popular and scientific press during the 1920s and 1930s.

19. The topics covered in the bulletin of the Netherlands Indies Eugenics Society give some sense of the range of themes included in these concerns: articles appearing in the 1920s and 1930s discussed, among other things, "biogenealogical" investigations, the complementarity between Christian thought and eugenic principles, ethnographic studies of mestizo populations, and, not least importantly, the role of Indo-Europeans in the anti-Dutch rebellions (*Ons Nageslacht* 1928–32).

20. See Mosse (1985) for an examination of the relationship between manliness, racism, and nationalism in the European context.

21. The relationship between physical appearance and moral depravity was not confined to evaluations of European colonials. Eugenic studies abounded in speculations on the specific physical traits signaling immorality in the European lower orders, while detailed descriptions of African and Asian indigenous populations paired their physical attributes with immoral and debased tendencies.

22. Adherence to the idea that "tropical neurasthenia" was a specific malady was not shared by all medical practitioners. Among those who suggested that the use of the term be discontinued, some did so in the belief that neurasthenia in the tropics was a pyschopathology caused by social, not physiological, maladjustment (Culpin [1926], cited in Price 1939:211).

23. On the social geography of hill-stations in British India and on the predominance of women and children in them, see King 1976:156–79.

24. European pauperism in the Indies at the turn of the century referred primarily to a class of Indo-Europeans marginalized from the educated and "developed" elements in European society (Blumberger 1939:19). However, pauperism was by no means synonymous with Eurasian status since nearly 80 percent of the "Dutch" community were of mixed descent, some with powerful political and economic standing (Braconier 1917:291). As Jacques van Doorn notes, "[I]t was not the Eurasian as such, but the 'Kleine Indo' [poor Indo] who was the object of ridicule and scorn in European circles" (1983:8). One could argue that it was as much Eurasian power as pauperism that had to be checked.

25. French government investigations, accordingly, exhibited a concern for "the *métis* problem" that was out of proportion with the numbers of those who fell in that category. While the number of "Indos" in the Indies was far greater, there was never any indication that this social group would constitute the vanguard of an anticolonial movement.

26. In colonial India, "orphanages were the starting-point for a lifetime's cycle of institutions" in which "unseemly whites" were secluded from Asian sight and placed under European control (Arnold 1979:113). In Indonesia, Pro Juventate branches supported and housed together "neglected and criminal" youth with special centers for Eurasian children.

27. See, for example, the contents of women's magazines such as the *Huisvrouw in Deli,* for which the question of education in Holland or the Indies was a central issue. The rise of specific programs (such as the Clerkx-methode voor Huisonderwijs) designed to guide European mothers in the home instruction of their children may have been a response to this new push for women to oversee directly the moral upbringing of their children.

28. I have focused on late colonialism in Asia, but the colonial elites' intervention in the sexual life of their agents and subjects was by no means confined to this place or period. See Nash (1980:141) on changes in mixed marriage restrictions in sixteenth-century Mexico and Martínez-Alier on interracial marriage prohibitions in relationship to slave labor supplies in eighteenth- and early nineteenth-century Cuba (1974:39).

29. See Adas (1989) for a discussion of major shifts in colonial thinking during this period.

REFERENCES

Abatucci. 1910. "Le Milieu Africain consideré au point de vue de ses effets sur le système nerveux de l'Européen." *Annales d'hygiène et de médecine coloniale* 13:328–35.

Adas, Michael. 1989. *Machines as the Measure of Men: Scientific and Technological Superiority and Ideologies of Western Dominance*. Ithaca, N.Y.: Cornell University Press.

Arnold, David. 1979. "European Orphans and Vagrants in India in the Nineteenth Century." *Journal of Imperial and Commonwealth History* 7/2:104–27.

———. 1983. "White Colonization and Labour in Nineteenth-Century India." *Journal of Imperial and Commonwealth History* 11/2:133–58.

Bajema, Carl, ed. 1976. *Eugenics Then and Now*. Stroudsburg, Pa.: Dowden, Hutchinson and Ross.

Ballhatchet, Kenneth. 1980. *Race, Sex, and Class under the Raj: Imperial Attitudes and Policies and Their Critics, 1793–1905*. New York: St. Martin's Press.

Baroli, Marc. 1967. *La Vie quotidienne des Français en Algérie*. Paris: Hachette.

Bauduin, D. C. M. 1941 [1927]. *Het Indische Leven*. The Hague: H. P. Leopolds.

Beidelman, Thomas. 1982. *Colonial Evangelism*. Bloomington: Indiana University Press.

Bérenger-Féraud, L. 1875. *Traité clinique des maladies des Européens au Sénégal*. Paris: Adrien Delahaye.

Blumberger, J. Th. Petrus. 1939. *De Indo-Europeesche Beweging in Nederlandsch-Indie.* Haarlem: Tjeenk Willink.

Blussé, Leonard. 1986. *Strange Company: Chinese Settlers, Mestizo Women and the Dutch in VOC Batavia.* Dordrecht: Foris.

Bock, Gisela. 1984. "Racism and Sexism in Nazi Germany: Motherhood, Compulsory Sterilization, and the State." In *When Biology Became Destiny: Women in Weimar and Nazi Germany.* New York: Monthly Review Press, 271–96.

Boutilier, James. 1984. "European Women in the Solomon Islands, 1900–1942." In *Rethinking Women's Roles: Perspectives from the Pacific,* ed. Denise O'Brien and Sharon Tiffany, 173–99. Berkeley: University of California Press.

Braconier, A. de. 1913. "Het Kazerne-Concubinaat in Ned-Indie." *Vragen van den Dag* 28:974–95.

———. 1917. "Het Pauperisme onder de in Ned. Oost-Indie levende Europeanen." In *Nederlandsch-Indie* (1st yr.), 291–300.

———. 1918. *Kindercriminaliteit en de Verzorging van Misdadiq Aangelegde en Verwaarloosde Minderjarigen in Nederlansch Indie.* Baarn: Hollandia-Drukkerij.

———. 1933. "Het Prostitutie-vraagstuk in Nederlandsch-Indie." *Indisch Gids* 55/2:906–28.

Brink, K. B. M. Ten. 1920. *Indische Gezondheid.* Batavia: Nillmij.

Brou, A. M. N. 1907. "Le Métis Franco-Annamite." *Revue indochinois* (July 1907):897–908.

Brownfoot, Janice N. 1984. "Memsahibs in Colonial Malaya: A Study of European Wives in a British Colony and Protectorate 1900–1940." In *The Incorporated Wife,* ed. Hilary Callan and Shirley Ardener. London: Croom Helm.

Butcher, John. 1979. *The British in Malaya, 1880–1941: The Social History of a European Community in Colonial Southeast Asia.* Kuala Lumpur: Oxford University Press.

Callan, Hilary, and Shirley Ardener, eds. 1984. *The Incorporated Wife.* London: Croom Helm.

Callaway, Helen. 1987. *Gender, Culture and Empire: European Women in Colonial Nigeria.* London: Macmillan.

Chailley-Bert, M. J. 1897. *L'Emigration des femmes aux colonies: Union Coloniale Française-Conférence, 12 January 1897.* Paris: Armand Colin.

Chenet, Ch. 1936. "Le Role de la femme française aux colonies: Protection des enfants métis abandonnés." *Le Devoir des femmes* (February 15, 1936): 8.

Chivas-Baron, Clotide. 1929. *La Femme française aux colonies.* Paris: Larose.

Clerkx, Lily. 1961. *Mensen in Deli.* Amsterdam: Sociologisch-Historisch Seminarium voor Zuidoost-Azie, publication no. 2.

Cock, J. 1980. *Maids and Madams.* Johannesburg: Ravan Press.

Cohen, William. 1971. *Rulers of Empire: The French Colonial Service in Africa.* Stanford, Calif.: Hoover Institution Press.

———. 1980. *The French Encounter with Africans: White Response to Blacks, 1530–1880.* Bloomington: Indiana University Press.

Cool, F. 1938. "De Bestrijding der Werkloosheidsgevolgen in Nederlandsch-Indie gedurende 1930–1936." *De Economist,* 135–47; 217–243.

Cooper, Frederick. 1980. *From Slaves to Squatters.* New Haven: Yale University Press.

Corneau, Grace. 1900. *La Femme aux colonies.* Paris: Librairie Nilsson.

Courtois, E. 1900. "Des Règles Hygiéniques que doit suivre l'Européen au Tonkin." *Revue indo-chinoise* 83:539–41, 564–66, 598–601.

Davin, Anna. 1978. "Imperialism and Motherhood." *History Workshop* 5:9–57.

Degler, Carl. 1971. *Neither Black nor White.* New York: Macmillan.

Delavignette, Robert. 1946. *Service africain.* Paris: Gallimard.

Dixon, C. J. 1913. *De assistent in Deli.* Amsterdam: J. H. de Bussy.

Douchet, P. 1928. *Métis et congaies d'Indochine.* Hanoi.

Dowd Hall, Jacquelyn. 1984. "'The Mind That Burns in Each Body': Women, Rape, and Racial Violence." *Southern Exposure* 12/6:61–71.

Drooglever, P. 1980. *De Vaderlandse Club, 1929–42.* Franeker: T. Wever.

Dupuy, Aimé. 1955. "La Personnalité du colon." *Revue d'histoire economique et sociale* 33/1:77–103.

Encyclopedie van Nederland-Indie. 1919. The Hague: Nijhoff and Brill.

Etienne, Mona, and Eleanor Leacock. 1980. *Women and Colonization.* New York: Praeger.

Fanon, Frantz. 1967 [1952]. *Black Skin, White Masks.* New York: Grove Press.

Favre, J. L. 1938. *La Vie aux colonies.* Paris: Larose.

Feuilletau de Bruyn, W. 1938. "Over de Economische Mogelijkheid van een Kolonisatie van Blanken op Nederlandsch Nieuw-Guinea." In *Comptes rendus du congrès international de géographie, Amsterdam*. Leiden: Brill, 21–29.

Fredrickson, George. 1981. *White Supremacy*. New York: Oxford University Press.

Gaitskell, Deborah. 1983. "Housewives, Maids or Mothers: Some Contradictions of Domesticity for Christian Women in Johannesburg, 1903–39." *Journal of African History* 24:241–56.

Gann, L. H., and Peter Duignan. 1978. *The Rulers of British Africa, 1870–1914*. Stanford, Calif.: Stanford University Press.

Gantes, Gilles de. 1981. *La Population française au Tonkin entre 1931 et 1938: Memoire*. Aix-en-Provence: Institut d'Histoire des Pays d'Outre Mer.

Gartrell, Beverley. 1984. "Colonial Wives: Villains or Victims?" In *The Incorporated Wife,* ed. H. Callan and S. Ardener. London: Croom Helm, 165–85.

Gilman, Sander L. 1985. *Difference and Pathology*. Ithaca, N.Y.: Cornell University Press.

Gordon, Linda. 1976. *Woman's Body, Woman's Right*. New York: Grossman.

Gordon, R., and M. Meggitt. 1985. *Law and Order in the New Guinea Highlands*. Hanover, N.H.: University Press of New England.

Grall, Ch. 1908. *Hygiène coloniale appliquée*. Paris: Baillière.

Grimshaw, Patricia. 1983. "Christian Woman, Pious Wife, Faithful Mother, Devoted Missionary: Conflicts in Roles of American Missionary Women in Nineteenth-Century Hawaii." *Feminist Studies* 9/3:489–521.

Hammerton, James. 1979. *Emigrant Gentlewomen*. London: Croom Helm.

Hansen, Karen Tranberg. 1986. "Household Work as a Man's Job: Sex and Gender in Domestic Service in Zambia." *Anthropology Today* 2/3:18–23.

Hardy, George. 1929. *Ergaste ou la vocation coloniale*. Paris: Armand Colin.

Hartenberg. 1910. *Les Troubles nerveux et mentaux chez les coloniaux*. Paris.

Harwood, Dorothy. 1938. *The Possibility of White Colonization in the Tropics: Comptes rendus du congrès int'l de géographie*. Leiden: Brill, 131–40.

Hermans, E. H. 1925. *Gezondscheidsleer voor Nederlandsch-Indie*. Amsterdam: Meulenhoff.

Hesselink, Liesbeth. 1987. "Prostitution: A Necessary Evil, Particularly in the Colonies: Views on Prostitution in the Netherlands Indies." In *Indonesian Women in Focus,* ed. E. Locher-Scholten and A. Niehof. Dordrecht: Foris, 205–24.

Het Pauperisme Commissie. 1901. *Het Pauperisme onder de Europeanen*. Batavia: Landsdrukkerij.

———. 1903. *Rapport der Pauperisme-Commissie*. Batavia: Landsdrukkerij.

Hobsbawm, Eric. 1987. *The Age of Empire, 1875–1914*. London: Weidenfeld and Nicholson.

Hunt, Nancy. 1988. "Le Bébé en Brousse: European Women, African Birth Spacing and Colonial Intervention in Breast Feeding in the Belgian Congo." *International Journal of African Historical Studies* 21/3.

Hyam, Ronald. 1986a. "Concubinage and the Colonial Service: The Crewe Circular (1909)." *Journal of Imperial and Commonwealth History* 14/3:170–86.

———. 1986b. "Empire and Sexual Opportunity." *Journal of Imperial and Commonwealth History* 14/2:34–90.

Inglis, Amirah. 1975. *The White Women's Protection Ordinance: Sexual Anxiety and Politics in Papua*. London: Sussex University Press.

Jaurequiberry, L. 1924. *Les Blancs en pays chauds*. Paris: Maloine.

Jordan, Winthrop. 1968. *White over Black: American Attitudes toward the Negro, 1550–1812*. Chapel Hill: University of North Carolina Press.

Joyeux, Ch., and A. Sice. 1937. *Affections exotiques du système nerveux: Précis de médecine coloniale*. Paris: Masson.

Kantoor van Arbeid, R. 1935. *Werkloosheid in Nederlandsch-Indie*. Batavia: Landsdrukkerij.

Kennedy, Dane. 1987. *Islands of White*. Durham, N.C.: Duke University Press.

Kennedy, Raymond. 1947. *The Ageless Indies*. New York: John Day.

Kevles, Daniel. 1985. *In the Name of Eugenics*. Berkeley: University of California Press.

King, Anthony. 1976. *Colonial Urban Development*. London: Routledge and Kegan Paul.

Kirkwood, Deborah. 1984. "Settler Wives in Southern Rhodesia: A Case Study." In *The Incorporated Wife,* ed. H. Callan and S. Ardener. London: Croom Helm.

Knibiehler, Y., and R. Goutalier. 1985. *La Femme au temps des colonies*. Paris: Stock.

————. 1987. *Femmes et colonisation: Rapport terminal au ministère des relations extérieures et de la coopération.* Aix-en-Provence: Institut d'Histoire des Pays d'Outre-Mer.

Koks, Dr. J. Th. 1931. *De Indo.* Amsterdam: H. J. Paris.

Kroniek. 1917. *Oostkust van Sumatra-Instituut.* Amsterdam: J. H. de Bussy.

Kuklick, Henrika. 1979. *The Imperial Bureaucrat: The Colonial Administrative Service in the Gold Coast, 1920–1939.* Stanford, Calif.: Hoover Institution Press.

Le Bras, Hervé. 1981. "Histoire secrète de la fécondité." *Le Débat* 8:76–100.

Loutfi, Martine Astier. 1971. *Littérature et colonialisme.* Paris: Mouton.

Lucas, Nicole. 1986. "Trouwverbod, inlandse huishousdsters en Europese vrouwen." In *Vrouwen in de Nederlandse Kolonien,* ed. J. Reijs et al. Nijmegen: SUN, 78–97.

Mackinnon, Murdoch. 1920. "European Children in the Tropical Highlands." *Lancet* 199:944–45.

Malleret, Louis. 1934. *L'Exotisme indochinois dans la littérature française depuis 1860.* Paris: Larose.

Mannoni, Octavio. 1964. *Prospero and Caliban.* New York: Praeger.

Mansvelt, W. 1932. "De Positie der Indo-Europeanen." *Kolonial Studien,* 290–311.

Martínez-Alier, Verena. 1974. *Marriage, Class and Colour in Nineteenth Century Cuba.* Cambridge: Cambridge University Press.

Mason, Philip. 1958. *The Birth of a Dilemma: The Conquest and Settlement of Rhodesia.* New York: Oxford University Press.

Maunier, M. René. 1932. *Sociologie coloniale.* Paris: Domat-Montchrestien.

Mazet, Jacques. 1932. *La Condition juridique des métis.* Paris: Domat Montchrestien.

Mercier, Paul. 1965. "The European Community of Dakar." In *Africa: Social Problems of Change and Conflict,* ed. Pierre van den Berghe. San Francisco: Chandler, 284–304.

Ming, Hanneke. 1983. "Barracks-Concubinage in the Indies, 1887–1920." *Indonesia* 35 (April):65–93.

Moore-Gilbert, B. J. 1986. *Kipling and "Orientalism."* New York: St. Martin's.

Mosse, George. 1978. *Toward the Final Solution.* New York: Fertig.

————. 1985. *Nationalism and Sexuality.* Madison: University of Wisconsin Press.

Muller, Hendrik. 1912. "De Europeesche Samenleving." In *Neerlands Indie.* Amsterdam: Elsevier, 371–84.

Nandy, Ashis. 1983. *The Intimate Enemy: Loss and Recovery of Self under Colonialism.* Delhi: Oxford University Press.

Nash, June. 1980. "Aztec Women: The Transition from Status to Class in Empire and Colony." In *Woman and Colonization: Anthropological Perspectives,* ed. Mona Etienne and Eleanor Leacock. New York: Praeger, 134–48.

Nieuwenhuys, Roger. 1959. *Tussen Twee Vaderlanden.* Amsterdam: Van Oorschot.

Nora, Pierre. 1961. *Les Français d'Algerie.* Paris: Julliard.

O'Brien, Rita Cruise. 1972. *White Society in Black Africa: The French in Senegal.* London: Faber and Faber.

Pollmann, Tessel. 1986. "Bruidstraantjes: De Koloniale Roman, de Njai en de Apartheid." In *Vrouwen in de Nederlandse Kolonien,* ed. J. Reijs et al. Nijmegen: SUN, 98–125.

Pouvourville, Albert de. 1926. *Le Métis: Le Mal d'argent.* Paris: Monde Moderne, 97–114.

Price, Grenfell A. 1939. *White Settlers in the Tropics.* New York: American Geographical Society.

Prochaska, David. 1989. *Making Algeria French: Colonialism in Bone, 1870–1920.* Cambridge: Cambridge University Press.

Pujarniscle, E. 1931. *Philoxène ou de la litterature coloniale.* Paris.

Raptschinsky, B. 1941. *Kolonisatie van Blanken in de Tropen.* The Hague: Bibliotheek van weten en denken.

Reijs, J., et al. 1986. *Vrouwen in de Nederlandse Kolonien.* Nijmegen: SUN.

Ridley, Hugh. 1983. *Images of Imperial Rule.* New York: Croom and Helm.

Ritter, W. L. 1856. *De Europeaan in Nederlandsch-Indie.* Leyden: Sythoff.

Rodenwalt, Ernest. 1928. "Eugenetische Problemen in Nederlandsch-Indie." *Ons Nageslacht,* 1–8.

Said, Edward W. 1979. *Orientalism.* New York: Vintage.

Sambuc. 1931. "Les Métis franco-annamites en Indochine." *Revue du Pacifique,* 256–72.

Schmidt, Elizabeth. 1987. "Ideology, Economics and the Role of Shona Women in Southern Rhodesia, 1850–1939." Ph.D. dissertation, University of Wisconsin.

Schneider, William. 1982. "Toward the Improvement of the Human Race: The History of Eugenics in France." *Journal of Modern History* 54:269–291.

Schoevers, T. 1913. "Het Leven en Werken van den Assistent bij de Tabakscultuur in Deli." In *Jaarboek der Vereeniging "Studiebelangen."* Wageningen: Zomer, 3–43.

Simon, Jean-Pierre. 1981. *Rapatriés d'Indochine.* Paris: Harmattan.

Sivan, Emmanuel. 1983. *Interpretations of Islam.* Princeton, N.J.: Darwin Press.

Smith-Rosenberg, Carroll, and Charles Rosenberg. 1973. "The Female Animal: Medical and Biological Views of Woman and Her Role in Nineteenth-Century America." *Journal of American History* 60/2:332–56.

Spear, Percival. 1963. *The Nabobs.* London: Oxford University Press.

Stepan, Nancy. 1982. *The Idea of Race in Science.* London: Macmillan.

Stoler, Ann. 1985a. *Capitalism and Confrontation in Sumatra's Plantation Belt, 1870–1979.* New Haven: Yale University Press.

———. 1985b. "Perceptions of Protest." *American Ethnologist* 12/4:642–58.

———. 1989. "Rethinking Colonial Categories: European Communities and the Boundaries of Rule." *Comparative Studies in Society and History* 13/1:134–61.

Strobel, Margaret. 1987. "Gender and Race in the 19th and 20th Century British Empire." In *Becoming Visible: Women in European History,* ed. R. Bridenthal et al. Boston: Houghton Mifflin, 375–96.

Stuurman, Siep. 1985. *Verzuiling, Kapitalisme en Patriarchaat.* Nijmegen: SUN.

Sutherland, Heather. 1982. "Ethnicity and Access in Colonial Macassar." In *Papers of the Dutch-Indonesian Historical Conference.* Leiden: Bureau of Indonesian Studies, 250–77.

Takaki, Ronald. 1977. *Iron Cages.* Berkeley: University of California Press.

Taylor, Jean. 1977. "The World of Women in the Colonial Dutch Novel." *Kabar Seberang* 2:26–41.

———. 1983. *The Social World of Batavia.* Madison: University of Wisconsin Press.

Tiffany, Sharon, and Kathleen Adams. 1985. *The Wild Woman: An Inquiry into the Anthropology of an Idea.* Cambridge, Mass.: Schenkman.

Tirefort, A. 1979. *"Le Bon temps": La Communauté française en Basse Cote d'Ivoire pendant l'entre-deux guerres, 1920–1940.* Paris: Centre d'Etudes Africaines.

Travaux du Groupe d'Etudes Coloniales. 1910. *La Femme blanche au Congo.* Brussels: Misch and Thron.

Van Doorn, Jacques. 1983. *A Divided Society: Segmentation and Mediation in Late-Colonial Indonesia.* Rotterdam: CASPA.

———. 1985. "Indie als Koloniale Maatschappy." In *De Nederlandse Samenleving Sinds 1815,* ed. F. L. van Holthoon. Assen: Maastricht.

Van Helten, J., and K. Williams. 1983. "'The Crying Need of South Africa': The Emigration of Single British Women in the Transvaal, 1901–1910." *Journal of South African Studies* 10/1:11–38.

Van Heyningen, Elizabeth B. 1984. "The Social Evil in the Cape Colony 1868–1902: Prostitution and the Contagious Disease Acts." *Journal of Southern African Studies* 10/2:170–97.

Van Marle, A. 1952. "De Group der Europeanen in Nederlands-Indie." *Indonesie* 5/2:77–121; 5/3:314–41; 5/5:481–507.

Van Onselen, Charles. 1982. *Studies in the Social and Economic History of the Witwatersrand 1886–1914.* Vol. 1. New York: Longman.

Veerde, A. G. 1931. "Onderzoek naar den Omvang der Werkloosheid op Java, November 1930–Juni 1931." *Koloniale Studien* 242–73, 503–33.

Vellut, Jean-Luc. 1982. "Materiaux pour une image du blanc dans la société coloniale du Congo Belge." In *Stéréotypes nationaux et préjuqés raciaux aux XIXe et XXe siècles,* ed. Jean Pirotte. Leuven: Éditions Nauwelaerts.

Vere Allen, J. de. 1970. "Malayan Civil Service, 1874–1941: Colonial Bureaucracy Malayan Elite." *Comparative Studies in Society and History* 12:149–78.

Wanderken, P. 1943. "Zoo Leven Onze Kinderen." In *Zoo Leven Wij in Indonesia.* Deventer: Van Hoever, 172–87.

Wertheim, Willem. 1959. *Indonesian Society in Transition.* The Hague: Van Hoeve.

Winckel, Ch. W. F. 1938. "The Feasibility of White Settlements in the Tropics: A Medical Point of View." In *Comptes rendus du congrès international de géographie, Amsterdam.* Leiden: Brill, 345–56.

Woodcock, George. 1969. *The British in the Far East.* New York: Atheneum.

Chapter 19
Age, Race, Class, and Sex:
Women Redefining Difference
Audre Lorde

Much of Western European history conditions us to see human differences in simplistic opposition to each other: dominant/subordinate, good/bad, up/down, superior/inferior. In a society where the good is defined in terms of profit rather than in terms of human need, there must always be some group of people who, through systematized oppression, can be made to feel surplus, to occupy the place of the dehumanized inferior. Within American society, that group is made up of black and Third World people, working-class people, older people, and women.

As a forty-nine-year-old, black, lesbian, feminist, socialist mother of two, including one boy, and a member of an interracial couple, I usually find myself a part of some group defined as other, deviant, inferior, or just plain wrong. Traditionally, in American society, it is the members of oppressed, objectified groups who are expected to stretch out and bridge the gap between the actualities of our lives and the consciousness of our oppressor. For in order to survive, those of us for whom oppression is as American as apple pie have always had to be watchers, to become familiar with the language and manners of the oppressor, even sometimes adopting them for some illusion of protection. Whenever the need for some pretense of communication arises, those who profit from our oppression call upon us to share our knowledge with them. In other words, it is the responsibility of the oppressed to teach the oppressors their mistakes. I am responsible for educating teachers who dismiss my children's culture in school. Black and Third World people are expected to educate white people as to our humanity. Women are expected to educate men. Lesbians and gay men are expected to educate the heterosexual world. The oppressors maintain their position and evade responsibility for their own actions. There is a constant drain of energy that might be better used in redefining ourselves and devising realistic scenarios for altering the present and constructing the future.

Institutionalized rejection of difference is an absolute necessity in a profit economy that needs outsiders as surplus people. As members of such an economy, we have *all* been programmed to respond to the human differences among us with fear and loathing and to handle those differences in one of three ways: (1) ignore them; (2) if that is not possible, copy the attributes of those who are dominant; or (3) destroy the attributes of those who are subordinate.

But we have no patterns for relating across our human differences as equals.

374

As a result, those differences have been misnamed and misused in the service of separation and confusion.

Certainly there are very real differences among us of race, age, and sex. But it is not those differences that are separating us. It is rather our refusal to recognize those differences and to examine the distortions that result from our misnaming them and their effects upon human behavior and expectation.

Racism, the belief in the inherent superiority of one race over all others and thereby the right to dominance. Sexism, the belief in the inherent superiority of one sex over the other and thereby the right to dominance. Ageism. Heterosexism. Elitism. Classism.

It is a lifetime pursuit for each one of us to extract these distortions from our living at the same time as we recognize, reclaim, and define those differences upon which they are imposed. For we have all been raised in a society where those distortions were endemic within our living. Too often, we pour the energy needed for recognizing and exploring differences into pretending those differences are insurmountable barriers or that they do not exist at all. This results in a voluntary isolation or false and treacherous connections. Either way, we do not develop tools for using human difference as a springboard for creative change within our lives. We speak not of human difference but of human deviance.

Somewhere, on the edge of consciousness, there is what I call a *mythical norm,* and within our hearts each one of us knows that we do not fit that norm. In America, this norm is usually defined as white, thin, male, young, heterosexual, Christian, and financially secure. Within this society, the trappings of power reside within this mythical norm. Those of us who stand outside that power often identify one way in which we are different, and we assume that to be the primary cause of all oppression, forgetting other distortions around difference, some of which we ourselves may be practicing. By and large within the women's movement today, white women focus upon their oppression as women and ignore differences of race, sexual preference, class, and age. There is a pretense to a homogeneity of experience covered by the word "sisterhood" that does not in fact exist.

Unacknowledged class differences rob women of one another's energy and creative insight. Recently a women's magazine collective made the decision for one issue to print only prose, saying poetry was a less "rigorous" or "serious" art form. Yet even the form our creativity takes is often a class issue. Of all the art forms, poetry is the most economical. It is the one that is the most secret, that requires the least physical labor, the least material, the one that can be done between shifts, in the hospital pantry, on the subway, and on scraps of surplus paper. Over the last few years, writing a novel on tight finances, I came to appreciate the enormous differences in the material demands between poetry and prose. As we reclaim our literature, poetry has been the major voice of poor, working-class, and colored women. A room of one's own may be a necessity for writing prose, but so are reams of paper, a typewriter, and plenty of time. The actual requirements to produce the visual arts also help determine, along class lines, whose art is whose. In this day of inflated prices for material, who are our sculptors, our painters, our photographers? When we speak of a broadly based women's culture, we need to be aware of the effect of class and economic differences on the supplies available for producing art.

As we move toward creating a society within which we can each flourish, ageism is another distortion of relationship that interferes with our vision. By ignoring the past, we are encouraged to repeat its mistakes. The "generation gap" is an important social tool for any repressive society. If the younger members of a community view the older members as contemptible or suspect or excess, they will never be able to join hands and examine the living memories of the community, nor ask the all-important question, Why? This gives rise to a historical amnesia that keeps us working to invent the wheel every time we have to go to the store for bread.

We find ourselves having to repeat and relearn the same old lessons over and over that our mothers did because we do not pass on what we have learned or because we are unable to listen. For instance, how many times has this all been said before? For another, who would have believed that once again our daughters are allowing their bodies to be hampered and purgatoried by girdles and high heels and hobble skirts?

Ignoring the differences of race between women and the implications of those differences presents the most serious threat to the mobilization of women's joint power.

As white women ignore their built-in privilege of whiteness and define "woman" in terms of their own experience alone, then women of color become "other," the outsider whose experience and tradition are too "alien" to comprehend. An example of this is the signal absence of the experience of women of color as a resource for women's studies courses. The literatures of women of color are seldom included in women's literature courses and almost never in other literature courses, nor in women's studies as a whole. All too often, the excuse given is that the literatures of women of color can only be taught by colored women, or that they are too difficult to understand, or that classes cannot "get into" them because they come out of experiences that are "too different." I have heard this argument presented by white women of otherwise quite clear intelligence, women who seem to have no trouble at all teaching and reviewing work that comes out of the vastly different experiences of Shakespeare, Molière, Dostoyevsky, and Aristophanes. Surely there must be some other explanation.

This is a very complex question, but I believe one of the reasons white women have such difficulty reading black women's work is because of their reluctance to see black women as women and different from themselves. To examine black women's literature effectively requires that we be seen as whole people in our actual complexities — as individuals, as women, as human — rather than as one of those problematic but familiar stereotypes provided in this society in place of genuine images of black women. And I believe this holds true for the literatures of other women of color who are not black.

The literatures of all women of color re-create the textures of our lives, and many white women are heavily invested in ignoring the real differences. For as long as any difference between us means one of us must be inferior, then the recognition of any difference must be fraught with guilt. To allow women of color to step out of stereotypes is too guilt-provoking, for it threatens the complacency of those women who view oppression only in terms of sex.

Refusing to recognize difference makes it impossible to see the different problems and pitfalls facing us as women.

Thus, in a patriarchal power system where white-skin privilege is a major prop, the entrapments used to neutralize black women and white women are not the same. For example, it is easy for black women to be used by the power structure against black men, not because they are men, but because they are black. Therefore, for black women, it is necessary at all times to separate the needs of the oppressor from our own legitimate conflicts within our communities. This same problem does not exist for white women. Black women and men have shared racist oppression and still share it, although in different ways. Out of that shared oppression we have developed joint defenses and joint vulnerabilities to each other that are not duplicated in the white community, with the exception of the relationship between Jewish women and Jewish men.

On the other hand, white women face the pitfall of being seduced into joining the oppressor under the pretense of sharing power. This possibility does not exist in the same way for women of color. The tokenism that is sometimes extended to us is not an invitation to join power; our racial "otherness" is a visible reality that makes that quite clear. For white women there is a wider range of pretended choices and rewards for identifying with patriarchal power and its tools.

Today, with the defeat of the Equal Rights Amendment, the tightening economy, and increased conservatism, it is easier once again for white women to believe the dangerous fantasy that if you are good enough, pretty enough, sweet enough, quiet enough, teach the children to behave, hate the right people, and marry the right men, then you will be allowed to coexist with patriarchy in relative peace, at least until a man needs your job or the neighborhood rapist happens along. And true, unless one lives and loves in the trenches, it is difficult to remember that the war against dehumanization is ceaseless.

But black women and our children know the fabric of our lives is stitched with violence and with hatred, that there is no rest. We do not deal with it only on the picket lines or in dark midnight alleys or in the places where we dare to verbalize our resistance. For us, increasingly, violence weaves through the daily tissue of our living — in the supermarket, in the classroom, in the elevator, in the clinic and the schoolyard, from the plumber, the baker, the saleswoman, the bus driver, the bank teller, the waitress who does not serve us.

Some problems we share as women, some we do not. You white women fear your children will grow up to join the patriarchy and testify against you; we fear our children will be dragged from a car and shot down in the street, and you will turn your backs upon the reasons they are dying.

The threat of difference has been no less blinding to people of color. Those of us who are black must see that the reality of our lives and our struggle does not make us immune to the errors of ignoring and misnaming difference. Within black communities where racism is a living reality, differences among us often seem dangerous and suspect. The need for unity is often misnamed as a need for homogeneity, and a black feminist vision mistaken for betrayal of our common interests as a people. Because of the continuous battle against racial erasure that black women and black men share, some black women still refuse to recognize that we are also oppressed as women and that sexual hostility against black women is not only practiced by the white racist society but implemented within our black communities as well.

It is a disease striking the heart of black nationhood, and silence will not make it disappear. Exacerbated by racism and the pressures of powerlessness, violence against black women and children often becomes a standard within our communities, one by which manliness can be measured. But these woman-hating acts are rarely discussed as crimes against black women.

As a group, women of color are the lowest paid wage earners in America. We are the primary targets of abortion and sterilization abuse, here and abroad. In certain parts of Africa, small girls are still being sewed shut between their legs to keep them docile and for men's pleasure. This is known as female circumcision, and it is not a cultural affair, as the late Jomo Kenyatta insisted — it is a crime against black women.

Black women's literature is full of the pain of frequent assault, not only by a racist patriarchy but also by black men. Yet the necessity for and history of shared battle have made us, black women, particularly vulnerable to the false accusation that antisexist is antiblack. Meanwhile, woman-hating as a recourse of the powerless is sapping strength from black communities and from our very lives. Rape is on the increase, reported and unreported, and rape is not aggressive sexuality — it is sexualized aggression. As Kalamu ya Salaam, a black male writer points out, "As long as male domination exists, rape will exist. Only women revolting and men made conscious of their responsibility to fight sexism can collectively stop rape."[1]

Differences among ourselves as black women are also being misnamed and used to separate us from one another. As a black, lesbian feminist comfortable with the many different ingredients of my identity, and a woman committed to racial and sexual freedom from oppression, I find I am constantly being encouraged to pluck out some one aspect of myself and present this as the meaningful whole, eclipsing or denying the other parts of self.

But this is a destructive and fragmenting way to live. My fullest concentration of energy is available to me only when I integrate all the parts of who I am, openly, allowing power from particular sources of my living to flow back and forth freely through all my different selves, without the restrictions of externally imposed definition. Only then can I bring myself and my energies as a whole to the service of those struggles that I embrace as part of my living.

A fear of lesbians, or of being accused of being a lesbian, has led many black women into testifying against themselves. It has led some of us into destructive alliances, and others into despair and isolation. In the white women's communities, heterosexism is sometimes a result of identifying with the white patriarchy, a rejection of that interdependence between women-identified women that allows the self to be, rather than to be used in the service of men. Sometimes it reflects a die-hard belief in the protective coloration of heterosexual relationships, sometimes a self-hate that all women have to fight against, taught us from birth.

Although elements of these attitudes exist for all women, there are particular resonances of heterosexism and homophobia among black women. Despite the fact that woman-bonding has a long and honorable history in the African and African-American communities, and despite the knowledge and accomplishments of many strong and creative women-identified black women in the political, social, and cultural fields, heterosexual black women often tend to ignore or discount the existence and work of black lesbians. Part of this attitude has come from an understandable terror of black male attack within the close confines of black society, where the punishment for any female self-assertion is still to be accused of being a lesbian and therefore unworthy of the attention or support of the scarce black male. But part of this need to misname and ignore black lesbians comes from a very real fear that openly women-identified black women who are no longer dependent upon men for their self-definition may well reorder our whole concept of social relationships.

Black women who once insisted that lesbianism was a white woman's problem now insist that black lesbians are a threat to black nationhood, are consorting with the enemy, are basically unblack. These accusations, coming from the very women to whom we look for deep and real understanding, have served to keep many black lesbians in hiding, caught between the racism of white women and the homophobia of their sisters. Often, their work has been ignored, trivialized, or misnamed, as with the work of Angelina Grimke, Alice Dunbar-Nelson, and Lorraine Hansberry. Yet women-bonded women have always been some part of the power of black communities, from our unmarried aunts to the amazons of Dahomey.

And it is certainly not black lesbians who are assaulting women and raping children and grandmothers on the streets of our communities.

Across this country, as in Boston during the spring of 1979 following the un-solved murders of twelve black women, black lesbians are spearheading movements against violence against black women.

What are the particular details within each of our lives that can be scrutinized and altered to help bring about change? How do we redefine difference for all women? It is not our differences that separate women but our reluctance to recognize those dif-ferences and to deal effectively with the distortions that have resulted from ignoring and misnaming those differences.

Women have been encouraged to recognize only one area of human difference as legitimate — those differences that exist between women and men. This has been done as a means of social control, but we have learned to deal across those differ-ences with the urgency of all oppressed subordinates. All of us have had to learn to live or work or coexist with men, from our fathers on. We have recognized and negotiated these differences, even when this recognition only continued the old dominant/subordinate mode of human relationship, where the oppressed must recognize the masters' difference in order to survive.

But our future survival is predicated upon our ability to relate within equality. As women, we must root out internalized patterns of oppression within ourselves if we are to move beyond the most superficial aspects of social change. Now we must recognize differences among women who are our equals, neither inferior nor superior, and devise ways to use one another's difference to enrich our visions and our joint struggles.

The future of our earth may depend upon the ability of all women to identify and develop new definitions of power and new patterns of relating across differ-ence. The old definitions have not served us, nor the earth that supports us. The old patterns, no matter how cleverly rearranged to imitate progress, still condemn us to cosmetically altered repetitions of the same old exchanges, the same old guilt, hatred, recrimination, lamentation, and suspicion.

For we have, built into all of us, old blueprints of expectation and response, old structures of oppression, and these must be altered at the same time as we alter the living conditions that are a result of those structures. For the master's tools will never dismantle the master's house.

As Paulo Freire shows so well in *The Pedagogy of the Oppressed*,[2] the true focus of revolutionary change is never merely the oppressive situations that we seek to escape but that piece of the oppressor that is planted deep within each of us and that knows only the oppressor's tactics, the oppressor's relationships.

Change means growth, and growth can be painful. But we sharpen self-definition by exposing the self in work and struggle together with those whom we define as different from ourselves, although sharing the same goals. For black and white, old and young, lesbian and heterosexual women alike, this can mean new paths to our survival.

> We have chosen each other
> and the edge of each other's battles
> the war is the same
> if we lose
> someday women's blood will congeal
> upon a dead planet
> if we win
> there is no telling
> we seek beyond history
> for a new and more possible meeting.[3]

NOTES

Paper delivered at the Copeland Colloquium, Amherst College, April 1980.

1. Kalamu ya Salaam, "Rape: A Radical Analysis, an African-American Perspective," *Black Books Bulletin* 6, no. 4 (1980).

2. Paulo Freire, *The Pedagogy of the Oppressed* (New York: Seabury Press, 1970).

3. From Audre Lorde, "Outlines," unpublished poem.

Chapter 20
Gender Is Burning: Questions of Appropriation and Subversion
Judith Butler

We all have friends who, when they knock on the door and we ask, through the door,
the question, "Who's there?," answer (since "it's obvious") "It's me." And we recognize
that "it is him," or "her."

Louis Althusser, "Ideology and Ideological State Apparatuses," emphasis added

The purpose of "law" is absolutely the last thing to employ in the history of the origin
of law: on the contrary, ... the cause of the origin of a thing and its eventual utility,
its actual employment and place in a system of purposes, lie worlds apart; whatever
exists, having somehow come into being, is again and again reinterpreted to new ends,
taken over, transformed, and redirected.

Friedrich Nietzsche, *On the Genealogy of Morals*

In Louis Althusser's notion of interpellation, it is the police who initiate the call or
address by which a subject becomes socially constituted. There is the policeman, the
one not only who represents the law but whose address "Hey you!" has the effect
of binding the law to the one who is hailed. This "one" who appears not to be in a
condition of trespass prior to the call (for whom the call establishes a given practice
as a trespass) is not fully a social subject, is not fully subjectivated, for he or she is
not yet reprimanded. The reprimand does not merely repress or control the subject
but forms a crucial part of the juridical and social *formation* of the subject. The call
is formative, if not *per*formative, precisely because it initiates the individual into the
subjected status of the subject.

Althusser conjectures this "hailing" or "interpellation" as a unilateral act, as the
power and force of the law to compel fear at the same time that it offers recognition at an expense. In the reprimand the subject not only receives recognition but
attains as well a certain order of social existence, in being transferred from an outer
region of indifferent, questionable, or impossible being to the discursive or social
domain of the subject. But does this subjectivation take place as a direct effect of
the reprimanding utterance, or must the utterance wield the power to compel the
fear of punishment and, from that compulsion, to produce a compliance and obedience to the law? Are there other ways of being addressed and constituted by the
law, ways of being occupied and occupying the law, that disarticulate the power of
punishment from the power of recognition?

Althusser underscores the Lacanian contribution to a structural analysis of this kind and argues that a relation of misrecognition persists between the law and the subject it compels.[1] Although he refers to the possibility of "bad subjects," he does not consider the range of *disobedience* that such an interpellating law might produce. The law not only might be refused but might also be ruptured, forced into a rearticulation that calls into question the monotheistic force of its own unilateral operation. Where the uniformity of the subject is expected, where the behavioral conformity of the subject is commanded, the refusal of the law might be produced in the form of the parodic inhabiting of conformity that subtly calls into question the legitimacy of the command, a repetition of the law into hyperbole, a rearticulation of the law against the authority of the one who delivers it. Here the performative, the call by the law that seeks to produce a lawful subject, produces a set of consequences that exceed and confound what appears to be the disciplining intention motivating the law. Interpellation thus loses its status as a simple performative, an act of discourse with the power to create that to which it refers, and creates more than it ever meant to, signifying in excess of any intended referent.

It is this constitutive failure of the performative, this slippage between discursive command and its appropriated effect, that provides the linguistic occasion and index for a consequential disobedience.

Consider that the use of language is itself enabled by first having been *called a name;* the occupation of the name is that by which one is, quite without choice, situated within discourse. This "I," which is produced through the accumulation and convergence of such "calls," cannot extract itself from the historicity of that chain or raise itself up and confront that chain as if it were an object opposed to me, which is not me, but only what others have made of me; for that estrangement or division produced by the mesh of interpellating calls and the "I" who is its site is not only violating but enabling as well, what Gayatri Spivak refers to as "an enabling violation." The "I" who would oppose its construction is always in some sense drawing from that construction to articulate its opposition; further, the "I" draws what is called its "agency" in part through being implicated in the very relations of power that it seeks to oppose. To be *implicated* in the relations of power, indeed, enabled by the relations of power that the "I" opposes, is not, as a consequence, to be reducible to their existing forms.

You will note that in the making of this formulation, I bracket this "I" in quotation marks, but I am still here. And I should add that this is an "I" that I produce here for you in response to a certain suspicion that this theoretical project has lost the person, the author, the life; over and against this claim, or rather, in response to having been called the site of such an evacuation, I write that this kind of bracketing of the "I" may well be crucial to the thinking through of the constitutive ambivalence of being socially constituted, where "constitution" carries both the enabling and the violating sense of "subjection." If one comes into discursive life through being called or hailed in injurious terms, how might one occupy the interpellation by which one is already occupied to direct the possibilities of resignification against the aims of violation?

This is not the same as censoring or prohibiting the use of the "I" or of the autobiographical as such; on the contrary, it is the inquiry into the ambivalent relations of power that make that use possible. What does it mean to have such uses repeated in one's very being, "messages implied in one's being," as Patricia Williams claims, only to repeat those uses such that subversion might be derived from the very conditions of violation? In this sense, the argument that the category of "sex" is the instrument or effect of "sexism" or its interpellating moment, that "race" is the instrument and effect of "racism" or its interpellating moment, that "gender" only exists in the service of heterosexism, does *not* entail that we ought never to make use of such terms, as if such terms could only and always reconsolidate the oppressive regimes of power by which they are spawned. On the contrary, precisely because such terms have been produced and constrained within such regimes, they ought to be repeated in directions that reverse and displace their originating aims. One does not stand at an instrumental distance from the terms by which one experiences violation. Occupied by such terms and yet occupying them oneself risks a complicity, a repetition, a relapse into injury, but it is also the occasion to work the mobilizing power of injury, of an interpellation one never chose. Where one might understand violation as a trauma that can only induce a destructive repetition compulsion (and surely this is a powerful consequence of violation), it seems equally possible to acknowledge the force of repetition as the very condition of an affirmative response to violation. The compulsion to repeat an injury is not necessarily the compulsion to repeat the injury in the same way or to stay fully within the traumatic orbit of that injury. The force of repetition in language may be the paradoxical condition by which a certain agency — not linked to a fiction of the ego as master of circumstance — is derived from the *impossibility* of choice.

It is in this sense that Luce Irigaray's critical mime of Plato, the fiction of the lesbian phallus, and the rearticulation of kinship in the film *Paris Is Burning* (1991) might be understood as repetitions of hegemonic forms of power that fail to repeat loyally and, in that failure, open possibilities for resignifying the terms of violation against their violating aims. Willa Cather's occupation of the paternal name, Nella Larsen's inquiry into the painful and fatal mime that is passing for white, and the reworking of "queer" from abjection to politicized affiliation will interrogate similar sites of ambivalence produced at the limits of discursive legitimacy.

The temporal structure of such a subject is chiasmatic in this sense: in the place of a substantial or self-determining "subject," this juncture of discursive demands is something like a "crossroads," to use Gloria Anzaldúa's phrase, a crossroads of cultural and political discursive forces, which she herself claims cannot be understood through the notion of the "subject."[2] There is no subject prior to its constructions, and neither is the subject determined by those constructions; it is always the nexus, the nonspace of cultural collision, in which the demand to resignify or repeat the very terms that constitute the "we" cannot be summarily refused, but neither can they be followed in strict obedience. It is the space of this ambivalence that opens up the possibility of a reworking of the very terms by which subjectivation proceeds — and fails to proceed.

Ambivalent Drag

From this formulation, then, I would like to move to a consideration of the film *Paris Is Burning*, to what it suggests about the simultaneous production and subjugation of subjects in a culture that appears to arrange always and in every way for the annihilation of queers but that nevertheless produces occasional spaces in which those annihilating norms, those killing ideals of gender and race, are mimed, reworked, resignified. As much as there is defiance and affirmation, the creation of kinship and of glory in that film, there is also the kind of reiteration of norms that cannot be called subversive and that leads to the death of Venus Xtravaganza, a Latina preoperative transsexual, cross-dresser, prostitute, and member of the "House of Xtravaganza." To what set of interpellating calls does Venus respond, and how is the reiteration of the law to be read in the manner of her response?

Venus, and *Paris Is Burning* more generally, call into question whether parodying the dominant norms is enough to displace them — indeed, whether the denaturalization of gender cannot be the very vehicle for a reconsolidation of hegemonic norms. Although many readers understood my book *Gender Trouble* to be arguing for the proliferation of drag performances as a way of subverting dominant gender norms,[3] I want to underscore that there is no necessary relation between drag and subversion and that drag may well be used in the service of both the denaturalization and the reidealization of hyperbolic heterosexual gender norms. At best, it seems, drag is a site of a certain ambivalence, one that reflects the more general situation of being implicated in the regimes of power by which one is constituted and, hence, of being implicated in the very regimes of power that one opposes.

To claim that all gender is like drag, or is drag, is to suggest that "imitation" is at the heart of the *heterosexual* project and its gender binarisms, that drag is not a secondary imitation that presupposes a prior and original gender, but that hegemonic heterosexuality is itself a constant and repeated effort to imitate its own idealizations. That it must repeat this imitation, that it sets up pathologizing practices and normalizing sciences in order to produce and consecrate its own claim on originality and propriety, suggests that heterosexual performativity is beset by an anxiety that it can never fully overcome, that its effort to become its own idealizations can never be finally or fully achieved, and that it is consistently haunted by that domain of sexual possibility that must be excluded for heterosexualized gender to produce itself. In this sense, then, drag is subversive to the extent that it reflects on the imitative structure by which hegemonic gender is itself produced and disputes heterosexuality's claim on naturalness and originality.

But here it seems that I am obliged to add an important qualification: heterosexual privilege operates in many ways, and two ways in which it operates include naturalizing itself and rendering itself as the original and the norm. But these are not the only ways in which it works, for it is clear that there are domains in which heterosexuality can concede its lack of originality and naturalness but still hold on to its power. Thus, there are forms of drag that heterosexual culture produces for itself — we might think of Julie Andrews in *Victor, Victoria* or Dustin Hoffman in *Tootsie* or Jack Lemmon in *Some Like It Hot,* where the anxiety over a possible homosexual consequence is both produced and deflected within the narrative trajectory of the films. These are films that produce and contain the homosexual excess of any given drag performance, the fear that an apparently heterosexual contact might be made before the discovery of a nonapparent homosexuality. This is drag as high het entertainment, and though these films are surely important to read as cultural texts in which homophobia and homosexual panic are negotiated,[4] I would be reticent to call them subversive. Indeed, one might argue that such films are functional in providing a ritualistic release for a heterosexual economy that must constantly police its own boundaries against the invasion of queerness and that this displaced production and resolution of homosexual panic actually fortifies the heterosexual regime in its self-perpetuating task.

In her provocative review of *Paris Is Burning,* bell hooks criticized some productions of gay-male drag as misogynist, and here she allied herself in part with feminist theorists such as Marilyn Frye and Janice Raymond.[5] This tradition within feminist thought has argued that drag is offensive to women and that it is an imitation based in ridicule and degradation. Raymond, in particular, places drag on a continuum with cross-dressing and transsexualism, ignoring the important differences between them, maintaining that in each practice women are the object of hatred and appropriation and that there is nothing in the identification that is respectful or elevating. As a rejoinder, one might consider that identification is always an ambivalent process. Identifying with a gender under contemporary regimes of power involves identifying with a set of norms that are and are not realizable and whose power and status precede the identifications by which they are insistently approximated. This "being a man" and this "being a woman" are internally unstable affairs. They are always beset by ambivalence precisely because there is a cost in every identification, the loss of some other set of identifications, the forcible approximation of a norm one never chooses, a norm that chooses us, but that we occupy, reverse, resignify to the extent that the norm fails to determine us completely.

The problem with the analysis of drag as only misogyny is, of course, that it figures male-to-female transsexuality, cross-dressing, and drag as male homosexual activities — which they are not always — and it further diagnoses male homosexuality as rooted in misogyny. The feminist analysis thus makes male homosexuality *about* women, and one might argue that at its extreme, this kind of analysis is in fact a colonization in reverse, a way for feminist women to make themselves into the center of male homosexual activity (and thus to reinscribe the heterosexual matrix, paradoxically, at the heart of the radical feminist position). Such an accusation follows the same kind of logic as those homophobic remarks that often follow upon the discovery that one is a lesbian: a lesbian is one who must have had a bad experience with men or who has not yet found the right one. These diagnoses presume that lesbianism is acquired by virtue of some failure in the heterosexual machinery, thereby continuing to install heterosexuality as the "cause" of lesbian desire; lesbian desire is figured as the fatal effect of a derailed heterosexual causality. In this framework, heterosexual desire is always true, and lesbian desire is always and only a mask and forever false. In the radical feminist argument against drag, the displacement of women is figured as the aim and effect of male-to-female drag; in the homophobic dismissal of lesbian desire, the disappointment with and displacement of men is understood as the cause and final truth of lesbian desire. According to these views, drag is nothing but the displacement and appropriation of "women" and hence fundamentally based in a misogyny, a hatred of women; and lesbianism is nothing but the displacement and appropriation of men, and so fundamentally a matter of hating men — misandry.

These explanations of displacement can only proceed by accomplishing yet another set of displacements: of desire, of phantasmatic pleasures, and of forms of love that are not reducible to a heterosexual matrix and the logic of repudiation. Indeed, the only place love is to be found is *for* the ostensibly repudiated object, where love is understood to be strictly produced through a logic of repudiation; hence, drag is nothing but the effect of a love embittered by disappointment or rejection, the incorporation of the other whom one originally desired, but now hates. And lesbianism is nothing other than the effect of a love embittered by disappointment or rejection and of a recoil from that love, a defense against it, or, in the case of butchness, the appropriation of the masculine position that one originally loved.

This logic of repudiation installs heterosexual love as the origin and truth of both drag and lesbianism, and it interprets both practices as symptoms of thwarted love. But what is displaced in this explanation of displacement is the notion that there might be pleasure, desire, and love that are not solely determined by what they repudiate.[6] Now it may seem at first that the way to oppose these reductions and degradations of queer practices is to assert their radical specificity, to claim that there is a lesbian desire radically different from a heterosexual one, with *no* relation to it, that is neither the repudiation nor the appropriation of heterosexuality and that has radically other origins than those that sustain heterosexuality. Or one might be tempted to argue that drag is not related to the ridicule or degradation or appropriation of women: when it is men in drag as women, what we have is the destabilization of gender itself, a destabilization that is denaturalizing and that calls into question the claims of normativity and originality by which gender and sexual oppression sometimes operate. But what if the situation is neither exclusively one nor the other; certainly, some lesbians have wanted to retain the notion that their sexual practice is rooted in part in a repudiation of heterosexuality, but also to claim that this repudiation does not account for lesbian desire and cannot therefore be identified as the hidden or original "truth" of lesbian desire. And the case of drag is difficult in yet another way, for it seems clear to me that there is both a sense of defeat and a sense of insurrection to be had from the drag pageantry in *Paris Is Burning,* that the drag we see, the drag that is after all framed for us, filmed for us, is one that both appropriates and subverts racist, misogynist, and homophobic norms of oppression. How are we to account for this ambivalence? This is not first an appropriation and then a subversion. Sometimes it is both at once; sometimes it remains caught in an irresolvable tension, and sometimes a fatally unsubversive appropriation takes place.

Paris Is Burning is a film produced and directed by Jennie Livingston about drag balls in New York City, in Harlem, attended by and performed by "men" who are either African-American or Latino. The balls are contests in which the contestants compete under a variety of categories. The categories include a variety of social norms, many of which are established in white culture as signs of class, like that of the "executive" and the Ivy League student; some of which are marked as feminine, ranging from high drag to butch queen; and some of which, like that of the "bangie," are taken from straight black masculine street culture. Not all of the categories, then, are taken from white culture; some of them are replications of a straightness that is not white; and some of them are focused on class, especially those that almost require that expensive women's clothing be "mopped" or stolen for the occasion. The competition in military garb shifts to yet another register of legitimacy, which enacts the performative and gestural conformity to a masculinity that parallels the performative or reiterative production of femininity in other categories. "Realness" is not exactly a category in which one competes; it is a standard that is used to judge any given performance within the established categories. And yet what determines the effect of realness is the ability to compel belief, to produce the naturalized effect. This effect is itself the result of an embodiment of norms, a reiteration of norms, an impersonation of a racial and class norm, a norm that is at once a figure, a figure of a body, which is no particular body, but a morphological ideal that remains the standard that regulates the performance, but that no performance fully approximates.

Significantly, this is a performance that works, that effects realness, to the extent that it *cannot* be read. For "reading" means taking someone down, exposing what fails to work at the level of appearance, insulting or deriding someone. For a performance to work, then, means that a reading is no longer possible or that a reading, an interpretation, appears to be a kind of transparent seeing, where what appears and what it means coincide. On the contrary, when what appears and how it is "read" diverge, the artifice of the performance can be read as artifice; the ideal splits off from its appropriation. But the impossibility of reading means that the artifice works; the approximation of realness appears to be achieved; the body performing and the ideal performed appear indistinguishable.

But what is the status of this ideal? Of what is it composed? What reading does the film encourage, and what does the film conceal? Does the denaturalization of the norm succeed in subverting the norm, or is this a denaturalization in the service of a perpetual reidealization, one that can only oppress, even as, or precisely when, it is embodied most effectively? Consider, on the one hand, the different fates of Venus Xtravaganza. She "passes" as a light-skinned woman but is — by virtue of a certain failure to pass completely — clearly vulnerable to homophobic violence; ultimately, her life is taken presumably by a client who, upon the discovery of what she calls her "little secret," mutilates her for having seduced him. On the other hand, Willi Ninja can pass as straight; his voguing becomes foregrounded in het video productions with Madonna et al., and he achieves postlegendary status on an international scale. There is passing and then there is passing, and it is — as we used to say — "no accident" that Willi Ninja ascends and Venus Xtravaganza dies.

Now Venus, Venus Xtravaganza, seeks a certain transubstantiation of gender in order to find an imaginary man who will designate a class and race privilege that promises a permanent shelter from racism, homophobia, and poverty. And it would not be enough to claim that for Venus gender is *marked by* race and class, for gender is not the substance or primary substrate and race and class the qualifying attributes. In this instance, gender is the vehicle for the phantasmatic transformation of that nexus of race and class, the site of its articulation. Indeed, in *Paris Is Burning*, becoming real, becoming a real woman, although not everyone's desire (some children want merely to "do" realness, and that, only within the confines of the ball), constitutes the site of the phantasmatic promise of a rescue from poverty, homophobia, and racist delegitimation.

The context (which we might read as a "contesting of realness") involves the phantasmatic attempt to approximate realness, but it also exposes the norms that regulate realness as *themselves* phantasmatically instituted and sustained. The rules that regulate and legitimate realness (shall we call them symbolic?) constitute the mechanism by which certain sanctioned fantasies, sanctioned imaginaries, are insidiously elevated as the parameters of realness. We could, within conventional Lacanian parlance, call this the ruling of the symbolic, except that the symbolic assumes the primacy of sexual difference in the constitution of the subject. What *Paris Is Burning* suggests, however, is that the order of sexual difference is not prior to that of race or class in the constitution of the subject; indeed, that the symbolic is also and at once a racializing set of norms; and that norms of realness by which the subject is produced are racially informed conceptions of "sex" (this underscores the importance of subjecting the entire psychoanalytic paradigm to this insight).[7]

This double movement of approximating and exposing the phantasmatic status of the realness norm, the symbolic norm, is reinforced by the diagenetic movement of the film in which clips of so-called real people moving in and out of expensive stores are juxtaposed against the ballroom drag scenes.

In the drag-ball productions of realness, we witness and produce the phantasmatic constitution of a subject, a subject who repeats and mimes the legitimating norms by which it itself has been degraded, a subject founded in the project of mastery that compels and disrupts its own repetitions. This is not a subject who stands back from its identifications and decides instrumentally how or whether to work each of them today; on the contrary, the subject is the incoherent and mobilized imbrication of identifications; it is constituted in and through the iterability of its performance, a repetition that works at once to legitimate and delegitimate the realness norms by which it is produced.

In the pursuit of realness this subject is produced, a phantasmatic pursuit that mobilizes identifications, underscoring the phantasmatic promise that constitutes any identificatory move — a promise that, taken too seriously, can culminate only in disappointment and disidentification. A fantasy that for Venus — because she dies, killed apparently by one of her clients, perhaps after the discovery of those remaining organs — cannot be translated into the symbolic. This is a killing that is performed by a symbolic that would eradicate those phenomena that require an opening up of the possibilities for the resignification of sex. If Venus wants to become a woman and cannot overcome being a Latina, then Venus is treated by the symbolic in precisely the ways in which women of color are treated. Her death thus testifies to a tragic misreading of the social map of power, a misreading orchestrated by that very map according to which the sites for a phantasmatic self-overcoming are constantly resolved into disappointment. If the signifiers of whiteness and femaleness — as well as some forms of hegemonic maleness constructed through class privilege — are sites of phantasmatic promise, then it is clear that women of color and lesbians not only are everywhere excluded from this scene but constitute a site of identification that is consistently refused and abjected in the collective phantasmatic pursuit of a transubstantiation into various forms of drag, transsexualism, and uncritical miming of the hegemonic. That this fantasy involves becoming in part like women and, for some of the children, becoming like black women, falsely constitutes black women as a site of privilege; they can catch a man and be protected by him: an impossible idealization that of course works to deny the situation of the great numbers of poor black women who are single mothers without the support of men. In this sense, the "identification" is composed of a denial, an envy, which is the envy of a phantasm of black women, an idealization that produces a denial. On the other hand, insofar as black men who are queer can become feminized by hegemonic straight culture, there is in the performative dimension of the ball a significant *reworking* of that feminization, an occupation of the identification that is, as it were, *already* made between faggots and women, the feminization of the faggot, the feminization of the black faggot, which is the black feminization of the faggot.

The performance is thus a kind of talking back, one that remains largely constrained by the terms of the original assailment: if a white, homophobic hegemony considers the black drag-ball queen to be a woman, that woman, constituted already by that hegemony, will become the occasion for the rearticulation of its terms; embodying the excess of that production, the queen will out-woman women and in the process confuse and seduce an audience whose gaze must to some degree be structured through those hegemonies, an audience who, through the hyperbolic staging of the scene, will be drawn into the abjection it wants both to resist and to overcome. The phantasmatic excess of this production constitutes the site of women not only as marketable goods within an erotic economy of exchange[8] but as goods that, as it were, are also privileged consumers with access to wealth and social privilege and protection. This is a full-scale phantasmatic transfiguration not only of the plight of poor black and Latino gay men but of poor black women and Latinas, who are the figures for the abjection that the drag-ball scene elevates as a site of idealized identification. It would, I think, be too simple to reduce this identificatory move to black male misogyny, as if that were a discrete typology, for the feminization of the poor black man and, most trenchantly, of the poor black gay man is a strategy of abjection that is already underway, originating in the complex of racist, homophobic, misogynist, and classist constructions that belong to larger hegemonies of oppression.

These hegemonies operate, as Antonio Gramsci insisted, through *rearticulation,* but here is where the accumulated force of a historically entrenched and entrenching rearticulation overwhelms the more fragile effort to build an alternative cultural configuration from or against that more powerful regime. Importantly, however, that prior hegemony also works through and as its "resistance" so that the relation between the marginalized community and the dominative is not, strictly speaking, oppositional. The citing of the dominant norm does not, in this instance, displace that norm; rather, it becomes the means by which that dominant norm is most painfully reiterated as the very desire and the performance of those it subjects.

Clearly, the denaturalization of sex, in its multiple senses, does not imply a liberation from hegemonic constraint: when Venus speaks her desire to become a whole woman, to find a man and have a house in the suburbs with a washing machine, we may well question whether the denaturalization of gender and sexuality that she performs, and performs well, culminates in a reworking of the normative framework of heterosexuality. The painfulness of her death at the end of the film suggests as well that there are cruel and fatal social constraints on denaturalization. As much as she crosses gender, sexuality, and race performatively, the hegemony that rein-scribes the privileges of normative femininity and whiteness wields the final power to *re*naturalize Venus's body and cross out that prior crossing, an erasure that is her death. Of course, the film brings Venus back, as it were, into visibility, although not to life, and thus constitutes a kind of cinematic performativity. Paradoxically, the film brings fame and recognition not only to Venus but also to the other drag-ball chil-dren who are depicted in the film as able only to attain local legendary status while longing for wider recognition.

The camera, of course, plays precisely to this desire and so is implicitly installed in the film as the promise of legendary status. And yet, is there a filmic effort to take stock of the place of the camera in the trajectory of desire that it not only records but also incites? In her critical review of the film, bell hooks raises not only the question of the place of the camera but also that of the filmmaker, Jennie Livingston, a white lesbian (in other contexts called "a white Jewish lesbian from Yale," an interpellation that also implicates this author in its sweep), in relation to the drag-ball community that she entered and filmed. In the review, hooks remarks that

> Jennie Livingston approaches her subject matter as an outsider looking in. Since her presence as white woman/lesbian filmmaker is "absent" from *Paris Is Burning,* it is easy for viewers to imagine that they are watching an ethnographic film documenting the life of black gay "natives" and not recognize that they are watching a work shaped and formed from a perspective and standpoint specific to Livingston. By cinematically masking this reality (we hear her ask questions but never see her) Livingston does not oppose the way hegemonic whiteness "represents" blackness, but rather assumes an imperial overseeing position that is in no way progressive or counterhegemonic.[9]

Later in the same essay, hooks raises the question of not merely whether or not the cultural location of the filmmaker is absent from the film but whether this absence operates to form tacitly the focus and effect of the film, exploiting the colonial-ist trope of an "innocent" ethnographic gaze: "Too many critics and interviewers," hooks argues, " . . . act as though she somehow did this marginalized black gay sub-culture a favor by bringing their experience to a wider public. Such a stance obscures the substantial rewards she has received for this work. Since so many of the black gay men in the film express the desire to be big stars, it is easy to place Livingston in the role of benefactor, offering these 'poor black souls' a way to realize their dreams."[10]

Although hooks restricts her remarks to black men in the film, most of the mem-bers of the House of Xtravaganza are Latino, some of whom are light-skinned, some of whom engage in crossing and passing, some of whom only do the ball, some of whom are engaged in life projects to effect a full transubstantiation into femi-ninity and/or into whiteness. The "houses" are organized in part along ethnic lines. This seems crucial to underscore precisely because neither Livingston nor hooks considers the place and force of ethnicity in the articulation of kinship relations.

To the extent that a transubstantiation into legendary status, into an idealized domain of gender and race, structures the phantasmatic trajectory of the drag-ball culture, Livingston's camera enters this world as the promise of phantasmatic fulfill-ment: a wider audience, national and international fame. If Livingston is the white girl with the camera, she is both the object and the vehicle of desire; and yet, as a lesbian, she apparently maintains some kind of identificatory bond with the gay men in the film and also, it seems, with the kinship system, replete with "houses," "mothers," and "children," that sustains the drag-ball scene and is itself organized by it. The one instance where Livingston's body might be said to appear allegorically on camera is when Octavia St. Laurent is posing for the camera, as a moving model would for a photographer. We hear a voice tell her that she's terrific, and it is unclear whether it is a man shooting the film as a proxy for Livingston or Livingston herself. What is suggested by this sudden intrusion of the camera into the film is something of the camera's desire, the desire that motivates the camera, in which a white lesbian phallically organized by the use of the camera (elevated to the status of disembodied gaze, holding out the promise of erotic recognition) eroticizes a black male-to-female transsexual — presumably preoperative — who "works" perceptually as a woman.

What would it mean to say that Octavia is Jennie Livingston's kind of girl? Is the category or, indeed, "the position" of white lesbian disrupted by such a claim? If this is the production of the black transsexual for an exoticizing white gaze, is it not also the transsexualization of lesbian desire? Livingston incites Octavia to become a woman for Livingston's own camera, and Livingston thereby assumes the power of "having the phallus," that is, the ability to confer that femininity, to anoint Octavia as model woman. But to the extent that Octavia receives and is produced by that recognition, the camera itself is empowered as phallic instrument. Moreover, the camera acts as surgical instrument and operation, the vehicle through which the transubstantiation occurs. Livingston thus becomes the one with the power to turn men into women who, then, depend on the power of her gaze to become and remain women. Having asked about the transsexualization of lesbian desire, then, it follows that we might ask more particularly: What is the status of the desire to feminize black and Latino men that the film enacts? Does this not serve the purpose, among others, of a visual pacification of subjects by whom white women are imagined to be socially endangered?

Does the camera promise a transubstantiation of sorts? Is it the token of that promise to deliver economic privilege and the transcendence of social abjection? What does it mean to eroticize the holding out of that promise, as hooks asks, when the film will do well, but the lives that they record will remain substantially unaltered? And if the camera is the vehicle for that transubstantiation, what is the power assumed by the one who wields the camera, drawing on that desire and exploiting it? Is this not its own fantasy, one in which the filmmaker wields the power to transform what she records? And is this fantasy of the camera's power not directly counter to the ethnographic conceit that structures the film?

hooks is right to argue that within this culture the ethnographic conceit of a neutral gaze will always be a white gaze, an unmarked white gaze, one that passes its own perspective off as the omniscient, one that presumes upon and enacts its own perspective as if it were no perspective at all. But what does it mean to think about this camera as an instrument and effect of lesbian desire? I would have liked to have seen the question of Livingston's cinematic desire reflexively thematized in the film itself, her intrusions into the frame as "intrusions," the camera *implicated* in the trajectory of desire that it seems compelled to incite. To the extent that the camera figures tacitly as the instrument of transubstantiation, it assumes the place of the phallus, as that which controls the field of signification. The camera thus trades on the masculine privilege of the disembodied gaze, the gaze that has the power to produce bodies, but that is itself no body.

But is this cinematic gaze only white and phallic, or is there in this film a de-centered place for the camera as well? hooks points to two competing narrative trajectories in the film, one that focuses on the pageantry of the balls and another that focuses on the lives of the participants. She argues that the spectacle of the pageantry arrives to quell the portraits of suffering that these men relate about their lives outside the ball. And in her rendition, the pageantry represents a life of plea-surable fantasy, and the lives outside the drag ball are the painful "reality" that the pageantry seeks phantasmatically to overcome. hooks claims that "at no point in Livingston's film are the men asked to speak about their connections to a world of family and community beyond the drag ball. The cinematic narrative makes the ball the center of their lives. And yet who determines this? Is this the way the black men view their reality or is this the reality that Livingston constructs?"[11]

Clearly, this *is* the way that Livingston constructs their "reality," and the insights into their lives that we do get are still tied in to the ball. We hear about the ways in which the various houses prepare for the ball; we see "mopping"; and we see the differences among those who walk in the ball as men, those who do drag inside the parameters of the ball, those who cross-dress all the time in the ball and on the street, and, among the cross-dressers, those who resist transsexuality and those who are transsexual in varying degrees. What becomes clear in the enumeration of the kinship system that surrounds the ball is not only that the "houses" and the "moth-ers" and the "children" sustain the ball but that the ball is itself an occasion for the building of a set of kinship relations that manage and sustain those who belong to the houses in the face of dislocation, poverty, homelessness. These men "mother" one another, "house" one another, "rear" one another, and the resignification of the family through these terms is not a vain or useless imitation but the social and discur-sive building of community, a community that binds, cares, and teaches, that shelters and enables. This is doubtless a cultural reelaboration of kinship that anyone outside of the privilege of heterosexual family (and those within those "privileges" who suf-fer there) needs to see, to know, and to learn from, a task that makes none of us who are outside of heterosexual "family" into absolute outsiders to this film. Signifi-cantly, it is in the elaboration of kinship forged through a resignification of the very terms that effect our exclusion and abjection that such a resignification creates the discursive and social space for community, that we see an appropriation of the terms of domination that turns them toward a more enabling future.

In these senses, then, *Paris Is Burning* documents neither an efficacious insur-rection nor a painful resubordination, but an unstable coexistence of both. The film attests to the painful pleasures of eroticizing and miming the very norms that wield their power by foreclosing the very reverse-occupations that the children nevertheless perform.

This is not an appropriation of dominant culture in order to remain subordinated by its terms but an appropriation that seeks to make over the terms of domination, a making over that is itself a kind of agency, a power in and as discourse, in and as performance, which repeats in order to remake — and sometimes succeeds. But this is a film that cannot achieve this effect without implicating its spectators in the act; to watch this film means to enter into a logic of fetishization that installs the ambivalence of that "performance" as related to our own. If the ethnographic conceit allows the performance to become an exotic fetish, one from which the audience absents itself, the commodification of heterosexual gender ideals will be, in that instance, complete. But if the film establishes the ambivalence of embodying — and failing to embody — that which one sees, then a distance will be opened up *between* that hegemonic call to normativizing gender and its critical appropriation.

Symbolic Reiterations

The resignification of the symbolic terms of kinship in *Paris Is Burning* and in the cultures of sexual minorities represented and occluded by the film raises the question of how precisely the apparently static workings of the symbolic order become vulnerable to subversive repetition and resignification. To understand how this resignification works in the fiction of Willa Cather, a recapitulation of the psychoanalytic account of the formation of sexed bodies is needed. The turn to Cather's fiction involves bringing the question of the bodily ego in Freud and the status of sexual differentiation in Lacan to bear on the question of naming and, particularly, the force of the name in fiction. Freud's contention that the ego is always a bodily ego is elaborated with the further insight that this bodily ego is projected in a field of visual alterity. Lacan insists that the body as a visual projection or imaginary formation cannot be sustained except through submitting to the name, where the "name" stands for the Name of the Father, the law of sexual differentiation. In "The Mirror Stage," Lacan remarks that the ego is produced "in a fictional direction," that its contouring and projection are psychic works of fiction; this fictional directionality is arrested and immobilized through the emergence of a symbolic order that legitimates sexually differentiated fictions as "positions." As a visual fiction, the ego is inevitably a site of *méconnaissance;* the sexing of the ego by the symbolic seeks to subdue this instability of the ego, understood as an imaginary formation.

Here it seems crucial to ask where and how language emerges to effect this stabilizing function, particularly for the fixing of sexed positions. The capacity of language to fix such positions, that is, to enact its symbolic effects, depends upon the permanence and fixity of the symbolic domain itself, the domain of signifiability or intelligibility.[12] If, for Lacan, the name secures the bodily ego in time, renders it identical through time, and this "conferring" power of the name is derived from the conferring power of the symbolic more generally, then it follows that a crisis in the symbolic will entail a crisis in this identity-conferring function of the name and in the stabilizing of bodily contours according to sex allegedly performed by the symbolic. *The crisis in the symbolic, understood as a crisis over what constitutes the limits of intelligibility, will register as a crisis in the name and in the morphological stability that the name is said to confer.*

The phallus functions as a synecdoche, for insofar as it is a figure of the penis, it constitutes an idealization and isolation of a body part and, further, the investment of that part with the force of symbolic law. If bodies are differentiated according to the symbolic positions that they occupy, and those symbolic positions consist in either having or being the phallus, bodies are thus differentiated and sustained in their differentiation by being subjected to the Law of the Father that dictates the "being" and "having" positions; men become men by approximating the "having of the phallus," which is to say they are compelled to approximate a "position" that is itself the result of a synecdochal collapse of masculinity into its "part" and a corollary idealization of that synecdoche as the governing symbol of the symbolic order. According to the symbolic, then, the assumption of sex takes place through an approximation of this synecdochal reduction. This is the means by which a body assumes sexed integrity as masculine or feminine: the sexed integrity of the body is paradoxically achieved through an identification with its reduction into idealized synecdoche ("having" or "being" the phallus). The body that fails to submit to the law or occupies that law in a mode contrary to its dictate thus loses its sure footing — its cultural gravity — in the symbolic and reappears in its imaginary tenuousness, its fictional direction. Such bodies contest the norms that govern the intelligibility of sex.

Is the distinction between the symbolic and the imaginary a stable distinction? And what of the distinction between the name and the bodily ego? Does the name, understood as the linguistic token that designates sex, only work to *cover over* its fictiveness, or are there occasions in which *the fictive and unstable status of that bodily ego trouble the name, expose the name as a crisis in referentiality?* Further, if body parts do not reduce to their phallic idealizations, that is, if they become vectors for other sorts of phantasmatic investments, then to what extent does the synecdochal logic through which the phallus operates lose its differentiating capacity? In other words, the phallus itself presupposes the regulation and reduction of phantasmatic investment such that the penis is either idealized as the phallus or mourned as the scene of castration and desired in the mode of an impossible compensation. If these investments are deregulated or, indeed, diminished, to what extent can having/being the phallus still function as that which secures the differentiation of the sexes?

In Cather's fiction, the name not only designates a gender uncertainty but produces a crisis in the figuration of sexed morphology as well. In this sense, Cather's fiction can be read as the foundering and unraveling of the symbolic on its own impossible demands. What happens when the name and the part produce divergent and conflicting sets of sexual expectations? To what extent do the unstable descriptions of gendered bodies and body parts produce a crisis in the referentiality of the name, the name itself as the very fiction it seeks to cover? If the heterosexism of the Lacanian symbolic depends on a set of rigid and prescribed identifications, and if those identifications are precisely what Cather's fiction works through and against the symbolically invested name, then the contingency of the symbolic — and the heterosexist parameters of what qualifies as "sex" — undergoes a rearticulation that works the fictive grounding of what only appears as the fixed limits of intelligibility.

Cather cites the paternal law, but in places and ways that mobilize a subversion under the guise of loyalty. Names fail fully to gender the characters whose femininity and masculinity they are expected to secure. The name fails to sustain the identity of the body within the terms of cultural intelligibility; body parts disengage from any common center, pull away from each other, lead separate lives, become sites of phantasmatic investments that refuse to reduce to singular sexualities. And though it appears that the normativizing law prevails by forcing suicide, the sacrifice of homosexual eroticism, or closeting homosexuality, the text exceeds the text, the life of the law exceeds the teleology of the law, enabling an erotic contestation and disruptive repetition of its own terms.

NOTES

1. Louis Althusser, "Ideology and Ideological State Apparatuses," 170–77; see also idem, "Freud and Lacan," 189–220, both essays in Althusser's *Lenin and Philosophy and Other Essays* (New York: Monthly Review Press, 1972).

2. Gloria Anzaldúa writes: "[T]hat focal point or fulcrum, that juncture where the *mestiza* stands, is where phenomena tend to collide"; and, "the work of *mestiza* consciousness is to break down the subject-object duality that keeps her a prisoner" ("La conciencia de la mestiza," in *Borderlands/La Frontera* [San Francisco: Aunt Lute, 1987], 79, 80).

3. Judith Butler, *Gender Trouble: Feminism and the Subversion of Identity* (New York: Routledge, 1990).

4. See Marjorie Garber, *Vested Interests: Cross-Dressing and Cultural Anxiety* (New York: Routledge, 1992), 40.

5. bell hooks, "Is Paris Burning?" *Z* (June 1991): 61.

6. Whereas I accept the psychoanalytic formulation that both the object and the aim of love are formed *in part* by those objects and aims that are repudiated, I consider it a cynical and homophobic use of that insight to claim that homosexuality is nothing other than repudiated heterosexuality. Given the culturally repudiated status of homosexuality as a form of love, the argument that seeks to reduce homosexuality to the inversion or deflection of heterosexuality functions to reconsolidate heterosexual hegemony. This is also why the analysis of homosexual melancholy cannot be regarded as symmetrical to the analysis of heterosexual melancholy. The latter is culturally enforced in a way that the former clearly is not, except within separatist communities that cannot wield the same power of prohibition as communities of compulsory heterosexism.

7. Kobena Mercer has offered rich work on this question and its relation to a psychoanalytic notion of "ambivalence." See "Looking for Trouble," in Henry Abelove, Michèle Barale, and David M. Halperin, eds., *The Lesbian and Gay Studies Reader* (New York: Routledge, 1993), 350–59 (originally published in *Transition* 51 [1991]); "Skin Head Sex Thing: Racial Difference and the Homoerotic Imaginary," in Bad Object-Choices, ed., *How Do I Look? Queer Film and Video* (Seattle: Bay Press, 1991), 169–210; "Engendered Species," *Artforum* 30, no. 10 (summer 1992): 74–78. On the relationship between psychoanalysis, race, and ambivalence, see Homi Bhabha, "Of Mimicry and Man: The Ambivalence of Colonial Discourse" *October* 28 (spring 1984): 125–33.

8. See Linda Singer, *Erotic Welfare: Sexual Theory and Politics in the Age of Epidemic* (New York: Routledge, 1992).

9. hooks, "Is Paris Burning?"

10. Ibid., 63.

11. Ibid.

12. For an argument against the construal of the Lacanian symbolic as static and immutable, see Teresa Brennan, *History After Lacan* (London: Routledge, 1993).

Chapter 21
Sisterhood: Political Solidarity
between Women
bell hooks

Women are the group most victimized by sexist oppression. As with other forms of group oppression, sexism is perpetuated by institutional and social structures: by the individuals who dominate, exploit, or oppress; and by the victims themselves, who are socialized to behave in ways that make them act in complicity with the status quo. Male supremacist ideology encourages women to believe we are valueless and obtain value only by relating to or bonding with men. We are taught that our relationships with one another diminish rather than enrich our experience. We are taught that women are "natural" enemies, that solidarity will never exist between us because we cannot, should not, and do not bond with one another. We have learned these lessons well. We must unlearn them if we are to build a sustained feminist movement. We must learn to live and work in solidarity. We must learn the true meaning and value of sisterhood.

Although the contemporary feminist movement should have provided a training ground for women to learn about political solidarity, sisterhood was not viewed as a revolutionary accomplishment women would work and struggle to obtain. The vision of sisterhood evoked by women's liberationists was based on the idea of common oppression. Needless to say, it was primarily bourgeois white women, both liberal and radical in perspective, who professed belief in the notion of common oppression. The idea of "common oppression" was a false and corrupt platform disguising and mystifying the true nature of women's varied and complex social reality. Women are divided by sexist attitudes, racism, class privilege, and a host of other prejudices. Sustained woman-bonding can occur only when these divisions are confronted and the necessary steps are taken to eliminate them. Divisions will not be eliminated by wishful thinking or romantic reverie about common oppression, despite the value of highlighting experiences all women share.

In recent years, "sisterhood" as slogan, motto, and rallying cry no longer evokes the spirit of power in unity. Some feminists now seem to feel that unity between women is impossible given our differences. Abandoning the idea of sisterhood as an expression of political solidarity weakens and diminishes the feminist movement. Solidarity strengthens resistance struggle. There can be no mass-based feminist movement to end sexist oppression without a unified front — women must take the initiative and demonstrate the power of solidarity. Unless we can show that barriers exist, we cannot hope to change and transform society as a whole. The shift away from an emphasis on sisterhood has occurred because many women, angered by the insistence on "common oppression," shared identity, and sameness, criticized or dismissed the feminist movement altogether. The emphasis on sisterhood was often seen as the emotional appeal masking the opportunism of manipulative bourgeois white women. It was seen as a cover-up hiding the fact that many women exploit and oppress other women. As early as 1970, Florence Kennedy, a black woman, activist, and lawyer, wrote an essay, published in the anthology *Sisterhood Is Powerful,* voicing her suspicions about the existence of solidarity between women:

> It is for this reason that I have considerable difficulty with the sisterhood mystique: "We are sisters," "Don't criticize a 'sister' publicly," etc. When a female judge asks my client where the bruises are when she complains about being assaulted by her husband (as did Family Court Judge Sylvia Jaffin Liese), and makes smart remarks about her being overweight, and when another female judge is so hostile that she disqualifies herself but refuses to order a combative husband out of the house (even though he owns property elsewhere with suitable living quarters) — these judges are not my sisters.[1]

Women were wise to reject a false notion of sisterhood based on shallow notions of bonding. We are mistaken if we allow these distortions or the women who created them (many of whom now tell us bonding between women is unimportant) to lead us to devalue sisterhood.

Women are enriched when we bond with one another, but we cannot develop sustaining ties or political solidarity using the model of sisterhood created by bourgeois women's liberationists. According to their analysis, the basis for bonding was shared victimization, hence the emphasis on common oppression. This concept of bonding directly reflects male-supremacist thinking. Sexist ideology teaches women that to be female is to be a victim. Rather than repudiate this equation (which mystifies female experience — in their daily lives most women are not continually passive, helpless, or powerless "victims"), women's liberationists embraced it, making shared victimization the basis for woman-bonding. This meant that women had to conceive of themselves as "victims" in order to feel that the feminist movement was relevant to their lives. Bonding as victims created a situation in which assertive, self-affirming women were often seen as having no place in the feminist movement. It was a logic that led many white women activists (along with black men) to suggest that black women were so "strong" they did not need to be active in the feminist movement. It was this logic that led many white women activists to abandon the feminist movement when they no longer embraced the victim identity. Ironically, the women who were most eager to be seen as "victims," who overwhelmingly stressed the role of victim, were more privileged and powerful than the vast majority of women in our society. An example of this tendency is some writing about violence against women. Women who are exploited and oppressed daily cannot afford to relinquish the belief that they exercise some measure of control, however relative, over their lives. They cannot afford to see themselves solely as "victims" because their survival depends on continued exercise of whatever personal powers they possess. It would be psychologically demoralizing for these women to bond with other women on the basis of shared victimization. They bond with other women on the basis of shared strengths and resources. This is the woman-bonding the feminist movement should encourage. This type of bonding is the essence of sisterhood.

Bonding as "victims," white women's liberationists were not required to assume responsibility for confronting the complexity of their own experience. They were not challenging one another to examine their sexist attitudes toward women unlike themselves or exploring the impact of race and class privilege on their relationships to women outside their race/class groups. Identifying as "victims," they could abdicate responsibility for their role in the maintenance and perpetuation of sexism, racism, and classism, which they did by insisting that only men were the enemy. They did not acknowledge and confront the enemy within. They were not prepared to forgo privilege and do the "dirty work" (the struggle and confrontation necessary to build political awareness as well as the many tedious tasks to be accomplished in day-to-day organizing) that is necessary in the development of radical political consciousness. The first task is honest critique and evaluation of one's social status, values, political beliefs, and so on, yet these women sought to avoid self-awareness. Sisterhood became yet another shield against reality. Their version of sisterhood was informed by a racist and classist assumption about white womanhood — that the white "lady" (that is to say, the bourgeois woman) should be protected from all that might upset or discomfort her and shielded from negative realities that might lead to confrontation. Their version of sisterhood dictated that sisters were to "unconditionally" love one another; that they were to avoid conflict and minimize disagreement; that they were not to criticize one other, especially in public. For a time these mandates created an illusion of unity suppressing the competition, hostility, perpetual disagreement, and abusive criticism (trashing) that were often the norm in feminist groups. Today many splinter groups who share common identities (e.g., WASP working-class women, white academic faculty women, anarchist feminists) use this same model of sisterhood, but participants in these groups endeavor to support, affirm, and protect one another while demonstrating hostility (usually through excessive trashing) toward women outside the chosen sphere. Bonding between a chosen circle of women who strengthen their ties by excluding and devaluing women outside their group closely resembles the type of personal bonding between women that has always occurred under patriarchy: the one difference being the interest in feminism.

To develop political solidarity between women, feminist activists cannot bond on the terms set by the dominant ideology of the culture. We must define our own terms. Rather than bond on the basis of shared victimization or in response to a false sense of a common enemy, we can bond on the basis of our commitment to a feminist movement that aims to end sexist oppression. Given such a commitment, our energies would not be concentrated on the issue of equality with men or solely on the struggle to resist male domination. We would no longer accept a simplistic good girls/bad boys account of the structure of sexist oppression. Before we can resist male domination we must break our attachment to sexism; we must work to transform female consciousness. Working together to expose, examine, and eliminate sexist socialization within ourselves, we can strengthen and affirm one another and build a solid foundation for developing political solidarity.

Between women and men, sexism is most often expressed in the form of male domination, which leads to discrimination, exploitation, or oppression. Between women, male-supremacist values are expressed through suspicious, defensive, and competitive behavior. It is sexism that leads women to feel threatened by one another without cause. While sexism teaches women to be sex objects for men, it is also manifest when women who have repudiated this role feel contemptuous and superior in relation to those women who have not. Sexism leads women to devalue parenting work while inflating the value of jobs and careers. Acceptance of sexist ideology is indicated when women teach that there are only two possible behavior patterns: dominance or submissiveness. Sexism teaches women woman-hating, and both consciously and unconsciously we act out this hatred in our daily contact with one another.

Although contemporary feminist activists, especially radical feminists, have called attention to women's absorption in sexist ideology, they have not stressed ways that women who are advocates of patriarchy, as well as women who uncritically accept sexist assumptions, could unlearn that socialization. It was often assumed that to support feminism was synonymous with repudiation of sexism in all its forms. Taking on the label "feminist" was accepted as a sign of personal transformation; as a consequence, the process by which values were altered was either ignored or could not be spelled out because no fundamental change had occurred. Sometimes consciousness-raising groups provided space for women to explore their sexism. This examination of attitudes toward themselves and other women was often a catalyst for transformation. Describing the function of rap groups in *The Politics of Women's Liberation,* Jo Freeman explains:

> Women came together in small groups to share personal experiences, problems, and feelings. From this public sharing comes the realization that what was thought to be individual is in fact common: that what was thought to be a personal problem has a social cause and a political solution. The rap group attacks the effects of psychological oppression and helps women to put it into a feminist context. Women learn to see how social structures and attitudes have molded them from birth and limited their opportunities. They ascertain the extent to which women have been denigrated in this society and how they have developed prejudices against themselves and other women. They learn to develop self-esteem and to appreciate the value of group solidarity.[2]

As consciousness-raising groups lost their popularity, new groups were not formed to fulfill similar functions. Women produced a large quantity of feminist writing but placed little emphasis on ways to unlearn sexism.

Since we live in a society that promotes fadism and temporary, superficial adaptation of different values, we are easily convinced that changes have occurred in arenas where there has been little or no change. Women's sexist attitudes toward one another are one such arena. All over the United States, women daily spend hours verbally abusing other women, usually through malicious gossip (not to be confused with gossip as positive communication). Television soap operas and nighttime dramas continually portray woman-to-woman relationships as characterized by aggression, contempt, and competitiveness. Feminists express sexism through abusive trashing of other feminists or through a total disregard and lack of interest in women who have not joined the feminist movement. The former is especially evident at university campuses where feminist studies, as a discipline or program, often seem to have no relationship to the wider feminist movement. In her commencement address at Barnard College in May 1979, black woman writer Toni Morrison told her audience:

> I want not to ask you but to tell you not to participate in the oppression of your sisters. Mothers who abuse their children are women, and another woman, not an agency, has to be willing to stay their hands. Mothers who set fire to school buses are women, and another woman, not an agency, has to tell them to stay their hands. Women who stop the promotion of other women in careers are women, and another woman must come to the victim's aid. Social and welfare workers who humiliate their clients may be women, and other women colleagues have to deflect their anger.[3]
>
> I am alarmed by the violence that women do to each other: professional violence, competitive violence, emotional violence. I am alarmed by the willingness of women to enslave other women. I am alarmed by a growing absence of decency on the killing floor of professional women's worlds.

To build a politicized, mass-based feminist movement, women must work harder to overcome the alienation from one another that exists when sexist socialization — for example, homophobia, judging by appearance, and conflicts between women with diverse sexual practices — has not been unlearned. So far, the feminist movement has not transformed woman-to-woman relationships, especially between women who are strangers to one another or from different backgrounds, even though it has been the occasion for bonding between individuals and groups of women. We must renew our efforts to help women unlearn sexism if we are to develop affirming personal relationships as well as political unity.

Racism is another barrier to solidarity between women. The ideology of sisterhood as expressed by contemporary feminist activists has not acknowledged that racist discrimination, exploitation, and oppression of multiethnic women by white women have made it impossible for the two groups to feel they share common interests or political concerns. Also, the existence of totally different cultural backgrounds can make communication difficult. This has been especially true of relationships between black and white women. Historically, many black women experienced white women as the white-supremacist group who most directly exercised power over them, often in a manner far more brutal and dehumanizing than that of white, racist men. Today, despite predominant rule by white-supremacist patriarchs, black women often work in situations where the immediate supervisor, boss, or authority figure is a white woman. Conscious of the privileges white men as well as white women gain as a consequence of racial domination, black women were quick to react to the feminist call for sisterhood by pointing to the contradiction in the idea that we should join with women who exploit us to help liberate them. The call for sisterhood was heard by many black women as a plea for help and support for a movement that did not address us. As Toni Morrison explains in her article "What the Black Woman Thinks about Women's Lib," many black women do not respect bourgeois white women and could not imagine joining a cause that would be for their benefit:

> Black women have been able to envy white women (their looks, their easy life, the attention they seem to get from their men); they could fear them (for the economic control they have had over black women's lives); and even love them (as mammies

and domestic workers can); but black women have found it impossible to respect white women. . . . Black women have no abiding admiration of white women as competent, complete people, whether vying with them for the few professional slots available to women in general, or moving in their dirt from one place to another, they regarded them as willful children, mean children, but never as real adults capable of handling the real problems of the world.

White woman were ignorant of the facts of life — perhaps by choice, perhaps with the assistance of men, but ignorant anyway. They were totally dependent on marriage or male support (emotionally and economically). They confronted their sexuality with furtiveness, complete abandon, or repression. Those who could afford it gave over the management of the house and the rearing of the children to others. (It is a source of amusement even now to black women to listen to feminist talk of liberation while somebody's nice black grandmother shoulders the daily responsibility of child rearing and floor mopping, and the liberated one comes home to examine the housekeeping, correct it, and be entertained by the children.) If Women's Lib needs those grandmothers to thrive, it has a serious flaw.[4]

Many women perceived that the women's liberation movement as outlined by bourgeois white women would serve the latter's interests at the expense of poor and working-class women, many of whom are black. Certainly this was not a basis for sisterhood, and black women would have been politically naive had we joined such a movement. However, given black women's historical and current participation in political organizing, the emphasis could have been on the development and clarification of the nature of political solidarity.

White females discriminate against and exploit black women while simultaneously being envious and competitive in their interactions with them. Neither process of interaction creates conditions where trust and mutually reciprocal relationships can develop. After constructing feminist theory and praxis in such a way as to omit a focus on racism, white women shifted the responsibility for calling attention to race onto others. They did not have to take the initiative in discussions of racism or race privilege but could listen and respond to nonwhite women discussing racism without changing in any way the structure of the feminist movement, without losing their hegemonic hold. They could then show their concern with having more women of color in feminist organizations by encouraging greater participation. They were not confronting racism. In more recent years, racism has become an accepted topic in feminist discussions not as a result of black women calling attention to it (this was done at the very onset of the movement) but as a result of white female input validating such discussions, a process that is indicative of how racism works. Commenting on this tendency in her essay "The Incompatible Ménage à Trois: Marxism, Feminism, and Racism," Gloria Joseph states:

> To date feminists have not concretely demonstrated the potential or capacity to become involved in fighting racism on an equal footing with sexism. Adrienne Rich's recent article on feminism and racism is an exemplary one on this topic. She reiterates much that has been voiced by black female writers, by the acclaim given her article shows again that it takes whiteness to give even Blackness validity.[5]

Focus on racism in feminist circles is usually directed at legitimating the "as is" structure of feminist theory and praxis. Like other affirmative-action agendas in white-supremacist, capitalist patriarchy, lengthy discussions of racism or lip service to its importance tend to call attention to the "political correctness" of the current feminist movement; they are not directed at an overall strategy to resist racist oppression in our society. Discussions of racism have been implicitly sexist because of the focus on guilt and personal behavior. Racism is not an issue simply because white women activists are individually racist. They represent a small percentage of women in this society. They could have all been antiracist from the outset, but eliminating racism would still need to be a central feminist issue. Racism is fundamentally a feminist issue because it is so interconnected with sexist oppression. In the West, the philosophical foundations of racist and sexist ideology are similar. Although ethnocentric white values have led feminist theorists to argue the priority of sexism over racism, they do so in the context of attempting to create an evolutionary notion of culture, which in no way corresponds to our lived experience. In the United States, maintaining white supremacy has always been as great a priority as (if not a greater priority than) maintaining strict sex-role divisions. It is no mere coincidence that interest in white women's rights is kindled whenever there is mass-based antiracist protest. Even the most politically naive person can comprehend that a white-supremacist state, asked to respond to the needs of oppressed black people and/or the needs of white women (particularly those of the bourgeois classes), will find it in its interest to respond to whites. Radical movement to end racism (a struggle that many have died to advance) is far more threatening than a women's movement shaped to meet the class needs of upwardly mobile white women.

It does not in any way diminish the value of or the need for a feminist movement to recognize the significance of antiracist struggle. Feminist theory would have much to offer if it showed women ways in which racism and sexism are immutably connected rather than pitting one struggle against the other or blatantly dismissing racism. A central issue for feminist activists has been the struggle to obtain for women the right to control their bodies. The very concept of white supremacy relies on the perpetuation of a white race. It is in the interests of continued white racist domination of the planet for white patriarchy to maintain control over all women's bodies. Any white female activist who works daily to help women gain control over their bodies and is racist negates and undermines her own effort. When white women attack white supremacy, they are simultaneously participating in the struggle to end sexist oppression. This is just one example of the intersecting, complementary nature of racist and sexist oppression. There are many others that need to be examined by feminist theorists.

Racism allows white women to construct feminist theory and praxis in such a way that they are far removed from anything resembling radical struggle. Racist socialization teaches bourgeois white women to think they are necessarily more capable of leading masses of women than other groups of women. Time and time again, they have shown that they do not want to be part of the feminist movement — they want to lead it. Even though bourgeois, white women's liberationists probably know less about grassroots organizing than many poor and working-class women, they are certain of their leadership ability, as well as confident that theirs should be the dominant role in shaping theory and praxis. Racism teaches an inflated sense of importance and value, especially when coupled with class privilege. Most poor and working-class women or even individual bourgeois, nonwhite women would not have assumed that they could launch a feminist movement without first having the support and participation of diverse groups of women. Elizabeth Spelmann stresses this impact of racism in her essay "Theories of Race and Gender: The Erasure of Black Women":

> [T]his is a racist society, and part of what this means is that, generally, the self-esteem of white people is deeply influenced by their difference from and supposed superiority to black people. White people may not think of themselves as racists, because they do not own slaves or hate blacks, but that does not mean that much of what props up white people's sense of self-esteem is not based on the racism which unfairly distributes benefits and burdens to whites and blacks.[6]

One reason white women active in the feminist movement were unwilling to confront racism was their arrogant assumption that their call for sisterhood was a nonracist gesture. Many white women have said to me, "[W]e wanted black women and other nonwhite women to join the movement," totally unaware of their perception that they somehow "own" the movement, that they are "hosts" inviting us as "guests."

Despite the current focus on eliminating racism in the feminist movement, there has been little change in the direction of theory and praxis. While white feminist activists now include writings by women of color on course outlines, or hire one woman of color to teach a class about her ethnic group, or make sure one or more women of color are represented in feminist organizations (they sometimes even acknowledge that this contribution of women of color is needed and valuable), more often than not they are attempting to cover up the fact that they are totally unwilling to surrender hegemonic dominance of theory and praxis, a dominance that they would not have established were this not a white-supremacist, capitalist state. Their attempts to manipulate women of color, a component of the process of dehumanization, do not always go unnoticed. In the July 1983 issue of *In These Times,* a letter by Theresa Funiciello was published on the subject of poor women and the women's movement that shows the nature of racism within the feminist movement:

> Prior to a conference some time ago on the Urban Woman sponsored by the New York City chapter of NOW, I received a phone call from a NOW representative (whose name I have forgotten) asking for a welfare speaker with special qualifications. I was asked that she not be white — she might be "too articulate" — (i.e. not me), that she not be black, she might be "too angry." Perhaps she could be Puerto Rican? She should not say anything political or analytical but confine herself to the subject of "what the women's movement has done for me."[7]

Funiciello responded to this situation by organizing a multiracial women's takeover of the conference. This type of action shows the spirit of sisterhood.

Another response to racism has been the establishment of "unlearning racism workshops," which are often led by white women. These workshops are important, yet they tend to focus primarily on cathartic, individual, psychological acknowledgment of personal prejudice without stressing the need for corresponding change in political commitment and action. A woman who attends an unlearning racism workshop and learns to acknowledge that she is a racist is no less of a threat than one who does not. Acknowledgment of racism is significant when it leads to transformation. More research, writing, and practical implementation of findings must be done on ways to unlearn racist socialization. Many white woman who daily exercise race privilege lack awareness that they are doing so (which explains the emphasis on confession in unlearning racism workshops). They may not have a conscious understanding of the ideology of white supremacy and the extent to which it shapes their behavior and attitudes toward woman unlike themselves. Often white women bond on the basis of shared racial identity without being conscious of the significance of their actions. This unconscious maintenance and perpetuation of white supremacy is dangerous because none of us can struggle to change racist attitudes if we do not recognize that they exist. For example, a group of white feminist activists who do not know one another may be present at a meeting to discuss feminist theory. They may feel they are bonded on the basis of shared womanhood, but the atmosphere will noticeably change when a women of color enters the room. The white women will become tense, no longer relaxed, no longer celebratory. Unconsciously, they felt close to one another because they shared racial identity. The "whiteness" that bonds them together is a racial identity that is directly related to the experience of nonwhite people as "other" and as a "threat." When I speak to white women about racial bonding, they often deny it exists; it is not unlike sexist men denying their sexism. Until white supremacy is understood and attacked by white women, there can be no bonding between them and multiethnic groups of women.

We will know that white feminist activists have begun to confront racism in a serious and revolutionary manner when they are not simply acknowledging racism in the feminist movement or calling attention to personal prejudice but are actively struggling to resist racist oppression in our society. We will know white feminists have made a political commitment to eliminating racism when they help change the direction of the feminist movement, when they work to unlearn racist socialization prior to assuming positions of leadership or shaping theory or making contact with women of color so that they will not perpetuate and maintain racial oppression or, unconsciously or consciously, abuse and hurt nonwhite women. These are the truly radical gestures that create a foundation for the experience of political solidarity between white women and women of color.

White women are not the only group who must confront racism if sisterhood is to emerge. Women of color must confront our absorption of white-supremacist beliefs, "internalized racism," which may lead us to feel self-hate, to vent anger and rage at injustice at one another rather than at oppressive forces, to hurt and abuse one another, or to refuse to communicate with other ethnic groups. Often women of color from varied ethnic groups have learned to resent and hate one another or to be competitive with another. Often Asian, Latina, or Native American groups find they can bond with whites by hating blacks. Black people respond to this by perpetuating racist stereotypes and images of these ethnic groups. It becomes a vicious cycle. Divisions between women of color will not be eliminated until we assume responsibility for uniting (not solely on the basis of resisting racism) to learn about our cultures, to share our knowledge and skills, and to gain strength from our diversity. We need to do more research and writing about the barriers that separate us and the ways we can overcome such separation. Often the men in our ethnic groups have greater contact with one another than we do. Women often assume so many job-related and domestic responsibilities that we lack the time or do not make the time to get to know women outside our group or community. Language differences often prevent us from communicating; we can change this by encouraging one another to learn to speak Spanish, English, Japanese, Chinese, and so on.

One factor that makes interaction between different ethnic groups of women difficult and sometimes impossible is our failure to recognize that a behavior pattern in one culture may be unacceptable in another, that it may have different signification cross-culturally. Through repeated teaching of a course titled "Third World Women in the United States," I have learned the importance of learning what we called one another's cultural codes. An Asian-American student of Japanese heritage explained her reluctance to participate in feminist organizations by calling attention to the tendency among feminist activists to speak rapidly, without pause, to be quick on the uptake, always ready with response. She had been raised to pause and think before speaking, to consider the impact of one's words, a characteristic that she felt was particularly true of Asian-Americans. She expressed a feeling of inadequacy on the various occasions she was present in feminist groups. In our class, we learned to allow pauses and appreciate them. By sharing this cultural code, we created an atmosphere in the classroom that allowed for different communication patterns. This particular class was peopled primarily by black women. Several white women students complained that the atmosphere in the class was "too hostile." They cited the noise level and the direct confrontations that took place in the room prior to class starting as an example of this hostility. Our response was to explain that what they perceived as hostility and aggression, we considered playful teasing and affectionate expressions of our pleasure at being together. We saw our tendency to talk loudly as a consequence of our often being in rooms where many people were speaking, as a consequence of cultural background: many of us were raised in families where individuals speak loudly. In their upbringing as white, middle-class females, the complaining students had been taught to identify loud and direct speech with anger. We explained that we did not identify loud or blunt speech in this way and encouraged them to switch codes, to think of it as an affirming gesture. Once they switched codes, they not only began to have a more creative, joyful experience in the class but also learned that silence and quiet speech can in some cultures indicate hostility and aggression. By learning one another's cultural codes and respecting our differences, we felt a sense of community, of sisterhood. Respecting diversity does not mean uniformity or sameness.

A crucial concern in these multiracial classroom settings was recognition and acknowledgment of our differences and the extent to which they determine how we will be perceived by others. We continually had to remind one another to appreciate difference since many of us were raised to fear it. We talked about the need to acknowledge that we all suffer in some way but that we are not all oppressed nor equally oppressed. Many of us feared that our experiences were irrelevant because they were not as oppressive or as exploited as the experiences of others. We discovered that we had a greater feeling of unity when people focused truthfully on their own experiences without comparing them with those of others in a competitive way. One student, Isabel Yrigoyei, wrote: "We are not equally oppressed. There is no joy in this. We must speak from within us, our own experiences, our own oppression — taking someone else's oppression is nothing to feel proud of. We should never speak for that which we have not felt." When we began our communication by focusing on individual experiences, we found them to be varied even among those of us who shared common ethnic backgrounds. We learned that these differences mean we have no monolithic experiences that we can identity as "Chicana experience," "black experience," and so on. A Chicana growing up in a rural environment in a Spanish-speaking home has a life experience that differs from that of a Chicana raised in an English-speaking family in a bourgeois, predominantly white New Jersey suburb. These two women will not automatically feel solidarity. Even though they are from the same ethnic group, they must work to develop sisterhood. Seeing these types of differences, we also confronted our tendency to value some experiences over others. We might see the Spanish-speaking Chicana as being more "politically correct" than her English-speaking peer. By no longer passively accepting the learned tendency to compare and judge, we could see value in each experience. We could also see that our different experiences often meant that we had different needs, that there was no one strategy or formula for the development of political consciousness. By mapping our various strategies, we affirmed our diversity while working toward solidarity. Women must explore various ways to communicate with one another cross-culturally if we are to develop political solidarity. When women of color strive to learn with and about one another, we take responsibility for building sisterhood. We need not rely on white women to lead the way to solidarity; all too often opportunistic concerns point them in other directions. We can establish unity among ourselves and with antiracist women. We can stand together united in political solidarity, in the feminist movement. We can restore to the idea of sisterhood its true meaning and value.

Cutting across racial lines, class is a serious political division between women. It was often suggested in early feminist literature that class would not be so important if more poor and working-class women would join the movement. Such thinking was both a denial of the existence of class privilege gained through exploitation as well as a denial of class struggle. To build sisterhood, women must criticize and repudiate class exploitation. The bourgeois woman who takes a less privileged "sister" to lunch or dinner at a fancy restaurant may be acknowledging class, but she is not repudiating class privilege — she is exercising it. Wearing secondhand clothes and living in low-cost housing in a poor neighborhood while buying stock is not a gesture of solidarity with those who are deprived or underprivileged. As in the case of racism in the feminist movement, the emphasis on class has been focused on individual status and change. Until women accept the need for redistribution of wealth and resources in the United States and work toward the achievement of that end, there will be no bonding between women that transcends class.

It is very apparent that the feminist movement so far has primarily served the class interests of bourgeois white women and men. The great majority of women from middle-class situations who entered the labor force (an entry encouraged and promoted by the feminist movement) helped strengthen the economy of the 1970s. In *The Two-Paycheck Marriage,* Caroline Bird emphasizes the extent to which these women (most of whom are white) helped bolster a waning economy:

Working wives helped families maintain that standard of living through inflation. The Bureau of Labor Statistics has concluded that between 1973 and 1974 the real purchasing power of single-earner families dropped 3 percent compared to 1 percent for families in which the wife was working.... Women especially will put themselves out to defend a standard of living they see threatened.

Women did more than maintain standards. Working women lifted millions of families into middle class life. Her pay meant the difference between an apartment and a house, or college for the children....

Working wives were beginning to create a new kind of rich — and ... a new kind of poor.[8]

Two decades later, it is evident that large numbers of individual white women (especially those from middle-class backgrounds) have made economic strides in the wake of the feminist movement's support of careerism and affirmative-action programs in many professions. However, the masses of women are as poor as ever, or poorer. To the bourgeois "feminist," the million-dollar salary granted newscaster Barbara Walters represents a victory for women. To working-class women who make less than the minimum wage and who receive few if any benefits, it means continued class exploitation.

Leah Fritz's *Dreamers and Dealers* is a fine example of liberal women's attempt to gloss over the fact that class privilege is based on exploitation, that rich women support and condone that exploitation, that the people who suffer most are poor, underprivileged women and children. Fritz attempts to evoke sympathy for all upper-class women by stressing their psychological suffering, their victimization in the hands of men. She concludes her chapter "Rich Women" with the statement:

Feminism belongs as much to the rich woman as to the poor woman. It can help her to understand that her own interests are linked with the advancement of all womankind; that comfort and dependency is a trap; that the golden cage has bars, too; and that rich and poor, we are all wounded in the service of patriarchy, although our scars are different. The inner turmoil that sends her to a psychoanalyst can generate energy for the movement which alone may heal her, by setting her free.[9]

Fritz conveniently ignores that domination and exploitation are necessary if there are to be rich women who may experience sexist discrimination or exploitation. She conveniently ignores class struggle.

Women from lower-class groups have had no difficulty recognizing that the social equality women's liberationists talk about equates careerism and class mobility with liberation. They also know who will be exploited in the service of this liberation. Daily confronting class exploitation, they cannot conveniently ignore class struggle. In the anthology *Women of Crisis,* Helen, a working-class white woman, who works as a maid in the home of a bourgeois white "feminist," expresses her understanding of the contradiction between feminist rhetoric and practice:

I think the missus is right: everyone should be equal. She keeps on saying that. But then she has me working away in her house, and I'm not equal with her — and she doesn't want to be equal with me; and I don't blame her, because if I was her I'd hold on to my money just like she does. Maybe that's what the men are doing — they're holding on to their money. And it's a big fight, like it always is about money. She should know. She doesn't go throwing big fat pay checks at her "help." She's fair; she keeps on reminding us — but she's not going to "liberate" us, any more than the men are going to "liberate" their wives or their secretaries or the other women working in their companies.[10]

Women's liberationists not only have equated psychological pain with material deprivation to deemphasize class privilege but also often have suggested it is the more severe problem. They have managed to overlook the fact that many women suffer both psychologically and materially and that for this reason alone changing their social status merits greater attention than careerism. Certainly the bourgeois woman who is suffering psychically is more likely to find help than the woman who is suffering material deprivation as well as emotional pain. One of the basic differences in perspective between the bourgeois woman and the working-class or poor woman is that the latter knows that being discriminated against or exploited because one is female may be painful and dehumanizing, but it may not necessarily be as painful, dehumanizing, or threatening as being without food or shelter, as starvation, as being deathly ill but unable to obtain medical care. Had poor women set the agenda for the feminist movement, they might have decided that class struggle should be a central feminist issue; that poor and privileged women should work to understand class structure and the way it pits women against one another.

Outspoken socialist feminists, most of whom are white women, have emphasized class, but they have not been effective in changing attitudes toward class in the feminist movement. Despite their support of socialism, their values, behaviors, and lifestyles continue to be shaped by privilege. They have not developed collective strategies to convince bourgeois women who have no radical political perspective that eliminating class oppression is crucial to efforts to end sexist oppression. They have not worked to organize with poor and working-class women who may not identify as socialists but do identify with the need for redistribution of wealth in the United States. They have not worked to raise the consciousness of women collectively. Much of their energy has been spent addressing the white male left, discussing the connection between Marxism and feminism, or explaining to other feminist activists that socialist feminism is the best strategy for revolution. Emphasis on class struggle is often incorrectly deemed the sole domain of socialist feminists. Although I call attention to directions and strategies they have not employed, I wish to emphasize that these issues should be addressed by all activists in the feminist movement. When women face the reality of classism and make political commitments to eliminating it, we will no longer experience the class conflicts that have been so apparent in the feminist movement. Until we focus on class divisions between women, we will be unable to build political solidarity.

Sexism, racism, and classism divide women from one another. Within the feminist movement, divisions and disagreements about strategy and emphasis have led to the formation of a number of groups with varied political positions. Splintering into different political factions and special-interest groups has erected unnecessary barriers to sisterhood that could easily be eliminated. Special-interest groups lead women to believe that only socialist feminists should be concerned about class; that only lesbian feminists should be concerned about the oppression of lesbians and gay men; that only black women or other women of color should be concerned about racism. Every woman can stand in political opposition to sexist, racist, hetero-sexist, and classist oppression. While she may choose to focus her work on a given political issue or a particular cause, if she is firmly opposed to all forms of group oppression, this broad perspective will be manifest in all her work irrespective of its particularity. When feminist activists are antiracist and against class exploitation, it will not matter if women of color, poor women, and so on, are present. These issues will be deemed important and will be addressed, although the women most person-ally affected by particular exploitations will necessarily continue in the forefront of those struggles. Women must learn to accept responsibility for fighting oppression that may not directly affect them as individuals. The feminist movement, like other radical movements in our society, suffers when individual concerns and priorities are the only reason for participation. When we show our concern for the collective, we strengthen our solidarity.

"Solidarity" has been a word seldom used in the contemporary feminist move-ment. Much greater emphasis has been placed on the idea of "support." Support can mean upholding or defending a position one believes is right. It can also mean serving as a prop or a foundation for a weak structure. This latter meaning had greater significance in feminist circles. Its value emerged from the emphasis on shared victimization. Identifying as "victims," women were acknowledging a help-lessness and powerlessness as well as a need for support, in this case the support of fellow feminist activists, "sisters." It was closely related to the shallow notion of sisterhood. Commenting on its usage among feminist activists in her essay "With All Due Respect," Jane Rule explains:

> Support is a much used word in the women's movement. For too many people it means giving and receiving unqualified approval. Some women are awfully good at withdrawing it at crucial moments. Too many are convinced they can't function without it. It's a false concept which has produced barriers to understanding and done real emotional damage. Suspension of critical judgement is not necessary for offering real support, which has to do instead with self-respect and respect for other people even at moments of serious disagreement.[11]

Women's legacy of woman-hating, which includes fierce, brutal, verbal tearing apart of one another, has to be eliminated if women are to make critiques and engage in disagreements and arguments that are constructive and caring, with the in-tention of enriching rather than diminishing. Woman-to-woman negative, aggressive behavior is not unlearned when all critical judgment is suspended. It is unlearned when women accept that we are different, that we will necessarily disagree, but that we can disagree and argue with one another without acting as if we are fighting for our lives, without feeling that we stand to lose all self-esteem if criticisms of one an-other emerge. Verbal disagreements are often the setting where women demonstrate their engagement with the win-or-lose competitiveness that is most often associated with male interactions, especially in the arena of sports. Women, like men, must learn how to dialogue with one another without competition. Jane Rule suggests that women can disagree without trashing if they realize that they do not stand to lose value or self-worth if they are criticized: "No one can discredit my life if it is in my own hands, and therefore I do not have to make anyone carry the false burden of my frightened hostility."[12]

Women need to come together in situations where there will be ideological disagreement and work to change that interaction so communication occurs. This means that when women come together, rather than pretend union, we would acknowledge that we are divided and must develop strategies to overcome fears, prejudices, resentments, competitiveness, and so on. The fierce negative disagreements that have taken place in feminist circles have led many feminist activists to shun group or individual interaction where there is likely to be disagreement that leads to confrontation. Safety and support have been redefined to mean hanging out in groups where the participants are alike and share similar values. While no woman wants to enter a situation in which she will be psychically annihilated, women can face one another in hostile confrontation and struggle and move beyond the hostility to understanding. Expression of hostility as an end in itself is a useless activity, but when it is the catalyst pushing us on to greater clarity and understanding, it serves a meaningful function.

Women need to have the experience of working through hostility to arrive at understanding and solidarity if only to free ourselves from the sexist socialization that tells us to avoid confrontation because we will be victimized or destroyed. Time and time again, I have had the experience of making statements at talks that anger a listener and lead to assertive and sometimes hostile verbal confrontation. The situation feels uncomfortable, negative, and unproductive because there are angry voices, tears, and so on, and yet I may find later that the experience has led to greater clarity and growth on my part and on the part of the listener. On one occasion, I was invited by a black woman sociologist, a very soft-spoken individual, to speak in a class she was teaching. A young Chicana woman who could pass for white was a student in the class. We had a heated exchange when I made the point that the ability to pass for white gave her a perspective on race totally different from that of someone who is dark-skinned and can never pass. I pointed out that any person meeting her with no knowledge of her ethnic background probably assumes that she is white and treats her accordingly. At the time the suggestion angered her. She became quite angry and finally stormed out of the class in tears. The teacher and fellow students definitely saw me as the "bad guy" who had failed to support a fellow sister and instead reduced her to tears. They were annoyed that our get-together had not been totally pleasurable, unemotional, dispassionate. I certainly felt miserable in the situation. The student, however, contacted me weeks later to share her feelings that she had gained insights and awareness as a result of our encounter that aided her personal growth. If women always seek to avoid confrontation, to be "safe," we may never experience any revolutionary change, any transformation, individually or collectively.

When women actively struggle in a truly supportive way to understand our differences, to change misguided, distorted perspectives, we lay the foundation for the experience of political solidarity. Solidarity is not always the same as support. To experience solidarity, we must have a community of interest, shared beliefs and goals around which to unite, to build sisterhood. Support can be occasional. It can be given and just as easily withdrawn. Solidarity requires sustained, ongoing commitment. In the feminist movement, there is need for diversity, disagreement, and difference if we are to grow. As Grace Lee Boggs and James Boggs emphasize in *Revolution and Evolution in the Twentieth Century:*

> The same appreciation of the reality of contradiction underlies the concept of criticism and self-criticism. Criticism and self-criticism is the way in which individuals united by common goals can consciously utilize their differences and limitations, i.e., the negative, in order to accelerate their positive advance. The popular formulation for this process is "changing a bad thing into a good thing."[13]

Women do not need to eradicate difference to feel solidarity. We do not need to share common oppression to fight equally to end oppression. We do not need anti-male sentiments to bond us together, so great is the wealth of experience, culture, and ideas we have to share with one another. We can be sisters united by shared interests and beliefs, united in our appreciation for diversity, united in our struggle to end sexist oppression, united in political solidarity.

NOTES

1. Florence Kennedy, "Institutional Oppression vs. the Female," in *Sisterhood Is Powerful,* ed. Robin Morgan (New York: Random House, 1970), 438–46.

2. Jo Freeman, *The Politics of Women's Liberation* (New York: David McKay Co., 1975), 118.

3. Toni Morrison, commencement address at Barnard College, May 1979.

4. Toni Morrison, "What the Black Woman Thinks about Women's Lib," *New York Times Magazine,* August 22, 1971, 15.

5. Gloria Joseph, "The Incompatible Ménage à Trois: Marxism, Feminism, and Racism," in *Women and Revolution,* ed. Lydia Sargent (Boston: South End Press, 1981), 105.

6. Elizabeth Spelmann, "Theories of Race and Gender: The Erasure of Black Women," *Quest* 5, no. 4 (1982): 36–62.

7. Theresa Funiciello, letter to the editor, *In These Times* (July 1983).

8. Caroline Bird, *The Two-Paycheck Marriage* (New York: Pocket Books, 1979), 9.

9. Leah Fritz, *Dreamers and Dealers: An Intimate Appraisal of the Women's Movement* (Boston: Beacon Press, 1979), 225.

10. See Robert Coles and John H. Coles, *Women of Crisis* (New York: Delacorte, 1979).

11. Jane Rule, "With All Due Respect," in *The Outlander* (Tallahassee, Fla.: Naiad Press, 1981).

12. Ibid.

13. Grace Lee Boggs and James Boggs, *Revolution and Evolution in the Twentieth Century* (New York: Monthly Review Press, 1974), 133.

Part IV

Postcolonial Theory

Chapter 22
Not You/Like You: Postcolonial Women and the Interlocking Questions of Identity and Difference
Trinh T. Minh-ha

To raise the question of identity is to reopen the discussion on the self/other relationship in its enactment of power relations. Identity as understood in the context of a certain ideology of dominance has long been a notion that relies on the concept of an essential, authentic core that remains hidden to one's consciousness and that requires the elimination of all that is considered foreign or not true to the self, that is to say, not-I, other. In such a concept the other is almost unavoidably either opposed to the self or submitted to the self's dominance. It is always condemned to remain in its shadow while making attempts at being its equal. Identity, thus understood, supposes that a clear dividing line can be made between I and not-I, he and she; between depth and surface, or vertical and horizontal identity; between us here and them over there. The further one moves from the core the less likely one is thought to be capable of fulfilling one's role as the real self, the real black, Indian, or Asian, the real woman. The search for an identity is, therefore, usually a search for that lost, pure, true, real, genuine, original, authentic self, often situated within a process of elimination of all that is considered other, superfluous, fake, corrupted, or Westernized.

If identity refers to the whole pattern of sameness within a being, the style of a continuing me that permeates all the changes undergone, then difference remains within the boundary of that which distinguishes one identity from another. This means that at heart X must be X; Y must be Y; and X cannot be Y. Those running around yelling "X is not X" and "X can be Y" usually land in a hospital, a rehabilitation center, a concentration camp, or a reservation. All deviations from the dominant stream of thought, that is to say, the belief in a permanent essence of woman and in an invariant but fragile identity whose loss is considered to be a specifically human danger, can easily fit into the categories of the mentally ill or the mentally underdeveloped. It is probably difficult for a normal, probing mind to recognize that to seek is to lose, for seeking presupposes a separation between the seeker and the sought, the continuing me and the changes it undergoes. Can identity, indeed, be viewed other than as a by-product of a manhandling of life, one that, in fact, refers no more to a consistent pattern of sameness than to an inconsequential process of otherness? How am I to lose, maintain, or gain a female identity when it is impossible for me to take up a position outside this identity from which I presumably reach in and feel for it? Difference in such a context is that which undermines the very idea of identity, differing to infinity those layers of totality that form I.

Hegemony works at leveling out differences and at standardizing contexts and expectations in the smallest details of our daily lives. Uncovering this leveling of differences is, therefore, resisting that very notion of difference that is defined in the master's terms and that often resorts to the simplicity of essences. Divide and conquer has for centuries been his creed, his formula of success. But a different terrain of consciousness has been explored for some time now, a terrain in which clearcut divisions and dualistic oppositions such as science versus subjectivity, masculine versus feminine, may serve as departure points for analytical purposes but are no longer satisfactory if not entirely untenable to the critical mind.

I have often been asked about what some viewers call the lack of conflicts in my films. Psychological conflict is often equated with substance and depth. Conflicts in Western contexts often serve to define identities. My response to questions about this "lack" is: let difference replace conflict. Difference as understood in many feminist and non-Western contexts, difference as foreground in my film work, is not opposed to sameness nor synonymous with separateness. Difference, in other words, does not necessarily give rise to separatism. This concept of difference can encompass differences as well as similarities. One can further say that difference is not what makes conflicts. It is beyond and alongside conflict. This is where confusion often arises and where the challenge can be issued. Many of us still hold on to the concept of difference not as a tool of creativity to question multiple forms of repression and dominance but as a tool of segregation used to exert power on the basis of racial and sexual essences. The apartheid type of difference.

Let me point to a few examples of practices of such a notion of difference. There are quite a few, but I'll select just three. First, there is the example of the veil as reality and metaphor. If the act of unveiling has a liberating potential, so does the act of veiling. It all depends on the context in which such an act is carried out or, more precisely, on how and where women see dominance. Difference should be defined neither by the dominant sex nor by the dominant culture. So when women decide to lift the veil, one can say that they do so in defiance of their men's oppressive right to their bodies. But when they decide to keep or put on the veil they once took off, they might do so to reappropriate their space or to claim a new difference in defiance of genderless, hegemonic, centered standardization.

Second, the use of silence. Within the context of women's speech, silence has many faces. Like the veiling of women, silence can only be subversive when it frees itself from the male-defined context of absence, lack, and fear as feminine territories. On the one hand, we face the danger of inscribing femininity as absence, as lack, and as blank in rejecting the importance of the act of enunciation. On the other hand, we understand the necessity of placing women on the side of negativity and of working in undertones, for example, in our attempts at undermining patriarchal systems of values. Silence is so commonly set in opposition with speech. Silence as a will not to say or a will to unsay and as a language of its own has barely been explored.

Third, the question of subjectivity. The domain of subjectivity understood as sentimental, personal, and individual horizon as opposed to objective, universal, societal, and limitless horizon is often attributed to women (the other of man) and natives (the other of the West). It is often assumed, for example, that women's enemy is the intellect, that their apprehension of life can only wind and unwind around a cooking pot, a baby's diaper, or matters of the heart. Similarly, for centuries and centuries we have been told that primitive mentality belongs to the order of the emotional and the affective, and that it is incapable of elaborating concepts. Primitive man feels and participates. He does not really think or reason. He has no knowledge, "no clear idea or even no idea at all of matter and soul," as Lucien Lévy-Bruhl puts it. Today this persistent rationale has taken on multiple faces, and its residues still linger, easily recognizable despite the refined rhetoric of those who perpetuate it.

Worth mentioning again here is the question of outsider and insider in ethnographic practices. An insider's view: the magic word that bears within itself a seal of approval. What can be more authentically other than an otherness by the other, herself? Yet every piece of the cake given by the master comes with a double-edged blade. The Afrikaners are prompt in saying, "You can take a black man from the bush, but you can't take the bush from the black man." The place of the native is always well-delimited. "Correct" cultural filmmaking, for example, usually implies that Africans show Africa; Asians, Asia; and Euro-Americans, the world. Otherness has its laws and interdictions. Since you can't take the bush from the black man, it is the bush that is consistently given back to him, and as things often turn out it is also this very bush that the black man shall make his exclusive territory. And he may do so with the full awareness that barren land is hardly a gift. For in the unfolding of power inequalities, changes frequently require that the rules be reappropriated so that the master be beaten at his own game. The conceited giver likes to give with the understanding that he is in a position to take back whenever he feels like it and whenever the accepter dares or happens to trespass on his preserves. The latter, however, sees no gift. Can you imagine such a thing as a gift that takes? So the latter only sees debts that, once given back, should remain his property — although land owning is a concept that has long been foreign to him and that he refused to assimilate.

Through audiences' responses and expectations of their works, nonwhite filmmakers are often informed and reminded of the territorial boundaries in which they are to remain. An insider can speak with authority about her own culture, and she's referred to as the source of authority in this matter — not as a filmmaker necessarily, but as an insider, merely. This automatic and arbitrary endowment of an insider with legitimized knowledge about her cultural heritage and environment only exerts its power when it's a question of validating power. It is a paradoxical twist of the colonial mind. What the outsider expects from the insider is, in fact, a projection of an all-knowing subject that this outsider usually attributes to himself and to his own kind. In this unacknowledged self/other relation, however, the other would always remain the shadow of the self. Hence not really, not quite all-knowing. That a white person makes a film on the Goba of the Zambezi, for example, or on the Tasaday of the Philippine rain forest, seems hardly surprising to anyone, but that a Third World person makes a film on other Third World peoples never fails to appear questionable to many. The question concerning the choice of subject matter immediately arises, sometimes out of curiosity, most often out of hostility. The marriage is not consummatable, for the pair is no longer outside/inside, that is to say, objective versus subjective, but something between inside/inside — objective in what is already claimed as objective. So, no real conflict.

Interdependency cannot be reduced to a mere question of mutual enslavement. It also consists of creating a ground that belongs to no one, not even to the creator. Otherness becomes empowerment, critical difference, when it is not given but re-created. Furthermore, where should the dividing line between outsider and insider stop? How should it be defined? By skin color, by language, by geography, by nation, or by political affinity? What about those, for example, with hyphenated identities and hybrid realities? And here it is worth noting, for example, a journalist's report, entitled "The Crazy Game of Musical Chairs," in an issue of *Time*. In this brief report attention was drawn to the fact that people in South Africa, who were classified by race and place into one of the nine racial categories that determined where they could live and work, could have their classification changed if they could prove they were put in a wrong group. Thus, an announcement of racial reclassifications by the home affairs minister once proclaimed that, in a certain time period, 9 whites became colored, 506 coloreds became white, 2 whites became Malay, 14 Malay became white, 40 coloreds became black, 666 blacks became colored, and the list goes on. However, said the minister, no blacks applied to become whites. And no whites became black.

The moment the insider steps out from the inside she's no longer a mere insider. She necessarily looks in from the outside while also looking out from the inside. Not quite the same, not quite the other, she stands in that undetermined threshold place where she constantly drifts in and out. Undercutting the inside/outside opposition, her intervention is necessarily that of both not quite an insider and not quite an outsider. She is, in other words, this inappropriate "other" or "same" who moves about with always at least two gestures: that of affirming "I am like you" while persisting in her difference and that of reminding "I am different" while unsettling every definition of otherness arrived at.

This is not to say that the historical I can be obscured and ignored and that differentiation cannot be made, but that I is not unitary; culture has never been monolithic and is always more or less in relation to a judging subject. Differences do not exist only between outsider and insider — two entities. They are also at work within the outsider herself, or the insider herself — a single entity. She who knows she cannot speak of them without speaking of herself, of history without involving her story, also knows that she cannot make a gesture without activating the to-and-fro movement of life.

The subjectivity at work in the context of this inappropriate other can hardly be submitted to the old subjectivity/objectivity paradigm. Acute political subject-awareness cannot be reduced to a question of self-criticism toward self-improvement nor of self-praise toward greater self-confidence. Such differentiation is useful, for a grasp of subjectivity as, let's say, the science of the subject or merely as related to the subject makes the fear of self-absorption look absurd. Awareness of the limits in which one works need not lead to any form of indulgence in personal partiality nor to the narrow conclusion that it is impossible to understand anything about other peoples, since the difference is one of essence. By refusing to naturalize the I, subjectivity uncovers the myth of essential core, of spontaneity and depth as inner vision. Subjectivity, therefore, does not merely consist of talking about oneself, be this talking indulgent or critical. In short, what is at stake is a practice of subjectivity that is still unaware of its own constituted nature, hence, the difficulty to exceed the simplistic pair of subjectivity and objectivity; a practice of subjectivity that is unaware of its continuous role in the production of meaning, as if things can make sense by themselves, so that the interpreter's function consists of only choosing among the many existing readings, unaware of representation as representation, that is to say, the cultural, sexual, political interreality of the filmmaker as subject, the reality of the subject film and the reality of the cinematic apparatus. And finally, unaware of the inappropriate other within every I.

NOTE

Lecture given at the Feminism and the Critique of Colonial Discourse Conference, University of California at Santa Cruz, April 25, 1987. First published in *Inscriptions* 3/4 (1988). Parts of this lecture have been published in Trinh T. Minh-ha, *When the Moon Waxes Red* (New York: Routledge, 1991).

Chapter 23
Is the "Post-" in "Postcolonial"
the "Post-" in "Postmodern"?
Kwame Anthony Appiah

> *You were called Bimbircokak*
> *And all was well that way*
> *You have become Victor-Emile-Louis-Henri-Joseph*
> *Which*
> *So far as I recall*
> *Does not reflect your kinship with*
> *Rockefeller.*[1]

Yambo Ouologuem, "À Mon Mari"

In 1987, the Center for African Art in New York organized a show entitled *Perspectives: Angles on African Art*.[2] The curator, Susan Vogel, had worked with a number of "co-curators," whom I list in order of their appearance in the table of contents of the exhibit's catalog: Ekpo Eyo, former director of the department of antiquities of the National Museum of Nigeria; William Rubin, director of painting and sculpture at New York's Museum of Modern Art and organizer of its controversial *Primitivism* exhibit; Romare Bearden, African-American painter; Ivan Karp, curator of African ethnology at the Smithsonian; Nancy Graves, Euro-American painter, sculptor, and filmmaker; James Baldwin, who surely needs no qualifying glosses; David Rockefeller, art collector and friend of the mighty; Lela Kouakou, Baule artist and diviner, from Ivory Coast (this a delicious juxtaposition, richest and poorest, side-by-side); Iba N'Diaye, Senegalese sculptor; and Robert Farris Thompson, Yale professor and African and African-American art historian. Vogel describes the process of selection of the art in her introductory essay. The one woman and nine men were each offered a hundred odd photographs of "African Art as varied in type and origin, and as high in quality, as we could manage" and asked to select ten for the show. Or, I should say more exactly, that this is what was offered to eight of the men. For Vogel adds that "[i]n the case of the Baule artist, a man familiar only with the art of his own people, only Baule objects were placed in the pool of photographs." At this point we are directed to a footnote to the essay, which reads:

> Showing him the same assortment of photos the others saw would have been interesting, but confusing in terms of the reactions we sought here. Field aesthetic studies, my own and others, have shown that African informants will criticize sculptures

420

from other ethnic groups in terms of their own traditional criteria, often assuming that such works are simply inept carvings of their own aesthetic tradition.[3]

I shall return to this irresistible footnote in a moment. But let me pause to quote further, this time from the words of David Rockefeller, who would surely never "criticize sculptures from other ethnic groups in terms of [his] own traditional criteria," discussing what the catalog calls a "Fante female figure":

> I own somewhat similar things to this and I have always liked them. This is a rather more sophisticated version than the ones that I've seen, and I thought it was quite beautiful. . . . [T]he total composition has a very contemporary, very Western look to it. It's the kind of thing that goes very well with contemporary Western things. It would look good in a modern apartment or house.[4]

We may suppose that David Rockefeller was delighted to discover that his final judgment was consistent with the intentions of the sculpture's creators. For a footnote to the earlier "checklist" reveals that the Baltimore Museum of Art desired to "make public the fact that the authenticity of the Fante figure in its collection has been challenged." Indeed, work by Doran Ross suggests this object is almost certainly a modern piece produced in my hometown of Kumasi by the workshop of a certain Francis Akwasi, which "specializes in carvings for the international market in the style of traditional sculpture. Many of its works are now in museums throughout the West, and were published as authentic by Cole and Ross"[5] (yes, the same Doran Ross) in their classic catalog *The Arts of Ghana*.[6]

But then it is hard to be *sure* what would please a man who gives as his reason for picking another piece (this time a Senufo helmet mask): "I have to say I picked this because I own it. It was given to me by President Houphouet Boigny of Ivory Coast."[7]

Rockefeller also remarks, "concerning the market in African art":

> [T]he best pieces are going for very high prices. Generally speaking, the less good pieces in terms of quality are not going up in price. And that's a fine reason for picking the good ones rather than the bad. They have a way of becoming more valuable.
>   I like African art as objects I find would be appealing to use in a home or an office. . . . I don't think it goes with everything, necessarily — although the very best perhaps does. But I think it goes well with contemporary architecture.[8]

There is something breathtakingly unpretentious in Mr. Rockefeller's easy movement between considerations of finance, of aesthetics, and of decor. In these responses, we have surely a microcosm of the site of the African in contemporary — which is, then, surely to say, postmodern — America.

I have given so much of David Rockefeller not to emphasize the familiar fact that questions of what we call "aesthetic" value are crucially bound up with market value; not even to draw attention to the fact that this is known by those who play the art market. Rather I want to keep clearly before us the fact that David Rockefeller is permitted to say *anything at all* about the arts of Africa because he is a *buyer* and because he is at the *center,* while Lela Kouakou, who merely makes art and who dwells at the margins, is a poor African whose words count only as parts of the commodification[9] — both for those of us who constitute the museum public and for collectors, like Rockefeller — of Baule art.[10] I want to remind you, in short, of how important it is that African art is a *commodity*.

But the co-curator whose choice will set us on our way is James Baldwin — the only co-curator who picked a piece that was not in the mold of the Africa of "primitivism," a sculpture that will be my touchstone, a piece labeled by the museum, *Yoruba Man with a Bicycle*. Here is some of what Baldwin said about it:

> This is something. This has got to be contemporary. He's really going to town. It's very jaunty, very authoritative. His errand might prove to be impossible. He is challenging something — or something has challenged him. He's grounded in immediate reality by the bicycle.... He's apparently a very proud and silent man. He's dressed sort of polyglot. Nothing looks like it fits him too well.

Baldwin's reading of this piece is, of course and inevitably, "in terms of [his] own . . . criteria," a reaction contextualized only by the knowledge that bicycles are new in Africa and that this piece, anyway, does not look anything like the works he recalls seeing in his earliest childhood at the Schomburg Museum in Harlem. And his response torpedoes Vogel's argument for her notion that the only "authentically traditional" African — the only one whose responses, as she says, could have been found a century ago — must be refused a choice among Africa's art cultures because he (unlike the rest of the co-curators, who are Americans and the European-educated Africans) will use his "own . . . criteria." This Baule diviner, this authentically African villager, the message is, does not know what *we*, authentic postmodernists, now know: that the first and last mistake is to judge the other on one's own terms. And so, in the name of this, the relativist insight, we impose our judgment: that Lela Kouakou may not judge sculpture from beyond the Baule culture zone because he will — like all the other African "informants" we have met in the field — read them as if they were meant to meet those Baule standards.

Worse than this, it is nonsense to explain Lela Kouakou's responses as deriving from an ignorance of other traditions — if indeed he is, as he no doubt is supposed to be, like most "traditional" artists today, if he is like, for example, Francis Akwasi, of Kumasi. Kouakou may judge other artists by his own standards (what on earth else could he, could anyone, do, save make no judgment at all?), but to suppose that he is unaware that there are other standards within Africa (let alone without) is to ignore a piece of absolutely basic cultural knowledge, common to most precolonial as well as to most colonial and postcolonial cultures on the African continent, the piece of cultural knowledge that explains why the people we now call "Baule" exist at all. To be Baule, for example, is, for a Baule, not to be a white person, not to be Senufo, not to be French.[11] The ethnic groups — Lele Kouakou's Baule "tribe," for example — within which all African aesthetic life apparently occurs, are the products of colonial and postcolonial articulations. And someone who knows enough to make himself up as a Baule for the twentieth century surely knows that there are other kinds of art.

But Baldwin's choice of *Yoruba Man with a Bicycle* does more than give the lie to Vogel's strange footnote; it provides us with an image of an object that can serve as a point of entry to my theme: it is a piece of contemporary African art that will allow us to explore the articulation of the postcolonial and the postmodern. *Yoruba Man with a Bicycle* is described as follows in the catalog:

Page 124
Man with a Bicycle
Yoruba, Nigeria 20th century
Wood and paint H. 35¾ in.
The Newark Museum

The influence of the Western world is revealed in the clothes and bicycle of this neo-traditional Yoruba sculpture which probably represents a merchant en route to market.[12]

And it is this word "neo-traditional" — a word that is almost right — that provides, I think, the fundamental clue.

•

But I do not know how to explain this clue without saying first how I keep my bearings in the shark-infested waters around the semantic island of the postmodern; and since narratives, unlike metanarratives, are allowed to proliferate in these seas, I shall begin with a story about a friend of mine, the late Margaret Masterman. Some-time in the mid-1960s Margaret was asked to participate at a symposium, chaired by Karl Popper, at which Tom Kuhn was to read a paper and then she, J. M. W. Watkins, Stephen Toulmin, L. Pearce Williams, Imre Lakatos, and Paul Feyerabend would engage in discussion of Kuhn's work. Unfortunately for Margaret, she de-veloped infective hepatitis in the period leading up to the symposium, and she was unable, as a result, to prepare a paper. Fortunately for all of us, though, she *was* able to sit in her hospital bed — in Block 8, Norwich Hospital, to whose staff the paper she finally did write is dedicated — and create a subject index to Kuhn's *The Struc-ture of Scientific Revolutions*. In the course of working through the book with index cards, Margaret identified no "less than twenty-one senses, possibly more, not less," in which Kuhn uses the word "paradigm." After her catalog of these twenty-one uses, she remarks laconically that "not all these senses of 'paradigm' are inconsistent with one another"; and she continues:

Nevertheless, given the diversity, it is obviously reasonable to ask: "Is there anything in common between all these senses? Is there, philosophically speaking, anything definite or general about the notion of a paradigm which Kuhn is trying to make clear? Or is he just a historian-poet describing different happenings which have occurred in the history of science, and referring to them all by using the same word 'paradigm'?"[13]

The relevance of this tale hardly needs explication, and the task of chasing the word "postmodernism" through the pages of Lyotard and Jameson and Habermas, in and out of the *Village Voice* and the *Times Literary Supplement* and even the *New York Times Book Review,* makes the task of pinning down Kuhn's "paradigm" look like work for a minute before breakfast.

Nevertheless, there *is,* I think, a story to tell about all these stories — or, of course, I should say, there are many, but this, for the moment, is mine — and, as I tell it, the Yoruba bicyclist will eventually come back into view.

Let me begin with the most obvious and surely one of the most often remarked features of Jean-François Lyotard's account of postmodernity: the fact that it is a metanarrative of the end of metanarratives.[14] To theorize certain central features of contemporary culture as *post* anything is, of course, inevitably to invoke a narrative, and, from the Enlightenment on, in Europe and European-derived cultures, that "after" has also meant "above and beyond," and to step forward (in time) has been ipso facto to *progress*.[15] Brian McHale announces in his *Postmodernist Fiction:* "As for the prefix POST, here I want to emphasize the element of logical and historical *consequence* rather than sheer temporal *posteriority*. Postmodernism follows *from* modernism, in some sense, more than it follows *after* modernism. . . . Postmodernism is the posterity of modernism, this is tautological."[16] My point, then, is not the boring logical point that Lyotard's view — in which, in the absence of "grand narratives of legitimation," we are left with only local legitimations, immanent in our own practices — might seem to presuppose a "grand narrative of legitimation" of its own, in which justice turns out to reside, unexcitingly, in the institutionalization of pluralism; it is, rather, that his analysis seems to feel the need to see the contemporary condition as over against an immediately anterior set of practices and as going beyond them. Lyotard's postmodernism — his theorization of contemporary life as postmodern — is *after* modernism because it rejects aspects of modernism. And in this repudiation of its immediate temporal predecessors (or, more especially, of their theories of themselves) it recapitulates a crucial gesture of the historic avant-garde: indeed, it recapitulates the crucial gesture of the modern "artist" in the sense of modernity characteristic of sociological usage, the sense in which it denotes "an era that was ushered in via the Renaissance, rationalist philosophy and the Enlightenment, on the one hand, and the transition from the absolutist state to bourgeois democracy, on the other";[17] this is that sense of the "artist" to be found in Lionel Trilling's account of Matthew Arnold's "Scholar-Gipsy," whose "existence is intended to disturb us and make us dissatisfied with our habitual life in culture."[18]

This straining for a contrast — a modernity or a modernism to be *against* — is extremely striking given the lack of any plausible account of what distinguishes the modern from the postmodern that is distinctively formal. In an essay, Fredric Jameson grants at one point, after reviewing recent French theorizings (Gilles Deleuze, Jean Baudrillard, Guy Debord), that it is difficult to distinguish formally the postmodern from high modernism:

> [I]ndeed, one of the difficulties in specifying postmodernism lies in its symbiotic or parasitical relationship to [high modernism]. In effect with the canonization of a hitherto scandalous, ugly, dissonant, amoral, antisocial, bohemian high modernism offensive to the middle classes, its promotion to the very figure of high culture generally, and perhaps most importantly, its enshrinement in the academic institution, postmodernism emerges as a way of making creative space for artists now oppressed by those henceforth hegemonic categories of irony, complexity, ambiguity, dense temporality, and particularly, aesthetic and utopian monumentality.[19]

Jameson's argument in this essay is that we must characterize the distinction not in formal terms — in terms, say, of an "aesthetic of *textuality*," or of "the eclipse, finally, of all depth, especially historicity itself," or of the " 'death' of the subject," or of the *"culture of the simulacrum,"* or of "the society of the spectacle"[20] — but in terms of "the social functionality of culture itself." He writes:

> [H]igh modernism, whatever its overt political content, was oppositional and marginal within a middle-class Victorian or philistine or gilded age culture. Although post-modernism is equally offensive in all the respects enumerated (think of punk rock or pornography), it is no longer at all "oppositional" in that sense; indeed, it constitutes the very dominant or hegemonic aesthetic of consumer society itself and significantly serves the latter's commodity production as a virtual laboratory of new forms and fashions. The argument for a conception of postmodernism as a periodizing category is thus based on the presupposition that, even if *all* the formal features enumerated above were already present in the older high modernism, the very significance of those features changes when they become a cultural *dominant* with a precise socio-economic functionality.[21]

It is the "waning" of the "dialectical opposition" between high modernism and mass culture — the commodification and, if I may coin a barbarism, the de-oppositionalization of those cultural forms once constitutive of high modernism — that Jameson sees as key to understanding the postmodern condition.

There is no doubt much to be said for Jameson's theorizing of the postmodern. But I do not think we shall understand what all the various postmodernisms have in common if we stick within Jameson's omni-subsumptive vision. The commodification of a fiction, of a stance, of oppositionality that is salable precisely because its commodification guarantees for the consumer that it is no substantial threat was, indeed, central to the cultural role of "punk rock" in Europe and America. But what, more than a word and a conversation, makes Lyotard and Jameson competing theorists of the *same* postmodern?

I do not — this will come as no surprise — have a definition of the postmodern to put in the place of Jameson's or Lyotard's: but there is now a rough consensus about the structure of the modern/postmodern dichotomy in the many domains — from architecture to poetry to philosophy to rock to the movies — in which it has been invoked. In each of these domains there is an antecedent practice that laid claim to a certain exclusivity of insight, and in each of them postmodernism is a name for the rejection of that claim to exclusivity, a rejection that is almost always more playful — though not necessarily less serious — than the practice it aims to replace. That this will not do as a *definition* of postmodernism follows from the fact that in each domain this rejection of exclusivity takes up a certain specific shape, one that reflects the specificities of its setting.

To understand the various postmodernisms this way is to leave open the question of how their theories of contemporary social, cultural, and economic life relate to the actual practices that constitute that life; to leave open, then, the relations between postmodern*ism* and postmodern*ity*. Where the practice is theory — literary or philosophical — postmodernism as a *theory* of postmodernity can be adequate only if it reflects to some extent the realities of that practice, because the practice is itself fully theoretical. But when a postmodernism addresses, say, advertising or poetry, it may be adequate as an account of them even if it conflicts with their own narratives, their theories of themselves. For, unlike philosophy and literary theory, advertising and poetry are not largely *constituted* by their articulated theories of themselves.

It is an important question *why* this distancing of the ancestors should have become so central a feature of our cultural lives. And the answer, surely, has to do with the sense in which art is increasingly commodified. To sell oneself and one's products as art in the marketplace, it is important, above all, to clear a space in which one is distinguished from other producers and products — and one does this by the construction and the marking of differences.

This is what accounts for a certain intensification of the long-standing individualism of post-Renaissance art production: in the age of mechanical reproduction, aesthetic individualism — the characterization of the artwork as belonging to the oeuvre of an individual — and the absorption of the artist's life into the conception of the work can be seen precisely as modes of identifying objects for the market. The sculptor of the bicycle, by contrast, will not be known by those who buy this object; his individual life will make no difference to its future history. (Indeed, he surely knows this, in the sense in which one knows anything whose negation one has never even considered.) Nevertheless, there is *some* thing about the object that serves to establish it for the market: the availability of Yoruba culture and of stories about Yoruba culture to surround the object and distinguish it from "folk art" from elsewhere. I shall return to this point.

Let me confirm this proposal by instances: in philosophy, postmodernism is the rejection of the mainstream consensus from Descartes through Kant to logical positivism or foundationalism (there is one route to knowledge, which is exclusivism in epistemology) and of metaphysical realism (there is one truth, which is exclusivism in ontology), each underwritten by a unitary notion of reason; it thus celebrates such figures as Nietzsche (no metaphysical realist) and Dewey (no foundationalist). The modernity that is opposed here can thus be Cartesian (in France), Kantian (in Germany), and logical positivist (in America).

In architecture, postmodernism is the rejection of an exclusivism of function (as well as the embrace of a certain taste for pastiche). The modernity that is opposed here is the "monumentality," "elitism," and "authoritarianism" of the international style of Le Corbusier or Mies.[22]

In "literature," postmodernism reacts against the high seriousness of high modernism, which mobilized "difficulty" as a mode of privileging its own aesthetic sensibility and celebrated a complexity and irony appreciable only by a cultural elite. Modernity here is, say (and in no particular order), Proust, Eliot, Pound, Woolf.

In political theory, finally, postmodernism involves, on the one hand, the rejection of the monism of capital-*M* Marxist (though not of the newer lowercase-*m* marxist) and liberal conceptions of justice and, on the other hand, their overthrow by a conception of politics as irreducibly plural, with every perspective essentially contestable from other perspectives. Modernity here is the great nineteenth-century political narratives, of Marx and Mill, but includes, for example, such latecomers as John Rawls's reconstruction of the liberal theory of justice.

These sketchy examples are meant to suggest how we might understand the family resemblance of the various postmodernisms as governed by a *loose* principle. They also suggest why it might be that the high theorists of postmodernism — Jean-François Lyotard, Fredric Jameson, Jürgen Habermas,[23] shall we say — can seem to be competing for the same territory: Lyotard's privileging of a certain philosophical antifoundationalism could surely be seen as underwriting (though not, I think, plausibly, as causing) each of these moves; Jameson's characterization of postmodernism as the logic of late capitalism — with the commodification of "cultures" as a central feature — might well account for many features of each of these transitions also; and Habermas's project is surely intended (though in the name of a most un-Lyotardian metanarrative) to provide a modus operandi in a world in which pluralism is, so to speak, a fact waiting for some institutions.

Postmodern culture is the culture in which all of the postmodernisms operate, sometimes in synergy, sometimes in competition; and because contemporary culture is, in certain senses to which I shall return, transnational, postmodern culture is global — though that does not by any means mean that it is the culture of every person in the world.

•

If postmodernism is the project of transcending some species of modernism — which is to say, some relatively self-conscious self-privileging project of a privileged modernity — our *neotraditional* sculptor of the *Yoruba Man with a Bicycle* is presumably to be understood, by contrast, as premodern: that is, traditional. (I am supposing, then, that being neotraditional is a way of being traditional; what work the *neo* does is a matter I shall take up again briefly later.) And the sociological and anthropological narratives of tradition through which he or she came to be so theorized is dominated, of course, by Max Weber.

Weber's characterization of traditional (and charismatic) authority *in opposition* to rational authority is in keeping with his general characterization of modernity as the rationalization of the world; and he insisted on the significance of this characteristically Western process for the rest of humankind. The introduction to *The Protestant Ethic* begins:

> A product of modern European civilization, studying any problem of universal history, is bound to ask himself to what combination of circumstances the fact should be attributed that in Western civilization, and in Western civilization only, cultural phenomena have appeared which (as we like to think) lie in a line of development having universal significance and value.[24]

Now there is certainly no doubt that Western modernity now has a universal *geographical* significance. The Yoruba bicyclist — like Sting and his Amerindian chieftains of the Amazon rain forest or Paul Simon and the Mbaqanga musicians of *Graceland* — is testimony to that. But, if I may borrow someone else's borrowing, the fact is that the Empire of Signs strikes back. Weber's "as we like to think" reflects his doubts about whether the Western imperium over the world was as clearly of universal *value* as it was certainly of universal *significance;* and postmodernism surely fully endorses his resistance to this claim. The bicycle enters our museums to be valued by us (David Rockefeller tells us *how* it is to be valued); but just as the *presence* of the object reminds us of this fact, its *content* reminds us that the trade is two-way.

I want to argue that to understand our — our human — modernity we must first understand why the rationalization of the world can no longer be seen as the tendency either of the West or of history, why, simply put, the modernist characterization of modernity must be challenged. To understand our world is to reject Weber's claim for the rationality of what he called rationalization and his projection of its inevitability; it is, then, to have a radically post-Weberian conception of modernity.

•

We can begin with a pair of familiar and helpful caricatures. Thomas Stearns Eliot is against the soullessness and the secularization of modern society, the reach of Enlightenment rationalism into the whole world. He shares Weber's account of modernity and more straightforwardly deplores it. Le Corbusier is in favor of rationalization — a house is a "machine for living in"; but he, too, shares Weber's vision of modernity. And, of course, the great rationalists — the believers in a transhistorical reason triumphing in the world — from Kant on, are the source of Weber's Kantian vision. Modernism in literature and architecture and philosophy — the account of modernity that, on my model, *post*modernism in these domains seeks to subvert — may be for reason or against it, but in each domain rationalization (the pervasion of reason) is seen as the distinctive dynamic of contemporary history.

But the beginning of postmodern wisdom is to ask whether Weberian rationalization is in fact what has happened. For Weber, charismatic authority — the authority of Stalin, Hitler, Mao, Guevara, Nkrumah — is antirational; yet modernity has been dominated by just such charisma. Secularization seems hardly to be proceeding: religions grow in all parts of the world; more than 90 percent of North Americans still avow some sort of theism; what we call "fundamentalism" is as alive in the West as it is in Africa and the Middle and Far East; Jimmy Swaggart and Billy Graham have businesses in Louisiana and California as well as in Costa Rica and in Ghana.

What we can see in all these cases, I think, is not the triumph of Enlightenment capital-*R* Reason — which would have entailed exactly the end of charisma and the universalization of the secular — not even the penetration of a narrower instrumental reason into all spheres of life, but what Weber mistook for that: namely, the incorporation of all areas of the world and all areas of even formerly "private" life into the money economy. Modernity has turned every element of the real into a sign, and the sign reads "for sale"; and this is true even in domains like religion where instrumental reason would recognize that the market has at best an ambiguous place.

If Weberian talk of the triumph of instrumental reason can now be seen to be a mistake, what Weber thought of as the disenchantment of the world — that is, the penetration of a scientific vision of things — describes at most the tiny (and in the United States quite marginal) world of the higher academy and a few islands of its influence. The world of the intellectual *is,* I think, largely disenchanted (even theistic academics largely do not believe in ghosts and ancestor spirits); and fewer people (though still very many) suppose the world to be populated by the multitudes of spirits of earlier religion. Still, what we have seen in recent times in the United States is not secularization — the end of religions — but their commodification; and with that commodification religions have reached further and grown — their markets have expanded — rather than dying away.

Postmodernism can be seen, then, as a new way of understanding the multiplication of distinctions that flows from the need to clear oneself a space; the need that drives the underlying dynamic of cultural modernity. Modernism saw the economization of the world as the triumph of reason; postmodernism rejects that claim, allowing in the realm of theory the same multiplication of distinctions we see in the cultures it seeks to understand.

•

I anticipate the objection that the Weber I have been opposing is something of a caricature. And I would not be unhappy to admit that there is some truth in this. Weber anticipated, for example, that the rationalization of the world would continue to be resisted, and his view that each case of charisma needed to be "routinized" was not meant to rule out the appearance of new charismatic leaders in our time as in earlier ones: our politics of charisma would, perhaps, not have surprised him.[25] Certainly, too, his conception of reason involved far more than instrumental calculation. Since much of what I have noticed here would have been anticipated by him, it may be as well to see this as a rejection of a narrow (if familiar) misreading of Weber as an argument against what is best in the complex and shifting views of Weber himself.

But I think we could also defend this misreading — which we find, perhaps, in Talcott Parsons — as in part a consequence of a problem with Weber's own work. For part of the difficulty with Weber's work is that, despite the wealth of historical detail in his studies of religion, law, and economics, he often mobilizes theoretical terms that are of a very high level of abstraction. As a result, it is not always clear that there really are significant commonalities among the various social phenomena he assimilates under such general concepts as "rationalization" or "charisma." (This is one of the general problems posed by Weber's famous reliance on "ideal types.") Reinhard Bendix, one of Weber's most important and sympathetic interpreters, remarks at one point in his discussion of one of Weber's theoretical distinctions (the distinction, as it happens, between patrimonialism and feudalism) that "[t]his distinction is clear only so long as it is formulated in abstract terms."[26] In reading Weber it is a feeling that one has over and over again. The problem is exemplified in Weber's discussion of "charisma" in *The Theory of Social and Economic Organization:*

> The term "charisma" will be applied to a certain quality of an individual personality by virtue of which he is set apart from ordinary men and treated as endowed with supernatural, superhuman, or at least specifically exceptional powers or qualities. These are...regarded as of divine origin or exemplary, and on the basis of them the individual concerned is treated as a leader.[27]

Notice how "charisma" is here defined disjunctively as involving *either* magical ("supernatural, superhuman," "of divine origin") capacities, on the one had, *or* merely "exceptional" or "exemplary" qualities, on the other. The first disjunct in each case happily covers the many cases of priestly and prophetic leadership that Weber discusses, for example, in his study *Ancient Judaism*. But it is the latter, presumably, that we should apply in seeking to understand the political role of Hitler, Stalin, or Mussolini, who, though no doubt "exceptional" and "exemplary," were not regarded as having "supernatural" powers "of divine origin." The point is that much of what Weber has to say in his general discussion of charisma in *The Theory of Social and Economic Organization* and in the account of "domination" in *Economy and Society* requires that we take its magical aspect seriously. When, however, we do take it seriously, we find his theory fails to apply to the instances of charisma that fall under the second disjunct of his definition. In short, Weber's account of charisma assimilates too closely phenomena — such as the leadership of Stalin, at one end of the spectrum, and of King David or the Emperor Charlemagne, at the other — in which magico-religious ideas seem, to put it mildly, to play remarkably different roles. If we follow out the logic of this conclusion by redefining Weberian charisma in such a way as to insist on its magical component, it will follow, by definition, that the disenchantment of the world — the decline of magic — leads to the end of charisma: but we shall then have to ask ourselves how correct it is to claim, with Weber, that magical views increasingly disappear with modernity. And if he is right in this, we shall also have to give up the claim that Weber's sociology of politics — in which charisma plays a central conceptual role — illuminates the characteristic political developments of modernity.

There is a similar set of difficulties with Weber's account of rationalization. In *The Protestant Ethic and the Spirit of Capitalism,* Weber wrote: "If this essay makes any contribution at all, may it be to bring out the complexity of the only super-ficially simple concept of the rational."[28] But we may be tempted to ask whether our understanding of the genuine complexities of the historical developments of the last few centuries of social, religious, economic, and political history in western Europe is truly deepened by making use of a concept of rationalization that brings together a supposed increase in means-end calculation (instrumental rationality); a decline in appeal to "mysterious, incalculable forces" and a correlative increasing confidence in calculation (disenchantment or intellectualization);[29] and the growth of "value-rationality," which means something like an increasing focus on maximiz-ing a narrow range of ultimate goals.[30] Here, seeking to operate at this high level of generality, assimilating under one concept so many, in my view, distinct and in-dependently intelligible processes, Weber's detailed and subtle appreciation of the dynamics of many social processes is obscured by his theoretical apparatus; it is, I think, hardly surprising that those who have been guided by his theoretical writings have ascribed to him a cruder picture than is displayed in his historical work.

•

That, then, is how I believe the issue looks from the perspective of the Euro-American intellectual. But how does it look from the postcolonial spaces inhabited by the *Yoruba Man with a Bicycle*? I shall speak about Africa, with confidence *both* that some of what I have to say will work elsewhere in the so-called Third World *and* that, in some places, it will certainly not. And I shall speak first about the pro-ducers of these so-called neotraditional artworks and then about the case of the African novel, because I believe that to focus exclusively on the novel (as theorists of contemporary African cultures have been inclined to do) is to distort the cultural situation and the significance within it of postcoloniality.

I do not know when the *Yoruba Man with a Bicycle* was made or by whom; Af-rican art has, until recently, been collected as the property of "ethnic" groups, not of individuals and workshops, so it is not unusual that not one of the pieces in the *Perspectives* show was identified in the "checklist" by the name of an individual artist, even though many of them are twentieth-century (and no one will have been surprised, by contrast, that most of them *are* kindly labeled with the name of the people who own the largely private collections where they now live). As a result, I cannot say if the piece is literally postcolonial, produced after Nigerian independence in 1960. But the piece belongs to a genre that has certainly been produced since then: the genre that the catalog calls *neotraditional*. And, simply put, what is distinctive about this genre is that it is produced for the West.

I should qualify. Of course, many of the buyers of first instance live in Africa; many of them are juridically citizens of African states. But African bourgeois consumers of neotraditional art are educated in the Western style, and, if they want African art, they would often rather have a "genuinely" traditional piece: by which I mean a piece that they believe to be made precolonially or at least in a style and by methods that were already established precolonially. And these buyers are a minority. Most of this art — which is *traditional* because it uses actually or supposedly precolonial techniques, but is *neo* (this, for what it is worth, is the explanation I promised earlier) because it has elements that are recognizably from the colonial or postcolonial in reference — has been made for Western tourists and other collectors.

The incorporation of these works in the West's world of museum culture and its art market has almost nothing, of course, to do with postmodernism. By and large, the ideology through which they are incorporated is modernist: it is the ideology that brought something called "Bali" to Antonin Artaud, something called "Africa" to Pablo Picasso, and something called "Japan" to Roland Barthes. (This incorporation as an official other was criticized, of course, from its beginnings: Oscar Wilde once remarked that "the whole of Japan is a pure invention. There is no such country, no such people.")[31] What *is* postmodernist is Vogel's muddled conviction that African art should not be judged "in terms of [someone else's] traditional criteria." For modernism, primitive art was to be judged by putatively *universal* aesthetic criteria; and by these standards it was finally found possible to value it. The sculptors and painters who found it possible were largely seeking an Archimedean point outside their own cultures for a critique of a Weberian modernity. For *post*modernisms, by contrast, these works, however they are to understood, cannot be seen as legitimated by culture- and history-transcending standards.

What is useful in the *neotraditional* object as a model — despite its marginality in most African lives — is that its incorporation in the museum world (while many objects made by the same hands — stools for example — live peacefully in non-bourgeois homes) reminds one that in Africa, by contrast, the distinction between high culture and mass culture, insofar as it makes sense at all, corresponds, by and large, to the distinction between those with and those without Western-style formal education as cultural consumers.

The fact that the distinction is to be made this way — in most of sub-Saharan Africa excluding the Republic of South Africa — means that the opposition between high culture and mass culture is available only in domains where there is a significant body of Western formal training: and this excludes (in most places) the plastic arts and music. There are distinctions of genre and audience in African musics, and for various cultural purposes there is something that we call "traditional" music, which we still practice and value; but village and urban dwellers alike, bourgeois and non-bourgeois, listen, through discs and, more importantly, on the radio, to reggae, to Michael Jackson, and to King Sonny Adé.

And this means that, by and large, the domain in which this distinction makes most sense is the one domain where it is powerful and pervasive: namely, in African writing in Western languages. So that it is here that we find, I think, a place for consideration of the question of the *post*coloniality of contemporary African culture.

•

Postcoloniality is the condition of what we might ungenerously call a *comprador* intelligentsia: of a relatively small, Western-style, Western-trained group of writers and thinkers who mediate the trade in cultural commodities of world capitalism at the periphery. In the West they are known through the Africa they offer; their compatriots know them both through the West they present to Africa and through an Africa they have invented for the world, for each other, and for Africa.

All aspects of contemporary African cultural life (including music and some sculpture and painting, even some writings with which the West is largely unfamiliar) have been influenced — often powerfully — by the transition of African societies *through* colonialism, but they are not all in the relevant sense *post*colonial. For the "post" in postcolonial, like the "post" in postmodern, is the "post" of the space-clearing gesture I characterized earlier: and many areas of contemporary African cultural life (what has come to be theorized as popular culture, in particular) are not in this way concerned with transcending — with going beyond — coloniality. Indeed, it might be said to be a mark of popular culture that its borrowings from international cultural forms are remarkably insensitive to — not so much dismissive of as blind to — the issue of neocolonialism or "cultural imperialism." This does not mean that theories of postmodernism are irrelevant to these forms of culture: for the internationalization of the market and the commodification of artworks are both central to them. But it *does* mean that these artworks are not understood by their producers or their consumers in terms of a postmodern*ism:* there is no antecedent practice whose claim to exclusivity of vision is rejected through these artworks. What is called "syncretism" here is made possible by the international exchange of commodities but is not a consequence of a space-clearing gesture.

Postcolonial intellectuals in Africa, by contrast, are almost entirely dependent for their support on two institutions: the African university — an institution whose intellectual life is overwhelmingly constituted as Western — and the Euro-American publisher and reader. (Even when these writers seek to escape the West — as Ngugi wa Thiong'o did in attempting to construct a Kikuyu peasant drama — their theories of their situation are irreducibly informed by their Euro-American formation. Ngugi's conception of the writer's potential in politics is essentially that of the avant-garde, of left modernism.)

Now this double dependence on the university and the Euro-American publisher means that the first generation of modern African novels — the generation of Chinua Achebe's *Things Fall Apart* and Camara Laye's *L'Enfant noir* — were written in the context of notions of politics and culture dominant in the British and French university and publishing worlds in the 1950s and 1960s. This does not mean that they were like novels written in Western Europe at that time: for part of what was held to be obvious both by these writers and by the high culture of Europe of the day was that new literatures in new nations should be anticolonial and nationalist. These early novels seem to belong to the world of eighteenth- and nineteenth-century literary nationalism; they are theorized as the imaginative re-creation of a common cultural past that is crafted into a shared tradition by the writer; they are in the tradition of Sir Walter Scott, whose *Minstrelsy of the Scottish Border* was intended, as he said in the preface, to "contribute somewhat to the history of my native country; the peculiar features of whose manners and character are daily melting and dissolving into those of her sister and ally." The novels of this first stage are thus realist legitimations of nationalism: they authorize a "return to traditions" while at the same time recognizing the demands of a Weberian rationalized modernity.

•

From the later 1960s on, these celebratory novels of the first stage become rarer: Achebe, for example, moves from the creation of a usable past in *Things Fall Apart* to a cynical indictment of politics in the modern sphere in *A Man of the People*. But I should like to focus on a francophone novel of the later 1960s, a novel that thematizes in an extremely powerful way many of the questions I have been asking about art and modernity: I mean, of course, Yambo Ouologuem's *Le Devoir de violence*. This novel, like many of this second stage, represents a challenge to the novels of the first stage: it identifies the realist novel as part of the tactic of nationalist legitimation and so it is — if I may begin a catalog of its ways of being *post* this and that — *postrealist*.

Now, postmodernism is, of course, postrealist also. But Ouologuem's postrealism is surely motivated quite differently from that of such postmodern writers as, say, Thomas Pynchon. Realism naturalizes: the originary "African novel" of Chinua Achebe (*Things Fall Apart*) and of Camara Laye (*L'Enfant noir*) is "realist." So Ouologuem is against it, rejects — indeed, assaults — the conventions of realism. He seeks to delegitimate the forms of the realist African novel, in part, surely, because what it sought to naturalize was a nationalism that, by 1968, had plainly failed. The national bourgeoisie that took on the baton of rationalization, industrialization, and bureaucratization in the name of nationalism turned out to be a kleptocracy. Their enthusiasm for nativism was a rationalization of their urge to keep the national bourgeoisies of other nations — and particularly the powerful industrialized nations — out of their way. As Jonathan Ngaté has observed: "*Le Devoir de violence...* deal[s] with a world in which *the efficacy* of the call to the Ancestors as well as the Ancestors themselves is seriously called into question."[32] That the novel is in this way postrealist allows its author to borrow, when he needs them, the techniques of modernism: which, as we learned from Fredric Jameson, are often also the techniques of postmodernism. (It is helpful to remember at this point how Yambo Ouologuem is described on the back of the Éditions Du Seuil first edition: "Né en 1940 au Mali. Admissible à l'École normale supérieure. Licenciéès Lettres. Licencié en Philosophie. Diplômé d'études supérieures d'Anglais. Prépare une thèse de doctorat de Sociologie." Borrowing from European modernism is hardly going to be difficult for someone so qualified — to be a Normalien is indeed, in Christopher Miller's charming formulation, "roughly equivalent to being baptized by Bossuet.")[33]

Christopher Miller's discussion — in *Blank Darkness* — of *Le Devoir de violence* focuses usefully on theoretical questions of intertextuality raised by the novel's persistent massaging of one text after another into the surface of its own body. The book contains, for example, a translation of a passage from Graham Greene's 1934 novel *It's a Battlefield* (translated and improved, according to some readers!); and borrowings from Maupassant's "Boule de Suif" (hardly an unfamiliar work for franco-phone readers; if this latter is a theft, it is the adventurous theft of the kleptomaniac, who dares us to catch him at it).

And the book's first sentence artfully establishes the oral mode — by then an inevitable convention of African narration — with words that Ngaté rightly describes as having the "concision and the striking beauty and power of a proverb"[34] and mocks us in this moment because the sentence echoes the beginning of André Schwartz-Bart's decidedly un-African 1959 holocaust novel *Le Dernier des justes,* an echo that more substantial later borrowings confirm:[35]

Nos yeux boivent l'éclat du soleil, et, vaincus, s'étonnent de pleurer. Maschallah! oua bismillah!...Un récit de l'aventure sanglante de la négraille — honte aux hommes de rien! — *tiendrait aisément dans* la première moitié de ce *siècle; mais la véritable histoire* des Nègres *commence* beaucoup plus *tôt,* avec les Säifs, en l'an 1202 de notre ère, dans l'Empire africain de Nakem.[36]	*Nos yeux* reçoivent la lumière d'étoiles mortes. Une biographie de mon ami Ernie *tiendrait aisément dans* le deuxième quart du xxe *siècle; mais la véritable histoire* d'Ernie Lévy *commence* très *tôt,* dans la vieille cité anglicane de York. Plus précisément: le 11 mars 1185.[37]

For this comparison I have made my own translations, which are as literal as possible:

Our eyes drink the flash of the sun, and, conquered, surprise themselves by weeping. Maschallah! oua bismillah!...An account of the bloody adventure of the niggertrash — dishonor to the men of nothing — *could easily begin in the* first half of this *century; but the true history of* the Blacks *begins* very much *earlier,* with the Säifs, in the year 1202 of our era, in the African kingdom of Nakem.	*Our eyes* receive the light of dead stars. A biography of my friend Ernie *could easily begin in the* second quarter of the twentieth *century; but the true history of* Ernie Lévy *begins* much *earlier,* in the old Anglican city of York. More precisely: on 11 March 1185.

The reader who is properly prepared will expect an African holocaust; and these echoes are surely meant to render ironic the status of the rulers of Nakem as descendants of Abraham El Héit, "le Juif noir."[38]

The book begins, then, with a sick joke at the unwary reader's expense against nativism: and the assault on realism is — here is my second signpost — postnativist; this book is a murderous antidote to a nostalgia for *Roots.* As Wole Soyinka has said in a justly well-respected reading, "[T]he Bible, the Koran, the historic solemnity of the griot are reduced to the histrionics of wanton boys masquerading as humans."[39] It is tempting to read the attack on history here as a repudiation not of roots but of Islam, as Soyinka does when he goes on to say:

A culture which has claimed indigenous antiquity in such parts of Africa as have submitted to its undeniable attractions is confidently proven to be imperialist; worse, it is demonstrated to be essentially hostile to the indigenous culture. . . . Ouologuem pronounces the Moslem incursion into black Africa to be corrupt, vicious, decadent, elitist and insensitive. At the least such a work functions as a wide swab in the deck-clearing operation for the commencement of racial retrieval.[40]

But it seems to me much clearer to read the repudiation as a repudiation of national history; to see the text as postcolonially postnationalist as well as anti- (and thus, of course, post-) nativist. (Indeed, Soyinka's reading here seems to be driven by his own equally representative tendency to read Africa as race and place into everything.) Raymond Spartacus Kassoumi — who is, if anyone is, the hero of this novel — is, after all, a son of the soil, but his political prospects by the end of the narrative are less than uplifting. More than this, the novel explicitly thematizes, in the anthropologist Shrobenius — an obvious echo of the name of the German Africanist Leo Frobenius, whose work is cited by Senghor — the mechanism by which the new elite has come to invent its traditions through the "science" of ethnography:

> Saiumlautf made up stories and the interpreter translated, Madoubo repeated in French, refining on the subtleties to the delight of Shrobenius, that human crayfish afflicted with a groping mania for resuscitating an African universe — cultural autonomy, he called it, which had lost all living reality; . . . he was determined to find metaphysical meaning in everything. . . . African life, he held, was pure art.[41]

At the start we have been told that "there are few written accounts and the versions of the elders diverge from those of the griots, which differ from those of the chroniclers."[42] Now we are warned off the supposedly scientific discourse of the ethnographers.[43]

Because this is a novel that seeks to delegitimate not only the form of realism but the content of nationalism, it will to that extent seem to us misleadingly to be postmodern. *Mis*leadingly, because what we have here is not postmodern*ism* but postmoderni*zation;* not an aesthetics but a politics, in the most literal sense of the term. After colonialism, the modernizers said, comes rationality; that is the possibility the novel rules out. Ouologuem's novel is typical of this second stage in that it is not written by someone who is comfortable with and accepted by the new elite, the national bourgeoisie. Far from being a celebration of the nation, then, the novels of the second stage — the postcolonial stage — are novels of delegitimation: rejecting the Western imperium, it is true; but also rejecting the nationalist project of the postcolonial national bourgeoisie. And, so it seems to me, the basis for that project of delegitimation is very much not the postmodernist one: rather, it is grounded in an appeal to an ethical universal; indeed, it is based, as intellectual responses to oppression in Africa largely are based, in an appeal to a certain simple respect for human suffering, a fundamental revolt against the endless misery of the last thirty years. Ouologuem is hardly likely to make common cause with a relativism that might allow that the horrifying new-old Africa of exploitation is to be understood — legitimated — in its own local terms.

Africa's postcolonial novelists — novelists anxious to escape neocolonialism — are no longer committed to the nation; and in this they will seem, as I have suggested, misleadingly postmodern. But what they have chosen instead of the nation is not an older traditionalism but Africa — the continent and its people. This is clear enough, I think, in *Le Devoir de violence;* at the end of the novel Ouologuem writes:

> Often, it is true, the soul desires to dream the echo of happiness, an echo that has no past. But projected into the world, one cannot help recalling that Saïf, mourned three million times, is forever reborn to history beneath the hot ashes of more than thirty African republics.[44]

If we are to identify with anyone, in fine, it is with the *la négraille* — the niggertrash, who have no nationality. For these purposes one republic is as good — which is to say as bad — as any other. If this postulation of oneself as African — and as neither of this-or-that allegedly precolonial ethnicity nor of the new nation-states — is implicit in *Le Devoir de violence,* in the important novels of V. Y. Mudimbe, *Entre les eaux, Le Bel immonde* (made available in English as *Before the Birth of the Moon*) and *L'Écart,* this postcolonial recourse to Africa is to be found nearer the surface and over and over again.[45]

•

There is a moment in *L'Écart,* for example, when the protagonist, whose journal the book is, recalls a conversation with the French girlfriend of his student days — the young woman on whom he reflects constantly as he becomes involved with an African woman:

> "You can't know, Isabelle, how demanding Africa is."
> "It's important for you, isn't it?"
> "To tell you the truth, I don't know. . . . I really don't. . . . I wonder if I'm not usually just playing around with it."
> "Nara, . . . I don't understand. For me, the important thing is to be myself. Being European isn't a flag to wave."
> "You've never been wounded like . . ."
> "You're dramatizing, Nara. You carry your African-ness like a martyr. . . . That makes one wonder . . . I'd be treating you with contempt if I played along with you."
> "The difference is that Europe is above all else an idea, a juridical institution, . . . while Africa . . ."
> "Yes? . . ."
> "Africa is perhaps mostly a body, a multiple existence. . . . I'm not expressing myself very well."[46]

This exchange seems to me to capture the essential ambiguity of the postcolonial African intellectual's relation to Africa. But let me pursue Africa, finally, in Mudimbe's first novel, *Entre les eaux,* a novel that thematizes the question most explicitly.

In *Entre les eaux* — a first-person narrative — our protagonist is an African Jesuit, Pierre Landu, who has a "doctorat en théologie et [une] licence en droit canon"[47] acquired as a student in Rome. Landu is caught between his devotion to the church and, as one would say in more Protestant language, to Christ; and the latter leads him to repudiate the official Roman Catholic hierarchy of his homeland and join with a group of Marxist guerrillas, intent on removing the corrupt postindependence state. When he first tells his immediate superior in the hierarchy, Father Howard, who is white, of his intentions, the latter responds immediately and remorselessly that this will be treason:

"You are going to commit treason," the father superior said to me when I informed him of my plans.
  "Against whom?"
  "Against Christ."
  "Father, isn't it rather the West that I'm betraying. Is it still treason? Don't I have the right to dissociate myself from this Christianity that has betrayed the Gospel?"
  "You are a priest, Pierre."
  "Excuse me, Father, I'm a black priest."[48]

It is important, I think, not to see the blackness here as a matter of race. It is rather the sign of Africanity. To be a black priest is to be a priest who is also an African and thus committed, willy-nilly, to an engagement with African suffering. This demand that Africa makes has nothing to do with a sympathy for African cultures and traditions; reflecting — a little later — on Father Howard's alienating response, Landu makes this plain:

Father Howard is also a priest like me. That's the tie that binds us. Is it the only one? No. There's our shared tastes.
  Classical music. Vivaldi. Mozart. Bach . . .
  And then there was our reading. The books, we used to pass each other. Our shared memories of Rome. Our impassioned discussions on the role of the priest, and on literature and on the mystery novels that we each devoured. I am closer to Father Howard than I am to my compatriots, even the priests.
  Only one thing separates us: the color of our skins.[49]

In the name of this "couleur de la peau," which is precisely the *sign* of a solidarity with Africa, Landu reaches from Roman Catholicism to Marxism, seeking to gather together the popular revolutionary energy of the latter and the ethical — and religious — vision of the former: a project he considers in a later passage, where he recalls a long-ago conversation with Monseigneur Sanguinetti in Rome. "The church and Africa," the Monseigneur tells him, "are counting on you."[50] Landu asks in the present:

Could the church really still count on me? I would have wished it and I wish it now. The main thing meanwhile is that Christ counts on me. But Africa? Which Africa was Sanguinetti speaking of? That of my black confrères who have stayed on the strait and narrow, or that of my parents whom I have already betrayed? Or perhaps he was even speaking of the Africa that we defend in this camp?[51]

Whenever Landu is facing a crucial decision, it is framed for him as a question about the meaning of Africa.

After he is accused of another betrayal — this time by the rebels, who have intercepted a letter to his bishop (a letter in which he appeals to him to make common cause with the rebels, to recover them for Christ) — Landu is condemned to death. As he awaits execution, he remembers something an uncle had said to him a decade earlier about "the ancestors":

"You'll be missed by them . . . ," my uncle had said to me, ten years ago. I had refused to be initiated. What did he mean? It is I who miss them. Will that be their curse? The formula invaded me, at first unobtrusively, but then it dazzled me, stopping me from thinking: "Wait till the ancestors come down. Your head will burn, your throat will burst, your stomach will open and your feet will shatter. Wait till the ancestors come down. . . ." They had come down. And I had only the desiccation of a rationalized faith to defend myself against Africa.[52]

Nothing could be clearer than the anti-Weberian thrust of this passage. In being postcolonial, Pierre Landu is against the rationalizing thrust of Western modernity. (That modernity here, in this African setting, is represented by Catholicism confirms how little modernity has ultimately to do with secularization.) And even here, when he believes he is facing his own death, the question, "What does it mean to be an African?" is at the center of his mind.

A raid on the camp by government forces saves Pierre Landu from execution; the intervention of a bishop and a brother powerfully connected within the modern state save him from the fate of a captured rebel; and he retreats from the world to take up the life of a monastic with a new name — no longer Peter-on-whom-I-will-build-my-church, but Mathieu-Marie de L'Incarnation — in a different, more contemplative order. As we leave him his last words, the last of the novel, are

. . . the humility of my abasement, what a glory for man![53]

Neither Marx nor St. Thomas, the novel suggests — neither of the two great political energies of the West in Africa — offers a way forward. But this retreat to the otherworldly cannot be a political solution. Postcoloniality has also, I think, become a condition of pessimism.

Postrealist writing; postnativist politics; a *transnational* rather than a *national* solidarity. And pessimism: a kind of *post*optimism to balance the earlier enthusiasm for *The Suns of Independence*. Postcoloniality is *after* all this: and its "post," like postmodernism's, is also a "post" that challenges earlier legitimating narratives. And it challenges them in the name of the suffering victims of "more than thirty republics." But it also challenges them in the name of the ethical universal; in the name of *humanism*, "le gloire pour l'homme." And on that ground it is not an ally for Western postmodernism but an agonist: from which I believe postmodernism may have something to learn.

•

For what I am calling humanism can be provisional, historically contingent, and antiessentialist (in other words, postmodern) and still be demanding. We can surely maintain a powerful engagement with the concern to avoid cruelty and pain while nevertheless recognizing the contingency of that concern.[54] Maybe, then, we can recover within postmodernism the postcolonial writers' humanism — the concern for human suffering, for the victims of the postcolonial state (a concern we find everywhere: in Mudimbe, as we have seen; in Soyinka's *A Play of Giants;* in Achebe, Farrah, Gordimer, Labou Tansi — the list is difficult to complete) — while still rejecting the master-narratives of modernism. This human impulse — an impulse that transcends obligations to churches and to nations — I propose we learn from Mudimbe's Landu.

But there is also something to reject in the postcolonial adherence to Africa of Nara, the earlier protagonist of Mudimbe's *L'Écart:* the sort of Manichaeanism that makes Africa *"a body"* (nature) against Europe's juridical reality (culture) and then fails to acknowledge — even as he says it — the full significance of the fact that Africa is also *"a multiple existence." Entre les eaux* provides a powerful postcolonial critique of this binarism: we can read it as arguing that if you postulate an either-or choice between Africa and the West, there is no place for you in the real world of politics, and your home must be the otherworldly, the monastic retreat.

•

If there is a lesson in the broad shape of this circulation of cultures, it is surely that we are all already contaminated by one another, that there is no longer a fully autochthonous, pure-African culture awaiting salvage by our artists (just as there is, of course, no American culture without African roots). And there is a clear sense in some postcolonial writing that the postulation of a unitary Africa over against a monolithic West — the binarism of self and other — is the last of the shibboleths of the modernizers that we must learn to live without.

Already in *Le Devoir de violence,* in Ouologuem's withering critique of "Shrobéniusologie," there were the beginnings of this postcolonial critique of what we might call "alteritism," the construction and celebration of oneself as other: "[T]hat's how Negro art was baptized 'aesthetic' and hawked — hey! — in the imaginary universe of 'life-giving exchanges'!"[55] Then, after describing the phantasmatic elaboration of some interpretative mumbo jumbo "invented by Saïf," Ouologuem announces that "Negro art created its patent of nobility from the folklore of mercantile spirituality, hey, hey, hey."[56] Shrobenius, the anthropologist, as apologist for "his" people; a European audience that laps up this exoticized other; African traders and producers of African art, who understand the necessity to maintain the "mysteries" that construct their product as "exotic"; traditional and contemporary elites who require a sentimentalized past to authorize their present power — all are exposed in their complex and multiple mutual complicities:

> "[W]itness the splendor of its art — the true face of Africa is the grandiose empires of the Middle Ages, a society marked by wisdom, beauty, prosperity, order, nonviolence, and humanism, and it is here that we must seek the true cradle of Egyptian civilization."
>
> Thus drooling, Shrobenius derived a twofold benefit on his return home: on the one hand, he mystified the people of his own country who in their enthusiasm raised him to a lofty Sorbonnical chair, while on the other hand he exploited the sentimentality of the coons, only too pleased to hear from the mouth of a white man that Africa was "the womb of the world and the cradle of civilization."
>
> In consequence the niggertrash donated masks and art treasures by the ton to the acolytes of "Shrobeniusology."[57]

A little later, Ouologuem articulates more precisely the interconnections of Africanist mystifications with tourism and the production, packaging, and marketing of African artworks:

> An Africanist school harnessed to the vapors of magico-religious, cosmological, and mythical symbolism had been born: with the result that for three years men flocked to Nakem — and what men! — middlemen, adventurers, apprentice bankers, politicians, salesmen, conspirators — supposedly "scientists," but in reality enslaved sentries mounting guard before the "Shrobeniusological" monument of Negro pseudosymbolism.

> Already it had become more than difficult to procure old masks, for Shrobenius and the missionaries had had the good fortune to snap them all up. And so Saïf — and the practice is still current — had slapdash copies buried by the hundredweight, or sunk into ponds, lakes, marshes, and mud holes, to be exhumed later on and sold at exorbitant prices to unsuspecting curio hunters. These three-year-old masks were said to be charged with the weight of four centuries of civilization.[58]

Ouologuem here forcefully exposes the connections we saw earlier in some of David Rockefeller's insights into the international system of art exchange, the international art world: we see the way in which an ideology of disinterested aesthetic value — the "baptism" of "Negro art" as "aesthetic" — meshes with the international commodification of African expressive culture; a commodification that requires, by the logic of the space-clearing gesture, the manufacture of otherness. (It is a significant bonus that it also harmonizes with the interior decor of modern apartments.) Shrobenius ("[c]e marchand-confectionneur d'idéologie" — this marketeer-manufacturer of ideologies), the ethnographer allied with Saïf (image of the "traditional" African ruling caste), has invented an Africa that is a body over against Europe, the juridical institution; and Ouologuem is urging us vigorously to refuse to be thus other.[59]

•

Sara Suleri has written, in *Meatless Days,* of being treated as an "Otherness-machine" — and of being heartily sick of it.[60] If there is no way out for the postcolonial intellectual in Mudimbe's novels, it is, I suspect, because *as* intellectuals — a category instituted in black Africa by colonialism — we are always at risk of becoming otherness-machines. It risks becoming our principal role. Our only distinction in the world of texts, to which we are latecomers, is that we can mediate it to our fellows. This is especially true when postcolonial meets postmodern; for what the postmodern reader seems to demand of his or her Africa is all too close to what modernism — as documented in William Rubin's *Primitivism* exhibit of 1985 — demanded of it. The role that Africa (like the rest of the Third World) plays for Euro-American postmodernism — like its better-documented significance for modernist art — must be distinguished from the role postmodernism might play in the Third World; what that might be it is, I think, too early to tell. And what happens will happen not because we pronounce upon the matter in theory but out of the changing everyday practices of African cultural life.

For all the while, in Africa's cultures, there are those who will not see themselves as other. Despite the overwhelming reality of economic decline; despite unimaginable poverty; despite wars, malnutrition, disease, and political instability — African cultural productivity grows apace: popular literatures, oral narrative and poetry, dance, drama, music, and visual art all thrive. The contemporary cultural production of many African societies — and the many traditions whose evidences so vigorously remain — is an antidote to the dark vision of the postcolonial novelist.

And I am grateful to James Baldwin for his introduction to *Yoruba Man with a Bicycle,* a figure who is, as Baldwin so rightly saw, polyglot — speaking Yoruba and English, probably some Hausa and a little French for his trips to Cotonou or Cameroon; someone whose "clothes do not fit him too well." He and the other men and women among whom he mostly lives suggest to me that the place to look for hope is not just to the postcolonial novel — which has struggled to achieve the insights of an Ouologuem or Mudimbe — but also to the all-consuming vision of this less anxious creativity. It matters little who it was made *for;* what we should learn from it is the imagination that produced it. *Yoruba Man with a Bicycle* was produced by someone who did not care that the bicycle is the white man's invention — it is not there to be other to the Yoruba self; it is there because someone cared for its solidity; it is there because it will take us farther than our feet will take us; it is there because machines are now as African as novelists... and as fabricated as the kingdom of Nakem.[61]

NOTES

1. See Yambo Ouologuem, "À Mon Mari":

> Tu t'appelais Bimbircokak
> Et tout était bien ainsi
> Tu es denvenu Victor-Émile-Louis-Henri-Joseph
> Ce qui
> Autant qu'il m'en souvienne
> Ne rappelle point ta parenté avec
> Roqueffelère.

2. Susan Vogel et al., *Perspectives.*
3. Ibid., 11.
4. Ibid., 138.
5. Ibid., 29.
6. Ibid., 143.
7. Ibid., 131.
8. I should insist this first time that I use this word that I do not share the widespread negative evaluation of commodification: its merits, I believe, must be assessed case by case. Certainly writers such as Kobena Mercer (e.g., in his "Black Hair/Style Politics") have persuasively criticized any reflexive rejection of the commodity form, which so often reinstates the hoary humanist opposition between "authentic" and "commercial." Mercer explores the avenues by which marginalized groups have manipulated commodified artifacts in culturally novel and expressive ways.
9. Once Vogel has thus refused Kouakou a voice, it is less surprising that his comments turn out to be composite also. On closer inspection, it turns out that there is no single Lela Kouakou who was interviewed like the other co-curators. Kouakou is, in the end, quite exactly an invention: thus literalizing the sense in which "we" (and, more particularly, "our" artists) are individuals while "they" (and "theirs") are ethnic types.
10. It is absolutely crucial that Vogel does not draw her line according to racial or national categories: the Nigerian, the Senegalese, and the African-American co-curators are each allowed to be on "our" side of the great divide. The issue here is something less obvious than racism.
11. Vogel, *Perspectives,* 23.
12. Margaret Masterman "The Nature of a Paradigm," 59n. 1, 61, 65.
13. Jean-François Lyotard, *The Postmodern Condition.*
14. "Post" thus images in modernity the trajectory of "meta" in classical metaphysics. Originating in the editorial glosses of Aristotelians wishing to refer to the books "after" the philosopher's books on nature (physics), this "after" has also been translated into an "above and beyond."
15. Brian McHale, *Postmodernist Fiction,* 5.
16. Scott Lash, "Modernity or Modernism?" 355.
17. Lionel Trilling, *The Opposing Self,* xiv.
18. Fredric Jameson, *The Ideologies of Theory,* vol. 2, *Syntax of History,* 195.
19. Ibid.
20. Ibid., 195, 196.
21. Ibid., 105.
22. Habermas is, of course, a theorist *against* postmodernism.
23. Max Weber, *The Protestant Ethic and the Spirit of Capitalism,* 13.

24. All that Weber was insisting was that these new charismatic leaders would have their charisma routinized also.

25. Reinhard Bendix, *Max Weber*, 360.

26. Max Weber, *The Theory of Social and Economic Organization*, 358–59.

27. Weber, *The Protestant Ethic and the Spirit of Capitalism*, 194.

28. See Max Weber, "Science as a Vocation," in *From Max Weber*, 155.

29. It is this tendency that leads (e.g., in the case of nineteenth-century British utilitarians, such as John Stuart Mill) to the view that we can identify a single goal — "the greatest good of the greatest number" conceived of as maximizing happiness or "utility."

30. Oscar Wilde, "The Decay of Lying: An Observation," 45.

31. Jonathan Ngaté, *Francophone African Fiction*, 59.

32. Christopher Miller, *Blank Darkness*, 218.

33. Ngaté, *Francophone African Fiction*, 64.

34. Ngaté's focus on this initial sentence follows Aliko Songolo, "The Writer, the Audience and the Critic's Responsibility: The Case of *Bound to Violence*," cited by Ngaté in *Francophone African Fiction*.

35. Yambo Ouologuem *Le Devoir de violence*, 9.

36. André Schwartz-Bart, *Le Dernier des Justes*, 11.

37. Ouologuem, *Le Devoir de violence*, 12.

38. Soyinka, *Myth, Literature and the African World*, 100.

39. Ibid., 105.

40. Yambo Ouologuem, *Bound to Violence*, 87. "Saïf fabula et l'interprète traduisit, Madoubo répéta en français, raffinant les subtilités qui faisaient le bonheur de Shrobénius, écrevisse humaine frappée de la manie tâtonnante de vouloir ressusciter, sous couleur d'autonomie culturelle, un univers africain qui ne correspondait à plus rien de vivant; ... il voulait trouver un sens métaphysique à tout. ... Il considérait que la vie africaine était art pur ..." (Ouologuem, *Le Devoir de violence*, 102).

41. Ouologuem, *Bound to Violence*, 6.

42. Here we have a literary thematization of Michel Foucault. This is also the theme of Valentin Mudimbe's important recent intervention, *The Invention of Africa*.

43. Ouologuem, *Bound to Violence*, 181–82. "Souvent il est vrai, l'âme veut rêver l'écho sans passé du bonheur. Mais, jeté dans le monde, l'on peut s'empêcher de songer que Saïf, pleuré trois millions de fois, renaît sans cesse a l'Histoire, sous les cendres chaudes de plus de trente Républiques africaines" (Ouologuem, *Le Devoir de violence*, 207).

44. It would be interesting to speculate on how to account for an apparently similar trend in African-American writing and cultural theory.

45. "Tu ne peux savoir, Isabelle, l'exigence de l'Afrique. — C'est important pour toi, n'est-ce pas? — A vrai dire, je ne sais pas ... — Nara ... Je ne comprends pas. Pour moi, l'important, c'est d'être moi. Etre européenne n'est pas un pavillon. — Tu n'as jamais été blessé comme.... — Tu dramatises, Nara. Tu portes ton africanité comme un martyre ... Ça donne àpenser ... Je te mépriserais si j'entrais dans ton jeu. — La différence, Isabelle, la différence, c'est que l'Europe est avant tout une idée, une institution juridique ... alors l'Afrique ... — Oui? ... — L'Afrique est peut-être surtout un corps, une existence multiple ... Je m'exprime mal ..." (Valentin Y. Mudimbe, *L'Écart*, 116).

46. Valentin Y. Mudimbe, *Entre les eaux*, 75.

47. Ibid., 18:

— Tu vas trahir, m'avait dit mon supérieur, lorsque je lui avais fait part de mon projet.
     — Trahir qui?
     — Le Christ.
     — Mon Père, n'est ce pas plutôt l'Occident que je trahis? Est-ce encore une trahison? N'ai-je pas le droit de me dissocier de ce christianisme qui a trahi l'Evangile?
     — Vous êtes prêtre, Pierre.
     — Pardon, mon Père, je suis un prêtre noir.

48. Ibid., 20:

Le Père Howard est aussi prêtre, comme moi. C'est là le lien qui nous unit. Est-ce le seul? Non. Il y a nos goûts communs.
     La musique classique. Vivaldi. Mozart. Bach. ...
     Et puis nos lectures. Les livres, nous nous les passions. Nos souvenirs communs de Rome. Nos discussions passionées sur le rôle du prêtre, comme sur la littérature et sur les romans policiers

que nous dévorions l'un et l'autre. Je suis plus proche du Père Howard que je ne suis de mes compatriotes, même prêtres.

Une seule chose nous sépare: la couleur de la peau.

49. "L'Église et l'Afrique comptent sur vous."

50. "L'Église pouvait-elle compter encore sur moi? Je l'aurais souhaité et je la souhaite. L'essentiel cependant est que le Christ compte sur moi. Mais l'Afrique? De quelle Afrique m'a parlé Sanguinetti? Celle de mes confrères noirs restés dans la bonne voie ou celle de mes parents pour qui j'ai déjà trahi? Ou même parlait-il de l'Afrique que nous défendons dans le camp?" (Mudimbe, *Entre les eaux*, 73–74).

51. "'Tu manqueras aux tiens...', m'avait dit mon oncle, il y a plus de dix ans. J'ai refusé d'être initié. Que voulait-il dire? Ce sont eux qui me manquent. Serait-ce leur malédiction? La formule m'envahit, discrète d'abord, plus éblouissante, m'empêchant de penser: 'Attends que nos ancêtres descendent. Ta tête brûlera, ta gorge éclatera, ton ventre s'ouvrira et tes pieds se briseront. Attends que les ancêtres descendent...' Ils étaient descendus. Et je n'avais que la sécheresse d'une Foi rationalisée pour me défendre contre l'Afrique" (ibid., 166).

52. "...[L]'humilité de ma bassesse, quelle gloire pour l'homme!" (ibid., 189).

53. See Richard Rorty, *Contingency, Irony and Solidarity*.

54. "...[V]oilà l'art nègre baptisé 'esthétique' et marchandé — oye! — dans l'univers imaginaire des 'échanges vivifiants'!" (Ouologuem, *Le Devoir de violence*, 110).

55. "L'art nègre se forgeait ses lettres de noblesse au folklore de la spritualité mercantiliste, oye oye oye..." (ibid., 110).

56. Ouologuem, *Bound to Violence*, 94–95. Ouologuem, *Le Devoir de violence*, 111:

"...[T]émoin: la splendeur de son art — la grandeur des empires du Moyen Age constituait le visage vrai de l'Afrique, sage, belle, riche, ordonnée, non violente et puissante tout autant qu'humaniste — berceau même de la civilisation égyptienne."
Salivant ainsi, Shrobénius, de retour au bercail, en tira un double profit: d'une part, il mystifia son pays, qui, enchanté, le jucha sur une haute chair sorbonicale, et, d'autre part, il explita la sentimentalité négrillarde — par trop heureuse de s'entendre dire par un Blanc que 'l'afrique était ventre du monde et berceau de civilisation."
La négraille offrit par tonnes, conséquemment et gratis, masques et trésors artistiques aux acolytes de la "shrobéniusologie."

57. Ouolguem, *Bound to Violence*, 95–96. Ouologuem, *Le Devoir de violence*, 112:

Une école africaniste ainsi accrochée aux nues du symbolisme magico-religieux, cosmologique et mythique, était née: tant et si bien que durant trois ans, des hommes — et quels hommes!: des fantoches, des aventuriers, des apprentis banquiers, des politiciens, des voyageurs, des conspirateurs, des chercheurs — "scientifiques," dit-on, en vérité sentinelles asservies, montant la garde devant le monument "shrobéniusologique" du pseudo-symbolisme nègre, accoururent au Nakem.
Déjà, l'acquisition des masques anciens était devenue problématique depuis que Shrobénius et les missionnaires connurent le bonheur d'en acquérir en quantité. Saïf donc — et la pratique est courante de nos jours encore — fit enterrer des quintaux de masques hâtivement executés à la ressemblance des originaux, les engloutissant dans des mares, marais, étangs, marécages, lacs, limons — quitte à les exhumer quelque temps après, les vendant aux curieux et profanes à prix d'or. Ils étaient, ces masques, vieux de trois ans, chargés disait-on, du poids de quatre siècles de civilisation.

58. Ouologuem, *Le Devoir de violence*, 111.

59. Sara Suleri, *Meatless Days*, 105.

60. I learned a good deal from trying out earlier versions of these ideas at a National Endowment for the Humanities summer institute on "the future of the avant-garde in postmodern culture" under the direction of Susan Suleiman and Alice Jardine at Harvard in July 1989; at the African Studies Association meeting (under the sponsorship of the Society for African Philosophy in North America) in November 1989, where Jonathan Ngaté's response was particularly helpful; and as the guest of Ali Mazrui, at the Braudel Center at the State University of New York at Binghamton in May 1990. As usual, I wish I knew how to incorporate more of the ideas of the discussants on those occasions. An earlier version of these arguments was published in *Critical Inquiry* 17 (winter 1991): 336–57; I am grateful to the editors of *Critical Inquiry* for their suggestions about that earlier essay.

BIBLIOGRAPHY

Bendix, Reinhard. *Max Weber: An Intellectual Portrait*. London: Methuen, 1966.

Jameson, Fredric. *The Ideologies of Theory: Essays 1971–1986*. Vol. 2, *Syntax of History*. Minneapolis: University of Minnesota Press, 1988.

Lash, Scott. "Modernity or Modernism? Weber and Contemporary Social Theory." In *Max Weber, Rationality and Modernity*. Edited by Scott Lash and Sam Whimster. London: Allen and Unwin, 1987.

Lyotard, Jean-François. *The Postmodern Condition: A Report on Knowledge*. Vol. 10, *Theory and History of Literature*. Translated by Geoff Bennington and Brian Massumi. Minneapolis: University of Minnesota Press, 1988.

Masterman, Margaret. "The Nature of a Paradigm." In *Criticism and the Growth of Knowledge*. Edited by Alan Musgrave and Imre Lakatos, 59–89. Cambridge: Cambridge University Press, 1970.

McHale, Brian. *Postmodernist Fiction*. New York: Methuen, 1987.

Mercer, Kobena. "Black Hair/Style Politics." *New Formations* 3 (winter 1987): 33–54.

Miller, Christopher. *Blank Darkness: Africanist Discourse in French*. Chicago: University of Chicago Press, 1985.

Mudimbe, Valentin Y. *Le Bel immonde*. Paris: Présence Africaine, 1976.

———. *Entre les eaux*. Paris: Présence Africaine, 1973.

———. *L'Écart*. Paris: Présence Africaine, 1979.

———. *The Invention of Africa: Gnosis, Philosophy, and the Order of Knowledge*. Bloomington: Indiana University Press, 1988.

———. *L'Odeur du Père*. Paris: Présence Africaine, 1982.

Ngaté, Jonathan. *Francophone African Fiction: Reading a Literary Tradition*. Trenton, N.J.: Africa World Press, 1988.

Ouologuem, Yambo. *Bound to Violence*. Translated by Ralph Mannheim. London: Heinemann, 1968.

———. *Le Devoir de violence*. Paris: Éditions du Seuil, 1968.

———. "À Mon Mari." *Presence Africaine* 57 (1966): 95.

Rorty, Richard. *Contingency, Irony and Solidarity*. Cambridge: Cambridge University Press, 1988.

Schwartz-Bart, André. *Le Dernier des Justes*. Paris: Éditions du Seuil, 1959.

Songolo, Aliko. "The Writer, the Audience and the Critic's Responsibility: The Case Of *Bound to Violence*." In *Artist and Audience: African Literature as a Shared Experience*. Edited by Richard Priebe and Thomas A. Hale, 126–40. Washington, D.C.: Three Continents Press, 1979.

Soyinka, W. *Myth, Literature and the African World*. Cambridge: Cambridge University Press, 1976.

Suleri, Sara. *Meatless Days*. Chicago: University of Chicago Press, 1989.

Trilling, Lionel. *The Opposing Self: Nine Essays in Criticism*. New York: Viking Press, 1955.

Vogel, Susan, et al. *Perspectives: Angles on African Art*. New York: Center for African Art, 1987.

Weber, Max. *From Max Weber: Essays in Sociology*. Edited by H. H. Gerth and C. Wright Mills. London: Kegan Paul, 1948.

———. *The Protestant Ethic and the Spirit of Capitalism*. Translated by Talcott Parsons. London: Unwin University Books, 1930.

———. *The Theory of Social and Economic Organization*. New York: Oxford University Press, 1947.

Wilde, Oscar. *Intentions*. London, 1909.

Chapter 24
The World and the Home

Homi K. Bhabha

In the house of fiction you can hear, today, the deep stirring of the unhomely. You must permit me this awkward word — "unhomely" — because it captures something of the estranging sense of the relocation of the home and the world in an unhallowed place. To be unhomed is not to be homeless, nor can the unhomely be easily accommodated in that familiar division of the social life into private and the public spheres. The unhomely moment creeps up on you as stealthily as your own shadow, and suddenly you find yourself, with Henry James's Isabel Archer, taking the measure of your dwelling in a state of "incredulous terror."[1] And it is at this point that the world first shrinks for Isabel and then expands enormously. As Isabel struggles to survive the fathomless waters, the rushing torrents, James introduces us to the "unhomeliness" inherent in that rite of "extra-territorial" initiation — the relations between the innocent American, the deep, dissembling European, the masked emigré — that a generation of critics have named his "international theme." In a feverish stillness, the intimate recesses of the domestic space become sites for history's most intricate invasions. In that displacement, the border between home and world becomes confused; and, uncannily, the private and the public become part of each other, forcing upon us a vision that is as divided as it is disorienting.

In the stirrings of the unhomely, another world becomes visible. It has less to do with forcible eviction and more to do with the uncanny literary and social effects of enforced social accommodation or historical migrations and cultural relocations. The home does not remain the domain of domestic life, nor does the world simply become its social or historical counterpart. The unhomely is the shock of recognition of the world-in-the-home, the home-in-the-world. In a song called "Whose House Is This?" Toni Morrison gives this problem of unhomely dwelling a lyric clarity:

> Whose house is this? Whose night keeps out the light in here? Say who owns this house? It is not mine. I had another sweeter.... The House is strange. Its shadows lie. Say, tell me, why does its lock fit my key?[2]

My earliest sense of the unhomely occurred in a prosaic house in Oxford, in a narrow street reserved for college servants and research fellows. It was a noisy, red-brick, terraced house haunted by the hydraulic regurgitations of the Victorian plumbing system, yet strangely appropriate to the task at hand, a thesis on V. S.

Naipaul. I was writing about *A House for Mr. Biswas,* about a small-time Trinidadian journalist, the son of an Indian indentured laborer, a devotee of Samuel Smiles and Charles Dickens, who was afflicted with the most noisy and public bouts of nervous dyspepsia. As I contemplated his tragic-comic failure to create a dwelling place, I wrestled with the wisdom of Iris Murdoch's laudable pronouncement, "A novel must be a house for free people to live in." Must the novel be a house? What kind of narrative can house unfree people? Is the novel also a house where the unhomely can live? I was straining nervously at the edges of Iris Murdoch's combination of liberalism and 'catholic' existentialism, while Mr. Biswas's gastric juices ran amok. The cistern churned and burped, and I thought of some of the great homes of English literature — Mansfield Park, Thrushcross Grange, Gardencourt, Brideshead, Howard's End, Fawlty Towers. Suddenly, I knew I had found, in the ruins of the Biswases' bungalows and their unlikely, unsettled lives, my small corner of the world of letters — a postcolonial place.

Working on *A House for Mr. Biswas*, I found that I couldn't fit the political, cultural, or chronological experience of that text into the traditions of Anglo-American, liberal, novel criticism. The sovereignty of the concept of character, grounded as it is in the aesthetic discourse of cultural authenticity and the practical ethics of individual freedom, bore little resemblance to the overdetermined, unaccommodated postcolonial figure of Mr. Biswas. The image of the house has always been used to talk about the expansive, mimetic nature of the novel; but in *Biswas* you have a form of realism that is unable to contain the anguish of cultural displacement and diasporic movement. Although the unhomely is a paradigmatic postcolonial experience, it has a resonance that can be heard distinctly, if erratically, in fictions that negotiate the powers of cultural difference in a range of historical conditions and social contradictions.

You can hear the shrill alarm of the unhomely at the moment when Isabel Archer, in *The Portrait of a Lady,* realizes that her world has been reduced to one, high, mean window as her house of fiction becomes "the house of darkness, the house of dumbness, the house of suffocation."[3] If you hear it thus at the Palazzo Roccanera in the late-1870s, then a little earlier, in 1873, on the outskirts of Cincinnati, in mumbling houses like 124 Bluestone Road, you hear the indecipherable language of the black and angry dead, the voice of Toni Morrison's *Beloved:* "the thoughts of the women of 124, unspeakable thoughts, unspoken."[4] More than a quarter-century later, in 1905, Bengal is ablaze with the Swadeshi or Home Rule movement when "home-made Bimala, the product of the confined space," as Tagore describes her in *The Home and the World,* is aroused by "a running undertone of melody, low down in the bass, ... the true manly note, the note of power." Bimala is possessed and drawn forever from the zenana, the secluded women's quarters, as she crosses that fated verandah into the world of public affairs, "over to another shore."[5] Much closer to our own times, in contemporary South Africa, Nadine Gordimer's heroine Aila emanates a stilling atmosphere as she makes her diminished domesticity into the perfect cover for gun-running: suddenly the home turns into another world, and the narrator notices that "it was as if everyone found that he had unnoticingly entered a strange house, *and it was hers.*"[6]

Gordimer's awkward sentence, with its rapid shift of genders and pronouns ("everyone" — "he" — "she"), provides the estranging syntax of the unhomely experience. Gordimer's sign of the woman's sense of possession and self-possession ("it was hers"), her ethical or historical transformation of the world, emerges retroactively, belatedly, *at the end of the sentence, toward the end of the book.* The historical or fictional subject is conscious of the meaning or intention of the act, but its transformation into a "public" symbolic or ethical realm demands a *narrative* agency that emerges after the event, often alienating intent and disturbing causal determinism. In *The Human Condition,* Hannah Arendt meditates on just such a perplexity in signifying the social sphere as a narrative process: "In any series of events that together form a story with a unique meaning," she writes, "we can at best isolate the agent who set the whole process into motion; and although this agent frequently remains the subject, the hero of the story, we can *never point unequivocally to [the agent] as the author of the outcome."*[7]

In order to appear as material or empirical reality, the historical or social process must pass through an aesthetic alienation or privatization of its public visibility. The discourse of "the social" then finds its means of representation in a kind of *unconsciousness* that obscures the immediacy of meaning, darkens the public event with an unhomely glow. There is, I want to hazard, an incommunicability that shapes the public moment, a psychic obscurity that is formative for public memory. Then the house of fiction speaks in tongues, in those indecipherable mumbling enunciations that emanate from *Beloved*'s "124" or the strange, still silence that surrounds Nadine Gordimer's Aila, whether she inhabits a house in the colored ghetto of Benoni (son of sorrow) or in a "gray area" of the Cape. And suddenly, literature asks questions at the very borders of its historical and disciplinary being: Can historical time be thought outside fictional space, or do they lie uncannily beside each other? Does the passage of power turn the agent of history into a stranger, a double agent living between the lines?

The process of the aesthetic that I am proposing for the grounds of historical "re-cognition," and as a reckoning with the historical event, must be clarified. The aesthetic as the obscuring of the historical event that refigures it through a temporal distancing or lag, as I've described it, must be distinguished from two familiar genealogies of the aesthetic. It must not be confused with the Kantian aesthetic that is a mediatory process that brings existence to its fullest being in a revelation of self-reflection. Nor do I prescribe to that tradition of a materialist aesthetic that sees art as the displaced or overdetermined symptom of social reification — a fetishism of phenomenal forms that conceals "real" ideological contradictions. Both these approaches to the aesthetic involve transcendent schemes of thought and art where the progressive movement of the dialectic at once poses the problem of difference, alienation, negation — at the ontological or epistemological level — but sublates or disavows it in the process of representation. For instance, although Louis Althusser is fully aware of the differential sites of the social formation and the displaced or overdetermined nature of ideology more generally, he sees the "subject" of cultural discourse as caught within the relatively homogenous, totalizing confines of the Lacanian Imaginary.

In contrast to this homogenous or transcendent temporality of the aesthetic, I want to suggest that the aesthetic process introduces into our reading of social reality not another reified form of mediation — the art object — but another temporality in which to signify the "event" of history. I take my lead from what Walter Benjamin describes as the "constructive principle" of materialist historiography, where the "historical materialist cannot do without the present which is not a transition, but in which time stands still and has to come to a stop. For this notion defines the present in which he himself is writing history." I locate the aesthetic in this time of inscription whose stillness is not stasis but a shock that Benjamin goes on to describe as "blasting a specific era out of the homogeneous course of history."[8] The present that informs the aesthetic process is not a transcendental passage but a moment of "transit," a form of temporality that is open to disjunction and discontinuity and that sees the process of history engaged, rather like art, in a negotiation of the framing and naming of social reality — not what lies inside or outside reality, but where to draw (or inscribe) the "meaningful" line between them.

The unhomely moment relates the traumatic ambivalences of a personal, psychic history to the wider disjunctions of political existence. Beloved, the child murdered by her own mother, Sethe, is a demonic, belated repetition of the violent history of black infant deaths, during slavery, in many parts of the South, less than a decade after the haunting of 124 Bluestone Road. (Between 1882 and 1895, from one-third to one-half of the annual black mortality rate was accounted for by children under five.) But the memory of Sethe's act of infanticide emerges through "the holes — the things the fugitives did not say; the questions they did not ask, . . . the unnamed, the unmentioned." As we reconstruct the narrative of child-murder through Sethe, the slave mother, who is herself the victim of social death, the very historical basis of our ethical judgments undergoes a radical revision.

In the denouement of her novel, Gordimer provides another example of the complexity of the unhomely when she describes what she calls "the freak displacement" that has afflicted the world of her characters. "The biological drive of Sonny's life which belonged to his wife was diverted to his white lover [Hannah]. . . . He and Hannah had begot no child. The revolutionary movement was to be their survivor. . . . But Aila, his wife, was the revolutionary now."[9] In the freak displacements of these novels, the profound divisions of an enslaved or apartheid society (negrification, denigration, classification, violence, incarceration) are relocated in the midst of the ambivalence of psychic identification — that space where love and hate can be projected or inverted, where the relation of "object" to identity is always split and doubled.

Such forms of social and psychic existence can best be represented in that tenuous survival of literary language itself, which allows memory to speak:

> while knowing Speech can (be) at best, a shadow echoing
> the silent light, bear witness
> to the truth, it is not.

Auden wrote those lines on the powers of poesis in "The Cave of Making," aspiring to be, as he put it, "a minor Atlantic Goethe." And it is to an intriguing suggestion in Goethe's final note on world literature, 1830, that I now turn to find a comparative method that would speak to the unhomely condition of the modern world. Goethe suggests that the possibility of a world literature arises from the cultural confusion wrought by terrible wars and mutual conflicts. Nations "could not return to their settled and independent life again without noticing that they had learned many foreign ideas and ways, which they had unconsciously adopted, and com[ing] to feel here and there previously unrecognized spiritual and intellectual needs."[10] Goethe's immediate reference is, of course, to the Napoleonic wars, and his concept of the feeling of "neighborly relations" is profoundly Eurocentric, extending as far as England and France. However, as an Orientalist who read Shakuntala at seventeen and writes in his autobiography of the "unformed and overformed"[11] monkey-god Hanuman, Goethe and his speculations are open to another line of thought.

What of the more complex cultural situation where "previously unrecognized spiritual and intellectual needs" emerge from the imposition of "foreign" ideas, cultural representations, and structures of power? Goethe suggests that the "inner nature of the whole nation as well as the individual man works...unconsciously."[12] When this is placed alongside his idea that the cultural life of the nation is "unconsciously" lived, then there may be a sense in which world literature could be an emergent, prefigurative category that is concerned with a form of cultural dissensus and alterity, where nonconsensual terms of affiliation and articulation may be established on the grounds of historical trauma. The study of world literature might be the study of the way in which cultures recognize themselves through their projections of "otherness." Where the transmission of "national" traditions was once the major theme of a world literature, perhaps we can now suggest that transnational histories of migrants, the colonized, or political refugees — these border and frontier conditions — may be the terrains of world literature. The center of such a study would neither be the "sovereignty" of national cultures nor the "universalism" of human culture but a focus on those "freak displacements" — such as Morrison and Gordimer display — that have been caused within cultural lives of postcolonial societies. If these were considered to be the paradigm cases of a world literature based on the trauma of history and the conflict of nations, then Walter Benjamin's homeless modern novelist would be the representative figure of an unhomely world literature. For he "carries the incommensurable to extremes in the representation of human life and in the midst of life's fullness, gives evidence of the perplexity of living."[13] Which leads us to ask: Can the perplexity of the unhomely, intrapersonal world lead to an international theme?

Gordimer places this very question at the center of literary narrative: "Love, love/ hate are the most common and universal of experiences. But no two are alike, each is a fingerprint of life. That's the miracle that makes literature and links it with creation in the biological sense."[14] To put Gordimer's point another way: the fingerprint of literature — its imagistic impulse, its tropic topos, its metaphoric medium, its allegorical voice — that these forms of narrative created from contingency and indeterminacy may provide historical discourse with its powers of narrative "beginning." For Michel de Certeau has suggested, in *The Writing of History,* that "beginnings" require an "originary nonplace," something "unspoken" that then produces a chronology of events.[15] Beginnings can, in this sense, be the narrative limits of the knowable, the margins of the meaningful. In what she calls her "in medias res" openings, Morrison stages such a narrative "nonspace" and turns it into the performative time of the experience of slavery — no native informant, she writes that she snatches the reader "as the slaves were from one place to another, . . . without preparation or defense."[16] Her opening sign — "124 was spiteful" — offers no respite, no immediate meaning, because the house of slave-memory is not a resting place, not a Wordsworthian "spot of time." Number "124" is the unhomely, haunted site of the circulation of an event not as fact or fiction but as an "enunciation," a discourse of "unspeakable thoughts unspoken" — a phrase that circulates in the work and comes closest to defining its mode of utterance, the uncanny voice of memory.

To "unspeak" is both to release from erasure and repression and to reconstruct, reinscribe the elements of the known. "In this case too," we may say with Freud, "the *Unheimlich* is what was once *heimisch*, home-like, familiar; the pre-fix 'un' is the token of repression." Morrison turns her narrative to just such an "affect" of distancing, obscuring the "referent," repeating and revising the "unspoken" in order to make the act of narration an ethical act:

> A few words have to be read before it is clear that 124 refers to a house...a few more...to discover why it is spiteful.... *By then it is clear that something is beyond control, but it is not beyond understanding since it is not beyond accommodation by both the women and the children....* The fully realized haunting...is a sleight of hand. One of its purposes is to keep the reader preoccupied with the nature of the incredible spirit-world while being supplied a controlled diet of the incredible political world.[17]

If we are seeking a "worlding" of literature, then perhaps it lies in a critical act that attempts to grasp the sleight of hand with which literature conjures with historical specificity, using the medium of psychic uncertainty, aesthetic distancing, or the obscure signs of the spirit-world, the sublime and the subliminal. As literary creatures and political animals we ought to concern ourselves with the understanding of human action and the social world as a moment when *"something is beyond control, but it is...not beyond accommodation."* This act of writing the world, of taking the measure of its dwelling, is magically caught in Morrison's description of her house of fiction — art as "the fully realized presence of a haunting" of history. Read as an image that describes the relation of art to social reality, my translation of Morrison's phrase becomes a statement on the political responsibility of the critic. For the critic must attempt to fully realize, and take responsibility for, the unspoken, unrepresented pasts that haunt the historical present.

Our task remains, however, to show how historical understanding is transformed through the signifying process, represented in a language that is *somehow beyond control.* This is in keeping with Hannah Arendt's suggestion that the author of social action may be the initiator of its unique meaning, but as agent he or she cannot control its outcome. The issue is not simply what the house of fiction contains or "controls" as *content.* What is just as important is the metaphoricity of the houses of racial memory that both Morrison and Gordimer construct — those subjects of the narrative that mutter or mumble like 124 or keep a still silence in a "gray" Cape Town suburb.

Each of the houses in Gordimer's *My Son's Story* is invested with a specific secret or a conspiracy, an unhomely stirring. The house in the ghetto is the house of "colored" collusion; the lying house is the house of Sonny's adultery; then there is the silent house of Aila's revolutionary camouflage; there is also the nocturnal house of Will, the narrator, writing of the narrative that charts the phoenix rising in his home, while the words must turn to ashes in his mouth. But each house marks a deeper historical displacement. And that is the condition of being colored in South Africa, or as Will describes it, "halfway between, . . . being not defined — and it was this lack of definition in itself that was never to be questioned, but observed like a taboo, something which no-one, while following, could ever admit to."[18]

This halfway house of racial and cultural origins bridges the "in-between" diasporic origins of the colored South African and turns them into the symbol for the disjunctive, displaced everyday life of the liberation struggle — "like so many others of this kind, whose families are fragmented in the diaspora of exile, code names, underground activity, people for whom a real home and attachments are something for others who will come after." Private and public, past and present, the psyche and the social develop an interstitial, intimacy. It is an intimacy that questions binary divisions through which such spheres of social experience are often spatially opposed. These spheres of life are linked through an "in-between" temporality that takes the measure of dwelling at home, while producing an image of the world of history. This is the moment of aesthetic distance that provides the narrative with a double edge that, like the colored South African subject, represents a hybridity, a difference "within," a subject that inhabits the rim of an "in-between" reality. And the inscription of this border existence inhabits a stillness of time and a strangeness of framing that creates the discursive "image" at the crossroads of history and literature, bridging the home and the world.

Such a strange stillness is visible in the portrait of Aila. Her husband, Sonny, now past his political prime, his affair with his white revolutionary lover in abeyance, makes his first prison visit to see his wife. The wardress stands back; the policeman fades; and Aila emerges as an unhomely presence, on the opposite side from her husband and son:

> [B]ut through the familiar beauty there was a vivid strangeness. . . . It was as if some chosen experience had seen in her, as a painter will in his subject, what she was, what was there to be discovered. In Lusaka, in secret, in prison — who knows where — she had sat for her hidden face. *They had to recognise her.* (230)

Through this painterly distance a vivid strangeness emerges; a partial or double "self" is framed in a climactic political moment that is also a contingent historical event: "some chosen experience . . . who knows where? . . . or what there was to be discovered." They had to recognize her, but *what* do they recognize in her?

The history of Aila's hidden face emerges at the moment of her framing. She begins to speak, "like someone telling a story," but soon we find it "difficult to follow. . . . You leave so much out." In her inability to articulate her intention, to demonstrate a clear causality of commitment, or even a rational, responsible political ideology, we are confronted with the novel's poignant and ambivalent interrogation of agency: *"Aila, Aila a revolutionary responsible for her acts"* (239). There is no giddy suggestion that Aila's revolution is instinctive, part of her gendered *jouissance,* nor that it is the displaced symptom of her domestic oppression or some fatal return of the repressed knowledge of Sonny's adultery. The political lesson Aila has to teach speaks through her narrative refusal to "name" her choice. With a certain obduracy and greater obscurity, she herself becomes the "image" of historical agency that the narrative is trying to wrench from her as an intention for her actions, an origin for her events, a "cause" for her consciousness. Literature, through its distancing act, frames this stillness, this enigmatic historical event:

> "The necessity for what I've done." She placed the outer edge of each hand, fingers extended and close together, as a frame on either side of the sheets of testimony in front of her. And she placed herself before him, to be judged by him. (241)

Words will not speak, and the silence freezes into the images of apartheid: identity cards, police frame-ups, prison mug shots, the grainy press pictures of terrorists. Of course, Aila is not judged, nor is she judgmental. Her revenge is much wiser and more complete. In her silence she becomes the unspoken "totem" of the taboo of the colored South African. She displays the unhomely world, "the halfway between, not defined" world of the colored, as the "distorted place and time in which they — all of them — Sonny, Aila, Hannah — lived" (241). The silence that doggedly follows Aila's dwelling now turns into an image of "interstices," the in-between hybridity of the history of sexuality and race.

Aila's hidden face, the outer edge of each hand, these small gestures through which she speaks describe another dimension of "dwelling" in the social world. Aila, as colored woman, defines a boundary that is at once inside and outside, the insiders' outsideness. The stillness that surrounds her, the gaps in her story, her hesitation and passion that speak between the self and its acts — these are moments in which the private and public touch in contingency. They do not simply transform the content of political ideas; the very "place" from which the political is spoken — the "public sphere" itself — becomes an experience of liminality that questions, in Sonny's words, what it means to speak "from the centre of life."

The central political preoccupation of the novel — until Aila's emergence — is the "loss of absolutes," the meltdown of the Cold War, the fear "that if we can't offer the old socialist paradise in exchange for the capitalist hell here, we'll have turned traitor to our brothers" (214). The lesson Aila teaches requires a movement away from a world conceived in binary terms, away from a notion of the peoples' aspirations sketched in simple black and white. It also requires a shift of attention from the political as a theory to politics as the activity of everyday life. Aila leads us to the "homely" world where, Gordimer writes, the banalities are enacted — "the fuss over births, marriages, family affairs with their survival rituals of food and clothing" (243). But it is precisely in these banalities that the unhomely stirs, as the violence of a racialized society falls most enduringly on the details of life: where you can sit, or not; how you can live, or not; what you can learn, or not; who you can love, or not. Between the banal act of freedom and its historic denial rises the silence: "Aila emanated a stilling atmosphere; the parting jabber stopped. It was as if everyone found he had unnoticingly entered a strange house, and it was hers; she stood there."

In Aila's stillness, its obscure necessity, we have glimpsed what Emmanuel Levinas has magically described as the twilight existence of the aesthetic image — art's image as "the very event of obscuring, a descent into night, an invasion of the shadow."[19] The "completion" of the aesthetic, the distancing of the world in the "image," is precisely not a transcendental activity. The image — or the metaphoric, "fictional" activity of language — makes visible "an interruption of time by a movement going on on the hither side of time, in its interstices."[20] The complexity of this statement becomes clearer when we remember the "stillness" of time through which Aila surreptitiously and subversively interrupts the ongoing presence of political activity, using her interstitial role in the domestic world to both "obscure" her political role and to articulate it the better. The continual eruption of "indecipherable languages" of slave-memory in *Beloved* obscures the historical narrative of infanticide only to articulate the "unspoken," that ghostly discourse that enters the world of 124 from the outside in order to reveal the profound temporal liminality of the transitional world of the aftermath of slavery in the 1870s — its private and public faces, its historical past, and its narrative present. The aesthetic image discloses an ethical time of narration because, Levinas writes, "the real world appears in the image as it were between parenthesis."[21] Like the outer edges of Aila's hands holding her enigmatic testimony, like 124, which is a fully realized presence haunted by indecipherable languages, Levinas's parenthetical perspective is also an ethical view. It effects an "externality of the inward" as the very enunciative position of the historical and narrative subject, "introducing into the heart of subjectivity a radical and an-archical reference to the other which in fact constitutes the inwardness of the subject."[22] Is it not uncanny that Levinas's metaphors for this unique "obscurity" of the image should come from those unhomely places in Dickens — those dusty boarding schools, the pale light of London offices, the dark, dank secondhand clothes shops?

For Levinas, the "art-magic" of the contemporary novel lies in its way of "seeing inwardness from the outside," and for us, it is this ethical-aesthetic positioning that returns us, finally, to the community of the unhomely:

> 124 was spiteful. . . . The house on the veld was silent.
> The women in the house knew it and so did the children.

Why, in particular, the women? Carole Pateman argues that the continual "forgetting" of domestic life in the definition of the private/public distinction introduces a negation at the very center of social contract theory. Domestic life becomes, by virtue of its disavowal, a problematic boundary of civil society. It can be reoccupied by those who have taken up the position of the "inwardness from the outside." This has indeed happened in the work of black American theorists like Patricia Hill Collins, who names the experience "the outsider-within status"; and in the work of Patricia Williams, who sees the possibility of deploying this status to describe an ambivalent, transgressive, fluid positioning (of herself and her work) "that moves back and forth across a boundary which acknowledges that I can be black and good and black and bad and that I can also be black and white."

It is Toni Morrison, however, who takes this ethical and aesthetic project of seeing inwardness from the outside furthest or deepest — right into Beloved's naming of her desire for identity: "I want you to touch me on my inside part and call me my name." There is an obvious reason why a ghost should want to be so realized. What is more obscure — and to the point — is how such an inward and intimate desire would provide an "inscape" of the memory of slavery. For Morrison, it is precisely the historical and discursive boundaries of slavery that are the issue. Racial violence is invoked by historical dates — 1876, for instance — but Morrison is just a little hasty with the events in themselves: "the true meaning of the Fugitive Bill, the Settlement

Fee, God's Ways, antislavery, manumission, skin voting. . . ." What has to be endured
is the knowledge of doubt that comes from Sethe's eighteen years of disapproval
and a solitary life in the unhomely world of 124 Bluestone Road. What finally causes
the thoughts of the women of 124, "unspeakable thoughts to be unspoken," is the
understanding that the victims of violence are themselves "signified upon": they are
the victims of projected fears, anxieties, and dominations that do not originate within
the oppressed and will not fix them in the circle of pain. The stirring of emancipation
comes with the knowledge that the belief "that under every dark skin there was a
jungle" was a belief that grew, spread, and touched every perpetrator of the racist
myth, and was then expelled from 124.

With this knowledge comes a kind of self-love that is also the love of the "other."
Eros and agape together. This knowledge is visible in those intriguing interstitial
chapters that lay over one another, where Sethe, Beloved, and Denver perform a
ceremony of claiming and naming: "Beloved, she my daughter"; "Beloved is my sister"; "I am Beloved and she is mine." The women speak in tongues, from a space
"in-between each other," which is a communal space. They explore an interpersonal
reality: a social reality that appears within the poetic image as if it were in parenthesis. It is difficult to convey the rhythm and the improvisation of those chapters,
but it is impossible not to see in them the healing of history, a community reclaimed
in the making of a name:

Who is Beloved?

Now we understand: she is the daughter that returns to Sethe so that her mind will
be homeless no more.

Who is Beloved?

Now we may say: she is the sister who returns to Denver and brings hope of her
father's return, the fugitive who died in his escape.

Who is Beloved?

Now we know: she is the daughter made of murderous love who returns to love and
hate and free herself. Her words are broken, like the lynched people with broken
necks; disembodied, like the dead children who lost their ribbons. But there is no
mistaking what her live words say as they rise from the dead despite their lost syntax
and their fragmented presence:

My face is coming I have to have it I am looking for the join I am loving my face
so much I want to join I am loving my face so much my dark face is close to me
I want to join.

My subject has been the nest of the phoenix, not its pyre. I have attempted to
illuminate the world forcibly entering the house of fiction in order to invade, alarm,
divide, dispossess. But I have also tried to show how literature haunts history's more
public face, forcing it to reflect on itself in the displacing, even distorting, image
of art. When the publicity of the "event," or the certainty of "intention" encounters
the silence of the word or the stillness of art, it may lose control and coherence,
but it provides a profound understanding of what constitutes human necessity and

agency. I have focused this argument on the woman framed (Gordimer's Aila) and the woman renamed (Morrison's Beloved). In both their houses great world events erupted — apartheid and slavery — and their coming was turned into that particular obscurity of art. In that unhomely second coming, both Aila and Beloved embody the "freak displacements" of their times. It could be said of these moments that they are of the world but not fully in it; that they represent the outsideness of the inside that is too painful to remember. "This is not a story to pass on," Morrison insistently repeats at the end of *Beloved* in order to engrave the event in the deepest resources of our amnesia, of our unconsciousness. When historical visibility has faded, when the present tense of testimony loses its power to arrest, then the distortions of memory offer us the image of our solidarity and survival. This is a story to pass on, to pass through the world of literature on its thither side and discover those who live in the unhomely house of fiction. In the house of fiction, there is a stirring of the unspoken, of the unhomely, . . . today.

NOTES

This is the transcript of a lecture given by Homi Bhabha at Princeton University. A number of historical and theoretical elaborations that were inappropriate to the occasion and format of the lecture were developed in an essay that was based on this lecture.

1. Henry James, *The Portrait of a Lady* (New York: Norton, 1975), 360.
2. Toni Morrison, "Honey and Rue" (from song-cycle for Kathleen Battle), *Carnegie Hall Stagebill* (January 1992): 12c.
3. James, *Portrait,* 360.
4. Toni Morrison, *Beloved* (New York: Knopf, 1987), 198–99.
5. Rabindranath Tagore, *The Home and the World* (New York: Asia Book Corporation, 1985), 70–71.
6. Nadine Gordimer, *My Son's Story* (London: Bloomsbury, 1990), 241–42.
7. Hannah Arendt, *The Human Condition* (Chicago: University of Chicago Press, 1958), 185.
8. Walter Benjamin, *Illuminations* (New York: Schoken Books, 1969), 262.
9. Gordimer, *My Son's Story,* 241–42.
10. *Goethe's Literary Essays,* ed. J. E. Spingarn (New York: Harcourt, Brace, 1921), 98–99.
11. *The Autobiography of Goethe,* ed. John Oxenford (London: Henry G. Bohn, 1948), 467.
12. Ibid.
13. Benjamin, *Illuminations,* 86.
14. Gordimer, *My Son's Story,* 275.
15. Michel de Certeau, *The Writing of History* (New York: Columbia University Press, 1988), 90–91.
16. Toni Morrison, "Unspeakable Thoughts Unspoken," *Michigan Quarterly Review* (fall 1990): 32.
17. Ibid.
18. Gordimer, *My Son's Story,* 21–22; further references to this work will be given in the text.
19. Morrison, "Unspeakable Thoughts," 32.
20. Ibid.
21. Emmanuel Levinas, "Reality and Its Shadow," in *Collected Philosophical Papers* (Dordrecht: Martinus Nijhoff, 1987), 1–13.
22. Ibid.

Chapter 25
Reading Africa through Foucault:
V. Y. Mudimbe's Reaffirmation of the Subject
Manthia Diawara

> *Everyone knows the famous words of the Sun-King to his godson, Aniaba, The Black Prince. On the eve of Aniaba's departure for his states, as he was saying his farewell to the king, Louis XIV is said to have told him: "Prince, the only difference between you and me is the difference between black and white." We interpret: after the education that we have provided you at our court, you have become a Frenchman with a black skin.*
>
> Léopold Sédar Senghor, "Vues sur l'Afrique noire, ou assimiler, non être assimilés"

> *Michel Foucault, because of his influence, his originality, and the significance of his work, may be considered a noteworthy symbol of the sovereignty of the very European thought from which we wish to disentangle ourselves.*
>
> V. Y. Mudimbe, *L'Odeur du Père*

Mudimbe posits here, in a rather blunt manner, the place that Western thought occupies in non-Western discursive formations. For him, it is necessary for the theorist in Africa to appreciate what it takes to create an authentic statement that reflects African sociocultural practices and takes as its condition of possibility a local discursive space. Such a project must distinguish what is still Western in the discourse that denounces the West. Likewise, the non-Western theorist, in search of the enabling elements inside the Western canon, must be aware of the traps and reversibilities embedded in that same canon.

Mudimbe's theoretical books, *L'Autre Face du royaume* and *L'Odeur du Père,* and his novels, *Entre les eaux* and *L'Écart,* engage as their subject the enabling as well as the regressive elements in Western discourse, thereby liberating spaces in Africa from which more empowered discourses can be uttered. In this essay, I will show how Mudimbe follows Michel Foucault's definition of the rules that subjugate discourse and then apply a Foucauldian critique to negritude in order to reveal the presence of the Western *ratio* in the first African literary movement; next I will show that Mudimbe's transformation of Foucault's thought is a necessary step in the creation of African essentialisms that in turn become targets for criticism.

Foucault's archaeological approach to discourse is doubly enabling: first, for thinking against the grain within the Western canon, and, second, for proposing alternative discursive formations outside the West. On the one hand, Mudimbe uses Foucault's method to unmask and unmake the Western *ratio* that dominates the human sciences and, under the guise of universalism, duplicates Western man in Africa. On the other hand, Mudimbe creates a postcolonial and postimperialist discourse that posits a new regime of truth and a new social appropriation of speech, thereby raising the question of individual subjugation in postcolonial discourse.

Out of Foucault's subversive uncovering of the rules that govern discourse in the West, Mudimbe unmasks the Western *ratio* in the African literary canon. But first, let's read Foucault through Mudimbe. In *L'Odeur du Père,* Mudimbe argues that, for Foucault, societies control discourse by first positing external rules. These include the construction of forbidden speech, a construction that bans certain words from certain statements; the designation of madness that opposes reason to insanity; and a regime of truth that determines the desire to know and practices a principle of discrimination based upon access to "education, books, publishing houses, and libraries, as well as the secret societies before and the libraries today."[1]

Next there comes an internal system for tying down discourse. This internal system is aimed at classifying, ordering, and distributing discursive materials so as to prevent the emergence of the contingent, of the other in all its nakedness. This internal system of discursive subjugation involves the concept of authorship, which serves to rarefy the quantity of statements that can be made; the construction of the organization of disciplines as a delimiting force; and a notion of commentary that organizes discursive statements according to temporal and spatial hierarchies.

The third system for mastering the movements of discourse that Mudimbe finds in Foucault consists of positing the conditions of possibility for putting discourse into play through the subjugation to rules of the individuals involved in discursive deployment. The object, however, is neither to neutralize the return of that which was repressed nor to conjure out the risk of it appearing in discursive practices, but to make sure that "no one will enter the discursive space unless certain prerequisites are satisfied and one is qualified to do so."[2]

It is this last system of control through discourse that serves to distribute and specialize the speakers. It involves four rules: (1) the discursive rituals that place constraints on the manner of delivering a discourse; (2–3) the discursive norms that, through their deployment in certain spaces, have the double function of linking the speakers to those spaces and of distributing them into specialized groups; and (4) the social appropriation of discourse that binds together discursive statements with such nondiscursive spaces as institutions, class interest, and political events.

For both Foucault and Mudimbe, societies put into play these discursive rules to repress the interruption of discontinuities, disorders, and the vengeful return of discourse as nonsense. At the same time, Foucault points out, the deployment of the rules coincides with the creation and the positioning of Western man, with all his positivity, at the center of discourse. Because Western man has been creating and re-creating his positivity through discourse, a problem concerning traps and reversibilities arises whenever an African theorist uses the dominant canon to represent African realities. Paradoxically, then, African theorists who assume a violence toward the West run the risk of unwittingly reasserting the superiority of the Western notion of rationality if they lose themselves in a discourse derived from Western ethnocentric canons. As Foucault puts it, "There is a certain position of the Western *ratio* that was constituted in its history and provides a foundation for the relation it can have with all other societies."[3]

Mudimbe's reading of the Foucauldian criticism of the discursive rules reveals both the position of the Western subject and the condition of possibility for its removal from the center of African discourse. The founders of negritude, for example, while aware of the duplication of French canons in their poetic statements, did not question the dangers of reproducing a French *ratio* in Africa that repressed the logical epistemologies as its other (i.e., "nos ancêtres les Gaulois").

The word *négritude* was coined by Aimé Césaire in the 1930s to conceptualize a black literary movement in Paris that was committed to freeing blackness from the pathological and evil space reserved for it in Judeo-Christian discourse. The negritude poets such as Léopold Sédar Senghor, Aimé Césaire, David Diop, and Léon-G. Damas wanted to restore to the word "black" a "true" meaning and a sense of "dignity" that would correspond to the lived experiences, cultures, and civilizations of black people throughout the world. For Senghor there is an objective and subjective level to negritude: on the one hand, it stands for an inventory of the sum total of black civilizations; and, on the other, it describes the way in which people of the African dispersion articulate their blackness in their contact with the material and spiritual worlds. The negritude writers believed in a complementary relation between civilizations and saw as their task the definition of black values that were necessary for the creolization (Senghor's word) of the world.[4] Negritude was a literature of emancipation that addressed itself to the oppressor in the language of the Parisian elite.

Negritude was invariably an exotic literature. It was exotic both because it was written by Africans and Caribbeans who came from different places and because the movement was inscribed in a tradition of exoticism that runs from Charles Baudelaire's West Indian poems, to Victor Ségalen's *Les immémoriaux,* and to Arthur Rimbaud's identification with blackness in "Mauvais Sang." However, the exoticism of the negritude writers differs from that of the French symbolists, who appropriated the distant object and described it in a familiar language. With poets such as Senghor, we face a reverse exoticism: the "barbarian" assumes the position of the writer and defamiliarizes the French language for French readers. Thus the newness of the writings: the negritude poems are "authentic" and "unmediated" because they represent the primitive's own subjectivity. On the ideological level, the negritude writers' participation in the tradition of exotic literature only complicates further the definition of the movement.

Negritude vacillated between black nationalism, which found its expression in French theories considering Marxism as methodology for action, and the need to assimilate the black world to the universal (i.e., French) culture. In short, the negritude poets, even as they sang about the "total sum of black values" and denounced European ethnocentrism, were reasserting the superiority of the West over Africa. As Mudimbe puts it, negritude was "a product of a historical moment proper to Europe, more particularly to the French thought which marked it."[5]

Perhaps this is best seen by the way in which Léopold Sédar Senghor, in a 1945 text that is formative for the ideas in negritude, addressed the manner in which the African canon may be constituted out of the study of French letters. For Senghor, just as such French writers as Racine shaped French language and styles out of their mastery of Greek fables and techniques of representation, Africans, too, must "discover their Blackness and a style to express it through the study of French letters."[6] For Senghor, the knowledge of Africa must pass through a knowledge of France recorded in literature. A mastery of "the most humane authors such as Corneille, Racine, Molière, and Hugo" imparts universal values like honesty to the African student and provides him with a language and a style to express them. The French writers are not only the masters with which to think: they are also the masters of language and style. Senghor recommended them for an essential French quality, a French way of doing things that he was later known to call *la francité:* the "clarity, order, harmony of ideas" that the African needs in order to describe his feelings and the world around him.[7] Senghor defended the principle of *la francité* as recently as 1985 against Captain Thomas Sankara, who staged a coup d'état and changed the name of Haute-Volta to Burkina Faso. Senghor saw some originality in the name change itself but was offended by the official adoption of "Burkinabe" instead of "Burkinais" or "Burkinois" as a way of referring to the people of Burkina Faso, for the latter would have "obeyed the rules of French grammar." Senghor concludes that, in this day and age, "on aura tout vu," but the refusal "to render adjectives and subjectives in French [*franciser*] shows an inferiority complex."[8]

To create the "African humanities," Senghor desired the assimilation of French classics to be accompanied by a teaching of ethnology that would make Africa known to Africans. The works of such European ethnologists as Leo Frobenius and Maurice Delafosse were necessary in the classroom "because they are our ancestors who saved us from despair by revealing our rich tradition to us."[9] Thus, ethnologists showed the world, too, that Africans, too, had an art, a philosophy, and a history. With the tools and the disciplines thus imported from Europe, Africans could begin a new humanities with an African style, which Senghor defines "not so much as a technique, but a state of mind which takes its nourishment from the deep sources of the Black soul; it is found in the traditional qualities, i.e., the warmth, the tension, and the rhythm."[10] For Senghor, the black is, before everything else, a lyrical person with a strong sense of verbal imagery, rhythm, and the musicality of words. Finally, following Frobenius's opposition between the Hamite and the Ethiopian, Senghor posited Africa as the primitive contemporary of Europe and argued that the former could help the latter to rediscover ancient values that had been deformed by the loss of natural feelings since the industrial revolution.[11]

Note that Senghor's defense of assimilation rests on a view of the world centered around France. This is understandable given that he wished to transcend what he called the "false antinomy" between the terms of assimilation and association. According to Senghor, the concept of assimilation has always been embodied within French civilization. Moreover, it is a Cartesianism that transcends human passions in order to emphasize reasoning as the glue that unites all men, regardless of their skin color. "French universalism speaks of Man, not men." When this Cartesian notion is applied to politics and colonialism, it results in the "Declaration of Human Rights," the creation of La Société des Amis des Noirs, the abolition of slavery, and the assimilation of Africans into the universal French civilization.[12]

For Senghor, the concept of assimilation that requires Africans to espouse the

French language as the universal does not contradict the concept of association that implies a relationship between two autonomous states. The doctrine of association seeks to undo hierarchies and to create the possibility for cultures and nations, diverse in origins, customs, religion, and race, to work together. It was a concept used by the opponents of assimilation during the period of the French Imperial Community, and it is used today by those in the Organization of Francophone Countries to denounce France's cultural imperialism within the organization.

Senghor defends himself against the proponents of association by drawing an evolutionist scheme that has equality as its goal. To become uncolonizable, Africans must first assimilate that which would enable them to be as educated as their colonizers. By posing the problem in this manner, Senghor wishes to show that the proponents of association, in their radical demand for equality between Africans and French, are against much needed education in Africa.[13] In place of the concept of association, Senghor prefers terms like "universalism," "creolization," "symbiosis," "grafting" — all of which posit France in the center and Africa on the margins.[14]

Let's now read this Senghorian statement through Mudimbe (and Foucault). To apply a Mudimbean reading to these Senghorian passages is not to deny the merit of negritude, which participated in the modernist movement of the 1930s and 1940s and helped to undermine the dogmatic claims of the canons of Western civilization. In short, the goal of this approach is not to criticize assimilation as a bad object, but to show that assimilation is an unattainable goal because of the barriers inherent in the French discourse between the West and Africa. Following Mudimbe, one reads Senghor in order to reveal the structures that create ambiguity and contradictions in the discourse and to posit the conditions of possibility necessary for getting rid of those structures. Thus, Senghor's intention to create the "African humanities" through assimilation is debunked by the emergence of a French *ratio* at the center of the text that forces Senghor to construct the African as the European's other.

Given that Senghor's only audience at that time was in France, it can be argued that he had no choice but to speak in an appropriated discourse that could recognize the African only as other. Even his categories of the black as warm, rhythmic, musical, and emotional come from a well-established source in French literature, extant since the Enlightenment and rethematized in the nineteenth century by the arch-racist Joseph-Arthur de Gobineau. As Christopher Miller has shown, Gobineau and other writers stripped the black of reasoning faculties and depicted him as one who is moved only by a blind sensorial desire. Gobineau's *Essai sur l'inégalité des races humaines*

> is at the origin of a notion that gained wide acceptance: that Blacks are endowed with a greater "imagination" than whites and are thus the source of the arts. From the *Essai* through Guillaume Apollinaire's theories on "fetish-art" to Sartre's "Orphée noir," this assumption continually endows the Black with a type of thinking that simultaneously robs him of the ability to think as a fully reflexive intellect. The *Essai* often reads as a caricature of other, subtler texts.[15]

The negritude of Senghor, because it was only addressed to French People, and because it was removed from Africa, constituted a black that never existed except as the other in the unconscious of the French. Nevertheless, it was an other that was presented as real, human, and beautiful. But the result of such a discourse is not only the impossibility of beautifying the other — that is, of making it exotic and French — but also the impossibility of speaking of Africa without reasserting the superiority of the West over it. To paraphrase Mudimbe, this discourse has internal constraints, so that even if Senghor's discussion of African beauty leads one to believe that he is against Western ethnocentrism, he nonetheless maintains the binary oppositions that separate European and African, civilized and primitive, rational and emotional, religious and idolatrous.

This brings us to my initial epigraph — namely, that the only difference between prince Aniaba and Louis XIV is one of skin color. Senghor's assimilationist discourse, far from making the African the European's equal, and therefore uncolonizable, participates in a universalist concept of man that posits Western man as the model and the African as its aberration. Africa, according to the Senghorism described above, is the primitive contemporary of the West; and as such, it can help Europe to rediscover its lost traditional values. According to a Mudimbean reading, however, this overstatement of universalism at the expense of difference leaves unstated a construction of Africa that sees it as "the infancy of humanity which, when studied carefully, reveals certain traumas repressed in Western societies."[16]

A Mudimbean/Foucauldian analysis of discourse also reveals the way in which negritude duplicates themes and motives that are always already appropriated by social conditions in the West. As Mudimbe puts it, "Western discourse defines its space and takes its order from a specific socio-economic and cultural structure. It can address other societies only in reference to itself, and never to specific systems that cannot be reduced to it."[17] Senghor, in an attempt to find African equivalents for European art and to valorize African culture in order to bring the West to respect it, has forced a reading upon Africa that aestheticizes and deforms it by making it conform to the gaze of the West. That negritude, in the name of a French universalism, unleashes on the surface of Africa Europe's regime of truth (*la volonté de vérité*), its notions of authorship, and its disciplines. Negritude, for Mudimbe, "simply and faithfully takes categories, concepts, schemas and systems from the West, and runs them into African entities."[18]

Following this Mudimbean/Foucauldian reading of some of the original claims of negritude, let us now turn to the other aspect of Mudimbe's work that transforms Foucault's thought. As I have shown, Mudimbe's critique of negritude is intended to name the paradoxical presence of the Western *ratio* in it, so that it can be removed, circumvented, or surpassed by a more liberated discourse. It is here that Mudimbe stands Foucault on his head.

Foucault is well known for his criticism of the use of discourse merely to indicate a structure of language put into play in order to produce meaning. For him, discourse is not simply there to mediate between thought and speech or to legitimize original experiences through the constitution of subjects. Foucault calls for the resurgence of discourse without signification; for a world of discontinuity between the speaking subject and the discourse he or she produces; for a pure discourse criticism divorced from the type of sentence criticism that is enthralled by the analysis of latent meaning and propositional statements. He draws our attention to the exteriority of discourse by delineating the condition of possibility for its materiality.[19]

To obtain this pure discursive analysis, Foucault proposes to remove from discourse the regime of truth and to return to discourse its aleatory and subversive elements. In this effort, he debunks classical notions of creativity, unity, originality, and signification in discursive analysis, and he emphasizes in their stead the notion of reversibility that reveals the negative side of subjugating discourse; the notion of discontinuity, which posits discursive statements as discontinuous practices that intersect each other, address each other, or exclude each other; and the notion of specificity, which conceives of discourse as a violence practiced upon other bodies. It is in these practices that contingencies and chance assume their regular recurrence and the notion of materiality comes to define the exterior "body" of discourse and its condition of possibility.[20]

If we suppose that Foucault is to Mudimbe what the French anthropologists were to Senghor — in the sense that the Africans have been empowered by the Europeans to carry on a discourse about themselves — the next question raised by Mudimbe's *L'Odeur du Père* is how to get rid of the father's abusive smell. For Mudimbe, "really to escape the supremacy of Western thought presupposes an exact appreciation of what it means to rid ourselves of it. It presupposes a knowledge of how far the West, perhaps cunningly, has re-created itself in us. It presupposes also a knowledge of the Western in what has enabled us to denounce the West."[21]

The West cannot talk about Africa outside the Western text, just as Africans cannot form canons with texts that reflect European sociocultural conditions. I have tried to show in this essay how Foucault's work influenced Mudimbe's critique of discursive formations in Africa. Moreover, when conceived in another manner, it is possible to argue that Mudimbe contradicts the French thinker; Foucault's thought properly belongs to a specific region in Western discourse that gives it its condition of possibility as a necessarily counterhegemonic statement. In short, the Foucauldian system, too, under whatever ideological and methodological metamorphoses it appears, belongs to the history of Western culture. Even Foucault's call for a pure discourse criticism, for a discourse unconstrained by social appropriations, leaves unsaid the repression of non-Westerners by Western discourse. Additionally, I would like to suggest that what is feared most in the West is not the emergence of the discourses of Foucault, Marx, Freud, or Nietzsche, which are always already appropriated; what is feared is the emergence of (an)other discourse, one that excludes the Western *ratio*. This means the breakdown of hierarchies between the West and the other; the end of conquest and the removal of the self from the other's space; the breakdown of the security and comfort to which one was accustomed when one was able to predict the other's actions in one's discourse. In essence, the West fears the fear of the unknown. Accordingly, Foucault's call for the removal of the subject and the return of pure discourse criticism posits the condition of possibility for the deployment of a new Western *ratio* and the repression of other subjectivities. The pure discourse criticism, which is part of a particular culture, enables non-Westerners to denounce the domineering presence of the West in their texts but paradoxically does not allow them to move forward and create a discourse outside of the Foucauldian system.

Mudimbe, in contrast, calls for a reformation of discourse in Africa. He argues that we Africans must invest in the sciences, beginning with the human and social sciences. We must reanalyze the claims of these sciences for our own benefit, evaluate the risks they contain, and their discursive spaces. We must reanalyze for our benefit the contingent supports and the areas of enunciation in order to know what new meaning and what road to propose for our quest so that our discourse can justify us as singular beings engaged in a history that is itself special.[22]

For Mudimbe, Africans must rid themselves of the smell of an abusive father, of the presence of an order that belongs to a particular culture but that defines itself as a fundamental part of all discourse. In order to produce differently, they must practice a major discursive insurrection against the West.

For Mudimbe, the most radical break with the West can be obtained only through a linguistic revolution in which European languages are replaced by African languages. Just as the originators of Greek thought set into motion a reorganization of knowledge and life through their transformation of ancient Egypt's use of science and methodologies, the West dominates the rest of the world today because it has appropriated Greek thought in its languages. In like fashion, for Mudimbe, at least a "change in the linguistic apparatus of science and production would provoke an epistemological break and open the door for new scientific adventures in Africa."[23]

Mudimbe further argues that the other insurrection against the abusive father is practiced through the excommunication of Western *ratio* from African discursive practices that take place in European languages. In other words, Mudimbe calls for a reformulation of disciplines inherited from the West and a subtle discursive technique aimed at deconstructing Western control over the rules that govern scientific statements. While working within Western languages, the new practice nevertheless departs from the traditional duplications of the Western canon in Africa and moves toward the construction of an African regime of truth and socially appropriated sciences. The new and cannibalizing discourse swells, disfigures, and transforms the bodies of Western texts[24] and establishes its order outside traditional binary oppositions such as primitive/civilized, (neo)colonized/colonizer, slave/master, receiver/donor. This uncovers the centrality of Althusserian notions of ideology in Mudimbe's work, which are beyond the scope of the present essay.

I will now turn to the novel *L'Écart* in order to show Mudimbe's discursive practice of unmaking the Western *ratio* and of building the African regime of truth. *L'Écart* is about Ahmed Nara, an African student in Paris working on a history dissertation on the Kouba people. Nara meets two Africans, Salim and Aminata, who are archivists at the Bibliothèque Nationale. Aminata and Nara become lovers. Other important characters in the story are Soum, an internationalist Marxist; Isabelle, Nara's French girlfriend; and Dr. Sano, a psychoanalyst.

The novel takes as its subject the questions of existence, history, and ideology. Its narrative strategy consists of describing African images in French discourse as a projective construction in order to reveal the modes of existence of the "real" contours of Africa. Nara finds his individual freedom trapped by Sartre's influential designations of negritude in "Orphée noir," the famous introduction to Senghor's *Anthologie de la nouvelle poésie nègre et malgache de langue française* (1948). As Mudimbe argues in *L'Odeur du Père,* Sartre's intent to theorize negritude for negritude's sake was defeated by a master text: that is, that of existentialist Marxism. Sartre blots out the irreducible part of the negritude movement, manipulates its operational system, and constructs the black man as an androgynous character — that ambiguous figure already common in Western literature. For Mudimbe, Sartre "modified, in fact, the ascension of the first manifestations [in negritude], fixed the ways of interpreting the writings, named the rules and the modulations of the action, articulated, at last, the claims of the Black race, and proposed a Universalist strategy [identification with the proletariat] for its struggle."[25] "Orphée noir" has influenced in a fundamental manner not only the criticism of negritude but also the creative writing that followed it.

In *L'Écart,* Nara tries to undo Sartre's re-creation of androgyny in Africa and the limitation of his freedom as constrained by the Sartrean construction of the personae of negritude. Nara realizes that, for Isabelle, his French girlfriend, he is one-half of the androgynous figure (i.e., the animal) while she herself is the other half (i.e., the human). Their sexual encounter is therefore symbolic of the encounter between Africa and Europe, between the primitive and the civilized. As Nara puts it, "I was a phallus...could only be that...and the gasps that I was to hear, these cries that I want never to have heard were supposed to come from the junction of two reigns, the human and the animal."[26] Nara and Isabelle are incapable of reaching true love because of the barrier that Western literature constructs between the "emotional African" and the "rational European" — concepts that are thematized in Senghorian negritude and made to trap the lovers' freedom in their text. According to Nara, Isabelle sees him in every erotic poem she reads and tells him, "You are my totem," to which he answers, "I am not an animal."[27]

In the novel, Mudimbe also illustrates the manner in which universalist Marxism debunks the freedom of Africans by assimilating their struggle into that of the proletariat. Mudimbe, in *Entre les eaux* (1973), a novel that was awarded the Grand Prix Catholique Littéraire, had already exposed the violence inflicted by Catholicism and classical Marxism on African spaces, which were outside the societies and class relations that produce these systems of thought. Likewise in *L'Écart,* Soum, the socialist-realist friend of Nara, believes that "to be a black, that is nothing exceptional in itself. To be a proletarian, yes."[28] Blotting out the differences of culture and history and emphasizing class alone, Soum states that history begins the moment Africa joins the proletarians in the fight against the Euro-American capitalists and their puppets. Soum points out to Nara that to celebrate his African heritage is to indulge in false consciousness: "For thirty years [since independence] they have tried to divert us. They sing the richness and the complexity of our culture.... What a farce! When you think about the fact that the majority of our people do not have one full meal a day."[29]

Nara, however, is not satisfied with Soum's deterministic positivism and tabula rasa approach to African culture and history. He thinks to himself, "How could our people live all their desires if they could not have, in addition to the architects and the engineers, culturally impassioned people who could, if need be, look for and find the secret keepers of our traditions?"[30] Elsewhere he states, "How am I to tell Soum? When I tried to communicate my doubts to him on the universality of his practice, he quoted Marx to me: The relations of production form a whole; that does not imply at all that history is a totality, but that there are totalities in it."[31]

As a student of history, Nara is not convinced by Soum's "scientific" method, which pushes aside as insignificant the ambiguities, the contradictions, and the challenges that African societies present to Western discourse. Nara argues against the anthropologists and historians who project images of their own desires onto the surface of Africa and posits as an imperative for himself the need to be more sensitive to the specificity of local knowledge. For him, the question of archives is not limited only to "the particular expressions actualized by the brief history of Europe."[32] The new historian must also question the oral traditions, reformulate the symbols in local cultures, and avoid easy conclusions about rituals. Nara, who spends most of his time ruminating about the mode of existence of a discourse not held hostage by a Western regime of truth, states:

> It is Aminata, boiling with cold anger, who gave me last year a good lesson: "Watch the dead, some things can make them move in the grave." No other image could have been stronger for me. She forced me to be cautious, and I stopped entertaining Salim about the primitive aspects of Nyimi funerals. I found the itinerary of silence and sympathy. The contact with tradition and its rigorous practice subjected me to its norms, and *my speech bent faithfully before it.*[33]

Defining history from the perspective of oral tradition, Nara compares it to memory, to a thought understanding itself at the root of its own consciousness. He says, "Science was, in my mind, a memory. I could dig it up, read it in my own way; if need be, find it in error and discard it."[34] Clearly what Nara is doing at the Bibliothèque Nationale is appropriating the archives and constructing his own regime of truth. For him, the anthropologists have either dismissed the rigid norms of African tradition as primitive or aestheticized them beyond their sociocultural limits. He therefore calls for a critical practice that will reveal the meaning of people's lives to themselves instead of using them to form a metadiscourse on the West.

So far I have shown that Nara in *L'Écart,* like Mudimbe in his books of criticism, creates a distance between himself and Western master texts by moving toward the construction of a discourse that can be socially and culturally appropriated by Africans. The comparison of the fiction to Mudimbe's theoretical works also helps us to understand *L'Écart* within the social context that gave it theme and structure. When dealing with an elusive character such as Nara, an easy way out, inherited from traditional Western criticism of the novel, would be to label him as insane. I will call to the reader's attention here Foucault's criticism of the division of insanity, discussed above, as a means of controlling discursive deployments. The blurb on the back of *L'Écart,* for example, describes Nara in the following terms: "Mudimbe is most certainly interested in a character who is a neurotic; he lives on the margins [*il vit l'écart*] of society. He is schizophrenic and it is killing him." Certainly the story of *L'Écart* can be twisted to fit the classic case of a character who is mad. As a child, Nara was locked up in a rat-infested cellar overnight. The following morning he was told of his father's death. When Nara is a student in Europe, his fear of rats and the dark becomes obsessive. And in Paris, Nara's women play simultaneously the ambivalent roles of lover and mother. It is convenient for a critic of thematology — the Geneva school of criticism for example — to find here a network of obsessive objects that are linked to a primal repression.

But such an interpretation only represses the revolutionary aspects of the text. Nara's power consists of being able to construct his text on the outer limits of Western discourse. He slips out of Soum's deterministic construct of history, Isabelle's image of the African as a totem, and the use of an Oedipus *universalis* to explain his desires. To put it in his own words, "I slipped out of bed, oozed out of the embrasure of the door, and took the first train to leave behind, forever, the torment of being loved."[35]

Nara's reformulation of discourse on Africa, like any form of essentialism, raises questions of discursive subjugation that Mudimbe addresses in *L'Odeur du Père*. As we have seen, however, Mudimbe's criticism of essentialism and identity does not mean a rejection of the concepts. It is necessary for Africans, too, to construct temporary totalities and to be allowed to raise questions of individual freedom within these totalities. For example, such categories as African history and African literature, by assuming the cultural unity of Africans, leave unstated the diversity of traditions and, since the era of independence, the emerging nationalist discourse of the authors. Since the 1960s, works of art and the lives of people have become reorganized according to new needs. They respond no longer to the need to struggle for independence or to the horrors committed by the white man. For Mudimbe, nowadays, "there is a diversification of themes, and, like all literatures, African literature, too, tends to occupy new spaces of enunciation. Each text is thus particularized according to the ideological and the literary inclination of its author. To a certain degree, the author's nationality also counts."[36]

The social context that provides the writer with the elements of his or her text is no longer the same from country to country; "the father to kill or to celebrate, when such is the case, is no longer the same from Senegal to the Congo."[37]

The unanimist tendency that one sees in Nara and also in Mudimbe, although necessary, can therefore be posited only momentarily. It is necessary and convenient for signifying Europe's discursive violence against Africa and the need for Africans to call for a discourse that can represent their history, their lives, and their literature. But once Africans stand up and speak, a new discursive violence takes place, and this has to be constantly challenged.

In summary, I have tried to show Mudimbe's original contribution to African and contemporary discourse. His texts address the condition for the existence of literary canons in Africa and the issues of epistemological breaks both with the West and with traditional Africa. Mudimbe also raises questions concerning identity and difference in postcolonial discourse, and he thus reformulates the Foucauldian definition of discourse and transforms negritude.

NOTES

1. V. Y. Mudimbe, *L'Odeur du Père: Essai sur des limites de la science et de la vie en Afrique noire* (Paris: Présence Africaine, 1982), 39. This and subsequent translations are my own, unless otherwise specified.

2. Ibid., 40.

3. Michel Foucault, *The Order of Things* (New York: Vintage Books, 1973), 377.

4. See Léopold Sédar Senghor, *Liberté,* vol. 1, *Négritude et humanisme* (Paris: Éditions du Seuil, 1964), 7.

5. V. Y. Mudimbe, *L'Autre Face du royaume: Une introduction à la critique des langages en*

folie (Lausanne: L'Age d'Homme, 1973), 101. Mudimbe argues that, ironically, the relativist discourse of European anthropologists such as Leo Frobenius gave fuel to the negritude poets to sing about the beauty of blackness. See my essay, "The Other('s) Archivist," *Diacritics* 18 (spring 1988).

6. Léopold Sédar Senghor, "Vues sur l'Afrique noire, ou assimiler, non être assimilés," in *La Communauté impériale française,* ed. Robert Lemaignen et al. (Paris: Éditions Alsatia, 1945), 95.

7. Ibid., 93.

8. Senghor, "Négritude et Vaugelas," in *Le Monde,* August 18–19, 1985.

9. Cited in Mudimbe, *L'Odeur du Père,* 36.

10. Senghor, "Vues sur l'Afrique," 92.

11. Ibid., 98.

12. Ibid., 57–65.

13. Ibid., 63–74.

14. See also Léopold Sédar Senghor, "Pierre Teilhard de Chardin et la politique africaine," *Cahiers Pierre Teilhard de Chardin* 3 (1962).

15. Christopher Miller, *Blank Darkness: Africanist Discourse in French* (Chicago: University of Chicago Press, 1985), 88.

16. Mudimbe, *L'Autre Face du royaume,* 81.

17. Mudimbe, *L'Odeur du Père,* 44.

18. Ibid., 43.

19. See Diawara, "The Other('s) Archivist."

20. Mudimbe, *L'Odeur du Père,* 42.

21. Ibid., 44.

22. Ibid., 35.

23. Ibid., 47.

24. For more on the reorganization of Western texts by discourse in Africa, see Christopher Miller, "Trait d'union: Injunction and Dismemberment in Yambo Ouologuem's *Le Devoir de violence,*" *L'esprit créateur* 23 (winter 1983): 62–73.

25. Mudimbe, *L'Odeur du Père,* 139.

26. V. Y. Mudimbe, *L'Écart* (Paris: Présence Africaine, 1982), 34.

27. Ibid., 170.

28. Ibid., 45.

29. Ibid., 44.

30. Ibid., 45.

31. Ibid., 149–50.

32. Ibid., 67.

33. Ibid., 28.

34. Ibid., 68.

35. Ibid., 30.

36. Mudimbe, *L'Odeur du Père,* 143.

37. Ibid.

Chapter 26
Teaching for the Times
Gayatri Chakravorty Spivak

This essay was originally written for the annual convention of the Midwestern Modern Language Association in the United States. I have not removed the signs that show that I am speaking to fellow teachers; in other words, it is a practical piece. I have also kept its local flavor. I think these signs and marks can be of some interest to readers from various parts of the world, if only because their presence might then produce some effort to work out how, in readers' own contexts, the teaching of literature can be transnational.[1]

The word "transnational" now bears the weight of the untrammeled financialization of the globe in the recent post-Soviet years. I will not offer a detailed discussion of this abundantly discussed phenomenon here, except to remark that, in this dispensation, the integrity of particular states has become much more fluid, especially in the South, and especially since capitalism is being reterritorialized as "democracy." It seems obvious that the always precarious hyphen between nation and state is now rather more so; and that this hyphen is being inhabited by multifarious mobilizers of identity politics. It is within this broad context that the words were first uttered; the exhortation was for new immigrant American college and university teachers of English to locate themselves in it: and that effortful location was called transnational literacy.[2] It would, I think, be less useful to read "transnational" only by the rules of an older lexicon, where it stands for a globality in conflict with the nation-state, although that lexicon is by no means obsolete.

It should also be kept in mind that we are speaking here of college and university teaching of English, not of subaltern projects of literacy or pedagogy of the oppressed. In an effort to understand how diversified yet related transnational teaching must be, I have attempted to travel the course, starting from rural or specifically aboriginal literacy under different national circumstances, all the way to international conferences — again under various national determinations, with situations of national(ized) education systems somewhere in the middle. If it has taught me anything, it is that nothing applies everywhere. I speak of the invention of unity for the new immigrant teacher in the body of the piece. That is a strategic unity. I do not believe we can have any more globalized a vision within the boundaries of the varieties of academic practice.

When I wrote the piece, we in the United States were still caught between "liberal multiculturalism," on the one hand, and white cultural supremacy — the anti–"politically correct" (pc) — on the other.[3] If the reader wishes to tease out a presupposition from the following pages, here is one: at a certain limit, the two sides of the debate feed each other. The lines have now become somewhat blurred in this fast-moving arena. "Contingency" has invaded "unity"-talk on the other side: "Our task is to combine due appreciation of the splendid diversity of the nation with due emphasis on the great unifying Western ideas of individual freedom, political democracy, and human rights" (Arthur M. Schlesinger Jr., 1992).[4] "Recognition both of the complexity and the contingency of the human condition thus underlines the *political* need for shared moral consensus in the increasingly congested and intimate world of the twenty-first century" (Zbigniew Brzezinski, 1993).[5] One is writing with rousing confidence in the American dream, the other with alarm about the world. Now more than ever it seems right for good teaching to turn from emphasis upon our contingent histories to the invention of a shared and dynamic present — as the continuous unrolling of an ungraspable event with consequences that might as well be called "global" in its minute detail.[6]

Another item about the effort to teach multicultural English in the United States might be of interest here. Among many of the participants in that effort, teachers and students, there is talk of something called postcolonial*ism*. These pages may be seen as an elaboration of a response to that trend: given the role of the United States in what has been called "recolonization," if there is to be a U.S. postcolonial*ism,* it can only be a transnational literacy; for postcolonial*ity* is a failure of decolonization. Is decolonization possible? In the broadest possible sense, once and for all, no; but this is what it shares with everything else.[7] Yet, given the situation of the self-representation of multicultural teaching of literature in the United States, it seems more canny to stop (or start) with prospects for decolonization, presumably a condition before *post*coloniality (or ism) can be declared. As far as I can tell, and for all practical purposes, a general condition of postcoloniality is a future anterior, something that will have happened, if one concerned oneself with the persistent crafty details of the calculus of decolonization, in the sphere in which one is contractually engaged, not excluding tacit affective contracts, of course.

Since its inception, the United States has been a nation of immigrants. The winners among the first set of European immigrants claimed, often with violence, that the land belonged to them, because the industrial revolution was in their pocket. And the story of its origin has been re-presented as an escape from old feudalism, in a general de Tocquevillian way. It is well known that in the founders' Constitution, African slaves and the Original Nations were inscribed as property in order to get around the problem of the representation of slaves as wealth: "The key slogan in the struggle against the British had been 'no taxation without representation. . . .' The acceptance that slaves as wealth should entitle Southern voters to extra representation built an acknowledgement of slavery into the heart of the Constitution."[8]

Here we have extreme cases of marginalization where the term itself gives way: dehumanization, transportation, genocide. I will not begin in that scene of violence at the origin, but rather with the phenomenon that has gradually kicked us — marginal voices — from opposition to the perceived dominant in the U.S. cultural space: new immigration in the new world order.

Let us rewrite "cultural identity" as "national-origin validation." Let us not use "cultural identity" as a permission to difference and an instrument for disavowing that Eurocentric economic migration (and eventually even political exile) persists in the hope of justice under capitalism. That unacknowledged and scandalous secret is the basis of our unity. Let us reinvent this basis as a springboard for a teaching that counterpoints these times. This is what unites the "illegal alien" and the aspiring academic. I am arguing that this is all the more important because "we" — that vague, menaced, and growing body of the teachers of culture and literature who question the canon — are not *oppositional* any more. We are being actively opposed because what used to be the dominant literary-cultural voice — the male-dominated, white, Eurocentric voice — obviously feels its shaping and molding authority slipping away. We seem to be perceived as the emerging dominant. What is the role and task of the emerging dominant teacher? Since one of the major functions of professional organizations in the United States is to facilitate employment, let us also consider the problems of educating the educators of the emerging dominant field: in other words, let us consider both the undergraduate and the graduate curriculum.

Access to the Universal/National-Origin Validation on the Undergraduate Curriculum

In a powerful paper entitled "The Campaign against Political Correctness: What's Really at Stake?" Joan Wallach Scott lays bare the shoddy techniques of what was the opposition at the beginning of the 1980s:

> Serious intellectuals have only to read the self-assured, hopelessly ill-informed, and simply wrong descriptions of deconstruction, psychoanalysis, feminism, or any other serious theory by the likes of D'Souza, Richard Bernstein, David Lehman, Roger Kimball, Hilton Kramer, George Will — and even Camille Paglia — to understand the scam.... [T]heir anger at the very scholars they long to emulate...seems to have worked in some quarters. That is partly because the publicists have assumed another persona beside that of the intellectual: they pretend to represent the common man — whom, as elitists, they also loathe.[9]

This brilliant and shrewd paper focuses on the contemporary American scene. And as such its writer shows that the opposition is desperately claiming a "universality" that, in my view, has already slipped out of their grasp. She quotes S. P. Mohanty who "calls for an alternative to pluralism that would make difference and conflict the center of a history 'we' all share." She quotes Christopher Fynsk as offering "the French word *partage,* [meaning]...both to divide and to share," as an informing metaphor of community. I will keep these suggestions in mind in this first section, most specifically confined to the undergraduate curriculum in the United States.

Emergence into an at best precarious dominant does not for a moment mean that our battle for national-origin validation in the United States is over. First, we as new immigrants must rethink the battle lines. Since the "national origins" of new immigrants, as fantasized by themselves, have not, so far, contributed to the unacknowledged and remoter historical culture of the United States, what we are demanding is that the United States recognize *our* rainbow as part of its history of the present. Since most of our countries were not *territorially* colonized by the United States, this is a transaction that relates to our status as new Americans, not primarily to the countries of our origin. (In this respect our struggle is similar to as well as different from that of the new European immigrants.) Second, we must realize that, in the post-Soviet, post-Fordist world, we as a specific part of the collective of marginals are currently fighting from a different position. We face the need to consolidate ourselves in new ways, which I have tried to indicate in my opening words. Being reactive to the dominant is no longer the only issue. I agree with Scott's and Mohanty's and Fynsk's general point: conflict, relationality, dividing, and sharing. In the American context these are good marching orders. But difference and conflict are hard imperatives. Difference becomes competition, for we live and participate — even as dissidents — within institutions anchored in a transnational capitalist economy. Our "limited physical supply of what is at stake makes it easy to overlook the fact that the functioning of the economic game itself presupposes adherence to the game and *belief in the value of its stakes.*"[10]

The stakes in question are not just institutional but generally social. Eurocentric economic migration as a critical mass is based on hope for justice under capitalism. The task of the teacher is as crucial as it is chancy, for there is no guarantee that to know it is to be able to act on it (especially since our self-representation as marginal in the United States might involve a disavowed dominant status with respect to our countries of national origin). To continue with the quotation above:

> [H]ow is it possible to produce that minimal investment which is the condition
> of economic production without resorting to competition and without reproducing
> individuation? As long as the logic of social games is not explicitly recognized (and
> even if it is . . .), even the apparently freest and most creative of actions is never more
> than an encounter between reified and embodied history, . . . a necessity which the
> agent *constitutes* as such and for which [s]he provides the scene of action without
> actually being its subject.

"Reified history" is in this case our monumentalized national-cultural history of origin combined with ideas of a miraculated resistant hybridity; "embodied history" our disavowed articulation within the history of the present of our chosen new nation-state.[11] This "encounter" does not translate to the scene of violence at the origin — slavery and genocide, black and red — that I laid aside at the opening of my essay.

In the U.S. classroom I spend some time on Pierre Bourdieu's caution: "and even if it is [recognized] . . ." I draw it out into the difference between knowing and learning. Without falling into too strict an adherence to the iron distinction between the constative and the performative, I still have to hang on to a working difference between knowing about something and learning to do something. The relationship between knowing and learning is crucial as we move from the space of opposition to the menaced space of the emerging dominant.

An anthology piece in an international collection will not allow the meditative tempo of the classroom. Let me therefore ignore Bourdieu's parenthesis and emphasize the point Bourdieu makes, keeping myself, for the moment, confined to our role within the academic institution. I will return to the more general social point of new-immigration-in-capitalism later.

As long as we are interested, and we *must* be interested, in hiring and firing, in grants, in allocations, in budgets, in funding new job descriptions, in *publishing* radical texts, in fighting for tenure and recommending for jobs, we are *in* capitalism, and we cannot avoid competition and individuation. Under these circumstances, essentializing difference, however sophisticated we might be at it, may lead to unproductive conflict among ourselves. If we are not merely the opposition any more, we must not lose the possibility of our swing into power by crumbling into interest groups in the name of difference. We must find some basis for unity. It is a travesty of philosophy, a turning of philosophy into a direct blueprint for policy making, to suggest that the search for a situational unity goes against the lesson of deconstruction. If we perceive our emergence into the dominant as a situation, we see the importance of inventing a unity that depends upon that situation. I am not a situational relativist. No situation is saturated. But imperatives arise out of situations, and, however unthinkingly, we act by imagining imperatives. We must therefore scrupulously imagine a situation in order to act. Pure difference cannot appear. Difference cannot provide an adequate theory of practice. "Left to itself, the incalculable and giving idea of justice [here as justice to difference] is always very close to the bad, even to the worst, for it can always be reappropriated by the most perverse calculation."[12]

In the interest of space I am collapsing a few philosophical moves needed to make this argument acceptable. I can only ask you to take it on trust that those moves can be made.[13] What is important for me, in order, later, to pass into the second part of my remarks, is simply the conviction: we, the new immigrant teachers of so-called oppositional discourses in the United States, must today find a practical basis for unity at this crucial moment.

Consider this good passage from Jonathan Culler, also quoted by Joan Scott:

> A particular virtue of literature, of history, of anthropology is instruction in otherness: vivid, compelling evidence of differences in cultures, mores, assumptions, values. At their best, these subjects make otherness palpable and make it comprehensible without reducing it to an inferior version of the same, as a universalizing humanism threatens to do.[14]

I repeat, good words, words with which we should certainly claim alliance. Yet, today in particular, we must also ask: Who speaks here? Who is the implied reader of this literature, the researcher of this history, the investigator of this anthropology? For whose benefit is this knowledge being produced, so that he or she can have *our* otherness made palpable and comprehensive, without reducing it into an inferior version of *their* same, through the choice of studying literature, history, and anthropology "at their best"? Shall we, today, be satisfied with the promise of liberal multiculturalism that these disciplines will remain "at their best," with a now-contrite universal humanism in the place of the same, and us being studied as examples of otherness? Or should we remind ourselves of Herbert Marcuse's wise words in the 1960s? I will speak of our difference from the 1960s in a while, but Marcuse's words are still resonant over against the promises of liberal multiculturalism: "Equality of tolerance becomes abstract, spurious. . . . The opposition is insulated in small and frequently insulated groups who, even when tolerated within the narrow limits set by the hierarchical structure of society, are powerless while they keep within these limits."[15]

This does not mean that we should be opposed to small victories: it is certainly important that some Third World literature job descriptions — "global" rather than "insular" English — now appear on the job lists issued by our national professional organization, the Modern Language Association of America. Yet it is possible that we will remain powerless collaborators in repressive tolerance if, in higher education in the humanities, we do not rethink our agency. Predictably, my agenda in the end will be the persistent and shifting pursuit of the global history of the present.

Other voices are asking questions similar to mine. I would cite here Aihwa Ong's piece "Colonialism and Modernity: Feminist Re-presentations of Women in Non-Western Society," which ends with these important words: "We begin a dialogue when we recognize other forms of gender- and culture-based subjectivities, and accept that others often choose to conduct their lives separate from our particular vision of the future."[16] To claim agency in the emerging dominant is to *recognize* agency in others, not simply to comprehend otherness.

A distorted version of this recognition is produced in liberal multiculturalism. Yet we have to claim some alliance with it, for on the other side, as the article by Joan Scott that I have already cited will make abundantly clear, are the white-supremacist critics of "political correctness," a major phenomenon on the U.S. scene. It is no secret that liberal multiculturalism is determined by the demands of contemporary transnational capitalisms. It is an important public relations move in the apparent winning of consent from developing countries in the dominant project of the financialization of the globe. (I am arguing that, having shifted our lives from those nations to this, we become part of the problem if we continue to disavow its responsibility.) Procter and Gamble, a large U.S. multinational corporation, sends students specializing in business administration abroad to learn language and culture. Already in 1990, the National Governors' Association report queried: "How are we to sell our product in a global economy when we are yet to learn the language of the customers?"[17] If we are to question this distorting rationale for multiculturalism while utilizing its material support, we have to recognize also that the virulent backlash from the current *racist* dominant in this country is out of step with contemporary geopolitics. *We* are caught in a larger struggle where one side devises newer ways to exploit transnationality through a distorting culturalism and the other knows rather little what transnational script drives, writes, and operates it. It is within this ignorant clash that we have to find and locate our agency and attempt, again and again, to unhinge the clashing machinery.

What actually happens in a typical liberal-multicultural classroom "at its best"? On a given day we are reading a text from one national origin. The group in the classroom from that particular national origin in the general polity can identify with the richness of the texture of the "culture" in question, often through a haze of nostalgia. (I am not even bringing up the question of the definition of culture.) People from other national origins in the classroom (other, that is, than Anglo) relate sympathetically but superficially, in an aura of same difference. The Anglo relates benevolently to everything, "knowing about other cultures" in a relativist glow.

What is the basis of the sympathy and the feeling of same difference among the various national origins in such a best-case scenario? Here the general social case writes our script. To pick up on my earlier argument, the basis for that feeling is that we have all come with the hope of finding justice or welfare within a capitalist society. (The place of women within this desire merits a separate discussion.)[18] We have come to avoid wars, to avoid political oppression, to escape from poverty, to find opportunity for ourselves and, more important, for our children: with the hope of finding justice within a capitalist society. Strictly speaking, we have left the problems of postcoloniality, located in the former colony (now a "developing nation" trying to survive the ravages of colonialism), *only* to discover that the white-supremacist culture wants to claim the entire agency of capitalism — recoded as the rule of law within a democratic heritage — *only* for itself; to find that the *only* entry is through a forgetfulness or a museumization of national origin in the interest of class mobility. In the liberal-multicultural classroom we go for the second alternative, thinking of it as resistance to forgetfulness, but necessarily in the long-term interest of our often disavowed common faith in democratic capitalism: "a necessity [as Bourdieu reminded us] which the agent *constitutes* as such and for which [s]he provides the scene of action without actually being its subject." This necessity is what unites us, and unless we acknowledge it ("and even if we do...") we cannot hope to undertake the responsibility of the emerging dominant.

Let me digress for a moment on a lesson such an acknowledgment can draw from history. If by teaching ourselves and our students to acknowledge our part and hope in capitalism we can bring that hope to a persistent and principled crisis, we can set ourselves on the way to intervening in an unfinished chapter of history that was mired in Eurocentric national disputes.

•

"The Law is the element of calculation, and it is just that there be Law, but justice is incalculable, it requires us to calculate with the incalculable."[19] Now that the Bolshevik experiment has imploded, we cannot afford to forget that the incalculable dreams of the vestiges of Second International Communism (rather than the overt history of its demise in national competition), placed within the calculus of the welfare state, are daily eroded by the forces of what is politely called "liberalization" in the Third World and the new Second World (the old Eastern bloc) — and by privatization in the First.

(In the first version of this essay, delivered in the United States and addressed to teachers of the humanities, I used the term "Second International" in rather a loose way. In a European and social-scientific context, the steps leading to this loose use should be spelled out.

In *Imperialism,* Lenin writes: "The boom at the end of the nineteenth century and the crisis of 1900–03. Cartels become one of the foundations of the whole of economic life. Capitalism has been transformed into imperialism."[20] The description sounds old-fashioned in its terms precisely because the transformation has moved into spectacular determinations. The post-Soviet world order is an example of the timeliness of Lenin's harsh proposition. His scathing critique of Karl Kautsky and the Second International in the same text, in contrast, has lost some of its point precisely because of the astuteness of his judgment that imperialism does not resemble its nineteenth-century lineaments today. Today the United States left turns toward "radical democracy" rather than socialism because the project is a transformation of capitalist imperialism everywhere, not a claim to the culture of postcoloniality in the multicultural United States of Europe and America.[21] When liberalism claims its revolution in the name of capitalism in the social sciences [see my discussion of Bruce Ackerman in note 6], it is time for us, humanist academics marked by recent other-national origin but integrated into developed civil societies, to take note; for we teach a large sector of the growing electorate the uncertain grounds of choice: the singular and unverifiable witnessing of literature.

I will quote Immanuel Wallerstein because the narrative here is conveniently put together, not because I necessarily subscribe to his position on world-systems or movements of ethnic identity. I should also mention that the invocation of specifically the *Second* International was to distinguish myself from those academic leftists in the United States who were concentrating on a Trotskyist critique of the Soviet system, precisely because such a concentration did not seem productive of a specific plan of action for the new immigrant academic. Given the absence of a serious state-level left in the United States, I must confess I did not see the need, in a hortatory piece, to distinguish carefully between the Second International as such and the specific party positions and histories of social democracy and democratic socialism. It should be also be remembered that the closest thing to a serious left party in the United States had been the Democratic Socialists of America under the leadership of Michael Harrington. With regard to new immigrants the point is that, whereas the original Second International Socialist movement had come to an end in European nationalisms, and the Third International Communist movement now shows itself to have had, in many respects, the lineaments and problems of a species of colonialism in the name of internationalism, this particular U.S. group, with what I am calling its "negotiable" national sentiments straddling the periphery and the center, can, especially through its contingent of radical humanist teachers, teach not only for a nostalgic culturalism but also for a progressivist socialism. Here is the passage from Wallerstein:

> [D]uring the period between the First and Second World Wars [there] exist[ed] . . . two rival and fiercely competitive Internationals, the Second and the Third, also known as the conflict between Social Democrats and Communists. . . . It is less that the social-democratic parties came to be seen as one of the alternating groups which could legitimately govern than that the main program of the Social Democrats, the welfare state, came to be accepted by even the conservative parties [of northwestern Europe], even if begrudgingly.[22]

I now return to the original essay.)

The calculations with the incalculable dream of communism are concealed in many passages of the later Marx, the most memorable being the long paragraph at the end of the chapter entitled "The Illusion Created by Competition" in *Capital,* vol. 3, where, in a series of five massive "ifs" (the rhetorical bulwark of the element of calculation), Marx comes to the conclusion: "*[T]hen* nothing of these [capitalist] forms remains, but simply those foundations of the forms that are common to all social modes of production."[23] If, if, if, if, if. The line between "democratic" capitalism and democratic socialism is here being undone, with a certain set of impossible conditions. Persistent critique is being replaced by blueprint. The new immigrant ideologue today acts out the impossibility of that blueprint. It is in the face of that impossibility that she must persistently investigate the possibility of the push from democratic capitalism into a globally responsible democratic socialism, the only struggle that fits the post-Soviet scene.[24] It is no secret that, in the developing countries, it is the forces of feminist activism and the non-Eurocentric ecology movement that are attempting to regenerate the critical element into that dream of displacement from capitalism to socialism. Ethnicity, striking at the very heart of identity, is the incalculable and mystical principle that is open for the "most perverse calculation" in that larger field. The role and agency of the U.S.-based marginal movement and its claims to ethnicity are therefore up for reinvention. That is indeed my theme. But by sounding this motif too soon, I am short-circuiting into my second movement, where I will speak of educating the educators. Let us return to the undergraduate classroom.

•

In spite of our commonsense estimation of the best-case scenario, national-origin validation in the general multicultural classroom remains crucially important, *for* the various national origins, if only to undermine the symbolic importance, all out of proportion to its content and duration, of the test in American history and civilization administered by the Immigration and Naturalization Services (INS) for new citizens, which establishes that, from now on, the history of the racial dominant in the United States is the migrant's own.

I have already suggested that the place of women within the desire for justice under capitalism may be different. Amy Tan's controversial *Joy Luck Club* animates this difference in every possible way.[25] The competitive difference among marginal groups, the difference between economic migration (to the United States) and political exile (in China), the necessity and impossibility of the representation of the "culture of origin," culture as negotiable systems of representation between mothers and daughters, the role of the university and corporatism in "moving West to reach the East" (*JLC* 205), the extreme ungroundedness of identity in the obsessive pursuit of perspectives, all thematized in this first novel, can be used for political pedagogy in the invention of unity.

Let me indicate the inaugural staging of the economic argument, rehearsed many times in the novel:

> After everybody votes unanimously for the Canada gold stock, I go into the kitchen to ask Auntie An-mei why the Joy Luck Club started investing in stocks.... "We got smart. Now we can all win and lose equally. We can have stock market luck. And we can play mah jong for fun, just for a few dollars, winner take all. Losers take home left-overs! So everyone can have some joy. Smart-hanh?" (*JLC* 18)

Contrast this egalitarian "joy luck" by way of investment to the original Joy Luck Club, four women attempting to contain political exile by force of spirit. This is the frame-narrator remembering the reminiscence of her recently dead mother. The women are refugees from the Japanese, in Kweilin:

> I knew which women I wanted to ask. They were all young like me, with wishful faces.... Each week we could forget past wrongs done to us. We weren't allowed to think a bad thought. We feasted, we laughed, we played games, lost and won, we told the best stories. And each week, we could hope to be lucky. That hope was our only joy.... I won tens of thousands of *yuan*. But I wasn't rich. No. By then paper money had become worthless. Even toilet paper was worth more. And that made us laugh harder, to think a thousand-*yuan* note wasn't even good enough to rub on our bottoms. (*JLC* 10, 12)

In this perspectivized field of identity, only the Polaroid produces the final ID. Here is the last scene of the novel, where the Chinese-American frame-narrator meets her long-lost Chinese half-sisters. No attempt is made to provide interior representations of their memories:

> I look at their faces again and I see no trace of my mother in them. Yet they still look familiar.... The flash of the Polaroid goes off and my father hands me the snapshot.... The gray-green surface changes to the bright colors of our three images, sharpening and deepening all at once. And although we don't speak, I know we all see it: Together we look like our mother. Her same eyes, her same mouth, open in surprise to see, at last, her long-cherished wish. (*JLC* 331, 332)

It is at her peril that the reader forgets the authoritative cherished wish that is given in the opening epigraphic tale:

> The old woman remembered a swan she had bought many years ago in Shanghai for a foolish sum. This bird, boasted the market vendor, was once a duck that stretched its neck in hopes of becoming a goose.... When she arrived in the new country, the immigration officials pulled her swan away from her, leaving the woman ... with only one swanfeather for a memory.... For a long time now the woman had wanted to give her daughter the single swan feather and tell her, "This feather may look worthless, but it comes from afar and carries with it all my good intentions." And she waited, year after year, for the day she could tell her daughter this in perfect American English. (*JLC* 3–4)

Tan's risk-taking book offers us a timely concept-metaphor: the dead mother's voice achieves perfect American English in the regularizing graph of the Polaroid. It is left to us to decode the scandal with sympathy and responsibility.

The Earlier Scene

Since Reconstruction and the first major change in the Constitution after the Civil War, the various waves of immigrants have mingled with one of the supportive, original agents of the production of American origins: the African-American (not the Original Nations). But even here, the emphasis on assimilation given in the melting-pot theory followed the pattern of Anglocentrism first and a graduated *Euro*centrism next, with the lines of dominance radiating out of that presumptive center. Indeed, this is why the older immigrant elements in the multicultural classroom may or may not strengthen the undermining of the INS test, if the issue is the invention of unity rather than difference. This is the pedagogic imperative, the persuasive force-field of the classroom, to change the "may not" to "may," among the descendants of the older white immigrants, in the interest of a different unity. We are not disuniting America. If we are not aware of this as participating agents, the tremendous force of American ethnicity can be used in the service of consolidating the new world order out of the ashes of the Soviet Union, simply by recoding capitalism as democracy.

I have so far put aside the uprooting of the African and the redefining of the Original Nations in the interest of the new (and old) immigrants. Also to be placed here is the itinerary of the Chicano/Latino, unevenly straddling the history of two empires, the Spanish and the U.S., one on the cusp of the transition to capitalism, the other active today.

For me, an outsider who came to the United States in 1961, the voice that still echoes from the civil rights/black power movement is from the Ocean Hill–Brownsville School District Struggle of 1968.[26] I had received my Ph.D. the previous year. My own school days in India, a newly independent country attempting to decolonize its curriculum, were not far behind. Perhaps this is why words from that less famous struggle have been retained by the force of my memory. I am not even sure who it was that said them. It may have been the Reverend Galamaison: "This is a struggle against educational colonization." The other day I caught a voice on television, of an African-American women who had been a student in that school district, now a mature woman who spoke of her experience and remarked: "We became Third World. We became international."

Let me propose what may at first sight seem odd: in the struggle against *internal* colonization, it is the African-American who is *post*colonial in the United States. To imply that postcoloniality is a step beyond colonialism is the new immigrant's reactive and unexamined disavowal of the move (however justified) away from the postcolonial scene to embrace the American dream — the civilizing mission of the new colonizing power. In its own context, postcoloniality is the achievement of an independence that removes the legal subject-status of a people as the result of struggle, armed or otherwise. In terms of internal colonization, the Emancipation, Reconstruction, and civil rights were just such an achievement. Furthermore, postcoloniality is no guarantee of prosperity for all but rather a signal for the consolidation of recolonization. In that respect as well, the condition of the African-American fits the general picture of postcoloniality much more accurately than the unearned claims of the Eurocentric well-placed migrant. Paradoxically, the rising racist backlash is an acknowledgment of this. In the so-called postcolonial countries, postcoloniality is not a signal for an end to struggle but rather a shifting of the struggle to the persistent register of decolonization. Here, too, the situation of the African-American struggle offers a parallel. The second wave of backlash rage is on the rise. With an awareness of that register Joan Scott asks her astute question and makes her judgments in terms of class:

[T]he special treatment that came with high social status never seems to have been seen as a compromise of university standards. (One has to wonder why it was that, for example, the test scores of blacks are stolen from the admissions office at Georgetown Law School and published by disgruntled conservatives, while those of alumni children of influential politicians were not. One can only conclude that the call for a return to a meritocracy that never was is a thinly veiled manifestation of racism.)[27]

I am claiming postcoloniality for the African-American, then, not because I want to interfere with her self-representation but because I want to correct the self-representation of the new immigrant academic as postcolonial, indeed as the source of postcolonial theory.

In terms of internal colonization in the United States, the original three groups have not emerged equally into postcoloniality. If I read the signs right (and I may not), the Latino/Chicano segment has, on one side, been moving for some time toward a recognition, in literary-cultural studies, of "our America" in the entire (North-Central-South) American continental context, not contained within *internal* U.S. colonization, as the African-American must be. The *différance* of unity and difference between African and African-American Pan-Africanism is the authoritative text here.[28] The Latino/Chicano move toward "our America" may be read as a move toward globality. This is particularly interesting today because, given U.S. economic policy toward Latin America, "illegal immigration," especially in the case of Mexico, *is* transnationality. *On that level* — the level of the subaltern *as* "illegal immigrant" under limited surveillance by the border patrol — the local *is* the global.[29] By contrast, specifically the Chicano engagement in the restoration of the major voices within internal colonization belongs within diasporic discourse studies.[30]

The thought of sublating internal colonization (another description of postcoloniality) is articulated differently in the context of the Original Nations.

At a recent conference on the literature of ethnicity, John Mohawk anguished that Native American writing was not yet stylistically competitive with the kind of sexy postmodernism that some of our best-known colleagues celebrate in the name of postcoloniality.[31] The embattled phrase "stylistically competitive" was not his. But I will use that phrase again before I end.

Since the Native American voice has been most rigorously marginalized even within marginality, I want to spend some time on the work of a Native American scholar, Jack D. Forbes, who is claiming a new unity with African-Americans. Unity in this sphere cannot be based on an initial, often disavowed, *choice* for justice under capitalism, as in the case of the new immigrants; but rather it must be based in the investigation of the institution of the so-called origins of the white-supremacist United States: a sublation of internal colonization.[32] Before making the claim to this divided unity, Forbes lays bare the mechanics of constructing another unity, in another political interest. He gets behind dictionaries to capture the elusive lexical space in-between meaning shifts, by sheer empirical obstinacy. He teases out usage to show the emergence of juridico-legal practice and rational classification. This is an invaluable quarry, on the level of aggregative apparatuses (power) and of propositions (knowledge), for a future Foucauldian who will dare to try to take these further below, into the utterables (*énoncés*) that form the archival ground-level (not ground) of knowledge and the nonsymbolizable force-field that shapes the shifting ground-levels of power.[33] I cannot readily imagine such a person, for the *pouvoir-savoir* (ability to make sense) in question involves

> 300 to 400 years of intermixture of a very complex sort, [and] varying amounts of African and American ancestry derived at different intervals and from extremely diverse sources — as from American nations as different as Narragansett or Pequot and the Carib or Arawak, or from African nations as diverse as the Mandinka, Yoruba, and Malagasy. (*BA* 270–71)

For the perceptive reader, then, Forbes's book at once opens the horizons of Foucault's work, shows the immense, indeed perhaps insuperable complexity of the task once we let go of "pure" European outlines, and encourages a new generation of scholars to acquire the daunting skills for robust cultural history. This work is rather different from the primitivist patronage of orality. It is in the context of this complexity that a new "unity" is claimed:

> In an article published in the *Journal of Negro History* [James Hugo] Johnston remarked: "Where the Negro was brought into contact with the American Indian the blood of the two races intermingled, the Indian has not disappeared from the land, but is now part of the Negro population of the United States." The latter statement might offend many Indians today, who still survive, of course, in great numbers as Native Americans, but nonetheless the significance of Johnston's thesis as regards the extent of Native American–African intermixture remains before us. (*BA* 191)

This point of view is to be contrasted with the persuasive and representative usual view of the substitution of one collective identity by another: that the Indian population dwindled, was exported, and was replaced by Africans and imported slaves from the West Indies.[34] It is in the pores of such identity-based arguments that Forbes discovers the survival of the Native American, in the male and female line. By focusing on the vast heterogeneity and textuality of the description of mixed groups, Forbes shows that the emergence of the "other," as the other of the white, may be, at best, an unwitting legitimation by reversal of the very dominant positions it is supposed to contest. My argument thus is a corollary of Forbes's. Forbes points out what we caricature by defining ourselves as the "other (of the white dominant in metropolitan space)": "It would appear that both Americans and Africans began to appear in exotic pageants and entertainments staged in London during the seventeenth century. It is not always possible to clearly ascertain the ethnicity of the performers, since Africans were sometimes dressed up as Americans, or perhaps vice versa" (*BA* 56).

In the discontinuous narrative of the development of racism, how are we to compute the relationship between that usage and the 1854 California State Supreme Court statement that "expresses a strong tendency in the history of the United States, a tendency to identify two broad classes of people: white and non-white, citizen and non-citizen (or semi-citizen)" (*BA* 65)? Are we, once again, to become complicit with this tendency by identifying ourselves, single ethnic group by group, or as migrant collectivity, only as the "other" of the white dominant? Shall we, "like so many Europeans, [remain] utterly transfixed by the black-white nexus either as 'opposites' or as real people" (*BA* 172)? Given that, in the literally postcolonial areas like Algeria or India, white racism is no longer the chief problem, Forbes's historical reasoning is yet another way of bringing together the intuitions of global resistance.[35]

Yet even in this work, where isolationist concerns broaden out into the global de-colonization of scholarship, one must note the absence of a feminist impulse. The Native American woman, being legally free, was often the enslaved man's access to "freedom" in the United States. And slavery itself is "matrilineal." These two facts provide the motor for a great deal of Forbes's narrative of interaction. Yet *Black Africans and Native Americans,* so resourceful and imaginative in probing the pores of the hide of history, never questions the gender secrets hidden in them. It is correctly mentioned that Native American practices included the thought of "individual free-dom and utopian socialism" (*BA* 266). But it is not noticed that there is feminism in those practices as well. What is it to define as "free" — *after* enslavement, genocide, colonization, theft of land, and tax-imposition — women who had, before these acts (masquerading today as social cohesion), been culturally inscribed as "freer"? What is it to become, then, a passageway to freedom after the fact? What is the "mean-ing" of matrilineage-in-slavery, mentioned in parentheses — "(generally slavery was inherited in the female line)" (*BA* 240) — where lineage itself is devastated?[36]

The Global Field/Transnational Literacy on the Graduate Curriculum

With the name of "woman" I pass from "access to the universal" into "the global field" of uneven decolonization and make an appeal to decolonize feminism as it studies feminism in decolonization. With plenty of help from feminist historians and social scientists, I teach myself to teach a course entitled "Feminism in De-colonization." From personal experience, then, I know how much education an educator (in this case myself) needs in this venture. "Feminism in Decolonization" is a political re-writing of the title "Women in Development." I am encouraged to see that a critique of the metropolitan feminist focus on women in development is one of the main premises of the piece by Aihwa Ong that I have already cited. This gives me an opportunity to recite once again that, in this effort, we have to *learn* interdis-ciplinary teaching by supplementing our work with that of the social scientists, and supplementing theirs with ours.

It is through the literature of ethnicity that we customarily approach the question of globality within literary-cultural studies when they are defined along humanist disciplinary lines. The Greek-English Lexicon tells us that the word *ethnos* meant "a number of people accustomed to live together" — one's *own* kind of people, in other words — and therefore, after Homer, "nation." Side-by-side with the Greek word *ethnos* was the word *ethnikos* — other people, often taken to mean "hea-then, pagan, foreign." It is not hard to see how the New Testament would use these already available words to mean "all but Jews and Christians." Like many ideas be-longing to Christianity, these words were pressed into pejorative service in English, to mean "other (lesser) peoples," in the Age of Conquest. In the nineteenth century, as conquest consolidated itself into imperialism, the word becomes "scientific," es-pecially in the forms "ethnography" and "ethnology." We are aware of the debates between the British ethnologist-ethnographers, on the one hand, and anthropologists, on the other, as to whether their study should be based on language or on physical characteristics. In any event, the discipline concerned itself, of course, with ideas of race, culture, and religion. The connections between *national* origin and "ethnicity" are, at best, dubious and, at worst, a site of violent contestation. In the cultural politics of the United States, they are now firmly in place without question.

I think the literature of ethnicity writes itself between *ethnos* — a writer writing for her *own* people (whatever that means) without deliberated self-identification as such — and *ethnikos*, the pejoratively defined other reversing the charge, (de)anthropologizing herself by separating herself into a staged identity. The literature of ethnicity in this second sense thus carries, paradoxically, the writer's signature as divided against itself, for the staging of the displacing of the dominant must somehow be indexed there. A woman's relationship to a patriarchal or patriarchalized ethnicity makes her access to this signature even more complex.

The standard world-system estimation of ethnicity, not unrelated to the failures of systemic communism, is something like the following: "Seen in long historical time and broad world space, [nations and ethnic groups] fade into one another, becoming only 'groups.' Seen in short historical time and narrow world space, they become clearly defined and so form distinctive structures."[37] Although I am in general sympathy with the resistance to "the intellectual pressure to reify groups," I cannot work with this world-system view of ethnicities in globality. The long view and the broad space are so perspectivized that to learn to acquire them in order to produce correct descriptions may be useful only if supplemented unceasingly, not just by way of the popular U.S. T-shirt slogan, "Think globally act locally," although it is not bad for a start.

Sublimation (and what Lacan calls the symbolic circuit) stands over against what Freud represents as cultural-ethical pathogenic repressions that may be represented as movements against the individual or social-psychic system. On the literary-critical side, Fredric Jameson represents such representations. And therefore he has been reading Third World literature for some time now as *allegories* of transnational capitalism. It is because I agree with Jameson in a general way that I would like to insist here upon a different definition of allegory, one that sees it as not just a symbolic order of semiosis. Otherwise, caught between accusations of political correctness and liberal multiculturalism, we are denied the right to say, "Heresy by itself is no token of truth."[38]

I take as my motto the opening words of *Abarodh-bāshini* (Lady-Prisoner), a critique of veiled female life published by Rokeya Sakhawat Hossain, an Indian Muslim woman, between 1915 and 1917. She shows that not only the signature of the writer of ethnicity, but also the signature of the patriarchally imprisoned woman, is self-separated: "We have become habituated after living for so long in prison; therefore, against the prison we, especially I myself, have nothing to say. If the fishwife is asked, 'Is the stink of rotten fish good or bad?' what will she respond? Here I will make a gift of a few of our personal experiences to our reader-sisters, and I hope they will be pleased."[39]

Hossain allows me to produce a more responsible sense of allegory: the fishwife-as-feminist who, like Hossain, admits to being unable to distance herself from her own imprisonment, "admits," in other words, "to the impossibility of reading [her] own text, . . ." and can only produce, as she herself says, fragmentary instances "against the inherent logic which animate[s] the development of the narrative [of imprisonment], and disarticulates it in a way that seems perverse."[40] On that model, since *we* are imprisoned in and habituated to capitalism, we might try to look at the *allegory* of capitalism not in terms of capitalism as the source of authoritative reference but in terms of the constant small failures in and interruptions to its logic, which help to recode it and produce our unity. "Allegory" here "speaks out with the referential efficacy of a praxis."

Learning this *praxis* that may produce interruptions to capitalism from within requires us to make future educators in the humanities transnationally literate, so that they can distinguish between the varieties of decolonization on the agenda, rather than collapse them as "postcoloniality." I am speaking of transnational *literacy*. We must remember that to achieve literacy in a language is not to become an expert in it. I am therefore not making an impossible demand upon the graduate curriculum. Literacy produces the skill to differentiate between letters, so that an articulated script can be read, reread, written, rewritten. Literacy is poison as well as medicine. It allows us to sense that the other is not just a "voice" — others also produce articulated texts, even as they, like us, are written in and by a text not of our own making. It is through transnational literacy that we can invent grounds for an interruptive praxis from within our disavowed hope in justice under capitalism.

If we were transnationally literate, we might read sectors that are stylistically noncompetitive with the spectacular experimental fiction of certain sections of hybridity or postcoloniality with a disarticulating rather than a comparative point of view. Native American fiction would then allegorically intervene in reminding us of the economic peripheralization of the originary, communist, precapitalist ethnicities of the Fourth World. We can link it to the fact that, even as we admire the sophistication of Indian writing in English, we have not yet seen a non-Christian *tribal* Indo-Anglican fiction writer in English.[41] And we will also discover that all stylistically noncompetitive literature cannot be relegated to the same transnational allegory in the crude sense.

Take, for example, the case of Bangladesh. You will hardly ever find an entry from Bangladesh in a course on postcolonial or Third World literature. Its literature is stylistically noncompetitive on the international market. The UN has written it off as the lowest on its list of developing countries, its women at the lowest rung of development. Our students will not know that, as a result of decolonization from the British in 1947 and liberation from West Pakistan in 1971, Bangladesh had to go through a double decolonization; that as a result of the appropriation of its language by the primarily Hindu Bengali nationalists in the nineteenth century, and the adherence of upper-class Bangladeshis to Arabic and Urdu, the Bangladeshis have to win back their language inch by inch. Some of this may be gleaned from Naila Kabeer's essay on Bangladesh in Deniz Kandiyoti's *Women, Islam, and the State*.[42] But apart from a rather mysterious paragraph on "progressive non-government organizations" that would be incomprehensible to most graduate students of modern languages, there is no mention of the fact that, because of the timing and manner of Bangladesh's liberation, the country fell into the clutches of the transnational global economy in a way significantly different from the situation of both the Asia-Pacific *and* the older postcolonial countries.[43] The transnationallly illiterate student might not know that the worst victim of the play of the multinational pharmaceuticals in the name of population control is the woman's body; that in the name of development, international monetary organizations are substituting the impersonal and incomprehensible state for the older, more recognizable enemies-cum-protectors (the patriarchal family), a process broadly comparable, in women's history, to the transition from feudalism to capitalism.[44] In this situation, the most dynamic minds are engaged in alternative development work, not literary production. And class-fixed literary production as such in Bangladesh is concerned not with the place of the nation in transnationality but rather with a nation-fixed view that does not produce the energy of translation.[45]

About twelve years ago, in an essay that was refused entry into the Norton Critical Edition of *Jane Eyre* because it was allegedly too oppositional, I wrote these words:

> A full literary reinscription cannot easily flourish in the imperialist fracture or discontinuity, covered over by an alien legal system masquerading as Law as such, an alien ideology established as only Truth, and a set of human sciences busy establishing the "native" as self-consolidating Other.... To reopen the fracture without succumbing to a nostalgia for lost origins, the literary critic must turn to the archives of imperial governance.[46]

Over the last decade, I have painfully learned that literary reinscription cannot easily flourish, not only in the inauguration of imperialism but also in the discontinuity of recolonization. The literary critic and educator must acquire and transmit transnational literacy in a system that must be allegorized by its failures. There is a mad scramble on among highly placed intellectuals to establish their "colonial origins" these days. Such efforts belong with the impatience of world-systems literary theory, with portmanteau theories of postcoloniality, with the isolationism of both multiculturalism and antiracism; they cannot keep the fracture or wound open. This is the infinite responsibility of the emergent dominant engaged in graduate education in the humanities. Otherwise we side with the sanctimonious pronouncement of a Lynn Cheney: of course I support multicultural education; I want each child to know that he can succeed.[47] Woodrow Wilson had, I believe, suggested at some point that he wanted each American to be a captain of industry! Faith in capitalism gone mad in the name of individualism and competition.

Over against this superindividualist faith, let me quote the *Declaration of Comilla* (1989), drawn up in Bangladesh, by the Feminist International Network of Resistance to Reproductive and Genetic Engineering, under the auspices of UBINIG, a Bangladesh development-alternative collective, proposing once again an interruptive literate practice within development:

> We live in a limited world. In the effort to realise [the] illusion [of unlimited progress leading to unlimited growth] within a limited world, it is necessary that some people [be] exploited so that others can grow; Woman is exploited so that Man can grow; South is exploited so that North can grow; Animals are exploited so that people can grow! The Good Life of some is always at the expense of others. Health of some is based on the disease of others. Fertility of some is based on the infertility of others.... What is good for the ruling class should be good for everybody![48]

I can just hear world-system theorists murmuring, "moralism." But then, the un-examined moralism of liberal multiculturalism allows us to forget these women's admonition. Like the fishwife, we cannot tell if the stink of rotten fish is good or bad when we disavow our own part or hope in U.S. capitalism.

I heard a colleague say recently, only half in jest, that the newest criticism no longer considered the "literary" part of literature to be that important. On the contrary. We expand the definition of literature to include social inscription. Farida Akhter intervening angrily against "the agenda of developing countries enforcing population policies on others" at the third plenary of the World Women's Congress for a Healthy Planet on November 11, 1991, has something like a relationship with the absence of classy postcolonial women's literary texts from Bangladesh on the U.S. curriculum. If those of us who write dissertations and teach future teachers still peddle something called "culture" on the model of national-origin validation (crucial to the general *undergraduate* curriculum), we have failed to grasp the moment of the emerging dominant, to rend time with the urgency of justice. Indeed, in the era of global capital rampant, it is the new immigrant intellectual's negotiable nationality that might act as a lever to undo the nation-based conflict that killed the Second International.

Conclusion

I close with two passages I often quote these days, from Assia Djebar's novel *Fantasia*.[49] Algeria, like India, is an older postcolonial state. The old modes of de-colonization at the time of national liberation are crumbling in both. Transnational literacy allows us to recognize that we hear a different *kind* of voice from these countries, especially from singular women, from Mahasweta Devi, from Assia Djebar.

In the case of Djebar, that crumbling can be staged as a profound critique of Fanon's false hopes for unveiling in *A Dying Colonialism*. Here are Fanon's famous words: "There is the much discussed status of the Algerian woman...today...receiving the only valid challenge: the experience of revolution. Algerian woman's ardent love of the home is not a limit imposed by the universe....Algerian society reveals itself not to be the woman-less society that had been so convincingly described."[50]

And here is Djebar, in *Fantasia*. Staging herself as an Algerian Muslim woman denied access to classical Arabic, she gives a fragmented version of the graphing of her bio in French, of which I quote the following fragments:

> The overlay of my oral culture wearing dangerously thin...Writing of the most anodyne of childhood memories leads back to a body bereft of voice. To attempt an autobiography in French words alone is to show more than its skin under the slow scalpel of a live autopsy. Its flesh peels off and with it, seemingly, the speaking of childhood which can no longer be written is torn to shreds. Wounds are reopened, veins weep, the blood of the self flows and that of others, a blood which has never dried. (*F* 156, 178)

Identity is here exposed as a wound, exposed by the historically hegemonic imperial languages, for those who have learned the double-binding "practice of [their] writing" (*F* 181). This double-bind, felt by feminists *in* decolonizing countries rather than in Eurocentric economic migration, is not ours. The wound of our split identity is not this specific wound, for this wound is not necessarily, indeed rarely, opened by a hope in Anglo-U.S.-EEC–based capitalism.

One of the major motifs of *Fantasia* is a meditation upon the possibility that to achieve autobiography in the double bind of the practice of the conqueror's writing is not for the well-placed marginal to "tell her own story," but to learn, to learn to be taken seriously by the gendered subaltern, the woman in radical disenfranchisement, who has not had the chance to master that practice. And therefore, hidden in the many-sectioned third part of the book, there is the single episode where the central character speaks in the ethical singularity of the *tu-toi* to Zohra, an eighty-year-old rural *muj hida* (female freedom fighter) who has been devastated both by her participation in the nationalist struggle and by the neglect of woman's claims in decolonized Algeria. The achievement of the autobiographer-in-fiction is to be fully fledged as a storyteller to this intimate interlocutor. Telling one's own story is not the continuist imperative of identity upon the privileged feminist in decolonization.

Rokeya Sakhawat Hossain, an upper-class Indian woman, had not kept a journal, but spoke as the fishwife. Djebar's French-educated heroine attempts to animate the story of two nineteenth-century Algerian prostitutes, Fatma and Meriem, allegorically interrupting Eugène Fromentin's *Un été au Sahara,* a masterpiece of Orientalism. She succeeds, for Zohra's curiosity flares up: " 'And Fatma? And Meriem?' Lla Zhora interrupted, catching herself following the story as if it were a legend recounted by a bard. 'Where did you hear this story?' she went on, impatiently." The "I" (now at last articulated because related and responsible to "you") replies simply: " 'I read it!' I retorted. 'An eye-witness told it to a friend who wrote it down' " (*F* 166).

This unemphatic short section ends simply: "I, your cousin, translate this account into the mother tongue, and report it to you. So I try my self out, as ephemeral teller, close to you little mother, in front of your vegetable patch" (*F* 167). The central character shares her mother-tongue as instrument of translation with the other woman.

In the rift of this divided field of identity, the tale shared in the mother tongue forever interrupts (in every act of reading) and is forever absent, for it is in the mother tongue. The authority of the "now" inaugurates this absent autobiography in every "here" of the book: the fleeting framed moment undoes the "blank [*blanc*] in the memory" of the narrator's *personal* childhood, which only yields the image of an old crone whose muttered Qur'anic curses could not be understood (*F* 10).

The final movement of *Fantasia* is in three short bits, what remains of an autobiography when it has been unraveled strand by strand. First a tribute to Pauline Rolland, the French revolutionary of 1848, exiled in Algeria, as the true ancestress of the *mujāhidāt*.[51] Revolutionary discourse for women cannot rely upon indigenous cultural production. If the tale told to Zohra is a divided moment of access to autobiography as the telling of an absent story, here autobiography is the possibility of writing or giving writing to the other identifiable only as a mutilated metonym of violence, as part object. The interrupted continuous source is, once again, Eugène Fromentin. There is one unexplained Arabic word in the following passage, a word that means, in fact, pen:

Eugène Fromentin offers me an unexpected hand — the hand of an unknown woman he was never able to draw. He describes in sinister detail: as he is leaving the oasis which six months after the massacre is still filled with its stench, Fromentin picks up out of the dust the severed hand of an anonymous Algerian woman. He throws it down again in his path. Later, I seize on this living hand, hand of mutilation and of memory, and I attempt to bring it the *qalam*. (*F* 226)

Everything in this essay has been a meditation upon the possibility that, at this divided moment, we not only should work mightily to take up the pen in our own hands but should also attempt to pick up the *qalam* offered us in uneven decolonization and, with the help of our Polaroid, attempt to figure forth the world's broken and shifting alphabet.

NOTES

This essay was first published in *MMLA Quarterly* 25, no. 1 (1992): 3–22; reprinted with extensive revisions in Jan Nederveen Pieterse, ed., *The Decolonization of Imagination* (London: Zed Books, 1995), 177–202. This version has been further revised. I thank Thomas W. Keenan for reading the first and Vincent Cheng for reading the final versions.

1. Now that this essay is being reprinted stateside, I want to keep the contextual sedimentation intact. It is because the "U.S. as such" (it means something in capital logic) is also "local," not merely its multicultural neighborhoods or its municipal issues.

2. As always, by "new immigrants" I mean the continuing influx of immigrants since, by "[t]he Immigration and Nationality Act of October 1, 1965," Lyndon Johnson "swept away both the national-origin system and the Asia-Pacific Triangle"; these are precisely the groups escaping decolonization, one way or another. "That the Act would, for example, create a massive brain drain from developing countries and increase Asian immigration 500 per cent was entirely unexpected" (Maldwyn Allen Jones, *American Immigration,* 2d ed. [Chicago: University of Chicago Press, 1992], 266, 267). For purposes of definition, I have repeated this footnote in other writing. It goes without saying that, in the post-Soviet phase, the patterns of this "new" immigration have a fast-changing dynamic. The increasing legislative and electoral rage against immigrants should strengthen the argument in my essay. A superficial understanding of this rage has, however, exacerbated the unexamined culturalist competition that is my target.

3. Darryl J. Gless and Barbara Herrnstein Smith, eds., *The Politics of Liberal Education* (Durham, N.C.: Duke University Press, 1992), gives a sense of the debate. A great many documents can now be cited, but I am revising on press deadline.

4. Arthur M. Schlesinger Jr., *The Disuniting of America* (New York: Norton, 1992), 138.

5. Zbigniew Brzezinski, *Out of Control: Global Turmoil on the Eve of the Twenty First Century* (New York: Scribner's, 1993), 231.

6. As I revise the essay for publication, the issue of multiculturalism has become visible in the high waters of the academic mainstream, as witness Charles Taylor, *Multiculturalism and "The Politics of Recognition": An Essay* (Princeton, N.J.: Princeton University Press, 1992); Bruce Ackerman, *The Future of Liberal Revolution* (New Haven: Yale University Press, 1992); John Rawls, *Political Liberalism* (New York: Columbia University Press, 1993). These important books can obviously not be discussed in an endnote. Here suffice it to say that the three texts have something like a relationship with the civilizing mission of imperialism seriously credited. Ackerman's position is so muscle-bound with learning as to be least examined, and it is not surprising that, at the 1994 Pacific American Philosophical Association convention, he advanced his position as a justification both for foreign aid and for the emancipation of the women of developing nations. His book is specifically addressed to the needs of the new world order; "The Meaning of 1989" (113–23) is one of his chapters. Charles Taylor reduces the value of his thoughtful study by deducing the subject of multiculturalism (difficult for me to imagine as a unicity) from the "European" historical narrative of the emergence of secularism. And John Rawls, by far the most astute of the three, recognizes the limits of liberalism as politics in order to save it as philosophy. "The hearts of innumerable men and women respond . . . with idealistic fervour to [t]his clarion, because

it [goes]...without saying that it would be good for...anywhere...to be made [American]. At this point it might be useful to wonder which of the ideals that make our hearts beat faster will seem wrong-headed to people a hundred years from now" (Doris Lessing, *African Laughter: Four Visits to Zimbabwe* [New York: HarperCollins, 1992], 3; she is writing about Cecil Rhodes and "Southern Rhodesia"). I have not yet read Duncan Kennedy, *Sexy Dressing Etc.: Essays on the Power and Politics of Cultural Identity* (Cambridge, Mass.: Harvard University Press, 1993).

7. I insist upon this point, trivially but crucially true. It is so often neglected that I take the liberty of self-citation: "The fact that socialism can never fully (adequately) succeed is what it has in common with everything. It is *after* that fact that one starts to make the choices, especially after the implosion of the Bolshevik experiment" ("Marginality in the Teaching Machine," in Spivak, *Outside in the Teaching Machine,* New York, Routledge, 1993, 68). What follows in the text about the foundation of the United States is a condensed version of the final chapter of *Outside.* Mindful of Kathy E. Ferguson's critique of my apparent claim to authority in *The Man Question: Visions of Subjectivity in Feminist Theory* (Berkeley: University of California Press, 1993), 201, I controlled my habit of self-referencing for a while. Weighing this against many complaints of overburdened, cryptic, and incomprehensible writing, I have thought it best to revert to a modified version of my original practice.

8. Robin Blackburn, *The Overthrow of Colonial Slavery: 1776–1848* (London: Verso, 1988), 123, 124.

9. Joan Wallach Scott, "The Campaign against Political Correctness: What's Really at Stake?" *Change* 23, no. 6 (November/December 1991): 32–33. The passages from Mohanty and Fynsk are from pp. 39 and 43, respectively.

10. Pierre Bourdieu, "The Philosophical Institution," in Alan Montefiore, ed., *Philosophy in France Today* (Cambridge: Cambridge University Press, 1983), 2; emphasis added.

11. In this connection, the phrase "colonial subject" may be misleadingly laden with pathos. In my estimation, the constitution of the so-called colonial subject can also be described as the violent and necessary constitution of an abstract subject of a limited-access civil society — the core of the colonial infrastructure. Eurocentric economic migration and its struggle for full access to civil rights accompanied by a validated if phantasmatic national-cultural origin can then be seen as a document continuous with that constitution. For a Foucauldian elaboration of this theme, see Spivak, "Narratives of Multiculturalism," in Thomas W. Keenan, ed., *Cultural Diversities* (forthcoming); for an elaboration of this in terms of the old multicultural imperial formations in Eurasia, see "Response to Anahid Kasabian and David Kasanjian," *Armenian Review* (forthcoming).

12. Jacques Derrida, "Force of Law: the 'Mystical Foundation of Authority,'" in *Deconstruction and the Possibility of Justice,* vol. 11, nos. 5–6 of *Cardozo Law Review* (July–August 1990): 971.

13. Some of these philosophical moves are to be found, with reference to a general social context, in the discussion of the aporia between the experience of the impossible and the possibility of the political in Jacques Derrida, *The Other Heading: Reflections on Today's Europe,* trans. Pascale-Anne Brault and Michael B. Naas (Bloomington: Indiana University Press, 1992), 44–46; and, with reference to the academic institutional context, in Derrida, "Mochlos; or, The Conflict of the Faculties," in Richard Rand, ed., *Logomachia: The Conflict of the Faculties* (Lincoln: University of Nebraska Press, 1992), 3–34.

14. Scott, "Campaign," 43.

15. Herbert Marcuse, "Repressive Tolerance," in Robert Paul Wolff and Barrington Moore Jr., eds., *A Critique of Pure Tolerance* (Boston: Beacon Press, 1965), 116.

16. Aihwa Ong, "Colonialism and Modernity: Feminist Re-presentations of Women in Non-Western Societies," *Inscriptions* 3, no. 4 (1988): 90. Although I have some problems with the details of Ong's argument, I am fully in accord with her general point.

17. Much the most successful effort is from the great UN Women's Conferences (Nairobi 1985, Cairo 1994, Beijing 1995). I have discussed this in "Love, Cruelty, and Cultural Talks in the Hot Peace," *Parallax* (forthcoming) and "Who Claims Sexuality?" *New Literary History* (forthcoming).

18. I have attempted such a separate discussion in "Diasporas Old and New: Women in the Trans-national World," *Textual Practices* (forthcoming). Suffice it here to say that even within economic migration, women often remain exilic. The definition is, as usual, gender-sensitive.

19. Derrida, "Force of Law," 947.

20. V. I. Lenin, *Imperialism: The Highest Stage of Capitalism: A Popular Outline* (New York: International Publishers, 1939), 22.

21. Stanley Aronowitz, "The Situation of the Left in the United States," *Socialist Review* 93, no. 3 (January–March 1994): 5–79. See also the collection of responses in the subsequent issue.

22. Immanuel Wallerstein et al., *Antisystemic Movements* (New York: Verso, 1989), 32, 34–35.

23. Karl Marx, *Capital,* trans. David Fernbach (New York: Vintage, 1981), 3:1015–16.

24. For the argument that socialism and capitalism are each other's *différance,* see Spivak, "Supplementing Marxism," in Steven Cullenberg and Bernd Magnus, eds., *Whither Marxism?* (New York: Routledge, 1995).

25. Amy Tan, *The Joy Luck Club* (New York: Ivy Books, 1989). Hereafter cited in the text as *JLC,* followed by the page number(s). For specific criticism of this text and other "ethnic minority" texts from specific ethnic groups, see my description of the liberal multiculturalist classroom above. By contrast, I am speaking of the text's witnessing to the U.S. commonality of the migrant, "the same difference."

26. The fact that this struggle did not mean the same thing for the Jewish and the black sectors of the district brings forth both the element of competition and the pedagogically negotiable epistemic space of the old immigrants that I have touched on above. These examples make clear that abstract talk of the politics of difference and different histories does not go too far unless we consider only the "white" as dominant. For details of the event, see Maurice R. Berube and Marilyn Gittell, eds., *Confrontation at Ocean Hill–Brownsville: The New York School Strikes of 1968* (New York: Praeger, 1969). For a testament on the continuing struggle in the field of black-Jewish unity, consider Thurgood Marshall's choice of Jack Greenberg in 1949 (Jack Greenberg, *Crusaders in the Courts: How a Dedicated Band of Lawyers Fought for the Civil Rights Revolution* [New York: Basic Books, 1994]).

27. Scott, "Campaign," 36.

28. For an account of the party debate on the internal colonization of the African-American, see Philip S. Foner and James S. Allen, eds., *American Communism and Black Americans: A Documentary History, 1919–1929* (Philadelphia: Temple University Press, 1986), vii–xvi, 163–201; and Philip S. Foner and Herbert Shapero, eds., *American Communism and Black Americans: A Documentary History, 1930–1934* (Philadelphia: Temple University Press, 1991), xi–xxix, 1–50, 93–107. I thank Brent Edwards for making these volumes known to me. The debate plays out the difference between Lenin's notion of (capitalist) territorial imperialism and Stalin's notion of (precapitalist) multinational empires in another setting.

29. On limited surveillance by the border patrol, see Michael Kearney, "Borders and Boundaries of State and Self at the End of Empire," *Journal of Historical Sociology* 4, no. 1 (March 1991): 52–74. Illegal immigration is so volatile a public issue in California that descriptive generalizations may become obsolete rather quickly.

30. Diaspora and transnationality are investigated, respectively, in José Saldivar, *The Dialectics of Our America: Genealogy, Cultural Critique, and Literary History* (Durham, N.C.: Duke University Press, 1991), and *Border Matters* (Berkeley: University of California Press, forthcoming). For an appropriately gendered perspective, see Jean Franco, *Border Patrol* (Cambridge. Mass.: Harvard University Press, forthcoming).

31. With texts such as Leslie Silko, *Almanac of the Dead* (New York: Simon and Schuster, 1991) and the work of younger writers like Drew Taylor, such anguish seems slightly anachronistic as I revise, although it is still appropriate in the larger context.

32. Jack D. Forbes, *Black Africans and Native Americans: Color, Race and Caste in the Evolution of Red Black Peoples* (New York: Blackwell, 1988). Hereafter cited in the text as *BA,* followed by the page number(s).

33. It would, for example, be interesting to play this narrative in counterpoint with Hortense Spillers, "The Tragic Mulatta," in Elizabeth A. Meese and Alice Parker, eds., *The Difference Within: Feminism and Critical Theory* (Amsterdam: John Benjamin, 1989), or with the more extensive work in Deborah E. McDowell and Arnold Rampersad, eds., *Slavery and the Literary Imagination: Selected Papers from the English Institute, 1987* (Baltimore: Johns Hopkins University Press, 1989). Since this is a slightly idiosyncratic reading of Foucault, I am obliged to cite my own "More on Power/Knowledge," in Spivak, *Outside,* 25–95.

34. This argument is generally present in extant scholarship. For a random and superior example, I offer Russell R. Menard, "The Africanization of the Lowcountry Labor Force, 1670–1730," in Winthrop D. Jordan and Sheila L. Skemp, eds., *Race and Family in the Colonial South* (Jackson: University Press of Mississippi, 1987), 81–108.

35. Contrary to some established opinion, Forbes makes a convincing case that the crucial descriptive *mulat(t)o* is a displacement of the Arabic *muwallad-maula* (*BA* 141–42). The importance of Islam in discussions of imperial formations is illustrated here from below as elsewhere from above. For the general reader, the sourcebooks are Samir Amin, *Unequal Development: An Essay on the Social*

Formations of Peripheral Capitalism, trans. Brian Pearce (Boston: Monthly Review Press, 1976), and the last chapter of Perry Anderson, *Lineages of the Absolutist State* (London: New Left Books, 1974). To this must now be added Jan Nederveen Pieterse, *Empire and Emancipation: Power and Liberation on a World Scale* (New York: Praeger, 1989).

36. The portions on Forbes are excerpted from Gayatri Spivak, "Race before Racism and the Disappearance of the American," *Plantation Society* 3, no. 2 (summer 93): 73–91.

37. Wallerstein, *Antisystemic Movements,* 21; the following phrase is on 20.

38. Marcuse, "Repressive Tolerance," 91.

39. Begum Rokeya Sakhawat Hossain, *Abarodh-bāshini,* in *Rokeya-achanābali* (Dhaka: Bangla Akademi, 1984), 473; translation mine.

40. Paul de Man, *Allegories of Reading: Figural Language in Rousseau, Nietzsche, Rilke, and Proust* (New Haven: Yale University Press, 1979), 205; the following phrase is from 208–9.

41. Here I refer the reader to a more extended discussion of the cultural politics of Indian writing in English in Gayatri Spivak, "How to Teach a 'Culturally Different' Book," in Peter Hulme, ed., *Colonial Discourse/Postcolonial Theory* (Manchester: University of Manchester Press, 1994).

42. Naila Kabeer, "The Quest for National Identity: Women, Islam and the State in Bangladesh," in Deniz Kandiyoti, ed., *Women, Islam, and the State* (Philadelphia: Temple University Press, 1991), 115–43; the quoted phrase is on 138.

43. For a convenient description of the qualitative change in global exploitation to manage the recession of 1973, see David Harvey, *The Condition of Postmodernity: An Enquiry into the Origins of Cultural Change* (Cambridge: Blackwell, 1989), 141–72.

44. Woman's position within the patriarchal family as a feudal mode of production has been argued forcefully by Harriet Fraad et al., in *Bringing It All Back Home: Class, Gender and Power in the Household Today* (London: Pluto Press, 1994).

45. A striking exception is the poetry of Farhad Mazhar. A selection will be available in my translation, forthcoming from *Third Text.*

46. Gayatri Spivak, "Three Women's Texts and a Critique of Imperialism," in Henry Louis Gates Jr., ed., *Race, Writing, and Difference* (Chicago: University of Chicago Press, 1986), 272.

47. Discussion with National Press Club, broadcast on CSPAN, September 28, 1991.

48. *Declaration of Comilla* (Dhaka: UBINIG, 1991), xiii.

49. Assia Djebar, *Fantasia: An Algerian Cavalcade,* trans. Dorothy S. Blair (New York: Quartet Books, 1985); translation modified in all cited passages; hereafter cited in the text as *F,* followed by page number(s). This concluding passage is a modified version of the opening of "Acting Bits/Identity Talk," *Critical Inquiry* 28, no. 4 (summer 1992): 770–803.

50. Frantz Fanon, *A Dying Colonialism,* trans. Haakan Chevalier (New York: Grove Weidenfeld, 1965), 65–66, 67.

51. It would be interesting to work out the itinerary of Rolland's exile from the energetic analysis of 1848 by Marx, "The Eighteenth Brumaire of Louis Bonaparte," in *Surveys from Exile,* trans. Ben Fowkes (New York: Vintage Books, 1974), 143–249.

Chapter 27
**Postcolonial Criticism and
Indian Historiography**
Gyan Prakash

One of the distinct effects of the recent emergence of postcolonial criticism has been to force a radical rethinking and reformulation of forms of knowledge and social identities authored and authorized by colonialism and Western domination. For this reason, it has also created a ferment in the field of knowledge. This is not to say that colonialism and its legacies remained unquestioned until recently: nationalism and Marxism come immediately to mind as powerful challenges to colonialism. But both of these operated with master narratives that put Europe at the center. Thus, when nationalism, reversing Orientalist thought, attributed agency and history to the subjected nation, it also staked a claim to the order of reason and progress instituted by colonialism; and when Marxists pilloried colonialism, their criticism was framed by a universalist mode-of-production narrative. Recent postcolonial criticism, in contrast, seeks to undo the Eurocentrism produced by the institution of the West's trajectory, its appropriation of the other as History. It does so, however, with the acute realization that postcoloniality is not born and nurtured in a panoptic distance from history. The postcolonial exists as an aftermath, as an after — after being worked over by colonialism.[1] Criticism formed in this process of the enunciation of discourses of domination occupies a space that is neither inside nor outside the history of Western domination but in a tangential relation to it. This is what Homi Bhabha calls an in-between, hybrid position of practice and negotiation[2] or what Gayatri Chakravorty Spivak terms catachresis: "reversing, displacing, and seizing the apparatus of value-coding."[3] In the rest of this essay, I describe this catachrestic reinscription and the anxieties it provokes in the field of Indian historiography, where postcolonial criticism has made a particularly notable appearance.

The Ambivalence of Postcolonial Criticism

A prominent example of recent postcolonial criticism consists of the writings in several volumes of *Subaltern Studies* (edited and theorized most extensively by Ranajit Guha) that challenge existing historiography as elitist and advance in its place a subaltern perspective.[4] A collective of historians writing from India, Britain, and Australia, the *Subaltern Studies* scholars use the perspective of the subaltern to fiercely combat the persistence of colonialist knowledge in nationalist and mode-of-production narratives. It is important to note that their project is derived from Marxism or from the failure of the realization of the Marxist collective consciousness. For it is this failure of the subaltern to act as a class-conscious worker that provides the basis for representing the subaltern as resistant to the appropriation by colonial and nationalist elites or to various programs of modernity. The subaltern is a figure produced by historical discourses of domination, but it nevertheless provides a mode of reading history differently from those inscribed in elite accounts. Reading colonial and nationalist archives against their grain and focusing on their blind spots, silences, and anxieties, these historians seek to uncover the subaltern's myths, cults, ideologies, and revolts that colonial and nationalist elites sought to appropriate and that conventional historiography has laid to waste by the deadly weapon of cause and effect. Ranajit Guha's *Elementary Aspects of Peasant Insurgency in India* (1983) is a powerful example of this scholarship that seeks to recover the peasant from elite projects and positivist historiography. In this wide-ranging study full of brilliant insights and methodological innovation, Guha provides a fascinating account of the peasants' insurgent consciousness, rumors, mythic visions, religiosity, and bonds of community. From Guha's account, the subalterns emerge with forms of sociality and political community at odds with nation and class, and they defy the models of rationality and social action that conventional historiography uses. Guha argues persuasively that such models are elitist insofar as they deny the subaltern's autonomous consciousness and are drawn from colonial and liberal-nationalist projects of appropriating the subaltern. Although such readings were brilliantly deconstructive of the colonial-nationalist archives, the early phase of the project *Subaltern Studies* was marked by a desire to retrieve the autonomous will and consciousness of the subaltern. This is no longer the case in these scholars' more recent writings, but even in their earlier writings the desire to recover the subaltern's autonomy is repeatedly frustrated because subalternity, by definition, signifies the impossibility of autonomy.

The concept of a subaltern history, derived from its simultaneous possibility and impossibility in discourses of domination, exemplifies the ambivalence of postcolonial criticism: formed in history, it reinscribes and displaces the record of that history by reading its archives differently from its constitution (in Spivak's sense of catachresis). This ambivalent criticism is observable also in writings that, with a somewhat different focus than that in the *Subaltern Studies* volumes, subject forms of knowledge, culture, and "traditions," canonized by colonial and Western discourses, to searching scrutiny and radical reinscription. Examinations of the nineteenth-century reformist attempts to suppress and outlaw the practices of widow sacrifice (sati), for example, rearticulate them by revealing that the colonial rulers and Indian male reformers formulated and used gendered ideas to enforce new forms of domination even as they questioned the burning of widows; studies of criminality point to power relations at work in classifying and acting upon "criminal tribes" even as threats to life and property were countered; and inquiries into labor servitude depict how the free-unfree opposition concealed the operation of power in the installation of free labor as the natural human condition while it provided a vantage point for challenging certain forms of corporeal domination.[5] The aim of such studies is not to unmask dominant discourses but to explore their fault lines in order to provide different accounts, to describe histories revealed in the cracks of the colonial archaeology of knowledge.

In part, the critical gaze that these studies direct at the archaeology of knowledge enshrined in the West arises from the fact that most of them are being written in the First World academy, where the power of hegemonic discourses about India is so palpable. This is not to say that the reach of these discourses does not extend beyond metropolitan centers; but outside the First World, in India itself, the power of Western discourses operates through its authorization and deployment by the nation-state — the ideologies of modernization and instrumentalist science are so deeply sedimented in the national body politic that they neither manifest themselves nor function exclusively as forms of imperial power.[6] In the West, in contrast, the production and distribution of Orientalist concepts continue to play a vital role in projecting the First World as the radiating center around which others are arranged. It is for this reason that postcolonial criticisms produced in the metropolitan academy evince certain affinities with deconstructive critiques of the West.[7] In this respect, both Michel Foucault's and Jacques Derrida's critiques of Western thought intersect with postcolonial criticism. This is true for Foucault because his account of the genealogies of the West provides a powerful critique of the rule of modernity that the colonies experienced in a peculiar form. Derrida's relevance is not obvious but is no less important because, exposing how structures of signification effect their closures through a strategy of opposition and hierarchization that edits, suppresses, and marginalizes everything that upsets founding values, he provides a way to undo the implacable oppositions of colonial thought — East/West, traditional/modern, primitive/civilized. If these oppositions, as in his analysis of the metaphysics of presence, aim relentlessly to suppress the other as an inferior, as a supplement, then their structures of signification can also be rearticulated differently:

> Metaphysics — the white mythology which reassembles and reflects the culture of the West: the white man takes his own mythology, Indo-European mythology, his own *logos,* that is, the *mythos* of his idiom, for the universal form that he must still wish to call Reason.... White mythology — metaphysics has erased within itself the fabulous scene that has produced it, the scene that nevertheless remains active and stirring, inscribed in white ink, an invisible design covered over in the palimpsest.[8]

If the production of white mythology has nevertheless left "an invisible design covered over in the palimpsest," the structure of signification, of *différance,* can be rearticulated differently than the structure that produced the West as reason. For postcolonial theorists, the value of Derrida's insight lies in the disclosure, on the one hand, that the politics displacing other claims to the margins can be undone by rearticulating the structure of differences that existing foundations seek to suppress and, on the other hand, that strategies for challenging the authority and power derived from various foundational myths (history as the march of Man, of Reason, of Progress, of Modes-of-Production) lie inside, not outside, the ambivalence that these myths seek to suppress. From this point of view, critical work seeks its basis not without but within the fissures of dominant structures. Or, as Gayatri Chakravorty Spivak puts it, the deconstructive philosophical position (or postcolonial criticism) consists in saying an "impossible 'no' to a structure, which one critiques, yet inhabits intimately."[9]

For an example of this deconstructive strategy that rearticulates a structure that one inhabits intimately, let us turn to archival documents dealing with the abolition of sati, or Hindu widow sacrifice in the early nineteenth century. The historian encounters these as records documenting the contests between the British "civilizing mission" and Hindu heathenism, between modernity and tradition, and as records of previous readings about the beginning of the emancipation of Hindu women and about the birth of modern India. This is so because, as Lata Mani has shown,[10] the very existence of these documents has a history involving the fixing of women as the site for the colonial and the indigenous male elite's constructions of authoritative Hindu traditions. The accumulated sources on sati — regarding whether or not the burning of widows was sanctioned by Hindu codes, whether they went willingly or not to the funeral pyre, on what grounds the immolation of women could be abolished, and so on — come to us marked by early nineteenth-century colonial and indigenous-patriarchal discourses. And just as the early nineteenth-century encounter between colonial and indigenous elites and textual sources was resonant with colonial-patriarchal voices, the historian's confrontation today with sources on sati cannot escape the echo of that previous rendezvous. In repeating that encounter, how does the historian today *not replicate* the early nineteenth-century staging of sati as a contest between tradition and modernity (or different visions of tradition), between the slavery of women and efforts toward their emancipation, between barbaric Hindu practices and the British civilizing mission? Lata Mani accomplishes this task brilliantly by showing that the opposing arguments were founded on the fabrication of the law-giving scriptural tradition as the origin of Hindu customs: both those who supported and those who opposed sati sought the authority of textual origins for their beliefs. During the debate, however, the whole history of the fabrication of origins was effaced, as was the collusion between indigenous patriarchy and colonial power in constructing the origins for and against sati. Consequently, as Spivak states starkly, the debate left no room for the woman's enunciatory position. Caught in the contest over whether traditions did or did not sanction sati and over whether the woman self-immolated willingly or not, the colonized subaltern woman disappeared: she was literally extinguished for her dead husband in the indigenous patriarchal discourse or was offered the disfiguring choice of the Western notion of the sovereign, individual will.[11] The problem here is not one of sources (the absence of woman's testimony), but that the very staging of the debate left no place for the widow's enunciatory position: she is left no position from which she can speak. Spivak makes this silencing of the woman speak of the limits of historical knowledge, but the critic can do so because the colonial archive comes with a pregnant silence.[12]

Spivak very correctly marks the silencing of the subaltern woman as the point at which the interpreter must acknowledge the limits of historical understanding; it is impossible to retrieve the woman's voice when she was not given a subject-position from which to speak. But this refusal to retrieve the woman's voice because it would involve the conceit that the interpreter speaks for her does not disable understanding; rather, Spivak manages to reinscribe the colonial and indigenous patriarchal archive when she shows that the tradition-versus-modernization story was told by obliterating the colonized women's subject-position. Here, the interpreter's recognition of the limit of historical knowledge does not disable criticism but enables the critic to mark the space of the silenced subaltern as aporetic. The recognition of the subaltern as the limit of knowledge, in turn, resists a paternalist "recovery" of the subaltern's voice and frustrates our repetition of the imperialist attempt to speak for the colonized subaltern woman. This argument appears to run counter to the radical historians' use of the historiographical convention of retrieval to recover the histories of the traditionally ignored — women, workers, peasants, and minorities. Spivak's point, however, is not that such retrievals should not be undertaken but that they mark the point of the subaltern's silencing in history. The project of retrieval begins at the point of the subaltern's erasure; its very possibility is also a sign of its impossibility and represents the intervention of the historian-critic whose discourse must be interrogated persistently and whose appropriation of the other should be guarded against vigilantly.[13]

Capitalism and Colonialism

These directions of postcolonial criticism make it a disturbing and ambivalent practice, perched between traditional historiography and its failures, between the elite and the subaltern, within the folds of dominant discourses and seeking to rearticulate their pregnant silence — outlining "an invisible design covered over in the palimpsest." How do these strategies fare when compared with a powerful tradition of historiography of India that seeks to encompass its colonial history in the larger narrative of the development of capitalism? Does not the concern with rearticulating colonial discourses necessarily neglect the story of capitalist exploitation and imperialist profits?

Elsewhere, I have argued that we cannot thematize Indian history in terms of the development of capitalism and simultaneously contest capitalism's homogenization of the contemporary world. Critical history cannot simply document the process by which capitalism becomes dominant, for that amounts to repeating the history we seek to displace; instead, criticism must reveal the difference that capitalism either represents as the particular form of its universal existence or sketches only in relation to itself.[14] This argument has drawn the criticism that my position commits me to view capitalism as a "disposable fiction" and reveals a simplistic understanding of the relationship between capitalism and heterogeneity. It is suggested that we recognize the structure of domination as a totality (capitalism) that alone provides the basis for understanding the sources of historical oppression and formulating critical emancipatory positions.[15]

Does a refusal to thematize modern Indian history in terms of the development of capitalism amount to saying that capitalism is a "disposable fiction," and that class relations are illusory? Not at all. My point is that making capitalism the foundational theme amounts to homogenizing the histories that remain heterogeneous with it. It is one thing to say that the establishment of capitalist relations has been one of the major features in India's recent history but quite another to regard it as the foundation of colonialism. It is one thing to say that class relations affected a range of power relations in India — involving the caste system, patriarchy, ethnic oppression, Hindu-Muslim conflicts — and quite another to oppose the latter as "forms" assumed by the former. The issue here is not that of one factor versus several; rather, it is that, as class is inevitably articulated with other determinations, power exists in a form of relationality in which the dominance of one is never complete. For example, although colonial rule in India constructed the labor force according to the economy of the free-unfree opposition, this domestication of otherness (of "Hindu" and "Islamic" forms of "slavery") as unfreedom also left "an invisible design covered over in the palimpsest."[16] It is precisely by highlighting the "invisible design" that capitalism's attempts to either subsume different structures or polarize them can be shown as incompletely successful. Only then can we, as critics, examine the fault lines of this discourse and make visible the ambivalence and alterity present in the constitution of capitalism as a foundational theme. This means listening attentively when the culture and history that the critic inhabits make capitalism name and speak for histories that remained discrepant with it. To the extent that these discrepancies are made to speak in the language of capitalism — as "precapitalist" peasants, "unfree laborers," "irrational" peasants — its "foundational" status is not a "disposable fiction." But it is equally true that in domesticating all the wholly other subject-positions as self-consolidating otherness (*pre*capitalist peasants, *un*free laborers, *ir*rational peasants), capitalism is also caught in a structure of ambivalence it cannot master. This is why study after study shows that capitalism in the Third World, not just in India, was crucially distorted, impure, mixed with precapitalist survivals. To think of the incompleteness and failures of capitalist modernity in the Third World in critical terms, therefore, requires that we reinscribe the binary form in which capitalism's partial success is portrayed, that we render visible processes and forms that its oppositional logic can appropriate only violently and incompletely. Of course, historians cannot recover what was suppressed, but they can critically confront the effects of that silencing, capitalism's foundational status, by writing histories of irretrievable subject-positions, by sketching the traces of figures that come to us only as disfigurations not in order to restore the "original" figures but to find the limit of foundations in shadows that the disfigurations themselves outline.

To write of histories at the point of capitalism's distorted and impure development in India does not amount to disregarding class or abandoning Marxism. At issue here is the irreducible heterogeneity of metropolitan capital with the colonial subaltern, a heterogeneity that an unexamined Eurocentric Marxism would have us overlook. I am not suggesting that acknowledging Marx's Eurocentrism requires abandoning Marxism altogether. But students of Indian history, who know only too well the Eurocentricity of Marx's memorable formulation that the British conquest introduced a historyless India to history, cannot now regard the mode-of-production story as a normative universal. In fact, like many other nineteenth-century European ideas, the staging of the Eurocentric mode-of-production narrative as history should be seen as an analogue of nineteenth-century territorial imperialism. From this point of view, Marx's ideas on changeless India — theorized, for example, in his concept of the "Asiatic mode of production" — appear not so much as mistaken but as the discursive form produced by the universalization of Europe, by its appropriation of the absolute other into a domesticated other. Such a historicization of the Eurocentrism in nineteenth-century Marxism enables us to understand the collusion of capitalism and colonialism and to undo the effect of that collusion's imperative to interpret Third World histories in terms of capital's logic. To suggest that we reinscribe the effects of capitalism's foundational status by writing about histories that remained heterogeneous with the logic of capital, therefore, is not to abandon Marxism but to extricate class analysis from its nineteenth-century heritage, acknowledging that its critique of capitalism was both enabled and disabled by its historicity as a European discourse.

The alternative would have us view colonialism as *reducible* to the development of capitalism in Britain and in India. The conflation of the metropolitan proletariat with the colonized subaltern that this produces amounts to a homogenization of irreducible difference. Of course, it could be argued that capitalism, rather than homogenizing difference, is perfectly capable of utilizing and generating heterogeneity. But the notion that capitalism is a founding source responsible for originating and encompassing difference amounts to appropriating heterogeneity as a self-consolidating difference, that is, refracting "what might have been the absolutely Other into a domesticated Other."[17] This assimilation of difference into identity becomes inevitable when capitalism is made to stand for history; the heterogeneity of histories of the colonized subaltern with those of the metropolitan proletariat is then effaced, and absolute otherness is appropriated into self-consolidating difference.

The issue of the heterogeneity of social identities and cultural forms raised by the relationship of colonialism to capitalism is not one that can be resolved easily by the extension of the race-class-gender formula; the question of colonial difference is not one of the adequacy of a single (class) versus multiple factors, nor are we constrained to choose forms of sociality other than class. What is at issue in the articulation of class with race, caste, gender, nation, ethnicity, and religion is that these categories were not equal; woman as a category was not equal to worker; being an upper-caste Hindu was not a form of sociality equal with citizenship in the nation-state that the nationalists struggled to achieve. Thus, the concept of multiple selves, incorporating a variety of social identities and thus popular with the contemporary liberal multiculturalists, cannot be adequate for conceiving colonial difference. Instead, we have to think of the specificity of colonial difference as class overwriting race and gender, of nation overinscribing class, ethnicity, and religion, and so forth — an imbalanced process, but nevertheless a process that can be re-articulated differently. This is the concept of heterogeneity and cultural difference as it emerges from postcoloniality.

The Question of Heterogeneity

The postcolonial disruption of master narratives authorized by imperialism produces an insistence on the heterogeneity of colonial histories that is often mistaken for the postmodern pastiche. Though the present currency of such concepts as decentered subjects and parodic texts may provide a receptive and appropriative frame for postcolonial criticism, its emphasis on heterogeneity neither aims to celebrate the polyphony of native voices nor springs forth from superior value placed on multiplicity. Rather, it arises from the recognition that the *functioning* of colonial power was heterogeneous with its founding oppositions. Not only were colonies the dark underside, the recalcitrant supplement, that subverted the self-same concepts of modernity, civilization, reason, and progress with which the West wrapped itself, but the very enunciation of colonial discourses was ambivalent. Thus, the postcolonial insistence on heterogeneity emanates from the insight that colonial discourses operated as the structure of *writing* and that the structure of their enunciation remained heterogeneous with the binary oppositions that colonialism instituted in ordering the discursive field to serve unequal power relations. Homi Bhabha's analysis of colonial mimicry outlines the postcolonial critic's distinct notion of difference.

Writing of the stereotypes and pseudoscientific theories that were commonly used in colonial discourse, Bhabha suggests that these were attempts to normalize the ambivalence produced in the contradictory enunciation of colonial discourses. This ambivalence arose from the "tension between the synchronic panoptical vision of domination — the demand for identity, stasis — and the counter-pressure of the diachrony of history — change, difference."[18] Under these opposing pressures, the colonial discourse was caught up in conflict, split between "what is always 'in place,' already known, and something that must be anxiously repeated...as if the essential duplicity of the Asiatic or the bestial sexual license of the African that needs no proof, can never really, in discourse, be proved."[19] If, on the one hand, the colonial discourse asserted that the colonizers and the colonized were fixed, unchanging identities, then the repetition of this assertion, on the other hand, meant that discourse was forced to constantly reconstitute and refigure this fixity; consequently, the discourse was split between proclaiming the unchangeability of colonial subjects and acknowledging their changing character by having to reform and reconstitute them. If that discourse created the colonizer-colonized opposition, it also produced figures and processes that its structure of power relations could not easily accommodate.[20] Bhabha traces an example of such an ambivalent functioning of discourse in the construction of the colonial stereotype of mimic-men applied to English-speaking Indians. He argues that if the British portrayal of the resemblance of Anglicized Indians with Englishmen as mimicry was a "strategy of reform, regulation, and discipline, which 'appropriates' the Other," then the stereotype of mimicry was also the mark of a recalcitrant difference, *"a difference that is almost the same, but not quite."*[21] If the colonial discourse produced a "reformed" Other — the Anglicized Indian (the infamous "Babu") who resembled the English — then the strategy of assimilation acknowledged a recalcitrant difference: the Anglicized Indian was a brown Englishman, at best — "not white/not quite." To be sure, the acknowledgment of recalcitrant difference took the racist form of Thomas Macaulay's notorious formulation that these mimic-men were to be "Indian in blood and color, but English in taste, in opinions, in morals, and in intellect." But the use of racism also signifies a heterogeneity that could not be appropriated. Bhabha fastens on this blind spot of the discourse to show that the flat assertion of stereotypes was also the moment of fear and anxiety in the discourse because the recalcitrant difference of the reformed Babu turned mimicry into mockery; confronted with Englishness in the brown figure of the Indian, the authority of selfness was put under profound stress.

Bhabha's analysis of colonial discourse at the point of its stress departs from the strategy of reversal practiced by previous criticism. For, at these moments of indeterminacy, when the discourse can be seen to veer away from the implacable logic of oppositionality, the critic can intervene and, using historical work as a license for a strategy of critical reading, renegotiate the terms of the discourse. The cultural difference that emerges from the renegotiation of the discourse is not polymorphous diversity released from the straitjacket of binary oppositions; instead, it is a heterogeneity that the existing dichotomies themselves make simultaneously possible and impossible. Bhabha reads this heterogeneity in the native rewriting of the colonial text, in those "hybrid" moments when the colonized produce not a copy of the original but misappropriate it, thereby reformulating the master text, exposing its ambivalence, and denying its authority.[22] From this point of view, categories of racial, class, ethnic, gender, and national difference arise not as the result of a well-intentioned liberal gesture but as social identifications formed at the point of colonialism's conflictual and contingent mode of functioning.

•

History and colonialism arose together in India. As India was introduced to history, it was also stripped of a meaningful past; it became a historyless society brought into the age of History. The flawed nature of history's birth in India was not lost on the nationalists who pressed the nation-state's claim to the age of history, and Marxists struggled against capital's collusion with colonialism to make the worker the agent of history. Consequently, history, flawed at birth, has lived an embattled life in India. These factors constitute the point of departure for postcolonial criticism.[23] For postcolonial historiography, the embattled and anxious enunciation of history as a form of being and knowledge provides the opportunity to seize and reinscribe it catachrestically, not to restore lost forms of telling and knowing but to pick apart the disjunctive moments of discourses authorized by colonialism and authenticated by the nation-state and rearticulate them in another — third — form of writing history. It is from the "scene that nevertheless remains active and stirring, inscribed in white ink, an invisible design covered over in the palimpsest" that the colonial and the subaltern supplement reinscribes and revises the narratives of the modern, the West, and man — white mythology.

NOTES

1. Gayatri Chakravorty Spivak speaks of postcoloniality in similar terms: "We are always *after* the empire of reason, our claims to it always short of adequate" ("Poststructuralism, Marginality, Postcoloniality and Value," in *Literary Theory Today,* ed. Peter Collier and Helga Geyer-Ryan [London: Polity Press, 1990], 228).

2. Homi Bhabha, "The Commitment to Theory," in *Questions of Third Cinema,* ed. J. Pines and P. Willemen (London: BFI, 1989), 112–31.

3. Spivak, "Poststructuralism."

4. The writings of this group include: Ranajit Guha, ed., *Subaltern Studies,* vols. 1–6 (Delhi: Oxford University Press, 1981–89); Ranajit Guha, *Elementary Aspects of Peasant Insurgency in Colonial India* (Delhi: Oxford University Press, 1983); Partha Chatterjee, *Nationalist Thought and the Colonial World: A Derivative Discourse?* (London: Zed Books, 1986); and Dipesh Chakrabarty, *Rethinking Working-Class History: Bengal 1890–1940* (Princeton, N.J.: Princeton University Press, 1989).

5. Veena Das, "Gender Studies, Cross-Cultural Comparison and the Colonial Organization of Knowledge," *Berkshire Review,* 21 (1986); Lata Mani, "Contentious Traditions: The Debate on Sati in Colonial India," *Cultural Critique* 7 (fall 1987): 119–56. On criminality, see Sanjay Nigam, "Disciplining and Policing the 'Criminals by Birth,'" *Indian Economic and Social History Review,* 27, no. 2

(1990): 131–64 and 27, no. 3 (1990): 257–87. On the discourse of freedom, see my *Bonded Histories: Genealogies of Labor Servitude in Colonial India* (Cambridge: Cambridge University Press, 1990).

6. See Lata Mani, "Multiple Mediations: Feminist Scholarship in the Age of Multinational Reception," *Inscriptions* 5 (1989): 1–23.

7. On poststructuralism, postcolonial criticism, and the critique of the West, see Robert Young, *White Mythologies: Writing History and the West* (London: Routledge, 1990).

8. Jacques Derrida, *Margins of Philosophy*, trans. Alan Bass (Chicago: University of Chicago Press, 1982), 213.

9. Gayatri Chakravorty Spivak, "The Making of Americans, the Teaching of English, the Future of Colonial Studies," *New Literary History* 21, no. 4 (1990): 28.

10. Mani, "Contentious Traditions."

11. Gayatri Chakravorty Spivak, "Can the Subaltern Speak?" in *Marxism and Interpretation of Culture,* ed. Cary Nelson and Lawrence Grossberg (Urbana: University of Illinois Press, 1988), 271–313, esp. 299–307.

12. For a similar argument about the colonized woman caught between indigenous patriarchy and the politics of archival production, see also Gayatri Chakravorty Spivak's "The Rani of Sirmur: An Essay in the Reading of the Archives," *History and Theory* 24, no. 3 (1985): 247–72.

13. See Young, *White Mythologies,* 164–65.

14. See my "Writing Post-Orientalist Histories of the Third World: Perspectives from Indian Historiography," *Comparative Studies in Society and History* 32, no. 2 (1990): 383–408.

15. Rosalind O'Hanlon and David Washbrook, "After Orientalism: Culture, Criticism, and Politics in the Third World," *Comparative Studies in Society and History* 34, no. 1 (January 1992). My reply, "Can the 'Subaltern' Ride? A Reply to O'Hanlon and Washbrook," from which this essay draws, appears also in the same issue.

16. For a study of the process of this covering over in the context of "unfree" laborers, see my *Bonded Histories.* Nicholas Dirks's *The Hollow Crown: Ethnohistory of an Indian Kingdom* (Cambridge: Cambridge University Press, 1987), similarly traces the marks of a relationship between caste and power in the process that hollowed out the political space in a south Indian kingdom and filled it with colonial power.

17. Gayatri Chakravorty Spivak, "Three Women's Texts and a Critique of Imperialism," *Critical Inquiry* 12, no. 1 (1985): 253.

18. Homi Bhabha, "Of Mimicry and Man: The Ambivalence of Colonial Discourse," *October* 34 (fall 1985): 126.

19. Homi Bhabha, "The Other Question . . . ," *Screen* 24, no. 6 (1983): 18.

20. Bhabha, "The Other Question," 23–25.

21. Bhabha, "Of Mimicry and Man," 126.

22. Homi Bhabha, "Signs Taken for Wonders: Questions of Ambivalence and Authority under a Tree Outside Delhi, May 1817," *Critical Inquiry* 12, no. 1 (1985): 144–65.

23. For a related argument, see Dipesh Chakrabarty, "History as Critique and Critique(s) of History," *Economic and Political Weekly* 26, no. 37 (September 14, 1991): 2162–66.

Chapter 28
The Postcolonial Aura: Third World Criticism
in the Age of Global Capitalism
Arif Dirlik

"When exactly . . . does the 'post-colonial' begin?" queries Ella Shohat in a discussion
of the subject.[1] Misreading the question deliberately, I will supply here an answer
that is only partially facetious: "When Third World intellectuals have arrived in First
World academe."

My goal in the discussion below is to review the term "postcolonial," and the
various intellectual/cultural positions associated with it, within the context of contemporary transformations in global relationships and the reconsiderations these
transformations call for of problems of domination and hegemony, as well as of
received critical practices. "Postcolonial" is the most recent entrant to achieve prominent visibility in the ranks of those "post" marked words (seminal among them,
"postmodernism") that serve as signposts in(to) contemporary cultural criticism. Unlike other "post" marked words, "postcolonial" claims as its special provenance the
terrain that in an earlier day used to go by the name of "Third World" and is intended, therefore, to achieve an authentic globalization of cultural discourses: by
the extension globally of the intellectual concerns and orientations originating at the
central sites of Euro-American cultural criticism; and by the introduction into the
latter of voices and subjectivities from the margins of earlier political and/or ideological colonialism, which now demand a hearing at those very sites at the center.
The goal, indeed, is no less than the abolition of all distinctions between center
and periphery, and all other "binarisms" that are allegedly a legacy of colonial(ist)
ways of thinking, and to reveal societies globally in their complex heterogeneity
and contingency. While intellectuals who hail from one part of that terrain, India,
have played a conspicuously prominent role in its formulation and dissemination,
the appeals of "postcoloniality" would seem to cut across national, regional, and
even political boundaries, which on the surface at least would seem to substantiate
its claims to globalism.

My answer to Shohat's question is only partially facetious because the popularity
that the term "postcolonial" has achieved in the last few years has less to do with
its rigorousness as a concept, or the new vistas it has opened up for critical inquiry,
than it does with the increased visibility of academic intellectuals of Third World
origin within the area of cultural criticism. I suggest below that most of the critical
themes of which postcolonial criticism claims to be the fountainhead predated in

their emergence the appearance, or at least the popular currency, of the term "post-colonial" and, therefore, owe little to it for inspiration. Whether or not there was a "postcolonial consciousness" before it was so termed, a consciousness that might have played a part in the production of those themes, is a question to which I will return below. As far as it is possible to tell from the literature, however, it was only from the mid-1980s that the label "postcolonial" was attached to those themes with increasing frequency, and that in conjunction with the use of the label to describe academic intellectuals of Third World origin, the so-called postcolonial intellectuals, who themselves seemed to acquire an academic respectability they did not have before.[2] A description of a diffuse group of intellectuals, of their concerns and orientations, was to turn by the end of the decade into a description of a global condition, in which sense it has acquired the status of a new orthodoxy both in cultural criticism and in academic programs. Shohat's question above refers to this global condition; given the ambiguity imbedded in the term "postcolonial," to redirect her question to the emergence of "postcolonial intellectuals" seems to be justifiable in order to put the horse back in front of the cart. It is intended also to underline the First World origins (and situation) of the term.

My answer is also facetious, however, because pointing to the ascendancy in First World academia of intellectuals of Third World origin and to the role they have played in the propagation of "postcolonial" as a critical orientation begs the question of why they and their intellectual concerns and orientations have been accorded the respectability that they have. The themes that are now claimed for postcolonial criticism, both in what they repudiate of the past and in what they affirm for the present, I venture to suggest, resonate with concerns and orientations that have their origins in a new world situation that has also become part of consciousness globally over the last decade. I am referring here to that world situation created by transformations within the capitalist world economy — by the emergence of what has been described variously as global capitalism, flexible production, late capitalism, and so on — that has "disorganized" earlier conceptualizations of global relations, especially relations comprehended earlier by such binarisms as colonizer/colonized, First/Third Worlds, or the "West and the rest," in all of which, furthermore, the nation-state as the unit of political organization globally was taken for granted. It is no reflection on the abilities of "postcolonial critics" to suggest that they, and the critical orientations that they represent, have acquired respectability to the extent that they have answered to the conceptual needs of the social, political, and cultural problems thrown up by this new world situation. It is, however, a reflection on the ideology of postcolonialism that except for a rare nod in this direction,[3] postcolonial critics have been largely silent on the relationship of the idea of postcolonialism to its context in contemporary capitalism; indeed, they have suppressed the necessity of considering such a possible relationship by repudiating a "foundational" role to capitalism in history.

A consideration of this relationship is my primary goal in the discussion below. I argue, first, that there is a parallel between the ascendancy in cultural criticism of the idea of postcoloniality and an emergent consciousness of global capitalism in the 1980s and, second, that the appeals of the critical themes in postcolonial criticism have much to do with their resonance with the conceptual needs presented by transformations in global relationships due to changes within the capitalist world economy. This also explains, I think, why a concept that is intended to achieve a radical revision in our comprehension of the world should appear to be complicit in "the consecration of hegemony," as Shohat has put it.[4] If postcolonial as a concept has not necessarily served as a fountainhead for the criticism of ideology in earlier ways of viewing global relationships, it has nevertheless helped concentrate under one term what had been earlier diffuse criticisms. At the same time, however, postcolonial criticism has been silent about its own status as a possible ideological effect of a new world situation after colonialism. "Postcolonial" as a description of intellectuals of Third World origin needs to be distinguished, I suggest below, from "postcolonial" as a description of this world situation. In this latter usage, the term mystifies both politically and methodologically a situation that represents not the abolition but the reconfiguration of earlier forms of domination. The complicity of "postcolonial" in hegemony lies in postcolonialism's diversion of attention from contemporary problems of social, political, and cultural domination and its obfuscation of its own relationship to what is but a condition of its emergence: a global capitalism that, however fragmented in appearance, serves nevertheless as the structuring principle of global relations.

Postcolonial Intellectuals and Postcolonial Criticism

The term "postcolonial" in its various usages carries a multiplicity of meanings that need to be distinguished for analytical purposes. Three uses of the term seem to be especially prominent (and significant). (1) It is used as a literal description of conditions in formerly colonial societies, in which case the term has concrete referents, as in "postcolonial societies" or "postcolonial intellectuals." It should be noted, however, that colonies here include both those encompassed earlier in the Third World and settler colonies usually associated with the First World, such as Canada and Australia. (2) The term is employed as a description of a global condition after the period of colonialism, in which case the usage is somewhat more abstract in reference, comparable in its vagueness to the earlier term "Third World," for which it is intended as a substitute. (3) The word is used to describe a discourse on the above conditions that is informed by the epistemological and psychic orientations that are products of those conditions.

Even at its most concrete, the term "postcolonial" is not transparent in meaning because each meaning is overdetermined by the others. Postcolonial intellectuals are clearly the producers of a postcolonial discourse, but who exactly are the postcolonial intellectuals? Here the contrast between "postcolonial" and its predecessor term, "Third World," may be revealing. The term "Third World," postcolonial critics insist, was quite vague because it encompassed within one uniform category vastly heterogeneous historical circumstances and because it locked in fixed positions, structurally if not geographically, societies and populations whose locations shifted with changing global relationships. While this objection is quite valid, the fixing of societal locations, misleadingly or not, permitted the identification of, say, Third World intellectuals with the concreteness of places of origin. "Postcolonial" does not permit such identification. I wondered above whether there might not have been a postcolonial consciousness even before it was so labeled, by which I mean the consciousness that postcolonial intellectuals claim as a hallmark of post-coloniality. The answer is: probably there was, although it was invisible because it was subsumed under the category "Third World." Now that postcoloniality has been released from the fixity of Third World location, the identity of the postcolonial is no longer structural but discursive. "Postcolonial" in this perspective represents an attempt to regroup intellectuals of uncertain location under the banner of "post-colonial discourse." Intellectuals in the flesh may be the producers of the themes that constitute postcolonial discourse, but it is participation in the discourse that defines them as postcolonial intellectuals nevertheless. Hence it is important to delineate the discourse so as to identify postcolonial intellectuals themselves.

Gyan Prakash frames concisely a question that provides the point of departure for postcolonial discourse: How does the Third World write "its own history"?[5] Like other postcolonial critics, such as Gayatri Spivak, he finds the answer to his question in the model of historical writing provided by the work on Indian history of the *Subaltern Studies* group,[6] which also provides, although it does not exhaust, the major themes in postcolonial discourse.

These themes are enunciated cogently in an essay by Prakash that, to my knowl-edge, offers the most condensed exposition of postcolonialism currently available. Prakash's introduction to his essay is worth quoting at some length:

> One of the distinct effects of the recent emergence of postcolonial criticism has been to force a radical rethinking and reformulation of forms of knowledge and social identities authored and authorized by colonialism and Western domination. For this reason, it has also created a ferment in the field of knowledge. This is not to say that colonialism and its legacies remained unquestioned until recently: nationalism and Marxism come immediately to mind as powerful challenges to colonialism. But both of these operated with master-narratives that put Europe at its [*sic*] center. Thus, when nationalism, reversing Orientalist thought, attributed agency and history to the subjected nation, it also staked a claim to the order of Reason and Progress instituted by colonialism; and when Marxists pilloried colonialism, their criticism was framed by a universalist mode-of-production narrative. Recent postcolonial criticism, on the other hand, seeks to undo the Eurocentrism produced by the institution of the West's trajectory, its appropriation of the other as History. It does so, however, with the acute realization that postcoloniality is not born and nurtured in a panoptic distance from history. The postcolonial exists as an aftermath, an after — after being worked over by colonialism. Criticism formed in the enunciation of discourses of domination occupies a space that is neither inside nor outside the history of Western domination but in a tangential relation to it. This is what Homi Bhabha calls an in-between, hybrid position of practice and negotiation, or what Gayatri Chakravorty Spivak terms catachresis; "reversing, displacing, and seizing the apparatus of value-coding."[7]

It will be helpful to elaborate on these themes. (1) Postcolonial criticism repu-diates all master-narratives and, since the most powerful current master-narratives are Eurocentric, as the products of the post-Enlightenment European constitution of history, takes the criticism of Eurocentrism as its central task. (2) Foremost among these master-narratives to be repudiated is the narrative of modernization, both in its bourgeois and its Marxist incarnations. Bourgeois modernization (developmen-talism) represents the renovation and redeployment of "colonial modernity ... as economic development."[8] Marxism, while it rejects bourgeois modernization, never-theless perpetuates the teleological assumptions of the latter by framing inquiry within a narrative of modes of production in which postcolonial history appears as a transition (or an aborted transition) to capitalism.[9] The repudiation of the nar-rative of modes of production, it needs to be added, does not mean the repudiation of Marxism — postcolonial criticism acknowledges a strong Marxist inspiration.[10] (3) Needless to say, Orientalism, in its constitution of the colony as Europe's other, in which the other is reduced to an essence without history, must be repudiated. But so must nationalism, which, while challenging Orientalism, has perpetuated the essentialism of Orientalism (by affirming a national essence in history) as well as its procedures of representation.[11] (4) The repudiation of master-narratives is necessary to dispose of the hegemonic Eurocentric assumptions built into those master-narratives that have been employed in the past to frame Third World histo-ries. It is necessary also to resist all spatial homogenization and temporal teleology. This requires the repudiation of all foundational historical writing. According to Prakash, a foundational view is one that assumes "that history is ultimately founded in and representable through some identity — individual, class, or structure — which resists further decomposition into heterogeneity."[12] The most significant conclusion to follow from the repudiation of foundational historiography is the rejection of capitalism as a "foundational category" on the grounds that "we cannot thematize Indian history in terms of the development of capitalism and simultaneously con-test capitalism's homogenization of the contemporary world."[13] (Obviously, given the logic of the argument, any Third World country could be substituted here for In-dia.) (5) "Postfoundational history," in its repudiation of essence and structure and a simultaneous affirmation of heterogeneity, also repudiates any "fixing" of the "Third World subject" and, therefore, of the Third World as a category:

> [T]he rejection of those modes of thinking which configure the third world in such irreducible essences as religiosity, underdevelopment, poverty, nationhood, non-Westernness . . . unsettles the calm presence that the essentialist categories — east and west, first world and third world — inhabit in our thought. This disruption makes it possible to treat the third world as a variety of shifting positions which have been discursively articulated in history. Viewed in this manner, the Orientalist, nationalist, Marxist and other historiographies become visible as discursive attempts to constitute their objects of knowledge, that is, the third world. As a result, rather than appearing as a fixed and essential object, the third world emerges as a series of historical positions, including those that enunciate essentialisms.[14]

It might be noteworthy here that with the repudiation of capitalism and struc-ture as foundational categories, there is no mention in the above statement of a capitalist structuring of the world, however heterogeneous and "discrepant" the his-tories within it, as a constituting moment of history. (6) Finally, postfoundational history approaches "third-world identities as relational rather than essential."[15] Postfoundational history (which is also postcolonial history) shifts attention from "national origin" to "subject-position." The consequence is that

> the formation of third-world positions suggests engagement rather than insularity. It is difficult to overlook that all the third-world voices identified in this essay speak within

and to discourses familiar to the "West" instead of originating from some autonomous essence, which does not warrant the conclusion that the third-world historiography has always been enslaved, but that the careful maintenance and policing of East-West boundaries has never succeeded in stopping the flows across and against boundaries and that the self-other opposition has never quite been able to order all differences into binary opposites. The third world, far from being confined to its assigned space, has penetrated the inner sanctum of the First World in the process of being "third-worlded" — arousing, inciting, and affiliating with the subordinated others in the First World. It has reached across boundaries and barriers to connect with the minority voices in the first world: socialists, radicals, feminists, minorities.[16]

It will help to underline the affirmations in the above statement, which are quite representative of the postcolonial stance on contemporary global relations (and of its claims to transcending earlier conceptualizations of the world). (*a*) attention needs to be shifted from national origin to subject-position; hence a "politics of location" takes precedence over politics informed by fixed categories (in this case the nation, but quite obviously referring also to categories such as Third World and class, among others). (*b*) While First/Third World positions may not be interchangeable, they are nevertheless quite fluid, which implies a necessity of qualifying, if not repudiating, binary oppositions in the articulation of their relationship. (*c*) Hence local interactions take priority over global structures in the shaping of these relationships, which implies that they are best comprehended historically in their heterogeneity rather than structurally in their "fixity." (*d*) These conclusions follow from the "hybridness" or "in-betweenness" of the postcolonial subject which is not to be contained within fixed categories or binary oppositions. (*e*) Finally, since postcolonial criticism has focused on the postcolonial subject to the exclusion of an account of the world outside of the subject, the global condition implied by postcoloniality appears at best as a projection onto the world of postcolonial subjectivity and epistemology; this is a discursive constitution of the world, in other words, in accordance with the constitution of the postcolonial subject, much as it had been constituted earlier by the epistemologies that are the object of postcolonial criticism.

If postcolonial criticism as discourse is any guide to identifying postcolonial intellectuals, the literal sense of "postcolonial" is its least significant aspect, if not altogether misleading. Viewed in terms of the themes that I have outlined above, on the one hand, "postcolonial" is broadly inclusive; on the other hand, as intellectual concerns these themes are by no means the monopoly of postcolonial criticism, and one does not have to be post*colonial* in any strict sense of the term to share in them, for which the most eloquent evidence is that they were already central to cultural discussions before they were so labeled. Crucial premises of postcolonial criticism, such as the repudiation of post-Enlightenment metanarratives, were enunciated first in poststructuralist thinking and the various postmodernisms that it has informed.[17] Taking the term literally as "post*colonial*," some practitioners of postcolonial criticism describe societies such as the United States and Australia as postcolonial. It is pointed out that regardless of their status as First World societies and as colonizers themselves of their indigenous populations (to be fair, the latter could also be said of many Third World societies), these societies did, after all, start off as settler colonies. According to Bill Ashcroft, Gareth Griffiths, and

Helen Tiffin, three enthusiastic proponents of the postcolonial idea, postcolonial covers

> all the cultures affected by the imperial process from the moment of colonization to the present day, . . . so the literatures of African countries, Australia, Bangladesh, Canada, Caribbean countries, India, Malaysia, Malta, New Zealand, Pakistan, Singapore, South Pacific Island countries, and Sri Lanka are all postcolonial literatures. The literature of the USA should also be placed in this category. Perhaps because of its current position of power, and the neo-colonizing role it has played, its postcolonial nature has not been generally recognized. But its relationship with the metropolitan centre as it evolved over the last two centuries has been paradigmatic for postcolonial literatures everywhere. What each of these literatures has in common beyond their special and distinctive characteristics is that they emerged in their present form out of the experience of colonization and asserted themselves by foregrounding the tension with the imperial power, and by emphasizing their differences from the assumptions of the imperial centre. It is this which makes them distinctly post-colonial.[18]

At the same time, the themes of postcolonial criticism have been outstanding themes in the cultural discourses of Third World societies that were never, strictly speaking, colonies, and/or conducted successful revolutions against Euro-American domination, such as China. There are also no clear temporal boundaries to the use of the term because the themes it encompasses are as old as the history of colonialism. To use the example of China again, such themes as the status of native history vis-à-vis Euro-American conceptualizations of history, national identity and its contested nature, the national-historical trajectory in the context of global modernization, and even the subjectivity created by a sense of "in-betweenness" are as old as the history of the Chinese encounter with the Euro-American West.[19] One might go so far as to suggest that, if a crisis in historical consciousness, with all its implications for national and individual identity, is a basic theme of postcoloniality, then the First World itself is postcolonial. To the extent that the Euro-American self-image was shaped by the experience of colonizing the world (since the constitution of the other is at once also the constitution of the self), the end of colonialism presents the colonizer as much as the colonized with a problem of identity. The crisis created by the commemoration of the five-hundredth anniversary of Columbus's adventure comes to mind immediately. Indeed, some postcolonial critics have gone so far to claim for postcoloniality all of modern history, substituting postcoloniality as a condition for everything from imperialism to revolution. To quote Ashcroft, Griffiths, and Tiffin again:

> European imperialism took various forms in different times and places and proceeded both through conscious planning and contingent occurrences. As a result of this complex development something occurred for which the *plan* of imperial expansion had not bargained: the immensely prestigious and powerful imperial culture found itself appropriated in projects of counter-colonial resistance which drew upon the many indigenous local and hybrid *processes* of self-determination to defy, erode and sometimes supplant the prodigious power of imperial cultural knowledge. Post-colonial literatures are a result of this interaction between imperial culture and the complex of indigenous cultural practices. As a consequence, "post-colonial theory" has existed for a long time before that particular name was used to describe it. Once colonised peoples had cause to reflect on and express the tension which ensued from this problematic

and contested, but eventually vibrant and powerful, mixture of imperial language and local experience, post-colonial "theory" came into being.[20]

Never mind the awkward statements about "theory" in this passage. What is important is that "postcolonialism" is coextensive with "colonialism," which not only confounds what we might mean by these terms but also abolishes any possibility of drawing distinctions between the present and the past or the indigenous oppressed and the oppressor settlers. If postcoloniality is a set of discursive attributes, moreover, there is no reason why in its extension to the past we should stop with the beginnings of modernity. Indeed, a recent work has carried this logic to its conclusion, claiming for postcoloniality all of human history, since "hybridity" and "in-betweenness" have been characteristics of cultural formation throughout![21]

In contrast, the term "postcolonial," understood in terms of its discursive thematics, excludes from its scope most of those who inhabit post*colonial* societies or hail from them. It does not account for the attractions of modernization and nationalism to vast numbers in Third World populations, let alone those marginalized by national incorporation in the global economy. Prakash seems to acknowledge this when he observes that "outside the first world, in India itself, the power of Western discourses operates through its authorization and deployment by the nation-state — the ideologies of modernization and instrumental science are so deeply sedimented in the national body politic that they neither manifest themselves nor function exclusively as forms of imperial power."[22] It excludes the many ethnic groups in post*colonial* societies (among others) who, obviously unaware of their "hybridity," go on massacring one another. It also excludes radical "postcolonials," who continue to claim that their societies are still colonized and believe that the assertion of integrated identities and subjectivities is essential to their ability to struggle against colonialism. Of particular note are indigenous radical activists who refuse to go along with the postcolonial repudiation of "essentialized" identities. When faced with this kind of challenge, some postcolonial critics are quick to forget their claims to openness and playfulness, as in the following statement by a Canadian "postcolonial critic," Diana Brydon:

> While post-colonial theorists embrace hybridity and heterogeneity as the characteristic post-colonial mode, some native writers in Canada resist what they see as a violating appropriation to insist on their ownership of their stories and their exclusive claim to an authenticity that should not be ventriloquized or parodied. When directed against the Western canon, post-modernist techniques of intertextuality, parody and literary borrowing may appear radical or even potentially revolutionary. When directed against native myths and stories, these same techniques would seem to repeat the imperialist history of plunder and theft.... Although I can sympathize with such arguments as tactical strategies in insisting on self-definition and resisting appropriation, even tactically they prove self-defeating because they depend on a view of cultural authenticity that condemns them to a continued marginality and an eventual death.... Ironically, such tactics encourage native peoples to isolate themselves from contemporary life and full citizenhood.[23]

In other words, be hybrid or die! Brydon's attitude is also revealing of the tendency of most postcolonials to take for granted the present economic and political organization of the world.

The problem of the relationship between postcoloniality and power is not re-stricted to its manifestations in the response to postcoloniality of people, such as the indigenous peoples of Australia or the Americas, about whose continued oppression there is little question. Intellectuals in India ask Spivak to explain "questions that arise out of the way you perceive yourself ('The post-colonial diasporic Indian who seeks to decolonize the mind'), and the way you constitute us (for convenience, 'native' intellectuals)," to which Spivak's answer is: "[Y]our description of how I con-stituted you does not seem quite correct. I thought I constituted you, equally with the diasporic Indian, as the post-colonial intellectual!" The interrogators are not quite convinced: "Perhaps the relationship of distance and proximity between you and us is that what we write and teach has political and other actual consequences for us that are in a sense different from the consequences, or lack of consequences, for you." They express doubts in another sense as well: "What are the theories or expla-nations, the narratives of affiliation and disaffiliation that you bring to the politically contaminated and ambivalent function of the non-resident Indian (NRI) who comes back to India, however temporarily, upon the wings of progress?"[24] As phrased by Prakash, it is not clear that even the work of the *Subaltern Studies* collective, which serves as the inspiration of so much of the thematics of postcoloniality, may be in-cluded under "postcolonial." I have no wish to impose an unwarranted uniformity on *Subaltern Studies* writers, but it seems to be that their more radical ideas, chief among them the idea of class, are somewhat watered down in the course of their representation in the enunciation of postcolonial criticism.[25] It is also misleading, in my opinion, to mention in the same breath as "postcolonial critics" intellectuals as widely different politically as Edward Said, Aijaz Ahmad, Homi Bhabha, and Gyan Prakash (and even Gayatri Spivak and Lata Mani). In a literal sense, they may all share in postcoloniality, and some of its themes. Said's situation as a Palestinian in-tellectual does not permit him to cross the borders of Israel with the ease that his in-betweenness might suggest (which also raises the question for postcoloniality of what borders are at issue). Aijaz Ahmad, vehemently critical of the Three Worlds concept, nevertheless grounds his critique within the operations of capital, which is quite different from the denial of a foundational status to capitalism in the under-standing of postcoloniality by Prakash.[26] Spivak and Mani, while quite cognizant of the different roles in different contexts that in-betweenness imposes upon them,[27] nevertheless ground their politics firmly in feminism (and, in the case of Spivak, Marxism).

Finally, examining the notion of postcoloniality in a different geographical con-text, Africa, Kwame A. Appiah points to another pitfall in the literal use of postcoloniality as post*colonial,* this time a temporal one. Appiah shares in the under-standing of postcolonial as postmodernization, post–Third World, and postnationalist and points out that while the first generation of African writers after the end of colonialism were nationalists, the second generation of writers have rejected na-tionalism.[28] In a recent discussion (a response to the controversy provoked by his criticism of postcolonial Sub-Saharan Africa), Achille Mbembe hints at an answer as to why this should be the case when he states that "the younger generation of Af-ricans have no direct or immediate experience" of colonization, whatever role it may have played as a "foundational" event in African history.[29] "Postcolonial," in other words, is applicable not to all of the post*colonial* period but only to that period after colonialism when a "forgetting" of its memories has begun to set in, among other things.

What, then, may be the value of a term that includes so much beyond it and that excludes so much of its own postulated premise, the colonial? What it leaves us with is what I have already hinted at: postcolonial, rather than a description of anything, is a discourse that seeks to constitute the world in the self-image of intellectuals who view themselves (or have come to view themselves) as postcolonial intellectuals; to recall my initial statement above, these are Third World intellectuals who have arrived in First World academe and whose preoccupation with postcoloniality is an expression not so much of agony over identity, as it often appears, but of new-found power. Two further questions need to be addressed before I elaborate further on this proposition; one concerns the role intellectuals from India have played in the enunciation of postcolonial discourse; the other concerns the language of this discourse.

Spivak comments (in passing) in an interview that "in India, people who can think of the three-worlds explanation are totally pissed off by not being recognised as the centre of the non-aligned nations, rather than a 'Third-World' country."[30] This state of being "pissed off" at categorization as just another Third World country is not restricted to Indian intellectuals (and others in India) but could be found in any Third World country (my country of origin, Turkey, and the country I study, China, come to mind immediately), which speaks to the sorry state of Third World consciousness, if there is one. It is also impossible to say whether or not Indian intellectuals being "pissed off" at such categorization has anything to do with the themes that appear in postcolonial discourse, in particular the repudiation of Third World as a category. Nevertheless, intellectuals from India, as I noted above, have been prominent in identifying themselves as postcolonial intellectuals, as well as in the enunciation of postcolonial criticism. There is nothing wrong with this, of course, except in a certain confusion that has been introduced into the discourse between what are specific problems in Indian historiography and general problems of a global condition described as "postcolonial," and the projection globally of subjectivities that are (on the basis of the disagreements among Indian intellectuals to which I alluded above) representative only of very few among the intellectuals in India. Most of the generalizations that appear in the discourse of postcolonial intellectuals from India may appear novel in the historiography of India but are not novel "discoveries" from broader perspectives. It is no reflection on the historical writing of *Subaltern Studies* historians that their qualifications of class in Indian history, their views on the nation as contested category, and their injunction that the history of capitalism must be understood not just as a triumphal march of a homogenizing capital but also in terms of the resistance to it at both the national and the local level (which rendered its consequences quite fractured and heterogeneous) do not represent earth-shattering conceptual innovations; as Said notes in his foreword to *Selected Subaltern Studies,* these approaches represent the application in Indian historiography of trends in historical writing that were quite widespread by the 1970s, under the impact especially of social historians such as E. P. Thompson, Eric Hobsbawm, and a host of others.[31] All this indicates is that historians of India were participants in the transformations

in historical thinking in all areas — transformations in which Third World sensibilities were just one among a number of factors, which also included new ways of
thinking about Marxism, the entry into history of feminism, and poststructuralism.
To be sure, I think it very important that Third World sensibilities must be brought
into play repeatedly in order to counteract a tendency toward cultural imperialism
of First World thinkers and historians, who extend the meaning of concepts of First
World derivation globally without giving a second thought to the social differences
that must qualify those concepts historically and contextually, but this is no reason
to inflate a postcolonial sensibility, especially one that is itself bound by national and
local experiences, indefinitely. And yet such a tendency (for which *Subaltern Studies*
writers may themselves not be responsible at all) is plainly visible in the exposition
of postcoloniality by someone like Prakash who writes of Indian historiography in
one sentence and projects his observations globally in the very next one.

These observations are not intended to single out postcolonial intellectuals from
India, which would be misleading not only about Indian intellectuals in general but
also about postcolonial intellectuals in general; the appeals of postcoloniality are
not restricted to intellectuals of any one national origin, and the problems to which
I pointed above are problems of a general nature, born out of a contradiction between an insistence on heterogeneity, difference, and historicity and a tendency to
generalize from the local to the global, all the while denying that there are global
forces at work that may condition the local in the first place. What my observations
point to is a new assertiveness on the part of Third World intellectuals that makes
this procedure possible. Another example may be found among Chinese intellectuals, in the so-called Confucian revival in recent years. The latter obviously do not
describe themselves as postcolonial, for their point of departure is the newfound
power of Chinese societies within global capitalism, which, if anything, shows in
their efforts to suppress memories of an earlier day when China, too, suffered from
Euro-American hegemony (though not colonialism). In their case the effort takes the
form of articulating to the values of capitalism a "Confucianism" that in an earlier day
was deemed to be inconsistent with capitalist modernization; this Confucianism has
been rendered into a prime mover of capitalist development and has found quite a
sympathetic ear among First World ideologues who now look to a Confucian ethic
to relieve the crisis of capitalism.[32] While quite different from "postcoloniality" in its
urge to become part of a hegemonic ideology of capitalism, it does share with the
latter a counterhegemonic self-assertiveness on the part of another group of formerly
Third World intellectuals. And it may not be a coincidence that Chinese intellectuals
in First World academia have played a major part in the enunciation of this Confucian
revival, although it is by no means restricted to them.

A somewhat different but parallel observation could be made with regard to the
appeals of postcoloniality to intellectuals from settler colonies. A changing global
situation in recent years has transformed earlier identifications with Euro-America
in these societies to new kinds of regional affinities — most clearly in the case of
Australia, which seeks to remake itself as an "Asian" society, but also in Canada,
which seeks to become part of a new Asia-Pacific economy. While it would be er-
roneous to say that settlers earlier did not have an awareness of being colonized
or lacked all identification with the Third World (witness Canada's relationship with

the United States, for example), it is also misleading to erase memories of racist exclusion and oppression practiced by the settlers themselves toward nonwhite immigrants or the indigenous populations. It is difficult to escape the observation, in light of what I have written above, that in these societies "postcoloniality" serves to erase such memories — on the one hand, it allows the settlers to identify more explicitly than earlier with Third World victims of colonialism, and, on the other hand, it helps them to counteract indigenous demands for authenticity and, even more radically, for land and political sovereignty.

The second question that needs to be considered concerns the language of postcolonial discourse, which is the language of First World poststructuralism, as postcolonial critics readily concede themselves, although they do not dwell too long on its implications. Prakash's statement (which I quoted above) that "all the third-world voices identified in this essay . . . speak within and to discourses familiar to the 'West' " acknowledges this problem but goes on to conceal its implications in his conclusion that all this proves is that "the maintenance and policing of East-West boundaries has never succeeded in stopping the flows across and against boundaries," as if the flows in the two directions have been equal in their potency. This is important not just for the inequalities disguised by assertions of flows, hybridity, and so on. More importantly, I think, it enables us to place temporally a post-coloniality that otherwise may stretch across the entire history of colonialism. Here, once again, a comparison with China may be instructive, this time over the issue of Marxism. Postcolonial critics insist that they are Marxists, but Marxists who reject the "nineteenth-century heritage" of Marxism, with its universalistic pretensions that ignored historical differences.[33] This is a problem that Chinese Marxist revolutionaries faced and addressed in the 1930s: how to articulate Marxism to Chinese conditions (and vice versa). Their answer was that Marxism must be translated into a Chinese vernacular, not just in a national but, more importantly, in a local sense: the language of the peasantry. The result was what is commonly called "the Sinification of Marxism," embodied in so-called Mao Tse-tung Thought.[34] In the approach to a similar problem of postcolonial critics, the translation takes the form not of translation into a national (as that is rejected) or local (which is affirmed) vernacular but of a rephrasing of Marxism in the language of poststructuralism, where Marxism is "deconstructed," "decentered," and so on. In other words, a critique that starts off with a repudiation of the universalistic pretensions of Marxist language ends up not with its dispersion into local vernaculars but with a return to another First World language with universalistic epistemological pretensions. It enables us, at least, to locate postcolonial criticism in the contemporary First World.

This is not a particularly telling point. Postcolonial critics recognize that the "critical gaze" their studies "direct at the archeology of knowledge enshrined in the west arise[s] from the fact that most of them are being written in the first-world academy."[35] Rather, in drawing attention to the language of postcolonial discourse, I seek to "deconstruct" the professions of hybridity and in-betweenness of postcolonial intellectuals. The hybridity that postcolonial criticism refers to is uniformly a hybridity between the post*colonial* and the First World — never, to my knowledge, between one post*colonial* intellectual and another. But hybridity and in-betweenness do not serve very revealing purposes in the former case either. While postcolonial criticism quite validly points to the "overdetermined" nature of concepts and subjectivities (and I am quite sure that the postcolonial subjectivity is overdetermined, while less sure that it is "more" overdetermined than any other), it conveniently ignores how location in ideological and institutional structures gives direction to the resolution of contradictions presented by hybridity — and the consequences of location in generating vast differences in power.[36] If the language of postcolonial discourse is any guide to its ideological direction, in this case the contradictions presented by hybridity would seem to be given direction by the location of postcolonial intellectuals in the academic institutions of the First World. However much postcolonial intellectuals may insist on hybridity and the transposability of locations, it is also necessary to insist that not all positions are equal in power — as Spivak's interrogators in India seem to recognize in their reference to the "wings of progress" that brought her to India. To insist on hybridity against one's own language, it seems to me, is to disguise not only ideological location but also the differences of power that go with different locations. Postcolonial intellectuals, in their First World institutional location, are ensconced in positions of power not only vis-à-vis the "native" intellectuals back at home but also vis-à-vis their First World neighbors here. My neighbors in Farmville, Virginia, are no match in power for the highly paid, highly prestigious postcolonial intellectuals at Columbia, Duke, Princeton, or the University of California at Santa Cruz; some of them might even be willing to swap positions with the latter and take the anguish that comes with hybridity so long as it brings with it the power and the prestige it seems to command.[37]

"Postcoloniality," Appiah writes, "has become . . . a condition of pessimism,"[38] and there is much to be pessimistic about the world situation of which postcoloniality is an expression. This is not the message of postcolonialism, however, as it acquires respectability and gains admission in U.S. academic institutions. While this discourse shares in the same themes as postcolonial discourses everywhere, it rearranges these themes into a celebration of the end of colonialism, as if the only tasks left for the present were to abolish the ideological and cultural legacy of colonialism; this sounds convincing only to the extent that, with its gaze fixed on the past, it avoids confrontation with the present. The current global condition appears in the discourse only as a projection of the subjectivities and epistemologies of First World intellectuals of Third World origin; this is another way of saying that the discourse constitutes the world in the self-image of these intellectuals: which makes it an expression not of powerlessness but of newfound power. Postcolonial intellectuals have "arrived" in the First World academy not just because they have broken new intellectual ground (although they *have* rephrased older themes) but because intellectual orientations that earlier were regarded as marginal or subversive have acquired a new respectability. Postcoloniality, it has been noted, has found favor even among academic conservatives who prefer it to less tractable vocabulary that insists on keeping in the foreground contemporary problems of political division and oppression.[39]

Postcoloniality has already been the subject of some telling criticism. Critics have noted that, in spite of its insistence on historicity and difference, postcoloniality mimics in its deployment the "ahistorical and universalizing" tendencies in colonialist thinking.[40] "If the theory promises a decentering of history in hybridity, syncretism, multi-dimensional time, and so forth," Anne McClintock writes, "the *singularity* of the term effects a recentering of global history around the single rubric of European time. Colonialism returns at the moment of its disappearance."[41] In a world situation in which severe inequalities persist in older colonial forms or in their neocolonial reconfigurations, moreover, "the unified temporality of 'postcoloniality' risks reproducing the colonial discourse of an allochronic other, living in another time, still lagging behind us, the genuine postcolonials."[42] The spatial homogenization that accompanies a "unified temporality" not only fails to discriminate between vastly different social and political situations but also, to the extent that it "fails to discriminate between the diverse modalities of hybridity," may end up in "the consecration of hegemony."[43] Rosalind O'Hanlon and David Washbrook observe that divorced from such discrimination, and without a sense of totality, "postcoloniality" also ends up mimicking methodologically the colonialist epistemology that it sets out to repudiate:

> [T]he solutions it offers — methodological individualism, the depoliticising insulation of social from material domains, a view of social relations that is in practice extremely voluntaristic, the refusal of any kind of programmatic politics — do not seem to us radical, subversive or emancipatory. They are on the contrary conservative and implicitly authoritarian, as they were indeed when recommended more overtly in the heyday of Britain's own imperial power.[44]

Postcolonialism's repudiation of structure and totality in the name of history, ironically, ends up not in an affirmation of historicity, but in a self-referential "universalizing historicism" that reintroduces an unexamined totality by the back door by projecting globally what are but local experiences. The problem here may be the problem of all historicism without a sense of structure, a web of translocal relationships without which it is impossible in the first place to determine what is different, heterogeneous, and local. In his critique of "essentializing" procedures (of India, of the Third World), Prakash offers as a substitute an understanding of these categories in terms of "relationships" but does not elaborate on what these relationships might be. The critique of an essentialist fixing of the Third World is not novel; Karl Pletsch's eloquent critique of "Three Worlds" theory (without the aid of postcoloniality), published more than a decade ago, enunciated clearly the problem of ideological essentializing in modernization "theory."[45] Further, Prakash's conceptual "innovation" (i.e., relationships) is not novel. Pletsch himself pointed to the importance of global relationships to understanding problems of development (as well as in understanding the conceptual underpinnings of modernization theory); and an understanding of modern global history in terms of relationships, needless to say, is the crucial thesis of world-system analysis.

The difference between the latter and Prakash's postfoundational understanding of relationships rests on his rejection of foundational categories, chief among them capitalism. What O'Hanlon and Washbrook say on this issue is worth quoting at some length because of its relevance to the argument here:

> What his [Prakash's] position leaves quite obscure is what this category of "capitalist modernity" occupies for him. If our strategy should be to "refuse" it in favour of marginal histories, of multiple and heterogeneous identities, this suggests that capitalist modernity is nothing more than a potentially disposable fiction, held in place simply

by our acceptance of its cognitive categories and values. Indeed, Prakash is particularly disparaging of Marxist and social historians' concern with capitalism as a "system" of political economy and coercive instrumentalities. Yet in other moments Prakash tells us that history's proper task is to challenge precisely this "homogenization of the world by contemporary capitalism." If this is so, and there is indeed a graspable logic to the way in which modern capitalism has spread itself globally, how are we to go about the central task of comprehending this logic in the terms that Prakash suggests?[46]

Prakash's answer to his critics simply evades the issues raised in this passage (while coming close to acknowledging a central role to capitalism) because to recognize them would make his postfoundational history untenable.[47] The political consequences of postcolonialist repudiation of the totality implied by metanarratives have been drawn out by Fernando Coronil in his observation that the opposition to metanarratives produces disjointed mininarratives, which reinforce dominant worldviews; reacting against determinisms, it presents free-floating events; refusing to fix identity in structural categories, it essentializes identity through difference; resisting the location of power in structures or institutions, it "diffuses it throughout society and ultimately dissolves it."[48] It also relieves this "self-defined minority or subaltern critics," O'Hanlon and Washbrook note, of the necessity of "doing what they constantly demand of others, which is to historicise the conditions of their own emergence as authoritative voices — conditions which could hardly be described without reference of some kind to material and class relations."[49]

Finally, the postcolonial repudiation of the Third World is intimately linked with the repudiation of capitalism as constituting "foundational categories" and of the capitalist structuring of the modern world. Once again, essentialism serves as a straw man, diverting attention from radical conceptualizations of the Third World, which are not essentialist but relational, as in world-system approaches. The latter comprehends the Third World as a structural position within a capitalist world order — a position that changes with changing structural relationships — rather than "fixing" it ahistorically, as Prakash would have it. To be sure, world-system analysis is as discursive in its location of the Third World as one based on modernization, but, as I have argued above, so is postcolonialist analysis. The question then becomes one of the ability of competing discourses to account for historical changes in global relationships and the oppositional practices to which they point. I will say more on the former below. As for oppositional practices, postcoloniality by its very logic permits little beyond local struggles and, without reference to structure or totality, directionless ones at that. For all its contradictions, Shohat writes, "'Third World' usefully evokes structural commonalities of struggles. The invocation of the 'Third World' implies a belief that the shared history of neo/colonialism and internal racism form[s] sufficient common ground for alliances among...diverse peoples. If one does not believe or envision such commonalities, then indeed the term 'Third World' should be discarded."[50]

The denial to capitalism of "foundational" status is also revealing of a culturalism in the postcolonialist argument that has important ideological consequences. This involves the issue of Eurocentrism. Without capitalism as the foundation for European power and the motive force of its globalization, Eurocentrism would have been just another ethnocentrism (comparable to any other ethnocentrism from the Chinese and the Indian to the most trivial tribal solipsism). An exclusive focus on Eurocentrism as a cultural or ideological problem, which blurs the power relationships that dynamized it and endowed it with hegemonic persuasiveness, fails to explain why this particular ethnocentrism was able to define modern global history, and itself as the universal aspiration and end of that history, in contrast to the regionalism or localism of other ethnocentrisms. By throwing the cover of culture over material relationships, as if the one had little to do with the other, such a focus diverts the task of criticism from the criticism of capitalism to the criticism of Eurocentric ideology, which helps disguise its own ideological limitation but also, ironically, provides an alibi for inequality, exploitation, and oppression in their modern guises under capitalist relationships. I will say more below on the contemporary circumstances of capitalism that enable such a separation of capitalism from Eurocentrism (the deterritorialization of capital under global capitalism). Suffice it to note here that the postcolonialist argument projects upon the past the same mystification of the relationship between power and culture that is characteristic of the ideology of global capitalism — of which it is a product.

These criticisms, however vehement on occasion, do not necessarily indicate that postcolonialism's critics deny to it all value; indeed, critics such as Coronil, McClintock, and Shohat explicitly acknowledge some value to the issues raised by postcolonialism and postcolonial intellectuals. There is no denying, indeed, that "postcolonialism" is expressive of a current crisis in the conceptualization of the world — not just a crisis in the ideology of linear progress but a crisis in the modes of comprehending the world associated with such concepts as the "Third World" and the "nation-state." Nor is it to be denied that as the global situation has become blurred with the disappearance of socialist states, the emergence of important differences economically and politically among so-called Third World societies, and the diasporic motions of populations across national and regional boundaries, fragmentation of the global into the local has emerged into the foreground of historical and political consciousness. Crossing national, cultural, class, gender, and ethnic boundaries, moreover, with its promise of a genuine cosmopolitanism, is appealing in its own right.

Within the institutional site of the First World academy, fragmentation of earlier metanarratives appears benign (except to hidebound conservatives) because of its promise of more democratic, multicultural, and cosmopolitan epistemologies. In the world outside the academy, however, it shows in murderous ethnic conflict; continued inequality between societies, classes, and genders; and the absence of oppositional possibilities that, always lacking in coherence, are rendered even more impotent than earlier by the fetishization of difference, fragmentation, and so on.

The predicament to which this gap points is rendered more serious in the confounding of ideological metanarratives with actualities of power — that is, mistaking fragmentation in one realm with fragmentation in the other, ignoring the possibility that ideological fragmentation may represent not the dissolution of power but rather its further concentration. It is necessary, to account for this possibility, to retain a sense of structure and totality in the confrontation of fragmentation and locality; the alternative to this may be complicity in the consolidation of hegemony in the very process of questioning it. "Postcoloniality," while it represents an effort at adjusting to a changing global situation, for the same reason appears as an exemplary illustration of this predicament. Critics have hinted at its possible relationship to a new situation in the capitalist transformation of the world without examining this relationship at length. I would like to look at this relationship more closely.

Global Capitalism and the Condition of Postcoloniality

David Harvey and Fredric Jameson, among others, perceive a relationship between postmodernism and a new phase in the development of capitalism that has been described variously as late capitalism, flexible production or accumulation, disorganized capitalism, or global capitalism.[51] I would like to suggest here that as a progeny of postmodernism, postcolonialism is also expressive of the "logic" of this phase of capitalism, this time on Third World terrain.

First, fundamental to the structure of the new global capitalism (the term I prefer) is what F. Frobel and others have described as "a new international division of labor": in other words, the transnationalization of production whereby, through subcontracting, the process of production (of the same commodity even) is globalized.[52] The international division of labor in production may not be entirely novel, but new technologies have expanded the spatial extension of production, as well as its speed, to an unprecedented level. These same technologies have endowed capital and production with unprecedented mobility, so that the location of production seems to be in a constant state of change, seeking for maximum advantage for capital against labor, as well as to avoid social and political interference (hence, flexible production). For these reasons, analysts of capitalism perceive in global capitalism a qualitative difference from similar practices earlier — and a new phase of capitalism.

Second, there is the "decentering" of capitalism nationally. In other words, it is increasingly difficult to point to any nation or region as the center of global capitalism. More than one analyst (in a position of power) has found an analogue to the emerging organization of production in the northern European Hanseatic League of the early modern period — that is, the period before the emergence of nation-states (one of these analysts described the new situation as a "high-tech Hanseatic League"); in other words, this is a network of urban formations, without a clearly definable center, whose links to one another are far stronger than their relationships to their immediate hinterlands.[53]

Third, the medium linking this network is the transnational corporation, which has taken over from national markets as the locus of economic activity — not just as a passive medium for the transmission of capital, commodities, and production but as a determinant of the transmission and its direction. In other words, while the analogy with the Hanseatic League suggests decentralization, production is heavily concentrated — behind this facade — in the corporation. One articulate spokesman for the new economic order suggests that when it comes to decision making regarding production, the corporation has roughly 70 percent of the say-so, and the market has roughly 30 percent.[54] With power lodged in transnational corporations, which by definition transcend nations in organization and/or loyalty, the power of the nation-state to regulate the economy internally is constricted, while global regulation (and defense) of the economic order emerges as a major task. This is manifested not only in the proliferation of global organizations but also in efforts to organize extranational regional organizations to give coherence to the functioning of the economy.[55]

Fourth, the transnationalization of production is the source at once of unprecedented unity globally and of unprecedented fragmentation (in the history of capitalism). The homogenization of the globe economically, socially, and culturally is such that Marx's predictions of the nineteenth century, premature for his time, finally seem to be on the point of vindication. At the same time, however, there is a parallel process of fragmentation at work — globally, in the disappearance of a center to capitalism and, locally, in the fragmentation of the production process into subnational regions and localities. As supranational regional organizations, such as the European Economic Community, the Pacific Basin Economic Community, and the North American Free Trade Zone (to mention some that have been realized or are the objects of intense organizational activity), manifest this fragmentation at the global level, localities within the same nation competing with one another to place themselves in the pathways of transnational capital represent it at the most basic local level. Nations, themselves, it is arguable, represented attempts historically to contain fragmentation, but under attack from the outside (transnational organization) and the inside (subnational economic regions and localities), it is not quite clear how this new fragmentation is to be contained.[56]

A fifth important (perhaps the most important) consequence of the transnationalization of capital may be that for the first time in the history of capitalism, the capitalist mode of production appears as an authentically global abstraction, divorced from its historically specific origins in Europe. In other words, the narrative of capitalism is no longer a narrative of the history of Europe, so that, for the first time, non-European capitalist societies make their own claims on the history of capitalism. Corresponding to economic fragmentation, then, is cultural fragmentation or, to put it in its positive guise, "multiculturalism." The most dramatic instance of this new cultural situation may be the recent effort to appropriate capitalism for the so-called Confucian values of East Asian societies, which is a reversal of a long-standing conviction (in Europe and East Asia) that Confucianism was historically an obstacle to capitalism. I think it is arguable that the apparent end of Eurocentrism is an illusion, because capitalist culture as it has taken shape has Eurocentrism built into the very structure of its narrative, which may explain why even as Europe and the United States lose their domination of the capitalist world economy, culturally European and American values retain their domination. It is noteworthy that what makes something like the East Asian Confucian revival plausible is not its offer of alternative values to those of Euro-American origin but its articulation of native culture into a capitalist narrative. Having said this, it is important to reiterate nevertheless that the question of world culture has become much more complex than in earlier phases of capitalism. The fragmentation of space and its consequences for Eurocentrism also imply a fragmentation of the temporality of capitalism: the challenge to Eurocentrism, in other words, means that it is possible to conceive of the future in ways other than those based on Euro-American political and social models. Here, once again, it is difficult to distinguish reality from illusion, but the complexity is undeniable.

Finally, the transnationalization of production calls into question earlier divisions of the world into First, Second, and Third Worlds. The Second World, the world of socialism, is, for all practical purposes, of the past. But the new global configuration also calls into question the distinctions between the First and Third Worlds. Parts of the earlier Third World are today on the pathways of transnational capital and belong in the "developed" sector of the world economy. Likewise, ways of life in those parts of the First World marginalized in the new global economy are hardly distinguishable from what used to be viewed as Third World ways of life. It may not be fortuitous that the North-South distinction has gradually taken over from the earlier division of the globe into the three worlds, so long as we remember that "North" and "South" designate not merely concrete geographic locations but also metaphorical referents: "North" denoting the pathways of transnational capital; "South" denoting the marginalized populations of the world, regardless of their location (which is where "postcoloniality" comes in!).

Ideologues of global capital have described this condition as "global regionalism" or "global localism," adding quickly, however, that global localism is 70 percent global and only 30 percent local.[57] They have also appropriated for capital the radical ecological slogan, "Think globally, act locally."[58]

The situation created by global capitalism helps explain certain phenomena that have become apparent over the last two to three decades, but especially since the 1980s: global motions of peoples (and, therefore, cultures), the weakening of boundaries (among societies, as well as among social categories), the replications in societies internally of inequalities and discrepancies once associated with colonial differences, simultaneous homogenization and fragmentation within and across societies, the interpenetration of the global and the local, and the disorganization of a world conceived in terms of "three worlds" or nation-states. Some of these phenomena have also contributed to an appearance of equalization of differences within and across societies as well as of democratization within and between societies. What is ironic is that the managers of this world situation themselves concede the concentration of power in their (or their organizations') hands as well as their manipulation of peoples, boundaries, and cultures to appropriate the local for the global, to admit different cultures into the realm of capital only to break them down and remake them in accordance with the requirements of production and consumption, and even to reconstitute subjectivities across national boundaries to create producers and consumers more responsive to the operations of capital. Those who do not respond and the basket cases that are not essential to those operations — four-fifths of the global population by these managers' count — need not be colonized; they are simply marginalized. The new "flexible production" has made it no longer necessary to utilize explicit coercion against labor, at home or abroad (in colonies); those peoples or places that are not responsive to the needs (or demands) of capital or that are too far gone to respond "efficiently" simply find themselves out of its pathways. And it is now easier even than in the heyday of colonialism or modernization theory to say convincingly: "It's their own fault."

I began this essay with Shohat's question, "When exactly...does the 'post-colonial' begin?" I can now give it a less facetious answer consistent with her intention: It begins with the emergence of global capitalism, not in the sense of an exact coincidence in time, but in the sense that the one is a condition for the other.

There is little that is remarkable about this conclusion, which is but an extension to postcolonialism of the relationship Harvey and Jameson have established between postmodernism and developments within capitalism. If postcolonialism is a progeny of postmodernism, then these developments within capitalism are also directly or indirectly pertinent to understanding postcolonialism. Postcolonial critics readily concede the debt they owe to postmodernist poststructuralist thinking; indeed, their most original contribution would seem to lie in their rephrasing of older problems in the study of the Third World in the language of poststructuralism. What is remarkable, therefore, is not my conclusion here but that a consideration of the relationship between postcolonialism and global capitalism should be absent from the writings of postcolonial intellectuals; this is all the more remarkable because this relationship is arguably less abstract and more direct than any relationship between global capitalism and postmodernism, since it pertains not just to cultural/epistemological but to social and political formations.

Postcoloniality represents a response to a genuine need: the need to overcome a crisis of understanding produced by the inability of old categories to account for the world. The metanarrative of progress that underlies two centuries of thinking first in Europe and then globally with the expansion of Europe is in deep crisis; this is not just because of a loss of faith in progress or because of its disintegrative effects in actuality but more importantly because over the last decade in particular our sense of time has been jumbled up: as conservatism has become "revolutionary" (the "Reagan revolution") while revolutionaries have turned first into conservatives and then into reactionaries (as in formerly socialist countries such as the Soviet Union and China); as religious millenarianisms long thought to be castaways from the Enlightenment have made a comeback into politics, sometimes allied to high-tech revolutions, as in the United States; and as fascism has been reborn out of the ashes of communist regimes. The crisis of progress has brought in its wake a crisis of modernization, more in its Marxist than its bourgeois guise, and has called into question the structure of the world as conceived by modernizationists and radicals alike in the decades after World War II: that is, the structure of "the Three Worlds." The Three Worlds as fixed in social theory (bourgeois or Marxist) geographically or structurally are indeed no longer tenable, as the globe has become as jumbled up spatially as the ideology of progress is temporally: with the appearance of Third Worlds in the First World and First Worlds in the Third; with the diasporas of people that have relocated the self there and the other here, and the consequent confounding of borders and boundaries; and with the culture flows that have been at once homogenizing and heterogenizing, where some groups share in a common global culture regardless of location even as they are alienated from the culture of their "hinterlands," and others are driven back into cultural legacies long thought to be residual, to take refuge in cultural havens that are as far apart from one another as at the origins of modernity — even though they may be watching the same television shows.

Politically speaking, the Second and the Third Worlds have been the major casualties of this crisis. The Second World, the world of socialist states, is already, to put it bluntly, "history." What has happened to the Third World (the immediate subject of "postcoloniality") may be less apparent but no less significant. We may note here that the two major crises of the early 1990s that are global in implication are the crises occasioned by Iraq's invasion of Kuwait and the situation in Somalia. In the Gulf crisis, a Third World country appeared as the imperialist culprit against a neighbor (a socially and politically reactionary but economically powerful neighbor) and had to be driven back by the combined armies of the First, Second, and the Third Worlds, led by an imperial power now turned into a paradigm of righteousness. The "invasion" (I borrow the word from a television report) of Somalia, if anything, was more revealing: if in the case of the Gulf crisis one "Third World" country had to be saved from another, in Somalia a Third World country had to be saved from itself. The Third World, viewed by radicals only two decades ago as a hope for the future, now has to be saved from itself. The crisis could not get much deeper.

"Postcoloniality" addresses this situation of crisis that eludes understanding in terms of older conceptualizations,[59] which may explain why it should have created immediate "ferment" in intellectual circles. But this still begs the questions of Why now? and Why has it taken the intellectual direction it has? After all, there is more than one conceptual way out of a crisis, and we must inquire why this particular way has acquired immediate popularity — in First World institutions. To put it bluntly, postcoloniality is designed to *avoid* making sense of the current crisis and, in the process, to cover up the origins of postcolonial intellectuals in a global capitalism of which they are not so much victims as beneficiaries.

Postcoloniality resonates with the problems thrown up by global capitalism. As the crisis of the Third World became inescapably apparent during the 1980s, so did the effects of global capitalism: the Reagan (and Thatcher) revolution was not so much a revolution heralding a new beginning as a revolution aimed at reorganizing the globe politically so as to give free reign to a global capitalism straining against the harness of political restrictions that limited its motions. The overthrow of socialist states was one part of the program. Another part was taming the Third World, if necessary by invasion, preferably by encirclement: economically or by "Patriot" missiles. But these are at best options of the last resort. By far the best option is control from the inside: through the creation of classes amenable to incorporation into or alliance with global capital.

I use "control" here advisedly; under conditions of global capitalism, control is not to be imposed: it has to be negotiated. Transnational capital is no longer just Euro-American, and neither is modernity just Euro-American modernity. The complicated social and cultural composition of transnational capitalism makes it difficult to sustain a simple equation between capitalist modernity and Eurocentric (and patriarchal) cultural values and political forms. Others who have achieved success within the capitalist world-system demand a voice for their values within the culture of transnational capital; the East Asian Confucian revival to which I referred above is exemplary of this phenomenon. Eurocentrism, as the very condition for the emergence of these alternative voices, retains its cultural hegemony; but it is more evident than ever before that, in order for this hegemony to be sustained, its boundaries must be rendered more porous than earlier, to absorb in its realm alternative cultural possibilities that might otherwise serve as sources of destructive oppositions — the mutual "bashing" between Japan and the United States in recent years, which revives racist and Orientalist vocabulary, attests to the dangers of conflict among the very ranks of transnational capital. And who knows, in the end, what values are most functional to the needs of a changing "capital"? Commentator after commentator has remarked in recent years that the "communitarian" values of "Confucianism" may be more suitable to a contemporary managerial capitalism than the individualistic values of an entrepreneurial capitalism of an earlier day. What is clear is that global capitalism is (and must be) much more fluid culturally than a Eurocentric capitalism.

This is also the condition of postcoloniality and the cultural moves associated with it. Obscurantist conservatives, anxious to explain away cultural problems by substituting the machinations of subversives for systemic analysis, attribute the cultural problems that became apparent in the 1980s (most recently, multiculturalism) to the invasion of academic institutions (and politics in general) by Marxists, feminists, ethnics, and so on. What they ignore is the possible relationship between the Reagan economic revolution and these cultural developments — in other words, the cultural requirements of transnational corporations that, in their very globalism, can no longer afford the cultural parochialism of an earlier day. Focusing on "liberal arts" institutions, they conveniently overlook how much headway multiculturalism has made in business schools and among the managers of transnational corporations, who are eager all of a sudden to learn about the secrets in "Oriental" philosophies that might explain the East Asian economic success, who cannibalize cultures all over the world in order better to market their commodities, and who have suddenly become aware of a need to "internationalize" academic institutions (which often takes the form not of promoting scholarship in a conventional sense but rather of "importing" and "exporting" students and faculty). While in an earlier day it might have been Marxist and feminist radicals, with the aid of the few ethnics, who spearheaded multiculturalism, by now the initiative has passed into the hands of "enlightened" administrators and trustees who are quite aware of the "manpower" needs of the new economic situation. Much less than a conflict between conservatives and radicals (although that, too, is there, obviously), the conflict shapes up now as one between an older elite (and a small-business sector threatened from the inside and the outside) and the elite vanguard of international business. The *Harvard Business Review* is one of the foremost and earliest (in the United States) advocates of transnationalism — and multiculturalism.

The Reaganites may have been misled by visions of many Dinesh D'Souzas, who were not forthcoming. Their failure to grasp the social and political consequences of the economic victory for transnationalism they had engineered became apparent during the 1992 elections when, against the calls from right-wingers for a return to such "native" American values as Eurocentrism, patriarchalism, and racism, George Bush often looked befuddled, possibly because he grasped much better than right-wingers such as Pat Buchanan the dilemmas presented by the victory of transnationalism over all its competitors in the Second and Third Worlds. The result has been the victory of high-tech yuppies who are much better attuned to the new world situation and aware of the difficulties it presents. It is no coincidence that Robert Reich, frequent contributor to the *Harvard Business Review,* keen analyst of developments within the capitalist world economy, and an advocate of the "borderless economy," is a close confidant of President Clinton.

This is also the context for the emergence of postcoloniality and its rapid success in academic institutions as a substitute for earlier conceptualizations of the world. Postcoloniality, in the particular direction it has taken as a discourse, also resonates with the problems of the contemporary world. It addresses issues that, while they may have been issues all along in global studies, are now rephrased in such a way that they are in tune with issues in global capitalism: Eurocentrism and its relationship to capitalism; the kind of modernity that is relevant to a postmodern/postsocialist post–Third World situation; the place of the nation in development; the relationship between the local and the global; the place of borders and boundaries in a world where capital, production, and peoples are in constant motion; the status of structures in a world that more than ever seems to be without recognizable structure; interpenetrations and reversals between the different "worlds"; borderland subjectivities and epistemologies (hybridity); homogeneity versus heterogeneity; and so forth.

Postcoloniality, however, is also appealing because it disguises the power relations that shape a seemingly shapeless world and contributes to a conceptualization of that world that, while functional for the consolidation of hegemony, is also subversive of possibilities of resistance. Postcolonial critics have engaged in valid criticism of past forms of ideological hegemony but have had little to say about its contemporary figurations. Indeed, in their simultaneous repudiation of structure and affirmation of the local in problems of oppression and liberation, they have mystified the ways in which totalizing structures persist in the midst of apparent disintegration and fluidity. They have rendered concrete and material problems of the everyday world into problems of subjectivity and epistemology. Because capital in its motions continues to structure the world, refusing "foundational" status to capital renders impossible the "cognitive mapping" that must be the point of departure for any practice of resistance, while any cognitive mapping there is remains in the domain of those who manage the capitalist world economy.[60] Indeed, in projecting the current state of conceptual disorganization upon the colonial past, postcolonial critics have also deprived colonialism of any but local logic, so that the historical legacy of colonialism (in an Iraq or a Somalia or, for that matter, any Third World society) appears irrelevant to the present, which shifts the burden of persistent problems on to the victims themselves.

"Postcoloniality," Appiah writes, "is the condition of what we might ungenerously call a *comprador* intelligentsia."[61] I think this is missing the point because the world situation that justified the term *comprador* no longer exists. I would suggest, rather, that postcoloniality is the condition of the intelligentsia of global capitalism. Ahmad is closer to the mark when he states, with characteristic bluntness, that "postcoloniality is...like most things, a matter of class."[62] While the statement is not entirely fair in ignoring that postcoloniality also has its appeals for many among the oppressed who would rather forget past oppression in order to be able to live in the present,[63] it is an uncompromising reminder nevertheless of the continued importance, albeit reconfigured on a global basis, of class relations in understanding contemporary cultural developments. The question, then, is not whether or not this global intelligentsia can (or should) return to national loyalties but whether or not, in recognition of its own class position in global capitalism, it can generate a thoroughgoing criticism of its own ideology and formulate practices of resistance against the system of which it is a product.

NOTES

My being (more or less) one of the Third World intellectuals in the First World academy does not privilege the criticism of postcolonial intellectuals that I offer below, but it does call for some comment. It is not clear to me how important the views I discuss (or the intellectuals who promote them) are in their impact on contemporary intellectual life. "Postcolonial" has been entering the vocabulary of academic programs in recent years, and there have been a number of conferences/symposia inspired by this vocabulary ("Postcolonialism," "After Orientalism," etc.), as well as special issues devoted to the subject in periodicals such as *Social Text* and *Public Culture*. Given the small number of intellectuals directly concerned with "postcoloniality" and the diffuseness in their use of the term, it might make more sense to study the reception of the term. What makes it important to study as a concept, I argue in this essay, is that the ideas associated with postcoloniality are significant and widespread as concerns, even if they predate in their emergence the appearance of the term "postcolonial" itself. It is not the importance of these ideas that I question, in other words, but their appropriation for "postcoloniality." Meanwhile, a "Third World" sensibility and mode of perception have become increasingly visible in cultural discussions over the last decade. I myself share in the concerns (and even some of the viewpoints) of "postcolonial intellectuals," though from a somewhat different perspective than those who describe themselves as such; this is evident most recently in my *After the Revolution: Waking to Global Capitalism* (Hanover, N.H.: University of New England Press for Wesleyan University Press, 1994).

For their assistance with sources/comments, I would like to thank the following, while relieving them of any complicity in my views: Harry Harootunian, Roxann Prazniak, Rob Wilson, and Zhang Xudong. The present essay is a slightly revised version (to take account of recent literature) of an essay that was published first in *Critical Inquiry* 20:2 (winter 1994): 328–56. Since the essay was first published, I have had occasion to discuss the ideas in it in seminars at Duke University, the University of California at Santa Cruz, the University of Hawaii, Washington University in St. Louis, and the Humanities Institute at Stony Brook. It would be impossible to name the participants in these various seminars. I extend my gratitude to them all.

1. Ella Shohat, "Notes on the 'Post-colonial,'" *Social Text* 31/32 (1992): 103.

2. In 1985, Gayatri Chakravorty Spivak insisted in an interview that she did not belong to the "top level of the United States Academy" because she taught in the South and the Southwest whereas "the cultural elite in the United States inhabit the Northeastern seaboard or the West coast." See Gayatri Chakravorty Spivak, *The Post-colonial Critic: Interviews, Strategies, Dialogues,* ed. Sarah Harasym (New York: Routledge, 1990), 114. Since then Professor Spivak has moved to the northeastern seaboard.

3. Ibid., passim. See also Arjun Appadurai, "Global Ethnoscapes: Notes and Queries for a Transnational Anthropology," in Richard G. Fox ed., *Recapturing Anthropology: Working in the Present* (Santa Fe: School of American Research Press, 1991), 191–210. Aijaz Ahmad, whom I do not include among the postcolonial critics here, does an excellent job of relating the problems of postcoloniality to contemporary capitalism, if only in passing and somewhat differently from what I undertake in this essay. See his "Jameson's Rhetoric of Otherness and the 'National Allegory,'" *Social Text* 17 (fall 1987): 3–25 and his more recent book *In Theory: Classes, Nations, Literatures* (London: Verso Books, 1992).

4. Shohat, "Notes," 110.

5. Gyan Prakash, "Writing Post-Orientalist Histories of the Third World: Perspectives from Indian Historiography," *Comparative Studies in Society and History* 32:2 (1990): 383.

6. Ibid., 399. See also Gayatri Chakravorty Spivak, "Subaltern Studies: Deconstructing Historiography," in Ranajit Guha and Gayatri Chakravorty Spivak, eds., *Selected Subaltern Studies* (New York: Oxford University Press, 1988), 3–32.

7. Gyan Prakash, "Postcolonial Criticism and Indian Historiography," *Social Text* 31/32 (1992): 8. I use Prakash's discussions of postcoloniality as my point of departure here because he has made the most systematic attempts at accounting for the concept and also because his discussions bring to the fore the implications of the concept for historical understanding. As this statement reveals, Prakash himself draws heavily for inspiration on the characteristics of postcolonial consciousness delineated by others, especially Homi Bhabha, who has been responsible for the prominence in discussions of postcoloniality of the vocabulary of "hybridity" and other terms. Bhabha's work, however, is responsible

for more than the vocabulary of postcolonialism, as he has proved himself to be something of a master of political mystification and theoretical obfuscation, of a reduction of social and political problems to psychological ones, and of the substitution of poststructuralist linguistic manipulation for historical and social explanation — which show up in much postcolonial writing, but rarely with the same virtuosity (and incomprehensibility) that he brings to it. For some of his more influential writings, see "Of Mimicry and Man: The Ambivalence of Colonial Discourse," *October* 28 (1984): 125–33; "The Comment to Theory," in Jim Pines and Paul Willemen, eds., *Questions of Third World Cinema* (London: BFI, 1989), 111–32; "The Other Question: Difference, Discrimination and the Discourse of Colonialism," in F. Barker et al., eds., *Literature, Politics and Theory* (New York: Methuen, 1986), 148–72; his essays in Homi Bhabha, ed., *Nation and Narration* (New York: Routledge, 1990); and, most recently, *The Location of Culture* (New York: Routledge, 1994). Bhabha may be exemplary of the Third World intellectual who has been completely reworked by the language of First World cultural criticism. This is not to deny, to rephrase what I said above, his enormous linguistic talents, which may be inseparable from his conviction to the priority of language, his conversion of material problems into metaphorical ones, and his apparent concern for aesthetic playfulness over clarity in his writing.

8. Prakash, "Post-Orientalist Histories," 393.

9. Ibid., 395. See also Dipesh Chakrabarty, "Post-coloniality and the Artifice of History: Who Speaks for 'Indian' Pasts?" *Representations* 37 (winter 1992): 4.

10. Prakash, "Postcolonial Criticism," 14–15. See also Spivak, *Post-colonial Critic,* passim. As the term "subaltern" would indicate, Antonio Gramsci's inspiration is readily visible in the works of subaltern historians.

11. Prakash, "Post-Orientalist Histories," 390–91.

12. Ibid., 397.

13. Prakash, "Postcolonial Criticism," 13.

14. Prakash, "Post-Orientalist Histories," 13.

15. Ibid., 399.

16. Ibid., 403.

17. Indeed, Lyotard has "defined" postmodern as "incredulity toward metanarratives" (Jean-François Lyotard, *The Postmodern Condition: A Report on Knowledge* [Minneapolis: University of Minnesota Press, 1984], xxiv).

18. Bill Ashcroft, Gareth Griffiths, Helen Tiffin, *The Empire Writes Back: Theory and Practice in Post-colonial Literatures* (London: Routledge, 1989), 2. Note that in this instance, the postcolonial concerns itself with literature, although the implications obviously go beyond the literary realm, which is characteristic of much of these discussions. Also, in case the reader might wonder why Latin American literatures, which may be more "paradigmatic" than any, are not included in the list, it is noteworthy that in the writings of Australian and Canadian postcolonials, "postcolonial" more often than not is associated with the former Commonwealth countries, rather than with the Third World in general — and this in spite of immense differences economically and politically between countries comprising the Commonwealth. This is indicated by Stephen Slemon, "Unsettling the Empire: Resistance Theory for the Second World," in Bill Ashcroft, Gareth Griffiths, and Helen Tiffin, eds., *The Post-colonial Studies Reader* (New York: Routledge, 1995), 104–10; reprinted in abridged form from *World Literature Written in English* 30:2 (1990).

19. For discussions of similar problems in Chinese historiography, see Joseph Levenson, *Confucian China and Its Modern Fate* (Berkeley: University of California Press, 1968); Rey Chow, *Woman and Chinese Modernity* (Minneapolis: University of Minnesota Press, 1991); Arif Dirlik, *Revolution and History: Origins of Marxist Historiography in China, 1919–1937* (Berkeley: University of California Press, 1978); idem, "The Globalization of Marxist Historical Discourse and the Problem of Hegemony in Marxism," *Journal of Third World Studies* 4:1 (spring 1987): 151–64.

20. Ashcroft, Griffiths, and Tiffin, *The Post-colonial Studies Reader,* 1.

21. Frederick Buell, *National Culture and the New Global System* (Baltimore: Johns Hopkins University Press, 1994).

22. Prakash, "Postcolonial Criticism," 10.

23. Diana Brydon, "The White Inuit Speaks: Contamination as Literary Strategy," in Ashcroft, Griffiths, and Tiffin, *The Post-colonial Studies Reader,* 140–41; originally published in Ian Adam and Helen Tiffin, eds., *Past the Last Post: Theorizing Post-colonialism and Post-modernism* (New York: Harvester Wheatsheaf, 1991). Similar warnings toward Australian aboriginal claims to "authenticity," although phrased much more gently, are to be found in Ashcroft, Griffiths, and Tiffin, *The Empire Strikes Back,*

and Gareth Griffiths, "The Myth of Authenticity," in Chris Tiffin and Alan Lawson, eds., *De-scribing Empire: Post-colonialism and Textuality* (New York: Routledge, 1994), 70–85.

24. Spivak, *Post-colonial Critic,* 67–68.

25. This is at any rate a question that needs to be clarified. It seems to me that Prakash's denial of foundational status to class goes beyond what is but a *historicization* of class in the work of *Subaltern Studies* historians, in the same way that, say, E. P. Thompson historicizes the concept in *The Making of the English Working Class* (New York: Random House, 1966). For a note on the question of class, see Dipesh Chakrabarty, "Invitation to a Dialogue," *Subaltern Studies* 4 (1985). The procedure of generalization may also play a part in the deradicalization of *Subaltern Studies* ideas by removing them from their specific historiographical context, where they *do* play an innovative, radical role. For instance, the qualification of the role of colonialism in Indian history is intended by these historians to bring to the fore the mystifications of the past in nationalist histories, which is a radical act. Made into a general principle of "postcolonialism," this qualification turns into a downplaying of colonialism in history. For an acknowledgment of doubt concerning the "success" attributed to *Subaltern Studies* historiography, see Chakrabarty, "Postcoloniality and the Artifice of History."

26. Note not just the ideas but the tone in the following statement by Ahmad: "But one could start with a radically different premise, namely the proposition that we live not in three worlds but in one; that this world includes the experience of colonialism and imperialism on both sides of Jameson's global divide . . . ; that societies in formations of backward capitalism are as much constituted by the division of classes as are societies in the advanced capitalist countries; that socialism is not restricted to something called the second world but is simply the name of a resistance that saturates the globe today, as capitalism, itself does; that the different parts of the capitalist system are to be known not in terms of binary opposition but as a contradictory unity, with differences, yes, but also with profound overlaps" ("Jameson's Rhetoric of Otherness," 9).

27. Spivak, "Can the Subaltern Speak?" in Cary Nelson and Lawrence Grossberg, eds., *Marxism and the Interpretation of Culture* (Urbana: University of Illinois Press, 1988), 271–313; Lata Mani, "Multiple Mediations: Feminist Scholarship in the Age of Multinational Reception," in James Clifford and Vivek Dhareshwar, eds., *Travelling Theories Travelling Theorists* (Santa Cruz, Calif.: Center for Cultural Theory, 1989), 1–23.

28. Appiah, "Is the 'Post-' in 'Postmodernism' the 'Post-' in 'Postcolonial'?" *Critical Inquiry* 17 (winter 1991): 353.

29. Achille Mbembe, "Prosaics of Servitude and Authoritarian Civilities," *Public Culture* 5:1 (fall 1992): 137.

30. Spivak, *Post-colonial Critic,* 91.

31. Edward Said, foreword to Guha and Spivak, *Selected Subaltern Studies.*

32. For a sampling of essays, see Joseph P. L. Jiang, *Confucianism and Modernization: A Symposium* (Taipei: Freedom Council, 1987). Scholars such as Tu Wei-ming and Yu Ying-shih have played a major part in efforts to revive Confucianism, while the quasi-fascist regime of Singapore (especially under Lee Kuan Yew) has been a major promoter of the idea.

33. Prakash, "Postcolonial Criticism," 14–15.

34. For a discussion of this problem in detail, see Arif Dirlik, "Mao Zedong and 'Chinese Marxism,'" *Encyclopedia of Asian Philosophy* (London: Routledge, 1993).

35. Prakash, "Postcolonial Criticism," 10.

36. Althusser recognized this problem, with specific reference to Mao Tse-tung Thought. See his "Contradiction and Overdetermination," in *For Marx,* trans. Ben Brewster (New York: Vintage Books, 1970), 87–128. For the "molding" of ideology, see Althusser's "Ideology and Ideological State Apparatuses," in *Lenin and Philosophy,* trans. Ben Brewster (New York: Monthly Review Press, 1971), 127–86. Lata Mani gives a good (personal) account of the contextual formation of ideology in her "Multiple Mediations." The risk in contextual ideological formation, of course, is the transformation of what is a problem into what is a celebration: game playing. This is evident throughout in Spivak's "playfulness" in *The Post-colonial Critic* as well as in, say, James Clifford's approach to the question of ethnography and culture. For a brief example of the latter, among Clifford's many works, see "Notes on Theory and Travel," in *Travelling Theory Travelling Theorists,* 177–88. My objection here is not to the importance of immediate context in ideology formation (and the variability and transposability of roles it implies) but to the mystification that such emphasis on the local causes regarding the larger contexts that differentiate power relations and suggest more stable and directed positions. No matter how much the ethnographer may strive to change places with the native, in the end the ethnographer returns to the

First World academy and the native back to the "wilds." This is the problem with postcoloniality, and it is evident in the tendency of so much postcolonial criticism to start off with a sociology of power relationships only to take refuge in aesthetic phraseology.

37. Conversely, absence from powerful institutions may lead to silence. This is an explanation that Nicholas Thomas has offered for the obliviousness of postcolonial criticism to the problem of indigenous peoples who, to the extent that they are present in the academy, are only marginally so. See Thomas, *Colonialism's Culture: Anthropology, Travel, and Government* (Princeton, N.J.: Princeton University Press, 1994), 172.

38. Appiah, "Is the 'Post-' in 'Postmodernism' the 'Post-' in 'Postcolonial'?" 353.

39. See the example Shohat gives of his experiences at CUNY ("Notes," 99).

40. Ibid.

41. Anne McClintock, "The Angel of Progress: Pitfalls of the Term 'Post-colonialism,'" *Social Text* 31/32 (1992): 86. Recall the statement I quoted above from Diana Brydon.

42. Shohat, "Notes," 104.

43. Ibid., 110.

44. Rosalind O'Hanlon and David Washbrook, "After Orientalism: Culture, Criticism, and Politics in the Third World," *Comparative Studies in Society and History* 34:1 (January 1992): 166.

45. Karl Pletsch, "The Three Worlds, or the Division of Social Scientific Labor, circa 1950–1975," *Comparative Studies in Society and History* 23:4 (1981).

46. O'Hanlon and Washbrook, "After Orientalism," 147.

47. Prakash, "Postcolonial Criticism," 13–14.

48. Fernando Coronil, "Can Postcoloniality Be Decolonized? Imperial Banality and Postcolonial Power," *Public Culture* 5:1 (fall 1992): 99–100.

49. O'Hanlon and Washbrook, "After Orientalism," 165–66.

50. Shohat, "Notes," 111.

51. David Harvey, *The Condition of Postmodernity* (Cambridge, Mass.: Basil Blackwell, 1989), and, Fredric Jameson, "Postmodernism or, the Cultural Logic of Late Capitalism," *New Left Review* 146 (July/August 1984).

52. F. Frobel, J. Heinrichs, and O. Kreye, *The New International Division of Labour* (Cambridge: Cambridge University Press, 1980). The term "disorganized capitalism" comes from Claus Offe, *Disorganized Capitalism* (Cambridge, Mass.: MIT Press, 1985), while "global capitalism" is the term used by Robert J. S. Ross and Kent C. Trachte, *Global Capitalism: The New Leviathan* (Albany: State University of New York Press, 1990). Other noteworthy books on the subject are Leslie Sklair, *Sociology of the Global System* (Baltimore: Johns Hopkins University Press, 1991), which spells out the implications for the Third World of global capitalism, and, especially in light of what I say below about the Clinton presidency, Robert Reich, *The Work of Nations* (N.Y.: Alfred A. Knopf, 1991). Reich's book incorporates his contributions to the *Harvard Business Review* and contains pieces with suggestive titles like "Who Is US?" and "Who Is Them?" For "subcontracting," see Gary Gereffi, "Global Sourcing and Regional Divisions of Labor in the Pacific Rim," in Arif Dirlik, ed., *What Is in a Rim? Critical Perspectives on the Asia-Pacific Idea* (Boulder, Colo.: Westview Press, 1993).

53. Riccardo Petrella, "World City-States of the Future," *New Perspectives Quarterly* (fall 1991): 59–64. See also "A New Hanseatic League?" *New York Times,* February 23, 1992, E3.

54. Kenichi Ohmae, "Beyond Friction to Fact: The Borderless Economy," *New Perspectives Quarterly* (spring 1990): 21.

55. While I stress transnational corporations here, it is important to note that the functioning of corporations is made possible by a whole gamut of transnational organizations, from state-led ones, such as the World Bank and International Monetary Fund, to what might be described as organizations of a global "civil society," from nongovernmental organizations to professional associations. Taking note of these organizations also serves as a reminder that, in spite of the appearance of decentralization and the dispersion of power, the powerful of the First World, through their immense concentration of wealth as well as the influence they exert on these organizations, continue to dominate the world, albeit at a greater distance (especially in terms of social and public responsibility) from their own societies.

56. This phenomenon is addressed in most of the works cited above n. 52.

57. Ohmae, "Beyond Friction." See, also, James Gardner, "Global Regionalism," *New Perspectives Quarterly* (winter 1992): 58–59.

58. "The Logic of Global Business: An Interview with ABB's Percy Barnevik," *Harvard Business Review* (March–April 1991): 90–105.

59. See Achille Mbembe, "The Banality of Power and the Aesthetics of Vulgarity," *Public Culture* 4:2 (spring 1992): 1–30, and the discussion provoked by that essay in *Public Culture* 5:1 (fall 1992).

60. For "cognitive mapping," see Fredric Jameson, "Cognitive Mapping," in Cary Nelson and Lawrence Grossberg, *Marxism and the Interpretation of Culture* (Urbana: University of Illinois Press, 1988), 347–57. Jameson has been a forceful advocate of retaining a sense of totality and structure in a socialist politics. His own totalization of the global structure has come under severe criticism (see Ahmad, "Jameson's Rhetoric"). I should stress here that it is not necessary to agree with his particular mode of totalization to recognize the validity of his argument.

61. Appiah, "Is the 'Post-' in 'Postmodernism' the 'Post-' in 'Postcolonial'?" 348.

62. Aijaz Ahmad, "The Politics of Literary Postcoloniality," *Race and Class* 36:3 (1995): 16. See also Benita Parry, "Signs of Our Times: Discussion of Homi Bhabha's *The Location of Culture*," *Third Text* 28/29 (autumn/winter 1994): 3–24.

63. This is an aspect of postcoloniality, and of its appeals, that clearly calls for greater attention. A historian of the Pacific, Klaus Neumann, writes that "these days Papua New Guineans...do not appear overtly interested in being told about the horrors of colonialism, as such accounts potentially belittle today's descendants of yesterday's victims" ("'In Order to Win Their Friendship': Renegotiating First Contact," *The Contemporary Pacific* 6:1 [1994]: 122). Likewise, Deirdre Jordan notes the complaints of adult aboriginal students in Australia about emphasis on white oppression, "which seems designed to call forth in them responses of hostility and racism and which, they believe, causes a crisis of identity" ("Aboriginal Identity: Uses of the Past, Problems for the Future?" in Jeremy R. Beckett, ed., *Past and Present: The Construction of Aboriginality* [Canberra: Aboriginal Studies Press, 1994], 119). There are others, needless to say, who would suppress memories of the past for reasons of self-interest.

Contributors

Norma Alarcón is associate professor of ethnic/women's studies at the University of California at Berkeley. She is the author of *Ninfomania: The Feminist Poetics of Difference in the Work of Rosario Castellanos* and numerous essays on Chicano/a literature and culture.

Kwame Anthony Appiah is professor of Afro-American studies and philosophy at Harvard and the author of *In My Father's House: Africa in the Philosophy of Culture; Necessary Questions: An Introduction to Philosophy; For Truth in Semantics;* and *Assertion and Conditionals;* as well as of three novels, of which the latest is *Another Death in Venice.*

Homi K. Bhabha is professor of English and art at the University of Chicago. He is the editor of *Nation and Narration* and the author of *The Location of Culture.*

Judith Butler is professor of rhetoric and comparative literature at the University of California at Berkeley. She is the author of, among other works, *Gender Trouble: Feminism and the Subversion of Identity;* and *Bodies That Matter: On the Discursive Limits of "Sex."*

Hazel V. Carby teaches American studies and African-American Studies at Yale University. She is completing *Race Men: Genealogies of Race Nation and Manhood.*

Manthia Diawara is professor of comparative literature and film and director of African studies at New York University.

Arif Dirlik is professor of history at Duke University, where he specializes in Chinese history. His most recent publications include *After the Revolution: Waking to Global Capitalism;* as editor, *What Is in a Rim? Critical Perspectives on the Pacific Region Idea;* and, as editor with Rob Wilson, *Asia Pacific as Space of Cultural Production.*

Jean Franco is professor emerita at Columbia University. Her most recent book is *Plotting Women: Gender and Representation in Mexico.*

Stuart Hall was for many years director of the Birmingham Centre for Cultural Studies and is now professor of sociology at the Open University in England. He has published widely on cultural and social theory and cultural studies and is currently working on questions of cultural identity in the context of globalization.

Theresa Halsey is a member of the Hunkpapa Kavioth Nation, an educator, and a producer of a radio program. She is also a counselor and a community organizer and coordinator.

Michael Hanchard is assistant professor of political science in the Department of Government at the University of Texas at Austin. He is the author of *Orpheus and Power: Afro-Brazilian Social Movements in Rio de Janeiro and São Paulo, Brazil, 1945–1988.*

bell hooks is the author of twelve books — most recently *Art on My Mind: Visual Politics* and *Killing Rage: Ending Racism.*

M. Annette Jaimes is associate professor of women's studies at San Francisco State University.

Audre Lorde, a lesbian feminist and renowned writer, poet, and essayist, was a recipient of many honors and awards. She was the author of *Zami: A New Spelling of My Name; Sister Outsider: Essays and Speeches; The Cancer Journals; The Black Unicorn;* and *A Burst of Light,* among other texts. Lorde died in 1992.

Wahneema Lubiano is assistant professor of English at Princeton University. A book, *Messing with the Machine: Modernism, Postmodernism, and Black American Fiction,* is forthcoming.

Anne McClintock is associate professor of gender and cultural studies in the Department of English at Columbia University. She is the author of *Imperial Leather: Race, Gender, and Sexuality in the Colonial Contest.*

Kobena Mercer is a cultural critic based in London. He has written and lectured widely on the cultural politics of race and sexuality in visual culture and is the author of *Welcome to the Jungle: New Positions in Black Cultural Studies.*

Trinh T. Minh-ha is a writer, filmmaker, composer, and professor of women's studies and film at the University of California at Berkeley. Her more recent works include the books: *Framer Framed; When the Moon Waxes Red; Woman, Native, Other; En miniscules* (book of poems); and the films: *Shoot for the Contents; Surname Viet Given Name Nam; Naked Spaces;* and *Reassemblage.*

Chandra Talpade Mohanty teaches feminist, antiracist, and Third World studies at Hamilton College. She is coeditor of *Third World Women and the Politics of Feminism* and of *Movements, Histories, Identities: Genealogies of Third World Feminism.*

Aamir Mufti is assistant professor of English and comparative literature at the University of Michigan, Ann Arbor.

Rob Nixon is associate professor of English and comparative literature at Columbia University. He is the author of *London Calling: V. S. Naipaul, Postcolonial Man-*

darin; and *Homelands, Harlem and Hollywood: South African Culture and the World Beyond.*

Gyan Prakash is associate professor of history at Princeton University. The author of *Bonded Histories: Genealogies of Labor Servitude in Colonial India,* he has written extensively on the history of colonial India and on colonialism and history writing. The editor of *After Colonialism: Imperial Histories and Postcolonial Displacements,* he is currently writing a book on science and the imagination of modern India.

Madhava Prasad is an independent researcher/writer based in Bangalore.

Roberto Fernández Retamar is professor emeritus at Havana University and Doctor Honoris Causa of the Universities of Lima, Sophia, and Buenos Aires. He is the author of *Caliban and Other Essays.*

Edward W. Said is University Professor at Columbia University. His many works include *Orientalism; The Question of Palestine; The World, the Text, and the Critic; Culture and Imperialism; The Politics of Dispossession; Representations of the Intellectual;* and *Peace and Its Discontents.*

Ella Shohat is professor of cultural studies and women's studies at the City University of New York Graduate Center and is the coordinator of the cinema studies program at CUNY–Staten Island. She is the author of *Israeli Cinema: East/West and the Politics of Representation* and the coauthor (with Robert Stam) of the award-winning *Unthinking Eurocentrism: Multiculturalism and the Media.*

Gayatri Chakravorty Spivak is Avalon Foundation Professor in the Humanities at Columbia University. She has published *Of Grammotology,* a critical translation of Jacques Derrida's *De la grammatologie;* and *Imaginary Maps,* a critical translation of Mahasweta Devi's fiction. Her own books are *Myself Must I Remake; In Other Worlds; The Post-colonial Critic;* and *Outside in the Teaching Machine.*

Robert Stam is professor of cinema studies at New York University. He is the author of *Reflexivity in Film and Literature: From Don Quixote to Jean-Luc Godard; Subversive Pleasures: Bakhtin, Cultural Criticism, and Film;* with Randal Johnson, *Brazilian Cinema;* and with Ella Shohat, the award-winning *Unthinking Eurocentrism: Multiculturalism and the Media.*

Ann Laura Stoler is professor of anthropology, history, and women's studies at the University of Michigan. Her most recent works include *Race and the Education of Desire: A Colonial Reading of Foucault's History of Sexuality;* and an edited volume with Frederick Cooper, *Tensions of Empire: Colonial Cultures in a Bourgeois World.*

Gauri Viswanathan is associate professor of English and comparative literature at Columbia University. She is the author of *Masks of Conquest: Literary Study and British Rule in India.*

Publication History

Introduction, by Aamir R. Mufti and Ella Shohat. Essay first published here.

Part I. CONTESTING NATIONS

1. Edward Said, "Zionism from the Standpoint of Its Victims." Previously published in *Social Text* 1 (1979). Copyright Duke University Press, 1979. Reprinted with permission.

2. Ella Shohat, "Sephardim in Israel: Zionism from the Standpoint of Its Jewish Victims." Previously published in *Social Text* 19/20, vol. 7, nos. 1–2 (fall 1988): 1–36. Copyright Duke University Press, 1988. Reprinted with permission.

3. Rob Nixon, "Of Balkans and Bantustans: Ethnic Cleansing and Crises of National Legitimation." Previously published in *Transition* 60 (1983). Copyright 1993, W. E. B. Du Bois Institute. Reprinted by permission of Duke University Press.

4. Anne McClintock, " 'No Longer in a Future Heaven': Race, Gender, and Nationalism." Previously published in Anne McClintock, *Imperial Leather: Race, Gender, and Sexuality in the Colonial Contest* (New York: Routledge, 1995).

5. Gauri Viswanathan, "Currying Favor: The Beginnings of English Literary Study in British India." Previously published in *Social Text* 19/20, vol. 7, nos. 1–2 (fall 1988): 85–104. Copyright Duke University Press, 1988. Reprinted with permission.

6. Jean Franco, "The Nation as Imagined Community." Reprinted from *The New Historicism,* editor Aram Veeser (1989), by permission of the publisher, Routledge: New York and London.

Part II. MULTICULTURALISM AND DIASPORIC IDENTITIES

7. Madhava Prasad, "On the Question of a Theory of (Third World) Literature." Previously published in *Social Text* 31/32, vol. 10, nos. 2–3 (spring 1992): 57–83. Copyright Duke University Press, 1992. Reprinted with permission.

8. Roberto Fernández Retamar, "Caliban Speaks Five Hundred Years Later." First English-language publication in the present volume.

9. Stuart Hall, "The Local and the Global: Globalization and Ethnicity." Originally published in *Culture, Globalization, and the World System,* edited by Anthony D. King (Binghamton: Department of Art History, State University of New York at Binghamton, 1991). Reprinted with permission.

10. Robert Stam, "Multiculturalism and the Neoconservatives." First published here.

11. Wahneema Lubiano, "Shuckin' Off the African-American Native Other: What's 'Po-Mo' Got to Do with It?" Previously published in *Cultural Critique* 18 (spring 1991): 149–86. By permission of Oxford University Press.

12. Michael Hanchard, "Identity, Meaning, and the African-American." Previously published in *Social Text* 24, vol. 8, no. 2 (spring 1990): 31–42. Copyright Duke University Press, 1990. Reprinted with permission.

13. Kobena Mercer, "Just Looking for Trouble: Robert Mapplethorpe and Fantasies of Race." Originally published as "Reading Racial Fetishism: The Photographs of Robert Mapplethorpe," in *Sex Exposed: Sexuality and the Pornography Debate,* edited by Lynn Segal and Mary McIntosh (London: Virago, 1992). Reprinted with permission.

Part III. GENDER AND THE POLITICS OF RACE

14. Chandra Talpade Mohanty, "Under Western Eyes: Feminist Scholarship and Colonial Discourses." Originally published in *Third World Women and the Politics of Feminism,* edited by Chandra Talpade Mohanty, Ann Russo, and Lourdes Torres (Bloomington: Indiana University Press, 1991). Reprinted with permission of the publisher.

15. Norma Alarcón, "*Traddutora, Traditora:* A Paradigmatic Figure of Chicana Feminism." Previously published in *Cultural Critique* 13 (fall 1989): 57–87. Reprinted by permission of Oxford University Press.

16. M. Annette Jaimes with Theresa Halsey, "American Indian Women: At the Center of Indigenous Resistance in Contemporary North America." Originally published in *The State of Native America: Genocide, Colonization, and Resistance,* edited by M. Annette Jaimes (Boston: South End Press, 1992). Copyright South End Press. Reprinted with permission.

17. Hazel V. Carby, "'On the Threshold of Women's Era': Lynching, Empire, and Sexuality in Black Feminist Theory." Originally published in *"Race," Writing, and*

Difference, edited by Henry Louis Gates (Chicago: University of Chicago Press, 1986). Reprinted with permission.

18. Ann Laura Stoler "Making Empire Respectable: The Politics of Race and Sexual Morality in Twentieth-Century Colonial Cultures." Reprinted by permission of the American Anthropological Association from *American Ethnologist* 16:4 (November 1989).

19. Audre Lorde "Age, Race, Class, and Sex: Woman Redefining Difference." Originally published in *Sister Outsider: Essays and Speeches* (Freedom, Calif.: Crossing Press, 1984). Reprinted with permission.

20. Judith Butler, "Gender Is Burning: Questions of Appropriation and Subversion." Reprinted from *Bodies That Matter: Questions of Appropriation and Subversion* (1993) by permission of the publisher, Routledge: New York and London.

21. bell hooks, "Sisterhood: Political Solidarity between Women." Reprinted from *Feminist Theory: From Margin to Theory* (1984), with permission from the publisher, South End Press, 116 Saint Botolph Street, Boston, MA 02115.

Part IV. POSTCOLONIAL THEORY

22. Trinh T. Minh-ha, "Not You/Like You: Postcolonial Women and the Interlocking Questions of Identity and Difference." Excerpted and reprinted from *When the Moon Waxes Red,* by Trinh T. Minh-ha (1991), by permission of the publisher, Routledge: New York and London.

23. Kwame Anthony Appiah, "Is the 'Post-' in 'Postcolonial' the 'Post-' in 'Postmodern'?" First published here.

24. Homi K. Bhabha, "The World and the Home." Previously published in *Social Text* 31/32, vol. 10, nos. 2–3 (spring 1992): 141–53. Copyright Duke University Press, 1992. Reprinted with permission.

25. Manthia Diawara, "Reading Africa through Foucault: V. Y. Mudimbe's Reaffirmation of the Subject." Originally appeared in *October* 55 (winter 1990): 79–92, copyright 1990 by the Massachusetts Institute of Technology and October Magazine, Ltd.

26. Gayatri Chakravorty Spivak, "Teaching for the Times." Previously published in *The Decolonization of Imagination,* edited by Jan Nederveen Pieterse and Bikhu Parekh (London: Zed Books, 1995), 177–202. Copyright Zed Books, reprinted with permission.

27. Gyan Prakash, "Postcolonial Criticism and Indian Historiography." Previously published in *Social Text* 31/32, vol. 10, nos. 2–3 (spring 1992): 8–19. Copyright Duke University Press, 1992. Reprinted with permission.

28. Arif Dirlik, "The Postcolonial Aura: Third World Criticism in the Age of Global Capitalism." First published here.

Index

compiled by Eileen Quam
and Theresa Wolner